300
St. Louis

Merame
St. Louis Com
11333 Big
Kirkwood, MO 63122-5799
314-984-7797

The Idea of Galicia

THE IDEA OF GALICIA

History and Fantasy in Habsburg Political Culture

Larry Wolff

STANFORD UNIVERSITY PRESS

STANFORD, CALIFORNIA

2010

This book has been published with the assistance of New York University

Stanford University Press,
Stanford, California
© 2010 by the Board of Trustees of the
Leland Stanford Junior University
All rights reserved

No part of this book may be reproduced or transmitted in any form or by any
means, electronic or mechanical, including photocopying and recording, or in any
information storage or retrieval system without the prior written permission of
Stanford University Press.

Library of Congress Cataloging-in-Publication Data

Wolff, Larry.
    The idea of Galicia : history and fantasy in Habsburg political culture / Larry
Wolff.
        p. cm.
    Includes bibliographical references and index.
    ISBN 978-0-8047-6267-0 (cloth : alk. paper)
    1. Galicia (Poland and Ukraine)—Intellectual life. 2. Galicia (Poland and
Ukraine)—History. 3. Political culture—Galicia (Poland and Ukraine)—History.
I. Title.

DK4600.G344W65 2010
943.8'603—dc22   2009023870

Printed in the United States of America on
acid-free, archival-quality paper

Typeset at Stanford University Press in 11/13 Garamond

For Jim Cronin—

J'ai toujours fait une prière à Dieu, qui est fort courte. La voici: Mon Dieu, rendez nos ennemis bien ridicules! Dieu m'a exaucé.

(I have always made one prayer to God, a very short one. Here it is: "O God, make our enemies ridiculous!" And God granted it.)
   —Voltaire, 1767

Samoobrona, odwet. Przed śmiesznością bronić się śmiechem.

(Self-defense, revenge. Against the ridiculous defend yourself with laughter.)
   —Taduesz "Boy" Żeleński, *Znaszli ten kraj?* 1931

This what neglected topic?
This strangely what topic?
This strangely neglected what?
   —Kingsley Amis, *Lucky Jim*, 1954

Contents

Acknowledgments, ix

Introduction, 1

1. Inventing Galicia: The Josephine
Enlightenment and the Partitions of Poland, 13

2. Galicia Restored: The Politics of Metternich
and the Comedies of Fredro, 63

3. The Galician Childhood of Sacher-Masoch:
From Folk Songs to Massacres, 111

4. Galician Vertigo: The Meaning
of the Massacres, 158

5. After the Revolution: The Rise of *Czas* and the
Advent of Franz Joseph, 188

6. The Average Galician in the Age of Autonomy:
Fantasies and Statistics of the Slavic Orient, 231

7. Fin-de-siècle Galicia: Ghosts and Monsters, 280

8. The Land of Impossibilities:
Another Chapter Beginning, 308

9. Geopolitical Conclusion:
The Liquidation of Galicia, 351

10. Haunted Epilogue: Galicia after Galicia, 383

Notes, 421
Index, 465

Acknowledgments

I first began to study Galicia as a college student at Harvard in the 1970s, and, working on this project, I have found myself constantly thinking back to issues that I discussed with professors who profoundly shaped my intellectual development: Wiktor Weintraub (1908–88), who introduced me to Polish literature and culture, and with whom I read Boy's *Znaszli ten kraj?;* and Omeljan Pristak (1919–2006), who introduced me not only to Ukrainian history but to the whole history of Eastern Europe. It was Professor Weintraub who inspired my interest in Cracow, and Professor Pritsak who started me thinking about Lviv—thus, between them, presenting me with the intellectual panorama of Galicia.

As a graduate student I began to study Habsburg history and was lucky enough to work with three inspirational professors, all with very different perspectives on the Habsburg monarchy according to their own principal academic interests: Wayne Vucinich (1913–2005) and Gordon Craig (1913–2005) at Stanford, and William Slottman (1925–95) at Berkeley.

Academic work on Galicia has been pursued very actively over the last decade while I have been working on this book, and I have benefited tremendously from discussion and guidance inside and outside the former Galicia. In Cracow I was most grateful for the guidance of Jacek Purchla and Krzysztof Zamorski. In Lviv I have received every possible assistance from my friend Yaroslav Hrytsak, who has also thought and written profoundly about Galician issues. In Vienna I was delighted to meet with the Galician studies group at the university, to present my work and discuss it from historical, philological, and literary perspectives with Andreas Kappeler, Michael Moser, and Alois Woldan.

I am grateful to many friends, colleagues, and fellow scholars who have discussed with me my research and their own research about Galicia and the Habsburg monarchy, including Gary Cohen, Patrice Dabrowski, David Engel, Hugo Lane, Elżbieta Matynia, Keely Stauter-Halsted, Ostap Sereda, Tom Simons, Nancy Sinkoff, Philipp Ther, Daniel Unowsky, Iryna Vushko, and Nathan Wood. My gratitude to Anna Popiel, who, for many years, has helped me with the subtleties of the Polish language. Special thanks to Pieter Judson and David Frick for their careful readings of my manuscript and their invaluable criticisms and suggestions.

Norman Naimark and Nancy Kollmann invited me back to Stanford to present my Galician research at the Center for Russian and East European Studies—and watched with me the last game of the 2007 World Series. Ivo Banac and Laura Engelstein invited me, on two separate occasions, to present different parts of my Galician work at Yale, where I also had the chance to discuss this work with Tim Snyder, Marci Shore, and Alexander Schenker, a great Galician. Tony Judt at NYU has offered me both his insight and his encouragement and has twice permitted me to present my Galician research at the exceptionally stimulating lunchtime seminar of the Remarque Institute. My friend Omer Bartov has been following the Galician trail together with me ever since 2002, when we both won Guggenheim Fellowships for parallel Galician projects, and I have particularly benefited from presenting my research in his Borderlands project at Brown. Istvan Deak has been inspirational for me, as for so many others, pursuing research on the Habsburg monarchy. Frank Sysyn, I hope, will remember guiding my earliest experiences with *Czas*, back when he was the adviser for my undergraduate senior thesis about the Polish perspective on the Austro-Hungarian compromise of 1867.

My parents, Robert and Renee Wolff, have always given me their loving encouragement and support in my various endeavors, and my father has taken a special interest in this work, as his parents, my grandparents, were both born in Habsburg Galicia, and thought of themselves as Galicians even after many decades in America. My own children, several generations removed from Galicia, have been very indulgent with me in my Galician distraction over these last years, which have coincided with the rather intense period of moving our whole family from Cambridge to Manhattan. To Orlando, Josephine, and Anatol I can only say: "Wait, there's a guy on our team who dresses like a pirate?" And to Perri Klass, married to a large academic project on Galicia: isn't it what every woman dreams of? My thanks and love, as ever. Without her I would be a worthless creature.

Having changed cities and universities while working on this book, I must express my gratitude to both Boston College and New York University for the generous institutional support that they have given to me, and I am especially grateful for the assistance of many wonderful colleagues in both places. I also thank the Guggenheim Foundation and the International Research and Exchanges Board for their support.

For twenty years at Boston College I was always happy to have as my friend and colleague Jim Cronin—and surely no one ever had a colleague who made academics and scholarship seem like more fun. This big book is dedicated to him.

New York City
19 September 2007

The Idea of Galicia

Introduction

Galicia was created in 1772 at the historical moment of the first partition of
Poland, when the Habsburg monarchy applied that name to Vienna's territorial portion of the partition and conceived of Galicia as a new Habsburg
province. At the beginning of the century there had been an old Habsburg
province of Galicia in northern Spain, but it was taken, along with Spain, by
the Bourbons in the War of the Spanish Succession. The name was therefore available in 1772, serving as the Latin form of the medieval Rus principality of Halych, one of the successors of Kievan Rus in the thirteenth
and fourteenth centuries. The territories of medieval Halych coincided only
roughly with those that the Empress Maria Theresa took from Poland in
1772, but the name served its purpose and continued to be used even as the
Habsburg province was extended and revised during the later partitions of
Poland and the Napoleonic wars. The population of the province included
Poles, Ruthenians (today Ukrainians), Germans (including Austrians), and
Jews. Galicia, invented in 1772, enjoyed a historical existence of less than a
century and a half, from 1772 to the end of World War I and the abolition
of the Habsburg monarchy in 1918. Galicia was then removed from the map
of Europe, and today, almost a century later, it belongs to the category of
extinct geopolitical entities.

The territory of the former Galicia now lies divided between contemporary Poland and Ukraine, and, although the Galician Jews were almost entirely
annihilated in the Holocaust during World War II, the earlier emigration of
Galician Jews meant that they survived outside Galicia, especially in America
and Israel, where they continued to identify themselves as "Galitzianer" long
after leaving Europe and well into the twentieth century. My father's parents
were born in Galicia at the turn of the century, as subjects of Emperor
Franz Joseph, and they remembered both the province and the emperor all
the rest of their lives, which they spent in New York City. The emperor, my

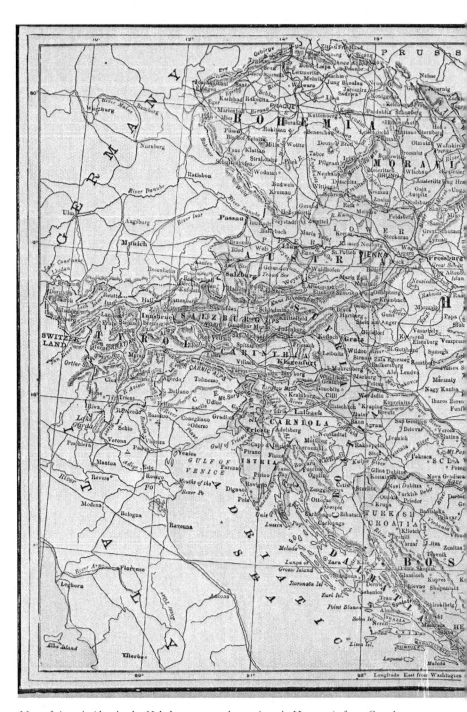

Map of Austria (that is, the Habsburg monarchy, or Austria-Hungary), from Cram's
Universal Atlas (Chicago, 1898). Galicia appears in the northeastern part of Austria-Hungary,
bordering Russia.

AUSTRIA

Geo. F. Cram,

ENGRAVER AND PUBLISHER,

Chicago Ill.

Population, ...37,741,413

Area, square miles, ...115,935

grandmother loyally believed, was good to the Jews. This conviction was at least as old as she was, since a Viennese folklore journal of 1903 already reported that in Galicia the emperor had become, in his own lifetime, "almost a legendary figure" as represented "in the fantasy of the Jewish people."[1] Legend and fantasy played a part in Galician political culture, dating back to the beginning, to the eighteenth-century reigns of Maria Theresa and her son Joseph II; the memory of Joseph was cherished by Galician peasants for generations after his death. Galician history, beginning so abruptly in 1772, was attended by messianic fantasies characteristic of the Habsburg Enlightenment, and when Galicia was abolished in 1918, that history became the haunted terrain of phantoms and fantasies. The Russian writer Isaac Babel came to the former Galicia in 1920, during the Polish-Soviet war, and recorded in his diary a vision of "spectral Galicians" passing through the scenes of wartime horror and brutality.[2] In 2007, when the very last native Galicians, born in 1918, were already almost ninety, there took place at the YIVO Institute for Jewish Research in New York a symposium under the title "Galicia Mon Amour"—a title that resonated with profoundly ambivalent emotions.

This book offers an intellectual history of the idea of Galicia—that is, the study of a place as an idea. Beginning almost as an ideological tabula rasa, a mere name applied to a stretch of annexed territory, Galicia acquired meaning over the course of its historical existence; indeed, it accumulated multiple and shifting layers of meaning. It meant different things to its diverse populations, and acquired complex significance in the observations of statesmen and the imaginations of writers. This book considers the meaning of Galicia for such political figures as Joseph II and Metternich, for writers such as the comic dramatist Aleksander Fredro and the notorious novelist Leopold von Sacher-Masoch, for modernist cultural leaders like Ivan Franko and Stanisław Wyspiański. At the same time, the meaning of Galicia was formulated in the journals of the public sphere, and may be traced in such leading newspapers as *Gazeta Lwowska* in Lviv and *Czas* in Cracow during the nineteenth century, as well as in specialized publications like the Viennese folklore journal that featured Galician Jewish fantasies of Franz Joseph. While the idea of Galicia embraced the entire province, from the Dniester River to the Vistula River, from the Carpathian Mountains to the Wieliczka salt mines, from great aristocratic estates to small Jewish shtetls, the production of culture was principally urban, and this book is, to some extent, a tale of two cities: Lviv and Cracow, exercising their urban perspectives upon Galicia as a whole. The third crucial city was Vienna, the imperial capital, with its own metropolitan perspective on provincial Galicia, a perspective alternately sustained and contested by

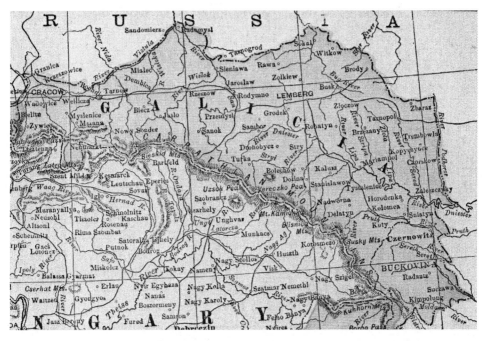

Galicia, on the map of Austria, from Cram's *Universal Atlas* (Chicago, 1898). Lemberg (Lwów, Lviv), the capital city of Galicia, appears in the center of the province. Cracow (Kraków, Krakau) appears in the far western corner. This map colors Bukovina as part of southeastern Galicia, though in fact they were separate crownlands after 1849. The Carpathian Mountains form the southern border of Galicia.

the ideas that emerged from Galicia itself. The meaning of Galicia was never stable but was always contested, negotiated, redeveloped, and redeployed over the course of its entire history.

Galicia was a province, a crownland of the Habsburg monarchy, sometimes called a country [*kraj*, in Polish], but it constituted neither a national community nor the basis for any sort of aspiring political state. Called into being by Habsburg dynastic exigency, Galicia remained dynastically defined as a province of the monarchy in a manner very different from that of Habsburg Bohemia or Hungary, crownlands in possession of historic crowns and traditions to accompany them. As national movements developed among the Poles, Ruthenians, and Jews of Galicia during the course of the nineteenth century, the idea of Galicia transcended nationality in the spirit of inclusive provincial integrity. That integrity, however, required its own work of conscientious cultural construction, as in the botany of Galicia published in 1809, followed over the course of the century by the flora, the fauna, the insecta, and in 1876 the physical anthropology of Galicia, thus transforming a geopolitical artifice of the eighteenth century into a natural space of the nineteenth century.

In 1792 an anonymous poet signed himself "Gallicjan," and from the eighteenth century to the twentieth century there were those who identified themselves as Galician, even if they simultaneously assumed other identities. Galician identity was fundamentally provincial, and its evolution suggests the importance of the provincial as an ideological force overlapping with the forces of the national and the imperial. "To see how administrative units could, over time, come to be conceived as fatherlands," Benedict Anderson has written, with particular reference to South America, "one has to look at the ways in which administrative organizations create meaning."[3] Galicia was first invented as an administrative unit in the eighteenth century and only then began to accumulate cultural meanings over the course of its provincial history in the context of the Habsburg empire. Edward Said, writing with particular reference to the English and French overseas empires, has emphasized the importance of "the general relationship between culture and empire," and suggested that imperial ideology was "completely embedded" in culture: "We must try to look . . . integrally at the culture that nurtured the sentiment, rationale, and above all the imagination of empire."[4] For the Habsburg empire, as for England and France, culture was marked by the tensions and pretensions of imperial rule, and culture was the site of those uncertain meanings and overlapping identities that defined provincial Galicia.

For the middle of the nineteenth century, based on the Habsburg census of 1857, the Galician population has been calculated as perfectly balanced between Greek Catholic Ruthenians at 44.83 percent and Roman Catholic Poles at 44.74 percent, with Jews completing the picture at 9.69 percent.[5] This exquisite decimal precision, however, was actually based on religious rather than national identification, and at that midcentury moment the great mass of the Galician peasant population would not have felt subject to the sentiments of modern nationalism. In 1894 the province offered a dramatic representation of itself at the General Provincial Exhibition in Lviv, which was even visited by Franz Joseph. The ethnographic pavilion, with costumed mannequins in full folkloric splendor, created a kaleidoscopic ensemble by which national divisions were dissolved into shifting patterns of color and ornament, dazzling to the eye of the spectator, including the emperor. Habsburg imperial rule in Galicia, as in the other provinces of the monarchy, sought the transcendence of national differences, and the provincial idea of Galicia remained fundamentally non-national.

Scholars of the Habsburg monarchy have sought to understand how national politics and national identities imposed themselves upon a hypothetically non-national society over the course of the nineteenth century. In the case of Galicia the "non-national" was as much an ideological construct as the "national"—alternative perspectives in conceptual tension with one another. In 1835 the greatest Galician writer of the age, the Polish comic dramatist Aleksander Fredro, was publicly denounced for creating "non-national [*nienarodowy*]" literary works. The idea of Galicia suggests the importance of the "non-national" for the construction of provincial identity.

This book stands closely related to previous work of my own. My study *Inventing Eastern Europe* (1994) led me to conclude that Eastern Europe, itself an intellectual artifice of the eighteenth century, was particularly fertile imaginative terrain for the devising of new geopolitical scenarios, such as that of Galicia in 1772. This moved me to consider further the problem of how an imagined or invented entity, like Galicia in the eighteenth century, became geopolitically real, meaningful, and historical in the nineteenth century—before receding again into the domain of fantasy in the twentieth century. My study *Venice and the Slavs* (2001) attempted to explore how the Enlightenment's ideas about Eastern Europe were deployed in an imperial context, on the Adriatic, where the political asymmetry of imperial power between Venice and Dalmatia seemed to align geographically with the emerging sense of continental differentiation. In the case of Galicia I have sought to understand how an ideology of empire, forged in the age of Enlightenment, persisted and developed over the course of the nineteenth century, and how evolving ideological tensions conditioned the end of empire in the twentieth century. In Galicia the imperial values of the Enlightenment took the particular form of Josephinism, named for Emperor Joseph II, with his commitment to revolutionary transformative absolutism, almost messianic in its application to the supposed redemption and "recasting" of Galicia. Most notably, the concept of supposed "civilization" was applied to the entire domain of Eastern Europe and the particular province of Galicia, from the reign of Joseph through the reign of Franz Joseph: Galician barbarism was to be reformed, and Galician backwardness was to be ameliorated. This book thus studies the ideological power and persistence of the Enlightenment's idea of Eastern Europe in modern Habsburg history.

The first chapter considers the accounts of the enlightened Josephine travelers who visited Galicia in the 1780s and very critically evaluated the province; their views were countered by the internal Galician perspective that emerged in 1790 with the so-called Magna Charta of Galicia. The second chapter, focusing on the post-Napoleonic period, juxtaposes the dominant political perspective of Metternich in Vienna with such internal Galician perspectives as the articles in *Gazeta Lwowska* and the comedies of Fredro on stage in Lviv. Chapter Three addresses the self-assumed Galician identity of the writer Sacher-Masoch, cultivated from the memories of his childhood as the son of the Lviv police chief in the 1830s and 1840s. Sacher-Masoch's literary sensibility developed in the context of emerging Ruthenian cultural currents and the folkloric exploration of the province, while his celebrated "masochism" was related to a specifically Galician sense of bondage. Chapter Four focuses on the pivotal and traumatic midpoint in Galician history, the massacre of 1846; the peasant massacre of insurrectionary Polish nobles, committed in Galician allegiance to the Habsburg dynasty, was the defining and unforgettable moment of the province's history ever after.

Chapters Five and Six make use of the Cracow newspaper *Czas* as the representative of a newly synthesized Polish-Galician hegemonic perspective, affirming Habsburg loyalty in exchange for Galician autonomy, beginning in the 1860s, such that the province became a truly meaningful geopolitical unit during the last third of the century. The hegemonic Polish-Galician perspective was, however, challenged by alternative Ruthenian-Galician and Jewish-Galician perspectives on the province, as in the literary work of Ivan Franko and Karl Emil Franzos, including the former's tales of the Boryslav oilfields and the latter's stories from *Halb-Asien*, the Galician Orient. Chapter Seven discusses fin-de-siècle Galicia in relation to broader fin-de-siècle currents inside and outside the Habsburg monarchy, considering especially Wyspiański's drama of 1901, *The Wedding (Wesele)*, as an artistic expression of Galicia's inner conflicts and contradictions at the turn of the century. Chapter Eight considers twentieth-century initiatives that sought to cut through those conflicts, such as the opening of the cabaret the Green Balloon in Cracow in 1905 (also the year of Franko's epic poem about Moses) and the assassination of the governor of Galicia in 1908 (also the year in which Martin Buber began to write about Hasidism). Chapter Nine analyzes how, semantically and ideologically, the province was removed from the map—"liquidated"—with the abolition of the Habsburg monarchy in 1918, while Chapter Ten traces the afterlife of Galicia in memory and fantasy, including the literary works of such Galician writers as Joseph Roth, Bruno Schulz, and Shmuel Yosef Agnon, in German, Polish, and Hebrew literature, respectively. While I have made every effort to consider a full variety of the perspectives on Galicia that emerged and evolved in the eighteenth, nineteenth, and twentieth centuries, the sampling remains inevitably incomplete, as every Galician political figure, public organ, and cultural work had something to say, implicitly or explicitly, about the nature of Galicia itself.

The history of the idea of Galicia is also the intellectual history of historical writing, for history was one of the crucial genres in which the idea and identity of Galicia was cultivated and developed. In 1817, only forty-five years after the invention of Galicia, Joseph Mauss, professor of history at the university in Lviv, was working on a full history of Galicia and trying to establish retrospectively its medieval antecedents; Mauss reported in a letter that he had reached the year 1347.[6] In 1853, the historian Walerian Kalinka published *Galicia and Cracow under Austrian Rule*, and went on to become one of the founding figures of the Cracow historical school. Later historians of the Cracow historical school would also become leading ideologues and statesmen of Galician autonomy—such as Józef Szujski, who published *The Poles and Ruthenians in Galicia* in 1882, and Michał Bobrzyński, who became the viceroy, or *namiestnik*, of Galicia in 1908.[7] Their Ruthenian or Ukrainian contemporaries, such as Stefan Kachala and Mykhailo Hrushevsky, likewise looked to history as a means of articulating the idea of Galicia, the identity of Galician Ruthenians, and their relationship to a larger Ukrainian nation. Historians like Kachala did not hesitate to connect contemporary Galicia to medieval Halych, bridging a gap of centuries in order to affirm the continuously Ruthenian nature of the province.[8] In the early twentieth century, Majer Bałaban in Lviv was publishing histories of the Jews of Galicia, conceived as a distinctive historical subject. These historians all contributed to a discourse of Galicia by writing the history of Galicia and Galicians while the province itself still existed.

For this reason history and historiography in this project have not always been easy to disentangle. I myself first began thinking about the history of Galicia as a student in the 1970s, half a century after the abolition of the province, when the lived experience of Galicia was already a very remote, but still surviving, memory. One pioneering work that made a great impression on me was Jan Kozik's book on the Ukrainian national movement in Galicia, published in Polish in the 1970s and in English in the 1980s. Similarly stimulating, at that time, was the collection on Galicia edited in 1982 by Frank Sysyn and Andrei Markovits.[9] Also in the 1980s, John-Paul Himka began to publish his work on Galicia, resulting in a number of important monographs on Galician politics, society, and religion. In 1983, Paul Robert Magocsi published an invaluable book-length bibliographic guide to Galicia.[10]

There was new interest in Galicia in the 1990s, after the collapse of communism in Poland and the achievement of independence in Ukraine. The important scholarly work of Maria Kłańska on Galicia "in the eyes" of

German-language writers, published in Cracow in 1991, pointed toward a new way of understanding the cultural representation of the province. Two edited collections have featured new angles of scholarship on Galicia: one edited by Antony Polonsky and Israel Bartal in 1999 as a volume of *Polin: Studies in Polish Jewry*, the other edited by Christopher Hann and Paul Robert Magocsi, *Galicia: A Multicultured Land*, in 2005.[11] Young American scholars have recently turned to Galicia with important new works: Keely Stauter-Halsted's book on the nationalization of the peasantry in Galicia (2001), Alison Fleig Frank's book about Galician oil (2005), and Daniel Unowsky's book on Habsburg patriotism, including an analysis of the emperor's official visits to Galicia (2005). In 2006 there appeared Daniel Mendelsohn's compelling family memoir, *The Lost*, about returning to Galicia to discover the story of his grandfather's family, murdered in the Holocaust. In recent years new research on Galicia has been encouraged by the "Borderlands" project at Brown University, directed by Omer Bartov, and in 2007, Bartov published a remarkable travel account of the vanishing traces of Jewish Galicia.[12]

In Rzeszów, since 1994, there have been published a series of volumes under the general title *Galicia and Its Legacy* (*Galicja i jej dziedzictwo*). In Cracow the International Cultural Center, under the direction of Jacek Purchla, has played an important role in the study of Galicia, including the publication of a volume on Cracow and Lviv edited by Purchla in 2003. In Lviv, Yaroslav Hrytsak has trained a new generation of students in the history of Galicia, while himself writing a series of pioneering articles that culminated in the publication of his book on Ivan Franko in 2006. Hrytsak has played a leading role in making the journal *Ukraina Moderna* and the Western-oriented website www.zaxid.net into important forums for Galician research and discussion; likewise significant is the Center for Urban History of East Central Europe, recently founded by Harald Binder in Lviv. At the University of Vienna a special interdisciplinary doctoral program has been established for the study of Galicia. In 2007 historians Andreas Kappeler and Christoph Augustynowicz, both faculty members of the Vienna program, published an edited collection on the Galician border region, while philologist Michael Moser, also a member of that faculty, published a book on the Ruthenian language in Galician primers. In 2007, further new works on Galicia included Hans-Christian Maner's study of Galicia conceived as a Habsburg borderland, and Michael Stanislawski's book, *A Murder in Lemberg*, about tensions and violence within the Galician Jewish community. In 2008, Danuta Sosnowska published a study that explored Ruthenian and Czech perspectives from inside and outside Galicia, and in 2009, Markian Prokopovych published a pioneering work on architecture and public space in Lviv.[13]

Historical reflection still today continues to preserve and revise the cultural meaning of Galicia in its phantom form, almost a century after its geopolitical demise in 1918. In the spirit of politically purposeful nostalgia, the 170th birthday of Emperor Franz Joseph was celebrated in Lviv, Lwów, Lemberg, in 2000, suggesting that Galicia still survived in memory and in fantasy. Indeed, a cultural circle of "Galician autonomists" has self-consciously cultivated that memory in Lviv. In 2001 international controversy surrounded the Galician legacy of Bruno Schulz, when murals that he had painted in his native Galician town of Drohobych, today in Ukraine, were removed to the Yad Vashem Museum in Jerusalem. This book attempts to trace the idea of Galicia from its initially figmentary conception in the eighteenth century to its phantom haunting of contemporary consciousness in the twenty-first. The history of the idea of Galicia may offer some insight into how cultural and ideological meanings have evolved in relation to geopolitical space in Eastern Europe.

In the 1780s the Polish writer Julian Niemcewicz traveled from Poland to the newly created province of Galicia—"not without heartache at seeing such a beautiful region broken off from the Polish kingdom."[14] At that moment Galicia was lamented as a loss to Poland, a territory whose significance lay only in its fractured condition. In the middle of the nineteenth century Sacher-Masoch dedicated a novel to his "countrymen," his fellow Galicians. "Far from the homeland [*Heimat*] I send you this greeting," he wrote. "I greet you all, for it was one land, Galicia, that gave us all birth: Poles, Ruthenians, Germans, and Jews!"[15] Already a long-established Habsburg crownland, Galicia now possessed an emotional significance of its own; the province was no longer just a broken off piece of Poland, but a homeland that transcended nations and religions. In the 1930s, when Joseph Roth was writing about Galicia, it had vanished from the map of Europe and was again evocative of loss and longing, a homeland preserved only in memory. In *The Emperor's Tomb* Roth described the plan for a Viennese expedition to Galicia to visit a particular town. "Gradually this journey became for us a passion, even an obsession," wrote Roth. "We were convinced that we were painting an entirely false portrait of it, yet could not stop picturing this place which none of us knew. In other words we furnished it with all sorts of characteristics which we knew from the start were deliberate creations of our own fantasy."[16] From the 1780s to the 1930s, from heartache, to homeland, to passion and obsession and fantasy, the idea of Galicia has left its mark on the European map and the European mind.

CHAPTER ONE

Inventing Galicia

The Josephine Enlightenment and the
Partitions of Poland

∽

INTRODUCTION: "ALTRI GUAI!"

"Je vais partir pour la Galicie; *altri guai!* [I am going to depart for Galicia; more problems!]" wrote Emperor Joseph II to his brother Leopold, Grand Duke of Tuscany, in July 1773.[1] Joseph had never been to Galicia before, and neither had Leopold—nor indeed had any but a very small number of recent travelers. For Galicia did not exist until 1772, when it was constituted and named as the Habsburg share in the first Polish partition. If there was some sense of occasion in Joseph's French announcement of his imminent departure, it was because Galicia was truly a new world, newly created the year before, invented in the rational spirit of enlightened statecraft. Joseph himself was one of its principal creators, now to become also one of its first discoverers and explorers, and certainly its most grandly distinguished visitor. Yet, the Italian exclamation *altri guai!* suggested something less than perfect imperial solemnity in his anticipation of the voyage, something more like irony or even comedy—opera buffa—in the Habsburg perspective on the newly annexed, newly named, newly invented, and newly problematic province of Galicia.

The province was designated on the map, a specified area of territory, an administrative entity subject to Habsburg authority, but this geopolitical formulation of Galicia offered only an outline of the province that was coming into being. This brand new Galicia posed a cultural challenge to make sense out of, and inject meaning into, its suddenly undeniable geopolitical contours. In the first generation of Galicia's existence from the 1770s to the

1790s, the age of the Polish partitions, the province was defined and established on the map and in the public sphere. Conceived as a figment of the Habsburg imperial imagination, Galicia was made into a plausible provincial entity whose cultural representations confirmed its territorial reality.

The imperial corulers—Joseph and his mother, Maria Theresa—gave the enterprise its initial political impulse, and the Habsburg chancellor, Prince Wenzel Kaunitz, along with the first Habsburg governor of Galicia, Count Johann Anton Pergen, attended closely to the province in pursuit of its ultimate administrative integration within the Austrian state in the 1770s.[2] The 1780s, the decade of Joseph's sole rule, brought to Galicia the Josephine travelers, including Franz Kratter and Alphons Heinrich Traunpaur, taking stock of the province according to the values of the Enlightenment. Their published travel accounts attempted to offer a summation of provincial economy, ethnography, and social structure. Such accounts located Galicia according to the enlightened cultural geography that distinguished Eastern Europe from Western Europe, measuring the gap between social backwardness and presumptive civilization. In 1790, at the death of Joseph and during the course of the French Revolution, political tensions within Galicia reflected contemporary European ideological currents, as local elites, who could be alternatively characterized as Polish or Galician, attempted to affirm provincial political prerogatives.

Finally, with the abolition of the Polish-Lithuanian Commonwealth in 1795 and the western extension of Galicia, the province began to play the part of a forum for preserving Polish culture in the absence of the Polish state. When in 1796 the dramatist Wojciech Bogusławski presented in Lviv his recently created national opera, *Krakowiacy i Górale*, the context of the performance gave the work itself a Galician, as well as Polish, significance. After 1772 the administrative coherence of the province required the designation of a capital: Lwów in Polish, Lemberg in German, Leopolis in Latin, today Lviv in Ukrainian. After 1795, Galicia came to include also the urban center of Cracow: Kraków in Polish, Krakau in German. Between the visit of Joseph in the 1770s and the arrival of Bogusławski in the 1790s, the invention of Galicia was politically consolidated, and the cultural construction of Galician provincial identity was just beginning.

JOSEPH IN GALICIA: "AMONG THE SARMATIANS"

Maria Theresa was uncomfortable with the first partition of Poland, which she clearly recognized as the illegitimate appropriation of territory from its legitimate sovereign. Nevertheless, she had been urgently advised to seize a share of Poland, and thus to preserve the balance of power by matching the aggrandizement of Russia and Prussia. "I do not understand the policy," she recorded, "that allows, in the case when two take advantage of their superiority to oppress an innocent, that the third can and must imitate and commit the same injustice, as a pure precaution for the future and convenience for the present."[3] It certainly did nothing to ease her conscience or pacify her scruples to know that she was acting complicitly with both Catherine and especially her archrival Frederick, while he, in turn, mocked what he perceived as Maria Theresa's hypocrisy, offering the barbed witticism: "The more she weeps, the more she takes." In fact, the Habsburg share of Poland—that is, Galicia—would turn out to be larger than either the Russian or Prussian annexations.

Kaunitz, like Joseph, accepted the logic of the balance of power, and therefore the inevitability of Austrian participation in the partition. In troubled discussion with Kaunitz in 1772, Maria Theresa noted, "The word partition repels me [*Ce mot de partage me répugne*]."[4] It was her imperial repugnance that paved the way for the introduction of the name "Galicia" into the Habsburg calculations concerning Poland. Kaunitz as chancellor had already encouraged research into the historical claims of the medieval Hungarian crown, and now, in 1772, the names of the medieval Rus principalities of Halych and Vladimir were suddenly floated in Habsburg discussions of Poland. The medieval Hungarian crown laid claim to those dominions as early as the twelfth century, while Poland acquired territory in the region only later in the fourteenth century; therefore, Maria Theresa, as queen of Hungary in the eighteenth century, could nominally claim title to the "Kingdom of Galicia and Lodomeria," which could be construed as approximately covering Austria's share in the Polish partition.[5] As Habsburg troops occupied portions of Poland in 1772, Vienna affirmed the "revindication" of the medieval claim and thus evaded the repugnant word "partition," which offended the empress.

Maria Theresa herself did not use the name Galicia in the letter that she wrote to Joseph in 1773, attempting to dissuade him, for the sake of her own maternal "tranquillity," from making "this terrible voyage." She needed Joseph in Vienna beside her, so that they could attend jointly to political affairs: "Here is your place, and not *in den Carpathischen Gebürgen*."[6] Shifting from French into their native German, she thus placed a particular emphasis on the Carpathian Mountains, perhaps to suggest that they were wild and remote. The reference to the mountains also gave a topographic character to the province that Maria Theresa could not yet casually designate as "Galicia."

Joseph summed up the situation for her in a letter from Lviv on 1 August 1773: "I already see in advance [*je vois déjà d'avance*] that the work will be immense here. Besides the confusion of affairs there already reigns here a partisan spirit that is frightful." He was, from the beginning, particularly concerned about the condition of the peasants, who seemed to him to possess "nothing but the human form and physical life."[7] The immense work that he claimed to foresee was, presumably, his own revolutionary engagement in the 1780s on behalf of the enserfed peasants and against the oppressive nobility, in Galicia as elsewhere in the Habsburg monarchy. He would return to Galicia in 1780, in 1783, and in 1786.[8] At the first glance, in 1773 the province already appeared to him in the light of his own Josephine sense of imperial mission, confirmed by his prophetic vision: *je vois déjà d'avance*. Imperial knowledge of the provincial Galician circumstances was produced by the privileged Habsburg gaze. "I try to be quite polite [*assez poli*] toward everyone," he assured his mother, affirming his own detachment.[9]

On the same day, 1 August, Joseph wrote to his brother Leopold in Florence: "Here I am then among the Sarmatians [*Me voilà donc au milieu des Sarmates*]. It is incredible everything that has to be done here; it is a confusion like no other: cabals, intrigues, anarchy, finally even an absurdity of principles."[10] The Sarmatians were, supposedly, ancient inhabitants of the region, whose name had been adopted by the Polish nobility in the seventeenth century as valorous ancestors: Sarmatian style, as reflected in long coats and curved swords, was considered to be distinctively Polish. Yet, for Joseph to declare himself "among the Sarmatians" was an attribution of comical barbarism to the inhabitants of Galicia, denominating them as if they were the natives of some parable by Voltaire: like Candide among the Bulgars and the Avars. Indeed, Joseph's discovery of the characteristic "confusion" of Galicia was entirely consistent with Voltaire's enlightened vision of Eastern Europe. For Voltaire wrote to Catherine, also in 1773, that he hoped she would bring about "the unscrambling of all this chaos in which the earth is plunged, from Danzig to the mouth of the Danube."[11] Such was the supposed chaos of Eastern Europe, and the confusion of Galicia, as discerned by Joseph, fitting within the geographical terrain whose contours Voltaire suggested. The Josephine mission in Galicia would similarly involve the unscrambling of chaos, bringing order out of confusion.

To order the province meant, first of all, constituting the newly appropriated territories as a coherent administrative unit: Galicia. The inaugural program for governing the province involved the appointment of a governor, Pergen, the protégé of Kaunitz. At the end of August 1772, Pergen was still uncertain about the name of the territory he would govern, and actually proposed calling it the Grand Duchy of Lemberg.[12] By October, however, when Pergen presided over the ceremonial Habsburg assumption of power in the province, there was posted in the streets and squares of Lviv the imperial patent on the revindication of the "Kingdom of Galicia and Lodomeria" by the Hungarian crown. Kaunitz had already planned the whole event in Vienna, specifying even the trumpets, the drums, and the cannon salutes. It was Pergen, however, who paraded to the cathedral in Lviv for a solemn Te Deum, after deploying Austrian troops in the city to guarantee that the occasion would be orderly.[13]

Pergen's assignment was the creation of a new administration, displacing the remnants of the former Polish government and establishing a province that could be aligned and integrated with the other Habsburg lands. This fantasy of enlightened statecraft—the perfect displacement of old forms and institutions by new—was encouraged by the ideological implications of the "revindication" of Galicia. Kaunitz proposed that since the Habsburgs were, in fact, reclaiming a Hungarian province, illegitimately obtained by Poland in the Middle Ages, then all intervening Polish developments could be considered null and void.[14] In particular, the extensive privileges and prerogatives of the Polish gentry in local government, along with Polish law and custom, could be simply canceled, producing a tabula rasa—Galicia—which the new Habsburg masters might cover with their own formulas. Pergen, arriving in Lviv in 1772, had to deal with the practical fact that Galicia was neither a blank slate nor a new world, but a thoroughly inhabited territory with persistent social, economic, and political circumstances that could not be simply abolished.

Galicia's territory, taken from the Commonwealth in 1772, combined a large part of what had formerly constituted the Ruthenian voivodship [*województwo ruskie*], centered on Lviv, with a part of Małopolska or Little Poland, whose principal city, Cracow, just barely remained in Poland, right across the border from Galicia. While Małopolska belonged to the Polish state from its beginnings in the late tenth century, Ruthenia was originally affiliated with the medieval domain of Kievan Rus and was annexed to Poland by King Casimir the Great only in the fourteenth century. Thus the population in western Galicia was more heavily Polish and that of eastern Galicia more heavily Ruthenian, though the landowning nobility, or *szlachta*, was generally Polish by language and culture throughout the province. "Polish" and "Ruthenian" should not be understood as modern national terms for describing the population in 1772, especially the enserfed peasantry, but rather as categories of language, or groupings of dialects, that roughly corresponded to the crucial religious and cultural distinction between Roman Catholicism and Uniate

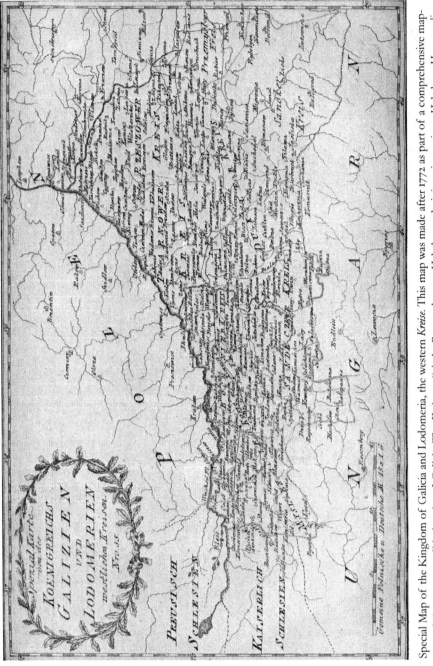

Special Map of the Kingdom of Galicia and Lodomeria, the western *Kreise*. This map was made after 1772 as part of a comprehensive mapping of the new geopolitical entity of Galicia. The *Kreise*, or "circles," were the new Habsburg administrative regions. Habsburg Hungary lies to the south of Galicia, Poland to the north, with Krakau (Cracow) shown still in Poland, just across the Galician border.

or Greek Catholicism. The Jewish population in this region also dated back to the reign of Casimir the Great, and was greatly influenced by the rise of Hasidism in the eighteenth century, as the founding figure of that movement, the Baal Shem Tov, lived in an area that later became part of Galicia.

In May 1773, Pergen set about trying to divide Galicia into administrative "circles [*Kreise*]" and districts, to match the structure of the rest of the Habsburg monarchy. He had some thoughts about trying to make the new units match the ethnographic composition of the province—for instance, creating a circle of Ruthenians—but ultimately he lacked both detailed maps and accurate information. He therefore found himself wrestling with proposals that actually corresponded closely to the older Polish administrative divisions, though such resemblances would permit precisely the sorts of political continuities that the Habsburg government sought to suppress.[15] In 1773, Pergen sought to raise revenues from the Jews of Galicia, and also to reduce their number, by placing a special tax on Jewish marriages. Later in the 1770s the Habsburgs would seek to deal more comprehensively with the social, judicial, and political autonomy that Jews had enjoyed in the Polish Commonwealth. The Habsburg reorganization of the Jews of Galicia in 1776—*Allgemeine Ordnung für die gesamte Judenschaft der Königreiche Galizien und Lodomerien*—involved administrative reform subordinating Galician Jews to a single body of elders, including a single rabbi, *Landesrabin*, directly responsible to the Habsburg government. Joseph would continue to reform the institutions of the Galician Jews in the 1780s, as he pursued a system of administrative absolutism throughout the Habsburg monarchy.[16]

When Joseph came to Galicia in 1773 he was already inclined to be dissatisfied with Pergen for an inadequate commitment to the radical overhaul of Galician society and administration. Joseph prepared for Pergen an agenda of 154 questions about Galicia, and Pergen therefore quickly compiled an account of the province—*Beschreibung der Königreiche Galizien und Lodomerien (Description of the Kingdoms of Galicia and Lodomeria)*—at the moment of its "revindication" by the Habsburgs.[17] This account made it very clear that Galicia was not a void in which the Habsburgs could act with complete disregard for current circumstances. Yet, even in the context of exchanging questions and answers, producing descriptions and information, Joseph would nevertheless, at the first glance of his own imperial eye, conclude that Galicia was at best a domain of confusion. Really, it was what he had expected all along, had known that he would discover from the moment that he set out on his voyage: *altri guai!*

Kratter's Letters: "The New and the Strange"

In 1780, Joseph visited Galicia again, spending three weeks there on his way to meet with Catherine in Russia. His journal account of Lviv was innocuous enough, recording attendance at Mass in various churches and recreational walks in various gardens, which he found "very pretty." A typical journal entry, from 16 May, reported simply: "In the morning I worked until eleven, then heard Mass in the ex-Jesuit church, gave several audiences, ate, gave dictation, and then went strolling with the nobles." Joseph was presumably "polite" with the nobles, as he was in 1773, but in the letter to his mother, dated 19 May from Lviv, he wrote that "up to the present there has been too much indulgence [*complaisance*] toward these great lords"—that is, toward the Polish nobility.[18] The death of Maria Theresa in November 1780, and the beginning of Joseph's sole rule, would mark the end of imperial indulgence, perhaps even politeness, in Galicia.

The death of the empress occurred on 29 November 1780, six months after Joseph's visit to Galicia. Maria Theresa had reigned for forty years, and, even as she was laid to rest in the Kapuzinergruft in Vienna with her Habsburg ancestors, there were also requiems and eulogies in the Lviv cathedral. In one of the eulogies—delivered in Polish in Lviv, but also published in German in Vienna—the Poles were characterized as the youngest children of the Habsburg monarch, since they were brought into the empire most recently: "We are the youngest among the imperial subjects, the smallest in enlightenment and knowledge among all those whom the kindest of rulers governs and leads. We are children who have just reached the age of eight."[19] Thus, the newness of Galicia, invented in 1772, was articulated through the metaphor of childhood in 1780. Joseph, ruling alone after 1780, would confront the tensions of adolescence.

In the Habsburg monarchy the 1780s were a decade of huge upheaval caused by Joseph's campaign for revolutionary enlightened absolutism, later labeled as Josephinism: the encouragement of administrative centralization from Vienna, the imposition of state control over religious life, the concession of religious toleration, the relaxation of censorship, the partial abolition of serfdom, and an assault on noble privileges. Such reforms were revolutionary everywhere in the monarchy, but the recent acquisition of Galicia, and the argument for its "revindication," meant that historic prerogatives had less weight there than in other Habsburg lands; Josephine reform was thus imposed all the more heedlessly, without regard for antecedent forms. Galicia, as an invented entity, could be considered to possess no proper history, and was therefore the perfect target for systematic enlightened transformation. At the same time, the Habsburg government in the Josephine decade continued to seek comprehensive information about Galicia, the official knowledge that facilitated imperial power. Such knowledge also began to find its place within the public sphere of the Enlightenment, as controversy over the emperor's reforms brought Galicia to the attention of German readers inside and outside the Habsburg monarchy. Provocative travel accounts were published in Leipzig and Vienna in 1786 and 1787. This German perspective on Galicia attributed to the province a particular identity and coherence in the context of general notions concerning Eastern Europe in the age of Enlightenment.

Franz Kratter, a young man from Swabia—within the Holy Roman Empire but outside the Habsburg dynastic lands—was living in Vienna in the 1780s, publishing pamphlets in the spirit of Josephine reform, and becoming controversially entangled in the factional disputes of the Viennese freemasons. He spent six months in Galicia in 1784, visiting his brothers who had established themselves selling wine in Lviv. Kratter's *Letters about the Present Situation of Galicia* (*Briefe über den itzigen Zustand von Galizien*) appeared anonymously in two volumes in Leipzig in 1786, and, for the first time, made Galicia into a subject for discussion in the public sphere, beyond the restricted circles and channels of the Habsburg government. Addressing the reader, by way of a preface to the first volume, Kratter remarked that travel accounts "have always been the favorite reading of the German public," because they appeal to "its taste, its inclination for the new and the strange."[20] Galicia was certainly something brand new to the reading public in the 1780s, but Kratter promised even more: not only new, but also strange. The travel accounts that fascinated the public of the eighteenth century were sometimes deeply exotic, as in the accounts of the Pacific islands—such as Tahiti and Hawaii—visited by Captain Cook between 1768 and 1779. Galicia was not nearly so remote from the German reading public, though it was similarly unfamiliar, and Kratter would seek to emphasize, indeed partly to impute, the requisite strangeness.

Kratter promised to present not only the positive aspects of Galicia but also "the bad, the ugly, the abominable [*das Schlechte, Hässliche, Abscheuliche*]." Strangeness would not necessarily take the attractive form of Tahitian exoticism, but rather Galician abomination. Indeed, Kratter anticipated that the bad, the ugly, and the abominable might overwhelm his enlightened public, and he pleaded for indulgence in advance:

> Friends of humanity, noble, gentle, amiable souls, I must beg your pardon if I sometimes offend the delicacy of your sensibility and make your heart bleed with terrible images of inhuman tyranny, with sad depictions of oppressed human misery. You will here become acquainted with completely alien classes of people.[21]

Thus Kratter established the chasm that separated his public of gentle German readers from the alien realm of Galicia. While he wrote in German,
and sometimes asserted a German standard of civilization in judging Galicia,
Kratter's perspective in the 1780s was not nationally German in a modern
sense, but rather included the multiple intimations of being German educated, Josephine enlightened, Habsburg imperial, and European civilized all
at once. His German readers were also his "friends of humanity." Kratter
would later settle in Galicia himself, soon after publishing his book, and he
would play a leading role in the theatrical life of the city, while his dramas,
written in German in Galicia, were also performed all over German-speak-
ing Central Europe. By the end of his life—he died in Lviv in 1830—he
probably considered himself Galician, but in the 1780s Galicia still seemed
altogether alien.

The nobility in Galicia appeared particularly detestable to Kratter, and he
aimed his account at a middle-class public who might be expected to approve
the Josephine assault on noble privilege: "The Galician nobility under the Austrian government naturally had to be given a turn quite opposed to its previous
constitution . . . to bend its unruly anarchic spirit to the yoke of monarchy."
The very notion of a "Galician nobility" was something new, the product of
Austrian rule; for the Habsburgs had annexed the lands of the Polish nobility,
who became Galician at the moment that they lost their Polish political status.
In its previous incarnation as the Polish nobility, this unruly class "robbed the
other part of the nation, made the people into slaves, ruled its subjects with
the lawless absoluteness of despotism, practiced all kinds of crimes and horrors [*Grausamkeiten*]."[22] The Enlightenment saw in Eastern Europe, in Russia
at least as much as in Poland, a pattern of social relations in which enserfed
peasants were virtually slaves.[23] In 1788, Joseph's nephew Franz, the future
emperor, traveled to Galicia at the age of twenty and commented in much the
same spirit as Kratter: "The people and the peasants especially have just begun
to recognize what great kindness they enjoy under our government, as before
they were slaves and now are free men."[24] In Josephine Galicia slavery was
remarked as one of the "horrors" that justified the imposition of Habsburg
power upon the nobility of the province.

The modern idea of "Eastern Europe" was formulated in the Enlightenment, as the eastern lands of the continent came to be seen as constituting
a domain of backwardness, awaiting the improvements of civilization. The
governing of Galicia was, accordingly, conceived as a civilizing project, and
Kratter cited "the barbarous wildness of the Polish nobility." The Polish
noble, before coming under Habsburg rule, was "the most inhuman, abominable wild thing [*Wildling*]" and was "remote from every mannered society,

from his youth destined for unlimited command, through coarse, wild and horrible actions hardened to the point of tigerish insensitivity." The mannered society of the civilized world, the world of the German reading public, was placed in clear opposition to the wild, coarse, and even bestial world of the tigerlike Polish noble in Galicia. Such wild things were, even as Kratter wrote, being transformed, civilized, melted down and "recast [*umgeschmolzen*]" as Habsburg Galician subjects.[25]

The Polish nobles, in Kratter's account, appeared as particularly barbarous in their conduct toward their serfs. There was, for instance, a certain Count M—known as "the wild" or "the horrible"—who whipped his peasants to death over trivialities. There was another Prince L. who arbitrated a dispute between a Jew and a nobleman in the following fashion:

> PRINCE: Hey, captain. [He comes.] Hang the Jew up in the next room.
> CAPTAIN: Right away. [He seizes the Jew and drags him away.]
> PRINCE: Servant, hey! Bring us some of my best Tokay! Sit down, nobleman, drink with me! [They drink. Soon after.]
> CAPTAIN: The Jew is hanging already!
> PRINCE: Bravo![26]

Kratter, who would compose literary dramas later in life, crafted this instance of barbarism into a playlet, exercising his dramatic imagination.

Further violent vignettes concerned the P. family (probably Potocki), who "murdered just to pass the time." Kratter reported that one member of the family sent a peasant up into a tree to clear away an owl's nest, then shot the man out of the tree, and laughed. There was also an account of a former bishop of Lviv, who supposedly ordered his serfs to be tortured and burned to death. "If a good painter were able to make use of this scene," commented Kratter, "he would have achieved a masterpiece of a laughing devil." Kratter himself was exercising his artistic liberty as he conjured the demonic figure of the bishop to dramatize the former "horrors" of Galicia. "By such despots was Galicia ruled when it came under Austrian rule," he observed.[27] In 1786 there was also published in Przemyśl an anonymous Polish work, *Geographia*, which offered an "exact description of the Kingdom of Galicia and Lodomeria" but denied the legitimacy of that geopolitical entity in the name of the Polish nobility.[28] Kratter's work, denouncing the Polish nobility, served the political purpose of Habsburg vindication. Maria Theresa had cherished the pretense to traditional legitimacy that derived from the medieval Hungarian claim to Halych and Vladimir. In the age of Joseph, in the 1780s, it was possible to articulate a more modern claim to legitimacy before the public, emphasizing the displacement of barbaric cruelty by enlightened government.

"Horror and Loathing"

Just as Joseph sought to restrict noble prerogatives throughout the Habsburg monarchy, he was simultaneously committed to striking down the privileges of the church, which he especially sought to subordinate to the state. Kratter's hostility to abominable bishops in Galicia was just as consistent with the spirit of Josephinism as his hatred of the nobility. Joseph was particularly committed to the suppression of monastic orders, and Kratter was passionately outraged against the monks of Galicia. For one thing, they were complicit in the sins of the nobles inasmuch as a monk could absolve a nobleman for all of his "unnatural, thieving, and murderous deeds." The absolved sinner would then reward the church with his financial patronage:

> That is why in Galicia there are so many churches, monasteries, and foundations with the most ridiculous purposes, and—I do not speak without basis—that is the origin of most monasteries, in this most devilish and blasphemous dealing in sins. That is why churches and monasteries are made into whorehouses and houses of public shame for the high nobility! That is why laymen and priests remain silent when a lustful, debauched monster, in church, has a penitent praying innocent removed from the foot of the altar, and amidst the most mysterious observance of Christian worship, surrounded by his followers, violates her in the clear sight of the people! My heart is outraged! My blood is in ferment, my soul filled with horror and loathing, and at this moment my conception of humanity and the church is lowered far beyond all ugliness.[29]

While such writing crudely served the political purpose of justifying Josephine measures against the clergy, Kratter's extravagant treatment of the subject went beyond the conventions of polemical engagement to achieve a blasphemously pornographic representation not altogether unlike the contemporary literary effusions of the Marquis de Sade. Kratter actually wrote himself into a passionate frenzy, describing his own clinical symptoms of heart and blood in a manner presumably intended to be infectiously communicated to susceptible readers. Moral outrage mingled with pornographic arousal, intended not just to instill enlightened anticlericalism but also to provoke an intensely emotional and even physiological response to Galicia.

Kratter roused himself to further vehemence in discussing the hygiene of the clergy and the cleanliness of the monasteries: "In German monasteries the pigsties are customarily cleaner than the kitchens and refectories here."[30] The "civilizing process" that Norbert Elias has described as the history of manners in early modern Europe provided a standard for measuring the gap between civilized refinement and barbarous uncouthness. Elias cites Erasmus from the sixteenth century on the propriety of blowing one's nose with a handkerchief instead of one's hand, and he cites La Salle from the eighteenth century, in *Les Règles de la bienséance*: "It is vile to wipe your nose with your bare hand, or to blow it on your sleeve or your clothes. It is very contrary to decency to blow your nose with two fingers and then to throw the filth onto the ground and wipe your fingers on your clothes."[31] In this cultural context of increasingly self-conscious propriety, Kratter reflected on the priests of Galicia:

> During the mass some blow their noses in their vestments, some in their hands, and fling the snot several paces away. One must be careful, standing near the altar, if one doesn't want to get a dose of priestly filth on one's clothing or in one's face. I have seen with my own eyes a priest at communion blow his nose right into his hand, and with the same shining filthy fingers he used to throw away the snot, he breaks the host, and sticks it in his mouth with holy appetite.[32]

This graphic account, intended to provoke the visceral disgust of the gentle reader and outrage his delicate sensibilities, revealed the particular twist of Kratter's anticlericalism in Galicia. He had put his finger, so to speak, on the civilizing pulse of the enlightened German public, invoking hygienic outrage as the motive for imperial presence. The issue of civilization was fundamental for enlightened perspectives on Eastern Europe, and Kratter's seemingly bizarre emphasis on snot in the churches of Galicia was only a frank expression of the crucial connection between manners and civilization.

Josephine assertion of state control over religion was generally experienced as a blow by the Roman Catholic Church in Galicia, but the Uniate Church, or the Greek Catholic Church as it came to be called by the Habsburgs, actually benefited in important respects from Habsburg rule. Based on the Union of Brest of 1596, preserving Orthodox ritual and Slavonic liturgy while recognizing the hierarchical authority of the pope, the Uniate Church of the Ruthenian population in the Polish Commonwealth had always suffered from the superior and favored position of Roman Catholicism. Both Maria Theresa and Joseph were far more balanced in their respective treatment of the two rites, and the creation of state seminaries, for instance, while instituting state control, were nevertheless experienced as highly beneficial to the Uniate Church.

Kratter too was even-handed in his anticlerical perspective toward both rites, though the Uniate parish clergy garnered some sympathy alongside his automatic contempt. Uniate parish priests often had to work the land, like peasants:

> It is not unusual in the country to see the priest in a ragged coat, the priestly collar around his neck, the tobacco pipe in his mouth, the whip in hand, waddling beside his horses or oxen. Most of them drink alcohol like water, are drunk almost every day, and then carry on all the filthy offenses characteristic of drunkards. I was very eager to get to know personally such a beast in priest's clothing.[33]

Kratter regarded this Galician ecclesiastical life with distaste, condescension, and perhaps some sense of incongruous comedy, declaring his journalistic intention of making the acquaintance of a typical specimen. Having obtained the desired interview, Kratter reported that the priest lived in a shabby room, wore dirty clothes, and was hopelessly ignorant: "I tried to turn the conversation to various subjects, to religion, morality, pastoral care, instruction, enlightenment, new regulations. He never understood me."[34] According to the presumed asymmetry of civilization, Kratter claimed to understand and explain Galicia, but insisted that Galicia could not understand him.

Joseph applied himself to clerical education among the Uniates with the opening of the General Seminary and the Ruthenian Institute in Lviv in the 1780s. Kratter regarded such institutions as fundamental for the civilizing of Galicia:

> Will the philosopher, the friend of humanity, ever be able to forgive the law for having abandoned the pitiable people during fourteen long, ruinous years of rapacity by these foxes, bears, and wolves, without once contemplating seriously the effective means of a salutary reform, until finally the wise Joseph promised the country better prospects for religion and the clergy through two educational institutions for the formation of the future teachers of the people in Lemberg?[35]

The fictional landscape of Eastern Europe in the 1780s, as in the popular novels about Baron Munchausen, often conveyed the savagery of the terrain through the presence of wild animals such as wolves and bears. For Kratter in Galicia, the human inhabitants appeared as predatory beasts, in this case members of the clergy, awaiting their domestication at the hands of the Habsburg emperor. The fourteen years between the creation of Galicia in 1772 and its literary representation by Kratter in 1786 seemed to him an epoch of mere anticipation, culminating not only in Joseph's reforms but also in the active engagement of the German public, his own philosophical readers.

Although Kratter was equally hostile to Roman Catholicism, the Uniate Church, with its preservation of Orthodox ritual, seemed even more alien. He was shocked to see a Uniate priest prostrate himself before the image of St. Nicholas: "He threw himself down, like a slave before his despot, and then looked at me with a very meaningful glance because I did not want to throw myself to the floor along with him before the great Nicholas."[36] In general, Kratter responded with ironic contempt to the elaborate, and to his mind excessive, ceremonial of the Uniate rite, and this was, in fact, precisely the moment when Josephine reform was seeking to simplify and streamline the ceremonial complications of Roman Catholicism. In this sense, the Josephine religious climate inevitably conditioned Kratter's dismissive perspective on Uniate ritual. He went so far as to describe that ritual as "low comic burlesque [*niedrigkomische Purleskerei*]," and was himself able to make it into comedy by the tone of his description. On one occasion in Lviv he went to Vespers and saw the Uniate bishop presiding over the ritual kissing of holy relics and sacred images:

> They lined up with their wares [*Kram*], and the rest of the clergy came in procession, and kissed what was to be kissed. Then came the people in a great mass, to kiss what was to be kissed. In the whole church I was the only outcast [*Verworfene*] who, from I know not what sort of unpardonable chilling of zeal, did not want to be kissing.[37]

The declaration of his own cool detachment, standing outside the comic circle of ritual kissing, clearly defined Kratter's sense of perspective on the strangeness of Galicia.

"THE PROMISED LAND"

Religiously stranger still were the Jews of Galicia, and Kratter was well aware of their very significant numbers in the population of the province, around 10 percent. Yet Kratter took little interest in the religious rituals of Galician Jews, while focusing considerable attention on their administrative and economic status. His ambivalence toward the Jews included a certain element of outspoken hostility on account of their economic relations with the nobles, from whom Jews leased various economic prerogatives. "Their leases extend to everything, whatever may be leased, Christian or non-Christian, Jewish or non-Jewish, holy or unholy," noted Kratter.[38] He particularly deplored the common Jewish leasing of the right to produce and sell alcoholic drinks on a noble estate or in a noble-owned town. Such a prerogative—called *propinacja*—placed the Jews of Galicia in a pernicious relation to the peasantry, according to Kratter, who described a market day in Galicia with peasants collapsing from drunkenness in the streets. He described a wedding at which everyone, including the bride and bridegroom, was drunk in church: "I can not easily think of a scene in which the dignity of humanity would be more debased." Peasant drinking, however, took place at the Jewish inn, and Kratter described Jewish innkeepers luring, indulging, and cheating their drinking customers, even giving drinks to children to induce the alcoholic habit. He also noted the role of Jewish pimps in Lemberg, and detailed the variety of their female offerings that reflected the variety of Galicia itself: Christians and Jews, Poles and Ruthenians.[39]

In 1785, Joseph sought to transform the economic situation of the Jews by restricting the possibility of obtaining leases from nobles—for instance, leases for operating mills or inns.[40] Previously, Jews had been made to pay extortionate fees to the nobles for the leases, and then had to try to make the leases profitable at the expense of the local population. The Jewish position in this system was always vulnerable and often desperate. The Jew in the playlet who was hung up in the next room by order of Prince L. was, in fact, holding one of the prince's leases. Kratter noted with general sympathy the poverty and misery of most Jews in Galicia.[41]

For Kratter the Josephine moment promised nothing less than the messianic transformation of the misfortunes of Jewish history.

> All Galicia wishes now to be placed in different relations with the Jews, with the depravation of the whole land. These general wishes have reached all the way up to the ears of the government, which now is ready to recast [*umzuschmelzen*] the whole Jewish system, because, after all, there is no Moses willing to take pity on his fellow Hebrews, free them from the yoke of despotism, and lead them into a promised land.[42]

Kratter implicitly spoke in the name of a nascent Galician public opinion: "All Galicia wishes [*Ganz Galizien wünscht*]." The Habsburg government supposedly responded to that Galician public and offered a "recasting [*Umschmelzung*]" of relations between Christians and Jews, just as it also sought a "recasting" of relations between nobles and peasants. The metallurgical metaphor suggested that what was being forged was nothing less than Galicia itself. Joseph would liberate the Jews from the Egyptian despotism of Polish noble domination, and offer them a promised land on the same terrain where they had lived for centuries, now socially and politically transformed: Habsburg Galicia.

Joseph's restriction of Jewish leases in 1785 was fundamental to this recasting, but the new regulation, Kratter recognized, would also be economically traumatic. He estimated that it would destroy the livelihood of thousands of families.

> That is now the decree that should offer a foretaste of the complete recasting of the Jewish system, which everyone looks to with fearful, anticipatory longing, but at the same time everyone, Jew and non-Jew, is put into panicking terror, because this appears in a quite different form from what one could ever have expected! The unfortunate Jews have been now, for centuries—God knows!—through some kind of curse of nature and heaven, placed in a relation with the rest of humanity, such that every private citizen, every society, every class, every nation, even the state itself, permits inhumanity toward the Jews, without self-reproach. People have thus abused a whole fraternal class of humanity [*ein ganzes, mitverbrüdertes Menschengeschlecht*].[43]

There was indeed a visionary tinge to Kratter's Josephine perspective. Although Jews might have been persecuted for centuries, and all over the world,

Galicia was to become the experimental domain for completely recasting relations between Christians and Jews. In all the Habsburg monarchy there was no more fitting province for such a program, inasmuch as there was nowhere else such a numerous population of Jews.

"What barbaric mistreatment!" Kratter commented, concerning the persecution of Jews. "Does the state owe any less to the Jew than to the Christian? The sun rises over one as it does over the other!" To remedy the barbarism of anti-Semitism thus became a part of Kratter's civilizing perspective on Galicia. His enlightened sentiments would find fulfillment in Joseph's decrees of toleration. While the edict of toleration of 1781 already prevailed for different Christian denominations, and lifted some restrictions on Jews, another decree of 1789 would give freedom of worship to the Jews of Galicia and the promise of equal treatment under the law: "in accordance with which the Jews are to be guaranteed the privileges and rights of other subjects."[44]

In principle, Joseph thus favored something very much like the emancipation of the Jews in the Habsburg monarchy, though this commitment was undermined by the imposition of special taxes for Jews, most notably the tax on kosher meat introduced in Galicia in 1784. In fact, Kratter himself, for a while, held a position in the administration of the kosher meat tax. The restriction on Jewish leases in 1785, while perhaps intended to remove the Jews from their awkward intermediary role in the feudal economy, had the immediate effect of causing economic dislocation and impoverishment. In 1787 the government sponsored an enlightened system of German schools for Jews in Galicia, organized by Herz Homberg, the Jewish reformer from Bohemia, but his proposals met with notable resistance from the rabbinical authorities in Galicia. Furthermore, in 1787, Joseph required the Jews of Galicia to take family names, usually German names, rather than the traditional patronymic designations.[45]

Most controversially, Joseph established the military conscription of Jewish subjects in 1788, against the advice of his own war council, and causing massive consternation to the traditional Jews of Galicia. Historian Michael Silber notes that Joseph, overriding pragmatic concerns about Sabbath observance and dietary restrictions, took his stand on principle: "The Jew as a man and as a fellow-citizen [*Mitbürger*] will perform the same service that everyone else is obliged to do. . . . He will be free to eat what he will, and will be required to work only on that which is necessary during the Sabbath, much the same as Christians are obligated to perform on Sundays." The freedom of worship affirmed in 1789 thus came at considerable social cost to traditional Jews in Galicia. By the end of Joseph's reign the Galician Jews were already profoundly polarized between, on the one hand, the enlightened principles of the Habsburg government and the Jewish reformers, and, on the other, the customary inclinations of Jewish religion and society, especially as endorsed by the increasingly influential force of Galician Hasidism. Historian Raphael Mahler has noted that for most Galician Jews—as for many Galician Christians—the enlightened Josephine reforms were experienced as something like persecution.[46]

Kratter, however, following Josephine principles, envisioned a process of imminent social assimilation: "In a few years the Jew will be no longer a Jew, as he would have to be according to the prescriptions of his religion; he would be a farmer, a citizen of the state, happy, social, and indispensable to humanity." Balthasar Hacquet, the scientific traveler from Brittany who became a professor in Lviv in the 1780s, considered what Galician Jews would have to give up—their distinctive clothing, their beards, the Hebrew language, the Saturday Sabbath—"so that people will not see any difference between Jew and Christian." The rhetoric of Josephinism ultimately imagined Galicia as the domain of religious and even ethnographic effacement, where Poles would cease to be Poles, and Jews would cease to be Jews. Kratter heralded the eventual liberation of the Jews from their condition as "the most unfortunate, most deplorable, most helpless class of men," and their recasting as "brothers of their fellow men" and "patriots in the bosom of the fatherland."[47] Such was the truly revolutionary Josephine fantasy of social transformation in Galicia.

Kratter affirmed that, under Habsburg rule, the city of Lviv was on the way to becoming "one of the most beautiful and excellent cities of the imperial-royal hereditary lands."[48] Before the advent of Austrian rule, he insisted, there was no public sanitation in Lviv: "All kinds of filth [*Unrath*] were poured out onto the street. In rainy weather the morass was so deep that one could sink in up to the waist. . . . The emperor, when he came to Lemberg for the first time, became stuck in the middle of the city with six horses."[49] The image of the emperor himself, bogged down in an excremental morass, may have been an exaggerated or even apocryphal memory, an urban legend. To be sure, the tale offers vivid context to Joseph's casual comment in his letter from Lemberg in 1773: "Here I am then among the Sarmatians. It is incredible everything that has to be done here." The Herculean Habsburg task before him was nothing less than the cleaning of the Augean Galician mess.

When Kratter gave his account of education in Galicia, he called for schools in which students would "unlearn forever the shameful vices of the Polish nation, that undermine propriety, health, and wealth." He hoped that some education in the German language would make the people of

Galicia "more familiar with our way of life and customs," so that the next generation would be "less coarse, less given to drink and idleness." Kratter summed up the project as nothing less than "the universal reformation of this people," a reformation in which a new Galician character would emerge from the encounter between Polish vices and German customs.[50] Although Lviv might be distressing with its urban problems of poverty and sewage, Kratter found that when he ascended the castle hill and looked away from the city, Galicia looked like the Garden of Eden: "Everything that a valley, an Eden, could have of beauty appears here in its greatness, its nature, its embellishment: blessed cornfields, rich and colorful meadows, ponds, woods, distant wilds, deceptive perspectives, unmeasurable prospects!" Kratter, after working himself up to a literary ecstasy, then enacted his own crushing disillusionment at the thought of "what a miserable, degenerate, wild people live in this country of nature and beauty."[51] The deceptive perspectives and unmeasurable prospects served as the perfect metaphors for the Habsburg project in Galicia, the universal reformation in the making. The people would have to be recast to fit the landscape.

In fact, the recasting of the population also involved an influx of German immigrants, encouraged by the government with a policy of exemption from taxation. An initial measure to attract foreigners in 1774 was made even more attractive in 1781, when Joseph, now ruling alone, was able to promise religious toleration for Protestants, in addition to ten years of tax relief and exemption from military service. By 1786, when Franz Kratter published his book, some three thousand German families had settled in Galicia.[52] He was well aware of this, since that number included his own family—that is, his two Swabian brothers with their successful wine business in Lviv. Ignaz Kratter came to Galicia soon after the Austrian annexation, opened an inn, and imported Hungarian and Austrian wines; he was joined in Lviv by his brother Johann. The author Franz Kratter decided to speak through his brother Johann in expressing the enthusiasm of a German in Galicia. "God showed Moses the promised land only from a distance," Johann supposedly declared, "but He led me all the way in." Habsburg Galicia was thus conceived as a promised land, not only for the Jews of the province but also for German settlers from beyond the provincial borders. Kratter described his brother Johann lifting a glass of wine to the health of the monarch he loved "to the point of fanaticism [*bis zur Schwärmerei*]," the monarch who had made Galicia into the Habsburg promised land: "*Vivat!* Long live the emperor."[53] In fact, Joseph visited Galicia again in 1786, the same year that Kratter published his account, and could have been saluted in person.

According to the *Wiener Zeitung*, Joseph in Lviv visited hospitals, convents, and seminaries, Roman Catholic and Uniate, and attended a ball in his honor. Polish nobles from the grandest families—Czartoryski, Potocki, Lubomirski—came to town to pay their respects to Joseph, and probably offered the appropriate toasts, though, in general, the nobility had less reason than the Kratter family to wish the emperor long life.[54] Actually, Joseph did not have long to live, just another four years, but Galicia itself, which he had revindicated, invented, and recast, would live on into the twentieth century.

When Kratter critically considered his own letters concerning Galicia, he conceded that some ideas might seem to be "the innocent dreams of a pleasantly occupied fantasy." Yet, dreaming and fantasy had their place in any consideration of Galicia. The province had to be imaginatively envisioned in the future; its creation was a work in progress. "The whole is near its recasting," he intimated, apocalyptically: *Das Ganze is seiner Umschmelzung nahe.* Yet, however near the recasting might appear, it would be always just out of reach, unattainable, eluding the best efforts of Habsburg reform. Kratter declared himself not altogether satisfied with his own writing about Galicia, inasmuch as he could not always bring all the aspects of the province "into proper order [*in gehöriger Ordnung*]."[55] It was an inevitable failing, for the very essence of Galicia, as he conveyed it, lay in its disorder; his unruly literary fantasy, following the emotional logic of Sturm und Drang, would never have submitted to the discipline of proper orderliness. Indeed, the ideological vindication of enlightened Habsburg rule in Galicia lay precisely in the literary evocation of disorderly confusion. Kratter reached out to the German public and conjured an image of Galicia to seduce his readers into dreaming, along with him, the dream of Habsburg universal reformation.

Robinson Crusoe in Galicia

Kratter's publication in 1786 immediately provoked another work in response in 1787, establishing the spirit of controversy, debate, and ongoing discussion concerning Galicia that generally characterized the nascent public sphere of the eighteenth century. Criticism, according to Jürgen Habermas, was the hallmark of the public sphere, and Kratter himself was inevitably criticized in the next publication concerning Galicia, even in the phrasing of the title: *Dreissig Briefe über Galizien: oder Beobachtungen eines unpartheyischen Mannes, der sich mehr als nur ein paar Monate in diesem Königreiche umgesehen hat* (*Thirty Letters about Galicia: Or the observations of a non-partisan man who has looked around this kingdom for more than just a few months*).[56] The work was published anonymously in German in 1787, in Vienna and Leipzig, and the author was Alphons Heinrich Traunpaur, Chevalier d'Ophanie, born in Habsburg Brussels. As an officer in the Habsburg army, he had been living in Galicia for eight whole years, which, he insisted, gave him greater credibility than Kratter with his visit of only several months.

While claiming greater authority based on longer experience in Galicia, Traunpaur also accused Kratter of producing an inaccurate account: "empty conjectures, superficial remarks, fictitious stories, offensive anecdotes, unconvincing proposals." Furthermore, the ultimate intention behind Kratter's dubious observations was, in Traunpaur's opinion, the disparagement of Galicia. "It is absurd to deny all worth to a whole vast land, capable in its situation of all culture, just because it has not come as far along as its neighbors," commented Traunpaur.[57] He thus fully accepted the Josephine logic of backwardness and development in Galicia.

Traunpaur's declaration of nonpartisanship in the title of his book was meant to suggest that Kratter was motivated by personal bias, that he was, in particular, nationally partisan in his hostility to the Poles. Traunpaur promised the public that he himself recognized "only two nations—good people and bad people."[58] He presented a "history of the land," affirming the "old claims" of the Habsburgs to Galicia: "The lands that came to Austria in the partition are those that now constitute a distinctive kingdom under the name of Galicia and Lodomeria." Traunpaur was aware of the element of artifice involved in staking a claim to the province—"under the name of Galicia," a convenient denomination. He clearly recognized the imperial dynamics of power when he suggested another name: "a new Peru." For thus it appeared to the treasure-seeking carpet-baggers who came to Galicia after 1772 "from every corner of the imperial lands."[59] Despite the pretensions to legitimate reacquisition, Galicia looked like some sort of colonial new world, a promised land that advertised the promise of opportune self-enrichment.

Although Traunpaur claimed to offer a more sympathetic portrait of Galicia than that of Kratter, the spirit of Josephinism shaped both accounts. Traunpaur was critical of the monastic clergy, citing the monks' pagan worship of Venus and Bacchus. Though he affirmed that noble manners were "polite, generous, and obliging," he could not resist including sensational instances of aristocratic vice and violence: incest, the violation of peasant virgins according to the *jus primae noctis*, and the case of a certain noble who made a Jew climb a tree, made him sing out "cuckoo," and then shot him dead, just for fun.[60] Traunpaur had clearly learned from Kratter what sort of tales of barbarism in Galicia would hold the attention of the German public.

At the heart of Traunpaur's book he inserted a travelogue of Galicia that

had been supposedly composed by another officer, Italian by origin, in the
Habsburg army. The unnamed Italian traveled around the province and narrated several Galician encounters fraught with allegorical significance. He
set out one day for a stroll without his uniform, so that he would be taken
for "what I really am—for a human being," rather than a Habsburg officer.
With some pretension he declared himself "a second Robinson"—that is,
Robinson Crusoe reduced to his most basic human qualities, cast up on an
unknown island far from civilization—in Galicia. Robinson, however, was
not alone on the island: "Suddenly I became aware that thirty paces in front
of me there was something black stretched out on the ground. I came closer,
and found that it was a Jew, who had fallen into a deep sleep, and beside
him lay an open book." When the Jew awakened, the Habsburg Robinson
engaged him in conversation and learned that he was a local rabbi. The conversation eventually came around to politics:

> ME: What do you say about the Emperor Joseph II?
> RABBI: Ach! Sir, do you love him?
> ME: Infinitely!
> RABBI: And I adore him as much as you love him. He has been chosen by Provi-
>   dence and has been loaned to the world.
> ME: How do you like the nation among whom you live?
> RABBI: I recognize only two nations in the world: good people and bad people.
> ME: Do you sincerely believe in the coming of the Messiah?
> RABBI: My duty obliges me to believe.[61]

This conversation was essential to the officer's travelogue of Galicia, touching upon issues that were profoundly related to contemporary conceptions
of the province: devout faith in the transformative powers of the Habsburg
emperor, enlightened philosophical interest in transcending distinctions of
nation, and messianic intimations of the dawning of a new epoch. Robinson
and the rabbi went on to speak about Moses Mendelssohn, the enlightened
Jewish philosopher who had died in Berlin the previous year, 1786, and about
the German dramatist Gotthold Ephraim Lessing, who had celebrated Mendelssohn in *Nathan the Wise* on the eighteenth-century stage. In fact, Traunpaur, operating through the Habsburg Robinson, presented the Galician
rabbi as just such a dramatic figure, the Galician incarnation of Lessing's
Nathan the Wise.

"How were the Jews treated before the partition of Poland?" asked Robinson. "We always suffered blows," replied the rabbi, and described scenarios in
which Jews were whipped and beaten in order to extort money from them.

> ME: These atrocities have vanished.
> RABBI: Our posterity will bless those who have made them vanish.[62]

Galizischer Jude, Galician Jew, from Julius Jandaurek, *Das Königreich Galizien und Lodomerien* (Vienna: Karl Graeser, 1884).

The dialogue sharply drew the line between old Poland and new Galicia, old atrocities and new beneficence. The Jews of Galicia, the rabbi implied with some aptness for prophecy, would bless the Habsburgs in future generations.

The Italian officer was looking forward to an enduring and edifying friendship with the rabbi, and went to visit him at home the very next day. The rabbi, however, had suddenly died, and the officer could only commiserate with the widow: "I could not restrain myself from mixing my tears with hers, thus honoring the memory of this rational and righteous Israelite."[63] Just as the Jew had saluted Joseph II as the messianic redeemer of Galicia, so now the rabbi himself appeared as precisely the sort of redemptive figure whose enlightened wisdom promised a hopeful future for the province. Travelogue became allegory, because Galicia was not merely topographical terrain, but the philosophical domain of enlightened fantasy.

Kratter's sweepingly negative presentation of "the barbarous wildness of the Polish nobility" was countered in Traunpaur by the conjuring of a virtuous nobleman. It was again the Italian officer who discovered the model specimen, by the name of Wikofski, living in the vicinity of Rzeszów.

> He does honor to his fatherland, Galicia, and combines intelligent humor with true manly beauty and the noblest way of thinking. His company is pleasant, and in his house there prevails order and unrestricted hospitality. Nothing is comparable to the harmony in which he lives with his charming wife, born Miretzka. If all Poles resembled this rare pair I would wish to live among them always.[64]

Such emphasis on a pair of virtuous nobles served to suggest that the rest of the nobility was in no way comparable; yet a single specimen held out hope for the future redemption of the entire caste. Most striking was the specification of the noble's fatherland: Galicia. The reader could infer that part of this nobleman's virtue was his sentimental forsaking of Poland, his former fatherland, in favor of a new Habsburg political affiliation.

Having encountered a virtuous Jew and a virtuous nobleman, the Habsburg Robinson made one more astonishing discovery on his desert island: the *Encyclopédie* of Diderot and d'Alembert, the literary totem of the Enlightenment. It was clearly the last thing that the traveler expected to find in Galicia, and the last thing that the German public would expect a traveler to find. Yet, there it was, in someone's provincial library. "I made a deep obeisance before it," declared the Italian officer, outlandishly. The presence of the encyclopedia, along with the specimens of righteous Judaism and honorable nobility, all testified allegorically to the promise of the Enlightenment for Galicia. Reverence for the enlightened Habsburg emperor Joseph II was accompanied by obeisances toward the literary texts of the Enlightenment, and the rabbi himself actually seemed to have stepped out of such a text—namely, Lessing's *Nathan the Wise*. Galicia, invented under the aegis of the Enlightenment, was envisioned as the redemptive domain of enlightened transformation.

THE "MAGNA CHARTA" OF GALICIA

In February 1790, Joseph II died, just fifty years old; he was succeeded by his brother, Leopold II. At the time of Joseph's death, after a decade of sole rule, there was widespread discontent with his reforms throughout the monarchy, and serious resistance in Hungary and the Austrian Netherlands. Resistance took the form of the defense of traditional noble privileges and provincial political prerogatives against the revolutionary absolutism of the emperor. Therefore, with Leopold's succession in 1790, the nobles of Galicia took the opportunity to formulate a defense of their traditional Galician prerogatives, though Galicia itself had no provincial tradition that antedated 1772. The ensuing controversy emerged in the published form of a volume entitled *Magna Charta von Galizien: oder Untersuchung der Beschwerden des Galizischen Adels pohlnischer Nation über die österreichische Regierung* (*The Magna Charta of Galicia: Or Examination of the Grievances of the Galician Nobility of the Polish Nation about the Austrian Government*). The "Magna Charta" referred to a Galician charter of political rights presented to Emperor Leopold. The "examination" undertaken in the volume, however, was a fierce Josephine rebuttal of the charter and its political presumptions. This anonymously published volume, though it purported to have appeared in Jassy in Moldavia, was probably produced in Lviv, and certainly circulated in the Habsburg monarchy and the Holy Roman Empire, conceived especially for a German public. It included three items: first, the Galician grievances as presented in the form of the charter addressed to Leopold (the so-called Magna Charta), written in French; second, the German translation of a Polish work that elaborated upon those grievances, *Uwagi nad rządem Galicyjskim* (*Considerations on the Galician Government*); and third, a German rebuttal of the Galician grievances.[65]

The "Magna Charta" claimed to speak for the collective Galician nobility, and its principal author was probably the Polish scholar and bibliophile Józef Maksymilian Ossoliński, the future founder of the Ossolineum Library in Lviv. He had family estates in Galicia, but in the 1790s he settled in Vienna to be closer to the court library. Ossoliński developed personal connections at the Habsburg court, while representing Polish noble interests in Galicia. Already in 1789, when Joseph was ailing, Ossoliński wrote to Kaunitz to protest against the Josephine limitations on feudal labor, the "urbarium" reform, which "far from advancing the prosperity of Galicia according to the wish of our gracious monarch is apt to plunge it into an abyss of irreparable evils." In 1790 it seems to have been Ossoliński who drafted the multiple points of the "Magna Charta" for presentation to Leopold, and he was probably also the main author of the anonymous *Considerations on the Galician Government*, which explained and endorsed the grievances of the "Magna Charta."[66]

The anonymous author of the rebuttal to the "Magna Charta," and the

figure behind the publication of the whole volume, was Ernst Traugott von
Kortum. Born in Silesia, educated in the spirit of the German Enlightenment
with a particular interest in the philosophy of Immanuel Kant, Kortum first
served the Polish king Stanisław August in Warsaw in the 1770s and then
moved to Lviv in 1783 to enter the administrative service of Joseph II in Galicia.[67] Kortum's volume explored the tensions between the Galician nobles and
the Habsburg monarchy at a moment of profound disappointment for enlightened Josephinism, inasmuch as the emperor's death became the occasion
for moderating and withdrawing some of his most controversial reforms.

Complicating the tensions that surrounded the death of Joseph and collapse of Josephinism in 1790 was the ongoing French Revolution, which
offered a whole new language and agenda for addressing political concerns.
The Galicians of 1790, whom Kortum bitterly rebutted, believed that they
possessed certain "rights," and spoke on behalf of their "nation." Yet,
though they might indulge in some of the phrases of the contemporary
revolution, they were far more attuned to the conservative reaction against
revolutionary France—which influenced the parallel reaction against revolutionary Josephinism. *Considerations on the Galician Government* seemed to
echo the title of Rousseau's *Considerations on the Government of Poland*, which
dated back twenty years to the period of the partition, but the views of
the Galicians of 1790 were actually closer ideologically to Edmund Burke's
Reflections on the Revolution in France, also published in 1790. The ideological
tensions of revolutionary politics and incipient modern conservatism thus
found expression in the controversy surrounding Galicia.

The first point of the Galician charter was entitled "Droit de la propriété,"
the right of property, as if taken from the French "Declaration of the Rights
of Man and the Citizen." Leopold was thus enjoined: "May it please Your
Majesty that property, this sacred right of man, the foundation of society
and the guarantee of the loyalty of subjects toward the state, may be forever
solidly established."[68] Yet, the Galician nobles invoked the right of property
in a spirit precisely opposite that of the French Third Estate: they were implicitly protesting against Joseph's efforts to limit their feudal right over lands
that were worked for them by their enserfed peasants. The fundamental conservatism of the charter was perfectly clear in its defense of the property of
the church and the power of the bishops, recent objects of drastic Josephine
reform. Still, the charter ambivalently deployed a few revolutionary phrases,
when proposing, for instance, that Jews should have "all the rights of the
citizen" (with some exceptions, such as the right to purchase land) and that
peasants should have security "against the oppression of their lords" (while
submitting, of course, to feudal obligations).[69]

Furthermore, the Galicians proposed the periodic summoning of the "estates general"—which, as everyone knew, had inaugurated the revolution in France; yet for Galicia the very idea of an estates general was a notable innovation, inasmuch as the land had never possessed any sort of distinctive political coherence before 1772. The Galicians now insisted that such an assembly, representing the whole province, should be "uniquely considered to be the general will of the nation."[70] The allusion to the "general will" was also a direct quotation from the "Declaration of the Rights of Man and the Citizen," which was quoting in turn from the *Social Contract* of Rousseau. Conservative nobles thus draped themselves in revolutionary rhetoric. They did not, however, specify exactly what "nation" would be represented in its general will through the estates general. If Galicia possessed a general will, then perhaps there was also a Galician nation.

Arguing that the estates general should formulate a code of laws for the province, the Galicians proposed that the laws should be such as "conform the most to the physical and moral aspects of the country [*pays*], to the character [*génie*] of its inhabitants, and finally to the present circumstances."[71] Such a bold proposal of provincial authority rested implicitly on the assumption that the province possessed a character of its own, that its physical and moral aspects formed a coherent whole: Galicia.

The Galicians proposed the use of Latin and the "national language" for administration, instead of German, and urged the assignment of Galician soldiers to "national regiments"—without ever using the word "Polish" to specify the nature of the "national." According to the charter, "nothing could better stimulate and recompense the courage of our compatriots, who have always been distinguished for military service, than if, when fighting for the interests of the august house of Your Majesty, they could rally to the name of their fatherland [*patrie*] and believe that they were shedding their blood to rekindle its glory." Yet, even in this tribute to the glorious name of their country, the Galicians did not actually name that name, as if to allow for the possibility that their fatherland might be Galicia, and their compatriots fellow Galicians, rather than fellow Poles. Indeed, soon afterward, the charter specified "Poland, the neighboring country to Galicia [*Pologne, pays limitrophe de la Galicie*]," as if those were clearly distinctive and easily distinguishable entities.[72] The appeals for "national" prerogatives played upon a carefully cultivated ambiguity about the character of the nation.

The charter notably accepted the Habsburg justification for annexing Galicia, and affirmed "the ancient union of Galicia and Lodomeria with Hungary."[73] This axiom then became the basis for the argument that Galician affairs should be assigned to the Hungarian chancellery in Vienna. This was a

delicate point for the Habsburgs, for it was perfectly logical in its consistency
with their own concocted claim to the province. Yet Joseph had written to
Maria Theresa from Lviv in 1780 that the very idea of joining Galicia administratively to Hungary was "absurd," and "even harmful."[74] Hungary was
already sufficiently weighty within the Habsburg monarchy, and emerged in
the 1780s as the most powerful force of resistance to Josephine reform and
centralization. The return of the crown of St. Stephen to Hungary in 1790
denoted the Hungarian victory over Habsburg absolutism, and the Galicians
were then eager to associate themselves with that triumphant resistance.
The Galician nobility, joined to the Hungarian nobility, would be able to
defend their interests even more effectively against the emperor in Vienna.
Therefore, the Galicians conceded the validity of the Habsburg claim to the
province, through the Hungarian crown, for the purpose of affirming Galician provincial prerogatives under Habsburg rule.

"Customs and Morals"

The anonymous *Considerations on the Galician Government* were translated
from Polish into German and published together with the "Magna Charta,"
but edited by Kortum with his own indignant annotations. He violently dis-
agreed with the arguments of the *Considerations* but seemed confident that he
could publish the work without risk of readers finding it politically convincing. Conceived from the same noble perspective as the charter, probably also
with Ossoliński as the principal author, the *Considerations* offered a political
agenda and, further, articulated a political philosophy of aristocratic conservatism. The work proposed to explore the reasons for Galicia's decline "to
this degree of abjectness [*do tego stopnia nikczemności*]," and the explanation
was found in the collapse of traditional relations between noble landowners
and peasant serfs. In accordance with "custom established over centuries,"
there had been achieved in Galicia a "tacit accord between the landowner
and his subjects," such as to "bind the well-being of the landowner most
closely to that of the subject" and thus achieve their mutual satisfaction.[75]
The *Considerations* thus matched the organic arguments of Edmund Burke
in favor of finely tuned social hierarchies sanctioned by venerable tradition,
though Ossoliński probably could not have read Burke's *Reflections on the Revolution in France*, which had just been published in November of 1790. Rather,
both works were conditioned by the ongoing revolutionary circumstances
in France, and, in the Galician context, philosophical conservatism became
the basis for an indictment of Josephinism.

The *Considerations* affirmed peasant content and even relative prosperity, which was attributed to harmonious social relations in the Polish Commonwealth:

> This so tightly fastened bond between landowners and subjects promoted agriculture and population, and lord and subject thus became rich. Both possessed the land communally. This was the situation of the province when it passed under the government of the house of Austria.[76]

The notion of communal ownership put the gentlest possible interpretation on feudal serfdom, an idyllic feudalism that supposedly existed right up until the partition of Poland in 1772. Whereas Kratter and Traunpaur had sought to demonstrate the miserable condition of Poland at the moment when Galicia was annexed by Austria, the author of the *Considerations* reversed that historical argument and insisted that the decline and fall of Galicia began from the moment of its creation as a Habsburg province: "This government initiated the violent transformation of all rights and the abrogation of all existing customs and morals," the *Considerations* affirmed, insisting, with Burkean fervor, that the Habsburgs should have respected that which had been "sanctified by centuries." Kortum here added a footnote to remark, in the true spirit of Josephinism, that "it is ridiculous to demand that one should leave things eternally unchallenged just because they are centuries old."[77] Thus the ideological stances of revolution and conservatism were applied to the circumstances of Galicia.

The *Considerations* described a struggle between the "strangers" who came to Galicia with the Habsburg occupation and the native "nation" that found itself suddenly despised and oppressed:

> The foreigners sent into the land to hold office faced the prejudice against them that they were strangers. They also attracted, however, the deserved hatred of the nation, because they portrayed the nation before the throne as a barbarous people, as men who recognized no social rights, as a nation that needed first to be educated. Their unfounded reports supported the bad opinion that Europe anyhow held about Polish disorder. Even the empress, otherwise so just, was too distant, and no Galician obtained access to her.[78]

Galician identity in 1790 was thus conditioned by a sense of resentment against Habsburg officials and observers who supposedly maligned "the nation"—that is, the Poles. The pointed reference to Maria Theresa, ten years dead in 1790, suggested that she had been deliberately misled about Galicia, but the glaring failure to mention Joseph implied that he was a fully witting participant in the Habsburg disparagement and degradation of the province. Kortum footnoted the reference to European opinion of Polish disorder: "And is this opinion then unfounded?"[79] Like Kratter and Traunpaur he pitched his appeal to the public, affirming the authority of public opinion.[80]

The lessons of the ongoing revolution in France suggested a socially conservative philosophical interpretation of what had occurred in 1772 with the partition of Poland. This was not simply a matter of the illegitimate dismemberment of a sovereign state, as might have been conceived from a patriotic Polish perspective, but rather the destructive dissolution of an entire society, as witnessed from a conservative Galician perspective.

> Political bodies resemble a chain that consists of many links. Its strength and survival rests upon the bond that connects the citizens to one another, partly for common advantage and partly for mutual need. If this bond is broken, society also ceases. The political bodies disappear, collapse into anarchy, and bring about by that downfall the ruin of the whole land.[81]

Such philosophizing was very close in spirit to Burke's condemnation of revolutionaries who, it seemed to him, were "not morally at liberty at their pleasure, and on their speculations of a contingent improvement, wholly to separate and tear asunder the bands of their subordinate community, and to dissolve it into an unsocial, uncivil, unconnected chaos of elementary principles."[82] In 1772 the powers that had partitioned Poland justified themselves partly by insisting on Poland's political "anarchy"; the Galician *Considerations* in 1790 reformulated this issue by insisting that it was the partitioners themselves who had brought about social anarchy in their formerly Polish lands.

Inevitably, however, the bond that was closest to their Galician hearts was that which bound their peasant serfs to feudal obligations. The Galicians argued that by interfering with "the holiness of property rights"—in regulating feudal ownership and confiscating church property—the Habsburg government had produced economic collapse in Galicia. Leopold was urged to respect the privileges of the noble estate, and cherish its sense of honor; the leveling of the estates was denounced as the path to Turkish despotism.[83]

"Now the new government transforms our despair into hope," declared the Galicians, saluting Leopold. They anticipated his imperial assistance "to restore to the land its former happiness and prosperity."[84] They urged him to look to the reign of Maria Theresa, "whose love of justice posterity remembers with reverence." The name of Joseph remained unmentioned. While the "Magna Charta" had proposed that Galician affairs should be assigned to the Hungarian chancellery, in deference to the Hungarian medieval claim, the *Considerations* went further in its full acceptance of the idea of Galicia and proposed an independent chancellery dedicated entirely to Galicia: "Why then should our fatherland be deprived of this favor?"[85] Galicia, invented only twenty years before, was now interpreted as not only a province but also a fatherland to its noble inhabitants.

The menace of revolution in France, coinciding with the imperial succession in Austria, provided the Galicians with their moment of political opportunity. "The nation is the guarantee of public peace," they declared. The bishops might be called upon to preach order and obedience to the people, and thus achieve "the appeasement of enraged spirits." The nobles of Galicia would volunteer to serve in the provincial administration, displacing the bureaucratic "strangers," and would thus serve their Habsburg sovereign, while presumably also pursuing their own noble class interests.[86] They would accept their own Habsburg Galician condition, in return for the imperial renunciation of Josephinism and the confirmation of feudal privilege.

In September 1790, Leopold was in Prague to be crowned as king of Bohemia, for Bohemia, unlike Galicia, possessed historic royal privileges. The very fact of the coronation was a political concession to the Bohemians, like the return of the Hungarian crown, and the Galicians, without a material crown and without a traditional coronation, were seeking some sort of similar concession to their provincial political prerogatives. Also in Prague that September was Mozart, to celebrate the occasion with the performance of his opera in Leopold's honor, *La Clemenza di Tito*. Leopold was honored, for his presumed clemency, in Titus's robes, while Mozart, unaware that he had only a year to live, must also have hoped to conciliate the new emperor's patronage for himself and his music.[87] The Galician *Considerations* participated similarly in the celebration of Leopold, and openly proclaimed Galician subjection to the Habsburgs: "The name of subject will be pleasing to the nation, because it will recall the happy reign of the monarch." The name of "subject" was closely related to the name of "Galicia," the provincial designation devised to establish subordination to the Habsburg dynasty. Eighteen years after the partition of Poland in 1772, the Galicians now claimed to anticipate a new epoch of happiness and prosperity, in which Leopold would assume "the sweet name of Titus."[88] Like Mozart in Prague, the Galicians sought the new emperor's favor in the spirit of operatic classicism and refulgent flattery. If Leopold would assume the ancient name of "Titus," they would accept the modern name of "Galicia."

"The Savage in the South Seas"

Kortum published both the charter in French, and the German translation of the *Considerations*, in the full conviction that a middle-class reading public would be as outraged as he was by the aristocratic presumption of the Galicians. In addition to annotating the *Considerations* with hostile counter-statements, he also wrote a long, independent essay of his own that headed the whole volume, his *Examination of the Grievances of the Galician Nobility of the Polish Nation*. It was dated 26 September 1790, penned approximately seven months after Joseph's death on 20 February, and only weeks before Leopold's coronation as Holy Roman Emperor on 9 October. This was an interval of tremendous uncertainty and political ferment as people all over the Habsburg monarchy waited to see whether Leopold was going to moderate the dramatic reforms of his older brother. By the time that Kortum wrote his *Examination* in September, Leopold's moderation was increasingly apparent, and the partisans of Josephinism were already feeling regretful at the passing of their revolutionary opportunity.

Joseph, according to Kortum, was an emperor far ahead of his time: "His people were still not ready for magnanimity and civic virtue. He himself came to the throne a century too soon." The proof of their unreadiness was their abuse of the slogan of freedom, and nowhere did that abuse seem more outrageous to Kortum than in Galicia. "Before 1772 three million people here were under the power and caprice of a few thousand others," he observed; eighteen years later those few thousand nobles were the ones who considered themselves oppressed, and they launched a campaign "to achieve freedom, without knowing freedom." They denied freedom to the millions in Galicia but demanded to be free from the authority of the emperor in Vienna. That was the basis of the Galician charter addressed to Leopold, which Kortum regarded with ironic disparagement: "the Magna Charta of Galicia—worthy indeed of the fourteenth century."[89] In fact, the English Magna Charta dated to the thirteenth century. There was perhaps some awkwardness in formulating a Habsburg charge of medievalism against the Galicians, when it was precisely the Habsburg revival of medieval claims that justified the annexation of Galicia.

Although Kortum included in his volume the full text of the Galician charter and the *Considerations*, he felt that those documents were so fundamentally dishonest about political motives and purposes that, in his own *Examination*, he permitted himself to ventriloquize Galician voices and articulate what he saw as their true meaning. The Galicians became stage villains, proclaiming their evil intentions through the lines that he wrote for them. Thus he imagined them in 1772, at the moment of the partition:

> We have lived till now in the fortunate situation of being able to regard every other sort of human being as insignificant, and the caste of our peasants as creatures born for subjection. Happy times! When the peasant awaited the commands

of his lord with trembling! How pleasant was life when we saw thousands of hands, without pay or reward, working for our convenience.[90]

Thus Kortum ripped the mask of piety from the Galician nostalgia for the ancien régime, as expressed in the *Considerations*.

Yet Kortum, who had been living in Galicia since 1783, had had time to form an unfavorable opinion of the Galician peasants as well as the Galician nobles. He blamed both classes for the failure of the Josephine experiment, though he did not attempt to ventriloquize the peasants.

A beautiful ideal was formed concerning the soul of a Galician helot. Magnanimously the emperor made a gift to this people—the greatest gift that could be made. He gave freedom and property, or wanted to give them. But just as the savage in the South Seas gazes in astonishment at the European ship, so gazed the Galician peasant at the gift that his beneficent monarch gave. Unacquainted with the value and the use of it, the peasant sold it to the Hebrews.[91]

Kortum, seeking to articulate his social vision at the threshold of modern European history, deployed allusions to Spartan helotry, to the island savagery of the South Pacific, and the biblical Hebrews still dwelling in Galicia. He produced an anthropological parable of a peasantry unprepared to assume the modern rights of humanity. In this regard, Kortum was closer than he might have liked to think to the Galician noble perspective, in the *Considerations*, which depicted the peasantry as incapable of living contentedly except on traditional feudal terms. Yet Kortum believed that the Josephine experiment might have worked, if only it had been more gradual:

If one had had the patience to let the peasant—at least the Galician peasant and others like him in coarseness—earn his freedom and property gradually, through industry, thrift, good morality, and enlightenment; if one had followed nature, which lets the child slowly awaken to manhood, then all the beautiful results that were promised by beneficence would have been more than a dream.[92]

The backwardness of Eastern Europe called for an antidote of gradual progress and development, articulated in conditional clauses. The struggle between absolute barbarism and perfect civilization could not be resolved in a single engagement of massive forces.

Kortum's vision of enlightenment by stages, analogous to the passage from childhood to adulthood, echoed Immanuel Kant's essay "What Is Enlightenment?" of 1784, which argued that enlightenment was man's gradual emergence from immaturity, only to be achieved slowly. Indeed, Kortum had studied in Kant's Königsberg in the 1760s and was always interested in Kantian philosophy. By his correlated negative verdicts on the enlightenment of both the peasantry and the nobility in Galicia, Kortum forged a unified perspective of enlightened disparagement concerning the whole province.

The charter, according to Kortum's title, represented only "the Galician nobility of the Polish nation," and therefore could not claim to speak for the whole Galician nation, if such a nation actually existed. For Galicia, he clearly recognized, was only a recent creation: "Galicia, which only a few years ago appeared in geography under that name."[93] If the nobles behind the charter really still belonged to the Polish nation, and, as Kortum suspected, harbored secret political ambitions to return to Polish sovereignty, then they absolutely could not claim to represent "the nation of Galicia." That nation was demographically more extensive, a nation of three million, and politically, almost by definition, determined by Habsburg sovereignty. "What is meant by the nation of Galicia?" asked Kortum, explicitly. Of course he answered the question himself: "The nation of Galicia would thus be the embodiment [*Inbegriff*] of all the different classes of people who, under the laws of the state of Austria, have their fixed residence, in some fashion or other, in this land with their families."[94] Kortum employed conditional clauses to suggest that the nation of Galicia was very much a work in progress. His serious philosophical concerns were evident in his wrestling with what it meant for a nation to embody, abstract, or epitomize different sorts of peoples.

Emphatically he rejected the idea that the Galician nation could be Polish in character, and he addressed the authors of the charter directly to let them know that he regarded them as Poles, not Galicians:

> You have been waiting right up to the present day for some sort of messiah who will liberate you from the domination of the heathens, that is, the Germans.
> You still can not get used to the thought that you now have another fatherland. Through a perhaps unconscious association of ideas you are always still thinking about the republic of Poland when you speak of patriotism. Language, clothing, and customs bring to recollection at every moment your former situation.[95]

Kortum understood in a very sophisticated way what it was that constituted a nation—language, clothing, customs—and he may have been reading Herder as well as Kant in the 1780s. The notion that the Poles were awaiting a national messiah actually seemed to anticipate by an entire generation the emergence of Polish romantic messianism in the early nineteenth century. Kortum believed that the Poles of Galicia were so thoroughly nationally formed as Poles, with their own sense of patriotism and fatherland, that they could not constitute a Galician nation.

"Is the Polish language really then the actual national language of Galicia?" asked Kortum. "Are then the Polish nation or the Polish nobility the original inhabitants of this land?"[96] Having insisted that the Polish nobles could not speak for the Galician nation, he went on to rebut the proposal for administration in the "national language," or rather to insist that the national language was not actually Polish. Kortum was himself a gifted linguist who, over the course of his career, learned many Habsburg languages, including Hungarian.[97] In 1790, after seven years in Galicia, he surely knew Polish well enough to know that it was linguistically distinct from the Ruthenian language in Galicia. Later in the 1790s, Johann Christian von Engel suggested the connection between the medieval history of the Rus principalities Halych and Vladimir (linked by name to the Habsburg Kingdom of Galicia and Lodomeria) and the modern history of Ukraine and the Cossacks. Engel's historical work, *Geschichte der Ukraine und der ukrainischen Cosaken wie auch der Königreiche Halitsch und Wladimir*, published in Halle in 1796, thus pointed toward the national connection and convergence of Ruthenians and Ukrainians while underlining the difference between Ruthenians and Poles.[98]

If the Galician nation was jointly Polish and Ruthenian, Kortum suggested—without mentioning the Jews—such a nation could be construed as linguistically and ethnographically heterogeneous. He addressed the Polish nobles directly:

> So you see, my lords, that you, with regard to Galicia, have never made Polish into the national language for this land, and you can not pass yourselves off as the original inhabitants of this province. You are no more and no less alien in Galicia than the Germans. You came as strangers into this land, and the long passage of time has made you forget your provenance.[99]

There was no reason to consider Polish the national language, and Kortum therefore argued for the administrative priority of German in the province. On the politics of language he quoted Gibbon, and the quotation was given ostentatiously in English: "So sensible were the Romans of the influence of language over national manners, that it was their most serious care to extend, with the progress of their arms, the use of the Latin tongue."[100] Thus the Habsburg civilizing "influence" in Galicia was construed as classical, and German as the language of imperial mission.

"Here I am then among the Sarmatians," Joseph had remarked, and Kortum also invoked the Sarmatians, who had been classified among the ancient barbarians by Tacitus. The Polish nobles of Galicia spoke through Kortum's ventriloquy:

> We have not ceased to be Sarmatians. . . . Look at our brothers in Poland, how they throw off foreign domination, how they take off foreign clothes, and stomp upon foreign enlightenment. . . . We want to participate in the merits of our brothers, who distinguish themselves from all the peoples of Europe, in order to turn back to their ancestors from the Orient.[101]

The ancient Sarmatians were regarded as Oriental, and therefore, with their self-styled Sarmatian identity—long robes and curved swords, shaved heads and dramatic moustaches—the Poles supposedly became Orientals. In 1790, however, when Poland, as Kortum noted, was seeking independence from foreign domination, the political style was anything but Sarmatian. That was the moment of the Four-Year Sejm, meeting from 1788 to 1792, overturning Russian domination in Poland and preparing the modern revolutionary constitution of 3 May 1791—comparable to the enlightened constitutions of the United States and France. Kortum's rhetoric of Sarmatian disparagement was therefore all the more revealing of his own cultural preconceptions.

Kortum saw Galicia as balanced between European civilizing elements and Oriental barbaric forces, and he proposed a hypothetical imaginative experiment:

> Imagine for a moment all the German inhabitants gone from Poland and Galicia, with their industriousness and business, and then imagine the image of those lands. Would one find any other counterpart except—Tartary, or at best [*höchstens*] Moldavia and Wallachia? Consider the Polish towns that once had, with their German inhabitants, a sort of prosperity, and would be now the sad residence of Jews, poverty, uncleanliness, and ignorance. Then deny my contention.[102]

With this extraordinary exercise in historical speculation, the Josephine view of Galicia imaginatively deployed the Enlightenment's perspective on Eastern Europe. The idea of Eastern Europe was created through a sort of demi-Orientalism that projected the otherness of the Orient onto lands that were indisputably European, characterizing them by a paradoxical combination of resemblance and difference from an implicitly Western sense of civilized Europe. In this case, Kortum's imaginative experiment stripped away the Western aspects of the supposed Galician amalgam in order to demonstrate that what remained would be both hopelessly backward and altogether Oriental.

Kortum's extraordinary geographical equation operated thus: Galicia minus the Germans equals Tartary. The best case—that is, the most Western conceivable comparison—was that of the Romanian principalities of Moldavia and Wallachia, which, though ruled by Greek Phanariot princes, were still ultimately under Ottoman sovereignty. Eliminating the Germans would leave the towns of Galicia in the hands of the Jews, whom Kortum regarded not only negatively in terms of poverty and ignorance but also as a biblically Oriental people, accentuating the Eastern character of Galicia. In the twentieth century Kortum's experiment would be executed in reverse, overturning the balance of elements in Galicia by the German elimination of the Jews. Kortum in 1790 envisioned Galicia as poised between Europe and the Orient, while Josephine reform and German influence wrestled with Sarmatian resistance. Galicia, as invented in 1772, was not only a political creation but also an ideological construction, and Kortum clearly demonstrated the instability of that construction when he hypothetically dissected its components in his thought experiment.

Difficile est satyram non scribere, noted Kortum in Latin, quoting Juvenal: It is difficult not to write satire. The presumption of the Galicians seemed to him so preposterous that he could barely contain his civilized Roman sense of sarcasm and satire, especially when he composed his first-person Galician monologues: "We have not ceased to be Sarmatians." Yet, in his concluding reflections, composed as a second-person lecture to the Galicians, Kortum wrote in a spirit of more earnest contempt:

> If you do not wish to follow the examples of other enlightened peoples; if you think the lessons of foreign wisdom are foolishness; and if you regard the beneficent intentions of your ruler as oppression; then the result will be the same twilight that is descending upon your brothers in Poland. You may approach the better part of the European peoples, but do not expect that those peoples, whom you are so far behind, should wait for you at your pleasure, or even turn backward to you.[103]

In these concluding reflections of his *Examination* Kortum revealed again how much he depended upon the Enlightenment's model of Eastern Europe—a model of backwardness and development—in order to articulate his perspective on Galicia. Europe consisted of more and less enlightened peoples, and while the former dwelled in the light of reason, the latter were doomed to grope around in the twilight of their own ignorance. The political creation of Galicia helped to make this dichotomous sense of enlightened cultural geography into an integral part of the Habsburg sense of imperial mission during the Josephine decade of the 1780s. Kortum, publishing his own *Examination*, bound together with the Galician "Magna Charta" and the related *Considerations*, was able to present to the public the dynamics of ideological engagement and resistance between Habsburg civilization and the forces of backwardness in Galicia.

"THE CONSEQUENCES OF THE WORKS OF VOLTAIRE"

In 1792 a Polish poem was published with the attribution "by a Galician [*przez Gallicyana*]." The unpoetic title of the poem was *The Consequences of the Works of Voltaire* (*Skutki dzieł Woltera*), and the message was one of clear hostility to the European Enlightenment as represented by the famous French philosophe. In France itself the consequences of the Enlightenment were evident in the abolition of the monarchy and declaration of the republic in 1792. Yet, like the Galician *Considerations* of 1790, the poem of 1792 established a distinctly Galician perspective for rejecting the Enlightenment and articulating the principles of ideological conservatism.

In the period leading up to the first partition of Poland, there was no more outspoken critic of the Polish state, no more enthusiastic partisan of annexation and partition, than the venerable philosophe Voltaire, writing from his estate at Ferney. Voltaire's hostility to Poland was simply a function of his enthusiasm for the partitioning monarchs, Frederick the Great in Prussia, and especially Catherine the Great in Russia. The substance of Voltaire's criticism of Poland concerned religious issues. He regarded Poland as a center of Roman Catholic fanaticism and intolerance, and published his outrage in an essay on "The Dissensions of the Churches of Poland" that appeared under the pseudonym of "Bourdillon" in 1767.

Voltaire died in 1778, but in 1781, in Lviv, there was published a German translation of his essay on religion in Poland, still attributed to "Bourdillon"—and "translated by a German Pole [*von einem deutschen Pollaken*]."[104] This was the year of Joseph's patent of toleration for the entire monarchy, and Voltaire's denunciation of Catholicism in Poland was clearly consistent with the Josephine assault on Polish fanaticism in Galicia. Kratter, for instance, described churches and monasteries "made into whorehouses," while conjuring irreverent images of sneezing priests and drunken monks. Voltaire had been the enemy of Poland during his lifetime, and could therefore be posthumously made into an advocate of Galicia in the 1780s.

Thus, in the 1790s, it was possible to articulate a Galician reaction to Josephinism by means of a rhymed poem denouncing Voltaire. The "Galician" who authored the poem declared an identity that required clarification, and his verse inevitably reflected upon what it meant to be Galician in 1792. Indeed, the poet of 1792 was perhaps the very first self-proclaimed Galician in the history of Polish culture. He began by defining his Galician identity with reference to the reign of Stanisław August, to whom the poem was dedicated and addressed:

> I was born, most illustrious lord,
> your subject, and of noble condition:
> and as the heavens have determined destiny at times,
> I had to seek my bread in Galicia [*Szukać musiałem w Galicyi chleba*].[105]

The invention of Galicia was attributed to providential destiny and accepted out of economic necessity. From 1772 to 1792, for twenty years, the poet had been Galician—"with my sons I am a subject of the emperor"—but also remained Polish:

> The blood in me declares that I am a true Pole [*Polak prawdziwy*],
> The heart of a Pole [*serce Polaka*] breathes and beats within me.
> I have taken an oath [*przysiągłem*]: to live loyal to the emperor.[106]

Physiology and sentiment of heart and blood thus formed the inner Polish dynamics of the Galician, while destiny made him, in his life and action, the loyal subject of the Habsburgs. He felt himself a Pole but lived as a Galician. His signature expressed the depth of his sincerity: "Z nayglębszych najglębszy, Gallicyan." He was "Galician" from the deepest depths, but the paradox was evident, for to be Galician was an externally lived relation to the viscerally experienced feeling of Polish heart and Polish blood.

Beyond the dedication, the poet attempted to demonstrate that the Enlightenment, led by Voltaire, had distorted and corrupted humanity with sacrilegious suggestions: "that there is no God, that people have no souls."[107] As in the Galician *Considerations*, here too the result of the Enlightenment was the radical disruption of traditional beliefs and the provocation of revolution. According to the Galician poet, the Enlightenment taught that "monarchs are only tyrants," and Voltaire believed that dogs were "equal" to humans.[108] In 1792 the French Revolution was in full swing, with the assault against the Tuileries in August followed by the September massacres. The poem made no mention of the revolutionary Polish constitution of 1791, which had been partly sponsored by Stanisław August himself; even as the poet composed his verses in 1792 the Russian army was stomping out enlightened constitutionalism in Poland.

In fact, the Galician poet believed that the Poles were uniquely immune to the dangerous sophistries of Voltaire and the Enlightenment.

> Not all of Europe is entangled in these errors,
> There are nations older than Voltaire;
> They know that this learning is perverse and feeble,
> They maintain faith in God, and loyalty [*wierność*] to the monarch.[109]

The Poles were thus one of the notable exceptions to Europe's intellectual decadence. If, however, one of the principles of glory was "loyalty to the monarch," along with the recognition that monarchs were not necessarily tyrants, then the Galicians had to be counted among the most honorable of Poles. For the condition of being Galician was defined precisely by an oath of loyalty to the Habsburg emperor, and the poet could thus proudly appropriate for himself a Galician identity.

HOMAGE IN WEST GALICIA

In 1790, Balthasar Hacquet began to publish in Nuremberg the volumes that summed up his geological exploration of the Carpathian Mountains in Galicia and Bukovina (the "Dacian and Sarmatian" Carpathians, according to his title). "I thought about the Carpathians, and so I went to Galicia," explained Hacquet. His account also included ethnographic observations, and he remarked that the Carpathians had been relatively understudied because of "the wildness of the inhabitants of these mountains." He noted that the Habsburg administration had produced a mapping of Galicia on twelve sheets, published in Vienna in 1790—but useless to him, because there were so many mistakes. In fact, Galicia itself was about to be transformed on the map in the 1790s.[110]

The Polish constitution of 1791 was affirmed at the Four-Year Sejm in Warsaw, and then overturned by the military intervention of Catherine the Great in 1792; the second partition of Poland ensued in 1793, with Russia and Prussia extending their Polish lands and Austria diplomatically excluded from any analogous aggrandizement of Galicia. The year 1792 also witnessed the sudden death of Leopold, whose accession two years before had seemed to offer such a promising political opportunity to the Galicians. He was succeeded by his son Franz, who found himself almost immediately at war with revolutionary France. What remained of Poland became the site of a great insurrection against Russian domination in 1794, under the leadership of Tadeusz Kościuszko, and the military suppression of the Polish forces led to the third and final partition of Poland in 1795, eliminating that country altogether from the map of Europe. This time the Habsburgs received their fair share, adding about a million and a half subjects in a stretch of Polish territory that was immediately designated as West Galicia, including the city of Cracow. West Galicia was regarded as an extension or completion of Galician territory, in spite of the fact that it bore no relation to the medieval vicinity of Halych and Vladimir.[111] Maria Theresa's scruples concerning legitimacy already belonged to the lost world of the ancien régime. West Galicia was established on the basis of Habsburg power in 1795, and it would be politically canceled purely on the basis of power by Napoleon fourteen years later, when he assigned it to the Grand Duchy of Warsaw, which lasted in turn only as long as Napoleonic power in Europe.

Without reference to the "revindication" of territory, the establishment of West Galicia required only the formalities of allegiance. When Austrian troops entered Cracow in January 1796, the Habsburg commanding officer was presented with the keys to the city. In April the newly appointed governor of West Galicia, Johann Wenzel Margelik, was formally welcomed to Cracow; his crucial qualification for the post was his Galician experience in the 1780s under Joseph. The Josephine project was now to be extended to a more broadly delineated Galicia. The Cracow welcoming ceremonies of 27 April, according to the *Gazeta Krakowska*, involved deputations of merchants, teachers, priests, and Jews, all greeting Margelik. The bells of St. Mary's, the Mariacki Church, rang out over the city as the governor proceeded to the castle cathedral on the Wawel hill above the city, where the bishop of Cracow presided over a celebratory Te Deum. There was further ceremonial surrounding formal acts of homage to the Habsburg emperor in August 1796. In February 1797, on the occasion of Emperor Franz's twenty-ninth birthday, there was singing in Polish and German of the newly composed Austrian anthem by Joseph Haydn: "Gott erhalte Franz den Kaiser!" "Boże zachowuj Cesarza!" In 1797, Franz authorized the creation of a Galician chancellery in Vienna, for the government of East and West Galicia together.[112] The staging of dynastic allegiance thus accompanied the political integration of the newly aggrandized Galician domain.

The poet Kajetan Koźmian recorded in his memoirs the experience of suddenly finding himself an inhabitant of Galicia after the abolition of the Polish state. He recognized the artifice involved in "the christening of this part of Poland under the name of western Galicia." He particularly resented the deployment of supposedly parasitical Habsburg bureaucrats, many of them sent directly from Lviv where they had already gained Galician experience: "Galicia as if breathed upon by death, displayed the image of a stiff corpse, which was filled with small and annoying worms [*drobne a dokuczliwe robactwo*] that tormented with unbearable itching." From the Habsburg perspective, of course, it was Poland that was the corpse, which could only be reanimated by the project of enlightened reform. "Not only was the name of Poland and every recollection about it erased [*wymazywano*] from official acts, from journals, from calendars, from gazettes," noted Koźmian, "but there was even issued a regulation forbidding that the Holy Virgin be called the Queen of Poland, and threatening punishment for whoever prayed to her under that motto."[113] Vienna prescribed the adaptation of church prayers, so that the phrase "Queen of Poland pray for us" was replaced by "Queen of Galicia and Lodomeria pray for us."[114]

In 1796, the same year that Margelik made his ceremonial entry into Cracow as the representative of Habsburg rule, there was published in Vienna an anonymous work: *Geographical-Historical Report about West Galicia or the newly acquired Austrian-Polish Provinces (Geographisch-historische Nachrichten von Westgalizien oder den neu erlangten österreichisch-polnischen Provinzen)*. Margelik's entry on 27

April was actually cited in the text, which described how on that occasion "the Polish eagles were everywhere taken down, and in their place the imperial eagles were affixed," a displacement that would have been noticeable from the fact that the Habsburg eagle had two heads.[115] The *Geographical-Historical Report*, however, was intended not only to mark the assumption of Habsburg political power but also to continue the intellectual work of Kratter and Traunpaur in placing Galicia before the public.

The Josephine ideology of Galicia was still clearly preeminent in this work, for the central argument affirmed that the territory had undergone a traumatic collapse under Polish rule and now awaited its restoration under beneficent Habsburg rule. The "devastation [*Verwüstung*]" of the city of Cracow had proceeded throughout the eighteenth century, now ending, and, according to the *Geographical-Historical Report*, the entry of Habsburg troops into the city in January 1796 was greeted with "manifestations of joy" by the inhabitants.[116] For now the resurrection of Cracow was about to begin: "Now, when Cracow has come under the Austrian government, it can become once again a brilliant center of commerce and one of the most flourishing cities." The better business conditions in the Habsburg monarchy would make urban progress inevitable—"as the example of East Galicia may notably convince us."[117] The intimately connected administrative domains of West Galicia and East Galicia were formulated in a relation of subtle asymmetry, since, just as Galicia had been presumed to be backward with respect to the Habsburg monarchy in 1772, now West Galicia was supposed to be a generation behind East Galicia, and in need of catching up. With the figleaf of medieval dynastic claims no longer even remotely relevant to the new territories, the Habsburgs were all the more insistent on the ideological justification that derived from a Josephine program of enlightened reform and economic progress.

The *Geographical-Historical Report* found a spiritual counterpart for Joseph by delving into medieval Polish history and discovering King Casimir the Great:

> He reigned in the fourteenth century, but his spirit was raised up far beyond his epoch. He greatly enlarged the possessions and the power of Poland, and, what is more important, he first gave the nation wise laws, and sought to draw it out of its wildness. . . . On account of his great sympathy for the humble classes of people, especially for the peasants, the nobles mockingly called him the peasant king, a title that only made him more precious in the eyes of every friend of humanity.[118]

Casimir the Great, extracted from the remote past of Polish history, was resurrected by a Habsburg apologist in 1796 and represented as the medieval twin of Emperor Joseph II. Casimir's alleged mission of civilizing the wild Poles and saving the peasants from the nastiness of the Polish nobility was, in fact, precisely the enlightened Josephine project in Galicia, now reformulated for West Galicia on the threshold of the nineteenth century.

BOGUSŁAWSKI IN GALICIA:
RESTAGING THE NATIONAL OPERA

In 1794, at the moment of the Kościuszko insurrection, the Polish dramatist Wojciech Bogusławski staged in Warsaw his opera *Krakowiacy i Górale*, with music by the Bohemian composer Jan Stefani. Bogusławski created a drama about regional tensions between villagers in the vicinity of Cracow and the highlanders [*górale*] who resided in the Tatra Mountains. With the encouragement of a scientifically minded student who improvised a "miracle" based on the principles of electricity, the villagers and mountaineers were eventually brought together in solidarity. This scenario proved particularly compelling to the Warsaw public at a time when Kościuszko was seeking to bring the Polish peasantry into the national insurrection against Russia. Bogusławski was himself a partisan of the insurrection, and, when it was defeated he decided to leave Warsaw and take refuge in Habsburg Galicia, in Lviv.

"I can not describe the joyful wonder which my heart felt at the sight of the Galician capital," recalled Bogusławski in his memoirs.

> I recognized there almost half of Warsaw. People of every class and dignity were gathered there, avoiding the temporary confusion in our country. This was in January at the beginning of 1795, in the month dedicated to carnival entertainments . . . and the Galicians [*Gallicyanie*], desiring to give proof of most sympathetic hospitality to their compatriots [*spółrodakom swoim*], with daily banquets and balls and every kind of amusements, sweetened the memories of freshly sustained losses and voluntary exile. The mild Austrian government seemed at that moment to share kindly the endeavor of brotherly love.[119]

This favorable view of both the Habsburg government and the Lviv inhabitants suggested that Bogusławski was inclined to settle down for a while in Galicia and become a Galician. He clearly felt that the "Galicians" constituted a recognizable category of identity, though they were at the same time "compatriots" of Poles from Poland.

Bogusławski intended to pursue in the new Galician context his old career as an actor, a dramatist, and theatrical impresario. He found in Lviv a busy winter theater season, around the time of carnival, and he also had the idea of next establishing a sort of summer festival.

> Though the demand of the public [*żądanie Publiczności*], foreseeing pleasant
> amusements in summertime, guaranteed a somewhat numerous attendance at the
> amphitheater, the most certain thing seemed to me the possibility of producing
> there the national opera: *Krakowiacy*, which was the only one of all Polish pieces
> forbidden in Galicia, and which the public most desired. I was almost certain that
> several repeated performances of that would pay entirely for the projected cost
> of building the structure. Encouraged not only by the granting of safe refuge
> in the country, but also by many other excellent proofs of the protection of the
> Austrian government, I ventured to submit a request for permitting the perfor-
> mance of this opera. . . . I placed a copy of *Krakowiacy* in the hands of the gover-
> nor of Galicia, Gallenberg, a man generally loved by both nations, and who was
> himself a lover of all the arts and sciences.[120]

The governor, Joseph Gallenberg, asked Bogusławski to make some changes
in the opera, which was then submitted for censorship in Vienna, and returned with government approval. "This news immensely delighted everyone," Bogusławski noted, "and increased affectionate gratitude to the government, which forbade nothing that increased the happiness of its subjects."
There were three performances in the summer of 1796—which "scarcely
satisfied the interest of everyone"—and the opera returned to the stage every year until Bogusławski left Lviv to return to Warsaw in 1799.[121] German
theater had been preeminent in Lviv in the 1780s, but Bogusławski provided
new energy for Polish theater, and it must have been the Polish public that
he particularly sought to satisfy with his "national" opera.

Bogusławski claimed that he had been asked by the government to make
only slight changes in the opera: "I can honestly confirm that I found only
several words underlined in the whole work." Yet, there must have been some
serious official deliberation about whether to permit the staging of a drama
that, only two years before, in Warsaw, had been closely associated with political insurrection. The scholar Jerzy Got has noted some of the changes in
the libretto from the Warsaw production of 1794 to the Lviv production of
1796.[122] For instance, in the song of Basia, the miller's daughter, there was a
notable variation, neutralizing any possible political interpretation:

> WARSAW: Where one lives in captivity [*w niewoli*],
>   There is no joy [*lubości*].
>   The dog on a leash will howl,
>   Everyone desires freedom [*wolności*].
> LVIV: Where the heart's ill-will deceives,
>   There you have no joy [*lubości*].
>   The world is built on romance [*na kochaniu*],
>   Everyone desires love [*miłości*].[123]

Romantic frustrations and community tensions were emphasized in Lviv, and
any potentially political allusions were eliminated by expedient revisions.

Yet the crucial difference between the two productions would have appeared not necessarily in the text of the libretto, but in the context of the performances. Bogusławski intended *Krakowiacy i Górale* as a national opera, conceived to dramatize the spirits and circumstances of Polish peasants and mountaineers. The Warsaw public of 1794 had hailed those characters as heroes of the Polish national cause, which was at that moment explosively engaged in the Kościuszko insurrection. Yet, the actual geographical setting of the opera, though it may have seemed Polish from the perspective of Warsaw in 1794, was about to become thoroughly Galician after the final partition of Poland: the Tatra range of the Carpathian Mountains, the peasant villages in the vicinity of Cracow, and finally Cracow itself. This terrain was mostly Galician after 1772, and entirely Galician after 1795. What appeared as a drama of Polish national unity in 1794 could also appear as a representation of Galician provincial unity in 1796.

Beyond the circumstances of geographical location, however, the political implications of *Krakowiacy i Górale* were notably transformed in the shift from the Polish context of 1794 to the Galician context of 1796, even without major alterations in the libretto. The celebration of peasant spirit, which seemed to encourage Kościuszko's insurrectionary purpose in Warsaw in 1794, could also have seemed entirely consistent with the Josephine ideology of Galicia. After all, Joseph had made the protection of the peasantry into the hallmark of his imperial career, while Kratter and Kortum had vindicated Habsburg rule in Galicia by emphasizing the victimization of the peasantry by the Polish nobility. The Galician peasants were the heroes of Bogusławski's drama, which the Habsburg government of Franz could therefore approve in the spirit of enlightened Josephine patronage. The student Bardos, whose part was performed by Bogusławski himself, soliloquized enthusiastically about peasant virtues.

> Oh, how with their sincerity [*swą szczerością*] these peasants
> Have taken possession of my soul![124]

Josephine ideology gave such paeans to the peasantry a particular political meaning in Galicia. Bogusławski insisted that his opera was produced at the demand of the public of Lviv, and the public, of course, could have taken away from the drama a variety of messages, even ambivalent or conflicting messages. The public could have applauded the work for its Polish national significance or for its Galician provincial significance.

Although Bogusławski claimed to be responding to a single "public," he was well aware that the public of Galicia was complex in composition. The tension between Polish and German consumers of culture was evident in the dancing regulations for public balls during carnival in Lviv in 1791:

> From the beginning [of the ball] until midnight one should dance a Polish and a
> German dance alternatively. From midnight until half past one (including half an
> hour rest), an English one. From half past one until three o'clock, a Polish and a
> German [dance]. From three to four an English quadrille. From four till half past
> four [there should be] a rest period and later, until the end of a ball, there should
> follow a Polish and a German [dance].[125]

Even in the wee hours of the night, there was no forgetting the distinction between Polish and German, in spite of the fact that dancing was entirely a matter of style with hardly any need for a spoken language, one or the other.

Bogusławski in Lviv presented dramas from both the German and the
Polish repertory. In 1797 he introduced his own exotic Polish melodrama, *Izka-
har King of Guaxara*, in which the Spanish conquest of the Incas could have
been interpreted by the public as an Aesopian account of the destruction of
Poland.[126] In that same year, however, he also staged Mozart's *Magic Flute*, in
which the trials and triumphs of Prince Tamino could have been interpreted
as an allegory for the enlightened education of young Franz, the Habsburg
emperor.[127] In 1796, Bogusławski staged Shakespeare's *Hamlet* in German in
Lviv, and in 1798 he offered the same drama, for the first time ever, in Polish—in his own translation from the German, starring himself in the title role.
Hamlet in German and Polish, as in English, was rich with possibilities for
political interpretation, as the prince sought to purge the royal government
of evil; he could have represented either an enlightened young Habsburg
prince or the national partisan of Poland's revenge. In any event there was no
need for Fortinbras to bring down the curtain, since, in this version, Hamlet
survived the final bloodletting and prepared to rule over the Danes in the
happy ending. Bogusławski believed that a play like Hamlet, "which in its
conclusion misses a moral goal by punishing with death both innocent and
guilty persons, should not be staged in this enlightened age without appropriate corrections."[128] While clarifying the moral message by adapting the drama,
Bogusławski allowed the political meaning to remain ambiguous.

The possibility of conflicting political interpretations in the dramatic
sphere went hand in hand with real political conflict during these same years.
Joachim Denisko launched a Polish insurrection in Galicia in 1797, quickly
crushed by the Habsburgs. Yet, Jan Henryk Dąbrowski, who established a
Polish legion in 1797 to fight alongside the French in Italy, considered the
possibility of Habsburg sponsorship of the Polish national cause: "Among all
the harm for which Poland reproaches its usurpers, the Austrian emperor has
perpetrated the least, and public opinion even among Poles is therefore least
opposed to him." Dąbrowski thought that a resurrected Polish state might
be ruled by the Habsburg archduke Karl, the brother of Franz. Jerzy Got
has proposed that Bogusławski himself may have held precisely that politi-

cal perspective and may have seen his theatrical work in Lviv as the cultural counterpart of Dąbrowski's political and military efforts.[129] On the occasion of Franz's birthday in 1797, Bogusławski illuminated the theater and had the actors sing the Haydn hymn "Gott erhalte," three times, with the audience joining in on the third round. According to the *Allgemeines Europaeisches Journal* in Brno, "Mister Bogusławski has earned our most ardent gratitude for this homage to our beloved monarch." In April, Bogusławski held a patriotic benefit performance and donated the box office receipts to Archduke Karl. In 1817, after the restoration of Galicia by the Congress of Vienna, there was a performance of *Krakowiacy i Górale* in Lviv that coincided with a visit to the city by Emperor Franz; for the occasion, a cantata in his honor was performed between acts.[130] Thus the Polish "national opera" of the 1790s, twenty years later, could be entirely domesticated as a Galician drama, even interposing the ceremonial celebration of Habsburg loyalty.

In 1796, Bogusławski presented in German the drama *Das Mädchen von Marienburg*, by none other than Franz Kratter, who was now living in Galicia after writing about it so critically ten years before. Chatinka, the maid of Marienburg, or Malbork, came originally from Poland, but she had been abducted by Russian troops and now found herself at the summer palace of Peter the Great, the Peterhof, outside St. Petersburg. In the play—Kratter's most successful drama, originally performed in Mannheim and Vienna in 1793—Peter fell in love with the virtuous maid, and, though tempted to wield his arbitrary power, finally resolved to respect her virtue, marry her, and make her his czarina. Peter's rule in Russia was represented in precisely the language that marked the invention of Eastern Europe in the age of Enlightenment. Peter had to struggle against "fanaticism that fears the light of day—ancient barbarity—and bloody insatiable oppression," laboriously striving "to bring a barbarous people from the yoke of superstition and savage customs to obedience through his wise laws."[131] This was absolutely consistent with the celebration of Peter in the age of Enlightenment, most famously by Voltaire, but it was also strikingly similar to the rhetoric in which Joseph had been celebrated by his admirers for his efforts in Galicia in the 1780s. Kratter himself had been one of the most prominent advocates of Josephinism in Galicia, and it would have been obvious to the public in Lviv, watching *Das Mädchen von Marienburg* in 1796, that the drama's reflections on Peter in Russia were also relevant to Habsburg Galicia. Bogusławski's presentation of Kratter's drama suggested the complexity of the encounter between the Polish national perspective, after the demise of the Polish state, and the crystallization of the Habsburg ideology of Galicia at the conclusion of the eighteenth century.

"Not without Heartache"

Julian Niemcewicz, the Polish dramatist and memoirist, traveled to Galicia in 1783, arriving in Lviv, coincidentally, at the moment of one of Joseph's imperial visits. Niemcewicz recalled the voyage in his memoirs: "From Podolia we went to Galicia, formerly known as Red Ruthenia, not without heartache [*nie bez boleści serca*] at seeing such a beautiful region broken off from the Polish kingdom."[132] Even in the retrospect of his memoirs, the name "Galicia" did not come naturally to Niemcewicz, who annotated it with a reference to a previous geographical designation that roughly fit the region. His sentimental heartache expressed the indissoluble connection between Galicia and Poland that would always exist for a patriotic Pole, in spite of the severance of political relations in the 1770s and the full abolition of Poland in the 1790s. The anonymous poet of 1792 sought to articulate the same sense of separation from Poland that nevertheless permitted him to remain nationally Polish while accepting a Galician identity.

The anonymous "Galician" poet noted that he had lived for twenty years as a subject of the Habsburg emperor, and it was certainly true that twenty years before, at the time of the first partition in 1772, it would have been unthinkable for anyone to assume the identity of a Galician. There was no Galicia before 1772, and the Habsburg efforts to legitimate their annexations with reference to medieval Halych and Vladimir only underlined the perfect artifice of the geopolitical coinage. A figment of the Habsburg imperial imagination, Galicia was simply invented as a name in order to vindicate and designate the newly acquired province.

Joseph's slogan of 1773—*altri guai!*—would, in the ensuing decades, became the hallmark of Habsburg ideology in Galicia. Joseph identified its many troubles and sought to apply his own program of enlightened reforms, while such Josephine writers and publicists as Kratter, Traunpaur, and Kortum sought to describe the process of development that, in their view, led from backward Poland through the progress of Galicia to the civilization of Europe. The supposedly Polish aspects of Galicia—a cruelly oppressive nobility, a brutalized alcoholic peasantry, fanatical and superstitious Roman Catholicism, and the alien presence of so many Jews—were dramatized all the more forcefully to vindicate and legitimate the Habsburg government and its program of enlightened Josephine reforms. "The whole is near its recasting," Kratter commented, but, though near perhaps, the recasting could never be fully achieved, for Galicia was, by definition, a work in progress.

In 1797 the partitioning powers—Russia, Prussia, and Austria—signed a secret agreement to abolish henceforth the very name of Poland: "The high contracting parties are agreed and undertake never to include in their titles the name or designation of the Kingdom of Poland, which shall remain suppressed as from the present and forever."[133] In this purposeful semiotic strategy of suppression, the Habsburgs were already well prepared with a new name and designation, having taken possession in 1772 of the Kingdom of Galicia and Lodomeria. After 1795 the logic of symmetry provided the necessary and sufficient explanation for dubbing the newly acquired territories as West Galicia, administratively and ideologically aligned with East Galicia. Once having staked their claim to the name of Galicia, the Habsburgs could adjust and revise the actual territorial domain according to the fluctuating political realities of the moment.

In fact, the twin pillars of West Galicia and East Galicia would stand for only fourteen years, pulled down by Napoleon in 1809. After Vienna itself capitulated to the French emperor in that year, Napoleon made over most of West Galicia to the Grand Duchy of Warsaw, the Polish principality that he had created two years earlier. East Galicia in 1809 was temporarily subject to the Napoleonic Polish army of Prince Józef Poniatowski. The leading figure of the Habsburg government in Lviv at this crucial moment was none other than Ernst Kortum, who received the Order of St. Stephen in reward for his loyal service to the dynasty after Habsburg rule was restored. "The day of 15 December 1809 will be remembered in the annals of Lwów, because the capital returned to the kind and clement rule of the Austrian emperor," commented one historical account, in Polish, published twenty years later. "At nine o'clock in the morning, deputies from the city municipal council, artisan guilds with their banners, and the municipal militia with Turkish [janissary] music, having gathered on the market place, walked up to the city's toll gates where they awaited the arrival of the imperial troops."[134] By 1809 the restoration of Galicia was already an occasion that called forth an array of ceremonial rites and, at least for some Galicians, a sentimental response. In that year the Habsburg archduke Ferdinand addressed them as "you loyal Galicians [*euch getreue Galizier*]," naming them as such, and acknowledging them as the "younger brothers" of the Habsburg community, which they had joined in 1772.[135]

In 1809 there was also published in Vienna a Latin botanical treatise on the native plants of Galicia: *Primitiae Florae Galiciae Austriacae Utriusque*, by Wilibald Swibert Joseph Gottlieb von Besser. The title specified "both" parts of Galicia, East and West, though West Galicia was abolished that same year and joined to the Grand Duchy of Warsaw. The book treated Galicia as a whole, with its two volumes divided not geographically between East and West but, rather, according to Linnaean principles of classification: the

first volume covered Monandria-Polyandria, based on the number of sta-
mens, while the second volume discussed Didynamia-Dioecia, based on the
principle of botanical sexual differentiation. Most remarkable, in historical
retrospect, was the completely casual acceptance by the author that Galicia,
which had been invented only in 1772, was of such self-evident coherence
that it was possible to discern and describe its native plants while treating the
province as a unified botanical domain. Besser noted the obstacles to botanical collection in Galicia: the Carpathian Mountains, the "most terrible forests
[*sylvarum horridissimarum*]," the "treacherous marshes [*paludum infidarum*]." He
paid tribute to Joseph II and also to Franz, as imperial patrons of science
at the university in Lviv.[136] As he collected scientific specimens and collated
botanical reports, Besser did not doubt the political, topographical, or botanical reality of Galicia, which, by 1809, already had a history that dated back a
whole generation.

Galicia would re-emerge in 1815, after the Congress of Vienna, with some
territorial revision. The post-Napoleonic restoration of Galicia, however,
was no great innovation, but simply an affirmation of continuity with the
Habsburg monarchy of the late eighteenth century. In 1772, the invention
of Galicia was accompanied by the fictive revindication of a province that
the Hungarian crown had failed to hold several centuries earlier. In 1815, the
re-establishment of Galicia looked back across the political lapse of a mere
decade to a name and domain that had acquired the historical texture of
cultural and political authenticity within the Habsburg monarchy. In 1792 the
Galician poet recalled that he and his sons had been subjects of the Habsburg
monarchy for twenty years. By 1815 he could already have spoken as a Galician
grandfather.

CHAPTER TWO

Galicia Restored

The Politics of Metternich and the Comedies of Fredro

⌒

Introduction: "Uncertainty of Possession"

In 1811, as Napoleon contemplated the fateful invasion of Russia and mobilized the Polish troops of the Grand Duchy of Warsaw, Metternich in Vienna worried over what remained of Habsburg Galicia. West Galicia had already been joined to the Grand Duchy two years earlier, and Napoleon's mystique was so great among Poles that the Habsburgs could hardly feel confident of Galician loyalty. Metternich acutely recognized that Galicia was, in fact, one of Napoleon's principal pressure points for preserving the Austrian alliance. "The great motive that dictated our conduct, the motive that he has put forward," noted Metternich to Emperor Franz, "was the uncertainty of possession of Galicia after the re-establishment of the kingdom of Poland." Napoleon meaningfully emphasized this: "He spoke of the possibility of insurrections which, in the course of the next war, could break out in our province of Galicia—and which he might find himself inclined to support in the interest of his Polish allies." Uncertainty of possession was further aggravated from the eastern side, where the movements of the Russian army, as Metternich noted, meant that "one day, given certain circumstances, the occupation of Galicia could well be brought about without our consent."[1] In 1811, as Europe prepared for what would turn out to be the decisive campaigns of the Napoleonic wars, there was every reason to be skeptical about the future of Galicia as a Habsburg province.

Although Galicia had been ruled by the Habsburgs since the first Polish partition of 1772, and its acquisition had been justified as the legitimate "revindication" of the medieval Hungarian claim, Metternich in 1811 did not indulge in futile protestations of legitimacy in the face of Napoleonic intimations of power. Rather, he readily prepared for the possibility of losing Galicia and asked, in the spirit of enlightened statecraft, the same pragmatic questions that Prince Kaunitz might have asked in the previous generation: "What does Napoleon understand as an equivalent for Galicia?" and "What, as an increase in territory, population, and revenues, is the equivalent that the Emperor of the French offers us for Galicia?"[2] In fact, the Josephine generation of the late eighteenth century had provided precisely the administrative knowledge and appreciation of Galicia that made it possible to evaluate the worth of the province in terms of territory, population, and revenues. Now Metternich was ready to trade it away, and his papers indicate that he was particularly interested in trading landbound Galicia for the Napoleonic provinces of Illyria, including the Adriatic coast of Dalmatia. Galicia's subterranean dimension, however, was of economic interest to Metternich, and he hoped to be able to avoid surrendering the salt mine at Wieliczka.[3]

As a consequence of Metternich's careful diplomacy and Napoleon's ultimate defeat, the Habsburgs would actually end up with both Galicia and Dalmatia at the Congress of Vienna in 1815. Cracow, however, was not restored to Austrian rule but established as a semi-independent urban republic—the Free, Independent, and Strictly Neutral City of Cracow—under the "protection" of Austria, Prussia, and Russia. Furthermore, most of West Galicia (acquired by Austria in the third partition of 1795) was now assigned to Congress Poland, to be ruled by the Russian czar. Galicia as restored in 1815 was close to the original Galicia of 1772 but was still a work in progress: Cracow would be effectively joined to Galicia after 1846, while Bukovina would be administratively separated from Galicia in 1849.

Metternich's Galicia would never rest securely on the eighteenth-century ideological foundations of dynastic revindication, as proposed by Maria Theresa, or enlightened messianism, as pursued by Joseph. Yet during the reign of Franz, who lived until 1835, Habsburg Galicia gradually achieved a renewal of legitimacy in the post-Napoleonic ideological context, deeply imbued with the conservatism of the Metternich era. The "uncertainty of possession," clearly discerned during the Napoleonic interlude, was later reflected in ideological ambivalence concerning the nature and identity of the province itself. Police and censorship, the hallmarks of the regime of Metternich and Franz throughout the Habsburg lands, defined the limitations of the emerging public sphere in Galicia, as journalistic ventures of modest ambition sought to address the measurable value of the province—territory, population, revenues—while also seeking a sentimental sense of provincial identity.

The uncertain nature of Galician identity remained a matter of tense ideological negotiation. The nascent competition between Polish and Ruthenian national claims upon the Galician cultural space led to the writing of Ruthenian textbooks for school use after 1815 and would finally result in the publication of the national poems of the Ruthenian Triad in the 1830s. Meanwhile, Galician Jewish reformers like Joseph Perl looked for an alliance with the Habsburg government to challenge the religious power of Hasidism in Galicia. At the same time there were concerted efforts to bridge the sometimes overlapping domains of German and Polish culture in the province, especially at the university in Lviv, and to articulate a common Galician culture in such public forums as *Gazeta Lwowska* (*The Lwów Gazette*) and *Pamiętnik Galicyjski* (*The Galician Journal*). The Ruthenian clergyman Ivan Lavrovsky sought to compile a Ruthenian-Polish-German dictionary as a sort of summation of Galician language, and Metternich wondered whether the government could synthesize its subjects to "make true Galicians."

Franz Xaver Wolfgang Mozart in Galicia, the great composer's son, regarded himself as a representative of Viennese culture in the provinces, while Józef Maksymilian Ossoliński in Vienna ambiguously represented both Polish national culture and Galician provincial concerns. His creation of the Ossolineum Library in Lviv was an important institutional step toward the cultural re-establishment of post-Napoleonic Galicia. The towering figure of Galician culture in the 1820s and 1830s was the dramatist Aleksander Fredro, whose comedies of Galician life, performed on stage in Lviv, reflected some of the ideological tensions of provincial identity. In 1835, Fredro was denounced by a Polish critic for writing "non-national" dramas, and that charge may be seen as closely related to his Galician circumstances. Post-Napoleonic Galicia, restored and governed by the imperial policies of Metternich and Franz, was also the Galicia of Fredro's provincial comedies, and political conservatism only barely contained the province's contradictory and combustible cultural elements.

"The Franco-Galician Army"

Under the reign of Joseph II, in a period of relative freedom from censorship, the *Lemberger Zeitung* was established in 1787 in Galicia, publishing the news in German. In 1811, while Metternich attempted to calculate the "equivalent" value of Galicia amid the upheaval of the Napoleonic campaigns, a semiofficial journal was founded in the Polish language, *Gazeta Lwowska*. The founding editor was Franz (or, in Polish, Franciszek) Kratter, who was not, it seems, the same Franz Kratter who had published his letters about Galicia in the 1780s—and was still alive and well and actually living in Galicia in 1811. These two men with the same name were probably cousins, one principally a writer, dramatist, and theater director, the other a Habsburg civil servant and newspaper editor. The Polish prospectus for the newspaper in 1811 proclaimed that "every country has newspapers according to its own needs, only Galicia does not have them," and promised to publish "whatever may be particularly useful for Galicia." A contemporary Viennese journal noted the appearance of "a Polish newspaper under the title *Gazeta Lwowska* (*Lemberger Zeitung*) that remedies the urgent need of a nation of more than three million souls."[4] There were three million Galicians, but certainly not three million Polish Galicians, so this designated "nation" was ambiguously national in character. The new newspaper—edited by a Habsburg civil servant with a German name and family origin—would seek to affirm the identity of Galicia before the Polish public at a moment when the very existence of the province was tenuously uncertain.

The national quality of *Gazeta Lwowska* was problematically conditioned by the need to reconcile the nationally incendiary Napoleonic news of the day with the legitimation of Habsburg imperial rule in Galicia. In the year 1812, as Napoleon's Grande Armée prepared for the invasion of Russia—to be launched from formerly Polish lands, with the cooperation of a hundred thousand Polish soldiers—Poles dared to imagine the possibility of national independence. This was the moment that would be immortalized in the Romantic epic poem *Pan Tadeusz* by Adam Mickiewicz, composed in Paris in the 1830s. The Galician perspective on the invasion of Russia, as articulated in *Gazeta Lwowska* during the course of 1812, offered a tensely wrought cultural representation of the mingled hopes, frustrations, anxieties, and uncertainties of the Habsburg government that sponsored the newspaper and the Polish public that read it.

In the early months of 1812, *Gazeta Lwowska* published foreign news from the Grand Duchy of Warsaw and from Napoleonic Paris—the same news that Metternich was worrying over in Vienna—while a steady supply of less disturbing domestic stories, from Lviv, from Vienna, and from the wider Habsburg realm, constituted the Galician news of the day. The weather in Lviv was reported with monthly summaries of barometric readings and inclement conditions: in January 1812 there were seventeen days of snow and sixteen of fog. In February the birthday of Emperor Franz was celebrated in Lviv with the presence on the Rynek, the Market Square, of a battalion of grenadiers, a division of hussars, and the local militia. In the afternoon the governor, Count Peter Goess, gave a dinner at which the emperor and em-

View of Lemberg (Lwów, Lviv). The tower of the Town Hall in the Market Square dominates the urban landscape. The tower collapsed in 1826 and was rebuilt in 1835. From Julius Jandaurek, *Das Königreich Galizien und Lodomerien* (Vienna: Karl Graeser, 1884).

press were ceremonially toasted, and in the evening, in the Municipal Theater, Haydn's imperial hymn was sung, and the members of the audience cried out, *"Vivat!"* The governor provided charity for the poor in honor of the emperor's birthday, and winners were announced for an essay contest on the improvement of agriculture in Galicia. Thus, the occasion of the emperor's birthday, as covered in *Gazeta Lwowska*, served to dramatize the dynastic element of Galician identity, the supposedly enthusiastic appreciation of the province for the supposedly beneficent Habsburg emperor.[5] Ironically, the festivities of dynastic celebration occurred in Lviv at the same time that Metternich in Vienna was actually thinking about trading Galicia for Dalmatia.

The essay contest on agricultural improvement looked back to the Josephine project of development in Galicia, which was in turn closely related to the Enlightenment's vision of backwardness as the defining characteristic of Eastern Europe in comparison with Western Europe. *Gazeta Lwowska* published some of the essays, for instance: "What means and industry does the English nation employ in the cultivation of the earth and the improvement of fertility, and how might we be able to imitate in this regard?" It was an article that meticulously counted 310,758 oxen and 527,519 cows in Galicia, "in our country [*w naszym kraju*]," and studiously neglected the ongoing international crisis.[6] No mention was made of the fact that England was thoroughly engaged in the struggle against Napoleon, whose campaigns were, at that very moment, exciting the Polish public with hopes of national independence. Counting cows was, in some sense, the prescribed Galician antidote for the Polish national fever.

In February 1812, *Gazeta Lwowska* included an article on how to obtain improved agricultural implements before spring, advertising especially items for farming potatoes, including a specialized potato hoe [*radło ziemniakowe*]. The notice was aimed at "lovers of higher cultivation in Galicia" at a moment when the potato crop may not have been uppermost in many Galician hearts and minds.[7] In March, *Gazeta Lwowska* celebrated the Sisters of Charity in Galicia, the originally French order of nuns who performed good works for the poor: "a pleasant and joyful subject of consideration for every friend of humanity." In fact, *Gazeta Lwowska* had in mind one particular friend of humanity and recalled that when Emperor Joseph II had visited Lviv in 1783, he had particularly praised the Sisters of Charity. *Gazeta Lwowska* fondly recalled "that great monarch, so solicitous for the good of humanity"—without needing to mention his general hostility to most other religious orders in the Habsburg monarchy.[8]

Gazeta Lwowska offered an even more forcefully explicit affirmation of Galicia with the publication in February of a prize-winning geological essay by Samuel Bredetzky, "A Glance at the Structure of the Galician Soil" ("Rzut oka na strukturę ziemi galicyjskiej"). Bredetzky was a Protestant pastor in Lviv, serving the German community. He wrote in German a travel account of Hungary and Galicia, published in Vienna in 1809; then, in 1812, which was also the year of his death, he published in Brno his *Historical-Statistical Contribution concerning the German Colonial Presence in Europe and a Short Description of the German Settlements in Galicia in Alphabetical Order*. His essay in *Gazeta Lwowska* offered a geological survey of Galicia, with particular attention to the relevance of geology to the quality of the soil. This description of the province affirmed the geological character, and even the agricultural destiny, of Galicia as a whole: "Nature has destined Galicia to be a granary [*Natura przeznaczyła Galicyę na kraj zbożowy*]."[9] The notion of Galicia as possessing any sort of natural providence was certainly striking in view of the fact that the province had been conceived as a completely artificial vindication of the partition of 1772, and that its dismemberment or dissolution was even now being contemplated in Vienna in exchange for equivalent value.

In March 1812, *Gazeta Lwowska* enthusiastically reported on the preparation of a new almanac for 1813, "The Poetic Almanac for Galicia." There would be two versions, one in Polish and one in German: "In this manner, we will refute in part the reproach that in our country, till now, learning has progressed too little." The almanac, intended thus as an antidote to allegations of backwardness, was being prepared by Professor Wacław Hann, who further sought to disprove the "so frequent and so unfounded opinion about the poverty of Polish literature."[10] In May 1812 the announcement of the almanac reached Vienna, and Hann's introduction was published in a journal devoted to art and literature in the Habsburg monarchy. He declared Polish to be "perhaps the queen among all Slavic languages" and therefore rejected the notion that "Galicia has no literature." During the previous year the same Viennese journal, in its "reports from Galicia," had suggested that "literary news from Sarmatia can only be scanty," further affirming that "the plurality of languages prevailing here is a principal obstacle to the promotion of literature in Austrian Galicia."[11] Now Hann proposed to overcome that obstacle.

Hann wanted Germans and Poles to know each other's poetry in Galicia. He claimed that almanacs had already served as vehicles of "enlightenment [*oświecenie*]" in German lands, including Austria: "Oh, that the day may likewise soon be light in the Galician sky, not with blinding brightness, but illuminated by the pleasant rays of the beneficent sun!"[12] Professor Hann was not without some poetic sensibility himself, as he seemed to invoke the spirit of the Enlightenment, even at the dawn of the age of European Romanticism. The publicity for the almanac appeared almost Masonic in its metaphors of light and illumination, as if inspired by Mozart's *Magic Flute*, which Bogusławski had, in fact, produced in Lviv in the 1790s. Hann's almanac affirmed that Galicia was a land of German and Polish poetry, with a provincial identity dependent upon the mutual relation of both languages and literatures.

Within the next generation the Ruthenians of Galicia would challenge the premise that Polish and German poetry were sufficient to define the cultural identity of the province. In the meantime, however, *Gazeta Lwowska* saluted the prospective almanac, noting that "Galicia lacks only opportunity and encouragement in order to be able to become equal with other lands."[13] Backwardness and development were still fundamental to the conception of Galicia in the early nineteenth century. *Gazeta Lwowska*, in the same issue that heralded the almanac, also transcribed a speech given by Metternich in Vienna on the importance of patriotism. He meant Austrian patriotism, of course, on behalf of the Habsburg monarchy. *Gazeta Lwowska*, however, nourished a sort of provincial patriotism, paradoxically self-conscious about Galicia's backwardness with respect to other lands but determined to achieve progress, prosperity, and illumination.

The year 1812 was the year of international destiny for Napoleon's ambitions of European conquest, overshadowing the provincial destiny of
Galicia as a land of grain, potatoes, and poetry. In 1812, *Gazeta Lwowska*
published assorted bits of news about Prince Adam Kazimierz Czartoryski.
In the 1790s he had been one of the Polish reformers in the Four-Year
Sejm in Warsaw, but in 1812 he was a Galician magnate, a field marshal in
the Habsburg army, who had been decorated with the Habsburg Order of
the Golden Fleece. *Gazeta Lwowska* reported in April that Czartoryski had
generously donated from his estate at Sieniawa supplies of potatoes for the
Habsburg army in Galicia. In May, *Gazeta Lwowska* saluted him again, this
time for demonstrating his model Galician spirit at Sieniawa by providing
grain to his starving peasants to make up for the previous year's bad harvest:
"true kindness for suffering humanity." Czartoryski, however, also maintained a political presence in the Grand Duchy of Warsaw, and in July 1812,
Gazeta Lwowska was quoting this allegedly Galician figure as he held forth
from Warsaw, as marshal of the Sejm, speaking a political language that was
altogether alien to Galicia: "Compatriots [*rodacy*] hold out their hands to
compatriots, fathers to sons, sons to fathers, brothers to brothers, they summon one another to the bosom of their single and common fatherland."[14]
Czartoryski thus heralded the imminent resurrection of the Polish state,
under the aegis of Napoleon, and he implicitly called upon compatriots to
reach out to one another across the borders of partitioned Poland, brother
to brother, from Warsaw to Galicia. If there was indeed only one single,
common Polish fatherland, then the significance of Galicia was ideologically uncertain and politically illogical. Czartoryski himself, even with his Order
of the Golden Fleece and his charitable donation of potatoes, made Galicia
seem momentarily meaningless.

Eventually the movements of the Grande Armée, with its Polish significance, would overwhelm any other news in the pages of *Gazeta Lwowska*. The
paper reported that Napoleon himself was in Vilnius, commencing the invasion of Russia and receiving a Polish delegation from Warsaw. Napoleon's
response to the delegation, though actually addressed to Warsaw, was quoted
in *Gazeta Lwowska* for the Polish reading public of Galicia: "If I were a
Pole, I would think and act just like you," declared Napoleon. "Love of the
fatherland is the first virtue of a civilized person." Then, as if aware of the
Galician public, he further remarked: "I must add that I have guaranteed to
the Austrian emperor the integrity of his state, and that I would not allow
any undertaking or disturbance, tending to trouble his peaceful possession
of the portion remaining to him of the Polish provinces."[15] Although *Gazeta
Lwowska* scrupulously quoted Napoleon's explicit reservation about the in-

tegrity of the Habsburg state, including Galicia, the cited words of Czarto-ryski and Napoleon on the Polish "fatherland" could not help provoking Polish hopes and passions in the province.

There were, in fact, many Galicians who participated in the invasion of Russia, including the youthful Aleksander Fredro. The future great writer was only nineteen in 1812, when as a Galician volunteer in the Grande Armée he was present at the fateful Battle of Borodino that turned the tide against Napoleon. While Lviv was celebrating the birthday of the Habsburg emperor in 1812, demonstrating Galician allegiance, Fredro was going into battle cry-ing out, *Vive l'Empereur!* The emperor for whom he fought, however, was the French emperor Napoleon, not the Habsburg emperor Franz. Fredro served in what he called "the Franco-Galician [*francusko-galicyjskiego*] army or the Galicio-French [*galicyjsko-francuskiego*] army (I no longer remember exactly which)."[16] Perhaps the most striking aspect of the "Franco-Galician" designation was the suggestion that Galician identity could exist apart from the Austrian affiliation, and even from the Polish association. Fredro, who first enlisted when he was only sixteen, was very much aware of himself as a teenage Pole during these fighting years, but he also maintained a sense of being Galician. At the same time, his unstable Galician identity was suscep-tible to unconventional hyphenations and recombinations.

In Fredro's memoirs, he observed that the Napoleonic campaigns had the effect of emphasizing differences within the population of Galicia, especially between Germans and Poles. Fredro offered a Linnaean summary of what he regarded as the distinctive species of the Galician German:

> Nota bene: The German of Galicia [*Niemiec galicyjski*] occupies, it is true, in natural history, the place of a race or a profession apart, like the race of French poodles or Tibetan goats, but in fact it is a debased race. Their hatred of Slav-dom, of these natives whose juices they live on, gives a more rapid course to their blood. . . .[17]

Fredro's disparaging sense of the distinctiveness of the Galician German, as a separate species of the Galician genus, expressed his mistrust of Galician German attitudes toward the Polish Napoleonic cause. He remembered the excitement at the arrival of Poniatowski's army in Lviv in 1809: "The whole population Christian and Jewish, with the exception of the German pencil pushers who trembled in their offices, the whole population, I say, boiled, so to speak, with Polish spirit. . . . People kissed the hands and feet of the soldiers, kissed the horses. The enthusiasm bordered on frenzy."[18] The Ger-man Habsburg bureaucrats constituted the unenthusiastic exception.

Fredro was also mistrustful of the supposed Napoleonic enthusiasm of the Jews in Galicia. "In 1809, in Lwów, the ardor of the Jews for our cause was immense," recalled Fredro. "In 1812 in Lithuania, and then in the Grand Duchy, the Jews became our principal enemies."[19] Yet, he did not articulate a cultural distinction between Galician Jews and Lithuanian Jews, insisting, rather, that "a Jew remains always a Jew," and that they cared only about money in the end. He mistrusted both Jews and Germans in Galicia, as they seemed to him clearly distinct from Poles and ultimately aloof from the Polish cause, but he recognized that they too had some claim to being Galician.

Young Mozart in Galicia

During the Napoleonic wars the musician Franz Xaver Wolfgang Mozart, the younger son of the great composer, was living in Galicia as a "Galician German," that "debased race" of Fredro's disparaging reflections. Young Mozart was born in 1791, the year of his father's death, and was already advertised as performing in Prague in 1797:

> By gracious request the small, just six-year-old Wolfgang, Mozart's younger son, will be presented to the admirable public of Prague, which displayed such manifold affection for his father. He will proffer a small token of thanks for this, and will attempt to follow the great example of his father singing the Aria "Der Vogelfänger bin ich" from *The Magic Flute*, accompanied on the pianoforte. One asks for forbearance at this first attempt to display his gentle talents.[20]

A decade later, in 1808, at the age of seventeen, he moved from Vienna to Galicia, hoping to earn his living as a music teacher. Himself a talented pianist and even a composer of some promise, he went by his father's name, Wolfgang, and found a position giving lessons in the noble family of Count Wiktor Baworowski. In the early nineteenth century the Galician spheres of German and Polish culture and society were not altogether separate and hostile. The career of Franz Xaver Mozart in and around Lviv suggested some of the nuances and complexities of cultural integration in Galicia.

Constanze Mozart, the great composer's widow, wrote to her older son Karl in 1808 to announce young Wolfgang's impending move: "Your brother has an engagement to go to Poland." The name "Galicia" did not seem to enter into her consciousness or correspondence. Young Wolfgang himself, however, knew exactly where he was, when he wrote to request copies of his father's music from the Leipzig publishers Breitkopf and Härtel: "I have already informed you from Lemberg about my arrival in Galicia."[21] At the beginning of 1809, the same year in which sixteen-year-old Fredro would join the Franco-Galician army, a year of Napoleonic upheaval in Galicia, eighteen-year-old Mozart gave an account of his situation to his brother in a letter that began, "How strangely destiny plays with men!" He did not mean the destiny of warring armies but rather the destiny of musical careers.

> For three months I have not been in our beloved native city, but in Galicia, several miles from Lemberg, employed by a count, to give his two daughters four hours of lessons daily. For that I get food, lodging, wood, light, laundry, etc. free. Here I will try my hardest to perfect my art, and then, when circumstances permit otherwise, I will undertake a journey.

He did not plan to remain in Galicia forever, but he declared himself for the moment "very satisfied," and ended up staying for a decade.[22] His career would eventually take him all over Europe, back to Galicia in the 1820s and 1830s, and finally home to Vienna. Although Mozart's son knew that a sojourn in Galicia might seem a strange turn of destiny, he thought it a plausible base for building his European career.

Constanze was skeptical, and she wrote to Karl about young Wolfgang in 1809: "Since he has gone to Poland, he has composed three sonatas for the flute and piano. I am not satisfied with that. All that is too little for a young man who should be training, who should be doing honor to himself and his father." She sent Karl a song that young Wolfgang had composed to a poem by none other than "Professor Hann of Lemberg," the illuminating sponsor of the almanac. It was a nature poem in German "To the Brooks" ("An die Bäche"). The musical setting of Hann's poem indicated that young Mozart was in some contact with the Lviv circle of *Gazeta Lwowska*, and especially with those forces committed to the rapprochement of German and Polish culture in Galicia. Young Mozart himself was writing to Breitkopf and Härtel in Leipzig in 1809 to request some music paper, "because there is none to be had in Lemberg, and the road to Vienna is obstructed."[23] Such was the young musician's minimal allusion to the great Napoleonic struggle that was taking place in Austria and Galicia.

He also complained about not having a really good piano to play upon, and it was just at this time that Constanze, preparing to marry again and move to Denmark, decided to dispose of Mozart's own piano and had to choose between his two sons for that precious legacy. She decided to send the piano to Karl—who was living in Milan—the older brother but the lesser musician, rather than to young Wolfgang in Galicia. The latter was already becoming more openly disenchanted with the Galician circumstances. He was living in the country with Count Baworowski, in the village of Podkamień, and wrote thus to a German friend in Weimar in 1810:

> Already since October 1808 I have been in Galicia, in the country, which can not compare with the charming environs of Vienna. Nevertheless I have already

become rather accustomed to my new situation, and would perhaps not feel so much the comical contrast (which is rather notable) between Vienna and a desolate Polish village, if I did not have to be completely deprived of the pleasure of seeing my friends, of hearing good music, and of reading the journals and intellectual productions that deal with my own art as well as literature in general.[24]

His was a powerfully negative idea of Galicia—no friends, no music, no journals, no literature—while the sense of contrast, conceived as "comic" in the true Mozartean spirit, represented the difference between Vienna and Podkamień, between the imperial metropolis and a provincial village. Young Mozart appealed to his correspondent for letters "in my loneliness [*in meiner Einsamkeit*]," a Galician loneliness in which the aloofness of the Enlightenment was flavored with the melancholy of Romanticism.[25] In 1810 he did actually compose a song entitled "Die Einsamkeit," but it was unexpectedly cheerful in musical spirit, and the words seemed to welcome solitude:

> My wish and my joy are you, solitude [*bist Einsamkeit du*],
> and domestic peace and country calm [*und ländliche Ruh*].[26]

This declaration of peace was perhaps wishful thinking in Napoleonic Europe, with the world at war, but the sentiment served to express a sense of Galician isolation.

Solitude, though welcome in the song, appeared as an obstacle to artistic creativity in young Wolfgang's letters. Writing to his brother Karl in 1810, he complained that he was simply unable to compose music in the provincial circumstances: "I compose—nothing. The sad and lonely life that I must lead here dulls my sensibility so much that I must often torment myself for an entire day in order to bring forth the smallest trifle." Thus, the son of the greatest genius of the previous generation attributed his creative crisis to the misfortune of living in Galicia. "As an artist I will profit little in a village, in a land where I am perhaps the first in my profession," he wrote to Karl, with remarkable presumptuousness as a composer who was composing nothing. "If you consider this exaggeration or vanity, I would ask you to come here yourself and become convinced."[27] Young Wolfgang thus found in Galicia the domain where he might consider himself unrivaled, the first among musicians, truly his father's heir, but only within the provincial Galician limits.

In 1811 young Mozart left his position with the Baworowski family and moved into the city of Lviv itself, where he would remain until 1818. While Napoleon invaded Russia from Lithuania, was driven back across Europe, and was ultimately defeated at Leipzig in 1813 and then Waterloo in 1815, young Wolfgang gave music lessons in Lviv and followed world affairs from the Galician perspective. He lived as music master with the Janiszewski family, giving his address in the care of Countess Janiszewska. According to the research of Walter Hummel, young Wolfgang also probably gave lessons for the grandest aristocrats, such as the Czartoryski family. He was particularly involved with the Habsburg bureaucratic family of Baroni-Cavalcabò, giving lessons to the daughter of the family, Julie, and probably becoming romantically involved with the mistress of the house, Josephine. While his lover in Lviv may have been the Italian wife of a Habsburg bureaucrat, young Mozart's friends there certainly included Poles. In 1811 he recommended to his publishers, Breitkopf and Härtel in Leipzig, music composed by his Lviv "friends [*Freunde*]" Lipiński and Kaszkowski (probably the violinist Karol Lipiński and the composer Joachim Kaczkowski, his name misspelled).[28] In any event, such names strongly suggest that young Mozart in Lviv moved easily in Polish social circles. When he was still living with the Baworowski family in the "Polish village," and claimed to be "the first in my profession," there was perhaps some sense of German superiority that conditioned his lonely arrogance. Yet, in Lviv, there was no mention of German identity in relation to the Polish patrons and friends whose names appeared in his correspondence. In recommending his Polish friends to his German publisher in 1811, young Mozart reflected the cultural rapprochement that Professor Hann sought to advance in 1812 with his literary almanac.

A letter to Breitkopf and Härtel in 1816 indicated what sort of music young Mozart was composing in Lviv. The publishers were printing copies of his music in Leipzig to send to him in Lviv, and he was impatient:

> The day before yesterday I finally received my so long-awaited polonaises, and I saw with no small amazement that the conditions by which I entrusted them to you must have been completely forgotten. Since these trifles in my eyes had too little worth to demand an honorarium in money, I requested forty copies and the exclusive right of sale in Lemberg for one year (understood to be one year calculated from the day that I would receive them). That you granted all this to me is proved by your esteemed letter of May 18, 1814, which I still have in hand. After two years I now finally receive seven, instead of forty copies.[29]

His "trifles," the scant products of his tormented creativity, were these "long-awaited polonaises," specifically Polish dances, for which he believed he would find a market in Lviv.

These particular trifles must have been the six polonaises mélancoliques for piano, numbered as opus 17 among the composer's works. Furthermore, since young Mozart was already requesting copies in 1814, they must have been completed in the preceding period—that is, at the culmination and collapse of the Napoleonic campaigns between 1812 and 1814, as Polish hopes were raised to the point of national ecstasy and then dashed by the disaster of the Grande Armée in retreat from Russia. The young Mozart, Viennese

by birth and German by language, was nevertheless sufficiently inspired by
the Polish context of Galicia to invest his painfully obstructed creativity in
the composition of six polonaises. He would compose four more by 1820,
dedicated to the countess Rzewuska, and two more by 1823, dedicated to the
countess Głogowska.[30] In the 1830s it would be Frédéric (Fryderyk) Chopin
who would transform the polonaise through his creative genius, infusing the
dance with the spirit of musical Romanticism and also the passion of Polish
nationalism. Young Mozart, in Galicia at the Napoleonic moment, already
responded to the same rhythms. In 1812, while Fredro, with the Franco-Galician troops, was on his way to Borodino, Franz Xaver Wolfgang Mozart was
perhaps contemplating the composition of a polonaise.

"A Flowering Oasis in the Sahara Desert"

The musical public in Lviv for young Mozart's polonaises would have
overlapped with the reading public for *Gazeta Lwowska*. In 1812, by the end of
the summer, the pages of the newspaper were increasingly filled with news
of the military campaign in Russia. In September, as the Battle of Borodino
was being fought near Moscow, *Gazeta Lwowska* was still reporting the news
of Napoleon's earlier victory at Smolensk. A notice on the "birthday of the
emperor" referred this time not to the Habsburg emperor Franz but rather
to Napoleon, whose birthday had been celebrated in France on 15 August in
his absence. The news of Napoleon's taking of Moscow was accompanied
by featured stories about Moscow itself. "The sight of the city of Moscow
seemed new and wild for every foreigner," remarked *Gazeta Lwowska*, at a
moment when a foreign army, including Galicians, was occupying Moscow.
Yet Galicia was not without wildness of its own, and the newspaper reported
that a young Greek Catholic villager was put to death in Galicia for murdering a fourteen-year-old boy in a dispute over a cap on the way home from
the market in Zolochiv.[31] With Napoleon in Moscow, everything Eastern,
including perhaps Greek Christianity, appeared under the sign of savagery
in the pages of *Gazeta Lwowska*.

The ultimate proof of Muscovite barbarism, however, was discovered in
the reports of Russian arson from the occupied city. *Gazeta Lwowska* translated into Polish the story from the *Journal de Paris* about the fires in Moscow,
thus synthesizing a Franco-Galician perspective on Russia: "There remains to
us the extremely painful obligation of mentioning one feature of barbarism,
an obligation which we would want to refuse, if it were not necessary to let
all Europe know the character and customs of this people, which has so

many times been presented as a civilized nation." *Gazeta Lwowska* outlined
the whole history of Moscow and reacted with horror to the burning of the
city:

> Such were the various vicissitudes of the city of Moscow up to the terrible mo-
> ment when monstrous barbarism, unworthy to be called human, gave it over to
> destruction. After seven centuries of existence, this splendid city would have
> been completely destroyed if the magnanimity of the Emperor of the French
> and the devotion of his courageous armies had not protected it.[32]

Gazeta Lwowska thus permitted its Galician public to adopt the perspective
of French civilization in its fierce contempt for Muscovite barbarism. Franz
Xaver Wolfgang Mozart might deplore the cultural poverty of a Galician village, but from the urban perspective of Lviv he might have joined the public
of *Gazeta Lwowska* in 1812 in deploring the monstrous barbarism of Russia.

By the end of the year the news from Russia was very different. The Russians were celebrating Napoleon's withdrawal from Moscow, and in Warsaw
there was issued a desperate appeal to the Poles to continue to fight for
Napoleon. This was reprinted in *Gazeta Lwowska* for Galician readers, but
Polish hopes of imminent national resurrection now seemed increasingly
implausible. On 23 December, Lviv celebrated the Christmas season with a
performance of Haydn's oratorio *The Seasons*, with the profits to benefit the
poor.[33] Thus the year 1812, with its stirring summer of Polish national passions, concluded on a Habsburg musical note in a winter of Galician charity
and resignation.

"With the decline of French power, the hopes of the Poles also declined,"
recalled Fredro in his Napoleonic memoirs. The Galician mood was one of
deep disillusionment over the dissipation of the Napoleonic mirage, and
after the Congress of Vienna in 1815, under Metternich's brand of Habsburg
absolutism, there was little opportunity for the pursuit of national politics.
Rather, according to Fredro, in the concluding sentence of his memoirs,
"The domestic happiness of the Pole is at present a flowering oasis in the
Sahara desert (*Szczęście domowe Polaka jest teraz oazą kwiecistą śród puszczy Sa-
hary*)."[34] In the political desert of Metternich's Galicia, Fredro himself would
discover his dramatic genius for domestic comedy.

For young Mozart, as for Fredro, the period after the Congress of Vienna
appeared as a moment for comedy. Mozart the son contemplated the great
opera buffa masterpieces of Mozart the father. "Recently I got much enjoy-
ment from the production of Figaro," wrote young Mozart in Lviv in 1817.
"What splendid music! Why did my father have to be torn away so soon from
us and from the world?"[35] Then, in 1818, young Mozart finally tore himself
away from Lviv, giving a farewell concert that received a negative review in

Vienna from the *Allgemeine musikalische Zeitung*. The principal performance
of the program was the composer playing his own piano concerto, which
left the Viennese reviewer "cold"—but was not actually criticized in detail,
"out of respect for the name Mozart." The opening piece of the program
was the overture to *Cosi fan tutte*, which the reviewer dismissed as "feebly"
done, and the concluding piece was the operatic finale from the same opera
buffa.[36] By 1818, Franz Xaver Wolfgang Mozart had succeeded in becoming
sufficiently Galician to receive a measure of dismissive Viennese contempt
for his provincial efforts in Lviv.

In the finale of *Cosi fan tutte* Ferrando and Guglielmo, who have been
courting in disguise each other's lovers, to test their fidelity, pretend to return
from combat in war, and surprise the unfaithful Fiordiligi and Dorabella. In
Lorenzo Da Ponte's libretto there was no real war, and the heroes were only
pretending to have been summoned to the army. Yet Mozart composed the
opera in 1790, when Habsburg soldiers really were at war against Ottoman
Turkey, and Franz Xaver Wolfgang Mozart presented the overture and finale
in Lviv in 1818, when the Napoleonic wars were only three years over. There
really had been soldiers, just recently, of the Franco-Galician army, who had
returned home to faithful or unfaithful wives or lovers. The finale of *Cosi fan
tutte* peculiarly fit the spirit of peacetime in Metternich's Galicia, but precisely
because the opera buffa made military service into a merely fictive pretext
for romantic comedy. The soldiers returned from a war that had never really
happened.

In 1825, Fredro looked back to the age of the Napoleonic wars for the
setting of his comedy *Ladies and Hussars* (*Damy i Huzary*). The hussars of
the title, including a major, a captain, and a young lieutenant, were all "on
leave" on a Galician estate in the country, and, though this was a drama set
in wartime, the war itself was extremely remote from the dramatic action.
The only action that the soldiers saw was the "invasion" of their masculine
company by a party of ladies, the major's sisters, intent upon "capturing" one
or more of the men for the purposes of marriage. Although the hussars were
described as handling guns in the opening scene, the audience immediately
learned that the weapons were intended for hunting. There was "a table covered with maps," a seeming allusion to the great international drama that was
being played out on the stage of history, but the hussars were not studying
the military situation, and the major, in the opening scene, querulously asked
one of his men, "Why do you leave my pipe here on the maps?"[37] Fredro,
though he himself had fought in the Napoleonic wars, and experienced the
bloody intensity of combat, nevertheless took the extreme dramatic liberty
of representing those wars in the spirit of domestic comedy.

The ladies' plan was to marry off the old major to his young niece, who had acquired the charming accomplishment of singing Rossini arias, though she might, in fact, have been taking piano lessons with Franz Xaver Wolfgang Mozart in Lviv. In the end she married the young lieutenant, and the old major declared that military operations were thus concluded: "Let it be enough for you ladies that you conquered hussars, that they were forced to capitulate and surrender one of their number to you in slavery, and—you will admit—the very best among them."[38] Though these hussars could perhaps have been the "Franco-Galician" troops, among which Fredro himself enlisted in 1809, Napoleon's name was never mentioned in the play, and the soldiers might actually have been in the service of the Habsburg emperor. In 1825, of course, any troops to be found in Galicia would have been wearing the Habsburg uniform, and a comedy performed at the height of the Metternich era in Galicia could hardly have posed the political problem of alienated military loyalties. Since the hussars were, anyway, on leave throughout the play, there was no need to specify whether they belonged to Franco-Galician or Austro-Galician regiments. Looking back to a historical moment when Metternich himself was uncertain about the future of Galicia, Fredro infused some of that spirit of uncertainty into the retrospectively comic scenario of Galicia in wartime.

"To Make True Galicians"

In April 1815, while the Congress of Vienna was in session, and the diplomats tensely awaited the military outcome of Napoleon's Hundred Days, Metternich met in the Austrian capital with Peter Goess, the Habsburg governor of Galicia, and then reported on Galician affairs to Emperor Franz. Metternich and Goess emphasized the importance of "secret police preparations"—a hallmark of the Metternich period throughout the monarchy—and also "political and administrative regulations in order to confirm more and more the dependence of the Galicians on the Austrian imperial state."[39] Galicia's nineteenth-century future would lie within the Habsburg monarchy after all.

In 1815, Metternich and Goess were also puzzling over the problem of identity in Galicia, involving the tension between Polish and German presences, much as the problem had been formulated in the Josephine decade of the 1780s. Yet Metternich and Goess, in the early nineteenth century, possessed a better appreciation of the potency of potentially national identities, and Metternich would spend the next generation trying to de-emphasize and even suppress them wherever possible in the Habsburg monarchy. In the case of Galicia there was every reason to recognize the latent force of Polish identity, especially after the Napoleonic interlude, which sent young Galicians like Fredro all the way to Moscow and back again because they believed in the Polish cause. Metternich thus gave the issue of identity due consideration in 1815.

> Concerning political applications Count Goess very rightly remarks that the tendency must principally be: not to make Poles into Germans all at once, but above all first to make true Galicians [*ächte Gallizier zu machen*], since only through this course of stages [*Stuffengang*] can one hope to achieve the ultimate goal [*End-zweck*], and any other conduct by the government would not only lead away from it, but could become at the present moment even dangerous.[40]

Metternich regarded national identity as potentially dangerous, but he was also sensitive to its possible plasticity. "True Galicians" could be "made" by means of government policy, but Poles could not be pressured to submit to the radical metamorphosis of becoming Germans without risk of a danger-ous reaction. Already in the 1780s, Kratter's letters articulated the concept of Galicia as a province to be purged of its Polish vices through Habsburg rule and German influence. Reciprocally, the anonymous Galician poet of 1792, author of "Consequences of the Works of Voltaire," claimed to possess the heart of a "true Pole" beating within his Galician exterior. To be truly Galician appeared as both a synthesis and an intermediary stage between the true Pole and the true German.

As Metternich sought to bring about "the dependence of the Galicians on the Austrian imperial state," he recognized the intermediary Galician identity as fitting for that purpose. A Galician identity might even serve to reconcile Polish and German with Ruthenian and Jewish elements within the province. The invention of Galicia in the eighteenth century called for the invention of Galicians in the nineteenth century.

For Metternich the crucial object of Habsburg government policy was "to win over the minds of the Galicians [*die Gemüther der Gallizier zu gewinnen*]." They had to be won over to the Habsburg government, but also, since they were still Galicians in the making, won over to being Galician. The empha-sis on *Gemüther* made it very clear that Metternich understood this to be a matter of interior conversion and metamorphosis, a matter of identity. To be Galician was not simply to reside on this side of the border rather than that side of the border. Metternich was willing to contemplate, as he wrote to the emperor, the possibility of some sort of constitution for the estates of Galicia, offering "national representation," the distribution of Habsburg offices among the most prosperous families of the province, and even, in the spirit of Joseph II, the alleviation of some of the burdens of the poor and oppressed. Metternich's final caution to the emperor concerned the newly reorganized Habsburg province of Lombardy-Venetia, warning that any imperial favors granted there might excite resentful jealousy in Galicia. The emperor should take care, "lest the Galicians also be left with the pretext for regarding themselves as less favored or even slighted."[41] Metternich's notion of the Galicians—their touchy sensitivity, rivalrous jealousy, and susceptibility to being won over with favors and offices—was curiously close to the comic vision that Fredro offered in his dramas during the ensuing decades. The statesman's manipulative political vision and the writer's comic dramatic vision were both premised upon a Galician dramatis personae without definitive national character, motivated by the mundane aspirations and anxieties of the human condition.

Metternich's letter of 1815 made clear that Galicia's integration within the Habsburg monarchy would be purposefully pursued, but he urged that this policy not be openly articulated: "Only there must not be, as Count Goess suggests, talk of any confirmation of the unification of Galicia with the Austrian imperial state, because such an utterance could easily give occasion for misunderstandings about the earlier relations of this land."[42] The resumption of Austrian rule in Galicia in 1815, following the interval of uncertainty during the Napoleonic period, was to obtain legitimacy precisely from its continuity with eighteenth-century Habsburg rule in the province. To speak of greater political integration in 1815 would encourage attention to the details of Galicia's earlier status, and would inevitably lead back to the moment of the first partition of Poland in 1772, when "Galicia" was simply invented. Only by the affirmation of perfect continuity, while at the same time encouraging political ambiguity about the previous and present political conditions of the province, could Metternich hope to win over the Galicians to being Galician.

In 1817, Galicia received a visit from Emperor Franz. In that same year, the condition of post-Napoleonic Galicia took shape with the renewal of the Galician Sejm, the refounding of the Lviv University, the establishment in that city of the Ossolineum Library, and the publication of a literary supplement to *Gazeta Lwowska*, called *Rozmaitości (Variety)*. The Sejm was a sort of estates general, in the spirit of the ancien régime, with precedents dating back to the time of Maria Theresa and Joseph, in 1775 and 1782, for the consolidation of Galician "estates" that would correspond to the social and political structures of other Habsburg provinces. As reconstituted in 1817, the Sejm was to consist of four estates, representing magnates, gentry, clergy, and towns, meeting once a year to discuss the affairs of the province but with very limited authority.

Before the Napoleonic interlude, such a body existed, according to historian Stanisław Grodziski, as a "useless political ornament," which now, after 1817, acquired somewhat greater, though still consultative, significance as an adjunct to the Habsburg administration in the province.[43] The Sejm had been the crucial legislative body of the Commonwealth of Poland and Lithuania up until its abolition in the final partition of 1795. The existence of a Sejm for Galicia now served to imply that Galicia was a historic Habsburg province with historic political prerogatives. Paradoxically, Habsburg absolutism had to insist on the reality of such prerogatives, indeed to invent them, for the purpose of overriding them on behalf of the imperial state.

The year 1817 also witnessed the refounding of the Lviv University. It had been first established by Joseph in 1784, and was noted with some condescension by Kratter two years later: "The university in Lemberg is still an infant [*Wiegenkind*], that needs careful, attentive, motherly nursing." The creation of Galicia in 1772 had had the effect of cutting off the population from the educational institutions of Poland, so Galicia's alleged provincial integrity called for a university just as it mandated some sort of Sejm. Demoted to lyceum status in 1805, during the Napoleonic wars, the Lviv University was re-established in 1817 as part of the institutional framework of Galicia. It was to be, as before, a German-language university, but in the spirit of Metternich's readiness to win over the Galicians, the government conceded the possibility of a chair in Polish language and literature. The chair was eventually filled in 1826 by Mikołaj Michalewicz, who was interested in both Polish and Ruthenian culture, and played a role in the editing of *Gazeta Lwowska* and *Rozmaitości*.[44]

Very much involved in the Viennese arrangements for the Lviv University, and particularly committed to the chair of Polish, was the literary scholar and collector Józef Maksymilian Ossoliński. He was probably the main author of the "Magna Charta" of Galician rights in 1790, and Ossoliński himself was sufficiently comfortable with Habsburg rule to establish a residence in Vienna at that time. Like Franz Xaver Wolfgang Mozart, he was convinced that cultural pursuits could be more gratifyingly pursued in the Habsburg capital than on a Galician country estate, and, unlike young Mozart, Ossoliński possessed the means to live in Vienna. He was well-connected in the Habsburg capital and enjoyed the friendship of Franz Thugut, the foreign minister in the 1790s. In Vienna, Ossoliński actually headed a Viennese-Galician Economic Institute as well as an Academy of Liberal Arts. Great bibliophile that he was, he amassed his tremendous collection in the Austrian capital and made books and manuscripts available to Polish students there, but the library was ultimately intended for Galicia. In 1809,

Ossoliński received a note from Emperor Franz expressing pleasure and satisfaction at the project of "a national library for Galicia." The emperor offered "the gratitude of the fatherland for your beneficent effort to enhance its intellectual culture."[45] The notion of a "national" library for Galicia suggested that, in the emperor's mind at least, Galicia might constitute a kind of nation within the Habsburg "fatherland."

Ossoliński himself returned to the subject with the return of peace in 1815, and wrote to a friend in Lviv, "For a long time it has been in my heart and on my mind to leave a memorial to my nation." Ossoliński's sense of his own nation was probably more Polish than Galician, but both sentiments were reconcilable in the library project. After living in Vienna for twenty-five years, he proposed to leave his library as a memorial in Lviv. "I care about this library as if I were giving in marriage an only daughter, whom I would not want to leave behind to a chance destiny," he wrote.[46] The Ossolineum Library—which was, in some sense, the daughter of the union between his Polish culture and his Viennese collecting—was to be purposefully settled in Galicia.

In May 1817, Ossoliński was notified of the emperor's approval of the library in a Latin letter from the Habsburg Hungarian chancellor Jozef Erdödy: *pro generosa bibliothecae publicae fundatione*. In June, Franz Krieg, a leading government official in Lviv, wrote to Ossoliński with the news that the emperor had also approved the Polish chair, and with a request for Ossoliński's assistance in framing the specifications of the professorial position. In August, Ossoliński wrote to the Roman Catholic archbishop of Lviv, and metropolitan primate of Galicia, Andrzej Ankwicz, discussing the establishment of the library and also the recently concluded visit of Emperor Franz to Galicia:

> I am immensely delighted that our good monarch convinced himself with his own eyes that our nation only needs to see the proofs of his good wishes and paternal feeling in order to become inflamed with the most lively affection for him. You gentleman have done great work in that you have removed the divide of prejudice, suspicion, and perverse insinuations that separated both sides. God grant that according to this model our nation, like the German nation, though partitioned among several rulers, may show itself to be always a free nation, having within itself its own particular quality and distinctive existence. Not the violation of nationality, but rather guiding it to the side of the ruling house would be at the same time both a bond for Galicia and a bait for the neighboring lands! May God grant it for the best that the coming generation may profit from good fortune, and the waning generation, to whose number I belong, may carry to the grave at least consolation from the happiness of the fatherland![47]

Ossoliński thus offered an unabashedly Galician conception of what it meant to be Polish at the beginning of the nineteenth century. Attachment to the

Habsburg monarch had to be stoked and stroked, beyond mere loyalty to flaming affection.

While some Poles were deeply disappointed by the defeat of Napoleon, Ossoliński, in the Galician spirit, believed that a future generation could expect better times to come, within the Habsburg monarchy. Indeed, he found consolation in hoping for "the happiness of the fatherland," without specifying whether the fatherland was Poland, whose political restoration he completely discounted, or Austria, whose good monarch was generating goodwill in Galicia. Ossoliński's fatherland [*ojczyzna*] was conceptually related to Franz's fatherland [*Vaterland*], with ambiguously overlapping Polish, Austrian, and Galician dimensions.

In September, Ossoliński wrote to the mathematician Jan Śniadecki in Vilnius, relating plans for the library in Lviv. Ossoliński would fund the whole thing himself with his Galician property, and he would participate in the selection of a curator to serve under the supervision of the newly reconstituted Galician Sejm. Also in September, another letter from Franz Krieg to Ossoliński expressed eagerness to have his advice on the selection of the professor for the Polish chair, but worried that the stipulated salary might be too high, and arouse jealousy among the other professors of the university.[48] All in all, 1817 was a year in which Ossoliński had played a prominent part in the renewal of Galician cultural life in the aftermath of the Napoleonic wars, and he was honored for his activities and contributions both with a Viennese decoration as a knight of the Order of St. Stephen and with a Galician title as a marshal of the Kingdom of Galicia.

In December, Ossoliński received congratulations on both honors as well as end-of-year greetings and warm wishes, in German, from Joseph Mauss, professor of history at the university in Lviv. Mauss offered a particular New Year's wish for Galicia itself:

> For the new year I wish our Galicia principally that its great ones in possession of great properties and much gold may, in the spending of it, increasingly take into consideration and imitate the example of the numerous wise ones of today and yesterday. Order and simple ornament bring forth beauty, but the waste on decorative or glittery or just noisy productions in home, clothing, and parade consumes everything, without bringing anything forth, and reinforces peacock pride [*Pfauensinn*] that is contrary to the public welfare as much as to educational national wisdom [*Nationalweisheit*].[49]

The model of magnanimous wisdom, spending money wisely, was surely intended to be Ossoliński himself, donating the funds and the collections for the creation of the library in Lviv. He was the paragon of "national wisdom"—but what was the nation to which Mauss alluded? Clearly, in this New

Year's wish for Galicia, the nation of which Mauss considered Ossoliński the model of wisdom could only have been the Galician nation.

Mauss's virtuous academic values dismissed even the glittery peacock pride of the ceremony that re-established his own university in 1817: "The ceremony took place in the presence of pretty ladies and misses who were very flatteringly invited with French invitations as *des personnes les plus distinguées*." Mauss was more concerned about the fact that the Polish chair remained unfilled. It was essential to his vision of relations between Polish and German literature in Galicia. He hoped to further "a lively and manifold literary connection between both nations which must have for both of them the noblest consequences." Mauss thus envisioned a convergence of nations in Galicia:

> Provocations and spitefulness, which only separate, and therefore hinder the two sides from achieving the common good, are to be left only for the masses. The intellectuals however love one another, and build together a common heaven, and honor each other eternally.[50]

In a revival of the Josephine spirit of messianism, Mauss's New Year's fantasy envisioned Galicia as heaven itself, at least for the intellectuals, and the temple of the new religion of brotherly love was to be none other than Ossoliński's library: "Parnassus Ossolinius." As for Mauss's own contribution, he was working on an epic history of Galicia, and reported that he had reached the year 1347.[51] It was a hopeless labor of dedicated national fantasy, probably never completed or published, for it involved projecting the history of Galicia back into the fourteenth century in search of medieval continuities. In 1817, Mauss cherished not only an interpretation of the historical past but also a vision of the utopian future in which the rites of Polish-German mutual love would be celebrated at the Parnassus Ossolinius—while Metternich imagined the remaking of Poles into Galicians.

"I Will Sing the Carpathians"

With the coming of the New Year, 1818, the newly created literary journal *Rozmaitości*, coming out every Saturday as the literary supplement to *Gazeta Lwowska*, offered the public of Galicia a glimpse of the "variety" of the wider world. One story reported that "Persia, about which we have such a beautiful fantasy, is, as we know it better now, an ugly desert, inhabited by hungry and unhappy people."[52] Another story offered a dramatic maritime narrative: "Journal of a Young Man of Massachusetts, who was Captured at Sea by the British in May 1813." This story originally appeared in Boston in 1816, but now, two years later in Lviv, *Rozmaitości* promised a "comparative glance at the national character of the English and the Americans," while noting that the young man of Massachusetts, naturally enough, revealed his "prejudice on behalf of his own nation [*uprzedzenie dla Narodu swoiego*]." National sentiment could most comfortably be treated at some global distance, and the most culturally relevant story of 1818 in *Rozmaitości* was a long, serially published essay taken from a Warsaw journal and entitled "Considerations on the Spirit of Polish Poetry." Without ever mentioning Galicia, and indeed barely alluding to Poland beyond the title, the article did emphasize the importance of the "national genius" and the "national language" for poetry. "Philosophers and scholars may work for the whole of human society," observed the essay, "but orators and poets should have their own nation particularly in mind."[53] Although such national emphases may have been unambiguously Polish when the essay was published in Warsaw, in the context of Lviv and Galicia the "national genius" could be construed multifariously—that is, multinationally.

Mauss, in his New Year's letter to Ossoliński of December 1817, stressed the importance of mutually appreciative cultural relations between Poles and Germans, but he also associated his own perspective more broadly "with the good people of the land and with the best people among my listeners of all three tongues [*aller drei Zungen*]."[54] With this allusion the Galician drama of Polish-German relations was alternately envisioned as a three-cornered affair, and though the third tongue was not named, Ossoliński would have certainly understood the reference to the Ruthenian language. The Ruthenian religion and language were present not only in Galicia but even in Vienna. Maria Theresa had created in Vienna in 1774 a Greek Catholic seminary, the Barbaraeum, and in the early nineteenth century there were sermons in the Ruthenian language at the seminary church of St. Barbara's. In 1806, Emperor Franz approved the creation of a Greek Catholic metropolitanate of Halych, thus constituting a distinctive ecclesiastical domain for the Uniate Ruthenians of Galicia; the dignity was assumed by Antin Anhelovych in 1808. In 1818, as *Rozmaitości* emphasized the importance of poetry in national languages, a Habsburg educational commission, sponsored by the governor of Galicia, Franz Hauer, ruled that Polish would be the preferred language of elementary education in Galicia, but Ruthenian would nevertheless be sometimes used, especially for Greek Catholic religious instruction.[55] The favored language of higher education remained German.

Lviv was the center of the Habsburg administration and Uniate Church in Galicia, but Przemyśl also became an important site for the emergence of a distinctive Galician Ruthenian culture. The Society of Greek Catholic Priests in Galicia, established in Przemyśl in 1816, mobilized clergymen to promote religious education in the Ruthenian language. The official approval of Ruthenian in 1818 for some limited use in school instruction stimulated the writing of basic texts in the language; Ivan Mohylnytsky, in particular, prepared Ruthenian textbooks with the sponsorship of the Society of Greek Catholic Priests. The society, according to historian Jan Kozik, was committed to "fostering patriotism and loyalty to the Austrian dynasty," and it was furthermore closely connected to Greek Catholic intellectual life in Vienna at the Barbaraeum, constituting a "Vienna-Przemyśl circle." One of Mohylnytsky's textbooks, which he actually translated from German into Ruthenian in 1817, was entitled *The Duties of Subjects* (*Povynnosty Podanych*) and inculcated the values of loyalty to the Habsburg emperor. Ivan Snihursky was the pastor of St. Barbara's in Vienna before becoming the Greek Catholic bishop of Przemyśl in 1818. Ivan Lavrovsky, on the other hand, moved from the Greek Catholic seminary in Lviv to the lyceum in Przemyśl, applying a part of his linguistic passion to the supremely Galician labor of compiling a Ruthenian-Polish-German dictionary. Both Snihursky and Lavrovsky together assembled significant library collections in Przemyśl, comparable on a smaller scale to the collections of Ossoliński.[56] Such libraries contributed notably to Galician culture while complicating the question of how that culture could best be identified. *Rozmaitości*, with its commitment to poetry in national languages, would eventually become one forum for publishing articles about Ruthenian language and culture.

The Ruthenian scholar Lavrovsky was also in contact with Polish scholar Zorian Chodakowski, who viewed the contemporary Ruthenians of Galicia as a resource for researching the historical circumstances of ancient Slavdom.[57] Chodakowski came to Galicia in 1818 under the patronage of the Czartoryski family at their estate of Sieniawa, and he wrote an essay "On Slavdom before Christianity" (*O Sławiańszczyźnie przed chrześcijaństwem*). Regretting the woeful historical ignorance of Slavic paganism, from the period before the medieval conversions to Christianity, he believed that he could find some answers in Galicia, and especially in the popular culture—the legends and folk songs—of the Ruthenian peasantry. Therefore, in 1818 he applied to the governor in Lviv for permission to travel around Galicia for the purpose of researching "Slavic mythology and antiquity" as revealed in "the songs of the country people." The research would involve the study of "songs, rituals, games, sorceries, and superstitions." He also hypothesized some sort of Slavic relation to Sanskrit—to be explored in Galicia—at a time when Sanskrit studies were becoming important in German universities. Chodakowski framed this research as a matter of provincial pride for "the government of the Galician Kingdom [*rząd Królestwa Halickiego*], friendly to science and protective of the village people."[58] Franz Xaver Wolfgang Mozart may have chafed at the conditions of Galician village life, but Chodakowski was eager to make the Galician countryside into the laboratory for his research into pre-Christian Slavdom: the further the village lay from the advantages of urban civilization, the more likely the possibility that it might have preserved some traces of Slavic antiquity in its popular culture.

In Chodakowski's scholarly conception, Galicia acquired an anthropological coherence, with backwardness as the guarantee of authenticity and the promise of a glimpse into the world of Slavic antiquity. He hoped to find the true Galicia, not in Lviv, not in Przemyśl, not even at Sieniawa, but in the villages of the province. "On Slavdom before Christianity" was published first in 1818 in *Ćwiczenia Naukowe* in Warsaw, but it was immediately republished in 1819 in the Galician journal, *Pamiętnik Lwowski*.

In 1821 the Habsburg neoclassical architect Pietro von Nobile completed a new governor's palace in Lviv, the architectural embodiment of imperial power in Galicia.[59] In that same year, the journal *Pamiętnik Galicyjski* (*Galician Journal*) appeared in Lviv, self-consciously seeking to give expression to the distinctive concerns of Galicia with a "journal dedicated to the history, literature, and industry of the country." The editors explained the project's particular purpose:

> Entering into the publication of a new periodical journal we feel the full importance of the obligation placed upon us. The editors of a periodical journal are in some sense interpreters of the public opinion of their own country [*swojego kraju*] . . . . The conferring of the new title upon our journal has no other purpose than to make the journal national. In Poland and in Lithuania various journals are coming out which are occupied mostly with matters of their own countries [*swoich krajów*]; likewise therefore we wish also to be occupied with our country, till now not completely known.[60]

The lexicon of the editors clearly suggested that Galicia was their "country [*kraj*]," and that country possessed a "national [*narodowy*]" aspect. The notion of the journal's being national, in fact, corresponded to Metternich's own idea of Galicia itself becoming national—that is, the inhabitants coming to identify as nationally Galician. That Galicia was less well "known" than Poland and Lithuania was hardly surprising inasmuch as the latter entities had existed for centuries as politically meaningful domains of the Polish-Lithuanian Commonwealth, while Galicia had been invented in 1772.

Pamiętnik Galicyjski began the year of 1821 with an article on "News about the Origins of the Slavic Nation," confirming the new importance of such studies in Galicia after Chodakowski's pioneering work. Articles about Slavic languages and literary culture would play an increasingly important part in *Pamiętnik Galicyjski*, often conceived in the spirit of Romanticism. A long Polish poem on the Carpathian Mountains, by Stanisław Jaszowski, celebrated the most prominent topographical feature of Galicia in the epic spirit: *Śpiewać będę Karpaty*...

> I will sing the Carpathians, giant mountains,
> Raised by the hand of the creator for our defense;
> May I succeed in grateful rhyme in expressing
> The precious grace of these mountains so picturesque.[61]

The picturesque perspective of the poet merged with a pragmatic Galician appreciation of the mountains providing "our defense." In Krystyna Poklewska's literary history of "Romantic Galicia," Jaszowski appears as a leading figure, representing a brand of Romanticism, contemporary with the early works of Mickiewicz in Lithuania, but rather different in its Galician focus on the provincial landscape. Jaszowski would later play a role in presenting the poetry of Mickiewicz, Pushkin, and Byron to the Galician public.[62]

Pamiętnik Galicyjski further explored the poetic possibilities of mountainous topography with an article on Slavic culture that looked farther afield to Montenegro for the poetry of "the wild mountaineer." The "Illyrian language" of the Montenegrins was celebrated as "noble, eloquent, violent, in a word, the language of heroes." The improvised oral poetry of the South Slavs demonstrated that "wild hordes, just like civilized society, have their own hymns, dances, and music."[63] It had been Herder who had first stressed the importance of folk poetry as the expression of the genius of each particular *Volk*, and now in *Pamiętnik Galicyjski* an article on "eastern" poetry presented Herder's passionate appreciation of Arabic, Persian, and Hebrew. While Arabia and Persia might have seemed remotely Oriental to the readers of *Pamiętnik Galicyjski*, Hebrew was regionally relevant as a recognizable aspect of Galician society with its large Jewish population.[64]

In 1821, *Pamiętnik Galicyjski* offered its readers "Fragments toward a History of the Jewish People in Europe," considering especially Jewish history as a case study in national identity. The article's opening lines introduced the issue:

> The Jewish people, even in dispersal, has so steadily preserved the uneffaced stamp of nationality [*niezatarte piętno narodowości*], a special kind of existence, a completely singular relation. Thus, they may share with us the common protection of the law and the advantages brought to Europe by the progress of enlightenment, the growth of industry and the improvement of education, but

they preserve all the marks of an individual tribe. Ultimately, there is the constant
resistance which governments today experience, resistance to the assimilation
of this people [*w przyswojeniu tego ludu*] with regard to various forms, resistance to
the imposition of equal obligations, resistance to a closer unification through the
bonds of a common fatherland and common destinies.[65]

The profound ambivalence of this observation was essentially Galician.
From a provincial Galician perspective, or from a Habsburg imperial perspective, the persistent national individuality of the Jews could be seen as an
obstacle to the state concerns of forming a common fatherland. At the same
time, from a nationally Polish perspective the Jewish resistance to assimilation
might have appeared as an inspirational example of the resistance that Poles
might hope to sustain in the face of foreign rule in Russia, Prussia, and even
Austria. Finally, the recognition of Jewish national persistence permitted
the contemplation of distinctive survival as a more general phenomenon:
considering the case of the Montenegrins, for instance, or, in the context of
Galicia, the case of the Ruthenians. If Metternich believed that identity was
plastic, that, for instance, the inhabitants of Galicia could be made into Galicians, the example of the Jews, as described in *Pamiętnik Galicyjski*, seemed
to suggest a less tractable model of identity.

In 1821, the same year as the article on Jewish identity, the Galician Jewish
reformer Joseph Perl received a medal from Emperor Franz. Perl's career
clearly indicated that the stubborn persistence of Jewish identity was sometimes perceived as problematic even within the Galician Jewish community.
Perl, born in Ternopil (Tarnopol) in 1773, was as old as Galicia itself, and represented the reforming perspective of the enlightened Haskalah movement,
which looked to the Habsburg government for support in transforming
Galician Judaism. In 1813, Perl created an enlightened German school for Jews
in Ternopil, and in 1819 he published anonymously in Vienna a novel written
in Hebrew, *Revealer of Secrets* (*Megalleh Temirin*), satirizing Jewish Hasidism
from the perspective of the Haskalah. Written as an epistolary novel among
Jews inside and outside Galicia, this work offered a conception of Galician
Hasidic Judaism characterized by foolishness and fanaticism. Perl was so
fiercely engaged against the Hasidim that he denounced them, at intervals, to
the Habsburg government for alleged criminal conduct, misuse of funds, and
interference with his own enlightened educational projects in Galicia. Metternich himself received Perl to hear about his plan, unrealized, for creating
a "Society for the Spread of Useful Industry and Employment among the
Jews of Galicia." The Galician Jewish community was thus highly polarized
and volatile at precisely the moment that *Pamiętnik Galicyjski* represented the
supposedly static nature of Jewish identity. Historian Raphael Mahler has

traced the conflict between Hasidism and the Jewish Enlightenment as the fundamental framework for the history of Galician Judaism.[66]

Pamiętnik Galicyjski was interested in Galicia's topographical features, such as the Carpathians, and its ethnographic communities, like the Jews, but also in the history of the province; in 1821 the journal undertook a "Short Sketch of the History of Galicia," published under the initials E.B., which denoted one of the editors, Eugeniusz Brocki. The article began with a Latin epigraph from Cassiodorus: *Turpe est, sua in patria peregrinum esse* ["Shameful it is, to be a stranger in one's own fatherland"]. Yet the inhabitants of Galicia might not have recognized Galicia as their fatherland, and might well have felt like strangers in a land whose very name was relatively new and whose political existence had seemed tenuously unstable during the recent Napoleonic wars. Brocki promised to provide "the statistics and history of those lands which form today's kingdom of Galicia."[67] To know Galicia was to affirm the validity of its existence as a Habsburg province, but the narration of its history was inherently problematic when the historian looked back before 1772.

Brocki, immersing himself in Galicia's medieval antecedents, found himself telling a tale of constantly changing names with little stable correspondence among names, places, and peoples. He began with the Scythians, reporting that they were later called Slavs. He described the Russian prince Vladimir conquering Red Ruthenia, which was footnoted with the explanation that "with this name was designated the lands where Halych, Vladimir, Chelm, Podolia, and Volhynia are found." Thus Galicia referred to Red Ruthenia, among other things, and Red Ruthenia referred to Halych, among other things, but the history of Galicia was difficult to discern clearly in the Middle Ages.[68] *Pamiętnik Galicyjski*, sketching the history of Galicia, could not fail to betray the issues of unstable signification that made such a history inevitably problematic.

THE DRAMA OF GALICIA

In 1821, *Pamiętnik Galicyjski* reviewed a notable new literary work, the drama *Zabobon (Superstition)*, also entitled *Krakowiacy i Górale*, a new installment on Bogusławski's national opera of the previous generation.[69] Although Bogusławski was still alive in 1821 and living in Warsaw, *Zabobon* was created by Jan Nepomucen Kamiński, who appropriated the original scenario in the spirit of Galician adaptation. Kamiński, whose enthusiasm for the enlightened legacy of the eighteenth century was evident in his numerous translations of Schiller, was a leading figure in Polish theatrical life in Lviv. Born

in 1777, Kamiński was present in Lviv when Bogusławski appeared on the
scene after 1795, and later, in the brief moment of Napoleonic occupation
in 1809, Kamiński actually staged a performance of *Krakowiacy i Górale* with
songs that celebrated Napoleon.[70] Like Fredro, Kamiński had to adjust to
the post-Napoleonic world of Metternich's Galicia, and in 1821 *Zabobon* was
a popular success that played upon the ambiguous relation between Galician
and Polish culture. The comedy adopted an enlightened Josephine tone of
mockery toward local superstitions—like the local belief in dragons—but
also a satirical perspective on the administration of noble estates in Galicia
by ignorant and irascible managers.

Kamiński's Galician scene showed the village of Mogiła, as in Bogusławski's
original setting, with the Vistula in the background and a view of Cracow
in the distance. Although Kamiński declared that he was compelled to create *Zabobon* by the "insufficiency of sincerely national dramatic works," the
"national" aspect of the drama was as much Galician as Polish; it focused
on the folkloric life of the peasantry with a sympathetic sensibility for local
dialect and local customs.[71] The economic administrator of the noble estate
was regarded with complete contempt by the peasants, and denounced as
"inhuman" by the virtuous student Bardos, who himself, in the denouement,
turned out to be the actual noble lord of the villagers. They submitted themselves to him as his enserfed subjects, but he invited them to live freely as his
brothers.

> KRAKOWIACY: We wish to die, my lord, as your subjects [*jak twoi poddani*]!
> BARDOS: Live as my brothers, free and beloved [*wolni, kochani*]![72]

The message of political equality and social emancipation was notably progressive for Metternich's Galicia, and presumably remained uncensored just
because the Polish nobles were the principal objects of government suspicion. With the drama published and performed in Lviv in 1821, there was,
in any event, little danger that any actually enserfed villagers would have the
opportunity to discover the emancipatory message.

While Kamiński's *Zabobon* was a notable success in 1821, an even more
important literary landmark of the moment was the performance of Fredro's
Husband and Wife (*Mąż i Żona*) in Lviv in 1822, the first of his important
Galician comedies. Set in the home of Count Wacław, in a town that was
presumably Lviv itself, *Husband and Wife* completely ignored the world of
the noble country estate, with its enserfed peasants—the dramatis personae
of *Zabobon*—and offered instead a representation of Galician urban society.
The drama depicted a society in which politics and economics were displaced by idle boredom that provoked the characters to compulsive romantic

infidelity. In the scenario of *Husband and Wife*, Wacław's wife, Elvira, was unfaithful to him with her lover Alfred, while both men were also involved with Elvira's servant, Justysia. Thus every one of the four characters in the play was romantically involved with every other one of the opposite sex, so that the drama seemed to propose a sort of law of maximal and universal heterosexual infidelity based on the supreme volatility and fragility of human love. Although the drama ended with the servant girl's being banished to a convent, and with the husband and wife reconciled after the mutual begging and granting of pardon, Fredro's devastating vision of marriage—even more cynical than *Così fan tutte*—could not be dramatically evaded by the happy ending of the comedy. Fredro, in his memoirs, would describe "domestic happiness" in Metternich's Galicia as a "flowering oasis in the Sahara desert," but in *Husband and Wife* he implied that such happiness was so unstable as to be almost unattainable, that the oasis was a mirage.

In 1822, in Vilnius, within the Russian Empire, Adam Mickiewicz published his *Ballads and Romances*, the opening salvo of Polish Romanticism. The poem whose title summed up the whole movement, "Romantyczność," was exactly contemporary with Fredro's *Husband and Wife*, composed in 1821, appearing before the public in 1822. The subject of the Mickiewicz poem was a girl speaking to her dead lover, faithful to him beyond life and death. The spirit of Polish Romanticism permitted contemporaries to appreciate the masked political implications of such fidelity, suggesting the possibility of loyalty to Poland itself beyond the grave of the partitions. Yet if the political interpretation of romantic fidelity in the poetry of Mickiewicz was meaningful in the context of Russian Poland, then it should also be possible to consider the political meaning of infidelity in the drama of Fredro in the context of Habsburg Poland. Beginning in the 1830s, Fredro would find himself the object of polemical denunciation from Romantic critics for his alleged social conservatism, political indifference, and literary frivolity. Yet Fredro himself began the nineteenth century as a Franco-Galician soldier in Napoleon's Grande Armée, fighting for the cause of Poland. *Husband and Wife*, which was considered to be profoundly influenced by the dramatic values of Molière, should itself be considered as the product of a Franco-Galician perspective.

Metternich's Galicia was founded on that condition of "uncertainty" that hovered over the province from the moment of the Napoleonic crisis: the uncertainty of Habsburg possession, the uncertainty of Galician identity, the uncertainty of Polish allegiance. Fredro himself experienced precisely such uncertainty in his own life as he passed from Napoleonic commitment to Galician resignation. His drama of infidelity, *Husband and Wife*, hardly seems intended as a moral lesson in the evils of inconstancy, but appears rather as an appreciation of the dynamics of infidelity, an acknowledgment of the universal principle of inconstancy that constitutes the comedy of domestic life. In *Husband and Wife* every romantic passion is inconstant, tenuous, and volatile, like the political loyalties of Fredro's contemporaries who lived through the Napoleonic age and into the era of Metternich's Galicia. The institution of marriage might cloak, but could never banish, the wayward impulses of the unfaithful heart, just as the inescapable political reality of Habsburg rule might dominate, but could never resolve, the volatile mix of sentimental uncertainties and ambivalent identities at play in Galicia.

In the first scene of *Husband and Wife* the audience learned of the adulterous romance between Elvira and Alfred. In the second scene the maid Justysia warned the lovers that Elvira's husband, Count Wacław, was about to come home early. So Alfred departed, Elvira hastily took up her sewing, and Wacław walked in upon his wife:

> WACŁAW: [Standing in front of Elvira] How is it that at least once a year you don't go out? Once in a while you should show yourself in the world. You're always at home; I always see you alone.
> ELVIRA: I like to be alone [*Lubię samotność*].
> WACŁAW: And I hate it. [Paces. A short pause.] Unusual taste, always sitting at home![73]

Fredro, after traveling far and wide in the Napoleonic wars, as far east as Moscow, as far west as Paris, stayed at home in Galicia after the wars were over, found refuge in the domestic oasis, and began to compose his comedies. Yet, the renunciation of the world was an ambivalent commitment in the Galician condition, and, as every member of the audience already knew, Elvira was deeply involved in worldly intrigue without leaving her home at all. She knew how to make the most of her Galician loneliness, *samotność*—the same condition that young Mozart described as *Einsamkeit*.

Elvira, who played the piano while her husband spoke to her, had at least one ostensible channel of intellectual access to the world outside her home. When she stopped playing the piano, she picked up a volume.

> WACŁAW: What kind of serious or amusing work is it that has caught your attention so?
> ELVIRA: The Journal [*Pamiętnik*].
> WACŁAW: Aha, the Journal—no joke. For two weeks it's lain there open, until at last it's lived to see a reading, I don't know whether out of boredom or desire.[74]

Husband and Wife, performed in 1822 but probably composed in 1821, was exactly contemporary with the inaugural volume of *Pamiętnik Galicyjski*, in which the editors prepared to attend to "our country, till now not completely known." Elvira herself, at that moment an unknown country to her own husband, might be imagined leafing through the poetic tribute to the Carpathians, the articles on the heroic Slavic poetry of Montenegro, on the stubborn persistence of Jewish identity, on the fluctuating affiliations of medieval Halych. Even within the restrictive censorship of the Metternich era she might have found enough to stimulate a sense of romance, a notion of relation to the wider world, and an idea of what it meant to be Galician. Even within her own home she found sufficient opportunity to exercise her extramarital impulses, while Wacław, with his susceptibility to the servant Justysia, was also able to enjoy a diversion of the passions without going out into the world. Fredro's comprehensive vision of ambivalent infidelities and fluctuating disloyalties suggested the dramatic uncertainties underlying the domestic oasis of Metternich's Galicia.

"Kennst du das Land?"

Metternich himself came to Galicia in 1823, on the way to Czernowitz in Bukovina, where Kaiser Franz was to meet with Czar Alexander; the crowned heads, as conservative pillars of the Holy Alliance, were to discuss the manifestations of revolution in Naples, Spain, and Greece. All was quiet, however, in Galicia, as Metternich discovered upon his arrival. He wrote to his wife from Rzeszów on 25 September: "The country is quite different from how I had imagined it [*tout autre que je ne me l'étais figuré*]. It is very beautiful and well cultivated. The entry into Galicia is very mountainous and resembles Upper Austria; then comes the plain, but it is varied, wooded, and very beautiful. What spoils the country [*ce qui gâte le pays*] is encountering Jews at every step. One sees only them, and they swarm [*ils pullulent*]."[75] On the one hand, Metternich claimed to like Galicia better than he had expected, and noted the beauty of the landscape and the cultivation of the fields. He himself, by the side of the emperor, had ruled over the province for a decade, but somehow expected it to appear as a wasteland. On the other hand the population of Galicia, especially the presence of so many Jews, ruined the good impression initially made by the landscape.

With a stop at Łańcut to visit the Potocki family palace, which he found satisfactory—"a large and beautiful country establishment"—Metternich was in Lviv on 28 September, but travel had taken a toll on the statesman, who now collapsed in bed with what was diagnosed as rheumatic fever. "I am in a continual sweat," wrote Metternich. "I can tell you nothing about Lemberg, for I have seen nothing of it." He would stay there for a month, recovering, but would have no chance to see Czernowitz, since the illness would prevent him from continuing his voyage and from being present at the meeting of the sovereigns in Bukovina. "Imagine my moral situation!" he exclaimed. "In bed in Lemberg, with the two emperors tête-à-tête in Czernowitz."[76] The future of Europe was in jeopardy, Metternich supposed, with characteristic lack of modesty, because he himself was too sick to travel. Metternich, however, dominated Europe systematically—or so he believed—and could therefore claim to have managed the meeting of the emperors, averting a Russian-Ottoman war, even from his sickbed in Lviv:

> I furthered affairs to such an extent before the meeting, that the force of circumstances was set to conclude without me. Peace was assured: everything was arranged in a miraculous manner, and the triumph is complete! This boon for all Europe is especially so for me; it offers me some chance of rest, that rest for which I sigh like a bird for the air.[77]

For the moment, the bird had no choice but to continue resting in Galicia.

Under these circumstances Metternich was unlikely to form a favorable impression of Lviv. There was a Potocki countess who "absolutely wanted to make me cross the Rubicon"—that is, who tried to force him to leave his sickbed and go to a ball. Metternich held his ground, and his bed, while reflecting on the economy of Galicia: "The country is excessively productive, but lacks all means of export." This spelled general poverty in the midst of agricultural plenty, because of the failure of distribution. "One must not make fun of such unfortunate people [*se moquer de gens aussi malheureux*]," commented Metternich.[78] In short, even from his sickbed, Galicia appeared to him as an object of ridicule, whether on account of the importunate countess or the dysfunctional economy.

"I thank you very much for the oranges that you had the inspiration to send me," wrote Metternich to his wife, after three weeks in Galicia. "It would have been impossible for me to procure them here. It is not in this land here that the lemon trees bloom."[79] He was alluding to Goethe's celebrated verse about Italy: "Kennst du das Land, wo die Zitronen blühn?" Do you know the land where the lemon trees bloom? Metternich now made Goethe's poem into the occasion for a witticism at the expense of Galicia, which, given its geographical situation, could hardly have been expected to enjoy a Mediterranean climate. A few days later he was well enough to be taken on a tour of Lviv, which he seemed to undergo with some reluctance. "They had me look all around Lemberg. I have never seen people so enamored of their city as these people here." The strong implication was that these were people who greatly overvalued the attractions of their city, as they urged

Metternich to notice that one view resembled Naples and another Vienna. He was resolutely unimpressed:

> If you look from up close, you see a city sunk in a hole, and the hole lacks water and trees. The city is half beautiful and half ugly. There are a lot of houses better constructed than those of Vienna, for they have architecture. Then come stretches, either empty, or encumbered with barracks. The Orient begins to reveal itself.[80]

Metternich, who once famously remarked that the Orient began with the Landstrasse, leading out of Vienna, revealed in Lviv that his mental geography was firmly grounded in the Enlightenment's idea of Eastern Europe, conceived as an intermediary zone of half and half. It was that same idea of Eastern Europe which originally contributed to the Josephine ideology of a Habsburg civilizing mission in Galicia.

"I don't know how to tell you, my dear, how happy I am to be leaving this place," wrote Metternich, finally able to travel. "Ennui consumes me. I will think all my life about the month of October 1823."[81] By 27 October he was already in Tarnów, having spent one night in Przemyśl and one night in Rzeszów, and he wrote boastfully about the lavish accommodations prepared for him at the emperor's special command. Still, the rooms were overheated, which gave him the pretext for ironic commentary on supposed Polish "politesse" and "urbanité"—in short, civilization. "There necessarily occurred some funny things," he remarked. "I will recount them to you, and they will make you laugh."[82] Metternich looked forward to inspiring laughter in Vienna when it came time to tell his story about Galicia.

On 30 October, Metternich exulted in having finally left Galicia behind him, and he permitted himself to generalize about the province as a whole.

> My dear, here I am in Moravia, that is, in a civilized country [*un pays civilisé*], and at a distance from Vienna that the courier will cross in thirty hours. I have never seen anything as striking as the passage from Galicia into Moravia. The land is the same, and very beautiful on the one side as on the other; but the first village on this side here gives the impression of being finally inhabited by humans. No more rags; the houses are clean and the inhabitants well-covered; no more Jews, no more mange, no more scurf, no more misery or death.[83]

Metternich had been miserable in Galicia through all of October, and now he took out his frustrations on the province itself, denouncing it as beyond the boundary of humanity and civilization. Metternich's idea of Galicia was summed up in the devastating list of negative attributes: rags, dirt, Jews, disease, misery, and death. He himself may have feared that his illness in Lviv was going to kill him, and may have persuaded himself that Galicia was to blame. While he had once, in the age of Napoleon, felt uncertain and ambivalent about the Habsburg possession of Galicia, he now regarded the

province as irrevocably Austrian and desperately in need of imperial absolutism. Although he had spent most of his time in bed in Lviv, Metternich
felt that he now knew Galicia well enough to generalize about its provincial
character. After the unforgettable month of October 1823, Galicia received
his unambivalent contempt.

"Pious and Loyal Physiognomy"

Gazeta Lwowska in the 1820s was shaped by the restrictions of bureaucratic absolutism and Metternich's censorship. The newspaper gave lots of
space to government edicts, in German and Polish, printed not as news but
as announcements: *Ankündigung, Obwieszczenie.* The paper also included rates
of exchange, market prices, and lottery notices. The first issue of January
1825 did report that Simon Bolivar had taken Lima, but that was revolutionary news from very far away. Likewise remote was the democratic news,
published later in January, that Andrew Jackson had been elected president
of the United States. Actually, it was a mistake and would be eventually cor-
rected: the new American president was John Quincy Adams.[84]

The only head of state who really mattered in *Gazeta Lwowska* was Emperor Franz, and the news of his birthday in February 1825 was given full
play. Galicians gathered in Lviv from all over the province, united in "one
spirit of joy, one rapture, and the most sincere attachment to the sanctified
person of the best of monarchs." The day began at ten o'clock with three
artillery salvos, followed by a parade with banners involving the civil and
military authorities in Lviv, culminating in a church ceremony with the singing of hymns in honor of the emperor. In the evening the town was illuminated, and throughout the celebrations there were incessant cries of "Long
live Franz! [Niech żyje Franciszek!]"[85] Simon Bolivar, with his message of
revolt and independence, would have seemed entirely irrelevant to the spirit
of Habsburg absolutism in Galicia. At Easter, *Gazeta Lwowska* reported that
Galician ladies of charitable spirit [*damy galicyjskie ducha dobroczynnego*] collected a handsome sum to benefit the poor and support the Order of the
Sisters of Charity.[86]

The appointment in 1826 of Prince August Lobkovic, a Bohemian nobleman, as Habsburg governor of Galicia, was attentively studied by the Galician nobility, who hoped to discover sympathetic intimations of imperial
favor for the province. Ossoliński in Vienna, now almost eighty, in the last
year of his life, wrote to Lobkovic immediately in German, soliciting his
support for the national library [*Nationalbibliothek*] that was being established

in Lviv, as the transfer of the Ossoliński collection was finally about to be completed and the library opened.[87]

Fredro, also appealing to the solidarity of the Habsburg nobility, and possibly courting the new governor's literary indulgence, sent Lobkovic the gift of a live Galician bear. The dramatist wrote to Lobkovic in French:

> My Prince! I hasten to send to Your Highness a bear from the Beskidy mountains, that I have just received from my brother Julian. The pious and loyal physiognomy promises much, and it is to be supposed that cubs will find in him a worthy preceptor. I believe that it would be well to be reassured for the future by the Italian manner of his sweetness and of his good conduct; there may thus also exist among his numerous talents that of singing.[88]

Hailing from the Beskidy range of the Carpathians, the bear would have handsomely represented Galician wildlife, and Fredro's humorous presentation may have also sought to represent an inward aspect of Galicia. The "pious and loyal physiognomy" of the bear seemed to suggest something about the population of the province, seemed to offer a promise of "good conduct." As for singing, the Galicians were already singing hymns of loyalty to the Habsburg emperor on his birthday.

In 1826, Franz Xaver Wolfgang Mozart was back in Lviv, where he established a choir and, in December, presented Mozart's *Requiem* at the Uniate Church of St. George—to mark the thirty-fifth anniversary of his father's death in Vienna in December 1791.[89] Galicians continued singing, and in 1828 there was published in Lviv "A Hymn Sung by the Actors of the Polish Theater on the Eve of the Birthday of His Highness the Emperor and King of Galicia and Lodomeria." In Lviv, also in 1828, the imperial hymn "Gott erhalte Franz den Kaiser" was first published in Ruthenian, in both the Cyrillic and Latin alphabets.[90] Emperor Franz, born in 1768, was sixty years old in 1828, just four years older than Galicia itself.

"Gin-Li-Kia-Bo-Bu, a Chinese Mandarin"

Even if the bear did not sing, the Ossolineum Library opened in Lviv in 1827, and Galicia as a whole remained loyal to the Habsburgs during the governorship of Lobkovic, though these were years during which loyalty was notably tested by the explosive example of insurrection and war against Russia in the Congress Kingdom of Russian Poland during 1830–31. Suddenly Galicians were given a glimpse of an alternative physiognomy that was anything but pious and loyal, and, as if in defiance of Metternich's intention to instill some sense of Galician provincial identity, the insurrection offered a dramatic demonstration of what it meant to be nationally Polish. Lobkovic was sufficiently sympathetic to Polish aspirations to permit some insurrectionaries to take refuge in Galicia after their defeat in 1831, and that indulgence was one reason for the dismissal of the governor in 1832.

The memoirs of Julian Horoszkiewicz described the politicizing influence of the November 1830 insurrection on an adolescent Galician. Horoszkiewicz was born in 1816, and, as a child, had only an unclear idea of what Galicia and Poland actually were. "I imagined that just as Brody belongs to the Potocki, and Lopatyn is the property of the Chołoniewski," wrote Horoszkiewicz, "so Galicia is the property of the Austrian emperor, and Poland the Muscovite property." Horoszkiewicz, whose father was an estate official in the service of the Chołoniewski family in Lopatyn, had every reason to be childishly familiar with feudal notions of possession, which therefore colored his conception of Galicia. Notably, he believed Galicia to be something somehow distinct from Poland. The naive political geography of a child lacked historical context: "About the violence and crimes committed upon our common fatherland, about the partitions of united Poland, at that time I heard nothing."[91] Not knowing about the demise of Poland, he could not know about the origins of Galicia, and therefore could not understand the relation between them. Educated in Lviv, Horoszkiewicz sang in the church choir, singing "Gott erhalte Franz den Kaiser" after every Mass.[92] The boy had lived in Habsburg Galicia all his life, and took its political existence completely for granted.

He was fourteen when the November Insurrection broke out in Russian Poland, and he registered the event from a Galician perspective.

> In the autumn quiet of 1830 at the end of November a thunderbolt suddenly struck in Warsaw, and its dull echo spread over Lwów only in the first days of December. This news very timidly, quietly, stealthily intruded into Polish homes, and did not all at once exercise a marked influence, did not call forth in the public the sign of any open sympathy. Nor could it have been otherwise. All government and municipal power was in the hands of the Germans or people brought up in German discipline, under the control of the prevailing discipline. In the schools it was just the same: German science, German prayers, German songs in church, including always at the end of mass, "Gott erhalte Franz den Kaiser." Ideas about the fatherland [*o ojczyźnie*] were held in common with the peoples of the whole of united Austria. . . . News about the uprising in Warsaw therefore did not awaken in me, nor could it awaken, any sentiment.[93]

If Metternich aspired "to make true Galicians" in 1815, then the child Horoszkiewicz, born in 1816, represented the fruit of that policy, singing "Gott erhalte" in a Galician choir that was supposedly tuned to the patriotism of all the peoples of the Habsburg monarchy, their common fatherland.

The insurrection in Russian Poland, however, would eventually contribute to the remaking of the adolescent Galician into a young Pole. "The news about the organizing of the uprising became ever louder, ever more accurate, and gripping," recalled Horoszkiewicz, who also remembered how that news was disseminated in Lviv. *"Gazeta Lwowska,* the official and only political newspaper, which was then being published in Lwów, very objectively, but faithfully gave the news from the field of battle. With eagerness we seized upon every newspaper." Just as in 1812 *Gazeta Lwowska* had reported upon the Polish participation in the Napoleonic invasion of Russia, while emphasizing Galicia's complete detachment, so during the uprising of 1830–31 the newspaper permitted its Galician readers a glimpse of the ongoing Polish-Russian struggle. At the same time Horoszkiewicz became aware of sudden disappearances in Lviv, young men, including his older brother, who had gone off "to the Poles [*do Polaków*]": as if they themselves were not Poles, but Galicians going to join the Poles.[94]

The historian C. A. Macartney has observed of Galicia in 1830–31 that "the province had in fact remained quiet, although a committee had formed itself in Lemberg to organize the dispatch of arms, ammunition and medical supplies to the Polish forces in Russia, and a few volunteers, but only a few, had crossed the frontier to join the fighting."[95] Yet the memoirs of Horoszkiewicz suggested that even the enlistment of a few young men could make a large impression on those left behind, including younger brothers. The memoirs also indicated that those young men could not necessarily be classified simply as "Poles" going off to join the Polish insurrection. Horoszkiewicz himself judged according to the empty seats in the Lviv gymnasium: "Academic youth, the higher classes of the gymnasium, Mazurians, Ruthenians, Hungarians, Germans disappeared from the benches, and the professor did not seem astonished that the sons of Germans, of high Austrian officials, like Vanroye, Osterman, and Reitzenheim, could not be restrained."[96] Metternich's idea had been to make Poles into Galicians rather than trying to make them into Germans, but that process also worked the other way around: Germans also became Galicians in Galicia, and were then susceptible to becoming Poles.

There was a distinctively Galician perspective on joining the Polish insurrection, and this was evident in the memoirs of Józef Reitzenheim, one of the "German" young men mentioned by Horoszkiewicz in his catalogue of those who disappeared from Lviv. Reitzenheim was born in 1812, and was thus eighteen in 1830, just old enough to go "to the Poles" and fight in the insurrection. His account of that time was published in Paris fifteen years later, in 1845, for his insurrectionary role had compelled him to emigrate; he

ended up playing a leading role in the Polish Emigration Committee, which
functioned as a kind of Polish government in exile in Paris in the middle
of the nineteenth century. His account of the insurrection was published in
1845 as *Galicia: Pamiętnik*—that is, *Galicia: A Memoir*, so that his Galician perspective was given particular emphasis as the defining feature of his autobiographical story. "I speak here about the parts of Podolia, Red Ruthenia,
and Little Poland known today as Galicia," wrote Reitzenheim. "Rank upon
rank her sons have appeared in battle among the national legions, for seventy years, and right up to the most recent times have constituted countless
victims in patriotic endeavors."[97] Galicia, originally formed from parts of
Poland, was now a distinctive geopolitical entity, making its own particular
contribution to the national Polish cause. Reitzenheim's chronology, which
counted seventy years of Galician participation in the Polish cause, was absolutely precise, since, counting back from the 1840s to the 1770s, he arrived
at the first partition of Poland and the creation of Galicia.

Reitzenheim wrote with provincial pride about Galicia, citing for instance
its charitable establishments for education, medical care, and agricultural
progress, such that "everyone in Galicia offers a hand in order to elevate
materially and morally the lower classes of society." The conservative Catholic Habsburg ethic of charity was evident, as cited by *Gazeta Lwowska*,
when Galician ladies at Eastertime raised money for the poor and for the
Sisters of Charity, but that ethic was also proudly recognized by a younger
generation of insurrectionaries like Reitzenheim as an aspect of Galician
character. He further boasted of Galicia's celebrated literary figures, including both Fredro and Kamiński. For Reitzenheim these were Galicians who
contributed to Polish "national" literature, and he identified himself as a
Galician along with them. "I who have spent a significant part of my life in
Galicia am painfully hurt by the complete lack of remembrance about this
part of Poland," he wrote. "It would be impossible in the end to narrate my
service in the Fifth Uhlan Regiment and its participation in the campaign
of 1831 without recalling the Galicians who, like me, were also active in the
Polish Kingdom."[98] Remembering thus the insurrection, a historic moment
for the rallying of national Polish sentiment, Reitzenheim chose to focus his
memoir on the role of Galicia and the Galicians.

Galicia, in Reitzenheim's representation, was a stronghold for preserving
Polish national memories:

> Constantly, always, at every step, traditions were nourished there, by the word, in
> bronze, and in stone, and they preserved like a sacred inheritance from father to
> son the passionate love of country. They elevated the remembrance of sacred
> battles of the Commonwealth against Tartars and Turks, when Poland was the
> *antemurale* of civilization. . . . Galicians remember this past all the better, the more

they are persuaded that to this day they stand, with all of Poland, in the vanguard, in the advanced guard, against the horde of Ruriks pressing toward Europe.[99]

The identity of Galicia, for Reitzenheim, writing in 1845, meant being European, engaged in a common European struggle against Russia.

At the time of the Kościuszko insurrection against Russia in 1794, wrote Reitzenheim, "the Galicians hastened to serve under his command," and in the Napoleonic Polish legions of Jan Henryk Dąbrowski, "the greatest number of soldiers was constituted of Galicians, such as had already passed through Austrian regiments." With the disappointment that followed the Napoleonic wars, Galicians took refuge in "country life and private life," but preserved their Polish sentiments "in the depths of their hearts and minds." Reitzenheim testified to the preservation of those sentiments in Metternich's Galicia by recalling how they sometimes bubbled to the surface, for instance in the theater: "As a child still I remember with what enthusiasm *Krakowiacy i Górale* was received."[100] Bogusławski's national opera, staged as a Polish national opera in Warsaw in 1794, became an ambiguously Galician and Polish work from the moment of its first performance in Lviv in 1796 with the dramatist's own revision and direction. Reitzenheim, born in 1812, might have been recalling the performance of 1817 that was given on the occasion of the visit of Emperor Franz to Lviv.

"The life of the Galicians went quietly, longingly [*tęskno*]," wrote Reitzenheim about Metternich's Galicia after the Congress of Vienna. He colored his account with the language of longing, from the vocabulary of Romanticism. For Reitzenheim the Galician response to the insurrection of 1830 in Russian Poland was already partly conditioned by certain less dramatic events in Galicia.

> The Austrian government addressed itself to the national sentiments of the Galicians. By command there was established in Lwów a professorship of Polish literature and language. The Czech Prince Lobkovic, whose family descends from Popiel, was sent as governor of Galicia. As a Slav, and an agreeable governor in relations with the citizens, he knew how to make them like him.[101]

Reitzenheim made the Slavic character of the Bohemian Lobkovic, even a supposed descent from the mythological Slavic king Popiel, into a bond between the governor and the Galicians. The Habsburgs, whose dynasty linked Bohemia to Galicia, were represented as ultimately sympathetic to the overlapping sentimental longings of subjects who were simultaneously Galicians, Poles, and Slavs.

Leaving Lviv to fight in the insurrection of 1830–31, Reitzenheim believed that all of Galicia supported him and his fellow volunteers: "As far as we went, everyone—whether Roman Catholics, Ruthenians, or Jews—blessed us on the road." He had no trouble conjuring an ecumenical Galician spirit of solidarity in what might have seemed a moment of particularly Polish commitment. Furthermore, within the Polish insurrectionary army, he immediately recognized his fellow Galicians: "When I arrived in Warsaw there were already Galicians sufficiently numerous in every army and almost in every regiment."[102] Thus Reitzenheim's tribute to the moment of Polish national solidarity also allowed for the recognition of a meaningful Galician identity. Entitling his memoir *Galicia*, he unhesitatingly described himself and his provincial fellows as "Galicians," and that identity tentatively took into account the religious and cultural variety of the province, including Ruthenians and Jews. Sympathy for the Polish national cause in 1830–31 was fully reconcilable with conserving a sentimental attachment to Galicia and the Habsburgs. In 1831 the Polish curator of the Ossolineum formally petitioned the court in Vienna for permission to hang in the library a portrait of Emperor Franz.[103]

With the Russian defeat of the insurrection in 1831, numerous Polish rebels fled across the Habsburg border into Galicia, and many ended up as émigrés in France, like Reitzenheim himself. According to Macartney, "The refugees, several thousand in number, who took shelter in Galicia, caused some trouble to the authorities, whose desire it was to combine a sympathetic attitude towards the Poles with a correct one towards Russia."[104] Lobkovic, as governor, was judged to have been too sympathetic to the Polish insurrectionaries, and he was replaced in 1832 by a member of the Habsburg imperial family, Archduke Ferdinand d'Este, who was more conservatively inclined. Fredro in 1832 wrote to a friend to express his political distress at the crushing of the insurrection in Russian Poland. Even the oasis of domestic happiness was insufficient to assuage altogether his political pangs: "I have a good wife, I have a little boy, I have books, and a peaceful home: in a word, I would be happy if I were not a Pole. When I have to write, how gladly I would sign myself today: Gin-Li-Kia-Bo-Bu, a Chinese Mandarin."[105] While Metternich claimed to discover intimations of the Orient in Galicia, for Fredro the Orient appeared as the realm of pure fantasy, the escape from an increasingly uncomfortable political reality. That political discomfort was not necessarily related to the provincial circumstances of Galicia, but rather to the personal problem of national identity, of being Polish in the 1830s. In Paris in the 1830s, émigré Poles like Mickiewicz and Chopin were about to give a powerful new Romantic dimension to Polish national identity. Fredro, though only five years older than Mickiewicz, would not be able to rediscover his Polishness in the refulgence of Romanticism. He fantasized about China, but remained fundamentally Galician.

After the insurrection of 1830–31, the Habsburg government in Galicia became increasingly attentive to the policing of conspiratorial discontent. Horoszkiewicz, age fourteen in 1830, sang the "Gott erhalte" in church and believed that Galicia was the personal property of the Habsburg emperor; by the end of the decade he was sufficiently politically engaged to be imprisoned in the Tyrolean fortress prison of Kufstein. By the agreement of Münchengrätz in Bohemia in 1833, Russia, Prussia, and Austria prepared to cooperate in their Polish policies, and one other Kufstein prisoner, Stefan Mułkowski, characterized Metternich as "the hangman of Poland," corrupted by "the handshake of Czar Nicholas," committed to "the devilish work of suppression and persecution."[106] If Metternich learned to despise Galicia in 1823, when he was confined to his sickbed in Lviv and missed the Austrian-Russian summit at Czernowitz, by the 1830s Galician antipathy toward Metternich was also on the rise.

"To Fly High amidst the Clouds"

In 1833, Mickiewicz in Paris composed an epistle to the Galicians, the poet already as much an apostle as Paul addressing the Galatians in Anatolia. The question was how to organize and advance the Polish national cause in the aftermath of the failed insurrection of 1830–31, and if St. Paul lectured to the Galatians against circumcision, Mickiewicz warned the Galicians against excessive circumspection: "Internal activity ought to have for its goal the preparation and gathering of forces and means for a future insurrection." Whereas St. Paul warned the Galatians against Jewish influences on Christianity, Mickiewicz urged an inclusive project of Galician political activity: "Priest, count, peasant, and Jew are equally necessary to us." Furthermore, he encouraged the landed elite "to protect the clergy of every confession, having particularly in mind the Ruthenian clergy, being careful to avoid quarrels and legal cases with them."[107] Mickiewicz thus took into account the particular details of Galician ethnography, as he contemplated organization to achieve eventual Polish national independence. He was already looking ahead to the next insurrection.

Jan Nepomucen Kamiński, author of *Zabobon* and director of the theater in Lviv, had by 1830 already created a Polish translation of Schiller's *Don Carlos*, with its harsh view of the Habsburgs in the sixteenth century, especially concerning their oppressive rule over Flanders. Later in the 1830s, after the suppression of the November Insurrection, Kamiński further undertook the translation of Schiller's *Wallenstein* trilogy, about the seventeenth-century Bohemian generalissimo whose loyalty to the Habsburgs was so suspect that the emperor finally had him murdered.[108] The dramatic meaning of dynastic loyalty in Habsburg history was clearly on the Galician agenda.

Fredro, on the other hand, continued to write comedies. In 1832, the year that Lobkovic was dismissed, the year that Fredro himself was in such despair that he wished he were a Chinese Mandarin, he saw the Lviv premiere of his comedy *Pan Jowialski*, about the most jovial of all possible Galician noblemen. Jowialski made everything into a joke, everything an occasion for the exercise of his eccentric humor. In 1833, the year of Münchengrätz, came the premiere of Fredro's *Maidens' Vows* (*Śluby panieńskie*), about two young women, Aniela and Klara, who, in a spirit of independence and idealism, resolved never to love or marry men. Aniela declared men to be "a race of crocodiles that lies in wait, yet rests easily, in order to gain our confidence and then betray us." Klara recognized the difficulty of resistance: "Scream, despise, hate—in hatred, anger, and contempt they find advantage, so that, finally, more than one of us, poor things, loses her patience, loses her head and, tired of fighting, pressed on all sides, has to fall in love in order to avoid trouble."[109] That, of course, described the eventual denouement of the drama itself. Fredro's conception of female resistance to the normal course of heterosexual relations might also describe the politics of resignation in Galicia in the 1830s. After the defeat of the insurrection in Russian Poland, and even more after Austria's accommodation with Russia at Münchengrätz, vows of eternal hatred were not enough to preserve the insurrectionary flame in Galicia. Eventually, tired of fighting, the Galicians would resign themselves to the routine patterns of everyday domesticity. In 1834 there followed the premiere of Fredro's *Revenge* (*Zemsta*), a comedy of hatred between rival Polish noble families that ultimately ended in reconciliation, marked by a wedding. *Pan Tadeusz*, published by Mickiewicz the same year in Paris, also involved details of petty noble rivalries, and also ended in reconciliation, though the message was distinctly more political, as the Poles joined together in enthusiasm for Napoleon's invasion of Russia. Reitzenheim, writing from a specifically Galician perspective, even in Paris, chose to quote from Fredro's *Revenge*—"all together [*wszyscy razem*]"—as a call to solidarity.[110]

In 1835 the painter Piotr Michałowski returned from Paris to Cracow, the city of his birth. Michałowski was born in 1800, a Habsburg subject of Emperor Franz. Seven years younger than Fredro, Michałowski experienced the Napoleonic interlude not as a fighting teenager but as a fascinated child. In the 1830s, with his return to Cracow, soon followed by the assumption of responsibility for his family's Galician estate, Michałowski commenced upon a life dedicated simultaneously to the land and to his art. While he managed his estate as a Galician subject of the Habsburgs, his art, beginning around 1835, was more and more focused on painting the figure of Napoleon and scenes of Napoleonic warfare. Known for his particular ability to paint horses, Michałowski also represented mounted Habsburg hussars, but he kept returning to the historically dramatic figure of Napoleon on horseback. Like Fredro he could not escape from the shadow of the Franco-Galician moment.[111]

Fredro was born in 1793, one year after Emperor Franz came to the throne, and had witnessed from childhood the celebration of Franz in Galicia. The playwright had never had any other sovereign. In 1835, Franz died, and in that year Fredro completed what was perhaps his last great comedy, the strange and bitter *Life Annuity* (*Dożywocie*), set in a town that was presumably Lviv. Metternich had been utterly bored in Lviv, but Fredro's Galician hero Leon Birbancki—"Leon the Reveler"—enjoyed the town's diversions only too well, and squandered his income on revels, on nightlife, and especially on gambling. That income came to him in the form of regular payments, an inherited life annuity, made over to him from some estate. He had to alienate his annuity in order to pay his debts, and the policy with its income fell into the hands of a nasty old miser, modeled by Fredro on Molière's miser. The Lviv miser therefore took an interest in protecting Leon from the medical consequences of his revelries, for fear that his premature death would cancel the annuity.

Leon's life thus became the miser's investment: "When I bought Leon Birbancki's life annuity I wanted someone clever who'd stay by him all the time, someone who'd keep watch over his esteemed health, over his life." Leon was aware that he had become the object of some sort of protective surveillance, but did not know why.

> For more than a year now some hidden power [*skryta władza*] that's always with me, guarding every step I take, helps me out of every trouble. When at public masquerades sometimes nasty brawls break out around me, I'm instantly surrounded by harlequins and doctors. If I'm somewhere and it's pouring, though I've said a word to no one, somehow a coach comes to fetch me. If I lose or damage something or get lost somewhere while traveling, someone comes from out of nowhere, eager just to be of service. Even when I come home late at night, sometimes not so steady on my feet, someone's hung a lantern for me, or an arm comes out to help me.[112]

The dramatic situation was strangely unsettling, for even as Leon felt himself to be living under benign guardianship, the audience was already aware that he was in fact caught in the web of surveillance spun by the miser's greed. Leon had the delusion of living under special protection, which was in fact a sort of supervised captivity, delicately administered to spare the sensibilities of the subject. He no longer owned his own life annuity, and therefore, in some sense, was no longer the master of his own life, which had become the parasitic object of someone else's financial interest.

Fredro, beyond the peculiar entertainment of the comedy, meant to satirize the miserly greed that pervaded modern life, and perhaps particularly the financial operations that deprived modern men and women of their natural independence. This hostility to finance was consistent with Fredro's conservative values as a member of the landed Polish gentry. Yet Fredro was also the provincial subject of a great empire, and Edward Said has suggested that modern European culture, especially literary culture, was marked by the tensions and contradictions of imperial rule. The alienated life annuity functioned as a metaphor for imperial relations, inasmuch as provincial Galicia existed under imperial protection, with imperial attention to its problems and ailments, while its care and preservation were intended to benefit the empire as a whole and further the interests of the Habsburgs. They profited by the preservation of the province in good condition, deriving regular income in the form of taxes. Metternich, who was famous for making use of police surveillance in modern administration, was the minister who protected the investment in Galicia of the Habsburg emperors. Franz was the ultimate possessor of the imperial annuity, right up until his own death in 1835, the year of *Life Annuity*.

That year also marked the end of Fredro's literary prime, for *Life Annuity* was the last of his great Galician comedies. In 1835, Fredro gave up writing comedy for many years, not just because the Galician circumstances may have seemed less humorous, but above all because he was confronted with a fierce public denunciation. The poet and critic Seweryn Goszczyński, who had participated in the November Insurrection in Russian Poland and then taken refuge in Galicia, published in 1835 an article on "The New Epoch in Polish Poetry," a salute to Romanticism that included a slashing attack on Fredro. He was criticized for the Frenchness [*Francuszczyzna*] of his style, and for exercising the shallow wit of a caricaturist, but Goszczyński's principal accusation concerned Fredro's alleged failure to create drama with national qualities:

> Comedy, written for the nation [*dla narodu*], should grasp and reveal the content of its life, from that perspective unique to the vocation, and on that everyone agrees who admits that comedy is not a childish toy but one of the most valiant means for the education and formation of the nation. That the comedies of Fredro do not correspond to that purpose, that they are non-national [*nienarodowe*], one may be convinced by reading them, better than by the longest lecture. Polish names are not the same as Polish characters; several national figures, sev-

eral national scenes, do not give a national coloring to the verses of four volumes. . . . The amorous side of the nation is a cosmopolitan feature—and that is really everything that constitutes the Polishness [*polskość*] of Fredro's comedy. But the virtues, faults, absurdities, unifying character, general physiognomy, whatever forms the true monuments of national individuality, you would seek in vain.[113]

The denunciation was crushing to Fredro. Though he lived for another forty years, until 1876, and wrote more plays in the 1850s and 1860s, his masterpieces belonged to the 1820s and 1830s, the age of Metternich's Galicia—when Fredro created a literary oasis in the political Sahara.

Goszczyński's denunciation was all the more devastating for containing elements of important insight. Although the critic failed to appreciate what made Fredro a great dramatist, the labeling of his work as "non-national" was plausible in the Polish cultural context of Romanticism in the 1830s. Fredro, of course, considered himself a Pole, had fought for the Polish cause in the Napoleonic wars, had sympathized with the Polish insurrection in 1830–31, and felt the misfortune of the national condition sufficiently to wish that he were anything but Polish in 1832. Fredro could never be a Chinese Mandarin, but he could be Galician, and the overlapping perspectives of Polish and Galician identity also shaped his dramatic vision. The non-national nature of Galician provincial life, muting nationality in the political conditions of Metternichian absolutism, transcending nationality in the cultural spirit of Habsburg heterogeneity, permitted Fredro to achieve a comedy of the human condition. The tensions of Polish identity and the contradictions of Galician identity were sublimated in the comedy of irresistible marital infidelities, untenable maidens' vows, perversely insistent joviality, and the existential alienation produced by an alienated annuity.

Leon Birbancki was excited to discover a poster for an Italian balloonist, issuing an open invitation to some brave member of the public, to ascend up into the skies.

What bliss! Even for a moment just to fly high amidst the clouds and cast a sage's quiet eye on so much stupidity and misery. As you fly on higher, higher, this mud-drop, the heart of our world, this whole anthill of ours—how small and petty it seems! and those splendid ants below, full of desire, wisdom, pride. . . . Where, in the grief of tears and blood, is the clamor of triumphant murders? Where is fame's resounding echo? Where are all those voices of praise which must strike the very heavens? There, on high, one can hear nothing . . . only silence . . . blissful silence. . . . There it's possible to breathe freely—far from people, closer to God! [Falls into reverie.][114]

The comedy of the scene derived from the fact that Leon's reverie about the balloon was being observed with horror by the secret owner of the annuity, who dreaded the risk to Leon's life, and regarded him as a raving madman.

For Fredro, the fantasy of escape into the skies was related to his own escapist fantasy of becoming a Chinese Mandarin. The reference to grief of tears and blood would have been easily interpreted by the public in Lviv in 1835 as a reference to the insurrection of 1830–31, and the allusion to triumphant murders was made at a moment when not only Czar Nicholas but also Metternich himself was being denounced as a "hangman of Poland." Fredro, as a dramatist, had dedicated himself to the comedy of the human anthill, revealing human beings in all their pettiness. Yet, he too could aspire to a more remote perspective on the human condition, such that it would be impossible to distinguish by eye the manifestations of stupidity and misery and perhaps even nationality. From the perspective of the balloon, after all, the quality of Polishness would also dissolve in the panorama of Galicia.

The highest point in the center of Lviv in 1835 was the spire of the newly rebuilt tower of the Town Hall in the Market Square.[115] The tower had collapsed in 1826 and was reconstructed in 1835 with the emblematic Lviv lion and Habsburg eagle at the top of the spire. If Fredro, like Leon, had ascended high enough in a balloon, higher than the Habsburg eagle, he might have discerned in the distance the topographical peaks of the Carpathian Mountains. Such was the native terrain of the live bear that Fredro had once presented to the Habsburg governor, with a Galician message about piety, loyalty, and good conduct. Fredro had lived in Galicia all his life, could not help regarding himself as Galician, and had long believed in Galicia as an oasis. Metternich had hopefully envisioned the emergence of a Galician identity, and Fredro, perhaps more than any other literary figure, had contributed to the non-national formation of a provincial Galician culture. Yet, by 1835, the year of the death of Emperor Franz, the oasis of Galicia had come to seem something like a mirage, unattainable except in fantasy. Indeed, the oasis seemed to be shrinking to the size of the basket of a balloon. The contradictions of Metternich's Galicia, which Fredro sought to reconcile in his comedies, might still be harmonized from an illusory and beguiling perspective, if the hero ascended in a balloon and looked down upon Galicia from a very great height.

CHAPTER THREE

The Galician Childhood
of Sacher-Masoch

From Folk Songs to Massacres

INTRODUCTION: GALICIAN SLAVERY

Leopold von Sacher-Masoch, the literary creator of modern masochism, was born in Galicia in 1836, the son of the Habsburg police chief in Lviv. Sacher-Masoch spent his childhood in Galicia, leaving the province only when his father was transferred to Prague in the turbulent revolutionary year of 1848. These first twelve Galician years of the writer's life were crucial for his personal and artistic formation, as is evident from the setting in Galicia of so many of his major literary works, including the most notorious "masochistic" text, *Venus in Furs*. At the same time, these were also crucially transformative years for Galicia itself, witnessing, between 1836 and 1848, the affirmation of Ruthenian cultural identity with the publication of *Rusalka Dnistrovaia* in 1837, the raising of the issue of peasant serfdom and forced labor in the Galician Sejm in 1843, the traumatic massacre of Polish insurrectionary nobles by Polish peasants in 1846, and the revolutionary manifestations of 1848 with competing Polish and Ruthenian agendas. Sacher-Masoch's childhood experience of Galicia, as reflected in his adult memoirs and fictions, may thus serve as a prism for analyzing the history of the province during these years, and especially for understanding what "Galicia" meant conceptually to Galicians of the 1830s and 1840s, as the defining political context for evolving cultural and national identities.

Sacher-Masoch was a Galician of the third generation, since his father, also Leopold von Sacher-Masoch, served as a Habsburg official in Lviv in the 1830s and 1840s, and his grandfather, Johann Nepomuk von Sacher, was a part of the Josephine Habsburg administration in eighteenth-century Galicia. The writer's Galician identity emerged from a family history of three generations in the province, dating back to the original invention of Galicia. Sacher-Masoch's own long lifetime spanned an entire epoch in Habsburg history: born in 1836, when Metternich still dominated Europe from the State Chancellery on the Ballhausplatz in Vienna, dying in 1895, when Freud was already analyzing patients at Berggasse 19. When Sacher-Masoch published his masterpiece *Venus in Furs* (*Venus im Pelz*) in 1870, he was in his thirties and living in Graz, but his literary imagination was looking back to the Galicia of his childhood.

The masochistic hero of the novella, Severin von Kusiemski, was introduced as "a Galician nobleman," while the whip-bearing heroine in furs, Wanda von Dunajev, was presented as a widow from Lviv. They met at a resort in the Carpathian Mountains, where she invited him to become her slave, and he passionately embraced his own slavery. This relationship was formally drawn up as a contract between them, including clauses of the utmost subordination:

> Frau von Dunajev may not only punish her slave as she thinks best for the least oversight or offense, but she also has the right to mistreat him as a whim or just to pass the time, however she likes, and even to kill him if she wishes. In short, he is her unrestricted property.[1]

This contractual relationship, and the inevitably ensuing scenarios, provided overwhelming sexual excitement to Severin, the Galician nobleman turned Galician slave. The happy couple actually departed from Galicia to pursue their complementary fantasies in Italy, bringing masochism to the heartland of Western civilization. Yet Galicia was unquestionably the formative environment that shaped their individual psyches and nourished their perverse romance. Galicia had seemed remote and uncivilized to Metternich, measuring by the imperial metropolitan standard of Vienna, and in Sacher-Masoch's literary imagination the wild and remote Carpathians harbored creatures of violently unconventional passions.

The fascination with slavery—its violence, its obligations, its humiliations—was also perfectly consistent with the Galician context of Sacher-Masoch's childhood in the 1840s. It was during that decade that the brutally oppressive conditions of serfdom in Galicia were being discussed in the Galician Sejm and within the Austrian administration, focusing especially on the contractual obligations to perform forced labor [*robot*]. Peasant rage erupted in the massacres of 1846 and was ultimately appeased with the emancipation of the serfs in 1848. Until then, it was not uncommon to describe the condition of serfdom in Galicia—but also in Russian Poland, and throughout the

Russian Empire—as a sort of slavery, comparable to contemporary African-American slavery in the United States. For Sacher-Masoch, then, slavery was neither an exotically or anachronistically remote subject of interest, but the burning issue of his own childhood's time and place, the issue that made an indelible mark on his developmental psyche. Furthermore, dating back to the 1780s, Josephine representations of Galicia had emphasized the exceptional brutality of Polish nobles toward their serfs, involving murder, torture, and incessant flogging. "It was something very usual," wrote Franz Kratter, "that people were left lying dead under the whip." This attention to the whip was consistent with the Enlightenment's whole view of Eastern Europe, a perspective that emphasized the arbitrarily violent treatment of serfs and the particular brutality of corporal punishment, especially punishment by the knout in Russia.[2] In Josephine ideology the abusive treatment of Galician serfs by Polish nobles pointed toward the vindication of Habsburg rule; Vienna would bring enlightened civilization to a land of barbaric cruelty. The whip thus left its semiotic mark on Habsburg consciousness in Galicia and became for Sacher-Masoch the sexual obsession of his life and his literature.

Sacher-Masoch eventually married a woman who took the name of Wanda von Dunajev, and she signed a contract of slavery with her husband, undertaking to beat him while wearing furs. "Not a day passed," wrote Wanda in her memoirs, "without my whipping my husband, without proving to him that I was keeping my part of the contract."[3] In the novella *Venus in Furs*, Wanda emphasized the arbitrariness, rather than the regularity, of punishment: "You will now for once have the whip in earnest—without having done anything to deserve it—so you will understand what to expect if you appear clumsy, disobedient, or rebellious." After the bloody beating he knelt down and kissed her foot, at her command.[4] Wanda's allusions to disobedience and rebelliousness echoed the social context of feudal oppression and class conflict in Galicia during Sacher-Masoch's childhood in the 1840s, a decade punctuated by violent insurrection and bloody massacres. In 1846 the Polish gentry rose against the Habsburgs, and the Polish peasants rose against the gentry. The notorious emblem of Galicia at midcentury was a parade of mutilated noble corpses, Polish nobles who had been murdered out of peasant loyalism to the Habsburg emperor. The massacres of 1846 constituted both the culmination and the collapse of the Josephine conception of Galicia polarized between nobles and peasants, while the memory and legacy of the massacres would condition the political and cultural dimensions of the province for the rest of its historical existence right up until World War I.

In 1890, the Austrian psychiatrist Richard von Krafft-Ebing coined a new clinical diagnosis for his *Psychopathia Sexualis*: "I feel justified in calling this sexual anomaly 'Masochism,' because the author Sacher-Masoch frequently made this perversion—which up to his time was quite unknown to the scientific world as such—the substratum of his writings."[5] By then Sacher-Masoch enjoyed a European reputation, and half a century had passed since his Galician childhood. While Galicia might have seemed only marginally relevant to the psychopathological concerns of Krafft-Ebing, there was, in fact, a Galician substratum that conditioned Sacher-Masoch's personal and literary anomalies. The years of his Galician childhood from 1836 to 1848 were formative and traumatic not only for him but also for the historical course of Galicia itself.

"Polish and Ruthenian Songs of the Galician People"

Sacher-Masoch, like Freud later on, placed considerable formative importance on the earliest experiences of infancy and childhood. While he never pronounced explicitly that his childhood in Galicia determined his masochistic sexual constitution, he did attribute developmental significance to the Galician village girl who nursed him as an infant. It was quite usual in the early nineteenth century for upper-class urban mothers to find poor girls from the countryside to serve as wet nurses, and the Habsburg bureaucratic Sacher-Masoch family in Lviv accepted the convention. While the population of Lviv, some fifty thousand people, included Poles, Jews, Germans, and Ruthenians, the surrounding countryside of eastern Galicia was overwhelmingly Ruthenian—and so, therefore, was the new baby's wet nurse. "With her milk I sucked in the love of the Russian people, of my province, of my homeland," declared Sacher-Masoch. "Through my nurse Russian became the first language that I commanded, though in my parents' house Polish, German, and French were primarily spoken. And it was she who told me the wondrously beautiful Russian fairy tales, or sang, while rocking me, those Little Russian folk songs that stamped themselves upon my existence, my emotional world, and also all my later works."[6] Imprecise in his ethnographic designations, alternating between "Russian" and "Little Russian" to describe the people who were then called "Ruthenian" and are today called "Ukrainian," Sacher-Masoch clearly identified with the eastern Slavs of Galicia.

When he affirmed his love "of the Russian people, of my province, of my homeland," the province could only be Galicia, and the homeland had to be the Habsburg monarchy. His identity—the "emotional world" of a man whose bizarre emotions became notorious all over Europe—was shaped by the parameters of nation, province, and empire. Sacher-Masoch wanted to be Ruthenian, remembering his wet nurse and her fairy tales, and so, perhaps fancifully, he claimed to be of noble Ruthenian descent on his mother's side, the Masoch side of the family. The exoticism of this ancestry was certainly intriguing to him, and he made his father's family no less exotic, tracing them back to the Spanish Moors: "The name Sacher, which people have so often taken for a Jewish name, is in reality of Oriental origin."[7] His fascination with the "Oriental" Judaism of Galicia became another component of his Galician identity.

> Among the inhabitants of Galicia and the different races living there, it is perhaps the Jews who claim the greatest interest. Nowhere do they dwell in greater number and in such authenticity as in Poland and Galicia. The Polish ghetto is a miniature Orient in the middle of Europe.[8]

The child of a Habsburg official in Galicia, Sacher-Masoch creatively dabbled in several ethnic identities native to the province. Although he wrote in German he was never eager to identify as a German by nationality, and he was never sympathetic to Polishness, which he regarded with the hostile eye of Josephine Galicians. It was the Jews and Ruthenians of Galicia who most notably populated his literary canvases of the Galician landscape. He allowed, and even tacitly encouraged, the belief that he was a Jew, while openly declaring himself to be of Ruthenian ancestry.

The heroes of his Galician tales were likely to be Ruthenian nobles, like the protagonist of *Don Juan von Kolomea* in 1866, though in Galician society the Ruthenians were actually much more likely to be peasants working on the estates of Polish nobles. The name of Severin von Kusiemski, the masochistic hero of *Venus in Furs*, seems to have been taken from Sacher-Masoch's correspondence in the 1860s with the Ruthenian political leader Mykhailo Kuzemsky. Living in Graz, Sacher-Masoch was received with enthusiasm there by the writer and critic Ferdinand Kürnberger, who was particularly interested in the young author's Ruthenian identity: "How would it be if, instead of the Great Russian Turgenev, we were to have a Little Russian, a Galician of the East, that is, an Austrian, that is, a German?" Such an author could reinvigorate German literature precisely because of his Galician origins. According to Kürnberger, "We would see German poets rising from the prairies of the Vistula and the forested mountains of the Dniester, poets who would not write books that come from books, but books that come from nature."[9] The Ruthenian aspect of Sacher-Masoch's identity thus served as a guarantee of originality, but it was also perceived in the richly overlapping contexts of Russian, Galician, Austrian, and German culture.

Sacher-Masoch's exotic cultivation of a Ruthenian identity coincided precisely with the emergence of an articulate Ruthenian national culture in Galicia during the nineteenth century. The 1830s, the decade of his birth, was a decade of cultural self-discovery for Ruthenians in Galicia: while he was still suckling with his Ruthenian wet nurse, in 1837, the landmark first collection of Ruthenian poetry was published, *Rusalka Dnistrovaia*, created in Lviv by the three writers of the Ruthenian Triad. In 1848, the year that the Sacher-Masoch family was transferred from Lviv to Prague, Galician Ruthenians articulated their first political program of national self-assertion in the context of the revolutionary upheaval in the Habsburg monarchy. Sacher-Masoch's childhood years in Galicia, therefore, belonged to a period when Ruthenian issues were being openly discussed as never before. Earlier, the most recognizable marker of Ruthenian distinctiveness had been religion: Uniate or Greek Catholic, rather than Roman Catholic. In the 1830s, this sense of religious difference was evolving toward a broader recognition of Ruthenians as the possessors of a distinctive national culture. According to Ivan Franko, looking back across the nineteenth century, "About the year 1830, the Poles could safely think that there is no Rus in Galicia, that there is only one Polish nation, oppressed by the Germans."[10] That view eventually became untenable in the period of Sacher-Masoch's childhood.

In 1830, when Poles in Russian Poland were launching their insurrection, Galician Poles were reaffirming their Galician identity with the publication of the literary almanac *Haliczanin*, edited by Walenty Chłędowski and published in Lviv. The title meant "Galician," but the spelling suggested a historical allusion to the medieval Rus principality of Halicz or Halych—which was also the original reason behind the Habsburg naming of "Galicia" in 1772. The sampling of Galician literature in *Haliczanin* included a poem by Leszek Dunin Borkowski, "The Cossack"; a novella by Eugeniusz Brocki, *Brigands in the Carpathians;* and even a drama by Fredro, *The Defense of Olsztyn.* There was a philosophical essay on language, emphasizing its importance for "the spirit of the nation," by Jan Nepomucen Kamiński—the author of the drama *Zabobon*—and his philosophical message was probably received with interest by both Poles and Ruthenians. Meanwhile, the literary supplement to *Gazeta Lwowska*—that is, *Rozmaitości*, especially under the editorship of Mikołaj Michalewicz, but also later, after 1835, under Kamiński—published articles by Ruthenian intellectuals on the Ruthenian language and on the Greek Catholic Church. Thus, literary publications in Polish affirmed the provincial identity of Galicia as the site of a specifically Galician literature, while suggesting that there might be a Ruthenian dimension to Galician identity.[11]

Haliczanin in 1830 included Ruthenian folk poetry translated into Polish.

In 1833, however, Wacław Zaleski—previously a contributor to *Rozmaitości* and later a governor of Galicia—published a full collection, *Polish and Ruthenian Songs of the Galician People* (*Pieśni polskie i ruskie ludu galicyjskiego*), with the Ruthenian songs transcribed into the Latin alphabet but otherwise untranslated.[12] Posing as an archaic collector, Zaleski took the pseudonym "Wacław z Oleska"—that is, Wacław from the eastern Galician town of Olesko. The introduction to the collection began with an epigraph from Herder on the importance of the people or the nation [*das Volk*] for poetry; indeed, it was Herder, with the publication of his *Volkslieder* in the 1770s, who put folk songs on the agenda of the European Enlightenment. It was Herder, furthermore, who had prophesied that "Ukraine will become a new Greece," celebrating the Ukrainians especially for "their musical nature."[13] That prophecy was not included in Zaleski's epigraph, but his publication of Ruthenian folk songs, with an appendix that also presented some songs in full notation on the musical staff, suggests that he believed in Ukrainian musicality.

Like Sacher-Masoch, Zaleski remembered the music of folk songs from his earliest childhood: "Born in the village, spending the first years of life in remote seclusion, I fell in love with these songs, which so pleasantly lulled my infant years, and remained in my early memory as the first impulses of developing emotion. This attachment was sucked in with milk, inhaled with air." As with Sacher-Masoch, the memory of folk songs was associated with infant milk, and exercised a formative influence on Zaleski's early character and emotions. He wrote down the songs that he remembered: "and that is the first germ of this collection."[14] The project was inspired by such recent efforts as the collection of Serbian folk songs by Vuk Karadžić and the Polish study of pre-Christian Slavdom by Chodakowski. Zaleski's conception of the project was not specifically Polish but Galician—"from all sides of Galicia I received assistance from young friends"—so that ultimately he produced, not a national collection of Polish folklore, but a provincial almanac that reflected the cultural complexity of Galicia with its Polish and Ruthenian aspects. Zaleski affirmed that folk songs had to be organically connected to the spirit of a nation: "They are true products of the earth on which they grew. Like the tree in the forest or the flowers in the valley, savagely luxuriant, they are the undeniably natural fruit of this land which produces them; thus the songs of the people are the natural poetry of the nation to which they belong, completely corresponding to nationality." This Herderian account of the folk song as the fundamental expression of the nation, environmentally conditioned by the land of the nation, was unusual in this case because the land was Galicia and the nation was plural: Polish and Ruthenian. Zaleski looked forward to the time when "the collection of Galician songs will be able to compete with the collections of songs of every nation."[15] For Za-leski as folklorist, "Galicia" was the environmental field for his collection, and therefore ambiguously significant, a provincial territory and a national homeland.

"Both the Pole and the Ruthenian, like every Slav in general, are always singing, singing from the heart," wrote Zaleski.[16] He recognized that treat-ing Poles and Ruthenians together required some justification, and began by explaining that the partitions of Poland necessitated a Galician framework for the study of folk songs.

> I do not deny that it would be better if we were to have a special individual col-lection of Polish songs, and another of Ruthenian songs; but in that event it would be necessary to collect songs over all of Poland and over all of Rus. The accomplishment of either one or the other seems to me in the present politi-cal circumstances to be an unlikely thing for one person. We can only partially move toward such collections. I have undertaken to collect and publish Galician folk songs; since Galicia is inhabited by Polish and Ruthenian people, I have therefore collected and published Polish and Ruthenian songs. I have published them together, because the collection of just one or the other individually would have been too thin. I have mixed them together, since in Galicia the Polish and Ruthenian people live mixed together. To separate them sharply did not seem to me necessary. . . . Every Ruthenian will understand Polish songs, and a Pole will understand Ruthenian songs, if only he wants to.[17]

Thus Zaleski justified his joining of Polish and Ruthenian songs as the work of necessity, dictated by political conditions and pragmatic considerations. He also, however, offered folkloric reasons for considering these songs to-gether on Galician terrain: first, that they were mutually intelligible, forming a unitary poetic domain, and second, that they were geographically "mixed [*pomieszany*]" on the terrain of Galicia and therefore also in the pages of the published collection. The alleged pretext of joining Poles and Ruthenians so that the book would not be too "thin" was belied by the book itself, which was dramatically fat: 50 pages of preface, 500 pages of songs, and almost 200 pages of musical notations in the appendix. Evidently Zaleski, in spite of his protestations and justifications, joined the Polish and Ruthenian songs in a Galician collection because he believed that they belonged together.

Zaleski even offered a Polish national justification for joining the Polish and Ruthenian songs. He pointed out that, elsewhere in the world of Slavic literature, the Czech tradition was coming to include Moravians and even Slovaks, and suggested that Polish culture had some stake in being similarly inclusive. He posed the question in nationally provocative terms: "Do we really wish the Ruthenians to have their own literature?" Yet Zaleski himself made a fundamental contribution to establishing an independent Ruthenian literature. He remarked about Ruthenian songs: "The transfer of them to paper involved no small difficulties: some had never before been written down. I note once more the difficulties. The Ruthenian language has no grammar and no dictionary. In pronunciation the manner is preserved differently in different places."[18] Zaleski therefore, while allegedly seeking to attach Ruthenian songs to Polish literature, was actually contributing to the establishment of Ruthenian as a literary language by recording the folk songs that served as a basis for Ruthenian literature. That did not go unappreciated, and Ivan Franko, much later, would remark about Zaleski's collection: "This book was the first harbinger of our national rebirth. Only then did lettered Ruthenians become convinced that in their very midst, in the mouths of the simple, enserfed peasants, there lived songs and tales of which they could be proud before the world."[19] Sacher-Masoch, born in 1836, discovered the beauty of Ruthenian folk poetry in the traditional "oral" fashion, from the songs of his Ruthenian wet nurse, but, in fact, after Zaleski's collection of 1833, those songs were also available to the general Galician reader in published form, including musical notation.

In the 1780s, Joseph II established a Greek Catholic seminary in Lviv, as part of his general campaign to promote state authority over religion and religious education in the Habsburg monarchy. Fifty years later, in February 1835, Markiian Shashkevych, a Ruthenian student in the seminary, paid his respects to the dynasty with a tribute in honor of Emperor Franz on his sixty-seventh (and last) birthday—composed and presented in the Ruthenian language, published at the Stavropygian Greek Catholic press. The use of Ruthenian was unprecedented for a formal tribute. The title, however, did not characterize the tribute as Ruthenian: "A Galician Voice in Honor of Emperor Franz I."[20] To express oneself in Ruthenian could be represented as a matter of Galician identity, and, certainly, to honor the emperor in Lviv was always a manifestation of being Galician. In 1836, Shashkevych took a public position in favor of Ruthenian expression in the Cyrillic alphabet, rather than the Latin letters used for Polish; the article ("Azbuka i abecadło") was published in Przemyśl. When Zaleski published his Polish and Ruthenian folk songs, mixed together, he did not feel obliged to alternate alphabets. When Shashkevych, however, along with Iakiv Holovatsky and Ivan Vahylevych, forming together the Ruthenian Triad, published their collection of Ruthenian literary writing, *Rusalka Dnistrovaia*, they employed not only the Galician Ruthenian vernacular but also the modern Cyrillic alphabet.

Rusalka Dnistrovaia (*The Dniester Nymph*), named for the Dniester River that ran through eastern Galicia, was actually produced in Budapest in 1836, though it bore the publication date of 1837 and was entirely conceived and created in Lviv. The book included folk poems and also original Ruthenian poetry by the young seminarians. The publication in Budapest circumvented government censorship in Lviv, which, for Ruthenian books, was executed by authorities of the Greek Catholic Church. To the conservative Uniate hierarchy, accustomed to the traditional liturgy in Old Church Slavonic, the work's vernacular language and modern orthography were unsettling; at the same time, the invocation of some Slavic pagan mythology—like the titular nymph, Rusalka—seemed suspiciously un-Christian. In fact, the prefatory essay on Ruthenian folk songs did emphasize a seamless transition from paganism to Christianity, and noted the preservation of popular culture and customs: "People were not deprived of their former customs, the sentiments sucked in with their mothers' milk were not wiped out, and the uprooting of paganism did not implant any foreign spirit in the nation." In the end, *Rusalka Dnistrovaia*, the founding work of modern Ruthenian or Ukrainian literature in Galicia, was permitted to circulate in the Habsburg monarchy but was banned in Galicia itself. The members of the Ruthenian Triad were summoned before the authorities of the Greek Catholic seminary and formally reprimanded.[21]

The very nature of Galicia was at stake with the publication of *Rusalka Dnistrovaia*, which, because of its long-term literary influence, made it possible to reconceive Galicia as fundamentally multinational, not just multiconfessional. The idea of Galicia would have to embrace both Polish and Ruthenian cultures, at the very least, and both would be qualified and inflected by the Galician context. In fact, the newly articulated Ruthenian perspective was conditioned by a powerful sense of being Galician. Shashkevych, after all, participated in *Rusalka Dnistrovaia* almost immediately after affirming his "Galician Voice" in honor of the emperor. The tensions within this Galician-Ruthenian perspective were eventually evident in the divergent courses of the Triad members: Shashkevych looking for solidarity with Ukrainians in the Russian Empire, Vahylevych working ever more closely with the Poles of Galicia, and Holovatsky ultimately immigrating to Russia.

Sacher-Masoch's birth in 1836 coincided precisely with the composition and publication of *Rusalka Dnistrovaia* by the Ruthenian Triad. His early memory of his Ruthenian nurse made her seem hardly less mythological than the nymph Rusalka.

> The first apparition that emerges from the mist of my past is a great and beautiful female form with the face of a Raphael Madonna. Still today I have the image clearly before me, with her great blue eyes and warm smile, a white shawl wrapped around her head, as she bends over my cradle to stroke me: Handscha, my nurse.[22]

He explained that he was such a delicate and nervous child at birth that finding the right nurse had been a matter of life and death. Handscha was found

The Dniester River, in Galicia. The *Dniester Nymph* (*Rusalka Dnistrovaia*) was an important Galician Ruthenian literary event in 1837. From Julius Jandaurek, *Das Königreich Galizien und Lodomerien* (Vienna: Karl Graeser, 1884).

in a village near Lviv, Winniki, which was famous for a wonder-working image of the Madonna. Sacher-Masoch's mother wrapped herself in heavy furs and drove by sleigh to the village, to plead with the girl to take the job. Handscha did not want to leave home, because she was nursing her own child. "I would never abandon my child," she declared, "not even for the crown of the czarina." In Sacher-Masoch's retelling of this episode from his own infancy, the Ruthenian heroine looked east to the Romanovs, not west to the Habsburgs. Sacher-Masoch's mother, however, wept as she pleaded in her furs, and the girl was moved by the tears. She would go to Lviv after all. With tears of her own, Handscha left her child to be nursed by a neighbor, put on a peasant sheepskin coat, in contrast to the Sacher-Masoch furs, and departed for the city. At her first sight of the sickly city infant, Handscha declared, "This child needs me more urgently than my own. I am a Christian and will do my duty. I will stay as long as the child needs a nurse."[23] She stayed for several years, long enough to make her mark on Sacher-Masoch's earliest memories, long enough to make Ruthenian his first language and earliest imaginative world.

She was able to offer him a taste of that same peasant oral culture—legendary tales and folk poetry—that became the basis for modern Ruthenian literature in the 1830s. Sacher-Masoch took it all in with the milk of infancy, which was also the prevailing metaphor for the transmission of folk culture, even in *Rusalka Dnistrovaia*. Ruthenian culture thus made an indelible impression on the Habsburg bureaucrat's delicate child.

> The fairy tales that my nurse told me, the folk songs that she sang for me, influenced my way of thinking, my emotional life, and my character more deeply than all my later studies. They made a stronger impression on my imagination than classical literature, the Greek and Roman authors, stronger also than the music of Beethoven and Mozart, than the pictures of Raphael and Rubens. On the long winter evenings we children sat in a circle around the pretty peasant girl and listened devotedly and full of attention, while she let the remarkable images, born of the fertile fantasy of the East Slavic people, march past us. There is scarcely any other people that possesses so great a treasury of fairy tales, legends, and folk songs as the Little Russian people.[24]

The spirit of European Romanticism encouraged the young Sacher-Masoch to relish the folk songs of the Galician Ruthenians in the privacy of his family home in Lviv, just as the Ruthenians themselves were beginning to make such songs into the basis of a modern national literature in the public sphere.

Sacher-Masoch would remember those songs as the music of Galicia and use them to set the mood for his Galician tales. At the beginning of *Don Juan von Kolomea*, the narrator found himself detained at a Jewish inn in eastern Galicia, where he would soon make the acquaintance of the libertine protagonist. In the meantime he listened to the local peasants singing:

> Everything was quiet, serious, and dignified, and outside the peasants were singing a melancholy song whose melody seemed to come from a great distance. The notes floated around the tavern like ghosts, and it seemed as if they were afraid to come inside and join the living, whispering people. . . . My boredom also turned into melancholy, the melancholy that is so peculiar to us Little Russians. . . .[25]

Long after he had left Galicia, Sacher-Masoch remembered the emotionally compelling power of Ruthenian song, and, though he wrote his Galician tale in German, he made his narrator a Ruthenian, writing about "us Little Russians" in the first-person plural.

Sacher-Masoch's Ruthenianism was a lifelong passion and affectation, the most important aspect of the Galician identity that underlay his entire literary career, even though he left Galicia at the age of twelve. His authentic Ruthenian counterpart and exact contemporary, the Ruthenian twin brother he never knew, was the child that his nurse left behind in the village when she went to Lviv. That child would have grown up in the generation after *Rusalka Dnistrovaia*, a true Galician Ruthenian of the nineteenth century.

"KNOWLEDGE OF OUR GREAT AND BEAUTIFUL PROVINCE"

In the 1840s a new German-language publication appeared in Lviv under the title *Galicia*. It described itself as the "Newspaper for the Maintenance and News of the Fatherland, of Art, of Industry, and of Life." Although the "fatherland" [*Vaterland*], in a German-language newspaper, might refer to the Habsburg monarchy as a whole, the title of the newspaper, *Galicia*, suggested that the province itself could also be conceived as a sort of fatherland. The New Year's issue of 1841 featured a poem of greetings from the editors of *Galicia* to their Galician readers, invoking, for the province,

> The motto that gladly upon the brow
> Galicia bears as a guiding star . . .
> Yes! God, the Emperor, and the Fatherland![26]

This patriotic verse was probably adapted from Hoffmann von Fallersleben's poem of 1839, "Mein Vaterland," expressing German national sentiment. The Galician poem attempted to represent the character of Galicia—both the province with it inhabitants, and the eponymous newspaper with its reading public—in terms of Habsburg loyalty that transcended individual national identities. Such a journal, with its three-word ideological slogan (*Gott, Kaiser, Vaterland*), might have had a limited linguistic and sentimental appeal to the Poles and Ruthenians of Lviv, but was surely required reading for a prominent bureaucratic household like that of the Sacher-Masoch family.

The appearance of *Galicia* in Lviv was also noted in Vienna, in an article in the *Allgemeine Theaterzeitung* in 1841. The absence, hitherto, of a good Galician journal in German was pronounced the reason that "Galicia, this great beautiful province, one of the richest pearls in the Austrian imperial crown, was till now, to us and to all parts of the common fatherland, an almost unknown land." Austrians had been uninformed about "the extraordinary progress which Galicia has made under the silent beneficent effects of the government." Now, finally, with the thrice-weekly publication of *Galicia*, "this sensitive gap concerning the public activity of such an important province has been decisively and honorably filled." The editor, Joseph Mehoffer, was qualified as "one of the best informed and most knowledgeable literary figures in the province," while even the paper and print of the journal were extravagantly praised with metropolitan condescension: "print more beautiful than any that has ever been seen in Lemberg."[27] In Vienna, *Galicia* seemed to offer valuable imperial knowledge of an important province.

In January 1841, *Galicia* published bits of news from far and near, including William Henry Harrison's election as president of the United States and the Habsburg emperor Ferdinand's selection of a clergyman for the

Przemyśl Greek Catholic cathedral chapter. There were agricultural reports from the country about growing beets for the manufacture of sugar, and there were theatrical accounts from the city about opera performances in Lviv of Donizetti's *Belisario* and Rossini's *Tancredi*, both hailed as novelties (though *Tancredi* was almost thirty years old). *Galicia* regretted the "sterility" of opera in Lviv, and the previous year's monotonous repetitions of Bellini's *Norma, La Sonnambula,* and *I Puritani,* along with Donizetti's *L'Elisir d'Amore.*[28] Although *Galicia* celebrated Galicia, there was no suppressing the concern that the province was, in some respects, provincial.

By the end of January, the Sacher-Masoch family would have found its own name in the newspaper. There was to be a carnival ball on the last night of the month, *Faschingsabend,* with costumes and dominoes, so that "unforced entertainment, spirit, and humor may freely unfold." The implicit limits of such carnivalesque freedom in the Metternich era were suggested by the notice about obtaining tickets from the police director, Sacher-Masoch—that is, the writer's father. The ball was afterward pronounced a great success, with the proceeds charitably benefiting the poor people of the city. *Galicia* saluted "this beautiful purpose, so important for Lemberg," and gave special credit to Police Director Sacher-Masoch for the success of the occasion. Thirteen hundred people attended and enjoyed themselves until three in the morning.[29] Five-year-old Sacher-Masoch was presumably left at home, while his parents attended this carnival occasion that took place under his father's benevolent sponsorship and watchful authority.

"I spent my childhood in a police residence," recalled Sacher-Masoch much later in the nineteenth century.

> Few people still know what that meant in Austria before 1848: Police soldiers, who bring in vagabonds and bound criminals, employees of dark appearance, a thin and creeping censor, spies who dare look no one in the face, the flogging station, barred windows from which smiling painted prostitutes sometimes stared, and sometimes pale and melancholy Polish conspirators. It was, God knows, not a cheerful environment.[30]

Spies, censorship, and police were closely associated with the Metternich era, and, given Sacher-Masoch's celebrated inclinations, it is possible that the darker side of police work—bondage, imprisonment, punishment, and especially flogging—may have made a particular impression on his youthful imagination.

Yet, in his literary portrait of his father the police chief, Sacher-Masoch described a man of varied interests, including especially natural history. The police director had a herbarium, a collection of minerals, and specimens of mammoth bones and elephant teeth. On his desk were little statues of Frederick the Great and Napoleon, but also Socrates, Virgil, and Goethe. On the walls of his office were paintings, tapestries, antique weapons, and bearskins—probably from Carpathian bears. In the corner of the police chief's office was a life-size mannequin dressed as a Carpathian bandit, with a stuffed and glass-eyed owl overhead.

> Here my father sat when his serious charge, the uninterrupted struggle against Polish conspirators, gave him a free hour, and untroubled by the death sentence that someone had posted on the gate, he organized his treasures, that he had collected in the woods, meadows, swamps, and quarries around Lemberg; he took the beetles out of the alcohol flasks to stick them on needles and exhibit them in the cork-lined cases, like soldiers in formation; he worked on the stones with a hammer, and pasted the dried and pressed plants on white paper.[31]

The 1830s and 1840s were, in fact, years of ongoing and unsuccessful Polish conspiracy in Galicia, stimulated in part by the refugees from the defeated insurrection of 1830–31 in Russian Poland. Julian Horoszkiewicz, who was a schoolboy in Lviv in 1830, was a political prisoner in Kufstein by 1840.[32] The attentive surveillance of Police Director Sacher-Masoch would not be adequate to forestall the disastrous Polish insurrection of 1846 or the briefly triumphant Revolution of 1848 in Galicia.

The Galician surveillance by police chief Sacher-Masoch also extended to the Jews of the province, and he was particularly concerned about the politically subversive implications of Hasidism. He was in contact with Joseph Perl, the *maskil* reformer, a man of the Jewish Enlightenment and fierce opponent of Hasidism; Perl's denunciations of the Hasids to the Habsburg government would come to the desk of the police chief in Lviv. In 1838, Perl was outraged about Hasidic disturbances in his own town of Ternopil, where the Hasids not only obstructed his program for German Jewish education but also rallied against the Ternopil appointment of the enlightened rabbi Solomon Judah Rapoport, vandalizing his synagogue. Perl denounced the Jewish institutions of the *bet ha-midrash* and the *mikva*, the house of study and the ritual bath house, arguing that these had become Hasidic sites for illegal assembly, subversive reading, and even sexual license. Perl further urged the strict enforcement of the Josephine requirement of German education for Galician rabbis, and warned that the Hasids were seeking to dominate Galician Judaism and to flout Habsburg law in the province.[33]

Police chief Sacher-Masoch issued a report on the pernicious role of the Hasidic leaders, the *zaddikim*, who allegedly controlled their followers by manipulation and failed to respect the law of the land. The Habsburg government, after due consideration in 1838, agreed that Hasidic leaders were seeking to "fetter the spirit of Jewry in chains of superstition" but declined to legislate against them, precisely because the Hasids were such a pervasive presence in the province. The surveillance of the police chief made him aware of the activities of Polish conspirators and Hasidic *zaddikim*, but he could not achieve the transformation of Galician society any more than Jo-seph could fifty years before. Indeed, such tensions had become integral to Galicia's provincial character, and when Joseph Perl died in 1839 the Hasids of Ternopil danced on his grave.[34]

"My father seldom spoke even a few words to me," recalled the writer Sacher-Masoch of his childhood in Lviv, "but I was glad to be around him, and as silent as a mouse, for fear of disturbing him."[35] The Habsburg police chief may also have appeared fearsome to restive Poles and pious Hasids in the 1840s, in spite of his charitable sponsorship of the carnival ball. The journal *Galicia*, subject to the censorship of the Metternich era, did not report on any burblings of Polish conspiracy, but, much later, the fiction of Sacher-Masoch conveyed a sense of pervasive suspicions in Galicia. Don Juan of Kolomea (or Kolomiya) was introduced to the reader as someone suspected of Polish conspiracy by a peasant patrol, though he himself claimed to be actually Ruthenian. "But friends, just do me the favor of recognizing me! Am I an emissary of the Polish revolt?" he expostulated when detained. "Am I a Pole? Do you want my parents to spin in their graves at the Russian cem-etery in Chernelytsya? Didn't my ancestors fight with the Cossack Bogdan Khmelnytsky against the Poles?" Sacher-Masoch recalled a Galician world in which peasants, whether Polish or Ruthenian, were automatically suspicious of noblemen, and every suspicion was immediately formulated as "conspir-acy" and "revolution." Don Juan of Kolomea was indeed a dangerous man, sexually dangerous as a libertine, not politically problematic as a conspirator. Detained at the inn, he immediately exercised his hypnotic charms upon the Jewish innkeeper's wife. The innkeeper warned the narrator in a whisper: "He's a dangerous man, a dangerous man."[36] For Sacher-Masoch, whose fa-ther tracked Polish conspirators in Galicia in the 1840s, sexual menace would always seem most exciting in the context of potential violence.

The life-size figure of the Carpathian bandit in the police chief's office might also have seemed menacing to the child. As an item of decor, however, it was probably intended as a folkloric token of general Galician interest in the Carpathian Mountains in the 1830s and 1840s. Eugeniusz Brocki wrote about "Brigands of the Carpathians" in *Haliczanin*, and Markiian Shashkevych wrote a story, "Olena," about brigands violently avenging the peasants against the nobles of Galicia. Members of the Ruthenian Triad were aware that Ruthenian folk songs sometimes glorified the brigands of the mountains.[37] In 1841, *Galicia* offered a published account of a journey in the "majestic" Carpathians, which had so much to offer to "the friend of nature."[38] In 1843 there was published in Vilnius, and in 1844 performed on the stage in Lviv, a romantic tragedy in Pol-ish entitled *Carpathian Mountaineers* (*Karpaccy Górale*), by Józef Korzeniowski, set with anthropological precision among the pastoral mountain Ruthenians,

Górale, mountaineers of the Tatra range of the Carpathians. The Górale became the objects of literary and folkloric interest in Galicia in the 1830s and the 1840s. They were also featured in Bogusławski's *Krakowiacy and Górale*, in the 1790s. From Julius Jandaurek, *Das Königreich Galizien und Lodomerien* (Vienna: Karl Graeser, 1884).

called Hutsuls. The detailed descriptions of Hutsul appearance included long hair, feathered caps, broad belts, hatchets, and pistols. The plot concerned a certain Antos, a young highlander, who deserted from the Habsburg army and became a bandit in the mountains, with tragic consequences. "For me there is no home," declared Antos. "My home is the cavern and the forest, and my kinsmen the brigands."[39] Thus the mannequin in the Sacher-Masoch police residence was brought to life on the stage of Lviv, an object of both police responsibility and romantic folklore.

The costumed mannequin might also have been considered a part of the police chief's natural history collection. Like his cases of minerals and plants, collected in the vicinity of Lviv, like the bearskins on the wall, the bandit represented a specimen of the Galician environment. *Galicia* in 1841 took particular notice of the publication of a book on *The Fauna of the Galician-Bu-kovinian Vertebrates*. The author, Aleksander Zawadzki, was a professor based in Przemyśl and Lviv, and the book was published in German in Stuttgart. *Galicia* wrote enthusiastically about "the richness of Galicia in the animal kingdom," and boasted that "we possess animals that in other provinces exist no more, or are very rarely present, like bears, chamois, and beavers." The newspaper noted that "the need for a systematic overview of the fauna of Galicia was all the more notable inasmuch as until now there had not even been published a name index of the native animals." The new book thus filled "a significant gap in the literature" while providing "knowledge of our great and beautiful province."[40] Knowledge of the province may be considered to be one of the imperatives of modern imperial mastery, and in the case of Galicia that was particularly true, since the recognition of its provincial coherence was an implicit vindication of Habsburg rule. The police chief's natural history collection could thus be considered a microcosmic token of his own crucial political role in the imperial administration of the province, while the figure of the bandit in his office represented a vertebrate type of particular relevance to his responsibilities.

The Habsburg ideology of Galicia in the 1840s still meant trying to envision some sort of rapprochement between Polish and German culture, and in 1841 the editors of *Galicia* accordingly reported on Polish literature to their German readers: "We certainly believe we would not be going too far in saying that Polish literature has remained until now, not just for the most part, but almost completely alien to German literature. The obstacle that always occurred, and still stands, is language." Police Director Sacher-Masoch kept a little statue of Goethe on his desk, but nothing suggestive of an interest in Polish literature—though in fact the bandit figure was relevant to such contemporary works as Korzeniowski's *Carpathian Mountaineers*. In *Galicia*, the commentary on Polish literature noted "the present tendency toward folk culture, the attempt to collect and preserve the spiritual monuments of this nation, to put them together in a mausoleum of folk poetry." *Galicia* saluted "the collections of folk songs and music, tales and legends."[41] In fact, the journal was interested in precisely the genres of songs and legends that were, just at that same moment, seizing the imagination of the five-year-old Leopold von Sacher-Masoch.

Galicia insisted that Polish journalism was "by no means so scant, and does not stand at such a low level of style, as one might believe." The editors mentioned *Rozmaitości* in Lviv, as well as other journals from Russian and Prussian Poland. Clearly, the German readers were presumed to harbor notably condescending attitudes toward Polish culture, while *Galicia* was determined to affirm a cultural "elective affinity [*Wahlverwandtschaft*]" between Poles and Germans. Fredro had been denounced by Goszczyński in 1835 for writing "non-national" comedies in the French style, and *Galicia* now also censured the Gallicisms in Polish culture, insisting that the greater Polish affinity was for German, rather than French, culture. "German language and culture [*Gesittung*] are native [*heimisch*] here," wrote the newspaper.[42] This meant not that Galicia was a German province, but that its culture transcended the difference between German and Polish. Zaleski's collection of folk songs in 1833 had similarly suggested that the culture of Galicia transcended the difference between Polish and Ruthenian. Correspondingly, in Przemyśl in 1838, Goethe's poem "Der Erlkönig" was published in a Ruthenian translation alongside the original German.[43]

In 1842 there appeared in Warsaw a journal that affirmed the relation between Polish and Russian culture, *Dennitsa-Jutrzenka (Morning Star)*, with parallel Russian and Polish versions of the same stories. One such story came from a member of the Ruthenian Triad, Iakiv Holovatsky, giving his account of a "Voyage in Galician and Hungarian Rus." He set out from Lviv to explore the Ruthenian countryside.

> You know with what delight a person born and raised on a modest village farm breaks away from the constricting walls of a great city. You know me well, and know my attachment to our unhappy ancestors. You recall with what longing [*z jakiem utęsknieniem*] I remembered the village, with what eagerness I anticipated that blissful moment when I would abandon the dust of the town. . . . You can guess with what feelings I was inspired when, after separating from Lviv, distasteful to me, I flew out into the free air like a bird from a cage.[44]

From the perspective of *Galicia*, Lviv, with its Habsburg officials, German publications, Italian operas, and masked balls, was essentially Galician, transcending nationality through urban cosmopolitanism. From the perspective of *Dennitsa-Jutrzenka* in Warsaw, Lviv appeared as a corruptive urban blight upon the authentic rural attractions of the eastern Galician countryside with its Ruthenian peasants. The motto of *Dennitsa-Jutrzenka*, with its parallel Russian-Polish columns, was, in Latin, a variation on Terence: *Slavus sum, nihil slavici a me alienum esse puto* ["I am a Slav, and I consider nothing Slavic alien to me"]. The stirrings of Russian-sponsored pan-Slavism were altogether alien to a newspaper like *Galicia,* which envisioned an elective affinity between Germans and Poles.

In 1842 there was also a proposal, originating in Vienna, for the creation of a state-sponsored Ruthenian journal, to counter the insinuations of Russian pan-Slavism. The proposed editor, Ivan Holovatsky, the brother of Iakiv, noted that the journal was to be published in the "Galician Ruthenian language" with contributors from Galicia. The project ultimately collapsed over Viennese insistence on the Latin alphabet, instead of Cyrillic, and there was some suspicion that Vienna wanted not only to counter Russian influence among the Ruthenians but also to distinguish the Ruthenians of Galicia from the Little Russians or Ukrainians of the Russian Empire.[45] This would not have been inconsistent with Metternich's earlier thoughts about making "true Galicians." In fact, in 1843, with the encouragement of the Uniate metropolitan, Vienna officially adopted the classification of "Ruthenians [*Ruthenen*]" for describing this population in Galicia, and would continue to use that name until the abolition of Galicia and the Habsburg monarchy in 1918.[46]

GALICIAN RAILWAYS

In Sacher Masoch's *Venus in Furs*, the lovers left Galicia by train. Wanda took a first-class compartment, while Severin, as her slave, traveled third class, but he had the more vivid Galician experience:

> I breathe the same onion-scented air with Polish peasants, Jewish peddlars, and common soldiers, and, when I mount the steps to her compartment, she is lying stretched out on the cushions, in her comfortable fur, covered with animal hides, like an Oriental despot.[47]

The train that brought Severin and Wanda from Galicia to Vienna, on the way to Italy, was taken quite for granted by the author of the novella, published in 1870, but no such train had existed when Sacher-Masoch himself was born in Lviv one generation earlier. The period of Sacher-Masoch's childhood was the very moment in European history when the building of railways was first being contemplated in Europe, and Galicia figured prominently in the Habsburg railroad program.

In 1836, the year of Sacher-Masoch's birth, Emperor Ferdinand granted to the Rothschilds the imperial privilege of constructing the first stretch of Habsburg railroad. It was to connect Vienna to the town of Bochnia in Galicia and would be known as the Vienna-Bochnia railroad, or the Kaiser-Ferdinands-Nordbahn. Bochnia was rich in salt mines, as was nearby Wieliczka, and therefore economically interesting as the endpoint of the northern line, and the tracks were also supposed to continue to the south of Vienna and end at Trieste on the Adriatic Sea. In 1836 there was published in Vienna a pamphlet on "The Project of the Vienna-Bochnia Railroad in Its Technical, Commercial, and Financial Aspects."[48] The railway project involved an element of political interest in binding together the provinces of the monarchy, including Galicia, through better communication and economic integration.

Cracow, though it was then a theoretically independent urban republic, was included on the Habsburg railroad route, but Lviv, and all of eastern Galicia, lay far beyond the anticipated rails. According to the record of the Galician Sejm in 1839, "Two well-known citizens submitted to the high authority of the royal court the idea of continuing the railway from Vienna to Bochnia, further along in Galicia, below Lwów to Brzeżany. The importance of this idea is striking to the eye."[49] One of the two citizens was Prince Leon Sapieha, who had participated in the November Insurrection and then taken refuge in Galicia; in the 1840s he became an important Galician political figure, participating in such practical ventures as a credit society, an economic society, an agricultural school, the establishment of fire insurance, and the expansion of the railways. The other well-known citizen was actually well known for reasons other than his steady political participation in the Sejm—none other than Aleksander Fredro. This was the period of his literary silence, after the denunciation by Goszczyński, and the playwright, while not writing plays, gave institutional support to the Polish theater and the Ossolineum Library in Lviv, while also attending to economic and political issues in the Galician Sejm. He worked closely with Sapieha to formulate railroad proposals in the late 1830s, and the two men would also collaborate in the 1840s in an unsuccessful effort to bring about some sort of reform of peasant serfdom. The Galician Sejm, like the other provincial diets of the monarchy, had only very restricted powers in Metternich's age of absolutism, but Fredro was actively involved in helping to shape and articulate the opinion of his peers for presentation to the Habsburg authorities in Lviv and Vienna.

Fredro in 1839 was on cordial terms with the Habsburg administration in Galicia. In October he was invited, along with his brother Henryk, to join an autumn hunting party with the governor, Archduke Ferdinand d'Este. It was the top-level Habsburg official Franz Krieg who wrote to Fredro, in German, on behalf of the governor: "His Royal Highness the illustrious Archduke General Governor intends in the coming week to dedicate himself to the pleasures of the hunt in the region of Dolina."[50] Fredro had sent a live Carpathian bear to the previous governor Lobkovic, but Ferdinand d'Este was not as popular with the Polish gentry, and Krieg even less so. "He was a true bureaucrat, a parvenu [*dorobkiewicz*]," noted Sapieha of Krieg, snobbily. "His wife was the daughter of a former tailor in Lwów, a German. Both were highly detestable to Poles, but the Poles concealed their distaste with great politeness."[51] Sacher-Masoch's father, the police chief, belonged to Krieg's official world.

Fredro, however, was on sufficiently polite terms with this world to receive hunting invitations that were certainly marks of favor. The dramatist, at this time, was hoping to use such favor to further the aims of the Galician Sejm. A letter of December 1839 suggested that he was counting on Krieg for Galician banking concerns, while the railway was also on Fredro's mind:

> Our Credit Society needs only the last and highest confirmation, and since Baron Krieg is in Vienna, we hope that everything will soon be successfully concluded. . . .In recent days we have given our opinion concerning the projected railway from Bochnia to Brzeżany. It would be without doubt a great benefit for the country [*dla kraju*]; it is only a question of who has to open the purse—a bagatelle![52]

Railroads were not bagatelles, of course, and the question of finance would weigh heavily on the project, intersecting with the plans for the credit society. The problem of the purse was posed airily, almost as if it might have come out of one of Fredro's comedies; purse-strings played a role, for instance, in the miserly calculations of *Life Annuity* in 1835. Yet Fredro was earnestly engaged in matters of credit and finance, and regarded the railway as something to benefit the country, *dla kraju*: in other words, for Galicia.

In 1840, Fredro's brother Henryk was in Paris, enjoying Donizetti at the opera—*Lucia di Lammermoor* and *Lucrezia Borgia*—while Lviv was still repeating Bellini favorites. One woman in Paris asked Henryk Fredro whether he was a poet, "the Polish Lamartine," and he replied that he was not: "We only have a Molière in our family, and that is my brother Aleksander."[53] Meanwhile, back in Lviv, the Polish Molière was studying the map of Galicia, and measuring the distances from one possible train station to another, estimating costs, making proposals to Franz Bretschneider, the engineer who was working on the Nordbahn, and corresponding with Leon Sapieha about all of the above. Sapieha, who had taken up arms in the November Insurrection of 1830, now wrote to Fredro in December 1840 in an unmartial spirit: "I am constantly thinking over the choice of direction for our railway, whether to go toward Brody and Podolia or whether to keep to the Dniester valley. Each of these has many arguments pro and contra." Fredro wrote to Sapieha in the same month without the slightest comic flair: "I have proposed to Bretschneider a course as a correction to his first project. We have all agreed that the line connecting the San and the Dniester is highly desirable—only Lwów, which can neither be left out, nor made into a great deviation from the commercial line, remains a problem to be resolved. In this regard I am searching for the middle point between Lwów and the Dniester."[54] Both men were deeply preoccupied with the map of Galicia, and focused on the creation of the means of communication and transport that would reinforce with iron the unity and coherence of the province.

Henryk Fredro in Paris may have actually had a better perspective on Polish national concerns than his brother did in Lviv. Henryk wrote in December 1840 about the arrival of the corpse of Napoleon in Paris, twenty years after his death on St. Helena in 1821, for ceremonial reburial in the Invalides. There were Polish officers present, shouting, *Vive l'Empereur! Vivent les Polonais!* ["Long live the Emperor! Long live the Poles!"]. Reports of the ceremony also reached Lviv and appeared in Polish in *Gazeta Lwowska* and in German in *Galicia*.[55] Along with the dead body of Napoleon, Poles in Paris could also witness the living presence of the nation's greatest poet, Adam Mickiewicz, who in 1840 began to lecture at the Collège de France as professor of Slavic literature. Henryk Fredro reported without great enthusiasm: "Mickiewicz holds lectures twice a week on Tuesday and Friday, but it is very difficult for him to express himself in French. I have only gone once so far. . . . I don't know him, but people say that he is very wild and disagreeable." While Polish Romantics attacked Aleksander Fredro for being too French, and therefore non-national, the Fredro brothers took some small revenge in relishing the idea that Mickiewicz was weak in the French language and perhaps French manners as well. Émigré life in Paris was perhaps the center of national Polish political and cultural life in the 1840s, not least because of the presence of Mickiewicz, but Henryk was distinctly reserved: "The émigrés here constantly do stupid things, but I do not become involved in anything."[56] Henryk's was a Galician perspective on the Polish national community in Paris, the perspective that corresponded to Aleksander's intense and pragmatic focus on Galician finances and railroads.

The Polish Molière composed for the Galician Sejm in 1840 a memorandum "About the Possibility and Need for Establishing a Bank and a Railroad in Galicia." He saw the two projects as closely related and mutually enhancing. Proposing a central railway axis running through the province from Auschwitz to Lviv, Fredro offered a vision of economic benefits based on Galicia's special position between east and west. "The lines which draw Oriental trade to Vienna, and from there push into the heart of Europe, will infallibly have supremacy over all others," observed Fredro ambitiously, aware that Galicia could act as a link to Russia and Moldavia, and thus to the trade of the Black Sea. Yet this was not merely the program of the conservative Galician gentry, eager to be able to transport their agricultural products. Fredro hailed the advent of a new economic epoch in Galicia: "Daily experience convinces us that Galicia can no longer be content with its agriculture, but must summon industry for assistance if it wishes to make forward progress with its own prosperity."[57] The premise of Galician backwardness, formulated almost from the founding of the province in the eighteenth century, became the basis for an ideology of progress in which provincial economic coherence was accepted as the corollary of the imperial political structure.

For Fredro the future of Galicia was not romantically entangled in the Polish myth of Napoleon and the Polish mysticism of Mickiewicz but was pragmatically provincial. "The railway will bring our land [*nasz kraj*] closer to other lands of rooted and diffused industry," he wrote. "The railway is important not as a necessity adapted to the present condition of Galicia, but as the means enabling it to change significantly and profitably." Such a vision of the future was indeed non-national in comparison with the Polish Romantic prophecies of Mickiewicz. The Galician bank and Galician railway were projects whose "existence would promise significant benefits, and whose neglect would promise even twice as significant damages to the country."[58] For Fredro "the country" was always Galicia. He himself appeared thoroughly Galician from the perspective of Vienna, and when, in 1843, the *Allgemeine Theaterzeitung* reported on "Galicia and the Literature of that Land," it was noted that "Count Fredro (Alexander) has written five volumes of greatly valued comedies."[59] In fact, five volumes were published by the Pichler house in Vienna itself from 1825 to 1838, the age of Fredro's Galician prime.

Fredro left the Sejm in 1842, for reasons of health, family, and some dissatisfaction with public life. He wrote to the Sejm from Vienna, regretting that his health and strength no longer permitted him to fulfill his duty "to serve the country [*służyć krajowi*]."[60] In November 1841 he had written a letter that suggested some larger personal crisis of frustration in both his literary career and his public life in Galicia. He was writing to Józef Załuski, who had been a friend ever since they both participated in the Napoleonic campaigns, thirty years before. Załuski had fought in the November Insurrection of 1830 and then settled in Galicia, and the two old friends were corresponding about the leasing of a farm on Fredro's estate. Fredro began to play with rhymes for *dzierżawa* [lease], such as *wrzawa* [clamor], *krwawa* [bloody], and *sława* [glory]. Many of Fredro's greatest comedies had been written in rhyming verse, but now, he regretfully remarked, the age of poetry had been succeeded by an epoch of mundane prose, neither clamorous, glorious, or bloody. This was perhaps more true in Galicia than elsewhere, for Mickiewicz in Paris was being hailed as the greatest of Polish poets, the superstar of Romantic poetry, while Fredro worried prosaically over railways and farm leases. He wrote to Załuski in a spirit of immobility:

We must stick to prose, for just as ice immobilizes a floating twig on the river, so cold prose presses upon our lives from every side. The fates knock us over at that very point where we are placed by creative fantasy and the power of taking in external beauty. From that point the hopes of man reach farthest: beyond one's grave, the grave of one's grandchildren, of one's great-grandchildren, of whole generations, as far as somewhere, somewhere, the wreath of immortality.[61]

While the sentiment was somewhat cryptic, Fredro seemed to express his own sense of literary frustration in the face of hostile fates, and seemed to renounce the wreath of poetic glory in favor of a more prosaic vision of the future. Creative fantasy gave way to a vision of the future in which railways would bring tangible benefits.

Fredro therefore questioned the value of his vocation as a writer, making use of a Polish pun on the common noun *żyd* (meaning "blotch") and the proper noun *Żyd* (meaning "Jew") :

Today if someone wants to write he just shakes the pen—probably a blotch (*żyd*)—and that's why there are so many dirty pages in contemporary works. Also, speaking truthfully, it is difficult to get along without the blotch—the blotch (*żyd*) on the paper, the Jew (*Żyd*) in the corridor, always with Jews: without the Jew the vodka dries up and the grain goes bad. There is already little difference between them and us. Like them—removed from public life, pushed around, despised— we creep about like the weeds that cover the earth in order to make it soft for the foreign foot. So the fashion of growing a beard, though dirty, is at any rate appropriate. Now then, as a Galician deputy, I write this nonsense.[62]

Fredro, writing explicitly as a representative in the Galician Sejm, a role which he was even then preparing to resign, noted not only the prosaic quality of the Galician experience but also the disquieting relation between prose and Jews. It was the Jews who attended to the everyday economic details of Galician life, and Fredro himself, as a Galician deputy, had to attend to similarly unpoetic affairs, like the bank and the railway. He was not alone in noting the omnipresence and indispensability of Jews in the Galician economy, but he was perhaps more original in observing the convergence: "between them and us." For the Jews pursued their economic interests while remaining aliens in Christian society, and Galician nobles like Fredro, even if they hunted with Habsburg archdukes, were cultivating fields, and building railroads, that lay ultimately beneath the foreign foot. Indeed, the very essence of Galicia, its subjection to Habsburg rule, made the Galicians into non-national aliens in their own country. Fredro recognized that in this regard the Jews were quintessential Galicians, non-national subjects who pursued prosaic economic interests under foreign rule.

Even after leaving the Sejm, Fredro remained involved in the discussions surrounding the Galician railway, and in 1844 he joined with several others, including Sapieha, to address a letter in German to Archduke Ferdinand d'Este, the governor, requesting permission to form a society for building the railway line from Bochnia to Lviv—with an additional route on the side to the Dniester River.[63] The government, however, was not forthcoming, and Fredro, together with Sapieha, ended up paying a visit to Salomon Rothschild in Vienna, who was financing the Vienna-Bochnia line. Sapieha recalled the meeting with Rothschild: "He received us politely, but with the feeling of superiority that his financial position gave him." With grating condescension Rothschild invited them to dinner, where he "smiled with satisfaction" when he was flattered, and dropped the names of government ministers who had supposedly given him his bottles of wine as friendly gifts. Sapieha claimed to have found Rothschild comical, but Fredro, apparently, was not amused. Sapieha described Fredro's anti-Semitic reaction: "I laughed heartily at the arrogance of the financial king, and also at the anger of Fredro who was constantly repeating: What does this scabby Jew think [*co sobie ten żyd parch myśli*], that we need his influence?"[64] For Fredro the infuriating irony was the dependence of a Galician aristocrat, himself, upon a Jew, but, especially in view of Sapieha's amusement, there may have been greater irony in the fact that the greatest Polish comic writer of his age was apparently incapable of appreciating the farcical aspect of his own situation.

The Polish Molière, after all, should have been able to appreciate the comic pretensions of a Jewish *bourgeois gentilhomme*. Furthermore, Fredro's own comedies, such as *Life Annuity*, often involved the convoluted financial circumstances of patronage and dependence. Yet Fredro, as he pursued the construction of a Galician railway, was unable to find amusement in the metropolitan entanglements of Viennese finance and politics. Although he claimed to be eager for a railway that would bring Galicia "closer to other lands," he was also obviously troubled by some of the contacts and encounters that might develop beyond the boundaries of provincial life. Ultimately, the railway would be slow in coming to Galicia, and the main east-west line between Lviv and Cracow was not completed until 1861.

"The Progress of Demoralization in Galicia"

In the early 1840s, when the railroad issue loomed so large for Fredro and Sapieha, they were also both concerned with the controversially urgent issue of peasant reform. Sapieha especially looked toward the moderation, if not the full abolition, of feudal serfdom in Galicia. Joseph II in the 1780s had instituted important legal limitations on serfdom in the Habsburg monarchy, providing peasant serfs with some protection and some legal redress against the arbitrary power of noble landowners. Yet forced labor contributions—*robot*—were still a characteristic feature of Galician agriculture, and the oppressiveness of the peasant condition still appeared as a sort of slavery. In fact, the peasants of Galicia would mesmerize all of Europe with their massacre of the Polish nobles in 1846, and would then be emancipated from serfdom by the Habsburg government in the Revolution of 1848.

Sacher-Masoch's childhood in Galicia, before 1848, belonged to an economic epoch dramatically different from the world of 1870, when his fantasies of slavery found expression in *Venus in Furs*. Severin passionately longed to become Wanda's slave:

> "And why is it impracticable?" I began.
> "Because we don't have slavery in our country."
> "Then let us go to a country where it still exists, to the Orient, to Turkey," I said eagerly.
> "You want to—Severin—seriously," replied Wanda. Her eyes were burning.
> "Yes, I seriously want to be your slave," I continued. "I want your power over me to be consecrated by the law, so that my life is in your hands. I want there to be nothing in the world that can protect me or save me from you. Oh, what voluptuousness to feel dependent entirely on your arbitrariness, your mood, a wave of your finger!"[65]

Serfdom no longer existed in Galicia in 1870, but before 1848 it was widely perceived to be as oppressive and arbitrary as Severin masochistically imagined. Both Severin and Wanda, fully consensual adults, were old enough to remember, like Sacher-Masoch, that something like slavery had existed in their own country and within their own lifetimes. Indeed, for Sacher-Masoch the intimations of slavery in Galicia before 1848 fit perfectly with his conception of the province's Oriental character.

"One of the most important matters raised in the Galician Sejm was the abolition of feudalism," remarked Sapieha, recalling the Sejm of 1843. "For several years it was the subject of conversations in private circles. Everyone acknowledged the harmfulness of feudalism, which was the reason for the wastefulness of labor." As long as the serfs were required to perform labor on noble estates, "the peasant's aim was to accomplish the least work in the most time."[66] Yet proposals for reform were complicated by the question of compensation to the landowners, and the Habsburg government did not encourage reforms that would differentiate Galicia from the rest of the monarchy. According to historian Stefan Kieniewicz, "The net result of the Sejm's proceedings was stories in the countryside that the noble lords had again discussed compulsory labor but had done nothing for the peasants."[67] This perception would seem much more important a few years later in 1846, when the peasants stood loyally alongside the Habsburg emperor and turned violently against the insurrectionary Polish nobility.

In 1844, Fredro wrote a memorandum on peasant reform to submit to Franz Krieg, and ultimately to the emperor. Composed in French, the memorandum from the Polish Molière addressed "The Progress of Demoralization in Galicia." Fredro introduced his work with basic principles of political philosophy: "There is no government without a social order. There is no order without laws." What Fredro called "demoralization" involved the failure of the law, such that "all the vices became social vices," general currents of social corruption rather than individual legal violations.[68]

While the newspaper *Galicia* celebrated the province for carnival balls held under the sponsorship of the chief of police for the charitable benefit of the poor, Fredro diagnosed progressive demoralization. Venality, drunkenness, and poverty were the particular consequences of hostility among the social classes: "The nobility, the clergy, the government employees, the peasants—they are all tacitly and incessantly at war." If the Habsburg government justified itself as an agent of civilization in Galicia, Fredro held up that same standard of civilization to call the government to account:

> For civilization to spread, it is necessary that reciprocal relations be benevolent, that there be mutual confidence. And everything has been done for twenty years to destroy that. There have been officials, even district heads, who make themselves into *agents provocateurs*—inciting the peasants against their lords—forcing them, so to speak, by every possible means to bring grievances against the existing order. Nothing is more praiseworthy than the protection accorded by the law to the weak against the strong, and who would be so shameless as to complain about that? But all those who have seen things from up close must admit that the infinite number of cases brought by peasants against lords has done more harm than good to both parties.[69]

Half a century before, in 1790, Ossoliński had helped to compose, also in French, the Magna Charta of Galicia, to be presented to the new emperor Leopold, who had just succeeded his brother Joseph. Then, too, the Habsburg government had been charged with sowing social dissension to destroy the social harmony of the Polish ancien régime. Now, in the 1840s, Fredro evaluated the Josephine legacy in just the same way.

Beyond the destruction of mutual confidence among social classes in Galicia, Fredro identified a particular and pernicious Habsburg imagery of the Galician nobility and peasantry, first formulated in the Josephine decade and still current half a century later. In the nineteenth century that imagery acquired a new significance from the rise of abolitionism in Europe and the United States. Galicia was viewed as a land of slavery, and Fredro censured Habsburg officials for propagating that jaundiced view.

They brought with them their prejudices concerning the tyranny of the lords and the slavery of the peasants, prejudices which it was impossible to vanquish, given their complete ignorance of the character of the social relations of the parties. The lord in Poland had never been a tyrant, and if the order that was entrusted to him by the government, the lack of civilization of his subordinates, sometimes obliged him to be despotic, it was a patriarchal despotism whose rigor never attained the level of feudal lords elsewhere in the same century. The slavery of the peasants was considered to be proved by the *corvée*—but the *corvée*, far from being such a proof, is on the contrary the first step from slavery toward individual liberty. The slave has no day, no hour to himself; like a beast of burden he moves at the stroke of the master's whip—but he who has a cottage, a field, who is master in his own home, on condition of limited work, is no longer a slave.[70]

The forced labor of corvée, or *robot*, was recognized by Fredro as harmful, to peasants, lords, and the Galician economy as a whole. Yet it did not constitute slavery, and was harmful because its abuses were wastefully detrimental to the economy of the province.

These abuses needed to be addressed by the Galician Sejm and the Habsburg government so that the social relations and economic conditions of the province might be ameliorated. The ideology of empire in Habsburg Galicia endorsed the advancement of "civilization" through the administrative tempering of "tyranny" and "slavery." In Fredro's view, however, this formulation pointed the way toward demoralization by countenancing a hostile mythology of Galicia. The Habsburg horror of "slavery" prevented the realistic appraisal of possible agrarian reform. This same mythology, still current in the childhood of Sacher-Masoch, and probably implicit in his father's official perspective, provided the impressionable child with the formative elements for his famous future perversion: slavery, despotism, and the stroke of the master's whip. There was a historical etiology of masochism by which the vices of provincial demoralization, as described by Fredro, also metamorphosed into the aberrational vices of Severin von Kusiemski, the Galician paragon of demoralized perversity.

Fredro discussed various Galician arenas in which Habsburg law remained inconsistently executed, concerning Jews, the clergy, army recruitment, and the sale of horses—but his larger point addressed the awkward inapplicability of general laws to the particular province. "There are ordinances made for the whole empire," he noted, "but since the empire is composed of heterogeneous provinces, it is clear that what might be good for Austria might hardly be good at all for Galicia and vice versa." Even the laws that applied only in Galicia were often ill conceived by the "foreign provincial government" of the Habsburg administration—"given that very often they were dictated only by theory."[71] The Habsburg government could still be considered foreign to

Galicia, seventy years after its establishment in 1772. Certainly the governor, Archduke Ferdinand d'Este, was foreign to the province, as were top officials like Franz Krieg. "One may be born in a province and still be completely a foreigner there," noted Fredro.[72] He might have been thinking of bureaucratic families like the Sacher-Masoch family, which had been present in the province dating back to the eighteenth century.

The masked ball in Lviv at the end of January 1841, a charitable benefit for the poor—proudly reported in the journal *Galicia*—seemed to counter Fredro's concern about demoralization. It reconciled the interests and well-being of different Galician social classes, under the sponsorship and authority of the government police director, Sacher-Masoch. At the end of February another masked ball was scheduled to mark the end of the carnival period, this time to benefit a charitable school for little children—perhaps the same age as the child Sacher-Masoch, age five in 1841. *Galicia* saluted the occasion of the second masked ball with extravagant provincial pride:

> With pleasure *Galicia* dedicates its pages to such a noble institution on any occasion, and may it succeed in inspiring the generous participation of the residents of Lemberg, as well as the other equally noble inhabitants of our great and beautiful province, and thus to show to the other provinces of our common fatherland that there is so much of public utility that occurs in our province, though it has remained until now unknown beyond our borders, because the language of our public communications was foreign to the other provinces.[73]

The affirmation of Galician identity meant making the province better known throughout the Habsburg monarchy. The journal's positive presentation of Galicia also served as a rejoinder to those, like Fredro, who diagnosed social demoralization.

The news of the nursery school was even reported in Vienna, and became the occasion for the New Year's Eve reflections of Dr. Wilhelm Turteltaub in Rzeszów, published as "Some Words from Galicia" in the Viennese journal *Der Humorist* in January 1842. Turteltaub, a completely enlightened Galician Jew of the Haskalah, had studied medicine in Vienna in the 1830s, returned to his hometown of Rzeszów in 1841, and continued to be involved in Viennese literary life. His New Year's Eve reflections, following his return to Galicia, observed that the only thing the Viennese took note of in the province was the theatrical life of Lviv, thus failing to appreciate the "giant steps" of ongoing Galician progress. Turteltaub wrote of his secret New Year's wish for Galicia: "The heart beating warmly for its fatherland harbors still one wish, the wish to see progress of the spirit and the heart also among the Jewish inhabitants of Galicia." He offered up a prayer to the *Zeitgeist* to grant this wish, hoping that, in Galicia, "everything will turn to gold."[74] This strange, perhaps satirically intended, effusion in the *Humorist* harkened back to the messianic fantasies of the Josephine age, with the Jews especially singled out for the modern transformation that would "recast" Galicia in the mold of modern Europe, recast it even in the precious metal of economic prosperity.

If Turteltaub suspected that the Viennese failed fully to appreciate progress in Galicia, Fredro believed that there prevailed a deeply prejudicial imagery of Galicia in the Habsburg government, a vision of the province as the domain of despotic nobles and enslaved peasants, a society governed by the crack of the whip. The news of Galicia—concerning masked balls and charitable campaigns—was evidently intended not only to make Galicia better known but also to combat negative conceptions of the province beyond its own borders. Yet the same issue of *Galicia* that announced the second masked ball as an inspirational manifestation of "our great and beautiful province" also contained the news of death sentences by hanging for two young men, Constantin Ciupka and Theodor Lozinski, ages twenty-three and twenty-five, identified as Greek Catholics, and therefore Ruthenians. They lived in the Galician village of Dobrosin and worked for the local landowner, participating in the supervision of forced labor, *robot*. Ciupka and Lozinski had just murdered another young man similarly employed, Onufrius Masluk, age nineteen, in order to steal the certificates of completed labor [*Robotzeichen*] that he was distributing.[75] Police Director Sacher-Masoch, even if distracted by the masked balls of carnival season, must have had to pay some attention to this criminal matter and its judicial consequences. Even as the tensions of Galician identity—noble and peasant, Polish and Ruthenian, German and Polish, Christian and Jewish, national and non-national—became increasingly complex, the tensions of economy and society were building toward the violent crisis of 1846. Galician demoralization was about to make itself dramatically known beyond the provincial borders in the language of blood.

"FRIGHTENING SCENES"

"The frightening scenes of 1846 remained unforgettable for me," recalled the writer Sacher-Masoch in his autobiographical essay.[76] He was only ten years old in 1846, when a Polish national insurrection broke out in Galicia. It was planned by émigrés in Paris and resulted in the declaration of an independent Polish national government in the little urban republic of Cracow, a government that lasted for nine days from 22 February until the taking of the city by Austrian troops on 4 March. The Polish leaders, Jan Tyssowski and Edward Dembowski, had hoped to extend the insurrection to Galicia—as envisioned by Mickiewicz in 1833—with the ultimate intention of moving next beyond Galicia to Russian Poland. The insurrection, however, encountered an unexpected and insurmountable obstacle in Galicia itself. The Polish nobility in Galicia rallied to the national cause, but the peasantry, whether Polish or Ruthenian, and in spite of the revolutionary promise of emancipation from serfdom, remained not only indifferent but actually hostile to the insurrectionaries, and loyal to the Habsburg emperor. In the western Galician area around the town of Tarnów, Polish peasants actually seized the opportunity to murder insurrectionary Polish nobles in the name of Habsburg loyalty, and the peasants brought to town the mutilated bodies of the massacred nobles as evidence of loyal conduct. Such conduct would have appeared to Fredro as the ultimate demonstration of "demoralization" in Galician social relations.

The national implications of the massacre were perhaps as shocking as the bloodshed itself, for it was suddenly clear that the supposedly "Polish" peasants of western Galicia—Polish by language and Roman Catholic by religion—scarcely considered themselves to be Polish at all, when it came to fighting for the national cause. Indeed, they were every bit as antipathetic as the Uniate Ruthenian peasants of eastern Galicia. Thus, peasant class resentment against the landowning nobility trumped any possible inkling of national solidarity, and the enserfed peasantry of Galicia was revealed to be unexpectedly "Galician"—that is, ultimately loyal to the Habsburg emperor in defiance of particular national claims upon their sympathy. In the 1780s the ideology of Josephinism in Galicia had denounced the brutality of the Polish nobles and sought to restrict their absolute power over the peasants, and that strategy of legitimation was dramatically vindicated in 1846, when the peasants massacred their noble masters in the name of the dynasty. Supposedly they murdered with the emperor's name on their lips: "Long live Emperor Ferdinand!"[77]

The exact number of nobles murdered in 1846 remains unknown, but historians have offered various body counts between one and two thousand, with more recent opinion tending toward the lower end of that range.[78] Sacher-Masoch, as a child in Lviv, could have witnessed only a minimal slice of the violence, but his position in the home of the police director would have permitted him to register some of the political intensity of the moment, as law and order in Galicia were challenged first by noble insurrectionaries and then by peasant vigilantes. The boy was ten in 1846, and later testified to his own budding dramatic imagination:

> I was about ten years old when, without any other intention than to give pleasure
> to my younger siblings, I undertook my first poetic efforts. I constructed pieces

which I produced in a small puppet theater, and I wrote down a story which I had heard from an old peasant, in order to communicate it better to my little sisters.[79]

Such childish literary efforts were entirely in character with the folk preoccupations of the period, including the transcription of peasant songs and tales, and Sacher-Masoch claimed to have been formatively shaped by a taste for Galician folk songs and folk tales. As a ten-year-old boy, however, collecting tales from an old peasant, perhaps a domestic servant, Sacher-Masoch in 1846 was in innocent contact with the Galician peasantry at the most violently dramatic moment in its entire social class history.

Sacher-Masoch did not specify precisely what sort of dramatic pieces he was staging in his puppet theater, but the "frightening scenes" of 1846 were enacted at roughly the same time, making a mark upon his susceptible dramatic sensibility.

> My father protected the east of the land from rebellion, as he discovered and arrested the leaders of the insurrection in Lemberg; when the Polish revolution broke out at the same time in the west, and the peasants, taking sides against the nobility, killed the insurgents, set fire to the noble manors, and produced a horrible blood bath, the precautions of my father were gratefully recognized even by the Poles. Only one leader of the insurrection escaped arrest in Lemberg. He gathered together in Gorozani the conspirators and the peasants, but the peasants here too turned their murderous scythes against the Poles. It was the only place in the east where blood flowed. I saw the insurgents arrive, some dead, some wounded, on an overcast February day, escorted by the armed peasants. The insurgents lay upon miserable little carts, the blood ran down from the straw, and the dogs licked it up.[80]

The year 1846 marked a turning point in the imaginative development of the child Sacher-Masoch, as in fact it also transformed the significance of Galicia in the provincial, imperial, and European imagination. Sacher-Masoch moved from folk tales and puppet theaters to the radically different poetry and puppetry of violence that manifested itself in the social explosions of 1846. This was a theatrically graphic historical moment that must have been shocking for a ten-year-old child, as indeed for everyone else in Galicia. For Sacher-Masoch, the drama of extreme and perverse violence would eventually become a central preoccupation of his adult emotional sensibility and mature literary creativity.

Sacher-Masoch's recollection of his own father's efforts against the Polish rebellion and in behalf of social order—"gratefully recognized even by the Poles"—touched on the most delicate of issues and was intended to exculpate his father from the most damning of suspicions. For the police chief, together with the entire Habsburg administration, while unambiguously opposed to

Polish rebellion, became immediately suspect of having tacitly or overtly encouraged the peasant massacre that checked the insurrection. Recent research
by Alan Sked suggests that, while Vienna was certainly not responsible for organizing or inciting the massacres, nevertheless there were Habsburg officials
in Galicia who not only urged the peasants to resist the noble insurrection
but who actually paid them for information and reimbursed them for time
and expense in the cause of resistance. Since massacre became one mode of
resistance, especially in the Tarnów region, some peasants might have supposed that they were being paid for killing in the name of the emperor. What
exactly was said orally between individual officials and particular groups of
peasants remains undocumented and partly unknown even to this day: hence
the rumors of Habsburg complicity that circulated at the time.[81]

There were also rumors, persistent among the Poles of Galicia for the
rest of the century, that the peasant leader of the violence around Tarnów,
Jakub Szela, was actually commended and rewarded by the Habsburg government for his instigating role. Szela, who had been previously engaged in
legal grievances against the noble Bogusz family, seemed to have bloodily
settled his personal scores while rallying the local peasants to the Habsburg
cause. The peasant massacre of the nobles offered both political advantage
and embarrassment to the government, and it was deemed convenient to
remove Szela from the Galician scene of his exploits and resettle him in
the adjoining region of Bukovina, though whether that was punishment or
reward was difficult to say for certain. In any event, his eastern removal from
Tarnów to Bukovina brought him through Lviv, where he was presented to
the police chief Sacher-Masoch.

Although Szela may have been known to some in Lviv as a notorious
murderer, he was apparently not kept away from the child of the police
chief for the sake of propriety. The adult writer Sacher-Masoch saluted Szela
as the "Galician Spartacus," and looked back forty years from the 1880s to
remember their single personal encounter:

> When he passed through Lemberg on the way to Bukovina, where the govern-
> ment exiled him, my father went to see him and brought me along. Szela received
> us with calm and courtesy. He was a small, lean man of sixty years, with a figure
> that did not correspond to the image that people formed of this peasant general
> with whom Europe was preoccupied for several months, whom the newspapers
> called "the peasant king," and whom Henryk Bogusz had accused of several
> murders. But in Szela's clear eyes were revealed great intelligence and energy.[82]

This positive view of Szela should be considered in the cultural context of
Galicia in the 1830s and 1840s, when literary Romanticism would have cast a
favorable light on the violence of Carpathian brigands.[83]

The Galician events of 1846, which were only glimpsed by the child Sach-er-Masoch, would radically destabilize and reconfigure the cultural meaning of Galicia for decades to come, crucially determining the provincial identity with respect to values of social class, national solidarity, political violence, and dynastic loyalty. For Sacher-Masoch the memory of the massacres, wit-nessed obliquely from the restricted perspective of a privileged bureaucrat's child, would remain sufficiently vivid to serve as the scenario for his first novel, published in 1858 when he was twenty-two, *A Galician History of 1846* (*Eine galizische Geschichte: 1846*). It would be republished in 1864 under the title *Graf Donski*, Count Donski, the name of the Polish noble protagonist who became a victim of the massacres. By the time Sacher-Masoch wrote his first novel he was already trained as a historian at the University of Graz, and in his *Galician History* he explored the historical dynamics of the uprising and massacres of 1846 while also revisiting the formative sentimental currents of his childhood in Galicia.[84]

In the novel, when the peasants were pressured to join the national in-surrection, they declared themselves loyal to the emperor. The Ruthenian peasant Onufry, described as a sort of peasant "giant," stood up to Count Donski and declared, "I am a peasant, but I have a memory . . . and my father was also a peasant and he also had a memory." Remembering back two generations Onufry reached back from the 1840s to the age of arbi-trary noble oppression in the Polish Commonwealth that had preceded the invention of Habsburg Galicia. Onufry recited an extraordinary anecdote of a Polish nobleman who made the peasant women lift up their dresses and then demanded that each peasant man identify his wife from behind: "and whoever failed to identify his wife, he was given a beating of fifty strokes from the gracious lord."[85] The combination of corporal punishment and sexual humiliation was peculiarly appealing to the literary imagination of Sacher-Masoch, who might have invented the anecdote. Onufry's other memories, however, were already extant tales during the reign of Joseph: "My father told me how the former master, the father of our count, made the peasants climb up into the trees and cry 'cuckoo' and then shot them down like forest birds." This was a story that Sacher-Masoch might have read in the published Josephine accounts from Galicia of the 1780s. Kratter had claimed to know of a Polish noble who sent a peasant up into a tree to retrieve an owl's nest, and then took shots at him just for fun. In the ac-count by Traunpaur it was a Jew who was compelled to climb the tree and cry "cuckoo"—and was then shot dead by the nobleman.[86] Sacher-Masoch's variant of this story, related by his Ruthenian giant, suggested the compel-ling power of the Josephine narrative of Galicia. The *Galician History*, composed in the 1850s and set in the 1840s, still responded in "memory" to the ideological dynamics of the 1780s.

"Deeply melancholy sounded the Ruthenian songs," wrote Sacher-Masoch, evoking the folk musical world of Galicia, the same songs that he remembered from his own childhood.[87] "We are not Lechi," cried out Onufry, using the derogatory Ruthenian term for Poles. "We are imperials." The cry of *Vivat Ferdinand* rallied the peasants, and provoked the nobles to strike the first blow, thus triggering the massacre. "Kill them, kill them!" cried Onufry, swinging his scythe. Sacher-Masoch, though he seemed to excuse the peasant violence as an expression of excessive imperial loyalty, was also able to relish the terrible details. His pen lingered over the perilous position of Wanda, the Polish noblewoman, in the midst of the massacre: "Wanda defended herself with success against several young lads, whose mouths were watering to take her captive. Again and again they fell back before her flaming gaze and the strong strokes that she dealt out with her riding whip."[88] A Galician noblewoman named Wanda would later become the heroine of *Venus in Furs*, and she would fiercely exercise her whip upon the quivering flesh of her victim and lover.

In the preface to his *Galician History*, Sacher-Masoch offered a personal Galician perspective: *Gruss an meine Landleute* ["Greeting to my Countrymen"]:

> Far from the homeland [*Heimat*] I send you this greeting. I do not choose, as in your songs, the tender nightingale, the proud swan, the lively lark, as messenger—but the printing press. It has not gleaming wings, but its thousands and thousands of paper pinions travel throughout the world, just as you are scattered, my countrymen! My messenger will find you and greet you on the boulevards, in the pallid splendor of the half moon, in the cabin of the prairie—as well as in the homeland. I greet you all, for it was one land, Galicia, that gave us all birth: Poles, Ruthenians, Germans, and Jews![89]

Now, living in Graz, gazing across the Habsburg monarchy from Styria to Galicia, and back across a decade to the 1840s, Sacher-Masoch discerned and celebrated the provincial unity of Galicia—what he perceived as the sentimental amalgamation of peoples formed by the same landscape, the same folk culture, and the same memories. His sense of Galicia as cultural construction was evident in his tribute to the printing press as the agent of imagined community, displacing the oral folk culture of tradition.

Sacher-Masoch's novel, with its brutal violence and horrific circumstances, was an effort to conjure the Galician landscape of his childhood memory:

> My longing draws me there to the mighty Vistula, to the lively Dunajec, to our ponds shimmering in the distance, to our woods, to our plains, to our people [*zu*

unserem Volk]. I greet you! It seems to me as if there were a greeting in response, an answer to the voices that address me from out of my own history. They sound so dear, so familiar. In the distance I think I hear the shepherds' pipes, like uncanny dreams. The melancholy Ruthenian melodies creep into my ear, the sounds of the fiery Mazur, the roguishly amorous Krakowiak, with the provocative clicking of heels and the bright clinking of spurs. The memories of my childhood come to me. . . .[90]

Such sentimental memories of childhood stood in strange contrast to the actual scenario of the novel, the massacres of 1846. In fact, Sacher-Masoch's childhood world of Galician melodies, dating back to his earliest memories, was traumatically interrupted and transmogrified by the outbreak of the Galician massacres in 1846. The sentimental calculus of Galician masochism was conditioned by a society of reciprocally violent tensions, poised between the master's whip and the peasant's scythe, between profound subjection and fierce self-assertion, between melancholy melody and savage massacre.

"THE VAST COMMUNIST CONSPIRACY"

Although Cracow had been initially joined to Galicia by the third partition of Poland in 1795, it was assigned to the Napoleonic Grand Duchy of Warsaw in 1809, and then made into a nominally autonomous urban republic with a sovereign senate after 1815: Wolne, Niepodległe, i Ściśle Neutralne Miasto Kraków—that is, the Free, Independent, and Strictly Neutral City of Cracow. The city remained under the watchful guardianship of the partitioning powers—Austria, Prussia, and Russia—but its relatively autonomous position seemed to make it an ideal point for the launching of a Polish insurrection in February of 1846. Before the end of that year the city would be punished for its insurgency by being restored to Habsburg rule and absorbed into Galicia.

In February 1846, Metternich wrote to his ambassador in Paris, Anton Apponyi, to let François Guizot and the French government know that the Habsburgs would occupy Cracow: "The vast communist conspiracy that covers the Polish territories seemed to have chosen this free city, a veritable free port open to adventurers and conspirators, to strike a blow contemplated and prepared for a long time by the Polish émigrés." Since those émigrés were based largely in France, Metternich wanted Apponyi to suggest in Paris that "that government would not want to be suspected of according a sort of moral protection to enterprises whose character is more antisocial than political."[91] While Karl Marx in 1848 discerned the specter of communism haunting Europe, Metternich had named the specter already in 1846 when he remarked that communism was haunting the Polish territories, including Galicia.

On 19 February the peasants appeared in Tarnów with the corpses of their aristocratic victims. On 20 February Metternich had already heard about murder and pillage in Galicia, and blamed the Polish nobles themselves for having fostered democratic impulses within the insurrectionary movement. "As democratic ideas are not at all applicable to a Slavic population like that of Poland," noted Metternich, "these ideas, put forward by a fraction of the émigrés, necessarily had to turn to communism, that is, to the pillage of properties and the murder of the proprietors."[92] He meant to suggest that the specter of Galicia was haunting all of Europe, that "communism" was being cultivated by misguided aristocratic revolutionaries, who would suffer the devastating consequences of their own irresponsibility. With his ethnographic focus on the "Slavic population" of the province, Metternich further suggested that the murder and pillage of "communism" in Galicia were more generally endemic in Eastern Europe. This conception of Eastern Europe, as unfit for democracy and properly destined for either absolutism or communism, would survive into the twentieth century.

On 22 February the Free, Independent, and Strictly Neutral City of Cracow reconstituted itself as the seat of the National Government of the Polish Commonwealth, "Poles! The hour of the rising has struck," announced the manifesto of the national government, as reported in the newspaper *Gazeta Krakowska*. There was "news from all sides" to confirm that "the rising is the will of God and the whole Polish nation."[93] This was whistling in the dark, for the grim news from Tarnów should have been sufficient to dispel such misplaced faith in Polish providence and national solidarity.

On 7 March, Metternich wrote to Paris with his considered analysis of what had just taken place in Galicia: an episode "without precedent in history." Since the national insurrection in Cracow had been encouraged by the Polish émigré movement in France, Metternich was particularly keen to have his ambassador represent to the French government, even to King Louis Philippe himself, the folly of tolerating Polish asylum in France.[94] Therefore, in order to clarify the unprecedented events of 1846, Metternich proposed to offer the French a lesson in the history of Galicia: "When Galicia passed under Austrian domination 74 years ago, the country found itself in the most barbarous condition," remarked Metternich, dating his history lesson back precisely to the first partition of 1772. "A just and paternal legislation and administration was introduced into the country."[95] Metternich himself, in Habsburg government service since the very beginning of the nineteenth century, seemed fully conversant with the Josephine ideology of bringing civilization to Galicia.

Metternich noted particularly that Maria Theresa and Joseph had limited the labor obligations of peasant serfs in Galicia, thus winning over their hearts and minds for the Habsburg dynasty.

> As a consequence of this, the people, far from suspecting either the intentions of the government toward them, or those of the immediate agents of sovereign authority, envisage them, on the contrary, as the veritable protectors of their rights, of their repose and their peaceful enjoyments. There exists no authority more generally respected by the people than that of the captains in their administrative circles; events have just proved this.[96]

The proof was written in blood, and Metternich, even as he affirmed the dynasty's commitment to upholding social order and tranquillity, found himself in the awkward position of vindicating Habsburg rule in Galicia by reference to the peasant massacre of the Polish nobles.

Such an ideology of empire could be sustained only by the unusual circumstance, as Metternich noted, that it was the "upper classes" who were "devoted to the cause of the Revolution," with a capital R. The people [*le peuple*] thus emerged as the enemies of the Revolution, motivated by their most compelling memory: "the memory of the miserable state in which the peasants found themselves under the Polish ancien régime."[97] In the Polish case, Metternich thus equated the Revolution with the nobles, rather than with "the people." In Galicia, Metternich took the side of the people, emphasizing their unhappy memory of the ancien régime, while passing over the awkward chronological fact that the Polish ancien régime had been displaced by Habsburg rule seventy-four years earlier, beyond the bounds of living memory. The peasants of Galicia in 1846 were reacting not to the memory of Poland, but rather to the history of Galicia itself. Metternich approved "the valorous and loyal resistance offered by the Galician people, opposed to the seduction of the upper classes."[98] Three-quarters of a century after the invention of Galicia, the peasants of the province had proved that they were Galician.

"Fresh Reports from Galicia"

While Metternich on 7 March was reporting to France on the recent Galician events, *Gazeta Krakowska* on 10 March was adjusting to the new political situation in Cracow and acknowledging the massacres in Galicia. The newspaper announced the formation of a "temporary civil administration" in Cracow, without necessarily knowing that the formerly free, independent, and strictly neutral government would never be restored. Now there were Russian troops in town, including Cossacks from Ukraine, Circassians from the Caucasus Mountains, and diverse peoples "from the depths of Asia." Their military exercises took place in the main square of Cracow, the Rynek, and *Gazeta Krakowska*, constrained to accept the new occupation, reported that the Cracovian public admired "their elegant and original uniforms, the agility of their horses, and the extraordinary accuracy in shooting." In fact, the editors must have known that such a Russian military presence in Cracow could only have been seen by the Polish residents as a horrific occupation by barbarians, however colorful the uniforms. Yet no less alarming were the reports "from over the border of Galicia" of the recent events that Cracovians could not have witnessed in the Rynek with their own eyes. "The most fresh reports from Galicia and Lwów," reported *Gazeta Krakowska* on 10 March, when the reports were already more than two weeks old, "communicate unfortunately that it was attempted there to stir the people to unrest under the cloak of communism," and that the "Galician people" had responded with violence.[99]

Further details were provided to Cracow readers in a report about Tarnów that was taken and translated from the *Oesterreichische Beobachter* in Vienna:

> The day of February 18th and the following night passed peacefully, and only on the 19th at half past nine in the morning was a crowd of villagers observed, acting as a convoy for several carts filled with corpses; they were the landowners, the private officials, and estate administrators, nineteen in number, whom, as the destroyers of order and tranquillity, were seized by the villagers and turned over to the authorities. From questioning the peasants and other witnesses it emerged that the conspirators tried to induce crowds of villagers by threats and means of violent compulsion, to which several peasants fell victim, to cooperate in the riots that were supposed to break out on February 18, and then to take over Tarnów, plunder it, and slaughter everyone who thought differently. How few loyal villagers gave in and joined with these rebellious intentions is demonstrated by their bloody proceedings against the conspirators.[100]

By 10 March the Cracovians would have already heard the story of the murders around Tarnów, but the public confirmation in the pages of *Gazeta Krakowska*, now publishing in Cracow under Habsburg occupation, amounted to a semiofficial warning about the consequences of insurrection. Tarnów was only fifty miles away from Cracow.

On 14 March a report from Galicia, arriving by way of Vienna and the *Oesterreichische Beobachter*, affirmed in *Gazeta Krakowska* that "peasants living everywhere are of good spirit, seizing the rebels, and giving them into the hands of the district authorities." Furthermore, a particular band of rebels from Cracow had recently surrendered in Wieliczka, ten miles away, just across the border in Galicia: "They were attacked and completely defeated by the army which was also joined by very many villagers."[101] This was the story of Cracow rebels defeated ten miles from Cracow in Wieliczka, but the report from Wieliczka was Galician news and was therefore forwarded from Galicia to Vienna, and transmitted from there to *Gazeta Krakowska*. The networking of Cracow, Galicia, and Vienna was becoming all the more intense in the transmission of the news of 1846.

On 16 March the word from Galicia, published in *Gazeta Krakowska*, was that wherever rebellion had occurred, "the villagers declared themselves un-conditionally for the government in spite of every allurement on the part of the rebels."[102] On 23 March, *Gazeta Krakowska* recognized the fundamental fact that would condition Polish national sentiment in Galicia for the rest of the nineteenth century: "The attempted Polish rebellion did not gain any general sympathy among the great mass of the nation." In spite of the general restoration of tranquillity in Galicia, "in many places there still exists fear [*obawa*]." The newspaper further noted that "in Brody the Jewish population has created among themselves a security guard."[103] It did not seem impossible that violence against the nobles might also be turned against the Jews.

The Austrian authorities had some reason to publicize such fears in Cra-cow in the spring of 1846, for after the demonstration of peasant violence in February the threat of further such violence became a potent means of dispelling any remaining Polish insurrectionary impulses. Metternich recog-nized this with characteristic self-satisfaction when he wrote to France about the proofs of peasant loyalty to the Habsburg dynasty. Yet Metternich could not altogether evade some inklings of ambivalence about the phenomenon of peasants who massacred their masters, even for the best of motives. When he reflected on the situation in Galicia as an issue for internal Habsburg policy, he identified the problem as Polish nationality, which, he believed, masked the most profoundly revolutionary purposes: "Polishness [*polonisme*] is nothing but a formula, a word behind which is hidden the Revolution in its most brutal form." Thus *polonisme*, according to Metternich, "preaches the overturning of all the bases upon which society rests."[104] The Polish insurrectionaries, he implicitly reasoned, in seeking to overturn the social order, succeeded in bringing upon themselves the murderous assaults of the peasantry. Metternich did not acknowledge that the massacres, committed in the name of the dynasty, also constituted a revolutionary overturning of the social order.

When he came to considering future policy, it was necessary to contem-plate measures that would diminish the likelihood of both noble insurrec-tions and peasant massacres. Metternich proposed both the creation of a regional gendarmerie and the construction of fortifications in Galicia, noting the long Russian border but also the danger of "interior agitations." At the same time, Metternich also looked for more fundamental alterations in Galicia's condition, seeking "to merge [*fondre*] Galicia with the monarchy."[105] The very idea of Galicia was a matter of ambivalence for Metternich at this moment, as he hinted at the need to merge, to melt, to dissolve its violent particularity into the orderly whole of the monarchy. He floated the possibility of dividing Galicia into two separate provinces, western and eastern, at the San River. Such a division would not only make Galicia easier to manage, Metternich thought, but would also correspond to Galician ethnography: "The race that inhabits the western bank is the Mazurs; that which occupies the eastern bank is the Rusniaks; they are separated by religion and by custom."[106] In this hypothetical fragmentation of Galicia the Polish nationality itself seemed to cease to exist for Metternich, with Poles rechristened as Mazurs in the western part of the province, while the eastern part was made over to the Ruthenians. Franz Anton Kolowrat, Metternich's rival in the Austrian government, proposed the elimination altogether of the name "Galicia," with the creation of two new provinces named for Cracow and Lviv.[107] The Galician Ruthenians would raise this issue of provincial division two years later in the Revolution of 1848, and the Habsburg government would use that proposal to manipulate Polish political concerns. Galicia, itself the product of the partitions of Poland, would remain under the shadow of possible partition for the rest of its political existence.

Yet, ultimately, Metternich fell back on the Josephine notion of Galicia conceived as the balance between German and Polish elements, reflecting the tension between the vectors of Western Europe and Eastern Europe. "That which is needed in Galicia," he declared, "is the development of the German element." He wanted to encourage the German bourgeoisie in Galicia, to enable Germans to acquire lands more easily, and to increase the use of the German language in the schools. The purpose was not to "Germanize" the Poles—"a race is only transformed after a long time"—but to balance one element with another, and thus to advance "civilization in the true sense of the word."[108] The imperial ideology of Galicia as the object of Habsburg civilizing policy seemed more urgent than ever in 1846, after the savage violence practiced by the peasantry upon their masters. Metternich's queasy intimation of barbarism was implicit in his appeal to the standard of civilization. In spite of his seeming celebration of peasant loyalty to the dynasty, he could not envision a future of Galicia based on its Slavic inhabitants, whether classified as Poles, Mazurs, or Rusniaks. Metternich was betting on the Germans with their alleged affinity for civilization.

The idea of Galicia was an unstable conception, from the beginning in 1772, envisioned as an arena of competing ethnographic forces that represented the opposed vectors of enlightenment and inhumanity, civilization and barbarism, progress and backwardness. These tensions could not be resolved one way or the other, because the ideology of empire in Galicia actually depended upon the political and cultural anxieties about civilization at risk and barbarism at bay. In 1846 the child Sacher-Masoch in Lviv saw the dogs licking up the blood of the victims. Metternich, from the more comfortable remove of Vienna, did not see anything so graphic or direct, but still he glimpsed the heart of darkness in Galicia.

"THE HECATOMB"

Gazeta Krakowska presented its most graphic account of the violence on 23 March, one month after the events in Galicia. That account was attributed to a German settler in Galicia—that is, precisely the social element that Metternich wanted to encourage as a matter of civilization. Thus, the "civilized" perspective of the German settler framed the narrative of savage violence in Galicia, as represented for the Polish public of Cracow. The German settler, a Habsburg loyalist, placed the blame for the violence squarely on the nobles: for pressuring the peasants to plunder the town of Tarnów, and proposing especially the "rich Jews" as a tempting target. The peasants, however, were impervious to such proposals, so that finally one of the nobles actually fired upon the peasants and killed one of them. After that, the German settler clearly believed, the nobles really deserved what was coming. "Immediately the desire for revenge overcame the peasants," he remarked. "The fury [*wściekłość*] of the peasantry at the sight of blood spilled was extremely wild [*rozhukana*]." The German settler offered details:

> Count Karol Kotarski, the leader of the mutiny: his completely naked body was brought to town; his twelve-year-old son was also murdered, when the manor was plundered on the estate of his father. Count Starzyński shot himself in order to escape a more cruel death.[109]

Such details were sufficiently graphic to dramatize both the barbarism of Galicia and the consequences of insurrection.

On 30 March, *Gazeta Krakowska* relayed the news from the Vienna: "Reports from every part of Galicia agree that tranquillity, shaken by the recent criminal commotions, has now been everywhere restored. The villagers have returned to their usual employments." Already, there was a hint of ambiguity about which commotions were actually criminal. The Cracow newspaper further included a report from Lviv that one of the leaders of the insurrection, Teofil Wiśniowski, had been seized by two peasants, presumably Ruthenians, in the district of Zolochiv. "Ivan Budnik found in his apiary an unknown person who seemed suspect, and seized him with the help of his relative Anastasz Budnik," reported the paper, mentioning also that this alert pair of peasants might expect to receive a reward.[110]

By the next week, however, on 6 April, *Gazeta Krakowska* was keen to clarify the fact that peasants had not been acting only in the expectation of rewards. Ugly rumors were circulating, perhaps aggravated by the capture of Wiśniowski, that the peasants in Galicia, from the beginning, were being paid by the government to murder the nobles. The Habsburg government had to try to make clear that it was not actually implicated in the bloody acts of violence committed in its name.

> The rebellious efforts of the mutineers were crushed because of the unshaken loyalty of the village people, not because of rewards which were supposed to be assigned for the delivery of the troublemakers dead or alive; it is an insolent and absurd lie, invented by the revolutionary party, in order to cover up the undeniable truth that the democratic and communist efforts were crushed because of the people, and in order to defame the people themselves. With monetary rewards it is possible to buy conspirators and assassins, but the government would never have been able to buy an entire people with such rewards, but only by the beneficent and loyal fulfillment of its obligations.[111]

The Polish cause was devastated by the hostility of the Galician peasantry in 1846, but the Habsburg government was compromised by the murderous peasant violence that carried the day. It was necessary to deny emphatically in the pages of *Gazeta Krakowska* that the government had paid for the corpses of the insurrectionary nobles in advance, even as public rewards were being offered for the capture of fugitives in the aftermath. It was essential to try to disentangle the strands of barbarism and civilization, lest the imperial image and mission be compromised by the massacres.

On 19 April, Emperor Ferdinand celebrated his birthday; he had been born in 1793, the same year as Fredro, and came to the throne in 1835, a year before Sacher-Masoch's birth. Habsburg birthdays were major Galician events in the nineteenth century, and Ferdinand's birthday, even in the year of the massacres, was not neglected. Indeed, the conduct of the Galician peasants in February was interpreted in April as evidence of the popular character of dynastic loyalty. The Viennese *Oesterreichische Beobachter* reported on the imperial birthday in Galicia: "It was a people's celebration [*Volksfest*] in the noblest sense of the word." The newspaper noted that "dark days had unfortunately preceded this celebration," that efforts had been made "to alienate the people from their holiest duties toward their prince and fatherland," but the Galicians had proven their loyalty to the emperor whose birthday they now celebrated.[112] Vienna thus looked to Galicia itself for the legitimation of Habsburg conduct.

As the political destinies of Cracow and Galicia seemed to converge, *Gazeta Krakowska*, after strategically publicizing the horrors of Galicia, began to publish more reassuring news from the province. On 30 May there was news of festivities in Lviv, relayed in the first person plural—"Today is for us a day of great ceremonial"—as Franz Krieg took office once again as president of the provincial government, celebrating his fiftieth year of Habsburg service. This was service that reached back into the eighteenth century, back to the earliest association of Cracow with Galicia in the 1790s, and over time Krieg had managed to make himself "detestable to the Poles," according to Leon Sapieha. In 1846, Krieg represented that German element upon which Metternich still hung his hopes for civilizing Galicia.

Krieg's anniversary was the only political news from Galicia, and that in itself was something worth noting, according to *Gazeta Krakowska*.

> From Galicia no political news reaches us, which is the most emphatic proof that proper order has been everywhere restored. In Lwów there appears again the inclination for entertainment. At the opening of a new café outside the city there were gathered a great number of the residents; everyone hurried to the new center of amusements; there were about forty vehicles. In Tarnów a certain Rutowski has set up a beautiful garden for the pleasure of the residents.[113]

The return of leisure pursuits in cafés and gardens, not only in Lviv but even in Tarnów, in spite of its recent horrors, signified the return of normality in Galicia. Later in the summer, the Galician Economic Society offered a prize for the best essay on the question "What is the most suitable way in the shortest time to increase the number and improve the quality of cattle in Galicia?"[114] This represented a comfortable reversion to the Galician formulas and rituals of economic development. The offering of an essay prize, in silver coins or as a gold medal, stood in striking contrast to the prices that the government had so recently placed on the heads of fugitive Polish insurrectionaries. Furthermore, the news of the essay contest in *Gazeta Krakowska* suggested that Cracovians were welcome to compete in this Galician contest, and that a broader public of Galicians, including Cracovians, was being constituted. While Metternich was thinking about "merging" Galicia with the Habsburg monarchy, there was also attention to the merging of Cracow with Galicia.

The consummation took place before the end of the year, on 16 November, when Cracow was formally subjected to Habsburg sovereignty, and the Free, Independent, and Strictly Neutral City of Cracow was definitively abolished as a political entity. Habsburg ceremonies [*uroczystości*] marked the end of the city's independence. Count Moritz Deym represented the Habsburg court by making a ceremonial entrance into the city, and he was met by the commander of the Habsburg troops in Cracow, Field Marshal Heinrich Castiglione; together they read in German and Polish the military manifesto and imperial patent by which Austria took possession of the city, with twenty-one artillery salvos from the Wawel Castle to announce that the deed was formally done. *Gazeta Krakowska* reported "joyful shouts of the people," but there must have been other, less joyous sentiments circulating in the city that day. In any event, there was a procession to St. Mary's, the Mariacki Church in the Rynek, for a celebratory Mass that concluded with the patriotic singing of the "Gott erhalte" for Emperor Ferdinand. The ceremonials of the day also included a military parade in the Rynek, a dinner hosted by Castiglione with a toast to the imperial family, and the illumination of the city by night: "by the free will of the residents," according to the awkward insistence of *Gazeta Krakowska*.[115]

On the very next day *Gazeta Krakowska* published the text of the imperial patent, presented in parallel columns of German and Polish. The patent also appeared in the same bilingual form as an official poster. Cracow was very explicitly being punished for hatching conspiracies against the Habsburg government back in February, and was therefore declared to be in violation of the treaty of 1815 that had set up the autonomous city republic. According to the Habsburg view in 1846, Austria was not annexing Cracow but rather repossessing the city, since it had belonged to them before 1809, when it had been made over to the Napoleonic Grand Duchy of Warsaw.[116] The seizure of Cracow in 1846 was represented as yet another act of Galician revindication.

The imperial patent of Emperor Ferdinand insisted that he was acting "to secure from the assaults and agitations of the revolutionary party the upright and order-loving part of the population of Cracow as well as our loyal subjects in Galicia." In the new political order the loyal subjects of Galicia would be protected from the revolutionary party in Cracow, while the upright citizens of Cracow would be guaranteed against violent Galician massacres. Ferdinand thus took possession of Cracow and "united it with our crown forever [*für ewige Zeiten, na wieczne czasy*]." He promised: "We will always be a gentle prince and merciful emperor to those who make themselves worthy through loyalty and attachment to our house."[117] Cracovians were thus admonished and encouraged to make themselves over as loyal Galicians.

The massacres of Galicia, however, were certainly not forgotten. When, in 1847, Italian nationalists published in Switzerland poems of hatred against the Habsburgs, who ruled over Lombardy and Venetia, it was natural to cite the case of Galicia as an example of imperial evil. One poem, by Gabriele Rossetti, was addressed to Metternich—*empio ministro, d'imbecille sire* ["the impious minister of an imbecile monarch"]:

> Unnatural man [*snaturato*]! upon the nobles themselves
> You unleash the wrath of the plebeians!
> In Galicia you show who you are
> By the hecatomb that burns for you.[118]

Here Ferdinand appeared not as a "gentle prince" but as the feeble-minded dupe of Metternich's machinations. Galicia was invoked as Metternich's hecatomb, his bloody sacrifice to himself—publicized by the Italians in order to discredit Habsburg rule throughout the empire. Children, like Sacher-Masoch, who had seen the dogs licking up the blood of the victims would never forget the sight, and Galicians, after 1846, would immediately set about trying to interpret the moral and political meanings of that fateful year. The memories and phantoms of 1846 would continue to haunt Galicia for the rest of the nineteenth century, and the bloody legend of the massacres would become the traumatic force that conditioned the ongoing evolution of Galician provincial identity.

CHAPTER FOUR

Galician Vertigo

The Meaning of the Massacres

While Metternich might exult over peasant loyalty in Galicia, and denounce the communist revolutionary agenda of *polonisme*, his perspective did not remain uncontested. The awkward contradictions and implicit hypocrisies of Metternich's position, especially his apparent endorsement of peasant violence, were vividly publicized by supporters of the Polish cause. "An invisible hand has written on the wall a judgment upon him in Galician blood," wrote Polish commentator Teodor Morawski about Metternich's public culpability. "He stands in the pillory of European public opinion, lashed by the revelations of a Polish nobleman."[1] The invisible hand belonged to Aleksander Wielopolski, who published anonymously in Paris in 1846 a French pamphlet entitled *Letter of a Polish Gentleman on the Massacres of Galicia addressed to Prince Metternich*. Wielopolski, whose family estate was located in West Galicia when he was born in 1803, was educated in Vienna, in Warsaw, and in Paris. As a young man he had represented the Polish insurrectionary government of 1830–31 in London, and his efforts there made him keenly aware of the importance to the Polish cause of public opinion in France and England. As a country gentleman attempting to reconstitute his patrician family estate in the 1840s, he reacted with predictable horror to the events of 1846, and, after penning his public letter to Metternich, he altogether repudiated the Habsburg monarchy, later emerging as a political reformer in Russian Poland, where he tried unsuccessfully to avert the insurrection of 1863.

Wielopolski's letter, dated 15 April 1846, denounced Metternich directly before the tribunal of European public opinion:

My Prince—More than a month ago Europe was moved by the story of the events of Galicia, and public opinion could not fathom them. Every day brought more terrible details than those that came before, and put to the test and exhausted all beliefs, all ideas of this century. . . . At the first news of this carnage, Europe turned its eyes to you, My Prince. Accustomed for a long time to revere in you one of the supports, one of the fathers, of the European order, Europe needed to hear your word.[2]

Metternich himself had hoped to justify himself in France through his ambassador, and Wielopolski formulated the Polish case against Metternich by writing in French and publishing in Paris. Both Metternich and Wielopolski insisted that "the events of Galicia" had implications that went far beyond the borders of the province, even beyond the Habsburg monarchy, and were meaningful for the continental order of Europe.

The Europe represented in Paris was, above all, Western Europe, gazing from afar at the eastern debacle of Galicia in 1846, and Wielopolski sought to engage the forces and values of civilization to validate his own Polish perspective. Metternich might pretend to be bringing civilization to Galicia, but Wielopolski called Metternich himself before the bar of civilized opinion:

You soon sensed that the accusations of the civilized world [*du monde civilisé*] were about to explode, and in order to avoid being accused, you hastened to make yourself the accuser. Grant that in the solemn debate that is opening before this tribunal of the civilized nations [*les nations policées*], of posterity and history, a voice may also arise in the name of that nobility executed without an executioner, without a defense, without an accusation, and without a crime.[3]

The Habsburg ideology of empire, dating back to the age of Joseph II, claimed to bring civilization to Galicia as a land of relative barbarism, but Wielopolski, in the aftermath of the massacres of 1846, was able to cast a glaring light on the implicit contradictions of such ideological posturing. He manipulated the conventional idea of Eastern Europe, with the alleged separation of Eastern and Western spheres, in order to appeal to the "civilized opinion" of supposedly civilized Western nations in a grievance that condemned Metternich himself as the accomplice of barbarism in Galicia.

Wielopolski's letter to Metternich articulated a self-consciously Polish perspective on the massacres, and he then turned his back on the Habsburg monarchy forever. Fredro, however, wrote about what had happened from the Galician perspective of a man who, for better or worse, conceived of himself as a subject of the Habsburg emperor. Years later, in 1863, Police Chief Sacher-Masoch published his memoirs of 1846, under the title *Polish Revolutions: Recollections from Galicia*. The retired police chief remained entirely committed to the Habsburg perspective, unapologetically justifying the massacres as a former official who was himself, at the time, indirectly implicated in the incitement to bloodshed. These accounts suggest the intellectual importance and complexity of contemporary efforts to interpret the meaning of the massacres. The significance of 1846 would influence, and in some ways even overshadow, the Revolution of 1848 in Galicia, and the contested meaning of the massacres would remain traumatically relevant to the politics of the province for the rest of the nineteenth century.

WIELOPOLSKI: "AFTER THE ORGIES OF CRIME"

Wielopolski insisted that the peasants of Galicia lived once upon a time— "under the Polish ancien régime"—in unity and community with the nobles, enjoying the benefits of an originally "patriarchal" society. It was only the partition of Poland and creation of Galicia that transformed social relations between nobles and peasants. The Habsburg government boasted of its "salutary influence upon the populations of Galicia," brought about by Austrian administration:

> And then, when it was a matter of explaining to a horrified Europe the brutalization of these masses, it was the Polish nobles whom you accused of having demoralized the people. If the Polish nobility is responsible for the moral state of the Galician peasant, if it is the nobility, through seventy years, that presided over the destinies of those populations, what then is the boasted excellence of your legislation? Your regime of seventy years, was it then impotent? . . . The nobility is not responsible for the current state of the peasants, and it is your regime that has made the people depraved, made their character unnatural, to the extent of being ungrateful, greedy, ferocious, and impious.[4]

Metternich claimed that, when Galicia was created in 1772, "the country found itself in the most barbarous condition," with peasants particularly oppressed, but Wielopolski reversed that judgment to insist that it was the Habsburgs who presided over the brutalization and depravation of the peasantry over the course of seventy years.

Habsburg ideology of empire was based upon the idea of backwardness in Galicia, backwardness always exposed to civilizing imperial influences, but never actually attenuated to the point of becoming civilized. If civilization could be achieved in Galicia, then empire would have no ideological vindication. Wielopolski cut right to the heart of this contradiction by insisting that, after seventy years, the Habsburgs had to accept responsibility for the unhappy condition and ferocious character of the peasantry.

Echoing the political theory of Burke, which also paralleled the arguments of the Galician "Magna Charta" of 1790, Wielopolski charged the Habsburgs with purposefully undermining the patriarchal harmony of the ancien régime in Galicia. Dating back to the reign of Joseph II, the government had intervened to regulate the terms of serfdom without actually abolishing it, and thus initiated an age of peasant discontent aggravated by bureaucratic corruption: "That which had been, in the former condition of the institution, an inexhaustible source of generous and elevated sentiments on the part of the master, and of filial respect, devotion, and trust on the part of the peasant, became gradually a source of reciprocal mistrust, cupidity, jealousy, and evil passions of every sort." The Habsburg officials in Galicia sought to "inspire in the peasants hostile sentiments toward their masters," as part of a purposeful policy of *divide et impera*. Wielopolski, well aware of the concerns of men like Sapieha and Fredro in the early 1840s, reminded Metternich that the Galician estates had actually tried to appeal to the Viennese government to reform the increasingly fraught character of Galician serfdom: "Why then did you not hasten to satisfy the demand of the estates of Galicia?"[5] Wielopolski did not doubt that Metternich had preferred to encourage agrarian discontent, so that it might be exploited in just such an eventuality as the insurrection of 1846. By this reasoning, Metternich was squarely responsible for the Galician massacres.

In conjuring the massacres for the public, Wielopolski focused on the murdered members of the Bogusz family and, in particular, the eighty-seven-year-old patriarch of the family, Stanisław Bogusz, who was older than Galicia itself.

> He knew Poland before the assaults committed upon it. He had never heard his fathers speak of a massacre of the nobles by the peasants of these regions. He had seen his country suffer and die, himself surviving after having personally served the last of its kings. The act by which Poland was condemned to death he had heard justified by the benefits which all classes were supposed to enjoy henceforth under the aegis of a strong, civilized, and paternal government. And in his old age, without any fault or reproach, at the end of a career marked with honor, he saw his children and all his household victimized, he saw that nobility, which honored him like a father, sacrificed to an idol that the assassins dared to call emperor.[6]

In Wielopolski's evocation of the perspective of the Bogusz patriarch, the massacres appeared as the barbarous rites of some sort of Aztec religion of blood, the misconceived worship of the Habsburg emperor. Never was supposedly "civilized" government so utterly exposed in its bloodthirsty hypocrisy. The rhetorical invocation of the doomed old man was calculated to denounce the very invention of Galicia, which Bogusz had been old enough to remember, with all its attendant Josephine justifications.[7]

Having spoken for the Bogusz family of victims, Wielopolski turned his attention to the man who had supposedly brought about their murder after years of grievances against them, Jakub Szela.

The exterminator of this whole house is the liberated convict who has acquired in these disorders such a deplorable renown as one of the principal leaders of the movement; between him and the authorities of the Tarnów district there were continual relations, and this man, boasting of the number of nobles who fell by his hand, has not ceased to be in conference with the imperial employees over a long time. By a reversal—I will not say of all principles, but of the most basic ideas, of common sense itself—a reversal which the words of language refuse to express, this Szela has been invested with the function of official assassin.[8]

Wielopolski thus insisted on the utmost complicity between Szela and the Habsburg officials in Galicia, though it was difficult to ascertain precisely the character or degree of encouragement that the peasantry received from Habsburg officialdom before the massacres. Afterward, Szela certainly conferred with no less an imperial employee than Police Chief Sacher-Masoch, as recalled by the latter's impressionable child. Wielopolski was determined to permit Metternich no pretense to the standard of civilization or even of conservatism. The shocking "reversal" was the unholy alliance between the Habsburgs and the peasant assassins, the world turned upside down with the seeming complicity of the dynasty itself.

The supposed loyalty of the peasants was countered with an affirmation of higher dynastic principles, as Wielopolski, who spent a part of his childhood in Vienna, invoked the Capuchin crypt that held the tombs of the Habsburg emperors, including the founders of Galicia.

My Prince, let us descend into those vaults where lie the bones of your monarchs; there, with the assurance of Christian conscience, let us risk this question: was it necessary at this price to preserve Galicia for their house? You hear these tombs stirring: the spirit of a great and pious empress rises up first of all, the frightening shade of Kaunitz also appears to you.[9]

This Gothic exercise in sepulchral fantasy served to suggest that Metternich, as the man behind the massacres, could no longer shroud himself, so to speak, in the ideology of dynastic service. Wielopolski notably did not conjure the shade of Joseph II, who crafted those very restrictions on serfdom that seemed, in retrospect, to have undermined "patriarchal" relations between nobles and peasants. It was enough for Wielopolski to remind Metternich that the cry *Vive l'empereur!* was the signal for the massacres in Galicia in 1846, a perversely conceived loyalty to Ferdinand that could be countered by summoning the spirit of Maria Theresa.

"What did you do then in Vienna?" asked Wielopolski, as he sought to establish Metternich's own perverse relation to the massacres of Galicia.

Not feeling master enough to repress the social disorder, you took the part of not condemning it, of recognizing it, of ratifying it. You published that memorable proclamation of the emperor, of March 12, by which you thanked the loyal populations of Galicia for their fidelity toward the sovereign, recommending simply that they return to their habitual occupations. This manifesto, like acts of indulgence toward the guilty, is more than an amnesty: and if the name is lacking, it is because in the face of Europe it would not have been decent to name the thing by its name. At the same time you thank your troops for their courage, your functionaries for their presence of mind. Even more, in the dispatch [of 7 March] to which we are responding, you offer an apologia for those massacres, you raise them to the height of great social principles, you show them as the celebration of the mysteries of legitimacy.[10]

Just as the fictive legitimacy of the revindication of Galicia camouflaged the ugly reality of the partitions of Poland, so the "mysteries of legitimacy" were perversely invoked to veil the violence of 1846. "In vain you wish to dissimulate," wrote Wielopolski, "the fact that what has just been consummated in Galicia is, since the partition of Poland, the most important event in the history of Eastern Europe."[11] The partitions concerned the territorial dismemberment of the state, but the massacres of 1846 represented the destruction of the nation.

The crucial question that hovered over the events of 1846 thus involved the relative and overlapping significations of Galicia and Poland. The peasant massacres of 1846 demonstrated either, as Wielopolski insisted, the vehemence of Habsburg hostility to the Polish nation in Galicia, or else, as Metternich affirmed, the tepid and tenuous nature of Polishness in Galicia. Ever since 1772, Habsburg ideology had insisted that Galicia was not an essentially Polish province, and the events of 1846 could be interpreted as the proof of that theorem. Galicia, territorially revindicated in 1772, was ideologically revindicated in 1846.

Polishness had been effaced, or perhaps transcended, by the Galician circumstances, though Wielopolski believed that it had been violently unraveled by Habsburg policy under Metternich's cynical direction.

> People say in Galicia that you like to see us die: so take our lives, but please, receive them as the ransom for that which you have taken from us; take our heads, but before you have them cut off, return to us the affection of our peasants, and when you kill us, do not do it again by their hands. We will not speak to you any more about our former fatherland, since you say that it is a crime for us to remember it. . . . But please, permit us to speak to you about that sole and unique nationality, or rather—if that word still frightens you—permit us to speak to you of that which you may call whatever you please.[12]

While Wielopolski mourned the fate of his own "unique nationality" in 1846, he also seemed to recognize the circumstantial contingency and semiological instability of national names and categories: "that which you may call whatever you please." Metternich, who once advocated the making of Galicians by weaning them away from their Polishness, took an even more historically contingent and politically plastic view of the evolution of nationality.

For Wielopolski the massacres of 1846 meant not only the perversion of Habsburg policy in Galicia, but also the subversion of the whole history of relations between Austria and Poland, the historical context of Galicia's political existence.

> An account with Austria is opening for us in the eternal pages of Providence; and the new page, My Prince, begins with your name. At the end of a long and glorious career, before descending into the tomb, your feet have slipped in blood. It is the blood of the descendants of the nobility that once gave its own blood under the ramparts of Vienna. From the towers of the ancient palace of our kings, that you are changing into a citadel, one still sees every night on the horizon bounded by the Carpathians the glimmering of the fires that consume our countryside. But in contemplating the future, do you not see another glimmering, the bloody trace that, coming from your own hands, descends upon the heads of the noble and ancient race of Rudolf of Habsburg and Maria Theresa, like a flaming cloud that presages lightning and conflagration? For those who have been the too docile instruments in this work, after the orgies of crime will come the calm solitude of remorse; they will encounter the ghosts of their victims, who will not have ratified the pardon accorded by you to their murderers.[13]

Wielopolski wrote in the spirit of Romanticism, conjuring ghosts from the recent crisis and the remote historical past, looking for Galicia in the light of strange and sinister hauntings, glimmerings, and portents, discerning an apocalyptic provincial landscape of flame and blood. These literary effects underlay his ideological purpose: the definitive rejection and refutation of the idea of Galicia.

Wielopolski turned his back on Galicia in the letter to Metternich, and signaled the opening of a new account. Viewed from the Wawel Castle in Cracow—"the ancient palace of our kings"—Galicia was a province in flames. The remains of the Polish rulers in the Wawel Cathedral suffered the ghostly spectacle of the Galician disaster, just as the remains of the Habsburg emperors in the Capuchin crypt of Vienna bore the ghostly burden of Metternich's criminal conduct. Wielopolski recognized that Galicia existed in the context of the historical encounter between Poland and Austria, looking back not just to the politics of partition in 1772 but further, to the military triumph of the Polish king Jan Sobieski, who saved Vienna from the Turks in 1683. Now, however, after the massacres of 1846, the idea of Galicia was bankrupt for Wielopolski. In Cracow, in February, there was terrible fear as the news of Galicia arrived in the city: "Against the horrors of Galicia, with which the return of your troops threatened the republic, people pleaded for the arrival of the Russians." The republic of Cracow would be annexed by the

Austrians, not the Russians, at the end of 1846, but Wielopolski declared that Polish sympathies forever after—and especially his own—would belong to Russia. "Like you, and with you, the Russians dethroned our king, our institutions, our liberties, but they left intact the social order," wrote Wielopolski to Metternich. "They have never turned over the authority of their czar to assassins."[14] The Russians were therefore, in some sense, more civilized than the Austrians. From the beginning, the anti-imperial thrust of Wielopolski's letter had suggested that the Habsburgs had lost the civilizing edge of their ideology of empire in Galicia, that they had shown themselves to be barbarians.

"The Polish nobility will prefer without doubt to march with the Russians at the head of Slavic civilization, young, vigorous, fully of the future," declared Wielopolski, "rather than being dragged along, despised, hated, and harmed, at the tail of your decrepit, anxious, and presumptuous civilization." Thus Wielopolski rejected the Habsburg world, and with it the idea of Galicia, in the name of "Slavic civilization." Wielopolski's French readers could have recognized the idea of Slavic civilization from the lectures at the Collège de France that Adam Mickiewicz delivered in the 1840s as professor of Slavic literature.

Wielopolski imagined the Polish nobility submitting themselves to the Russian czar, as "the most generous of our enemies," and appealing not to the czar's qualities of mercy but to his spirit of revenge: "Do not leave unpunished the crime committed by the foreigner against our brothers of Galicia with the shedding of their blood—and do not forget the Slavic blood [*sang slave*] that cries out for vengeance." In this same spirit Wielopolski prophesied disaster for the Habsburgs who had given the Galician peasants a taste of blood. He quoted Goethe's Mephistopheles, as if to remind Metternich that a Polish nobleman had mastered German culture, but now rejected it absolutely in the name of Slavic civilization: *Das Blut ist ein besonderer Saft.*[15] Blood is an extraordinary juice. The writer Sacher-Masoch also discovered the taste of blood in his Galician childhood, and would savor it again and again, with masochistic sensuality, in his fiction of punishment and revenge, for the rest of his literary life.

FREDRO: "SEIZED BY VERTIGO"

Wielopolski wrote anonymously as a "Polish noble [*gentilhomme polonais*]," and many Polish nobles may have shared his outrage over the massacres of 1846, but not every one of them came to the same conclusion of absolutely renouncing Galicia and anathematizing the Habsburgs forever after. Another Polish noble, none other than Aleksander Fredro, gave voice to his concerns in a series of semiprivate letters and a semipublic memorandum in the aftermath of the massacres. Fredro, who wrote in a spirit far from Wielopolski's language of blood and ghosts, remained ultimately Galician both in his reflections and in his recommendations. Wielopolski's letter to Metternich was dated 15 April, and, probably in late April or early May, Fredro wrote a letter, also in French, to Count Alfred Potocki, then residing in Vienna though he was the master of the great Potocki estate at Łańcut in Galicia. He was the son of Jan Potocki, author of the novel *The Saragossa Manuscript*, and Alfred Potocki, like Fredro, had fought for Napoleon at the Battle of Borodino. Potocki played a prominent role in Galician affairs during the Metternich era, and was in Vienna at the time of the massacres of 1846. Since Potocki had close connections to the Habsburg government, Fredro's letter could be considered a not altogether private document. "Monsieur le Comte!" he began. "The horrors of which our unhappy country has just been the theater and of which the complete extent is known only to those who have been the victims, are nothing in comparison with those that await us in the future, given the manner in which it has been undertaken to re-establish order."[16] The "theater" of horrors was very far from the spirit of Fredro's genius for comedy, and he himself reacted with deadly seriousness.

Fredro censured the Austrian government for pretending to re-establish order in April while ignoring the crimes that had been committed in February. The Austrian officials in Galicia, according to Fredro, were totally out of touch with reality: "They pretend that everything has returned to order. It is false: the tendency toward anarchy increases at every glance. The peasants everywhere dream only of massacre and pillage—they do nothing but speak about that, and the whole world can hear except for the government which does not want to."[17] Fredro in Lviv offered Potocki in Vienna a dose of reality, a report from the scene of the crime, as an antidote to the prevailing climate of delusion and fantasy: the government's deluded conviction of order and the peasants' bloody dreams of massacre and pillage. The reality that Fredro craved and recommended was the reality of punishment.

Fredro claimed to know that in eastern Galicia peasants were flaunting their pillaged gains by the purchase of cattle: "The impunity of their crimes encourages imitation." All over the province peasants had ceased to work the land according to their feudal obligations—"and how could it be otherwise when the approbation of their conduct has been proclaimed even where the greatest atrocities have been committed?" Fredro, like Wielopolski, deplored the "striking victory" of the "revolutionary spirit," and lamented the position of the Galician landowners. "We have been despoiled," he declared: "we great proprietors, despoiled of all moral and material power, of every consideration on the part of the peasants and of all confidence on the part of the government." The nobles were thus abandoned to suffer "under the blows of the whips and the lies [*les coups de fléaux et de faux*]."[18] The "blows of the whips" were perhaps intended figuratively by Fredro, but his imagery brought him very close to the scenarios of flagellation that Sacher-Masoch would later make into his literary trademark.

Fredro recognized that the feudal corvée would have to be abolished, and indeed, together with Sapieha, he had already advocated feudal reform during the early 1840s. He warned Potocki, however, that the government must not permit feudalism to lapse as a consequence of the unpunished massacres, since "this impunity will remain always a pernicious tradition for the future." Impunity would become precedent, and the precedent would lead to further massacres and ultimately to anarchy. "In the name of God, Monsieur le Comte," wrote Fredro, "try to make them understand in Vienna that the state of things in Galicia is desperate just because no one wants to know about it." No measures were being taken by the government for the security of the nobles, and at Easter in 1846 they were afraid to go to their estates, remaining in the towns. "You have no idea of the discouragement and demoralization, so to speak, that has spread among the proprietors," wrote Fredro. "Nothing but chaos is foreseen, and there are very few who would not wish to sell all that they possess to flee a country where they see only enemies set upon their ruin."[19] Fredro's interpretation of the events was no less dire than Wielopolski's, but he himself was not prepared to abandon Galicia, and he wrote to Potocki urging measures of punishment and security that would forestall both chaos and emigration. Above all, however, the difference between Fredro and Wielopolski was that the dramatist did not interpret Austrian policy as an assault on the Polish nation, but rather on the social order of the Galician nobility.

Potocki's reply from Vienna to Fredro's letter from Lviv has not survived as an original document, but a fragment from that reply, translated from French into Polish, was preserved. The correspondence between the two Galicians, carried on between the Habsburg imperial capital and the Galician provincial capital, constituted an epistolary negotiation of what it meant to be Galician in the immediate aftermath of the massacres of 1846. Potocki wrote to Fredro recommending Galician prudence: "Great prudence is necessary, so as not to excite the masses, and in general this is a moment appropriate for showing that the majority of the nobility, animated by conservative principles, desires to respect the legal order."[20] Potocki's phrase "conservative principles" meant not only deploring the peasant massacres, as Fredro did, but above all respecting the "legal order" of Habsburg rule in Galicia. While Wielopolski cursed the Habsburgs for purposefully inciting the massacre of the nobility, and Fredro criticized the government for failing to punish the peasants and preserve security, Potocki in Vienna could envision no way out of the crisis except through loyalty to the dynasty.

Fredro replied on 16 May from Lviv by insisting that there was no disloyalty in his criticism of the government.

> My letter was not at all one of those complaints that arrive from Galicia, of which people seem to be weary in Vienna; it was rather an opinion that I believed I had to pass on through you as intermediary . . . to indicate the errors of subaltern employees, that may become pernicious to the social order of the province and therefore to the whole monarchy.[21]

He insisted that he was every bit as devoted to social order as his correspondent, and no less committed to a policy of prudence.

> You say that great prudence is necessary so as not to excite the masses. But it is precisely to such prudence that I appeal. And it is not assuredly the rigor of justice toward the crime (of which every man, however barbarous he may be, feels the infamy in the depths of his heart), but rather its impunity that may excite the masses to deviate from the line of the laws and to despise in the end all authority. . . .[22]

Like Wielopolski, Fredro understood that the massacres of 1846 profoundly compromised Austria's self-assumed posture of civilization in Galicia, and he pointedly pronounced the word "barbarous" in his letter to Vienna.

Up to this point Fredro claimed to be in agreement with Potocki on matters of conservative principle, but, in fact, there was a profound distance that separated them, literally the geographical distance between Vienna and Lviv, between the ruling metropolis and the governed, or misgoverned, province. This distance could be represented with graphic clarity in the epistolary form that linked these two Galician nobles across the terrain of the Habsburg monarchy. Fredro believed that a Galician had to be present in Galicia in order to appreciate what had happened in 1846, and though he graciously offered "a thousand apologies for my frankness," he was emphatically frank. Fredro urged, even dared, Potocki to come to Galicia himself, to inspect the Potocki estate at Łańcut.

> Come see what has happened in your vast domains. And when you have seen the wheat distributed from your stores without any previous inquiry (which, parenthetically, can not be called "respect for the rights of property"), when you have been present at commissions where nothing occurs except to "excite the masses" by provoking complaints against the lords . . . when you have read with your own eyes the proclamations which give the peasants the right to deliver over to the

district every landowner who seems to them guilty of this or that crime, when, finally, convinced by a mass of actions suited to overturning the social order from top to bottom, you address the authorities and say to them: "I am of the majority that wishes to re-establish order. I am of this country [*je suis du pays*]. I know the character and relations of the inhabitants. I therefore warn you that you are proceeding along a path that is completely wrong." And when you have received a response that proves to you that they distrust you, that they do not wish to believe you, that your zeal for the public good, your loyal sentiments, are rejected, repulsed, despised, it is then, Monsieur le Comte, that I will take once again the liberty of asking you what should be the conduct of those who would gladly offer their own blood in case of need for the prosperity of their country.[23]

Fredro's frankness was almost intemperate in its blunt insistence that Potocki, in Vienna, was completely cut off from the reality of Galicia. What strikingly emerged from this challenge—"come see"—was that the whole discussion, for Fredro, turned on the question of being Galician, of who was qualified to step forward and say: *Je suis du pays.* I am of this country. That country was clearly neither Austria nor Poland, but Galicia. Furthermore, when Fredro uncharacteristically conjured with blood, it was not, as for Wielopolski, the blood of Poles murdered for their Polishness, but the blood of Galicians that they would gladly have given for the good of their country: Galicia.

Potocki's next reply, dated 25 May, recognized that Fredro was angry and tried to make amends: "I pray you, Monsieur le Comte, to believe that if my letter has wounded you, it is by my clumsiness, and that my intentions will always be to preserve the best relations with a compatriot for whom I profess sentiments of the highest esteem." At this point in the correspondence there could hardly be any doubt that the two counts, if they recognized each other as compatriots, could only be Galician compatriots. While Fredro had hoped to encourage Potocki's exercise of influence in Vienna, Potocki reciprocally insisted on the importance of Fredro's influence in Galicia. "It is just because I have the feeling that my opinion carries very little weight in our province," wrote Potocki, "that I would have desired to go along with you who would have influence if you wished." Potocki claimed that he could hardly know what to believe about Galicia when there arrived in Vienna a "heap of invented stories," and he himself received from Lviv "the strangest accounts." He was hoping to put together a balanced account, without assigning blame, let alone anathema, to the Habsburg dynasty. "At this moment there is reaction, perhaps as brutal as the action was criminal and stupid, but I repeat that the central government wants only for justice to be rendered to all: the peasant murderers will be hung, I do not doubt that."[24] Potocki thus suggested a balance between action and reaction, between the criminal stupidity of the Polish insurrectionaries and the possible complicity of some Habsburg bureaucrats in the peasant violence. The central government in Vienna was, however, absolved of all moral responsibility. In this sense, Potocki's position was absolutely opposed to that of Wielopolski, for Wielopolski explicitly indicted the central government in the person of Metternich himself.

Fredro wrote to Potocki in Vienna once again in July to let him know what was happening in Galicia: *Rien de bon*. Nothing good. There were still bureaucratic subalterns fomenting unrest among the peasants, and Fredro was "seized by vertigo [*saisi de vertige*]" as he tried to fathom the "enigma" of the government's intentions:

> That the bureaucracy should want to undo the nobility, the great landowners, that could be conceived—but that it should use the demoralization of the people in order to achieve this end is inconceivable . . . it is to wish to break one by one all the bonds of social order, to attack wealth and national civilization. And yet it is done, it is done systematically, for it is done throughout the country. One must truly believe that God in his anger is punishing us by striking with blindness those who govern us, and then there is nothing to be done.[25]

Again the civilizing Habsburgs were cited for condoning an assault on civilization. This paradox was a part of that enigma of reversals that Fredro found so dizzyingly vertiginous, overturning not only the social order but also his whole conception, consolidated over half a century, of what it meant to be Galician.

"We are persuaded of the good intentions of the central government," wrote Fredro, though this was perhaps no more than a courteous platitude: good intentions would not amount to much if the government was completely blind. The most hopeful sign was the dispatch to Galicia of Rudolf Stadion, the governor of Moravia, to report to Vienna on the Galician situation, offering his direct observations from the province to alleviate the prevailing blindness in the metropolis. His brother Franz Stadion would be named governor of Galicia in 1847, replacing Archduke Ferdinand d'Este, whose term was rendered irretrievably notorious by the events of 1846. Fredro warned Potocki that Rudolf Stadion's mission would be complicated by "many Gordian knots," and that the Habsburg government had to proceed immediately to "finish with anarchy" and "punish the assassins." This was the only way to begin to escape from the "vicious circle," which Fredro seemed to intend as a pun on the term for the Habsburg administrative districts in Galicia: *cercle* in French, *Kreis* in German. He blamed the bureaucrats at the level of the "circle" for every viciousness in 1846, and was shocked to learn that Joseph Breinl, the leading administrator in the Tarnów circle, who was allegedly in contact with Jakub Szela at the time of the massacres, was actually being rewarded by Vienna with an honorary Habsburg decoration. "At the moment at which I am writing to you," noted Fredro in his letter to Potocki, "I learn that Breinl has received a splendid recompense for his fine deeds. He has just been decorated."[26] For Fredro this was further evidence of blindness in Vienna, the failure to recognize that the Habsburg bureaucracy had been scandalously compromised by contacts with the peasant murderers. Police Chief Sacher-Masoch, in Lviv, did not decline to meet with Szela at the moment of the latter's removal from Galicia.

Fredro struck a sentimental note when he informed Potocki about the "thousands, yes, thousands of orphans whose parents have been executed without judgment," and about the charitable commitment of the Galician nobles to care for them. In fact, Fredro and his wife were caring for an eight-year-old girl, the daughter of a murdered forester from one of the noble estates around Tarnów. Yet the government was providing "not even a crumb" to support these orphans, and many were being raised "among Jews and bourgeois workers" with the risk of "poverty and perdition."[27] This response to the massacres with a charitable campaign on behalf of the orphans was a characteristically Galician gesture of the sort that had regularly been mentioned in the pages of *Gazeta Lwowska* during the preceding decades. Fredro, however, recognized that, beyond punishment for the assassins and charity for the orphans, a much more comprehensive response to the crisis was required. Accordingly, he prepared a memorandum, "Considerations on the Social Situation in Galicia [*Uwagi nad stanem socjalnym w Galicji*]," which was probably composed in the context of his correspondence with Potocki and was ultimately formulated as "Address to the Throne in the Year 1846 [*Głos do Tronu w Roku 1846*]." The memorandum may never have actually been presented to the throne, but it circulated in Galicia in manuscript form in 1846 and was even published anonymously in German in 1847.[28] The ideas elaborated in Fredro's semiprivate correspondence with Potocki thus found a semipublic outlet in the memorandum, and played a part in shaping a specifically Galician, as opposed to Austrian or Polish, reaction to the events of 1846.

"The events which covered part of Galicia with blood and destruction and still threaten similar misfortune, are not accidental," wrote Fredro. He traced their origins back to the creation of Galicia in the partitions of Poland, when Vienna faced a choice between two approaches to imperial rule: either to rule Galicia according to "civilization under the influence of nationality"—that is, Polish nationality—or to rule through bureaucracy. The Habsburgs chose bureaucratic rule, and thus set Galicia on the road to disaster. Carefully, Fredro explained what he meant by nationality, which stood opposed to bureaucracy in Galicia. He defined it with reference to the Commonwealth, defunct for half a century.

Nationality in Poland was, and is up until today, constituted of two parts. One, almost unconscious [*prawie nieświadoma siebie*], which results from the situation of the land, the climate, the food, the way of life, blood and language. The other, conscious of itself, which lives only with the life of the first, but grows with memories, relations, consolidated through centuries, with intellectual formation, and finally with power, which it possessed for a long time. The people [*lud*] are the representative of the first part. The nobility [*szlachta*] of the other.[29]

It was the self-consciously Polish *szlachta* that found itself embattled against the Habsburg bureaucracy. As for the unconsciously national peasantry, Fredro insisted that they could not have been motivated by Austrian patriotism; rather, they murdered the nobility to free themselves from their feudal obligations.[30] Yet the notion of a nationally "unconscious" people posed precisely the enigma that Fredro himself could not truly resolve, the mystery of the identity of the peasants of Galicia.

The memorandum, like the letters to Potocki, stressed the evil of impunity [*bezkarność*], as the fundamental obstacle to restoring social order. Fredro, however, went further to propose principles of ameliorative reform for the province. The first was a role for the representative estates of the province—as established by Joseph II and confirmed by the Congress of Vienna. Fredro himself had served in the Galician Sejm, and hoped it would play a role in guiding public opinion in the province. The second proposal was the introduction of Polish as the language of education and administration: "to open up a wider field for Galician youth to develop their abilities on the path of law and toward utility in the service of the country." Third, Fredro recommended an easing of censorship of the press, so that the business of the estates could reach all those concerned with "the general interest of the country." Finally, the estates would have to undertake a reform of the feudal subordination of the peasantry in the interest of "the security of the country [*bezpieczeństwo kraju*]."[31] While Fredro thus attended with concern to the condition of the Polish nation in Galicia, his every proposal was focused on "the country," on Galicia itself. Although implicitly critical of the Habsburg government, and frankly hostile to the Habsburg bureaucracy, Fredro's memorandum fully accepted the premise of the political order as well as the social order in Galicia. In this sense, Fredro's "Address to the Throne" of 1846 was the plausible descendant of the "Magna Charta" of 1790.

"These are the means which seem to us effective for restoring and preserving order in Galicia," he noted, and he attempted, in conclusion, to analyze what "Galicia" actually meant, and what it might come to mean in the future. "Under the broad wing of the law the various estates and various nationalities find their place, sufficient place," he wrote, suggesting the multinational nature of the province. Yet, like Wielopolski, he could also envision a sort of national coherence in Galicia as a "province of five million Slavs." Denominating the nationally unconscious mass of the people as "Slavs" rather than Poles or Ruthenians, Fredro still envisioned for the Polish nation the role of making those five million Slavs into a power "among Slavdom [*w Słowiańszczyźnie*]," the center of gravity of Eastern Europe, dominating the Slavic peoples of neighboring lands. Galicia would thus become the "antemurale and point of support for many Slavic generations, united under the paternal scepter of the Austrian house."[32] For Wielopolski the events of 1846 became the reason for abandoning Austria in favor of a Slavic alignment with Russia; for Fredro the idea of Galicia still offered the possibility of Slavic solidarity loyal to Austria and resistant to Russian magnetism.

In spite of his protestation of Galician loyalty, the bureaucrats he excoriated were not delighted with Fredro's memorandum, and the administration filed away a copy in German, noting that it was authored by Fredro and signed by forty-four nobles, for eventual presentation to the emperor in Vienna. The notation fairly summarized Fredro's perspective, in opposition to the Habsburg view of events: "The author attempts to attribute fundamentally, in spiteful tones, the hatred of the subjects for their feudal masters and the consequent atrocities to the bureaucratic endeavors of the official authorities."[33] At the time of the Revolution of 1848, Fredro made a speech that was similarly critical of the Habsburg bureaucracy, and in 1852, after the revolutionary epoch had passed, he found himself charged with treason on account of those criticisms. His delicate situation was already evident in the memorandum of 1846 as he attempted awkwardly to define what it meant to be Galician in the aftermath of the massacres.

"POLISH REVOLUTIONS"

In Prague in 1863, long after the Galician massacres, there was published an anonymous work in German that retrospectively expressed the bureaucratic perspective of the authorities, *Polish Revolutions: Recollections from Galicia*, generally considered to be the memoirs of Police Chief Sacher-Masoch. The father was sixty-six when he published these recollections, and the son had already begun a literary career both as a historian and a novelist, publishing in 1857 his academic dissertation about the insurrection of Ghent in the age of Charles V, and then, in 1858, anonymously, his novel about the insurrection and massacres of 1846 in Galicia. The son would eventually pay tribute to the father's narrative skill: "My father wrote well, though his style was the clear and dry style of a man of state; however, as soon as he began to speak, he became a poet: I have never heard anyone tell a story as well as he. As soon as he opened his mouth everyone was hanging upon his words, as if he had been a novelist of the first order."[34] In 1864 the son published another novel about Galicia, this time focusing on the Revolution of 1848, and the book appeared with the very same publishing house in Prague that had published the father's recollections in 1863. The son also republished in 1864 his first novel, about Galicia in 1846, this time casting aside anonymity and placing his own name on the title page. Thus, both father and son, long after the massacres of 1846, returned to that year in fiction and memoirs, and explored the themes of insurrection, violence, massacre, and retribution. The moment was ripe for public interest, on account of the contemporary Polish insurrection of 1863 in Russian Poland. In Galicia there was no such upheaval, but there was a literary revisiting of the historical scenario of 1846.

Police Chief Sacher-Masoch permitted himself some poetic flourishes in his recollections, including a tribute to Galicia as "a pearl in the crown of our monarchy" and the reciprocal formulation of the monarchy as "a true El Dorado for the Galician peasant."[35] The police chief was born in Galicia, himself the child of a Habsburg bureaucrat of Bohemian origin. "My grandfather Johann Nepomuk von Sacher was at one time imperial administrative official, when the Kingdom of Galicia was incorporated into Austria at the time of the Polish partition," wrote Sacher-Masoch the writer. "He was sent there, along with other officials, in order to bring order to the new province which had neither administration nor law." Police Chief Sacher Masoch recalled similarly the family's advent in Galicia: "My father, as he often told me later, did not willingly leave blessed Bohemia for the lands of the Sarmatians."[36] The authentic oral tradition, citing the grandfather's own words, thus reached back to the moment in 1772 when Galicia did not yet possess a name, and could be comically designated, even by Joseph II, as the land of the Sarmatians. By the time of the grandson's generation, the "Kingdom of Galicia" could be discussed as if it had always existed. All three Sacher-Masoch generations seemed to understand implicitly that it was the Habsburg administrative mission to bring order out of anarchy in Galicia, to polish the Polish pearl.

Habsburg officials, as exemplified by Police Chief Sacher-Masoch, might feel sentimental attachment and appreciation for Galicia, while at the same time emphasizing the negative provincial conditions that called forth their administrative labors. The police chief was the protégé of Franz Krieg, and described Krieg as an enlightened executor of the Josephine tradition, who entered Habsburg service as a young man from Württemberg: "In Galicia he found a second homeland [*Heimat*], and loved this land so much that he dedicated the greater part of his life to it." The police chief clearly respected Krieg, while acknowledging that he was not exactly likable, that "his physiognomy gave the impression of stiffness, coldness, and mockery."[37] Polish Galicians like Sapieha found Krieg "detestable," but Krieg himself, even as a Habsburg administrative official, could claim to adopt Galicia as his homeland and could represent himself as Galician. Police Chief Sacher-Masoch had an even greater claim to being Galician, as he already belonged to the second family generation of Habsburg administrators in the province.

In the *Polish Revolutions* the police chief wrote admiringly about the peasants of western Galicia, in the region where the massacres had taken place:

> The country people in this part of Galicia are thoroughly Polish. The peasants however do not call themselves Poles, but rather, in distinction from the Ruthenians of East Galicia, Mazurs, or else Austriaks, Austrians, more seldom Galicians. They are normally of middling size; broad shoulders, and dainty feet distinguish their body build. The form of the face is often beautiful, always intelligent and engaging; the brow more broad than high, the nose finely curved, the chin round and fleshy, the hair normally reddish brown. Among the female sex one finds here not striking beauty, as in the Carpathians, but much grace and almost always beautiful, expressive eyes, that very much distinguish the type of the Galician country people—particularly from the German type, inside and outside Austria.[38]

The police chief clearly considered himself an expert on ethnographic physiognomy, but the shifting deployment of labels—by which the population began as "thoroughly Polish" and ended as "Galician country people"—served to suggest an ambiguity of identity as background to the drama of 1846.

Polishness was deeply paradoxical in the national reflections of the police chief: "Everywhere there appeared a deeply rooted antipathy of the Polish peasants in Galicia against the strivings of the nobility, and hatred against everything connected to the Polish state or the Polish nationality."[39] Clearly the Polishness of such peasants was compromised indeed by their supposed hatred of all things Polish.

Habsburg Galicia appeared as "El Dorado" to the Galician peasantry by contrast with conditions under the Polish Commonwealth before 1772, when the nobility held absolute dominion: "A nobleman could strike a peasant dead, rob him, rape his wife, without having to worry about a bad word being spoken to any authority."[40] The alleged history of murder and violence against peasants in the Commonwealth served as an implicit vindication of the reversal of relations in 1846, when it was the peasantry that murdered the nobles with seeming impunity. In this sense, the massacres of 1846 might seem to be implicitly anticipated in the whole ideology of Galicia as it developed at the time of the partitions. "Immediately in 1772, when the first authorities, district offices, and courts were set up in Galicia," noted the police chief, "the situation of the peasant changed much to his advantage."[41] He acquired some security in his life and his property, and had some right of recourse against his feudal master.

Police Chief Sacher-Masoch was once again reciting his own family history, since it was his father, Johann Nepomuk von Sacher, who had come to Galicia in 1772 to bring about these reforms. The police chief himself was born in 1797, but he recalled the Josephine decade as the golden age of the Galician peasantry: "The most beautiful time for the Galician peasant was, however, the reign of Joseph II from 1780 to 1790."[42] Police Chief Sacher-Masoch believed that the reforms of Joseph had already determined in the 1780s that the peasantry of Galicia would remain loyal to the Habsburgs in 1846.

The police chief represented Galicia in two parts, west and east, on the Vistula and on the Dniester. The western part was where the Galician peasantry was "thoroughly Polish" but hated all things connected to Polish nationality. The eastern part was even more hostile to Polishness, for the Ruthenian population "showed such passionate and implacable hatred against the Poles, that one must look back into their history to understand it." The answer lay in the Middle Ages, when "the Ruthenians were governed by their own princes in Galicia, as far as Kiev, in all of southern Russia." This supposedly medieval "Galicia"—or Halych—was emphatically not Polish, but belonged to the Ruthenians: "far more fortunate and more cultured in the Middle Ages than the other peoples of Europe, especially the Poles." The police chief, like his son the writer, must have been moved by the discovery of Ruthenian folk poetry in Galicia in the 1830s, for he affirmed that in the Middle Ages the Prince Igor tale, which he attributed to the Galician Ruthenians, was superior to any poetry produced in Western Europe, including the German *Nibelungenlied*.[43]

The elder Sacher-Masoch emphasized the illegitimacy of the Polish annexation of Rus lands in the fourteenth century:

> From that time began the real misery of the Ruthenians. Induced by numerous advantages, the Ruthenian nobility and the towns became Polonized. So only the peasantry and the clergy remained to represent the Ruthenian nationality, and the inhabitants of small villages. They defended their language and church with the stubbornness of the Slavs, and maintained them in every storm against the Polish government and against clerical attacks of the Latin Church. With every century the Ruthenians lost more of their rights, and they preserved only their existence at the time when Galicia came to Austria in 1772. Like a shipwrecked man, who thanks God for having saved his naked life, the Ruthenian people came under the mild, just, and wise government of the Austrian monarchy.[44]

In Galicia the Ruthenian peasants in the east, like the Polish peasants in the west, allegedly recognized the Habsburgs as their saviors from a historical shipwreck.

The police chief offered physiognomic impressions of the Ruthenians as a group: they were melancholy, but also mistrustful, the men physically stronger than the Poles, the women more imposing in their beauty and less delicate than the Poles. The Hutsuls of the Carpathian Mountains he regarded as exotic Orientals of a "truly Circassian beauty."[45] Both Polish and Ruthenian males were evaluated as human military material: "In the Austrian army the Ruthenian, just like the Pole, in a word, the Galician soldier, is considered the best, most steadfast, most reliable soldier."[46] The police chief thus vacillated between an insistence on the difference between Poles and Ruthenians and an inclination to forge them into one Galician people: "in a word, the Galician soldier."

"The Ruthenians attached themselves ever closer to the Austrian monarchy and dynasty," wrote Police Chief Sacher-Masoch, and he observed that the Galician Jews were similarly loyal.

> The Jews first came with the Poles to Galicia, and their expansion was supported by the Polish kings who especially discovered a taste for pretty Jewesses. In general, however, the situation of Jews in the Polish realm was not much better than that of the Ruthenians; only a poor peasant might have been right to envy them. The Jews also received great beneficence from the Austrian government, and especially under the reign of Joseph II they witnessed the cessation of the most painful oppressions, and therefore have showed themselves scarcely less grateful than the peasants and Ruthenians. They have always proved themselves to be loyal, and with their actions and many sacrifices have always supported the government in Galicia. During the revolutions they performed the most important services as informers and agents of the authorities, and played this role much more often out of attachment to the government or to individual humane officials, rather than from greed and avarice.[47]

Furthermore, the Jews of Lviv were supposed to have donated supplies of alcoholic drink to the Habsburg army that restored order in the province.[48] With a casual allusion that simultaneously proposed and dismissed the anti-Semitic stereotype of the avaricious Jew, the police chief argued for sincere loyalty on the part of the Jews of Galicia. Presumably he himself was one such "humane official" who had relied on agents and informers, both Jews and non-Jews, in the course of his policing responsibilities in Lviv, and probably such services were remunerated.

To insist on the uncorrupted quality of Jewish loyalty was particularly pressing with reference to the events of 1846, because the government did not dare concede that financial incentives might have encouraged the massacre of the nobles. The affirmation of Jewish attachment to the Habsburgs thus resembled the discussion of peasants and Ruthenians, suggesting a triple solidarity of loyalism, that was, in every case, revealed to be historically rooted in the reign of Joseph II. The invention of Galicia in the eighteenth century still remained relevant, indeed central, to the ideology of Habsburg rule in the nineteenth century.

"GALICIAN ATROCITIES"

As he set the stage for narrating the events of 1846, Police Chief Sacher-Masoch introduced into his account the figure of a model Habsburg official in Galicia, none other than Police Chief Sacher-Masoch himself. Since he was publishing his work anonymously he could present himself as one of the historical actors in the crisis of 1846, guiding the Galician police. "At the head of that authority was the police chief Leopold Ritter von Sacher-Masoch," he wrote, introducing himself. "Descended from a noble family of the landed estate in the crownland of Galicia, he completed his studies there, and was brought into political service by Baron Krieg."[49] If Galicia was a second homeland for Krieg, it was clearly the true homeland of the police chief, born and educated there, as it would be for his son the writer. The elder Sacher-Masoch appeared in his own narrative as someone with the vision to foresee the terrible events of 1846: "The peasants were so disposed that he was convinced that in the event of an insurrection the nobles would be killed by them. But all warnings were in vain." In this sense, Sacher-Masoch became the hero of his own account, one of the few who understood Galicia well enough to predict the massacres, but doomed, Cassandra-like, to be disbelieved. He had been regarded as an "extreme pessimist [*übertreibender Schwarzseher*]," and so his account served not only as a vindication of the Habsburg government but also of himself and his own understanding of Galicia.[50]

Already in January of 1846, Police Chief Sacher-Masoch learned of a conspiracy to assassinate the governor, Archduke Ferdinand d'Este, on the occasion of a ball in Lviv at which Polish ladies would undertake to dance with Habsburg officers and distract them at the critical moment. This was to be the "Sicilian Vespers" of Galicia, the signal for general insurrection.[51] Five years earlier, in January 1841, the Lviv carnival ball was supposedly an occasion of "unforced entertainment, spirit, and humor"—organized under the watchful auspices of Police Chief Sacher-Masoch, whose office also controlled the sale of tickets. In 1846 it was he who took credit for forestalling the intended assassination of the archduke in Lviv in January, but he could not control the insurrectionary turn of events in the countryside in February.

Police Chief Sacher-Masoch did not seek to minimize the sensational horrors of the occasion, and he vividly described the arrival of the peasants in Tarnów on 19 February:

> Around nine-thirty in the morning, while the authorities and troops in Tarnów at any moment expected the attack of the Polish insurgents, the scene was suddenly and unexpectedly altered. There appeared several sleighs and carts, surrounded by peasants armed with pitchforks, pikes, muskets, and scythes, proceeding to the district office building. Upon one of the carts sat a man at the last gasp of life, and on his lap two lifeless half-dressed corpses, with multiple wounds and crushed heads. The other carts were likewise laden with corpses and with other persons still alive but horribly wounded, swimming in their own blood.[52]

These were the first in a procession of such carts that arrived in Tarnów that day with the bodies of the massacred nobles. "That terrible atrocities [*entsetzliche Greuelthaten*] were committed by the peasants, no one will deny," wrote the police chief, but he did deny that the government was in any way responsible. "We will narrate some of the frightful scenes of the bloodbath," he wrote, "so that it will not appear as if we wished to shroud them in silence and consign them to oblivion." He told of ears and noses cut from faces, eyes gouged out, nobles dragged to their deaths attached to the tails of horses, and the murder of pregnant women. He noted the "European fame of the Galician atrocities of those bloody days," a notoriety "exploited by the enemies of Austria."[53] The police chief's professional sangfroid made him unafraid to confront the excessive violence of 1846, and he was fully convinced that Austria would be vindicated if the facts were frankly presented. It is possible that he was not averse, even in 1863, to publicizing the terrible fate of the Polish rebels of 1846, as a warning to any potential insurrectionaries, and it is also possible that—like father, like son—he found some literary satisfaction in the detailed narration of horror, violence, and bloodshed.

Wielopolski had affirmed that Jakub Szela cooperated so closely with the Habsburg officials in Tarnów as to merit the strange designation of "official assassin." Yet the writer Sacher-Masoch described Szela as the "Galician Spartacus," and Police Chief Sacher-Masoch also offered praise and vindication: Jakub Szela was a man of true "humanity [*Menschlichkeit*]" and a model of "loyalty to Austria."[54] Szela, according to the police chief, "achieved European fame during the proceedings of the year 1846 in Galicia, but in a quite different sense than he deserved"—for "he was not involved in the atrocities."[55] The European notoriety of Szela in 1846 was symptomatic of the European celebrity at that moment of Galicia itself. There was no other

Tarnów, where Galician peasants brought the bodies of the massacred nobles in February 1846. From Julius Jandaurek, *Das Königreich Galizien und Lodomerien* (Vienna: Karl Graeser, 1884).

moment in the nineteenth century when Galicia compelled such European attention, exercising a grisly fascination through reports of the massacres.

Szela was sixty years old in 1846, almost as old as Galicia itself. "As a young man, he experienced the authoritative and transformative reforms of Joseph II," wrote the police chief, "and this made a very great impression on his youthful temperament and fantasy, which remained with him for his whole life." Szela was furthermore an "eyewitness [*Augenzeuge*]" of the ensuing improvement in the conditions of peasant life as a consequence of the Josephine reforms.[56] Those who were children during Joseph's reign became lifelong witnesses to the Habsburg achievement in Galicia, and their experience could be cited to explain peasant loyalism. Szela's vindication was also the vindication of the government in Galicia, and Szela's life story was the ontogenetic recapitulation of the history of the whole province from the moment of its conception. His supposed sense of "fantasy" reflected the Habsburg fantasy of Galicia.

Szela, because he appreciated the importance of the Josephine reforms for the protection of enserfed peasants, had studied the statutes and tried to explain to the peasants of the Tarnów district their rights as Habsburg subjects. In particular, he advised the peasants that they could appeal to the government authorities and courts against the arbitrary dispensations of noble landlords. Szela himself initiated a suit against the ill-fated Bogusz family, charging them with having required excessive *robot* labor from their peasants, and suing them for financial compensation. According to the police chief, Szela was guided by the Josephine conviction that "the Galician peasant generally can expect good from no one else but Austria, the emperor, and his officials."[57] This principle neatly summed up the Habsburg ideology of empire in Galicia, ever since the reign of Joseph II. In addition to affirming the axiom of the Galician peasant's loyalty to the Habsburg emperor, it further affirmed the existence of the social category of the "Galician peasant." For the Galician peasant was precisely that being whose legal status was defined by the Josephine reforms after the first partition of Poland, whose Galician identity was distinct from the Polish nationality of the noble lords, and whose direct attachment to the Habsburg emperor and his representatives in the province excluded any possible solidarity with insurrectionary Poles. If there was indeed a "Galician peasantry" in the province, defined according to these principles, then the massacres needed no further explanation.

When members of the Bogusz family were murdered by peasants in February 1846, the survivors blamed Szela for inciting the murders, amid further suspicions that the Habsburg district official Joseph Breinl might have encouraged Szela. Police Chief Sacher-Masoch denied such insinuations emphatically, insisting that neither Szela nor Breinl played any part in the massacres, and that "the Bogusz family collectively were not innocent, but on the one hand traitors, and on the other hand tyrants over the peasants."[58] Clearly, the police chief had little sympathy for the murdered nobles.

Fredro felt in 1846 that the government could not, at any cost, permit the massacres to go unpunished, but the police chief in 1863 had a very different perspective on impunity. He wrote in a spirit of ironic comedy that Fredro, the master of comedy, would certainly not have appreciated. According to the elder Sacher-Masoch, "It sounds almost comic, when the introduction of a great trial against the Polish peasants in Galicia is demanded from the government by Poles and foreign organs." The comic element was that those who were most eager to punish the peasants were also most inclined to pardon the Polish insurrectionaries, even though the insurrectionaries had been ready to countenance the murder of Habsburg soldiers and officials. "In the end if one should punish, whom does one want to punish?" asked the police chief, whose profession involved punitive considerations.[59] That same question would dominate the fantasies of his son the writer, who would answer in his literary work that the person one most wants to punish might ultimately be oneself. Those who recognized their own fantasies in his fiction would end up taking his name, identifying themselves as masochists.

Szela was not punished after the massacres but was removed from Galicia and given a farm in Bukovina (which would be officially detached from Galicia after the Revolution of 1848). According to Polish rumor, Szela was also given a Habsburg medal for his demonstrative loyalty. "Szela received a very pretty farm in Bukovina and had to leave his homeland [*Heimat*]," reported the police chief, who met with him in Lviv in 1846 and noted an expression of "melancholy" on his face. "The removal from his homeland had an unfavorable effect upon him, but he did not utter a word of protest, and died, as he had lived, a model of loyalty."[60] Galicia was Szela's homeland: his birth in the 1770s coincided with the creation of the province, and his childhood during the reign of Joseph made him a "Galician peasant" of the first generation.

In his final pages the police chief brought his story up to the current decade of the 1860s, and introduced a new model Galician, the governor Agenor Gołuchowski, who was soon to preside over the introduction of Galician political autonomy after 1866: "Descended from an old Polish noble family, Count Gołuchowski was one of the few chevaliers of Galicia who dedicated himself to state service. Gołuchowski, a Pole with all his soul, was attached with equal love to the Austrian state."[61] Wielopolski had ostentatiously turned to Russia after 1846, and actually participated in the government of Russian Poland. The Polish insurrection of 1863 marked the failure of everything Wielopolski had undertaken since 1846, while Gołuchowski, the Habsburg loyalist, was about to achieve the triumph of Galician autonomy.

"The hopes of Galicia are directed not toward Paris or Warsaw, but Vienna," wrote the police chief in 1863. "The Polish party in Galicia is in restless movement to give support to the bloody struggle against Russia, but Galicia will remain peaceful, because the peasant stands guard [*denn der Bauer wacht*]."[62] The retired police chief himself had long ago ceased to watch over law and order in Galicia. Others would fill his position in Lviv, but the lesson of 1846, as he understood it, almost suggested his own irrelevance. It was the peasants themselves who had preserved Galicia for the Habsburgs in 1846, without any encouragement or complicity from officials like himself.

The police chief did not deny the reality of the massacres of 1846. Quite the contrary, he described them in grisly detail, in order to preserve the memory of the episode. The massacres would determine the course of political life in Galicia for the rest of the nineteenth century, really for the rest of the province's political existence, and the crucial factor would be the general consciousness that "the peasant watches." In this peculiar panopticon it was the Galician peasantry, abstracted into a single Galician eye, that monitored and disciplined the political life of the province. The Habsburg government could only be deeply ambivalent about the massacres of 1846, which were both embarrassing to the dynasty and undeniably useful to the government, then and thereafter. Police Chief Sacher-Masoch explained the massacres in relation to the reforms of the Josephine era, and thus indicated how such violence could be intellectually integrated into the original Habsburg imperial ideology of Galicia.

FROM THE MASSACRES OF 1846 TO
THE REVOLUTION OF 1848

Police Chief Sacher-Masoch remained in Galicia until the spring of 1848, when, at the moment of revolution in the Habsburg monarchy, indeed in most of Europe, he was transferred to Prague with his family. Moving in May, they experienced the outbreak of revolution in Lviv and then the triumph of counter-revolution in Prague, as the Habsburgs regained political authority in the monarchy. The revolution that began in Paris in February arrived in Vienna in March, with the demonstrations that led to Metternich's dismissal; for Galicia this meant freedom of the press, the promise of constitutional government, and the resurfacing of Polish national demands. Such demands—the adoption of the Polish language in education and administration, the displacement of foreigners in the bureaucracy and army, the expansion of the powers of the Galician Sejm—were presented in an address to the governor, Franz Stadion, and, ultimately, to Emperor Ferdinand in Vienna. Some of these demands were as old as the Galician "Magna Charta" of 1790, and the Galician provincial framework remained the basis for constructing a Polish national agenda. In 1790, Polish proposals had been offered in a conservative spirit, but in 1848, with the promise of imminent constitutional government, the same concerns appeared more politically challenging, indeed revolutionary. At the same time, a Polish national committee, formed in Galicia, embraced a modern liberal program of civil liberties, equality before the law, more representative government, and the abolition of *robot* labor. In emigration, Adam Mickiewicz was preparing to form a Polish legion to fight against the Habsburgs in Italy, while even Fredro, the conservative "non-national" literary giant of Galicia, was sufficiently implicated in Polish political projects in 1848 to find himself later charged with treason against the Habsburgs.

If the Polish National Council [*Rada Narodowa*] was associated with potential Polish insurrection and therefore suspected of disloyalty, the unprecedented formation of a Supreme Ruthenian Council [*Holovna Rada Ruska*] was associated from its inception with the principle of Galician loyalty to the Habsburgs. The Ruthenian council was encouraged by the governor, Franz Stadion, as a counterweight to the Polish council, while the appearance of *Zoria Halytska* [*Galician Star*], the first Ruthenian political journal, was likewise encouraged by Police Chief Sacher-Masoch. Stadion proposed to make use of the Ruthenian committee as "a means of paralyzing the Polish influence and getting a backing for Austrian rule in Galicia," and there would even be satirical insinuations—possibly originating with the Viennese journalist Moritz Gottlieb Saphir—that the governor had "invented" the Ruthenians as a Habsburg political expedient.[63] In fact, the emergence of Ruthenian national awareness was related to the Habsburg invention and consolidation of Galicia itself. The province provided the political framework for articulating Ruthenian identity, while the ideology of Habsburg rule, with its fundamental rejection of Polish ascendancy, inevitably encouraged the general cultivation of cultural alternatives in Galicia.

The so-called Pillersdorf Constitution, issued by decree on 25 April, made the Habsburg state into a constitutional monarchy, while the April Laws in Hungary produced a model of Hungarian autonomy that Polish Galicians might have liked to emulate. Yet the Ruthenian political address, composed by Mykhailo Kuzemsky for presentation to Stadion in April 1848, countered Polish national claims by requesting a role for the Ruthenian language in education and administration in Galicia. The Ruthenian address not only affirmed unconditional loyalty to the dynasty but also appropriated the ideology of legitimacy in Galicia by affirming Ruthenian national entitlement in relation to the medieval principality of Halych. Just as the Habsburgs had invented Galicia in 1772 by discovering a medieval claim to Halych, the Ruthenians in 1848 made reference to Halych in order to identify themselves as the "original inhabitants" of Galicia, which constituted for them a "beloved homeland." It was therefore convenient for Stadion to affirm "the highest respect that I feel for the Ruthenian people, who distinguish themselves in faithful adherence to the emperor and the Austrian government." The Ruthenian council had no hesitation about addressing Emperor Ferdinand to declare "the unchanged feelings of fidelity and allegiance of the Galician Ruthenians to Your Highness and to the Exalted Imperial House," while Ferdinand replied with a "Manifesto to My Faithful Galicians."[64] The national claims of the Ruthenians in Galicia in 1848 were correlated with the provincial affirmation of a Galician identity. At the same time the Ruthenians began to rally around the cause of dividing Galicia into two separate Habsburg lands, a Polish Galicia in the west and a Ruthenian Galicia in the east.

The Ruthenian check on Polish national ambitions in Galicia was related to the broader Polish dilemma in 1848: how to approach the peasantry, which also included most Ruthenians. The bloody lesson of 1846 that the Galician peasantry did not regard itself as nationally Polish was reinforced by the affirmations of the Ruthenian Council in 1848, but it remained furthermore unforgettable that the clearly non-Ruthenian peasants around Tarnów had been the most active in the massacre of Polish nobles. There were therefore Polish proposals for the abolition of *robot* labor right from the start of the Revolution of 1848, in the hope of encouraging, or at least neutralizing, the peasantry for the national cause. Stadion, however, preempted this gambit with a Habsburg government proposal for abolition, to be enacted by Emperor Ferdinand for the welfare of the Galician peasants: "and this he does in a continuing expression of his promised favour for their loyalty shown in 1846."[65] The Habsburgs thus explicitly played upon the very recent memory of the massacres in Galicia.

Nowhere was that memory so vivid as it was in Tarnów, where the noble corpses and captives had been so dramatically delivered only two years before. On 27 March 1848, in the Tarnów cathedral, there was celebrated a ceremony of gratitude for the emperor's granting of freedom of the press and his promise of a constitution. According to the newspaper *Gazeta Tarnowska*, "Immediately after the service in the cathedral the public of Tarnów, around 2000 people, went to the cemetery where lay our fallen martyrs [*męczennicy nasi*] of February 1846; all those present knelt at the graves, and raised up fervent prayers to God."[66] As the celebration of political liberty in the cathedral was followed "immediately [*zaraz*]" by the ceremony in the cemetery, the freedoms of 1848 seemed to include, in Tarnów, the freedom to commemorate the Galician victims of 1846 as Polish national martyrs. Indeed, the new freedom of the press allowed for the freedom of *Gazeta Tarnowska* to designate the victims as martyrs, and report on the whole occasion at the cemetery.

This news was reported in the very first issue of *Gazeta Tarnowska*, dated 1 April, a journalistic manifestation of the revolutionary moment. Yet even in the giddy political excitement of that moment, the journal also articulated residual Galician anxieties. While greeting "a new era in national life," meaning Polish national life, *Gazeta Tarnowska* warned against excessive expectations: "A sad glance at the year 1846 and the division between the principal classes of public life . . . does not permit us to greet this first moment in heartfelt fraternal joy."[67] Fraternity would be a difficult ideal in the Galician context. In the next issue, one week later, on 8 April, *Gazeta Tarnowska* enumerated a list of anxious questions:

Is the promise of a constitution real? Is the dismissal of Prince Metternich from the helm of the government true? Why the arming of village people? Why the persistent propagation of disagreement between peasants and landowners? Why the preparation of the people for an uprising and for the horrors of the year 1846? Why does the administration look upon all this with such an indifferent eye?[68]

The initial question about the prospects for constitutional government, which might have been asked all over Europe in 1848, led immediately into a uniquely Galician agenda of anxieties. In Tarnów the unprecedented hopes of that celebrated springtime were relentlessly shadowed by the unprecedented terrors of the recent past. The revolutions of 1848 automatically provoked fear of the recurrence of the massacres of 1846.

On 15 May, the same day that *Zoria Halytska* published its first issue, articulating the Ruthenian political perspective, the government's abolition of the *robot* went into effect, causing the peasants to respond with grateful loyalty to the Habsburg dynasty. In May 1848, as Polish national aspirations were complicated by these political developments, Police Chief Sacher-Masoch was transferred to Prague, where he would continue to participate in the Habsburg official response to the Revolution of 1848. His twelve-year-old son was thus displaced from the province that he would always regard as his homeland, Galicia. Actually, the Galician revolution followed the Sacher-Masoch family to Prague, inasmuch as the Slavic Congress, meeting in Prague in early June, became the site for tense Polish-Ruthenian negotiations over the future of Galicia. A joint committee eventually reached the tentative agreement (never put into effect) to create a bilingual structure for administration and education in Galicia, though the delegates deferred the question of whether the province itself should be divided in two.[69] The congress was interrupted when Prince Alfred Windischgrätz arrived in Prague with the Habsburg army, marking the beginning of the triumph of the imperial reaction.

Wielopolski and Fredro made their cases against the Habsburgs in the aftermath of the massacres of 1846, and they must have felt vindicated in 1848 as Metternich was ignominiously dismissed, forced to flee from Vienna into foreign exile. Police Chief Sacher-Masoch retrospectively defended the conduct of the government in 1846 (including his own conduct as a government official), and he affirmed the legitimacy of Habsburg Galicia long after he himself had been removed from the province in 1848. Personal memories of Galician experience and historical constructions of Galician identity, as exemplified in the Sacher-Masoch writings, by both father and son, were inevitably tinged with sentiment and also with blood. The revolutions of

1848, so fundamental for politics and society all across Europe, were shadowed—perhaps overshadowed—in Galicia by the traumatic massacres of 1846. In 1901, when the Cracow dramatist Stanisław Wyspiański ushered in the age of Polish theatrical modernism with his Galician village drama *The Wedding (Wesele)*, he put the ghost of Jakub Szela on the stage, still able to inspire terror.[70] Szela and the events of 1846 would be indelibly remembered and inextricably involved in Galician visions and cultural anxieties right up until the threshold of the twentieth century.

CHAPTER FIVE

After the Revolution

The Rise of Czas and the Advent of Franz Joseph

Introduction: "Indivisible"

On 2 November 1848, a few days after the Habsburg army had retaken Vienna from the revolutionary democrats, the year of revolution also came to an end in Galicia as the army bombarded Lviv, defeated a Polish national uprising, and took control of the city. The very next day, on 3 November, there appeared in Cracow—two hundred miles to the west, on the other side of Galicia—the inaugural issue of a new daily newspaper: *Czas*, meaning "time."[1] Indeed, the destiny of *Czas* was all a matter of timing. Conceived in the context of revolution—of Habsburg constitutional upheaval, Polish national aspirations, and the unprecedented freedom of the press that followed upon the fall of Metternich—*Czas* would quickly become an unequivocally conservative newspaper, established at the conservative moment when absolutism and reaction, including renewed censorship, were making their historic comeback in Galicia. *Czas* would become the definitive organ of Galician conservatism during the age of Habsburg absolutism after 1848, the age of Galician autonomy after 1867, and the age of Polish independence after 1918, surviving continuously until the Nazi conquest of Poland in 1939. During the second half of the nineteenth century, *Czas* would articulate and advocate a Galician Polish identity in which the concerns of the Galician province [*kraj*] would subtly absorb and perhaps even subordinate those of the Polish fatherland [*ojczyzna*].

No less important for Galician identity in the second half of the nineteenth century was the Habsburg emperor Franz Joseph, who came to the throne at the age of eighteen on 2 December 1848, following the abdication of Ferdinand, his uncle. Franz Joseph maintained among his titles that of the Kingdom of Galicia and Lodomeria, up until his death in 1916, which preceded by only two years the abolition of Galicia itself in 1918 along with the Habsburg monarchy. His inaugural manifesto of 2 December paid lip service to "liberty" and looked toward "a salutary transformation and rejuvenation of the monarchy as a whole." At the same time he declared himself "determined to maintain the splendor of the crown undimmed and the monarchy as a whole undiminished, but ready to share our rights with the representatives of our peoples." He hoped to succeed "in uniting all the regions and races of the monarchy in one great state."[2] The monarchy would, in fact, undergo multiple constitutional adaptations over the course of the next generation, and the initial yoking of Galicia to Vienna under centralized absolutism in the 1850s would give way to the Galician provincial autonomy that followed from the pivotal Austro-Hungarian compromise of 1867. The transformation of the monarchy in 1867 created the so-called special position of Galicia within the monarchy, and thus, almost a full century after the invention of Galicia in the partition of 1772, would provide the province with the most definitive validation of its own historical existence.

In the inaugural issue of 3 November, *Czas* declared, in the spirit of Polish nationalism, that "the only goal for us is to work toward the recovery of a free and independent fatherland [*ojczyzna*]." Yet the moment for such aspirations was already passing, and on 9 November the newspaper observed that "Lwów and the whole of our country [*kraj nasz*] has encountered terrible misfortune." Galicia—our country—was occupied by the Habsburg army under a state of siege.[3] The revolutionary moment of *Czas* had proved to be entirely ephemeral, and on 30 November the newspaper made one last sympathetic allusion to Poland's national fate, by recalling the national uprising of 30 November 1830, eighteen years before, "a day of dear memory" that brought to mind thoughts of "martyrdom" and "Golgotha."[4] Such was the newspaper's farewell to Polish Romanticism and the Revolution of 1848, and when Franz Joseph assumed the throne on 2 December, *Czas* stood ready to salute him in the spirit of postrevolutionary conservatism.

"To change the ruler on the throne is in any event a very solemn political occurrence, and all the more so at a moment of social dissolution and political transformation like the present," wrote *Czas*, observing the monarchical succession on 7 December 1848. "Never indeed has a young monarch entered upon a more difficult path than Franz Joseph." *Czas* brought its particular Galician perspective to bear upon the difficulties of 1848 by recalling the disasters of 1846. "The administrative-political organism, as in Galicia in 1846, so today in all of Austria," wrote *Czas*, "seeks a point of support in the masses—but that is a two-edged sword." The violent events of 1846 meant that Galicians might claim to possess some experience of benefit to the monarchy as a whole and to the young monarch in particular. In 1848, the same year that Karl Marx declared that a specter was haunting Europe, the specter of communism, Galicia was haunted by its own particular ghosts, and *Czas* warned Franz Joseph against "the spirit of anarchy."[5]

On 9 December, one week into the reign of Franz Joseph, *Czas* addressed the issue of the Ruthenians in Galicia: "We return to the consideration of our Ruthenian brothers." This affirmation of brotherhood was a direct response to the Ruthenian denial of kinship over the course of the revolutionary year, the Ruthenian affirmation of distinctive national identity through their own national council, Holovna Rada Ruska, and the reiterated Ruthenian proposals for the division of Galicia into two separate entities, east and west, Ruthenian and Polish. The Slavic Congress in Prague in June 1848 became the site for discussing this issue of provincial partition. There was tentative conciliation between Poles and Ruthenians in Prague, an agreement in principle on Ruthenian political, religious, and linguistic rights in Galicia. By July, however, there were petitions for partition circulating in eastern Galicia, in solicitation of peasant signatures, for submission to the Habsburg government in Vienna; it was estimated that two hundred thousand signatures were ultimately collected. The Ruthenian council addressed itself formally to the Austrian government on 28 October, advocating the partition of Galicia and denouncing the Polish oppression of Ruthenians in the province. "The partition of Galicia is a vital issue for the Ruthenians," declared the council. "Only in this way can the country be freed from the terrorism under which it now groans and the Ruthenians be permitted freely to develop their nationality." The Poles were further stigmatized as "revolutionaries," determined to obtain the restoration of Polish independence, and this was contrasted with Galician Ruthenian loyalty to the Habsburg emperor. The Ruthenians even had an audience with Emperor Ferdinand on 6 November, a month before his abdication on 2 December.[6]

Czas, on 9 December, addressed the issue of "our Ruthenian brothers" at a moment when all Galicians were deeply apprehensive about how the new teenage emperor would view the province. Acknowledging "the antagonism today dividing the Polish and Ruthenian population of Galicia," *Czas* suggested that Russian insinuations had stimulated Ruthenian separatism. *Czas* looked hopefully toward fraternal coexistence between Poles and Ruthenians: "Let the Ruthenian nationality develop in Galicia according to its own force and nature; not in antagonism, but in alliance, hand in hand, let us go forward together toward a better future."[7] In 1848 some Poles may have dreamed of Polish independence, but, at the end of the year, as the revolution foundered, *Czas* spoke for those who were rediscovering the importance of Galicia. In January 1849 the Constitutional Committee of the Reichstag, having moved from Vienna to Kremsier in Moravia, debated the future of the Habsburg monarchy; the Polish delegate, Florian Ziemiałkowski, supported a federal structure based on the existing crownlands, including Galicia, while the Ruthenian delegate, the Uniate bishop Hryhorii Iakhymovych, advocated the division of Galicia. Ziemiałkowski, in fact, denied the existence of the Ruthenians as a separate nation—"an artificial nation, invented last year," invented by Franz Stadion in 1848 as a counterweight to Polish national demands. The division of Galicia was rejected at Kremsier, though the work of the Constitutional Committee would anyway be preempted by the end of the revolution.[8]

Menaced by the Ruthenian threat of partition, the integrity of Galicia—an artificial province, invented in the last century—became the crucial object of Polish political attentions. Galicia now appeared not as a Habsburg artifice but as a native land worth fighting for in its historically defined entirety. The word "partition" was not a word that Poles could contemplate lightly. Mickiewicz, in *Pan Tadeusz*, sang: "O Lithuania! you are like health/ How much to be valued one only knows/ When you have been lost." Galicia was not yet lost in January 1849, but, facing the demand for partition, Polish Galicians began to value it as never before: O Galicia!

"What is to be done?" asked *Czas* on 13 January 1849, at the beginning of the new year that inaugurated the postrevolutionary era. "This is the question that everyone is asking in Galicia: what is to be done?" The article was entitled "About Galicia," and *Czas* posed its question as a provincial problem. Starting from the principle that "suffering, whether individual or national, flows undoubtedly in significant part from one's own mistakes," *Czas* then pursued an analysis that was neither individual nor national, but strictly provincial.

> We will not undertake a review of our national history in order to demonstrate the mistakes that led to ruin . . . but we will look more closely into our own times, into the events that have notably put Galicia in the condition in which it presently finds itself. The greatest disasters and misfortunes fell upon us after the year 1846. Who was the author? What was the reason?[9]

While noting that some responsibility might be attributed "to those benevolently [*łaskawie*] ruling over us"—the Habsburg government—*Czas* nevertheless insisted that Galicians had to accept some responsibility themselves. The political culprit could be identified in a single word:

> The reason for the ever renewed disasters of Poland and Galicia is the desire to recover independence [*niepodległość*]. Independence! the freedom of the nation! sacred slogan, sublime purpose, the everlasting aim of higher souls; who would dare to curse such sanctity?[10]

Czas itself, in its inaugural issue of 3 November 1848, had advocated the pursuit of "the recovery of a free and independent fatherland." Now, two months later, in the altered context of reaction, *Czas* dared to renounce the ideal of Polish independence—in favor of Galician provincial interests. The national was to be sacrificed to the provincial, Poland to Galicia, with the wishful, but far from self-evident, supposition that both might ultimately benefit. At the bottom of the front page, the newspaper reported on the discovery of gold in California and the feverish intensity of the California gold rush; the lead article, however, insisted on the political acceptance of Galicia as it was, and the renunciation of whimsical ambitions, the fool's gold of independence.[11]

On 5 March, *Czas* reported on the religious service in Cracow, in the Mariacki Church, for the soul of Wacław Zaleski, the recently deceased governor of Galicia. Ceremonious mourning, like ceremonious celebration, was to become one of the hallmarks of Galician Cracow, and the solemn commemoration of a Galician governor was in itself an affirmation of provincial identity. In this case the occasion appeared particularly significant for Galicia at a pivotal moment in Habsburg history. Zaleski had been the very first Polish governor of Galicia: "Through the course of eighty years when Galicia was under the Austrian scepter, only several Poles entered the higher administration, and none reached the governorship except for W. Zaleski alone."[12] When Franz Stadion was recalled from Lviv to Vienna in the midst of revolution in 1848, Zaleski was named to replace him as governor of Galicia, in part as a gesture to the Poles of the province, who were demanding their national rights. His term of service would be no more than a token matter of months, cut short by his premature death, though he had the opportunity to exercise influence in Vienna against the Ruthenian campaign for the partition of Galicia. The governor's affirmation of loyalty to the young emperor in December emphasized the importance of Galicia's "indivisible" integrity.[13]

Czas emphasized that the late Zaleski had advocated the cultural community of Poles and Ruthenians in Galicia. For he was none other than the very same "Wacław z Oleska" who had published in 1833 his collection of *Polish and Ruthenian Songs of the Galician People*. The pan-Galician nature of that collection served as an affirmation of provincial community, and Zaleski's literary career thus evoked a specifically Galician culture of the early nineteenth century. "His childhood years went by amidst the Ruthenian people, full of poetic longing," wrote *Czas*, "and his childish body sucked in almost with its milk that poetic element." This was the very same language that Sacher-Masoch used to describe his own infant relation to Ruthenian folk songs,

Cracow, with the Mariacki Church. Drawing by Włodzimierz Tetmajer, from Bolesław Limanowski, *Galicya przedstawiona słowem i ołówkiem* (Warsaw: Wydawnictwo Przeglądu Tygodniowego, 1892).

through his Ruthenian wet nurse, nourishing his Galician identity.[14] Zaleski's whole career could be summed up as an argument for the unity and coherence of the province, and his progress from the circles of Galician culture to the very apex of Galician politics followed a persuasively provincial logic.

His successor in 1849, Agenor Gołuchowski, would dominate the political life of the province for the next generation, remaining influential until his death in 1875. Gołuchowski, in 1851, welcomed Franz Joseph to Galicia, and later, in the 1860s, presided over the achievement of Galician autonomy within the Habsburg monarchy. *Czas* in the 1850s reaffirmed Galicia's relation to the dynasty in the context of the restoration of absolutism, and then in the 1860s celebrated autonomy as the most viable alternative to the self-destructive ambition of Polish independence. Over the course of the post-revolutionary generation *Czas* articulated a Galician ideology of provincial unity and integrity, artfully synthesizing Polish and Galician political concerns in the forging of a new Galician identity. That identity was also shaped by new perspectives on Polish and Galician history, emerging in the postrevolutionary decades with such historians as Walerian Kalinka and Józef Szujski, eventually leading to the consolidation of the revisionist Cracow historical school.

Cracow itself found a new urban identity through its leading role in forming a Polish Galician synthesis. The royal capital of Poland until the sixteenth century, Cracow then ceded its status as capital to Warsaw and played a secondary urban role. Joined to Galicia by the third partition of 1795, Cracow was separated from it again after the Congress of Vienna and was permitted to maintain a fragile urban autonomy. When Cracow was compelled to reunite with Galicia after 1846, the city seemed fated again to play a secondary role, for Lviv was emphatically the Galician capital. Yet, by drawing upon its Polish cultural resources—especially the Jagiellonian University—Cracow reinvented itself as the intellectual center of Polish Galician life and the ideological crucible of Polish Galician identity. Gołuchowski in Lviv as provincial statesman and *Czas* in Cracow as provincial organ of public opinion would be deeply implicated in the landmark Galician declaration of loyalty to Franz Joseph in 1866, in the aftermath of the Austro-Prussian War: "We stand with you, Your Majesty, and we wish to stand with you." The provincial autonomy of Galicia was achieved politically after 1866, but the meaning of "Galicia" had already been negotiated intellectually over the course of the preceding decades.

"In the Country through the Country"

In November 1848, at its founding, *Czas* had declared its "only goal" to be "the recovery of a free and independent fatherland." The fatherland [*ojczyzna*] was not named, because everyone knew that it could only be Poland. On 22 March 1849, *Czas*, having already renounced the goal of independence, articulated a brand new slogan of principle and practice: "In the country through the country [*w kraju przez kraj*], we acknowledge for us as the only true and strong activities, the country as the only natural field for us." The country was not named, because everyone knew that it could only be Galicia, no longer an artificial entity but the "natural field" for the political efforts of Galicians. On 31 March, *Czas* reported that there were Poles fighting in revolutionary armies all over Europe, especially against the Habsburgs in Italy. The newspaper, however, declared that "our stated opinion is unchanging: in the country, to be active on the path of organic work, for the country, to profit from the new laws."[15] The ideology of "organic work" emerged in Prussian Poland in the 1840s, with reference to the envisioned transformation and amelioration of a whole society. It would become the slogan of positivism throughout the Polish lands during the second half of the nineteenth century, cited as the only pragmatic alternative to doomed Romantic insurrections.[16] In 1849, when *Czas* advocated "organic work" on behalf of "the country," the clear implication was that Galicia itself constituted an indivisibly organic whole, that its social problems might be ameliorated within the Habsburg imperial framework.

In 1849 the organic coherence of Galicia was affirmed with the publication of Hipolit Stupnicki's *Galicia*, a "topographical-geographical-historical" account of the province, including a map; the book was first published in Polish in Lviv under the auspices of the Ossolineum, then republished in German in 1853, and finally reissued in a second Polish edition in 1869. Discussing geography, Stupnicki found the opportunity to express patriotic admiration for the province: "The chief character of the Galician mountains is the wild romantic, dark primeval forests, and rough stone formations alternating with magical valleys which can compete for beauty with any valleys on earth." Galicia was thus supposed to possess a natural and picturesque geographical coherence. "Nature has formed Galicia to be a grain-growing country," observed Stupnicki in 1849, three-quarters of a century after the partitions of Poland had formed Galicia to be an Austrian province in 1772.[17] Just as the province was the "natural field" for politics, according to *Czas*, so it could also be viewed as a natural ecological domain, and, following the natural history of Aleksander Zawadzki, Stupnicki counted the number of species of flora and fauna that inhabited the province, regretting that he could not precisely count the number of insect species.

In the same spirit, Stupnicki also enumerated the ethnographic categories: "No land of the Austrian monarchy is inhabited by such different peoples as Galicia. Poles, Ruthenians, Germans, Armenians, Jews, Moldavians, Hungarians, Gypsies . . ." He also mentioned Hutsuls, the Carpathian Ruthenian mountaineers, and Karaites, the heretical Jews who were guided only by the Bible and rejected the Talmud along with rabbinical Judaism. In spite of such heterogeneity, it was possible to make some human generalizations across the province, and Stupnicki remarked that "the customs of the Galician peasantry," though variable, were "collectively still very coarse." This coarseness extended to feasting, drinking, and the singing of songs. Thus, the collective character of the ethnographically diverse peoples was marked by a coarseness that also corresponded to the provincial geography of wild, primeval forests. The Krakowiak villagers and the Góral mountaineers, the protagonists of Bogusławski's Polish national opera in the 1790s, now appeared in Stupnicki as Galician ethnographic types: the Krakowiak with "great suppleness and grace in body movements," and a four-cornered crimson cap; the Góral a "strongly built, physically agile, inventive, creative, often cunning and crafty breed," in a long collarless shirt.[18] Galician history, according to Stupnicki, could be divided into three periods: after 1772, the Austrian period; from 1340 to 1772, the Polish period; and from 981 to 1340, a medieval period of Ruthenian and Hungarian princes. Thus Galicia was endowed not only with natural coherence but also with historical continuity, retrospectively antedating the Austrian annexation.

Czas, on 3 October 1849, greeted Stupnicki's *Galicia* with interest—"a book with such a promising title"—but pedantically regretted that there were too many mistakes, both historical and topographical. "The geography of our province is something very interesting," wrote *Czas*, "very necessary for educating young people," for providing them with a "national education [*narodowe kształcenie*]."[19] Yet, the sort of "national education" that might be provided by a book with such a promising provincial title—*Galicia*—was unconventionally national at best, and might be more plausibly interpreted as "non-national," in the spirit of Goszczyński's assault on Fredro in 1835. *Czas*, however, had already proclaimed "country" to be the fundamental domain of its journalistic mission, so that provincial topography, geography, and history might provide the new contours for a national education with mingled Galician and Polish aspects.

In autumn 1849, *Czas* reported on the death of Chopin on 17 October in Paris: "Chopin is dead! The musical world has lost its most poetic master; we have lost no small share of our living national glory. Almost every day we become more impoverished." The passing of the Romantic generation meant the dimming of national glory, which was therefore naturally displaced by a different sort of national project, the organic work of provincial culture. Chopin himself, in *Czas*'s obituary tribute, scarcely seemed to be the composer of a revolutionary or military polonaise: "Chopin did not discard his

"Krakowiak" peasant from the region around Cracow. Stupnicki cited the Krakowiak for his "great suppleness and grace in body movements" in the 1850s. The Krakowiak was also featured in Bogusławski's *Krakowiacy and Górale* in the 1790s. From Julius Jandaurek, *Das Königreich Galizien und Lodomerien* (Vienna: Karl Graeser, 1884).

heated love for his poor orphaned Poland; amidst the adoration of all Paris, amidst everything to which vanity and the love of glory could aspire, he never stopped grieving and longing for that poor land, for that northern air and sky, and for those village songs which lulled him to sleep in his childhood."[20] Curiously, the obituary of Chopin seemed to converge with the obituary of Zaleski, earlier in 1849, harkening back to a childhood surrounded by folk songs. Chopin became a kind of honorary Galician, longing for the organic satisfactions of the postrevolutionary era that was only just commencing at the time of his death.

By the following spring of 1850, *Czas* was attending to the less poetic, less romantic, less nationally Polish project of "The Railway in Galicia." *Czas* recognized the revolution in transport and communications, noting that "today in Cracow with the help of the railway we are nearer to Paris and London, from which we have letters and newspapers in four or five days, than we were, not so many years ago, to Warsaw, Vienna, or even Lwów."[21] The western horizon may have seemed to come closer to Cracow, but Galicia, as a whole, was not yet integrated into modern European transport.

> Steam communication in the western direction, as we see, responds lavishly to all private and public requirements. Why can we not say this about the eastern direction? Why is our Galicia, so far, excluded from that chain of railways which embraces all of Europe? . . . To this day communication in Galicia remains in the state of nature.[22]

Backwardness was governed by laws of relativity, and, in an age of steam progress in transportation all over Europe, Galicia's "state of nature" was not just an absolute technological minimum, a fixed point of economic backwardness, but a relatively receding condition of underdevelopment. Galicia was behind, and falling further behind, and that was all the more problematic inasmuch as an underdeveloped economy had particular need of modern transport. "Galicia is an exclusively agricultural country," observed *Czas*—and the province therefore needed to export agricultural products, and import manufactured goods.[23] Stupnicki might seek to evoke the picturesque charm of primeval forests—unspoiled by railway tracks—but *Czas* recognized that the state of nature was not an economically advantageous environment.

Looking back to an earlier era of Galician history, *Czas* recalled that in 1842 the Sejm had considered the importance of railway development, encouraged by such men as Prince Leon Sapieha. In fact, Sapieha and Fredro had met with Salomon Rothschild in Vienna to lobby for a railway connection to Lviv. The revolutions of 1846 and 1848 had derailed such economic concerns, but in 1850, in the postrevolutionary era, *Czas* was ready to put them back on track. Nevertheless, the railway connection between Cracow and Lviv—integrating Galicia, west and east, as one unitary province—would not be completed until 1861.

In October 1850, *Czas* welcomed to Galicia the new *namiestnik*, the viceroy or governor, Agenor Gołuchowski.

> The long and impatiently awaited return of His Excellency the *namiestnik* of the crownland took place the day before yesterday. He was greeted joyously, because

in him may be seen the announcement of the nearing moment when our country [*nasz kraj*] will pass from its hitherto provisional condition into a provincial government organized in the spirit of the constitution of March 4 . . . .[24]

The constitution of 4 March 1849 codified the restoration of Habsburg absolutism under Franz Joseph, and was written under the guidance of Franz Stadion after he was recalled from Galicia and became the minister of the interior in Vienna. It was a strongly centralizing constitution, giving great power to the emperor in Vienna, but, from a Galician point of view, it had the virtue of preserving the structure of the monarchy as an assemblage of crownlands, with their respective diets, including the Galician Sejm.[25]

Gołuchowski, born in Galicia at the moment of Napoleonic upheaval in 1812, would come to define what it meant to be Galician over the course of his lifetime. He was just the right age to join the insurrection in Russian Poland in 1830—but he did not. Instead he entered Habsburg governmental service in the 1830s and rose through the bureaucracy in Galicia. As mayor of Lviv in 1848 he worked closely with Stadion, and then with Zaleski, before succeeding them as governor in 1849. Historian Józef Buszko has summed up Gołuchowski's career at that time: "In a word, he moved together with the government against the revolution and his own society." In fact, Gołuchowski was negotiating the ambiguous relation between Polish and Galician interests and identities at this turning point in the history of the Habsburg monarchy. According to Buszko, "In his frequent journeys to Vienna he represented to the emperor that the Polish *szlachta* could become in Galicia a mainstay of the throne against revolutionary and separatist tendencies."[26] Winning the confidence of the young emperor, and moving easily between Vienna and Lviv, Gołuchowski could be welcomed "joyously" home to Galicia, because his every journey, back and forth, further consolidated the persevering political reality of the province in the postrevolutionary era.

On 25 October 1850, *Czas* reported on Gołuchowski's triumphal progress through Galicia to Lviv:

> The much heralded arrival of the *namiestnik* was an exceptionally important event for Galicia: every reasonable and unreasonable hope, every great and small ambition, awaited his arrival with the greatest intensity. He was greeted everywhere with cries of joy, received with cannon salutes, and every little town in which His Excellency stopped offered him serenades and torchlight processions. Lwów however distinguished itself among all others. Representatives of the town institutes, the clergy, and the guilds appeared corporatively before the palace of the *namiestnik*, who gave a speech of gratitude to them from the balcony, assuring them that Galicia lay as close to the heart of His Majesty as any other province, and Lwów as much as any other loyal town. The banner which is only raised for the arrival of the emperor was waving for three days at the town hall as a sign of joy.[27]

Gołuchowski thus claimed to construct—almost to constitute in his vice-regal person—the most intimate reciprocal relations between Galicia and Franz Joseph. If the map of Galicia was engraved on the heart of the emperor, then its provincial integrity was certainly secure. Although the banner reserved for the emperor was already waving for Gołuchowski, *Czas*'s correspondent in Lviv reported that Franz Joseph himself was expected to visit in person in May of the following year, and that preparations were already under way: "The theater here, which in spite of a vast and beautiful hall is very ugly and very badly lit, is supposed to be newly restored for that ceremonial occasion." The arrival of Gołuchowski was thus a sort of ceremonial rehearsal for the even more anticipated advent of Franz Joseph himself.[28] At the same time, Gołuchowski's importance in Vienna would guarantee that Galicia received close consideration in the gradually evolving postrevolutionary Habsburg order.

"The state constitution of 4 March 1849, in paragraph one, inscribed [*wpisała*] the Kingdom of Galicia and Lodomeria, and the Duchies of Auschwitz and Zator, and the Grand Duchy of Cracow in the register of the crownlands of the hereditary constitutional Austrian monarchy," announced *Czas* on the front page on 11 November 1850. In 1772, when Galicia was incorporated into the monarchy, Maria Theresa herself had doubts about the legitimacy of the annexation; yet now, in 1850, the very same political circumstance, constitutionally reaffirmed, was being hailed by *Czas* as an important milestone. Beyond the obligatory dynastic loyalism implicit in this perspective, *Czas* had additional motivation for approving of Galicia's constitutional inscription in the register of Habsburg hereditary territories. The constitution, which was further clarified by separate patents for each of the crownlands, guaranteed "autonomy [*samoistność*]" to each of the "individual lands."[29] While provincial political autonomy might have seemed merely nominal in a constitution aimed at the restoration of centralized imperial absolutism, *Czas* was nevertheless interested in the fact that the crownlands were "individual," and therefore "autonomous" from one another, their integrity implicit in the constitution. If Galicia was inscribed as a hereditary crownland, governed by an imperially designated viceroy, then it was possible to argue that any partition of the province was unconstitutional.

"We have declared constantly and openly that we do not think of denying whatever right of development to whatever nationality," wrote *Czas*, "that indeed we judge that that may be sufficiently achieved without partition of the country; and as for partition we consider it to be harmful, weakening the strength of the country."[30] Such protests were necessary precisely because—especially in an age of new and revised constitutions—the partition of Galicia had been both widely advocated in the province and seriously considered in Vienna. Indeed, the postrevolutionary reinscription of the Habsburg possessions made Bukovina into a separate crownland, though it had been casually associated with Galicia ever since its annexation from Moldavia in 1775, coincidentally three years after the annexation of adjoining Galicia from Poland in 1772. Galicia itself, even after 1848, still required a patchwork assortment of titular designations—Galicia, Lodomeria, Auschwitz, Zator, Cracow—in order to preserve the pretense of historic claims that covered the entire territory. Yet, from the conservative Polish perspective of *Czas*, the Habsburg dynastic and constitutional claim to Galicia—to the integrity of Galicia's provincial existence—legitimated a Galician political identity and a programmatic resistance to provincial partition.

On 2 January 1851, greeting the new year, *Czas* reflected on the revolutions of the recent past, and looked toward the postrevolutionary political future. The new year was scheduled to include a visit to Galicia by the emperor himself, and *Czas* proposed a political path that emphasized provincial pragmatism instead of the frustrated national ideals of 1848. "We are thinking about ourselves," wrote *Czas*, in a spirit of frank political self-interest, "and to profit from the opportunities [*korzystać z sposobności*] that in any event have been given to us as a consequence of the events of 1848." The lessons to be learned, however, were specifically Galician lessons, and derived from a pair of revolutionary dates that, taken together, were relevant only to Galicia:

> In the years 1846 and 1848 something unprecedented occurred; in one nation, on one territory, the mass of the people rose up generally against those who not only raised the national standard but spoke in the supposed interest of that people. Neither the ideal of the past nor the charm of freedom nor material profits managed to attract the people. Why? Because the masses have an instinct of common sense, which shows them what is possible, and when—and they have a feeling that tells them who is worthy to lead them.[31]

While other nations in Europe might feel that reactionary monarchs had cheated them out of their revolutionary hopes in 1848, the Galicians had the additional lessons of 1846 to remind them that the people themselves—the masses—could play a violently decisive and ultimately counter-revolutionary role.

At New Year's 1851, *Czas* rejected the "loud patriotism" of Polish national advocates and proposed instead a conservative vision of reconciliation between the upper and lower classes, favoring the common sense of the latter:

> In order to join with the nation it is not enough to speak constitutionally about rights, but it is necessary to understand the instincts of the people, and the instincts of our people are orderly and hierarchical: it is therefore necessary to

assume a position of leadership in the community, in the various branches of administrative provincial service. The new organization of the province offers an opportunity for this . . . .[32]

According to *Czas*, the postrevolutionary politics of Galicia had to be specifically Galician, based on the provincial pragmatism of pursuing political opportunities in the Galician administration, according to the constitutional framework of the Habsburg monarchy: "In the country through the country." To accept the popular instincts for order and hierarchy meant accepting Galicia within the political context of Habsburg hierarchical rule. "We are thinking about the country [*myślimy o kraju*], so let us write for the country [*piszymy dla kraju*]," wrote *Czas* the next day, affirming its own Galician journalistic identity at the beginning of the new year.[33]

"Our Native Country"

In June 1851, Gołuchowski was traveling from Lviv to Vienna, and *Czas* reported on his passage through Cracow, where "his presence, anticipated with desire, was too short to allow the opportunity to demonstrate the honor with which the inhabitants of Cracow, expecting a longer stay, intended to greet him." The Galician identity of *Czas* reflected, in part, the political marginalization of Cracow itself, now a point of transit in the crucial Galician connection between Lviv and Vienna. *Czas* nevertheless expressed warm Galician sentiments in favor of Gołuchowski: "to which he has the undeniable right, on account of the honorable confidence of His Majesty the monarch, as well as his dedication to the good of our province."[34]

On 27 June, *Czas* reflected on the even more anticipated visit of the emperor himself, who had not come to Galicia in May, as initially expected, and whose date of arrival remained uncertain: "His Majesty is coming. His Majesty is not coming." Such were supposedly the contradictory exchanges of conversation in the Rynek, the Market Square of Cracow. On the road from Cracow to Lviv smaller towns were already involved in "the preparation of triumphal arches, illuminations, orations." In Lviv itself the arrival of the imperial guest was certain to call forth, "as if from underground, the most elegant coaches, the most beautiful teams of horses, and abundantly gold-braided liveries," as well as fashionable imported evening clothes for formal imperial occasions. *Czas* regretted that Cracow was too poor to rival Lviv in urban adornments.

How then to come forward here and seize the eye of His Majesty with some novel sight? In general, considering the contemporary physiognomy of Cracow, if we look over the preparations for the public festivities, it is possible to discern on people's faces an expression of anticipation, the approaching fulfillment of sweet hopes. There is no one who does not prophesy to himself a better future.[35]

What might catch the eye of the emperor was precisely that facial expression which *Czas* represented as the typical physiognomy of provincial politics, the characteristic Galician anticipation of the hierarchical Habsburg gaze.

In July, *Czas* inaugurated a series of "Letters from Galicia," in which readers were invited to become better acquainted with their own country, thus emphasizing the new importance of the provincial homeland. "One might dare to say that we know more about foreign lands than our native country [*kraj rodzinny*]," wrote *Czas*. As the journalist set about exploring a corner of the Carpathians, he deplored the lack of guidance in the published literature, particularly despising Stupnicki's recent effort as "drowning in errors." Reporting from Szczyrzyc, *Czas* described old castles and cloisters that might be considered points of provincial pride, and gave medieval historical annotations that long antedated the creation of Galicia itself. The cloister garden at Szczyrzyc was celebrated as the greatest "in the country [*w kraju*]."[36] In these "Letters from Galicia" (which were also, self-evidently, letters to Galicia and about Galicia), the province was represented as the "native country" of its inhabitants.

In October, after protracted anticipation, the emperor finally made his visit to Galicia and stayed for three weeks. *Czas*, on 13 October, reported on the imperial presence in Cracow, and the "joyful cries" of the Cracovians who lined the streets for the grand procession. In the Jewish suburb of Kazimierz representatives of the community "awaited the monarch with the Torah, according to custom." In Cracow military bands played Haydn's Austrian anthem, and the emperor was solemnly received in the Mariacki Church, which, in the touristic spirit of "Letters from Galicia," was described as "the most beautiful monument of Gothic architecture in this country [*w tym kraju*]." By night the great Renaissance Cloth Hall—the Sukiennice—"sparkled with multi-colored lights."[37]

The Cracow visit became a municipal celebration, while also contributing to the larger provincial celebration of Franz Joseph. He was in Cracow on 11 and 12 October, but on the thirteenth he was already visiting the salt mines at Wieliczka and setting out to cross Galicia on the road to Lviv. Historian Daniel Unowsky has observed that the imperial visit to Galicia of 1851 was received critically by some Polish nobles, including those who still harbored bitter national feelings from 1848 and those who merely felt they had been snubbed by exclusion from gala events. Gołuchowski himself resented the fact that during the visit Habsburg military authorities received precedence over his own civilian administration. Thousands of Galician peasants, how-

Emperor Franz Joseph on horseback in 1849. He came to the throne in December 1848, at the age of eighteen, and visited Galicia in 1851. From the author's collection.

ever, lined the route of the voyage to see the emperor pass by, and Franz Joseph received more than three thousand petitions for imperial assistance from his Galician subjects.[38] With a keen commitment to Galicia as a historic Habsburg crownland, at the moment of Franz Joseph's visit in 1851, *Czas* even reminisced about the visit to Galicia of Joseph II in 1773.[39]

In Tarnów, between Cracow and Lviv, the twenty-one-year-old emperor wrote to his mother on 12 October to express satisfaction at the ringing of church bells, the firing of cannon salutes, the keys to the city, "school children, guilds with their banners, Jews with rabbis carrying the Torah, clergy in pontifical attire at the cathedral . . . much shouting, especially the Jews, who made an unbelievable spectacle."[40] For the emperor, as for any visitor to Galicia, the dramatic presence of Jews—far more populous than in any other Habsburg province—was one of the most notable features of the Galician landscape. In Franz Joseph's letters from Galicia in 1851, as in Metternich's letters in 1823, the Galician Jews clearly made an impression on the Viennese visitor. For the Jews of Galicia the year 1851 also marked the end of an episode of violent conflict between the enlightened, reforming movement of the Haskalah and the traditionally religious Orthodox community: the Maskilim and the Mitnaggedim, both of which were also opposed to the mystical piety of the Hasidim. The enlightened Jews, who favored the German language and modern customs, had received encouragement from the Habsburg government since the age of Joseph, and achieved a triumph in 1844 when Rabbi Abraham Kohn was named to the leading position in the Great Synagogue of Lviv. In September 1848, however, in the middle of the revolutionary year, Kohn was murdered by his Orthodox opponents, who allegedly had someone slip arsenic into the Kohn family's soup. Historian Michael Stanislawski has analyzed how this murder reflected characteristic tensions within Galician Judaism. In 1851, the year of the emperor's voyage, the Supreme Court in Vienna rejected the widow's appeal against the Orthodox leaders suspected of complicity in the murder.[41] *Czas* noted none of these recent conflicts when representing the Jews as party to the general and unified Galician enthusiasm for Franz Joseph in 1851.

The leading figure in the conservative editorial direction of *Czas* during these early years of publication was Paweł Popiel, and another editorial participant was the young Walerian Kalinka, only twenty-five in 1851 and destined to become one of the founding fathers of the Cracow historical school. Kalinka had been involved in the disastrous Polish national insurrection in 1846, but he wrote as a Galician conservative when he joined *Czas* in 1849. In the postrevolutionary political climate Kalinka himself became the subject of investigation by the Austrian police, and he immigrated to Paris in 1852. There he dedicated himself to composing his first major historical work, *Galicia and Cracow under Austrian Rule*, published in 1853.[42] It was an indictment of Austrian rule in Galicia, but, at the same time, a work that fully accepted the authenticity and significance of Galicia as a subject of historical study and domain of political engagement. Born in 1826, educated in autonomous

Cracow, Kalinka regretted the limited educational opportunities available to "Galician youth," his own contemporaries.

> The Austrian government, which is accurately called a police state, exerted its watchfulness over every manifestation of public life and smothered them in embryo. Citizens under suspicion and surveillance closed themselves off in social circles necessary for amusement, but the needs of constant endurance, assistance, support, in a word, solidarity of interest, could not develop in them. That was and is the great misfortune of Galicia.[43]

Kalinka noted that Galicia—both in the Metternich era and, again, after the revolution—could not really develop a Galician civil society, a Galician public sphere.

His criticism of Austria, however, did not mean that Kalinka was nostalgic for Poland before the partitions. In fact, he would take the lead among Polish historians in reconsidering the whole history of Poland and the downfall of the Commonwealth. Rejecting the Romantic cult of Poland's victimization, Kalinka and the Cracow school would accept the partitions as historically explicable events, whose causes lay partly within Polish political and social life. The natural corollary of this historical revisionism was the implicit acceptance of Galicia as a legitimate subject for historians. Similarly, for *Czas*, Galicia was a meaningful sphere of political journalism: "in the country through the country."

Even as *Czas* articulated its commitment to Galicia after the revolution, Fredro, a dedicated Galician during the Metternich era, was now finding it difficult to sustain his Habsburg Galician identity. After playing a conservative role in the Galician Sejm in the early 1840s, Fredro participated in the Polish revolutionary movement of 1848, joining the National Council and the National Guard, while his son Jan, age nineteen in 1848, played an active military role fighting against the Habsburgs and for the revolution in Hungary. In fact, Jan in 1848 was the same age that his father had been when he fought for Napoleon in Russia in 1812. In the postrevolutionary years father and son were able to see each other in Paris, though Fredro, unlike his son, supposed that he could freely and safely return to Galicia when he wished. In 1852, however, the great dramatist was charged with treason against the Habsburgs on account of his revolutionary role in 1848, and especially for a speech denouncing the Austrian bureaucracy. He was acquitted of the charge in 1854 but hesitated to resume his residence and identity as a Galician in the aftermath of such political unpleasantness. Fredro was in Lviv in December 1855 but was seriously pursuing the purchase of an estate in Prussian Poland, where he would be able to see his son, Jan, who could not return to the Habsburg monarchy without facing arrest. With his most glorious period of literary success behind him, Fredro thus contemplated giving up Galicia forever.[44]

Emperor Franz Joseph, born in 1830, was just the same age as Jan Fredro, born in 1829, and the Fredro family was naturally interested in the emperor as a source of potential amnesty. In 1853, Zofia Fredrowa, the wife of the dramatist, responded emotionally to the news of the emperor's marriage to Elisabeth of Bavaria: "The news of the marriage of the emperor shook me, whether with joy or with fear—I myself do not know. There is no doubt that there is a chance of amnesty." Amnesty took a little longer in coming, but in 1856 Jan Fredro wrote to his parents from Spa, "I don't know how to explain, but, just as until now it always seemed that obtaining an amnesty was unlikely, now it seems to me that it is coming, and that soon I will return to Galicia." It finally came in 1857, and Aleksander Fredro reported in a letter from Lviv on 12 June: "It was a great day for me, the day of the return of my son. Now it will be possible to die peacefully."[45] Fredro did not die until 1876, in Lviv, a lifelong octogenarian Galician—but in the 1850s his commitment to Galicia faltered on the brink of absolute alienation.

In 1857, the same year that Jan Fredro returned to Galicia, another prodigal Galician son returned to his native land. Leopold von Sacher-Masoch, who had left Galicia as a twelve-year-old when his father was transferred to Prague in 1848, had now recently completed a degree in history at the University of Graz. He was beginning in Graz his career as a teacher, a writer, and a sensualist in dedicated pursuit of masochistic sexual satisfaction. In 1857, Sacher-Masoch had just completed his first novel, set in the Galicia of 1846, and with the payment from his publisher he was able to travel to the landscape that he had fictionally described from childhood memory.

> I used the first honorarium to hurry back to my homeland [*Heimat*]. It was the summer of 1857, and I shed tears as I saw the first Galician peasant, and now when the post carriage arrived in Lemberg—there was still no train at that time—and I recognized the streets, the houses, the trees along the wall, the promenade of Lemberg, I began to weep like a child. My grandmother was still alive. The old family house looked exactly as it had when I left it ten years before. It was like a fairy tale in which, after a thousand years' sleep, everything awakens exactly as it was before.[46]

Like Franz Joseph when he visited Galicia in 1851, the young author came to stake a kind of imperial claim, the sentimental and emotional claim of a writer upon the native landscape that would belong to him for the rest of his writing life.

Galicia, for Sacher-Masoch, was the fairy tale scenario of enchantment and superstition, of natural beauty and fierce cruelty, the province in which the semimythological backwardness of Eastern Europe permitted the fictional staging of childhood fantasy as adult perversion. In 1857 he exercised his claim upon Galicia by letting it exercise its power over him: "From Lemberg I roamed around the east of the province. Later in life I would often visit my homeland, but never again would I receive the same impression as then, when I returned, driven by overwhelming passion, and lived for two months with our people [*mit unserem Volke*]."[47] The overwhelming passion that dominated his psychic and creative life, the masochistic passion, was also nourished by his return to Galicia as a young adult. His fantasies were rekindled among "our people," the Galicians, and there was unmistakably an imperial insinuation in the use of the first-person plural. To the child of the Lviv police chief the people of Galicia were inevitably "our people," the subjects of the Austrian bureaucracy and the Habsburg monarchy.

Sacher-Masoch particularly recalled his encounter with Jewish Hasidism in Galicia in 1857. It was actually in the adjoining province of Bukovina (recently separated from Galicia) that Sacher-Masoch visited one of the Hasidic religious leaders, known as the Zaddik for his righteousness.

> In 1857, I visited Zaddik Liebmann of Sadagora in the company of my uncle, and I had the opportunity of observing and studying this miraculous man and the Hasidim myself. . . . Sadagora was a small town at that time, inhabited almost exclusively by Jews and Armenians. Narrow streets full of filth, streets with dark recesses that the sun's rays never entered.[48]

The Hasids, as Sacher-Masoch understood them, were mystics who had renounced asceticism, renounced the mortification of the flesh, seeking union with God through prayer, while allowing themselves "to avoid every torment, satisfy every allowable need, and even cultivate pleasure." The paradoxes of pleasure and pain were especially interesting to the youthful masochist, and he paid due respect to the "Columbus of Hasidism," known as the Baal Shem Tov—who, according to Sacher-Masoch, lived in the eighteenth century "in Galicia."[49] In fact, the Baal Shem Tov died in 1760, before Galicia was created in 1772, but the Hasids did afterward flourish in Galicia, and Sacher-Masoch was convinced that Hasidism was fundamentally Galician.

Sacher-Masoch left a vivid account of his visit to the Zaddik in Sadagora:

> A young Hasid with the face of a young fox led the way. We climbed the stairs, passed an anteroom, and found ourselves in a large room where the ladies of the house, the Zaddik's wife and daughters-in-law, his daughters and his nieces, were assembled. I felt as if I had been transported into the harem of the Sultan in Constantinople. All these women were beautiful, or at least pretty; both astonished and amused, they all looked at us with their big black-velvet eyes; they were all dressed in silk morning-gowns and long caftans made of silk or velvet, and trimmed and lined with expensive furs: yellow and pink silk, green, red, and blue

velvet, squirrel, ermine, marten, and sable. . . . Finally a large, heavy curtain was shoved aside, and we entered the large room in which the Zaddik usually received the petitioners. Along the wall across from the entrance stood an old Turkish divan on which the Zaddik was reclining.[50]

Evidently, the Galicia of the Hasidim was full of Oriental intimations for Sacher-Masoch, who claimed to find himself in the fairy tale world of the *Thousand and One Nights*, with harems, sultans, and divans. At the same time, for the future author of *Venus in Furs*, the most famous fur fetishist in history, the rabbi's "harem" must have been dramatically arousing, the fantasy scenario for multiple masochistic sexual scenarios, involving squirrel, ermine, marten, and sable.

It was Sacher-Masoch's conviction that Hasidism, with its fantastic and fanatic elements of mysticism, was characteristically Galician.

In order to understand the Hasidic sect, one has to understand the land where they live. One has to know Galicia. Think of a boundless plain covered with green sprouts in the spring, yellow fields of grain in the summer, and snow in the winter. . . . You know that the sailor who spends his life in the middle of a watery desert becomes taciturn, serious, melancholy; the Galician flatlands produce the same effect. Here people have a feeling of infinity that they cannot grasp, and they withdraw into themselves. . . . And now imagine, in a dull, sunless shed, in this wasteland, far from the world, far from civilization . . . a man who has a great mind, who has the need to investigate and discover the world, to penetrate its secrets to the depths, who has a burning imagination and a warm heart, and who is shut up within his four walls like a prisoner, like a dried flower in a herbarium, who has no well of knowledge to draw from other than his Talmud and his Kabbalah. You will understand that this man, constantly searching and brooding, will become a dreamer and a fanatic, will believe he hears the voice of God, and will be convinced that he converses with angels and demons. No, the Hasidim are not swindlers—they are all Hamlet and Faust, and you shouldn't be surprised when they end up a little crazy like Hamlet.[51]

Sacher-Masoch's sanity would often be questioned by those who knew him, or even knew his writings, and he would eventually lend his name and fame to a diagnosis in Krafft-Ebing's *Psychopathia Sexualis*. Galicia itself Sacher-Masoch regarded as the conditioning landscape of fantasy, fanaticism, and some degree of mental derangement—consistent with Shakespearean dignity. The character of that landscape was also, for Sacher-Masoch, a matter of Galicia's primitive remoteness from civilization.

During the first half of the nineteenth century the Habsburgs in Galicia attempted to come to imperial terms with the fact that the empire had acquired an enormous population of Jews by the partitions of Poland—that is, Polish Jews. During the second half of the nineteenth century, as the provincial integrity of Galicia was increasingly accepted, as its provincial features were carefully studied, it became more and more plausible to suggest, as Sacher-Masoch did, that Galician Jews constituted a distinctive community, different from other Jewish populations in Eastern Europe. Hasidism, though in fact it could be also found in Russian Poland, would be made into one of the characteristic markers of the Galician Jew, the Galitzianer.

Galician Autonomy: "Sanctuary"

Franz Joseph ruled in the spirit of imperial absolutism during the 1850s, with Alexander Bach as minister of the interior, but after Austria was defeated by Italian forces in the Battle of Solferino in 1859, and was compelled to cede the province of Lombardy to the newly united Kingdom of Italy, the decade of absolutism gave way to a decade of unstable constitutional adaptation in the 1860s. Gołuchowski as *namiestnik* in Galicia during the 1850s preserved the integrity of the province and resisted the claims of Ruthenian political movements. Within the imperial context of the Habsburg monarchy, however, he could do little more than submit to Vienna's bureaucratic absolutism, which was administered largely by Germans and in German, in spite of the precedence of the Polish viceroy. It was therefore all the more unexpected when in 1859, after Solferino, Gołuchowski was summoned from Lviv to Vienna to assume the office of minister of the interior for the whole monarchy. There was no precedent for a Polish Galician holding such a position of power in the central government, and the appointment testified not only to the emperor's personal confidence in Gołuchowski but also to the general sense that his Polish national identity was significantly modified by a Habsburg imperial, or Galician provincial, perspective. There was no doubt that his highest priority as a Galician would be loyalty to the Habsburg emperor.

Gołuchowski, however, was not selected for the purpose of re-establishing the absolutism of the 1850s, and he presided instead over the brief political interlude defined by the so-called October Diploma of 1860. The constitution of 1849 had recognized the crownlands as the basic constituent territorial elements of the monarchy, which ruled centrally over them, but the October Diploma provided for a far greater reservation of political competency to those crownlands, to be exercised by their respective legislative bodies, including the Galician Sejm. In other words, the October Diploma emphasized those federal aspects of the Habsburg constitution that had been most welcomed in Galicia by Polish conservative forces like *Czas*, and it was perfectly appropriate to put a Galician like Gołuchowski in charge of the implementation. Not just an individual Galician, but a generally Galician perspective, was suddenly influential in the Habsburg monarchy as a whole.

The October Diploma was immediately controversial, and was particularly opposed by German and liberal forces within the bureaucracy. According to historian C. A. Macartney, Gołuchowski in Vienna was "the target of particularly vehement and scurrilous attacks by the Liberal Press (who hated him alike as an aristocrat, a federalist, a clerical, and a Pole)."[52] In December, two months after the issuing of the October Diploma, Gołuchowski was abruptly compelled to resign, and two months later, in February 1861, the so-called February Patent effectively reversed the October Diploma and re-established a system of centralization. Yet, as minister of the interior in Vienna, and previously as *namiestnik* in Galicia, Gołuchowski had offered a glimpse of how the constitutionally sanctioned crownlands might become potentially significant politically. The consolidation of Galicia as a coherent whole was also meaningfully advanced with the opening of the railway between Cracow and Lviv, at long last, in 1861.

The great testing of Galicia took place in 1863, when the national insurrection in Russian Poland inevitably attracted the sympathy of Galician Poles, but Habsburg military and police pressure in the province—a state of emergency and a plethora of arrests—limited the expression of that sympathy. There was a Supreme Galician Council to organize support for the insurrection, and the representative in Galicia of the insurrectionary government, Seweryn Elżanowski, critically evaluated the Galician scene. "We must consider Galicia as one of the most ancient provinces of Poland, and therefore an inseparable part of it," he wrote, but he was disappointed in the response to his appeals for support. He claimed to discern a "less heated patriotic disposition in Galicia than in other regions of Poland," noted a "niggardliness of monetary offerings brought to the altar of the fatherland," and flatly concluded that "nowhere else have the authorities constituted by the national government found such cool and unenthusiastic support as in Galicia."[53] Elżanowski attributed this defective patriotism to a lack of national organization, but it was also perhaps due to the evolving sentimental dualism of Galicians. Patriotism in Galicia meant not only national allegiance to the fatherland, to Poland, but also provincial dedication to the crownland, to Galicia itself.

In 1865, after the insurrection in Russian Poland had been brutally crushed, Galicia was still proceeding along the path of provincial self-affirmation. Stupnicki in 1853 had counted Galician species of flora and fauna but regretted that he could not offer a precise count of Galician insects. In 1865 the problem was remedied with Maksymilian Nowicki's *Insecta Haliciae*, published in Cracow by the Jagiellonian University, giving a complete provincial taxonomy with names in Latin and Polish: *vespa, osa* [wasp]. In that same year, he published a more specialized work on the butterflies of Galicia, appearing in Polish and German, in Lviv and Vienna, for the delight and edification of lepidopterists in the province and in the capital. In future years he would also turn his attention to piscine matters, making another comprehensive Galician contribution, published in Cracow in 1889, one year before his death: *On the Fishes of the Vistula, Styr, Dniester and Prut Rivers in Galicia.*[54]

In 1865 the publication of *Insecta Haliciae* coincided with a summoning of the Sejm, as the Habsburg monarchy prepared to adapt its political structure once again, modifying the February Patent in pursuit of a somewhat less centralized system, and therefore involving the diets of the crownlands. The challenge of Bismarck and the advent of the Austro-Prussian War in 1866, ending with Austria's defeat at Königgrätz, made Franz Joseph suddenly very vulnerable to pressures for political change within the monarchy. The result was the Austro-Hungarian compromise of 1867, which politically separated the Kingdom of Hungary from the Empire of Austria, while Franz Joseph embodied their dynastic union. The "Austrian" or "Cis-Leithanian" half of the empire (now demarcated by the Leitha River) received a new and liberal constitution that applied to fifteen crownlands, including Upper and Lower Austria, Tyrol, Bohemia, Moravia, Styria, Carinthia, Carniola, Dalmatia, and Galicia. Yet Galicia, on the map, did not neatly fit together with the other Cis-Leithanian lands, most of which formed a geographically coherent grouping, west of the Leitha. Especially the eastern territories of Galicia were remote from such Cis-Leithanian centers as Vienna, Prague, and Ljubljana.

Politically, Galicia enjoyed an even more pressing claim to some separate status, inasmuch as the imperial government calculated that it would depend upon the support of Galician Poles in the new constitutional parliament in Vienna. Therefore, the historic compromise with Hungary was supplemented by a more modest compromise in Galicia, which was allowed a large degree of autonomous self-government, with the promise of priority for the Polish language in education and administration. Thus, in the same decade that witnessed the crushing of the Polish insurrection in Russian Poland, the Galicians received comprehensive political autonomy under Polish auspices within their provincial borders. Insects might freely fly across state frontiers, and fish might swim down the Vistula from Cracow to Warsaw, but the political boundaries of Galician autonomy marked the province as a distinctive entity more emphatically than ever before.

The Austrian defeat at Königgrätz took place on 3 July 1866, and on 11

August, *Czas*, in Cracow, was already anticipating major political changes in the monarchy. "Three systems are open to Austria: centralization, dualism, and the autonomy of the crownlands," wrote *Czas*. "Austria must say to itself: I am not a German state; I am not a half-German half-Hungarian state; rather I am a collective state whose strength and power rests on all the people who form the composition of the monarchy."[55] The Galician perspective on Austrian political transformation was focused, above all, on the crownlands, which naturally included Galicia itself. It was a political perspective that *Czas* identified with the figure of Gołuchowski, who had been living in relative retirement on his Galician estates for five years, ever since resigning as the emperor's minister in December 1860. In 1865 he participated in the Sejm in Lviv, and in 1866 he was busy in Vienna discussing with Franz Joseph, and with the minister president Richard Belcredi, the future of Galicia in the context of a dualist Austro-Hungarian monarchy. It was Gołuchowski, more than anyone, who negotiated Galicia's special autonomous position, not as one among many autonomous crownlands but rather as the uniquely autonomous crownland within Cis-Leithania.

On 26 September, *Czas* reported that Gołuchowski was on his way from Vienna to Lviv, having just received Franz Joseph's appointment to a new term as *namiestnik*.

> Our country [*kraj nasz*], which has constantly sought from the minister of state the satisfaction of its own needs in a national and autonomous spirit, receives today the first token of those wishes in the person of the *namiestnik*. This nomination is indeed the proof that from now on Galicia will be governed in a spirit corresponding to its own interests and that the good of the province will be in agreement with the good of the monarchy. We will therefore greet our *namiestnik* with all good wishes and hope, and show him that the confidence that surrounds him is fully shared in Cracow.[56]

He would be in Cracow for just a few hours, since now the railway to Lviv was complete, and he only needed to change trains on the way from Vienna. At the station Gołuchowski's viceregal person—reflecting the power of the emperor in the province and, reciprocally, the unity of the province in loyalty to the emperor—became in itself a kind of manifestation of Galicia's special position within the monarchy. Galicia was "our country," a unified and coherent whole, with its own interests and its own good, conceptually inseparable from the Habsburg empire, and now, through the mediation of Gołuchowski, entirely in harmony with the Habsburg emperor.

"The autonomy of every crownland must constitute the whole and also be an individual unit of the whole of the monarchy," wrote *Czas* on 29 September. "Well known are the tendencies and efforts of a certain party toward the partition of Galicia." The lesson of 1848 remained relevant for *Czas* still in 1866. Ruthenian demands for the partition of the province made the integrity of Galicia, and therefore the very idea and identity of Galicia, all the more significant from the Polish perspective, which was paradoxically compelled to efface its Polishness in the name of an alternative Galician perspective, the perspective of the "whole country [*kraj cały*]." For *Czas*, Gołuchowski was the quintessential Galician and the province's most appropriate political actor: "We too are certain that he will overcome difficulties, because he will find the support of the whole country. The whole country feels the need for self-government and desires strong authority."[57] Cracow conservatism offered an organic political philosophy of general harmony, denying the validity of dissenting views by insisting on the political and social integrity of the "whole country," a political philosophy that could be summed up in the name Galicia.

These reiterated affirmations of provincial unity would have been completely undercut by any frank recognition of authentic Ruthenian opposition to Galician autonomy, and for that reason *Czas* preferred to insist that the real opposition originated outside Galicia, indeed outside the Habsburg monarchy: in Russia. If Galicia was to be considered as an integrated whole—*kraj cały*—then fractious Ruthenians had to be construed as the objects of Russian manipulation and foreign interference. On 8 November, *Czas* charged that "in eastern Galicia Russia uses the St. George party as its own organ and tool." This St. George party [*sviatoiurtsi*], associated with the Greek Catholic Church and also known as the "Old Ruthenians," was the conservative Ruthenian party most hostile to the Poles, most loyal to the Habsburgs, and most inclined to regard Galician Ruthenians as a distinctive national community. In the 1860s, as *Czas* suspected, this party was also becoming increasingly sympathetic to the Ruthenian Russophiles. Furthermore, in that same decade, within the Greek Catholic Church there was a movement toward "ritual purification," favoring the elimination of Roman Catholic influences on traditional ritual among the Uniates and harboring inclinations toward Orthodoxy. After the death of the Ukrainian poet Taras Shevchenko in St. Petersburg in 1861, there emerged an increasing interest in his work among Galician Ruthenians, who thus looked across the Habsburg border to Ukrainian culture within the Russian Empire.[58] Any such manifestations of Ruthenian interest in Orthodoxy or Ukraine were crudely interpreted by *Czas*, from a Polish perspective, as matters of Russian manipulation.

Opposition to Galician autonomy in the 1860s was thus regarded by *Czas* as potentially treasonous to Austria, while support of autonomy was essentially loyal and patriotic. This last axiom required a rather delicate analysis of loyalism and patriotism with their intersecting and overlapping references to Galicia, Austria, and Poland.

> One of the most important benefits which, in our opinion, is created for Galicia by its relation to the government is that we can legally acknowledge our national feelings and legally put demands in the spirit of national needs. . . . The demands of the country do not violate the limits of possibility. Galicia feels [*Galicya czuje*] how far the Austrian government can go, and does not demand, nor will it demand, what goes beyond the power and possibility of the state, and what would not be consistent with the interests of the state.[59]

The word "Polish" was not even mentioned in this passage, evading the question of whether Galicia's "national feelings" or "national needs" should be analyzed as Polish or Galician. *Czas*'s political theory of the relation between province and state recognized the limits of political possibility. Those limits reflected, implicitly, the boundaries of the province within the Habsburg monarchy, and also the boundaries of the monarchy that separated Galicia from the other Polish lands. Galicia possessed a political perspective of its own [*Galicya czuje*] within its own limitations and boundaries.

Yet Galicia was not unaware of the other Polish lands, and *Czas* formulated with remarkable prescience what was to become the Galician sense of mission for the rest of its provincial existence up until World War I.

> While in other Polish regions, brutal force crushes the signs of national life and the slightest breath of freedom, and elsewhere only the dominant nationality has the privilege of existence and public freedoms, Galicia is destined to be a sanctuary for the preservation of national elements in immaculate purity, and likewise, the faith of our fathers and their treasures. It is not necessary to hide them from the evil eye or deny possession, for no one aims at their extermination; on the contrary the government promises to share in their protection and defense. That is also the reason for the feeling of loyalty in the country.[60]

The notion of autonomous Galicia as a national sanctuary for the preservation of Polish national culture would be ideologically developed over the course of the next generation. This articulation of a provincial mission was also, in its origin, an ideology of self-exculpation, for only by renouncing the revolutionary cause of Polish political insurrection and resurrection, by withdrawing within the provincial borders, was it possible to establish Galicia as the Polish national sanctuary.

Loyalty to the emperor was both the most potent guarantee and, at the same time, the ultimate limitation on Galician autonomy, the ideological frontier that could not be crossed. *Czas* articulated that loyalty in its own editorial voice: "Never has Galicia been more loyal than now, never have there been heard or seen such general signs of that loyalty, and completely spontaneous signs, not administratively prepared."[61] During the first half of the nineteenth century, and even as recently as the visit of Franz Joseph in 1851, the Habsburg bureaucracy in Galicia may have helped to stage demonstrations of loyalty on appropriate occasions. Beginning in the 1860s, however, and under the influence of public organs like *Czas*, the culture of ritualized affirmations of loyalty to Austria would become increasingly integral to general Galician identity. As *Czas* recognized with paradoxical insight, every affirmation of loyalty to Franz Joseph was, at the same time, a testimonial to the autonomy of Galicia.

Loyalty: "We Stand with You"

Czas's declaration of 8 November—"Never has Galicia been more loyal than now"—preceded by a month the famous and formal declaration of loyalty issued by the Galician Sejm in Lviv on 10 December 1866. At a moment when the Habsburg monarchy was maximally vulnerable, in the aftermath of military defeat by Prussia, the Galicians did not raise the Polish question of national independence, but, instead, affirmed their loyalty to the emperor. "During the days of bloody battles, gracious lord," declared the Sejm to Franz Joseph, "our country [*nasz kraj*] brought the blood of its own sons in contribution, and—in heated popular participation, with demonstrated readiness for dedication—warmed and confirmed the courage of the many troops, coming from its bosom, who formed a significant part of your army."[62] These were Galician soldiers who fought for Austria against Prussia in 1866, a very different struggle from that of the Polish soldiers who fought for Polish independence against Russia in 1863.

"Austria should be strong and powerful," affirmed the Sejm. "Its entirety will be secure, its prosperity and power will increase, in proportion as the autonomous establishment of the crownlands develops and increases on historical and national foundations their moral and material forces." The emphasis on the desirable autonomy of the crownlands was the implicit statement of quid pro quo in a declaration of seemingly unconditional loyalty. The Sejm invoked "providential destiny," which, in this case, was also provincial destiny.

> We conclude, most gracious lord, in the true and deep conviction . . . [that] Austria, in order to flourish with greater strength than ever, will be in its internal organization the most powerful expression of respect for freedom, and in its external organization the shield of the civilization of the West, the rights of nationality, humanity, and justice. . . . Without fear, then, of abandoning our national idea [*bez obawy więc odstępstwa od myśli naszej narodowej*], with faith in the mis-

sion of Austria, and with confidence in the decisiveness of change which your monarchical word has pronounced as an unchangeable intention, we affirm from the depths of our hearts that we stand with you, Your Majesty, and we wish to stand with you [*przy tobie, najjaśniejszy panie, stoimy i stać chcemy*].[63]

The Galicians' somewhat defensive insistence that they were not abandoning their national commitment suggested that some Poles would see the declaration of loyalty to the Austrian emperor in precisely that unpatriotic light.

The declaration was based not only on the implicit understanding of imminent Galician autonomy but also on an ideological interpretation of Galicia's relevance to Austria's "mission." In the late eighteenth century, after the creation of Galicia, the Habsburgs had ideologically vindicated their annexation of the province with reference to a civilizing mission, formulating an Austrian role to remedy the supposed backwardness of the province. This was understood in terms of the broader enlightened conception of the difference between Western Europe and Eastern Europe. In 1866, as the Sejm affirmed its loyalty to the emperor, without allusion to the eighteenth-century partitions, the civilizing mission of the Habsburgs was adapted to establish Galicia as an outpost, not an outcast, of Western civilization. For the idea of civilization in the nineteenth century could be construed to include the rights of nationality, humanity, and justice, and the corollary rights of the crownlands to provincial autonomy. Unspoken was the implicit opposition between Western civilization and the Russian Empire, whose shadowy influence on the Ruthenians was supposed to threaten both Galician and Austrian integrity.

On 11 December, the day after the Sejm's adoption of the address, *Czas* placed the Habsburg constitutional crossroads in the context of worldwide political change in the 1860s: the end of the Civil War in the United States, the extension of the franchise in England, the creation of a new Germany by Bismarck. On 20 December, *Czas* could report on Franz Joseph's favorable reply to the Galician address: "His Majesty the Emperor pronounces that the connection of Galicia with the ruling house and the Austrian monarchy assures the material and moral good of the province, and guarantees its free development."[64] Galician autonomy was now just a matter of working out the details. Galician identity was fully confirmed and consummated after almost a century of political ambiguity and ambivalence. Jakub Szela, the terror of Galicia in 1846, died in Bukovina in 1866, at the moment of the birth of Galician autonomy.

On 19 January 1867, *Czas* was already looking toward the meeting of the Reichsrat in Vienna, at which the Galician delegation was expected to be decisively influential in the restructuring of the monarchy. It was widely

anticipated that the Poles would support Austro-Hungarian dualism in exchange for Galician autonomy, and *Czas* was determined to demonstrate that
this was not merely a matter of provincial self-interest. This involved a long
view of Galician, Austrian, and Polish history, beginning with a reference to
the pragmatic sanction by which the Hungarian and Bohemian crowns were
bound to the dynasty in the eighteenth century in anticipation of the female
succession of Maria Theresa.

> Galicia knows no pragmatic sanction to which it may refer, and which it would
> defend; incorporated into Austria by force of conquest, there is no personal
> crown to be revindicated; it indubitably possesses historic rights, but can only
> demand autonomy on the basis of the equal rights of all the peoples of the mon-
> archy. . . . It has been forgotten, it seems, that Galicia was a part of the former
> Polish Commonwealth, participating through a great state in the vicissitudes of
> all Christian Europe, so joined together that, although effaced from the political
> map everywhere and always, in every parliament where Poles are seated as Poles,
> their delegation, by its own character, as in this Austrian case, will have a Europe-
> an perspective. Nothing can counter this, for the past bequeaths a tradition which
> history records as law, and the contemporary world, willingly or unwillingly, ac-
> knowledges it. It is not possible to efface a nation from Europe.[65]

The Sejm had insisted that it was not deserting the Polish national idea,
and *Czas* now purposefully invoked both the Polish Commonwealth and
the Polish partitions. Galicia as a crownland could not possess any historic
crown—like those of St. Stephen and St. Wenceslas for Hungary and Bohemia—since it had been simply a part of the Polish Commonwealth before
1772. Yet Galicia claimed its "historic rights," as a land of the Habsburg
monarchy and of Christian Europe.

   Czas in January 1867 sought to reconcile Galician loyalty to Austria with the
history of Poland as a state and a nation. Likewise in January 1867 the journal
Przegląd Polski, which had just begun publication in Cracow in 1866, featured
an article by one of its editors, the young historian Józef Szujski: "Several
Truths from Our History" ("Kilka prawd z dziejów naszych"). Szujski was
born in Tarnów in 1835, a contemporary of Sacher-Masoch, and was present
as an impressionable child in Tarnów itself in 1846, supposedly catching a
glimpse of the peasants who came to town with the corpses of the murdered
nobles. He was still a student in Tarnów when Franz Joseph visited Galicia
in 1851, but then in 1852 Szujski shifted his studies to Cracow, attending there
the gymnasium of St. Anne and the Jagiellonian University.[66] In 1863, he was
sympathetic to the insurrection in Russian Poland, but after its defeat, he
turned his back on insurrectionary adventures and embraced a lifelong Galician loyalism among a cohort of like-minded young Cracovians, including
Stanisław Tarnowski and Stanisław Koźmian; all of them were close to the

editorial board of *Czas*.[67] Following some of the traces of Kalinka's work, Szujski would become the real founder of the Cracow historical school, which flourished in the age of Galician autonomy. He became professor of Polish history at the Jagiellonian University in 1869, and general secretary of the Academy of Learning [Akademia Umiejętności] in 1872, making him one of the institutionally preeminent Galician intellectuals of his generation.

Szujski's several truths began with "the great truth that if a nation has fallen as a state, that is its own fault, and if it rises up again, that will happen by its own work, its own understanding, its own spirit."[68] Rejecting the long tradition of cultural lamentation over Poland as a tragic historical victim—most dramatically expressed by Mickiewicz in the gospel of Poland as the crucified Christ among nations—Szujski heretically proposed that the partitions of Poland were not just the evil predations of foreign aggressors but the consequences of Poland's own historical faults and weaknesses. Poles themselves, he suggested, had to accept some responsibility for Poland's national demise.

Looking back to the late sixteenth century, Szujski claimed to discern the origins of the historical decline of the Commonwealth that would culminate in the partitions at the end of the eighteenth century. Poles had to reflect on their own historical "contempt" for government, their inclination toward "anarchy," and their "oppression" of the population. All of this had produced a "crazy disharmony in national society, which ended with the partition of Poland." The end of the Commonwealth, according to Szujski, resulted from its own internal problems and should therefore be considered definitive: "The Commonwealth died, I say, and new times began." Revolutionary uprisings for the resurrection of the Commonwealth were therefore pointless, and this was a lesson that his own generation had finally learned from the insurrection of 1863. "The year 1863 has closed forever the epoch of conspiracy," wrote Szujski, who heralded "the road of normal organic national development." Just as the gentry prerogative of the *liberum veto* had helped to destroy the Commonwealth, so the *liberum conspiro*—as he called it—had been thoroughly self-destructive in the nineteenth century.[69] To be sure, his childhood experience of Tarnów in 1846 would have helped him to reach that conclusion.

The lesson of the insurrection of 1863 in Russian Poland, though it compelled Szujski to reject the path of conspiracy, also persuaded him that Russia was the supreme enemy of all Poles. The alternative was Galicia: "Whoever today stands opposed to the course of the Poles in Austria, against the course of organic work at any time in the future, stands directly on the side of Moscow, whether intentionally or not." Austria now represented the only option for the Polish nation. In the context of the Habsburg constitutional transformation of 1867 it was possible to make Galician autonomy into the basis of Galician identity: "We become, by circumstance [*przypadkowo*], not only Polish, but also true Austrian patriots."[70] *Czas*, favorably reviewing Szujski's "Several Truths," noted that he "knows how to draw from history such positive truths for the country [*dla kraju*]." The newspaper endorsed him as a future candidate for the Galician Sejm.[71]

As the details of Habsburg dualism emerged over the course of 1867, *Czas* followed and reported the news from Vienna, often as discussed in the Viennese press. On 9 February, *Czas* mentioned for the first time, somewhat ingenuously, that there were rumors in Vienna of a "special position [*Sonderstellung*]" for Galicia within the monarchy. It was Gołuchowski, "fervent advocate before the throne," who negotiated the special position, while *Czas* publicly insisted that Poles wanted all the crownlands of the monarchy to enjoy autonomy. "We also dream of a triad for Austria," wrote *Czas*, "but a triad of three crowns under the Austrian scepter of the Habsburg dynasty." *Czas* dreamed that the Habsburg emperor might someday wear a Polish crown, alongside those of St. Stephen and St. Wenceslas. Such a fantasy, which allowed for the possibility of a reunited Poland under Habsburg rule, reflected the strange reconciliation of Polish and Galician sentiment at the moment of the emergence of autonomous Galicia in the 1860s.[72]

The provincial contours of ecological and economic life became increasingly important with the emergence of political autonomy. On 9 February 1867, Czas published an article on Galician natural history, affirming the autonomy of the province as a reptile habitat by discussing the characteristics of provincial snakes [*charakterystyka wężów krajowych*]. On 1 May, a Galician mortgage bank was established in Lviv, and the names of the founders, listed in the advertisement that appeared in *Czas*, included a member of the Gołuchowski family. On 14 May, *Czas* published not only the advertisement but also a front-page editorial endorsing the mortgage bank as an institution calculated to meet "the pressing needs of the country" and certain to bring "profit for the country [*korzyść dla kraju*]."[73]

On 19 June 1867, the younger brother of Franz Joseph, Emperor Maximilian of Mexico, was executed by Mexican republican forces, and when the news reached Cracow, *Czas*, on 3 July, took the opportunity to reiterate its principles of Habsburg loyalism. "This is already the second member of the imperial family in Austria to die on the scaffold, Marie Antoinette and Maximilian," wrote *Czas*, exercising a remarkable memory for Habsburg history that long antedated the establishment of the newspaper itself. "History has rehabilitated the memory of the first; the rehabilitation of the second commenced even before the pronouncement of the sentence that condemned him to death."[74] The somewhat unusual analogy made sense only from an ideologically conservative perspective that still excoriated the French Revolution as the source of destructive revolutionary political impulses. In this case, the invocation of the death of Marie Antoinette in 1793 brought the readers of *Czas* back three-quarters of a century to the early decades of Habsburg Galicia, indeed to a moment that actually preceded the annexation of Cracow in the third partition of 1795. At the same time that *Czas* expressed its due respect for Marie Antoinette in the article about Maximilian, the paper also published a series of articles that evoked the Habsburg ghosts of her mother, Maria Theresa, and her brother Joseph II. In Vienna the scholar Alfred Ritter von Arneth published in 1867, for the first time, the correspondence between Maria Theresa and Joseph II, and those letters included some from the period of the first partition of Poland and the creation of Galicia. *Czas* published excerpts from the letters, supplemented by historical commentary.

Czas found Maria Theresa, in her letters, admirably distressed at the possibility of Polish partition: "All these mysterious political intrigues made the heart of Maria Theresa bleed." Joseph's letters showed him much more actively interested in Galicia after the partition. *Czas* reported on his visit to Galicia in 1773: "An ample field for reforms opened up in a notorious land considered to be a nest of disorder and the most monstrous social relations. The emperor was convinced, in his understanding, that he would bring true happiness to this part of the carved up nation." There were citations from Joseph's letters on the poverty of Galicia and the misery of the peasantry, but *Czas* insisted that the peasants found no satisfaction in Joseph's reforms and regarded Habsburg bureaucrats as oppressors.[75] Clearly there were limits to *Czas*'s readiness to rethink Polish history, and there were exceptions to its enthusiasm for Habsburg emperors. Joseph's policy of detailed imperial intervention in Galicia was precisely what Galician autonomy was supposed to prevent in the future.

STAŃCZYK: "DIFFERENT DEGREES OF NATIONAL EXISTENCE"

On 8 August, *Czas* responded indignantly to the intervention of the Viennese press, which had published an article about Galicia under the title "Poles, Ruthenes, and Jews." The title itself, with its analytical division of Galicia into separate components, was offensive to *Czas*, which criticized the Viennese press for having "represented the Ruthenians as if they were a special oppressed race of the peasantry, not enjoying the same rights as

other peasants in Galicia, west as well as east." Likewise, it was wrong to see
the Jews as separately oppressed: "as deprived of all security, as if they were
excluded from the law."[76]

While Polish conservatives were preparing to assume power in autonomous Galicia, under a Polish viceroy, with electoral laws that favored the
landed Polish gentry, with educational and administrative reforms that favored the Polish language, it was all the more ideologically important to insist
that there were no serious cultural chasms dividing the province:

> Social relations may be settled only through institutions adapted to the religions,
> nationalities, manners, customs, and traditions of the inhabitants. It will not help,
> however, to seek out differences that do not exist, or represent those that do ex-
> ist in exaggerated and irritable colors. Among the peoples who have lived for so
> many centuries in agreement with one another, it is not right to take artificially
> evoked or temporarily occurring oppositions as insurmountable obstacles to
> further coexistence, especially to regard partisan intrigues as popular movements.
> On the field of freedom, any true freedom, they will find opportunities for un-
> derstanding and mitigating those differences which exist in reality, and they will
> disappear in proper and mutual satisfaction.[77]

Galician autonomy and Habsburg constitutionalism would provide that field
of freedom in which, as *Czas* optimistically imagined, cultural differences
would be resolved in the provincial coherence of Galicia. The Galician formulation offered a hopeful vision for the Habsburg monarchy as a whole:
a vision of transcendence to counter the so-called nationalities problem
that would embitter Habsburg politics for the next half-century and finally
destroy the monarchy.

On 23 January 1868, *Czas* reported on the news from England wherein
supposedly "prudent minds" envisioned a peaceful resolution of violent
Anglo-Irish hostilities based on the "legal foundation" of a separate administration for Ireland. This formula for home rule in Ireland was, in fact, the
Polish prescription for autonomy in Galicia. On 15 February, *Czas* saluted
the creation of a provincial school board for Galicia—*Rada Szkolna Krajowa*—noting "with what heated feeling, deep hope, and full confidence the
whole country has greeted this long desired institution."[78] The journalistic
representation of public opinion—the opinion of "the whole country"—
was a convenient artifice. Galicia was to be politically autonomous, and *Czas*
correspondingly invented, and spoke for, an allegedly unified Galician public
opinion, in which social and cultural differences were conveniently dissolved.
In fact, the educational council would refashion education in Galicia based
on Polish language and Polish concerns, and the supposed enthusiasm of
the whole country would become an increasingly tenuous fiction.

When the Sejm met in Lviv in 1868 to discuss issues of autonomy, Szujski was an elected representative and claimed to feel a powerful sense of responsibility to Galicia as a whole: "The country demands from us that in this chamber we step forward as fighters against the ills of the country, not against one another." At the same time, as Galicians fought for their own country within the Habsburg monarchy, they would also, Szujski believed, advance the Polish national cause. "The eyes of all Poland are watching Galicia," he declared in the Sejm.[79] A resolution of the Sejm in September 1868 called for the most comprehensive autonomy and the most extensive prerogatives for itself, even seeking to make the viceroy responsible to the Sejm. While Vienna refused to accept this fully, Polish control over Galician education and administration were conceded in 1869, leading to the dominance of Polish in schools above the elementary level and making Polish the principal language of internal administration in Galicia.[80] Szujski himself was appointed to both Sejm committees on education and administration.

In 1869 and 1870, Szujski, together with his Polish conservative colleagues, Tarnowski and Koźmian, gave a name to their own political perspective by publishing in *Przegląd Polski* a series of anonymous satirical articles known collectively as the *Portfolio of Stańczyk (Teka Stańczyka)*. It was Koźmian, writing satirically under the name "Optymowicz," who summed up the whole Polish tradition that the Stańczyk perspective rejected:

> I do not need to prove to you that for an oppressed nation, oppressed by three powers, there is only one way to salvation, one possible policy, which is—to sum it up in two words—continuous insurrection. All compromise, diplomacy, considerations of this or that—they are nonsense, reactionary inventions. We alone, believing only in the efficacy of the great means, have preserved since 1772 the sacred fire, we the vestals of the Polish idea.[81]

The Polish idea that was being flagrantly ridiculed by Koźmian was radically different from the kind of Polishness that Szujski advocated in the Sejm. Szujski was a man of pragmatic compromise and measured considerations—which some might have characterized as essentially Galician. The Cracow revision of Polish history and the Stańczyk rejection of Polish insurrection led to a Galician redefinition of Polishness, the invention of a new Polish idea that could be summed up in a single word: Galicia.

Koźmian would come to regard the 1860s as a historical turning point: "This epoch may be called the rebirth of Galicia." The rebirth was related to a new sense of Polish patriotism, and a new notion of national existence, in the aftermath of the failed insurrection of 1863. "Of course there must be different degrees of national existence [*różne stopnie bytu narodowego*]," reflected Koźmian, "and the highest security is independence." Yet it was also true, he affirmed, that national existence could "exist and flourish under conditions very different and remote from independence." *Czas*, back in 1849, had renounced the "sacred slogan" of independence as a pernicious delusion: "The reason for the ever renewed disasters of Poland and Galicia is the desire to recover independence." For Koźmian, the rebirth of Galicia in the 1860s involved recognizing that national existence was not concerned only with political independence, that it was possible to cultivate "Polish national existence, without regard to the form which it assumes or can assume."[82] In the 1860s it was possible to discern a paradoxical renewal of national existence in the non-national form of Galicia.

In 1869, as Galician Poles pursued their administrative and educational goals, *Czas* acted as a watchdog, guarding Galicia from its enemies abroad and rebutting them in the spirit of Cracow conservatism. The most notorious enemy of Galicia was always identified as Russia—which *Czas*, on 17 January, called "the most valiant leader of brutal Asiatic force"—and the Russian menace to Galicia was framed in terms of the global chasm between East and West. "Just as politically only Austria and Poland can constitute a bulwark," wrote *Czas*, "so economically the final outcome of the conflict between the two currents may hang upon the strengthening of these points."[83] The historical mission of the Commonwealth as the "antemurale," the military bulwark of Western Christianity against both Turks and Russians, was transformed into an imperative of economic development in Galicia. Organic work in Galicia thus became essential, not only to the preservation of the Polish nation but also to the defense of Western civilization.

In the aftermath of the Austro-Prussian War, it seemed increasingly evident to military planners in the Habsburg government that Galicia's future strategic significance lay in the eventuality of some future war with Russia. Historian Hans-Christian Maner has argued that this became one fundamental meaning of Galicia as a Habsburg imperial borderland during the last third of the nineteenth century, with planners already noting as early as 1868 that "all army routes out of Russia toward Vienna and Budapest lead through Galicia." In 1873 a report on the hypothetical theater of future military operations [*Kriegsschauplatz*] concluded that Galicia, with its narrow and extended contours, would be "easier to attack than defend."[84] Viennese military concerns thus matched the Galician Polish hostility to Russia, as expressed in *Czas*.

On 19 February 1869, *Czas* was once again venting its indignation at the Viennese press, for the *Neue Freie Presse* had dared to publish an article under the byline "A German Voice from Galicia." *Czas* mocked the German correspondent for voicing his nostalgia for "the lost El Dorado" of bureaucratic German rule in Galicia. Calling him "the colonist," *Czas* noted his suggestion that the Sejm should be dissolved because it contained too few Ruthenians and no Germans at all. "The voice of the German colonist," wrote *Czas*, "would concern us little, because as his own beloved poet says: Against stupidity even the gods themselves struggle in vain."[85] It was, however, necessary to denounce the Viennese organ that published such stupidities, and *Czas*, armed with a quotation from Schiller, recorded the defamation of Galician autonomy.

Czas monitored not only Vienna, the capital of the monarchy, but also Paris, one of the capitals of Western civilization, and noted with awkward ambivalence on 25 February that the French publisher and politician Casimir Delamarre was petitioning the Senate to revise the French historical curriculum and to recognize the difference between Ruthenians and Russians. His pamphlet "A European People of Fifteen Million Forgotten by History" ("Un peuple européen de quinze millions oublié devant l'histoire") was troubling to *Czas*, since two and a half million of those alleged fifteen million lived in eastern Galicia, and two hundred thousand had petitioned for the partition of the province in 1848.[86]

Czas initially applauded Delamarre for his hostility to Russia, but then, a few days later, decided to present some further considerations with reference to the Union of Lublin in 1569, noting that 1869 was the year of its three-hundredth anniversary. The Union of Lublin was the political instrument that bound together all the lands of the Polish-Lithuanian Commonwealth, including the Ruthenian lands of Rus, as a single republican state with an elective monarchy and a unitary parliament. Ever since the partitions of Poland, the lands of Rus and the Ruthenians (or Ukrainians) had been divided between the Habsburg monarchy and the Russian Empire. Within Austria the Ruthenians were, for the most part, residents of Galicia.

> Not only the celebration of the memory of the Union in Galicia but also the preservation of its moral and even in part political importance must be desirable for the Austrian government, and upon that rests also the unity of Galicia, the unity of the Sejm and the viceroyalty, the unity of institutions. . . . For that reason also, in spite of the raising several times of the idea of the partition of Galicia, that is, the tearing apart of the Lublin Union, a healthy political understanding has always prevailed. . . . Tear apart in Galicia the bond sealed in Lublin, and Austria will find itself with two small crownlands on its northern border, too weak to guard its integrity.[87]

In the ongoing revisionist analysis of Polish history, the Union of Lublin was historically reconceived by *Czas* as the rationale for preserving the unity of Galicia. Historical anniversary commemorations would play an important part in Galician cultural life during the next half-century, and the discussion of the Union of Lublin on the front page of *Czas* in 1869 suggested the strategy by which events from Polish history might be reinterpreted in a contemporary Galician context.

Galician history itself was no less carefully monitored in *Czas*. When, in 1869, Moritz Ritter von Ostrow published in Vienna a book on the "peasant war" [*Bauernkrieg*] of 1846 in Galicia, *Czas* was offended even by the title, which represented the massacres as authentic class warfare. Ostrow had been a Habsburg bureaucrat in Galicia, and his book presented the Habsburg bureaucratic perspective, as did the *Polish Revolutions* of Police Chief Sacher-Masoch in 1863. Now, at the moment of Galician autonomy in 1869, *Czas* found Ostrow's book deeply disturbing.

> Unwillingly, and with a certain psychological aversion, we receive the subject of this book which we have picked up with mistrust. The title alone is inconsistent with reality . . . and the subject awakened memories which today one would rather conjure away than call forth. . . . Just the tale is terrifying to children, moves women to pity, and is depressing to men. Every truth or principle that can be drawn from it becomes so bitter that for some it poisons peace of mind, for others it shakes the faith. . . .[88]

Czas, for all its interest in history, might have preferred not to revisit this "terrible catastrophe," and certainly preferred not to hear about it from a Viennese perspective. While *Czas* seemed to suggest that the harshness of "Providence [*Opatrzność*]" in permitting the massacres of 1846 was such as to shake the religious faith of a Galician Pole, the editors may have meant to suggest that a different sort of faith [*wiara*] was also at stake—that is, Galician loyalty to the Habsburg government.[89]

Once upon a time, *Czas* knew, the Habsburg government had regarded the Galician peasantry as a political counterforce to the national conspiracies of the Polish gentry: "But those times have already passed, irretrievably [*bezpowrotnie*]; the most suspicious police agent today must be free of fears of Polish inclinations against the integrity of the state." Galician loyalism in the 1860s was in part the consequence of the massacres of 1846, for the cost of disloyalty had been terrifyingly high. Now, *Czas* declared, the age of national conspiracies and peasant massacres was irretrievably over. To some extent, the whole history of Galician autonomy for half a century would be founded on the political and cultural neutralization of the historical memory of 1846. Szujski, the leading figure in Galician intellectual life in the first decades of autonomy, had been a boy himself in Tarnów at the moment of the massacres.

"Galicia, or Austrian Poland, is not at all striving to tear itself away from the monarchy," wrote *Czas* in April 1869, "but on the other hand it does not renounce its national community with the rest of the Polish lands, for it is necessary to differentiate between political existence and national existence."[90] This differentiation was an essential aspect of Galician ideology during the decades of the 1860s as the province sought and ultimately attained autonomy within the Habsburg monarchy. The nationally Polish sphere—which transcended the Habsburg borders—was carefully distinguished from the political domain of Galicia within those borders.

In June 1869, during restoration work in the Wawel Cathedral in Cracow, the mortal remains and royal regalia of Casimir the Great were accidentally discovered, brought to light for the first time since his death in the fourteenth century. In July, therefore, he received a ceremonial reinterment with religious services and public appreciation. It was a Polish national event, of course, but Casimir's career also had some particular relevance for Galicia: he reigned from Cracow, he conquered Ruthenia, and he encouraged Jewish settlement in Poland. The commemorative reinterment took place just in time for the five-hundredth anniversary of Casimir's death in 1370.[91]

Historical commemorations would become one of the ways that Galicia affirmed its cultural solidarity with the other Polish lands. The Union of Lublin, already invoked by *Czas* earlier in 1869, was commemorated particularly on 11 August, the three hundredth anniversary of the precise date when the Sejm of 1569 concluded its work of unification in Lublin. *Czas* took note of the date:

> This day of sacred history across the whole extent of Poland, wherever the work of unity was achieved, does not call forth happiness but rather feelings of contrition before the tribunal of history, of dignity before the majesty of misfortune, of faith and hope before Providence. To set apart Galicia which accidentally finds itself in happier circumstances in the matter of the common national jubilee, to differentiate it in this celebration from the silent feelings with which Lithuania, Rus, and the Polish kingdom must celebrate their national marriage, would contradict the national commonality, would deny the suffering and bondage of our brothers. But if to feast and rejoice would be unworthy of us, it would be right for us to enhance greatly that internal contrition, that concentration of the spirit. By the spoken and written word, by thought and action, to demonstrate that if there has fallen to us, out of the entire disempowered nation, the possibility of action in a certain sphere, we know how to do it, and wish to fulfill for ourselves the obligation of internal work, the reckoning with the past and the future of the nation.[92]

The politically "special position" of Galicia within Austria was now interpreted as a culturally special position by which Galicia was "set apart" from the other Polish lands.

Even in Galicia the public celebration of the Lublin tricentennial was officially discouraged, lest it provoke external Russian hostility or internal

Ruthenian discontent. There were thirty-two services celebrated in Roman Catholic churches in Galicia (but only two in Greek Catholic churches), and in Cracow the Mass in the Mariacki Church was followed by a showing of Jan Matejko's history painting of the Lublin Union. In Lviv, Franciszek Smolka, a leading Polish political figure in the Reichsrat in Vienna, led a procession past Ruthenian protests to lay the foundation for a monument on Castle Hill—actually Franz Joseph Hill ever since his visit in 1851. In some Galician cases, the commemoration of the Lublin Union, dated 11 August, was conveniently connected to the celebration of the birthday of Franz Joseph on 18 August.[93] The tricentennial of the Union of Lublin was celebrated both for its Polish national and Galician provincial significance, recalling the Polish national unity of the past and affirming the Galician provincial unity of the present.

On 15 August 1869, the centennial birthday of Napoleon Bonaparte passed without great fanfare, even in France. In Cracow, however, *Czas* took note of the occasion, recalling that Napoleon had exercised a special mystique in the Polish lands, and that many Poles—including Galician Poles like Fredro— had participated in Napoleon's invasion of Russia in 1812. *Czas* marked Napoleon's centennial by drawing a Galician lesson from Napoleonic history: "Looking to an external power, which almost miraculously is supposed to raise us up from internal impotence, must always bring disappointment, for external help succeeds only together with internally cultivated strength." From the perspective of the Cracow historical school, the Union of Lublin was more worthy of commemoration than the birthday of Napoleon.

On 1 September, after recalling the major commemorations of the year, Lublin and Napoleon, *Czas* remarked on a more peculiar centennial that was being observed in Austria. It was a hundred years ago, supposedly, that Joseph II, traveling in Moravia, had put his imperial hands to the plow in order to help a peasant work his field. *Czas* had no patience for the legend of Joseph and his alleged love for the peasantry. Rather, from the Polish perspective, this was a story with a more complicated ideological message: "The German emperor brings German culture into the savage Slavic lands of the east." Assisted perhaps by the published letters of Joseph and Maria Theresa, *Czas* ironically registered the civilizing implications of Josephine ideology.[94] In the decade of the 1860s, with the achievement of autonomy, Galician Poles rejected this aspect of the Josephine perspective and affirmed the historical Polish affiliation with Western civilization. The conservative preservation of Western civilization thus became the ideological underpinning of Galicia's "special position" within the Habsburg monarchy. Galicia had been invented by the Habsburgs, but it was now being reinvented by Polish Galicians on their own terms.

Coda: An Orphan in Galicia

In 1869, Apollo Korzeniowski died in Cracow, leaving an eleven-year-old orphan son, Józef Teodor Konrad Korzeniowski; the boy was known as Konrad and destined to become the great English writer Joseph Conrad, the literary master of the complications of empire. Apollo Korzeniowski was himself a writer, a Polish poet, dramatist, and nationalist, who left Russian Poland for Galicia in 1868 and spent the last year of his life in Lviv and Cracow. His letters suggest that already in 1868, when Galician autonomy was established, there was a significant divergence between Polish and Polish Galician political perspectives. He was determined to bring up his son "as a Pole," but was skeptical, in March 1868, about whether that could really be done in Lviv:

> I doubt whether that is the intention behind the present educational system in Lwów. . . . What keeps me in Lwów is that this is a providential city where, although Polishness is lacking today, it may still find its expression. . . . Will you believe me that at twenty public meetings here I heard the word "Poland" only once?[95]

Czas, of course, would have understood this Galician syndrome perfectly, as the newspaper was one of the principal Galician public organs in which concepts like "Poland" and "Polish" were often just ambiguously implied. Korzeniowski was eager to found a newspaper of his own in Galicia, precisely because he was so dissatisfied with the current state of the press. In emphatic contrast to the editors of *Czas*, he believed that Galicia had to become prepared for a national uprising:

> Is not this calm before the storm the right time to prepare Galicia for the good? When she is taken unawares by the hurricane, stupidity, baseness, and treachery will appear, ruining everything: God grant I may be wrong, but neither at home nor at school nor at church do I see any evidence of sacrifice and readiness for the opportune moment.[96]

In fact, 1868 was the opportune moment for achieving Polish predominance and political autonomy in Galicia, but such Galician opportunism appeared to Korzeniowski as something altogether non-national and therefore deplorable.

In October 1868, Korzeniowski exploded in an epistolary diatribe against the Galicians, noting their fundamental frivolity and national indifference to the fate of Russian Poland:

> All of them have such a fear of Moscow that they would let her devour their own children providing she would not interfere in Galicia with their parading of

horses, leading of dances at balls, founding of partnerships, etc. They have forgotten what it is to feel—they know not how to speak—they read nothing. Customs, language, religion mean nothing to them. . . . Galicia weighs on me heavily
like a presentiment of my tombstone; and should my grave have no stone, I expect to feel there less oppressed than I do today in Galicia. . . . The very mention
of Warsaw or Varsovians makes my heart beat faster: I have never met people
more alive and honest. The time I spent there I count as the most beautiful moments in my life as man and Pole. For one Varsovian I could give away many
many Galicians and the rest besides.[97]

Apollo Korzeniowski did die in Galicia, in Cracow in 1869, and his son Konrad later tried and failed to obtain citizenship in Galicia within the Habsburg
monarchy. Still liable to Russian conscription, he left Galicia in 1874 to go to
sea, and followed the destiny that would eventually transform Konrad Korzeniowski into Joseph Conrad.[98] Indeed, his father would hardly have been
happy to see the boy grow up as a Galician, a Habsburg subject for whom
the meanings of Polish customs, language, and religion were subtly revised
and reinterpreted. The letters of Apollo Korzeniowski in 1868, at the moment of the achievement of Galician autonomy, testify to the existence of a
distinctive way of being Galician, an idea of Galicia that appeared altogether
alien to the Polish observer from beyond the provincial borders.

CHAPTER SIX

The Average Galician
in the Age of Autonomy

Fantasies and Statistics of the Slavic Orient

INTRODUCTION: ALLEGORICAL GALICIA

In 1868 an announcement appeared in Lviv inviting subscriptions to a tremendous work in progress, a multivolume encyclopedia—*The Encyclopedia of Expertise on Galicia (Encyklopedya do krajoznawstwa Galicyi)*—to appear in monthly installments and to cover every aspect of the province, including geography, history, statistics, topography, agronomy, and economy. This ambitious project was basically the work of a single man, Antoni Schneider, who himself stood ready to collect the addresses of interested subscribers as he prepared to write and issue the first installments. In the announcement Schneider wrote of his hopes for "this almost thirty-year labor of mine, in which I have been guided till now only by the fervent and undiscouraged desire to serve the fatherland," his hopes that his own dedication and "the value of this work" would receive "strong support from the honorable public."[1] In 1868, with the consolidation of Galician autonomy, the notion of a comprehensive encyclopedia must have seemed politically plausible, even practical: knowledge of the country [*krajoznawstwo*], the intellectual and touristic accompaniment to the emerging administrative and educational provincial framework.

Schneider's encyclopedia of Galicia was a Polish project, conceived in the Polish language and politically calculated to appear in the 1870s, the first decade of Polish predominance in the autonomous province. Yet the project would founder, producing only two published volumes, in 1871 and 1874, respectively, alphabetically covering the letters A and B in Galician lore. The Galician encyclopedia would not find the supportive Galician public that Schneider envisioned, and, in fact, the very notion of a Galician public became increasingly

Palace of the Galician Sejm, in Lviv, completed in 1881 (today the university). The allegorical sculpture of Galicia is on top of the Sejm. Author's photograph.

uncertain, as Polish predominance in the 1870s called forth the increasingly
articulate dissidence of Jewish and Ruthenian perspectives in the province.

While the Polish conservative perspective of *Czas* enjoyed a measure
of ideological hegemony during the early decades of autonomy in Galicia,
seeking to legitimize the dominant Polish position in the province, the liberal

Allegorical sculpture of Galicia, between the Vistula and Dniester rivers, created for the Galician Sejm in Lviv. Author's photograph.

constitutional framework of Habsburg Cis-Leithania after 1867 encouraged the emergence of alternative perspectives. Both Galician Ruthenian and Galician Jewish perspectives would offer variant views of what it meant to be Galician. Just as Józef Szujski continued to play a leading intellectual role in articulating the Polish perspective on Galicia, so Ruthenian intellectuals like Stefan Kachala and Ivan Franko articulated an ideological alternative to the hegemonic Polish perspective on Galician autonomy. At the same time, the fiction of Karl Emil Franzos publicized the conditions and concerns of Galician Jews and emphasized their specifically Galician character.

The consolidation of the Galician provincial framework in the age of autonomy meant that not only Poles but also Ruthenians and Jews had to negotiate their particular Galician relation to broader religious and national communities beyond the borders of the province. Galician intellectual efforts, however, also sought to affirm provincial coherence, as in Schneider's ultimately futile attempt to create a multivolume encyclopedia of Galicia. Architectural efforts could play a similar role, as in the construction of a building in Lviv for the Sejm, the crucial political institution of unitary Galician autonomy. The architect, Juliusz Hochberger, built a neo-Renaissance palace, completed in 1881, topped by a grand allegorical female figure of Galicia herself, a stone goddess, flanked by the allegorized geographical figures of the Vistula and Dniester rivers, representing the west and the east of the unpartitioned province.[2]

In 1868, the year that Schneider's encyclopedia was announced, the Galician Sejm, embarking upon the age of autonomy, voted a resolution seeking to maximize its own prerogatives: for instance, insisting that the *namiestnik* should be responsible to the Sejm, rather than to the emperor. Franz Joseph did not accept the resolution, and responded by canceling a scheduled imperial visit to Galicia, two days before it was supposed to begin. "Unfortunately I have had to give up the trip to Galicia," he wrote in a letter. "The provincial diet, in genuine Polish irresponsibility, just now commits such incomprehensible foolishness that it is impossible for me to visit the province at this time."[3] The delicate correspondence of Polish, Galician, and Habsburg interests and identities would be a matter of ongoing negotiation and renegotiation during the last decades of the nineteenth century. Franz Joseph himself recognized that the identity of Galicia, even in the age of autonomy, was ideologically dependent upon the figure of the emperor. He would finally reschedule the imperial visit in 1880.

Franz Joseph would live and rule until 1916, almost until the end of Galicia. His mustachioed imperial person, reigning from Vienna and occasionally visiting Galicia, would remain a crucial point of reference for Galician identity, channeling the sentimental affiliations of Poles, Ruthenians, and Jews alike. The grand allegorical goddess of Galicia who presided over the Sejm in Lviv aspired to a similarly transcendent charismatic precedence. The grandeur of allegory, however, was countered by the misery of sociological reality, and Galicia became proverbial for its poverty in 1888 with the publication of *The Misery of Galicia in Statistics* (*Nędza Galicyi w Cyfrach*) by Stanisław Szczepanowski. *The Misery of Galicia* accepted the provincial framework of the age of autonomy, and statistically analyzed the province, not by categories of national difference but according to the economic indices of poverty and backwardness. His statistical approach permitted Szczepanowski to synthesize the figure of "the average Galician" in order to represent the impoverished population of the province.

The Josephine ideology of Galicia, attuned to the enlightened conception of Eastern Europe in the 1780s, was thus reframed in the language and statistics of modern social science one hundred years later, in the 1880s. In 1848, Galicians were susceptible to the revolutionary insinuations of the *Emigracja*, the Emigration: the Poles in Paris, like Mickiewicz at the Collège de France, or Prince Adam Czartoryski at his palace headquarters, the Hotel Lambert. In 1888 a very different and vastly more numerous emigration had already begun: the mass emigration of impoverished Galicians—Poles, Ruthenians,

pulation of this third nationality in Galicia, though not native but im-
[*nie rodzima lecz napływowa*], and of a completely different breed [*całkiem
ego szczepu*], becomes an interesting and scientifically important subject
arch precisely on account of its own distinctiveness . . . for in spite of
enturies of existence in our country, this people, living in villages and little
–those we dealt with exclusively in our research—did not grow from the
o as to be able to distinguish themselves by any stamp of the locality. . . .[11]

any Jews had been living in Poland since the fourteenth century, en-
to settle there by Casimir the Great. The authors emphasized, how-
sh transience, of which they took a rather negative view—"avoiding
ultural work, and pursuing easier earnings, the Jews moved from
place"—in order to explain why Jews would not necessarily be
y regional characteristics. Yet, in the end, when the measurements
were analyzed, Jews turned out to be, on average, exactly as tall as
h both groups only slightly shorter than Ruthenians.[12]
evaluation of skin color each subject was judged as being "white
yellowish [*płowy*]," or "swarthy [*śniady*]." The researchers then con-
ratio of fair subjects to dark subjects for each of the three nation-
es and Ruthenians, with a ratio of three-to-two, were thus shown to
than Jews, with a ratio of two-to-one. For eyes—with each subject's
tered as grey, green, blue, or brown—the ratio of light-to-dark
variation among all three nationalities: Poles had the lightest eyes,
darkest, with Ruthenians intermediary. Hair color, evaluated light-
anked similarly: Poles, then Ruthenians, then Jews.[13] Skulls were
for height, width, and circumference; faces were judged to be short,
ng; and noses were evaluated as straight, flat, pug, and humped.
"scientific" discovery that Jews had statistically more "humped
noses than Poles or Ruthenians, the researchers felt that they had
t they had anticipated from the beginning. The Jews were different:
is regard are most clearly differentiated from the native population
, namely by humped noses."[14] The numerical tables that summed
ole study gave a positivist representation of the province.
nd Kopernicki thus affirmed the similarity of Poles and Ruthenians
rebutting Ruthenian aspirations for partition), and emphasized the
of the Jews, who lived in Galicia but could not be considered
Galicia. Yet perhaps the most important aspect of the study was
ing assumption that Galicia was a meaningful territorial unit for
ogical analysis in the age of autonomy. Earlier in the nineteenth
e plants, animals, and insects of the province had already been
d classified; now the human subjects were also to be analyzed, as
tory made way for modern anthropology. Majer and Kopernicki

and Jews—to America. After the achievement of autonomy in the 1860s, Galicia, taken as a coherent statistical whole, discovered its modern identity as a provincial homeland of extreme misery.

THE ENCYCLOPEDIA OF GALICIA

Antoni Schneider was born in 1825, the son of a Bavarian officer in the Habsburg army in Galicia. He attended the gymnasium in Lviv, joined the Hungarians in fighting against the Habsburgs in 1848, but then, renouncing revolution, entered the Habsburg bureaucracy in Galicia in the 1850s; he worked particularly in the road service, which enabled him to travel around the province. His background inevitably gave him a Galician perspective, even as he associated himself with Polish culture through the literary journal *Dziennik Literacki* in Lviv in the 1860s. There he sought financial support, as well as documents and materials, for his encyclopedia project. In fact, he received a free apartment, courtesy of the Ossolineum, a financial subvention from the Galician Sejm, and some sponsorship from Gołuchowski himself.[4] The first volume, appearing in 1871, offered an introductory apologia: "For many years voices have emerged on behalf of a broader description of our country, for the purpose of a more accurate recognition of its monuments and characteristics so dear to us. Alongside these voices, the progress of national knowledge also requires us to engage in rivalry with the other nations of Europe."[5] Schneider presumed that his public would feel, along with himself, a sentimental attachment to Galicia ("so dear to us") and that an encyclopedic account would satisfy "national" ambitions. The name Poland was not mentioned, and the very nature of the project seemed to suggest that Galicia itself was one of the nations of Europe, the subject of a national knowledge that cried out for representation and publication. The first volume, including the A subjects, contained articles on all the Lviv archbishoprics: Roman Catholic, Ruthenian, and Armenian. The second volume, with the B subjects, covered, among many other things, "Baba, babka: a kind of cake"—and the progress from A to B, from archbishoprics to bakeries, suggested the range of Schneider's eclecticism.

The B volume of 1874 was, in fact, the last to appear, but the state archive in the Wawel Castle in Cracow still today preserves the massive quantity of materials that Schneider had assembled for his project, extending all the way from A to Z. The Galician town of Żurawno on the Dniester, for instance, was covered by a file that contained materials in Polish, German, and Latin: notes on Jan Sobieski resisting the Turks in the seventeenth century, documents from the Jesuit college in the eighteenth century, nineteenth-century newspaper clippings from *Gazeta Lwowska* about the horse market.[6] Schneider's eclectic approach was conducive to representing the heterogeneity of the province, even as it compromised the coherence of the encyclopedic project.

Schneider had preserved a statistical account of Galicia from 1822, three years before his own birth, carried out under the bilingual Socratic slogan—*Kenne dich selbst* and *Znaj siebie samego* ("Know thyself")—with reflections on Galician heterogeneity in German. Who were the Galicians?

> According to descent they are partly Slavs—to which the Poles and Rusniaks belong, partly Moldavian, German, Armenian, Hungarian, and Szekler, partly a mix of several peoples, like the Lipovaners, partly Jews, and additionally a small number of Gypsies. . . . With regard to religion Galicia offers, like the Austrian monarchy as a whole, the image of a great and well-ordered family, in which the patriarch embraces all the branches with equal love and concern, regardless of the difference in their characters and mentalities.[7]

Schneider himself seemed similarly all-embracing in his files of data. The Latin declaration of Maria Theresa upon the partition of Poland in 1772 was accompanied by his penciled note, looking back to the fourteenth century, on the relevance of "the rights of Casimir the Great to Red Ruthenia." The file on the Jews of Drohobych included Polish documents concerning the *kahal*, the Jewish communal institution, from the period of the Commonwealth, but also German documents from the Josephine period of the 1780s, including correspondence with the government about the regulation of marriages and reform of *propinacja*, the leased monopolies on alcohol.[8]

Schneider, trying to understand Galicia comprehensively, could not fail to recognize the Jewish and Ruthenian aspects of the province that emerged all the more emphatically under Polish predominance in the age of autonomy. It was perhaps an impossible project to bring together all the aspects of the province in one coherent encyclopedia project, and the intellectual tensions of such a project also reflected the social and political tensions of the 1870s in Galicia. Having accumulated almost two thousand files of information, having published only two volumes of the whole encyclopedia, having recognized the indifference of the hypothetical Galician public, Schneider shot himself in 1880.

In spite of the impressive institutional support of the Sejm, the Ossolineum, and the *namiestnik*, Schneider's encyclopedia of Galicia came to a halt with the publication of the B volume in Lviv in 1874. In 1876 there appeared in Cracow, however, a very different sort of encyclopedic volume, sharply focused on the coherence of Galicia. Not in the least eclectic in its scope, *The Physical Characteristics of the Population of Galicia* was a supposedly scien-

tific effort to sum up the province according to of the new and modern discipline of physical Józef Majer and Izydor Kopernicki, were work logical Commission of the Jagiellonian Univers Academy of Learning (Akademia Umiejętnośc institutions of Galician autonomy in the 187c 1808, became a professor of physiology at th founding president of the academy from 1872 to have been related to Copernicus, was born in of Schneider. Majer participated as a doctor i while Kopernicki, younger, took part in the ir in Galicia only after the achievement of au was clearly an important Polish dimension t interests. As an anthropologist—one of the pline of anthropology at the Jagiellonian Uni himself to specific studies of Gypsies and hi involved in the contemporary projects, led l lection of folklore and folk songs all over Pc was, however, very specifically provincial in and anything but folkloric in its radically ant

The anthropological commission had spo: tions on living people"—that is, "the provir "the three main component nationalities— The study included 5,052 male subjects—re and examined by local doctors, with results ers—promising thus a representative cros: doctors were supplied with a set of instruc ments to be made. The researchers, Majer a of analysis between them, with Majer cons chest circumference, color of skin and eyes, while Kopernicki dealt with the formation research, conducted in the 1870s, was inten more detailed, more accurate, more scientif of autonomy. Similar sorts of examination science, would be conducted in Galicia, a under the auspices of Nazi Germany in th

On the criterion of height, Poles were fc 164 centimeters—"precisely the average he Ruthenians, including Hutsuls, were mea Jews were clearly expected to be different had succeeded, in their anthropological fashion, in representing Galicia as a coherent human domain—marked by differences and variations to be sure, but composed of interlocking, comparable, related elements. They published their work in Cracow in 1876, the same year that Aleksander Fredro died in Lviv, at the age of eighty-three. In the 1820s he had represented the society of Galicia on stage in his comic dramas; in the 1870s he would scarcely have recognized his own province as reflected in the measurements, ratios, and statistics of physical anthropology.

If proving the difference of the Jews was part of the Galician anthropological project in the 1870s, and contributed to the emergence of modern anti-Semitism, this took place in the context of the Habsburg constitutional reforms of 1867, which had made the Jews of Cis-Leithania equal to other citizens before the law. Although Jews had been emancipated once already in the revolution of 1848, the reaction of the 1850s had restored some civil restrictions, especially with regard to the ownership of land. The constitutional guarantees of 1867 not only emancipated them definitively but also created the postabsolutist political framework in which civic rights became more meaningful than ever before. While Jews acquired those rights all over the monarchy, there was nowhere such a large concentration of Jews as in Galicia, where emancipation thus appeared especially significant. Over the course of the next generation, large numbers of Galician Jews would move to Vienna, and during the 1870s the Jewish population of Vienna increased from 6.6 percent to fully 10 percent.[15] In 1869, Leiser (Eleazer) Erber was born in Galicia in Żurawno, among the first cohort of fully emancipated Jews born as citizens with equal rights in the Habsburg monarchy. Erber would later freely move to Vienna, where he ran a retail business in leather goods. His rights as a citizen lasted until the Anschluss in 1938, when Austria was joined to Nazi Germany. In 1942, Erber was deported from Vienna to Theresienstadt and then murdered in the Holocaust, a life story that was tragically typical for the Jews born in autonomous Galicia after 1867.[16]

The emancipation of the peasantry from feudal obligations in 1848, followed by the full emancipation of the Jews and the constitutional guarantee of civic rights to all citizens in 1867, theoretically demolished the ancien régime and laid the legal foundations for modern society in the Habsburg monarchy, including Galicia. While Galicia enjoyed a special autonomous position within Cis-Leithania, Galicians also enjoyed all the liberal rights of citizens in Cis-Leithania, as legislated by the Reichsrat in 1867, including freedom of speech, religion, and the press, and individual equality before the law. At the same time the Reichsrat legislated collective national rights, declaring that "all peoples [*Volksstämme*] of the state enjoy equal rights, and every people has an inalienable right to the maintenance and cultivation of nationality and language."[17] Language rights were specifically affirmed for administration and education, and the Polish domination of autonomous Galicia was thus contrived in tensely unacknowledged friction with the leg-islated principles of the state as a whole.

The whole concept of equality of rights after 1867—individual and col-lective, for different social classes, different religions, and different nationali-ties—was perhaps more radically unfamiliar in Galicia, a land of formerly huge inequalities, than elsewhere in the monarchy. The affirmation of such rights naturally intensified public awareness of their earlier absence and what it had meant to live without them. On 8 December 1869 the Galician writer Sacher-Masoch, then living in Graz, signed a formal contract to abdicate his human rights and make himself a slave in sexual bondage to the woman he masochistically loved: "Herr Leopold von Sacher-Masoch agrees on his word of honor to be the slave of Frau von Pistor and unconditionally fulfill her every wish and every order for a period of six months." She contractually received the right to punish him at will, and assumed only the obligation to wear furs—"as often as practical and especially when being cruel."[18] This contract, executed in real life, was replicated fictionally in *Venus in Furs*, which was published the next year, in 1870.

Venus in Furs not only made Sacher-Masoch notorious as a writer in the 1870s but also brought an ambiguous celebrity to Galicia itself, making it famous for private rites of violent slavery at precisely the moment when civic rights were, for the first time, legally guaranteed. In 1872 the preface to a French translation of Sacher-Masoch emphasized the Galician terrain of his fiction: "Realism begins to form a school in the Slavic Orient [*l'Orient slave*], where it has appeared in a new aspect, draped in that pessimistic resigna-tion, in that blind submission to the commandments of that nature which forms the basis of the moral philosophy of those pastoral peoples. The most curious and remarkable representative of this school is a Little Russian of Galicia, Monsieur Sacher-Masoch."[19] While Sacher-Masoch thus appeared as a Ruthenian representative of Galicia, the province itself was made to represent a "Slavic Orient" of primitive pastoralism and blind submission to curious commandments.

Sacher-Masoch thus became a famous Galician Ruthenian in the 1870s, all over Europe, though there were also those who concluded from his writ-ings that he must have been a Galician Jew. In the 1880s the writer Wilhelm Goldbaum, in Vienna, described Sacher-Masoch as someone "as much at home between Lemberg and Czernowitz as the most passionate Hasid who makes a pilgrimage five times a year on foot to the rabbi of Sadagora."

Sacher-Masoch could be summed up thus according to his national inclinations: "He hates the Poles, sympathizes with the Ruthenians, and loves the Jews."[20] In short, he was a Galician who embraced the dissident provincial perspectives that were becoming increasingly pronounced in the age of Galician autonomy.

Venus in Furs was published in 1870 as part of an overarching literary project that bore the weighty title *The Testament of Cain*, and Sacher-Masoch also catered directly to his Galician celebrity with such titles as *Galician Tales* (*Galizische Geschichten*) in 1875 and *Jewish Tales* (*Judengeschichten*) in 1878. In 1875, in the tale "Hasara Raba," Sacher-Masoch began with the Emperor Joseph II assigning family names to the Jews of Galicia, and proceeded to the dramatic tale of a Jewish family perversely involved with whips, adultery, kabala, and Oriental costumes—even including a formal contract by which a Polish nobleman purchased the nose of a Galician Jew. In the age of constitutional government in autonomous Galicia, as the province witnessed the evolving encounter between modernity and traditional society, the tales of Sacher-Masoch emphasized precisely those elements that made the province seem bizarre, exotic, primitive, and Oriental. He himself had left Galicia as a child in 1848, before the advent of emancipations or constitutions, and in his vivid literary fantasies his native province remained perversely resistant to the forces of modernity.

KARL EMIL FRANZOS: "EUROPEAN CULTURE AND ASIATIC BARBARISM"

The French preface of 1872 described Sacher-Masoch as the representative of a "school" of realism—though his realism was profoundly influenced by his fantasies. If there really was such a school, cultivating the Galician literary terrain, then its most notable figure in the 1870s, alongside Sacher-Masoch himself, was Karl Emil Franzos. Unlike Sacher-Masoch, Franzos actually was a Galician Jew, and would make the Jews of Galicia into his literary life's work. His grandfather owned a candle factory in Ternopil (Tarnopol), and his father was a doctor in Chortkiv (Czortków). Younger than Sacher-Masoch by twelve years, Franzos was born in the revolutionary year of 1848, and he spent the first ten years of his childhood in postrevolutionary Galicia, in Chortkiv, before his father died in 1858 and his mother moved the family to Czernowitz in neighboring Bukovina. Like Sacher-Masoch, Franzos was nursed as a baby by a Ruthenian peasant woman who also made him familiar with the Ruthenian language and culture; he even had a Slavic nickname, "Milko" for

Emil.[21] Yet his father was educated in a Vienna gymnasium and at German universities, so the boy was brought up in a family of German language and culture, combined with the spirit of enlightened Judaism that eschewed the traditional practices and proscriptions of most Galician Jews. Educated in a gymnasium in Czernowitz and the university in Vienna, Franzos was living in Graz in 1870 when Sacher-Masoch published *Venus in Furs*; they may have had some contact with each other, and the younger man would certainly have been aware of the sudden notoriety of the somewhat older writer.

During the 1870s, Franzos began to write stories about the Jews of Chortkiv, as he remembered them from his childhood, though he renamed the town as Barnow in his fiction. He moved to Vienna and became a contributor to the German liberal newspaper, the *Neue Freie Presse*, one of the papers that often offended the Polish conservatism of *Czas* in Cracow. The image of Galicia in the *Neue Freie Presse* in the 1870s would derive in part from the published contributions of Franzos himself. In 1876 he published in Leipzig the book whose title would sum up a distinctive cultural perspective on Galicia: *Aus Halb-Asien*. It was a collection of stories and sketches from "Half-Asia," the demi-Orient, specified on the title page as Galicia, Bukovina, South Russia, and Romania. Galicia, for Franzos, was the familiar childhood terrain that enabled him to sum up all of Eastern Europe with one hyphenated name. In fact, when *Halb-Asien* was republished in the 1880s, the subtitle was, broadly, "The Land and People of Eastern Europe," while the subject remained, fundamentally, Galicia.

The "Slavic Orient" invoked in the French preface to Sacher-Masoch in 1872 was the same domain of literary realism and exotic fantasy summed up in the title that Franzos adopted in 1876: *Halb-Asien*. Franzos himself attempted to explain the title in terms that echoed the Enlightenment's invention of Eastern Europe, the same terms that formulated the Josephine perspective on Galicia.

> Not just geographically are these lands placed between cultured Europe [*gebildete Europa*] and the barren steppe across which the Asiatic nomads move; not just by the language of their inhabitants . . . are they separated from the rest of Europe; and not just by the landscape do these distant plains and gently merging mountain chains . . . remind one of regions which lie closer to the Urals or in deep Central Asia. No! Also in political and social relations, European culture and Asiatic barbarism strangely encounter one another, European striving and Asiatic indolence, European humanity and such wild, such terrible conflict between nations and religious communities that it must appear to a resident of the West as not just unfamiliar but actually shocking, even unbelievable. The surface, the form, in these lands are in many ways borrowed from the West; the essence, the spirit are in many ways autochthonous and barbaric. . . .[22]

This characterization of Eastern Europe as the intermediary domain between Europe and Asia, between civilization and barbarism, was as old as the Enlightenment.

"When one enters Poland, one believes one has left Europe entirely," wrote the Frenchman Louis-Philippe de Ségur in the 1780s. Metternich invoked the same sort of Orientalism when he was in Galicia in the 1820s: "The Orient begins to reveal itself."[23] Franzos, with the phrase *Halb-Asien*, insisted on the continued relevance of such Orientalism—or rather demi-Orientalism—for evaluating Eastern Europe in general, and Galicia in particular, in the late nineteenth century. This perspective was in notable contrast to that of *Czas* and the Polish elite; for them, the crucial ideological foundation of Galician autonomy was the province's unqualified allegiance to Western civilization.

Franzos particularly emphasized the strangeness and primitiveness of Galician Jews—not without sympathy—and never doubting that the context of Galicia was one of the conditioning factors that made them strange and primitive. "Every land has the Jews that it deserves," wrote Franzos in *Halb-Asien*, suggesting that if Galician Jews were half-Asiatic it was because Galicia itself was half-Asiatic.[24] Majer and Kopernicki sought to confirm by their research in physical anthropology that the Jews were not "native" to Galicia, were anthropologically distinct, while Franzos in the 1870s suggested that the Jews of Galicia were truly Galician Jews, their character shaped by the Galician context.

Because the fiction of Franzos focused closely on one particular town that he called Barnow (modeled on Chortkiv), his work was a kind of anthropology, in which a complete microcosmic Galician community was re-created in careful literary detail. By the beginning of the twentieth century Chortkiv was a town of fifteen thousand people, divided almost evenly among Poles, Ruthenians, and Jews, with a railroad station close by the ruins of the Potocki family palace. During the childhood of Franzos the town would have been still undisturbed by the roar of locomotive engines. In the revolutionary year of his birth, 1848, the Ruthenians of the town gathered to hear Iakiv Holovatsky, of the Ruthenian Triad, speak to them about their national rights: "I spoke about the situation of our nation as the first master of this land from the most distant times, about the splendid period of Rus and our princes, about its collapse during the Tatar incursions, about how Poland lay in wait for Rus and conquered it, about its fate under the rule of the Polish *szlachta* and under Austria's reign up to this date."[25] Franzos, a Jewish child of Austria's reign, would assert his own literary claim to the town in the 1870s as he wrote his stories about "The Jews of Barnow," publishing a collection under that title in 1877 that achieved a worldwide public when it appeared in English translation in New York in 1883. For the Austrian and German reading public Franzos depicted the strangeness of the Galician Jews, conditioned by the backwardness of Galicia. In New York, Galician Jewish immigrants also made a strange impression, especially upon the earlier established community of "our crowd," the German Jews.

The story "Two Saviors of the People" was narrated by an old Jewish grandmother in Barnow with a very long memory. She claimed to be able to remember back as far as the Easter season of 1773, the first Easter after the creation of Habsburg Galicia in 1772. "The Easter festival was about to commence," related the old grandmother, "when it was rumored that the Empress-Queen at Vienna intended to deprive the Poles of their remaining power, and to govern the land hence-forward by means of her own officials. But so far as we could see, there was no sign of this intention being carried out." It was just at this time that a peasant woman—perhaps Polish, per- haps Ruthenian—secretly deposited the corpse of a child in a Jewish house, "in order that the hideous old story might be revived that the Jews were in the habit of killing Christian children before the feast of the Passover; and terrible would be the vengeance of the Christians of the neighborhood."[26] Therefore, a young Jewish woman claimed to have committed the murder herself, claimed that the dead child was her own, so that the whole Jewish community would not be destroyed, but only she would suffer punishment as the "savior" of her people. By the justice of the Polish feudal lord, she was promptly condemned to be broken on the wheel and then beheaded: "But Lea did not die on the scaffold; she died peacefully in her own house forty years later, surrounded by her children and grandchildren; for Austrian military law was proclaimed in the district before Graf Bortynski's people had time to execute the sentence pronounced upon Lea, and an Austrian government official, whose duty it was to try criminal cases, examined the evidence against her."[27] Judged innocent, she received her freedom from the Austrians. Thus, Franzos summed up the dramatic impact of the creation of Galicia in 1772, as Habsburg government began the gradual progress toward overruling the savage social relations of traditional society.

In 1872, a hundred years after the creation of Galicia, Franzos wrote "Es- terka Regina," about a Jewish girl in Barnow of such beauty that she could be compared to the biblical Esther who became queen of Persia, and to the legendary Esther who supposedly entranced Casimir the Great, the medieval king of Poland, and inspired his benevolence toward the Jews. "Esterka Re- gina! That was what we schoolboys used to call her when we returned home for the midsummer holidays from the gymnasium at Ternopil, or from that at Czernowitz," recalled the narrator, "and later on, when we were students at the University of Vienna, we called her by the same name whenever we talked of the girls at Barnow during any of our meetings with each other. Her real name was Rachel Welt."[28] The royal name, Esterka Regina, devised for a Galician Jewish girl, was quintessentially the creation of a generation of Galician Jewish boys with Habsburg educations. Who else could combine the Hebrew name, the Slavic diminutive, and the Latin sobriquet? Like the Emperor Joseph II, the schoolboys gave new names to Galician Jews.

The male admirers of Rachel Welt, Esterka Regina—the Barnow butcher's daughter—included not only Jewish students but also the broader Galician society of Barnow: Habsburg officers and Polish nobles, and even a Polish poet with long hair who had once studied philosophy in Lviv and now wrote verses for a women's magazine in Cracow. The tragic romance of Esterka Regina involved a Barnow boy who was studying at the university in Vienna. The romance began at a Barnow party at the home of a wealthy Jewish widow who herself comically reflected the complex cultural forces conditioning Galician Jews:

> Frau Klein lives like every other Jewess. She does not venture to wear her own hair, and can not bring herself to disobey the Levitical laws regarding food in the smallest particular. But as she once spent six months in Lemberg when she was a girl, she has a sort of Platonic love for "culture" and "enlightenment." She begins nearly every sentence with "When I was in Lemberg." She shows her Platonic love of enlightenment in strange ways. For instance, she delights in speaking High-German, and whenever she manages to pick up a foreign word, she continually drags it into her conversation by hook or by crook for the next week. You can easily imagine how the unfortunate foreign word suffers at her hands.[29]

As the Mrs. Malaprop of *Halb-Asien*, Frau Klein was caught between the conflicting worlds of a little Galician Jewish community and the prestigious attractions of Polish and German culture in Lviv and Vienna, just as Galician students in Vienna could still be subject to the Barnow beauty of Esterka Regina. Sacher-Masoch, of course, created in *Venus in Furs* the demonic apotheosis of a wealthy Galician widow with a more than Platonic commitment to extreme enlightenment.

In the story "Chane," from 1873, a Jewish woman underwent a Galician metamorphosis that led to her leaving her Jewish husband and remarrying the local Habsburg official. She was an Oriental beauty—"her appearance conjures up Zuleima and Zuleika, and the enchanted beauties of the East"—but forever isolated in Barnow society, whether Jewish or Christian: "How can one associate with such a person? Look at her card—why has she not had it printed in the proper way, with her maiden name in the usual place? Because it would not look well to put 'Christine von Negrusz, *née* Bilkes, *divorcée*

Silberstein.' Her real name is Chane."[30] Long after the original renaming of
the Galician Jews by Joseph II, Jewish names remained a complex marker of
Galician Jewish identity. In the case of Chane her Jewish husband Silberstein,
influenced by the poetry of Schiller, resolved to renounce his wife in deference to the power of love.

The notion of German culture as the civilizing principle in Galicia was as
old as the reign of Joseph II. Franzos, making his career as a German writer,
had no doubt that German culture remained the crucial force for enlightenment in *Halb-Asien*, that it could bring light to the primitive, fanatical, Oriental
Jews if only they could unblinker themselves to receive it. In fact, one of the
stories in the original edition of *Halb-Asien* in 1876 was entitled "Schiller in
Barnow"; it suggested the mystically elevating literary charisma of Schiller
for Poles, Ruthenians, and Jews alike. Ironically, this affirmation of German
culture came at exactly the historical moment when provincial autonomy
made Polish into the dominant language and culture of Galicia, paramount
in administration, education, and intellectual life. Up until the 1860s, Jews in
Galicia, if they strayed from traditional society, from Yiddish and Hebrew
culture, found access to education through German culture, and became,
in some sense, Germanized, like the family of Franzos. After the establishment of Galician autonomy, however, more and more Galician Jews would
discover their way to modernity through Polish culture, creating a social class
of Polonized Galician Jews, gradually increasing in numbers relative to the
class of Germanized Galician Jews.[31] In the last Galician Jewish generation,
which witnessed the dissolution of the Habsburg monarchy and the abolition
of Galicia itself, Bruno Schulz, born in 1892, became a great Polish writer,
and Joseph Roth, born in 1894, became a great German writer.

MEMOIRS OF A FORMER HASID

"Every age has a keyhole to which its eye is pasted," wrote Mary McCarthy
in the 1950s, commenting on the titillation of the public by the memoirs of
former communists. In 1874 there was published in Vienna an autobiographical work entitled *The Path of My Life: Memoirs of a Former Hasid*. The author,
Josef Ehrlich, was not a figure of particular importance, but the course of
the life that he had lived was of inevitable interest to the Habsburg public
in the 1870s, when the strangeness of Hasidism in Galicia appeared as one
of the primitive Oriental aspects of *Halb-Asien*. The same public that read
the stories of Franzos would have found in the memoirs of a former Hasid
matter for reflection on the civilizing mission of the monarchy in Galicia.

"My birthplace was Brody," wrote Ehrlich, putting himself immediately on the Habsburg map, "a free trade city by the Russian border of Galicia."[32] Born in 1842, he described himself as a child who displayed precocious enthusiasm as he reached out ahead of all the other children to kiss the Torah. Enthusiasm was the hallmark of a Hasid, and Hasidism would become closely associated with Galicia as the most striking religious aspect of Galician Jewry. "Whenever the prayer leader during worship concluded a blessing," recalled Ehrlich of his childhood, "I had to raise my voice with a resounding 'Umein [Amen].' But in my own enthusiasm I went so far as to ring out with that mighty 'Umein' before the end of the blessing."[33] It was a merely trivial illustration of childish Hasidic enthusiasm, but Ehrlich also indicated a sensitivity to pronunciation, to the particular sound of "Amen" in Brody during his childhood.

The issue of pronunciation came up again when Ehrlich related the encouragement that he received, from his Hasidic mentor, to contemplate a career as a Hasidic rabbi: "Now," continued Samuel, as he ran his fingers through his beard, "I am of the opinion that you will become a rabbi in one of the small towns of Galicia, like Belz for instance." Belz was not tiny and insignificant; by the beginning of the twentieth century it would have six thousand inhabitants, including thirty-six hundred Jews, and would possess "the most famous wonder-working rabbi in Galicia, to whom, several times a year, Jews in crowds of thousands made a pilgrimage, especially at the time of the Jewish New Year."[34] For young Ehrlich in Brody, however, in the middle of the nineteenth century, a small Galician town seemed like a narrow prospect, and he told Samuel that he thought he would not want to be a rabbi in such a town for his whole life.

> "Well then," said Samuel, as he held out the palms of his hands, "you can be the same thing in one of the great cities of Russia. There they are looking for good Jews." "Eh, Russia," I grimaced, "in Russia there are wild Cossacks." "No," Samuel interrupted, "on the contrary, Joschu, the Cossacks have respect for a rabbi; they open up the border-crossings for him, without even asking him for a passport, without even searching his trunks and bags, as they normally do with all other travelers." And I answered quite firmly: "I don't like Russia, for this reason, because the pronunciation of Russian Jews disgusts me [*weil mich die Aussprache der russischen Juden anwidert*], whenever I hear them speak; always "e" instead of "ei"—they just can not say "ei.""[35]

Young Ehrlich clearly embraced the Galician ideology of Western civilization, conceived as a bulwark against "wild Cossacks" and other unsettling Eastern forces. He also, however, seemed to have believed, even as an unknowledgeable child, in some sort of meaningful cultural difference between Galician Jews and Russian Jews.

As a boy in Brody, of course, Ehrlich had none of the resources or methodologies of the Anthropological Commission of the Jagiellonian University in Cracow, and he could offer only crude impressions rather than anthropometric measurements to distinguish between communities. As it happens, however, the details of pronunciation would become anthropologically meaningful for defining what it meant to be a Galician Jew, a Galitzianer. The difference between "ei" and "e"—between "Umein" and "Amen"—would become proverbial in American emigration, distinguishing the Galitzianer from his cultural countertype, the Litvak, or Lithuanian Jew.

Ehrlich's account in the 1870s may be the earliest observation of the dialectical distinction of Galician Jews, especially if the observation can, in fact, be dated back to his childhood in the 1840s and 1850s. Brody's location near the Russian border, and its status as a free trade town, made it possible for Ehrlich to encounter Russian Jews, and to hear them speak Yiddish, so as to form his own Galician identity in contrast to the Jews from beyond the border. That same process of identity formation would later be massively confirmed in New York, where Jews from Galicia encountered Jews from Russian Poland without any border to separate them in the tenements of the Lower East Side of Manhattan. In the 1870s, at the same time that Franzos was fictionally representing the world of Galician Judaism, Ehrlich suggested the crystallization of a distinct ethnographic category of Galician Jews, associated with Austria, with Hasidism, and even with a particular variant of the Yiddish language. By the time that George Bernard Shaw wrote *Pygmalion* in 1916, the Galician Jew, no less than the Cockney, existed as an ethnographic type embedded in his linguistic dialect: Umein!

Ehrlich remembered celebrations of the emperor's name day in the great synagogue of Brody. He recalled his eagerness at the age of seventeen in 1859 to enlist and fight in the war between Austria and Italy, his resignation to staying at home in Brody, his enthusiasm for singing the Austrian anthem, "Gott erhalte!" The autobiography ended with his leaving Galicia and Hasidism behind him, and setting out for Vienna. The memoirs of the former Hasid constituted a book about the cultural formation of a specifically Galician Jew.[36]

Born in Vienna in 1878, into a family of Galician Jews, was Martin Buber, who would become famous in the twentieth century as a German Jewish theologian and philosopher, noted especially for his fascination with Hasidism. In that same year, 1878, in Lviv, the young Ruthenian writer Ivan Franko, who would become famous as one of the leading figures of modern Ukrainian literature, published his novella *Boa Constrictor*, a landmark in the development of his literary career. He had been arrested the previous year for socialist activity, while a student at the university. *Boa Constrictor* offered a socialist perspective on the capitalist oppression of the Ruthenians who worked in the Galician oil fields of Boryslav—and an extremely critical picture of their capitalist oppressor, the Galician Jew.

Martin Buber, though born in Vienna, was actually brought up in the home of his grandfather in Lviv, Solomon Buber, himself a celebrated religious scholar of the Bible and the Talmud. Solomon Buber was born in Lviv in 1827, back in the age of Fredro, became a businessman as well as a scholar, and played a significant role in the capitalist development of Galician banking in the age of provincial autonomy after 1867. He sent his grandson back to Vienna in the 1890s to study at the university, and it was from Vienna that Martin Buber wrote in 1903 to Ivan Franko, to solicit from him for a Jewish journal an article to be entitled "The Jews in Galicia."[37]

Franko instead wrote a more personal essay under the title "My Jewish Acquaintances." He described his subjects with such phrases as "Galician Jewry [*galizische Judenschaft*]" and "Galician Jews [*galizische Juden*]," thus strongly suggesting that he regarded them as a distinctively Galician type.

> Galician Jewry is such a wondrous cultural-historical and national-psychological creation [*ein kulturhistorisch und völkerpsychologisch so wundersames Gebilde*], that neither from an outsider's nor from an insider's perspective can it be completely understood, because each sees a different physiognomy and judges it according to different values. Therefore, to the friendly invitation of the editor of this journal to write an article about Galician Jews, I have answered that I do not feel myself qualified to deal with this theme in its totality, but am willingly ready to depict my personal experiences and thoughts with respect to Jews and Jewish matters as a modest contribution to the knowledge of Galician Jewry. And even this I do only because, in my stories and poems, I have very often presented Jewish types and have sung Jewish melodies, and on that account have reaped from some Jews reproaches of anti-Semitism and from some of my own countrymen reproaches of philo-Semitism. I can only counter all these reproaches by saying that I have just depicted what I have seen and experienced, and as I have understood it, and that I have always tried, in depicting Jews, just as in depicting Ruthenians, Poles, and Gypsies, to see and depict human beings and only human beings.[38]

The human landscape that he represented—of Jews, Ruthenians, Poles, and Gypsies—was unmistakably a Galician landscape, and Franko clearly regarded Galician Jews as a distinct and specific ethnographic category: created by culture and history, motivated by national psychology.

Parallel to Franzos, who was born in 1848 and made his literary reputation in Vienna in the 1870s with stories about Galician Jews, Franko, born in 1856, made his literary reputation in Lviv in the 1870s with stories about Galician Ruthenians in the oil fields of eastern Galicia—in everyday relations with Galician Jews. In the essay "My Jewish Acquaintances," Franko looked back to his childhood, to eastern Galicia in the 1860s, and remembered his Christian mother bringing home unleavened bread to eat at the time of the Jewish Passover season, telling her children that some people said the Jews baked matzoh with the blood of Christian children, but that she considered such beliefs to be nonsense. Franko remembered a Jewish traveling salesman: "He was perhaps a fifty-year-old, gaunt man, a typical Jewish proletarian with a friendly, melancholy face—we children were afraid of him a little." Franko also recalled that in the village school he attended there were two Jewish boys, one of whom briefly became his friend: "He was a nature lover, and loved especially bird hunting and fishing. In these poetical extravagances I became his comrade and companion, and we crossed through the fields to capture young quail and wild doves."[39] Both fear and camaraderie conditioned the enmities and affinities of the different peoples of Galicia.

In the early 1870s, Franko was a student at the gymnasium in Drohobych, where he encountered both Jewish and Polish students. This was the period of the advent of Galician autonomy, which, Franko believed, contributed greatly to the aggravation of national tensions in the province as a consequence of Polish predominance. He remembered Poles and Ruthenians arguing over history and literature, while Jews remained aloof from those controversies. This was also the period of the oil boom at Boryslav, and Franko recalled that from Drohobych it was possible to walk to the oil fields: "I went to Boryslav many times on foot and could also observe in Drohobych, from the most immediate proximity, the activity of the Boryslav workers, entrepreneurs, and speculators."[40] He sorted out these roles according to his sense of the ethnography of Galicia, and according to the values of his own juvenile socialism. Franko's stories about Boryslav that began to appear in the later 1870s represented both Ruthenians and Jews in the social and economic context of contemporary autonomous Galicia.

Historian Alison Frank, writing about the Galician oil industry, has noted that the ethnographic distribution of labor involved relatively more skilled jobs for Poles than for Ruthenians, who often worked underground in the mines, while Jews were more often in the roles of the "tremendously unpopular overseers and foremen." Poor Jews did perform unskilled labor in the oil fields, but, according to Frank, "the existence of Jewish laborers was rarely acknowledged in contemporary sources that presented a stereotypical image of Jews as foremen, small business owners, and tavern-keepers."[41] In 1884 a fight between a Jewish overseer and a Ruthenian miner led to riots and retaliations, an escalating conflict between Christians and Jews that was called the Boryslav Wars.

The Jewish protagonist of Franko's *Boa Constrictor*, Herman Goldkramer, rose from poverty to become the owner of an oil well at Boryslav and a millionaire. Herman had spent his childhood in the village of Gubichi, and Franko lovingly described the Galician landscape:

> Gubichi was a large village on the bank of the Tismennitsa, half-way between Boryslav and Drohobych. A sloping plain rises to the north, the high hills to the south turn into another high plain, crowned by the lovely quadrangle of the Teptyuzh oak forest. The village lies in a hollow, about a thousand feet wide, that stretches along the Tismennitsa from the Boryslav hills to the Kolodruby, where it becomes part of the great Dniester Valley. The strange beauty of the environs of Gubichi is unique.[42]

For Franko, in this very specifically Galician fiction, his Jewish protagonist was a product of Galician geography, clearly native to the province, not somehow alien as suggested by Majer and Kopernicki in their physical anthropology.

Herman Goldkramer was sufficiently native to Galicia to feel nostalgic for the landscape of his childhood, a nostalgia aggravated by spiritual uneasiness over his rise to wealth and power in the oil fields. He felt some fleeting pangs of conscience over the conditions of his Ruthenian workers, and was caught in an ugly Oedipal struggle with his own son—a struggle that Franko, born in 1856, the exact contemporary of Freud, represented as frankly murderous. While Herman was stirred by the Galician landscape, there was also another landscape that haunted his imagination and appeared in his nightmares: the Oriental Bengali landscape of the boa constrictor. Herman had become obsessed with a painting purchased in Vienna, a painting of a boa constrictor attacking a gazelle in the Bengali forest. Bengal was thus brought to Galicia in Franko's fiction; *Boa Constrictor* was published in the same decade as *Halb-Asien*.

Franko did not specify whether Herman feared the boa constrictor, or feared, rather, that he himself had become the boa constrictor. The Ruthenian workers, on the other hand, were portrayed by the author as innocent and vulnerable, like the gazelles. These workers risked their lives to descend into the oil wells.

> Mikola was calmly loading a pickaxe and hoe into an iron tub that was hooked onto the end of the cable; Semyon went on working the pump, swaying to and fro like a drunkard, while Stepan tied a cord to a spring with a bell on the end, lit the lantern, and handed it to Grigory.
>
> "Why are you so slow?" Herman shouted again, enraged by the indifference and wooden calmness of the workers.
>
> "We're doing the best we can!" Semyon answered. "After all, we can't send him down if there's no air there! It's over five hundred feet, and that's no joke, you know!"
>
> "Here, Grisha, take the lantern, and God bless you!" Stepan said.[43]

Herman was still present when they raised up from the well the skeleton and skull of a Ruthenian man who had been killed two years before, perhaps not accidentally, and Herman wondered whether he himself was cursed.

In the essay on Jewish acquaintances that he later wrote for Buber, Franko recalled writing *Boa Constrictor*, and insisted, somewhat defensively, that Herman Goldkramer was not intended as a derogatory stereotype:

> At that time I sketched the story that critics have seen as my first not completely insignificant work, namely the already mentioned *Boa Constrictor*. What was new in it for Ruthenian literature was just the fact that the hero of the story was a Jew, and that this Jew was drawn completely as a man, without any trace of the caricature that was usual till then in Ruthenian (and also Polish) literature (or idealization, which is also caricature in the opposite direction).[44]

What made Galician literature Galician in the 1870s, whether in Franzos or in Franko, was the ways in which Jews, Ruthenians, and Poles appeared in one another's stories, appearing in patterns of conflict and coexistence that were governed by the Galician context, ever more compelling in the age of Galician autonomy.

"With Regard to Rus"

Franko became a young socialist in the later 1870s, and his university education in Lviv was interrupted when he was arrested in 1877. In 1879 he wrote a poem mocking Ruthenian representatives in the Reichsrat in Vienna for routinely supporting the government out of reflexive Habsburg loyalism:

> We are Austrian patriots—
> For Austria we're ready to sacrifice
> Not just money—but even blood,
> If blood is needed.[45]

Leonid Rudnytzky, analyzing "The Image of Austria in the Works of Ivan Franko," places this poem in the context of the poet's discontent with "overzealous loyalty," as Ruthenians sought to compete with Poles in their Habsburg loyalism, as if bidding for the favor of Vienna. Franko, in some of his stories, represented Ruthenian peasants who loyally remembered Emperor Ferdinand from before 1848, and even Joseph II from the eighteenth century—but were more ambivalent about Franz Joseph after 1848, and deeply hostile to his Polish viceroy Gołuchowski.[46]

Ivan Levytsky was also skeptical about the political consequences of unconditional Ruthenian loyalism when he published in Lviv in 1879 (in Polish, as Jan Lewicki) an essay on *The Ruthenian Movement in Galicia*. "For a hundred

Galician misery. In 1884, Galicia would be summed up in a little volume onging to the series of books on "The Lands of Austria-Hungary in d and Image," published under the imperial patronage of Crown Prince olf. In 1888, Galicia would be summed up again, this time in statistical nomic data, under the title *Misery of Galicia* (*Nędza Galicyi*), defining the ince as a coherent domain of extreme poverty.

he famine of 1880 called forth a publication, *Scarcity and Famine in Galicia urodzaj i głód w Galicyi*) by Roger Łubieński, emphasizing his interest in nic work and economic development. He remarked, and *Czas* seconded oncern, about the excessive emphasis on agriculture in Galicia and the esponding lack of development of industry, making the province more eptible to famine.[56] In March 1880, *Czas* noted that "the occurrence of ration of our peasants to America is increasing again," and the newspa-egretted the lack of "moral harmony" in village life—though it might been more apt to mention the lack of agricultural productivity.[57] In ineteenth century, the Kingdom of Galicia and Lodomeria—as listed g Franz Joseph's titles—was sometimes transformed by derogatory ing into "Golicia and Głodomeria": the land of the naked [*goły*] and ungry [*głodny*]. In Lviv in 1868, Apollo Korzeniowski irritably invoked hrase, as if it were a well-known witticism: "Oh, how selfish, selfish to nth degree are those inhabitants of the Kingdom of Głodomeria and ia!"[58] Galician poverty was already proverbial before the famine and ation of the 1880s.

n Franko was arrested again as a socialist in 1880 and imprisoned for months in Kolomiya. One of his poems from prison, "Spring Scene," 28 March, alluded to the famine conditions in Galicia:

> Down in the clear and quiet stream
> The silvery fishes sport and speed,
> While over last year's stubble brown
> The lean cows limp in search of feed.[59]

ranko, famine was not just a matter of economic backwardness, but onomic exploitation and oppression of the impoverished classes of
. He was also sensitive to national oppression, and in 1880 he created em that would become a popular national hymn among Ruthenians in a, though it implicitly rejected Galician Ruthenian identity in the name rainian nationalism:

> No longer, no longer should we
> The Russian or Pole meekly serve!
> Ukraine's ancient grievances lie in the past—
> Ukraine doth our whole life deserve.[60]

years the banner of the Rutheno-Galician leaders has been flying with a lack of faith in the worthiness of their own nationality," began Levytsky, marking one hundred years of Galician history in the 1870s. His own es-say, which focused on the first fifty years of Galicia, from 1772 until 1820, judged the failure of contemporary Rutheno-Galician leaders to make the Viennese government live up to its earlier commitment to the Ruthenians. "All the more comfortably have they relied upon Vienna for the realization of their own illusions, and truly they have been relying for a hundred years," wrote Levytsky. "They only remember the supposed good will of the Aus-trian government demonstrated at the first moment after the annexation of Galicia, having founded the university in Lviv with lectures in the Ruthenian language in the department of theology and philosophy, also the elevation of the Lviv bishopric to the status of metropolitan, which the Austrian govern-ment brought about for its own interest."[47] Beginning with Maria Theresa's establishment of the Barbaraeum seminary in Vienna for Uniate priests in 1774, Levytsky traced a critical history of what the Austrian government had achieved, and what it had failed to achieve, for the Ruthenians of Galicia.

By his definition of the subject and handling of the material, Levytsky clearly established the importance of Galicia as a coherent domain for the study of Ruthenian—or even Rutheno-Galician—national history and na-tional politics. He himself would go on to become extremely erudite and deeply pedantic about this domain as the leading Ruthenian bibliographer of his age. Between 1888 and 1895, Levytsky published in Lviv the components of his comprehensive *Galician-Ruthenian Bibliography* (*Halytsko-ruskaia bybliohrafiia*) with more than seven thousand entries. He also undertook the compilation of a Galician-Ruthenian biographical dictionary but, like Antoni Schneider with his encyclopedia of Galicia, never published beyond the letter B.[48]

Levytsky, perhaps grudgingly, acknowledged Habsburg beneficence to-ward the Uniate Church, at least during the early years of Galicia. The same theme was far more favorably and gratefully treated in the *History of the Union of the Ruthenian Church with Rome from the Oldest Times until the Present*, produced in Vienna in two volumes, in German, by the Ruthenian churchman Julian Pelesz between 1878 and 1881. Pelesz particularly contrasted the unhappy fate of the Uniate Church under the Russian Empire with the relative protection enjoyed under the Habsburgs. In 1886 he himself would become a powerful prelate in Galicia, bishop of Stanyslaviv (today Ivano-Frankivsk, named for Ivan Franko) and bishop of Przemyśl in 1891. In that year, at the Lviv Synod he unsuccessfully advocated the adoption of celibacy for the Uniate Church, which had preserved, like Orthodoxy, a married parish clergy.[49] The Uniate Church in the late nineteenth century was tensely divided over conflict between Vatican and Jesuit efforts to Romanize the Uniates, on the one hand, and Russophile Galician pressures to bring the Uniates closer to Orthodoxy. Indeed, the tense survival of the Uniate Church as a compromise between Roman Catholicism and Russian Orthodoxy was seen as reconciling the West and the East in the Slavic Orient.

In 1879 the Ruthenian Uniate priest Stefan Kachala published in Lviv, in Polish, a book about Poles: *The Politics of the Poles with Regard to Rus*. The book was written in Polish in partial recognition of the fact that Polish had become the predominant language of the public sphere in autonomous Galicia, and, as Kachala said, so that Poles might have the opportunity to appreciate the Ruthenian perspective on Poland and Galicia. While Slovenes and Germans might quarrel within the Habsburg monarchy, Kachala thought it even sadder that "in Galicia two nations of Slavic origin" should maintain such mutual antagonism.[50] Recognizing the importance of history for the formulation of the Polish ideology of Galicia—namely, the historical revisionism of the Cracow historical school—Kachala offered his own work as a similarly revisionist view of history, seen from the Ruthenian perspective. He criticized the "false historical views" of people "believing by tradition in the golden age of former Poland."[51] He rejected conventional Polish views of both the history of former Poland and the history of present Galicia.

Kachala reached back to the medieval era of Halych as a Rus principality, for the name of Galicia indubitably derived from an originally Ruthenian political domain. He noted that the territory of Halych was conquered by Poland, by Casimir the Great, in the fourteenth century, though Kachala did not think Casimir was so great:

> Casimir III, the Polish king, by the right of the stronger, invades Halychian Rus, besieges Lviv, and returns to Cracow with the conquest. Seeing moreover the weakness of the Ruthenians, he decides to conquer Red Rus; he gathers new forces and occupies the lands around Przemyśl, Sanok, and Lubachiv. The Ruthenians negotiate submission under one condition, that their rite and nationality not be violated or changed. Casimir promised not to restrict the faith of the Ruthenians and to respect their nationality, but later, made bold by his advances, he began to persecute the Greek Eastern rite.[52]

Kachala argued that "Halychian Rus" had been illegitimately acquired by Poland in the fourteenth century, and he emphasized the separateness of the Rus territories from the Polish lands of the kingdom. He noted the conditions that stipulated the preservation of a distinctive "nationality"—as he applied the nineteenth-century term anachronistically to the fourteenth century. Casimir's violation of his promise in the fourteenth century established the fundamental illegitimacy of Cracow's relation to Rus, still maintained in violation five cen-

turies later within Galicia. Indeed, Kachala's style of writ with present-tense verbs made him, and his readers, all th casually, and anachronistically, between past and present.

Reconsidering the history of Poland brought Kach that, in any event, confirmed his initial assumptions: " are distinguished from each other not only by habits a language, writing, and rite. In a word, both these Slav separate nations."[53] Kachala himself was born in 1815, a active in 1848. Writing about 1848, he remarked upon t understand Ruthenian national aspirations. Discussing Galician autonomy in the 1860s, Kachala quoted a Polish of 1868, who declared that "there are no Ruthenians, tha what is not Poland is Moscow." Kachala demonstrated rapid pace of Polonization in Galicia in the 1870s, and cla policy for "Halychian Rus" was nothing less than "to des [*zniszczyć Rusinów*]" through cultural warfare. He criticize for its dismissive perspective.[54] In the age of Galician articulated a Ruthenian perspective that challenged the within the context of Habsburg Galicia.

THE VISIT OF FRANZ JOSEPH: "A TRIUMPHAL

The year 1880 inaugurated the next decade with tw occurrences of portentous significance for how Galician ince. First, it was a year of famine: "There was famine in o for the fourth time in fourteen years!" wrote *Czas* on 18 record back to 1866, the pivotal year of Galicia's politica 1880 was the year of Franz Joseph's ceremonial visit to not repeated nearly so frequently, for though he might pa ince on the way to annual military maneuvers on the e had been no formal Galician voyage in the full spirit of solemnity since the postrevolutionary tour of 1851. Fra only twenty-one at that time, but he would be turning Galicia also had come of age after more than a decade the natural disaster of famine and the ritual celebratio visit to Galicia offered opportunities for provincial intr posite poles of self-criticism and self-congratulation. The reaffirmation of Galicia's identity in political terms of and the simultaneous articulation of a social identity ba

Looking beyond the borders of the Habsburg monarchy to Ukrainian brethren in the Russian Empire, Franko began to formulate the course that would lead the Galician Ruthenians to Ukrainian identity.

On 7 July 1880, when the famine was probably already being moderated by the growth of early summer crops, *Czas* announced the confirmation of the emperor's upcoming visit to Galicia. *Czas* welcomed Franz Joseph but warned that "the monarch visiting his own land must be prepared for all sorts of demands, all sorts of grievances against the government or provincial authorities."[61] The grievances of the Ruthenians were surely the principal ones that *Czas* thought the emperor should be prepared to hear when he came to Galicia—to hear and to ignore, for such grievances, according to the Polish perspective, were no more than grumbling expressions of incessant dissatisfaction. *Czas* had no doubt that the quarter of a century since the last visit of Franz Joseph in 1851 had established the credit of the Galician Poles as loyal Habsburg subjects, and that the visit would confirm the reciprocal bonds of provincial loyalty and imperial favor that underlay the "special position" of Galicia in the Habsburg monarchy. Franz Joseph had reigned as emperor for thirty-two years since 1848, and *Czas*, founded in 1848, had also grown old and distinguished over the intervening decades. The Cracow writer Tadeusz Żeleński, known as "Boy," would later remember "the venerable daily *Czas*, the aristocratic, conservative, and clerical organ," with its pervasive influence on the public: "*Czas* writes, *Czas* says, these were words that rang in my ears from my earliest childhood."[62] Boy was born in 1874, so his childhood dated back to the emperor's visit to Galicia in 1880, the moment of the newspaper's maximal prestige and impact.

Czas demonstrated its Galician loyalism the very next week, on 13 July, when the newspaper reacted to a manifesto that appeared in Lviv, calling for public observances in all the Polish lands to mark the fiftieth anniversary of the November Insurrection of 1830. "We judge that there will be no one who supposes that such a sad anniversary of the defeat of the whole nation can be otherwise observed than at home in silence, in the silence of hearts and in mourning," wrote *Czas*, rejecting all public demonstrations. Those behind the manifesto, according to *Czas*, were "incorrigible or unhealthy people [*ludzie niepoprawni lub chorobliwi*]" who "like to sanctify former political mistakes." Furthermore, with an implicit allusion to the emperor's upcoming visit, *Czas* remarked that "the moment for issuing such a manifesto in Galicia was fatally chosen."[63] It would have been better not to offer a trace of insurrectionary sentiment during the year that Franz Joseph was going to visit the province.

One month later, on 18 August, *Czas* demonstrated its preference for a very different sort of fiftieth anniversary—that is, the fiftieth birthday of

Emperor Franz Joseph, born on 18 August 1830. Noting that the whole monarchy was celebrating "joyfully," *Czas* particularly emphasized the Galician reasons for celebration: "For that of the Polish nation under the scepter of the emperor of Austria, this reign constitutes an important and decisive stage and the happiest epoch since the time that Galicia entered into the structure of the monarchy." Because Franz Joseph demonstrated his respect for the "rights" of nationality, "he created during his reign a moral foundation for the relation of Galicia to Austria which had not existed until then, a foundation which—we do not doubt it—has already become a tradition of his dynasty forever [*na zawsze*]."[64] Far from nostalgic for the insurrection of November 1830, *Czas* took the opportunity of the emperor's birthday to declare, in an extraordinary gesture, that Galicia's adherence to the Habsburgs was neither transitory nor expedient, but moral and eternal. The annexation of 1772 may have been a matter of power, with just a figleaf of ideological justification based on dynastic claims, but, according to *Czas*, the evolution of the Habsburg monarchy during the reign of Franz Joseph, and especially the acknowledgment of national rights through provincial autonomy, finally, and for the first time, created a moral basis for the existence of Galicia.

Meanwhile, the Ruthenians also looked back to the founding era of Galicia and affirmed their own Habsburg loyalism by preparing to celebrate the centennial of Joseph II, who became the sole ruler of the monarchy at Maria Theresa's death in 1780. Joseph's alleviations of serfdom made him particularly commemorable for peasant Ruthenians, and an emissary from Galicia placed a wreath on his coffin in the Capuchin crypt in Vienna: "Galician-Ruthenians—To Emperor Joseph II—1880."[65] The occasion thus affirmed both Ruthenian Habsburg loyalism and Ruthenian Galician identity.

On 22 August, *Czas* published Franz Joseph's schedule: his anticipated arrival in Galicia at the train station of Auschwitz (Oświęcim) on 1 September, the two weeks that he would spend mostly in Cracow and Lviv, with train stops in Tarnów, Rzeszów, and Przemyśl, the excursion to Drohobych, and the five days with the army on military exercises. Historian Patrice Dabrowski has further noted the significance of the emperor's visit to an ethnographic exhibit at Kolomiya that featured the Hutsuls as figures of Galician folklore. The emperor's presence at this exhibit, according to Dabrowski, represented the culmination of the nineteenth-century "discovery" of the Galician Carpathians.[66]

On 1 September, *Czas* greeted "the monarch whom our country has been anticipating with longing for years, to pay him grateful homage." There was no ulterior motive for the emperor's visit, no particular political issue on the table, no special occasion to be marked:

This will be a triumphal procession. It will be an unusual triumph, unique, of its own kind, because it is neither the celebration of bloody victories or new acquisitions, nor a procession to heroic and martial enterprises, but the solemn and peaceful ceremonial signifying the fruitful rebirth of society for the future and also the complete transformation of the meaning of the relation of a great country and the nation inhabiting it to a glorious dynasty and vast monarchy.[67]

Galicia was the "great country," which, in the careless account of *Czas*, was represented as the homeland of one single nation. The triumph of the emperor would thus be interpreted as a simultaneous triumph for the Polish Galician perspective, for its cultural hegemony in the autonomous province. The alleged triumph involved "victory without victors or vanquished," based upon "the community of culture, religion, and civilization, the reciprocal understanding of needs and purposes."[68]

Czas concluded its editorial by reciting the famous declaration of 1866, still pertinent in 1880: "under the motto which was put forward years ago, and has not ceased, and will never cease to be our slogan: We stand with you, Your Majesty, and we wish to stand with you!" The affirmation of loyalty was also the foundation of autonomy, and inspired *Czas* to envision the permanent Habsburg proprietorship of Galicia. The triumph of the imperial visit would override the misery of the famine, and the grumblers with their grievances—like the Ruthenians who believed that Galicia was a country of two nations—would not be heard above the triumphal fanfares. The records in the Cracow municipal archive preserve the forms with which the city ordered from Vienna an assortment of "balcony banners" for hanging out over the streets, in three sizes—small, medium, and large—as well as lamps with the image of the imperial crown, and golden candelabras to plant on balconies for nocturnal illumination.[69]

Historian Daniel Unowsky has found that the "triumph" was conditioned by the fact that the Galician conservatives, the same forces who governed the province and edited *Czas*, were permitted by the emperor to script a large part of the imperial visit. Whereas the visit of 1851 had been programmed strictly by Habsburg bureaucrats in the spirit of neoabsolutism, now, in the age of autonomy, the governing class of Galicia had autonomously staged some of the spectacle. According to Unowsky, "The Polish conservatives labored to orchestrate a series of public spectacles designed to communicate the Stańczyks' message of imperial loyalty and Polish achievement." One Galician official, who played a role in the orchestration, recorded that "our endeavor was, naturally, to avoid any kind of dissonance during the reception of the emperor, so that everything flowed smoothly."[70] Galicians thus articulated the significance of Galicia, presenting the province to the emperor, and presenting the emperor to the province, as fundamentally inseparable aspects of Galician identity.

The *namiestnik* Alfred Potocki was there to welcome the emperor at the Auschwitz train station on 1 September 1880. Potocki (whose father, also Alfred Potocki, was Fredro's friend) had served as the emperor's minister president in Vienna in 1870–71, and had been honored with the supreme Habsburg decoration of the Golden Fleece. In Lviv, *Gazeta Lwowska* celebrated the emperor's arrival in Galicia, "in our country [*w kraju naszym*]." The newspaper anticipated "thundering cries breaking out from thousands of breasts, offered with joyous echo from district to district, from town to town, from village to village, along the whole way through Galicia."[71] Although only just begun, the voyage had already, in anticipatory fantasy, unified Galicia into a welcoming whole, expressing its unanimous loyalty.

On 2 September in Cracow, the emperor ascended to the Wawel Castle and Cathedral to visit the tombs of the Polish kings, where the remains of Casimir the Great had been ritually reinterred in 1869. A delegation of the Sejm formally proposed to the emperor that he accept the Wawel Castle, the residence of the Polish kings, as his own imperial residence whenever he might happen to come to Cracow. Józef Szujski served on the Cracow welcoming committee, and Franz Joseph visited the Jagiellonian University and the Academy of Learning in Cracow, both institutions at which Szujski exercised his intellectual sway over the Polish Galician perspective. The president of the academy, welcoming the emperor, was Józef Majer, author with Kopernicki of *The Physical Characteristics of the Population of Galicia*.[72]

The busy schedule for the afternoon of 2 September involved hurrying the emperor to the university at two o'clock, the academy at 2:20, the Mariacki Church at 2:45, and the Czartoryski Museum at 3:10. This last museum had opened in 1878, when the Czartoryski family moved their celebrated artistic collection, including Leonardo Da Vinci's "Lady with Ermine," from Paris to Cracow, partly as a gesture of confidence in Galician autonomy. The emperor's schedule allowed for twenty-five minutes to visit the museum. The next day, on 3 September, he visited St. Anne's gymnasium school, where Szujski had been a student in the 1850s. Now the current classes of 1880 sang the Austrian anthem in Polish, earning the emperor's approval in German: *sehr schön gesungen* ["very prettily sung"].[73] Cracow had been singing that same old song for a long time, and with increasing conviction since the 1860s.

Czas lovingly described the emperor's last night in Cracow, when he passed in procession through the Rynek square, where he was residing at the Potocki palace "Pod Baranami," under the stone rams. People were dancing in the

Sukiennice with the festivities spilling out into the Rynek itself: "and among the dancers peasants were mixing with great nobles and men in *kontusz*." It was a scene to encourage historical amnesia, to efface all memories of the horrors of 1846 when peasants murdered nobles. The *kontusz* was the long coat worn by Polish nobles in centuries past, in the former Commonwealth, and *Czas*, as it declared the emperor's visit to Cracow a "triumph," was engaged in dialogue with the ghosts of Polish history: "This Cracow Rynek, in which at meditative moments we see so many figures from Casimir the Great to Kościuszko, so many centuries of historical scenes, preserves also the traces of the steps of Franz Joseph on his nocturnal procession."[74] This was Cracow historical revisionism at its most active, placing the Habsburg emperor in heroic succession to the greatest names of Polish national history, forging a Galician history alongside the Polish tradition.

There were a hundred thousand people gathered to greet Franz Joseph when he entered Lviv on 11 September. The *namiestnik* was there to welcome him, and the emperor visited such quintessentially Galician institutions as the Ossolineum Library. There was also, however, a separate Ruthenian reception committee in Lviv, which sponsored particular Ruthenian occasions for welcoming the emperor to the Uniate Church of St. George and the Ruthenian National Institute. Philologist Michael Moser has shown that Ruthenian primers, in editions of 1859 and 1871, actually preserved the memory of Franz Joseph's attentions to the Ruthenians on his earlier visit to Lviv in 1851.[75] In 1880, as in 1851, such attentions could become the occasions for subtle expressions of dissent, not because the Ruthenians were lacking in demonstrative loyalty to the emperor, but rather because they would not permit Ruthenian sentiment to be silently subsumed within a general manifestation of Galician loyalty, as orchestrated by the Polish ruling class. Commemorating the centennial of Joseph II, for instance, permitted Ruthenians to express their Habsburg loyalism with a dash of Josephine hostility to Polishness.

Franz Joseph's visit to Galicia produced multiple manifestations of loyalty, under the pretense of general Galician sentiment, but there nevertheless emerged tensions over the identity and representation of Galicia. With the visit already drawing to a close on 15 September, its significance for the idea of Galicia was articulated in *Czas*: "Galicia enjoying national rights and freedoms, Galicia morally in close conjunction with the monarchy, joined together with the Habsburg dynasty, loyal and grateful to the monarch who allows her to reconcile respect for the past with the needs of the present."[76] Galicia was to be ultimately vindicated by an ideology of reconciliation: imperial loyalty and national rights, the national past and the provincial present.

DON QUIXOTE AND SANCHO PANZA

In 1881 a Polish Roman Catholic order, the Brothers of the Resurrection, proposed the establishment of a boarding school for Ruthenian students in Galicia, in the interest of promoting reconciliation between the Roman and Greek Catholic rites. The order had been founded in Rome by émigré Poles in the aftermath of the November Insurrection of 1830, and one generation later, in 1868, the historian Walerian Kalinka decided to become a Resurrectionist. He stood behind the school project as a means to "resolve the Ruthenian question with love and not with hate."[77] Ruthenians, however, strongly opposed the school, seeing in it a stratagem to Romanize the Uniates, to Polonize the Ruthenians, and thus to advance Polish national predominance in Galicia.

Speaking against the school in the Galician Sejm in 1881 was Stefan Kachala. Thus, the debate over reconciliation in Galicia, turning on the proposed boarding school, brought into conflict two irreconcilable historical perspectives, that of Kalinka and that of Kachala. *Czas* looked for "harmony" in Galicia, but Kachala refused to play a harmonious part, and demanded Ruthenian national rights:

> If there is enmity between Ruthenians and Poles, it is because the Ruthenians are demanding their rights and the Poles refuse to grant them. As long as there are not equal rights, there will be no mutual harmony. For harmony to become consolidated, it has to be based not on boarding schools, but on justice.[78]

While *Czas* in 1880 had viewed the emperor's visit as the occasion for celebrating Galician autonomy based on national rights, Kachala offered pointed dissent in 1881, declaring that "this is not autonomy, but hegemony."[79] The alleged unity of Galicia, orchestrated in celebration of Franz Joseph, was almost immediately disproved by the controversy between Poles and Ruthenians over the boarding school.

In 1882, Józef Szujski published in Vienna, in German, a book on *The Poles and Ruthenians in Galicia*, appearing as a volume in a series on *The Peoples of Austria-Hungary: Ethnographic and Cultural-Historical Representations.* The work had been prepared for the series in particular conjunction with the visit of the emperor to Galicia in 1880, and was intended to illuminate a province that supposedly still remained little known outside its own borders.

> The Austrian fatherland of the Poles and the Ruthenians, Galicia, belongs to the most neglected areas of general and of Austrian geography. Handbooks and even larger works skip over this land as hurriedly as possible; travelers very rarely choose it as a destination for serious observations; more often, tendentious correspondents indulge in variously colored views of its circumstances which, far

from illuminating the darkness, combine truth and falsehood in Rembrandt-like shadow images. So it happens that the European public, even the Austrian public, indifferently permits itself to be told monstrous things [*manches Ungeheuerliche*] about Galicia in novellas, novels, and newspaper pages.[80]

No doubt the works of Sacher-Masoch and Franzos were among those that he indicted for spreading monstrous lies about Galicia, or rather for mixing truth and falsehood in shadowy confusion, putting perverse fantasies of Galicia before the European public. As a Galician Szujski stepped forward to offer a supposedly accurate representation of his "fatherland"—written in German to enlighten the public beyond the borders of Galicia, and especially in the imperial capital.

If Galicia was, as Szujski liberally defined it, the fatherland of both Poles and Ruthenians, then he was particularly qualified to represent it to the foreign public, since he could claim to be both Polish and Ruthenian. The Szujski/Shuisky family was one of the great princely families of medieval Rus, as clearly demonstrated by the family history: one branch had resided in the Lithuanian lands of the Polish-Lithuanian Commonwealth, while another branch had featured prominently in Russian history, and Vasily Shuisky was actually czar in Moscow from 1606 to 1610 during the Time of Troubles, after the death of Boris Godunov and before the accession of the Romanov Dynasty. Józef Szujski could thus claim from his medieval Rus ancestry a transcendent perspective upon the contemporary ethnographic controversies of Galicia.

Szujski surveyed the variety of peoples inhabiting the province, the various communities of mountaineers in their diversely colorful folk costumes. Yet he recognized the Poles and Ruthenians as the two principal ethnographic orders, and attempted to identify the boundaries between them:

> The opposite poles of Polishness and Ruthenianism in East Galicia are not strongly felt—either harmonized, or in a gentle adjacent coexistence—but they stand forth clearly even today at the ancient Ruthenian-Polish border in West Galicia, and the Rusniak demonstrates in his character, with respect to the neighboring Polish villager, many original, divergent ethnographic features. Of slender form, of delicate limbs, almost universally dark-eyed and dark-haired, slow and melancholy in his deportment . . .[81]

Szujski was interested in the metrics of physical anthropology, the coloring of eyes and hair, but also attempted to draw a more general contrast, while noting the convergence of types through centuries of adjacency.

The ethnographic boundary that Szujski discovered was marked spiritually by melancholy, and seemed to recapitulate the chasm between East and West in *Halb-Asien*. The Rusniak village with its wooden buildings might at first deceive the eye, and imply prosperity, but inside the houses Szujski found only poverty, "faces pale with hunger," no doubt suffering the consequences of recurrent famine in Galicia. "So melancholy, yes almost tragic, appears to us the Ruthenian at the first encounter," wrote Szujski, having carefully staged that encounter for his readers. The Ruthenian villages were primitive to the point of exoticism. "They appear picturesque in any event and original," he wrote, "comparable to African villages. Straw, twigs, clay, and a little wood form the building materials."[82] Orientalism was scarcely strong enough to convey the chasm of civilization that Szujski perceived—or attributed—when he contemplated Africa in the Ruthenian villages of Galicia.

Anthropologically, Galicia was an amalgam, according to Szujski: "In Galicia, for centuries, German blood has been mixing with Polish and Ruthenian blood." Of course, Galicia had not actually existed for centuries, only for one century, and Szujski was aware that Joseph II, with the establishment of Galicia, had introduced new German settlers in the 1780s. "But they too," observed Szujski, "the Protestants excepted, have lost some of their original Germanness, and are becoming amalgamated [*verschmelzen sich*] in many ways with the population of the province."[83] Amalgamation [*Verschmelzung*] was, in fact, one of the themes of Josephine writing about Galicia, dating back to the travelogue of Franz Kratter in the 1780s. The theme of amalgamation was relevant even to the Jews of Galicia, according to Szujski. He recognized Galicia as the fatherland of Poles and Ruthenes, but he noted that Jews made up 10 percent of the population. "The educated element, streaming toward German or Polish culture, follow the currents of general financial and business movements," he observed, suggesting the dynamics of cultural transformation, of Jews becoming Germans or Poles. As for the impoverished Jewish masses, they lived "among the impoverished Christian population," and their conditions also converged in poverty—"or now and then they sought the sea route to America or Australia."[84]

Szujski was further aware that the "Galician Jew" had achieved a kind of "European fame"—though this presumably resulted from the kind of novelistic sensationalism that he himself deplored. This category of the "Galician Jew" could be sorted into three major types: the "civilized Pole or German of Mosaic confession," in professional or business careers; the "half-civilized" Jews who were dressed "half modern, half old-fashioned" and presumably belonged to *Halb-Asien*; and finally the Hasids with their fur caps and inveterate traditionalism.[85] Szujski accepted that Jews were an integral part of Galician society, "an extremely active and energetic people in the Christian society of Galicia, in between two Slavic breeds, one rash Slavic, the other careless Slavic." In this rather casual anthropology of the Slavic spirit, the Jews actually served to integrate the divergent emotional characters of the two principal Slavic communities. According to Szujski, the erudite professor at the Jagiellonian University, the Galician Jew mediated between the noble Polish Don Quixote and the peasant Ruthenian Sancho Panza: "One could call this middle class almost beloved, so intimately has it grown together with the Christian society of Galicia."[86] So Jews were not actually aliens, and though some might be seen as half-civilized, that only confirmed their intermediary and integrating role in Galician society. That society was, in Szujski's vision, constituted by the integration and amalgamation of assorted Galician peoples.

The contrast between the Polish Don Quixote and the Ruthenian Sancho Panza was not intended to be flattering to the latter. The possibility of Ruthenian civilization was not seriously considered by Szujski, and when he wrote about the history of Rus—that is, the history of his own princely ancestors—he regretted that "the Halych empire could not leave behind some number of cultural sites and cultural works." The Rus world collapsed after the Tartar onslaughts, and there was nothing culturally meaningful that Galicia could have inherited from Halych. Casimir the Great, annexing Ruthenia in the fourteenth century, brought "the blessings of civilization from Poland to the land that was languishing under Tartar subjection."[87] Szujski, whose family was absorbed into Polish culture centuries before, himself brought the "blessings of civilization" to Galicia through such Polish cultural institutions as the Jagiellonian University and the Academy of Learning. The ideology of civilization had been fundamental to Galician autonomy ever since the declaration of 1866, and in 1882, Szujski invoked that ideology, historically and anthropologically, to clarify the Polish perspective on the Ruthenians of Galicia.

In fact, archaeological research of the early 1880s, in the region around Halych, uncovered some of the medieval remains of the Rus principality that gave Galicia its name, and therefore encouraged Ruthenian claims that the province was originally their own. In 1882 the Ruthenian journal *Zoria* lamented that the town of Halych had "lost its ancient, truly Ruthenian character," and complained of the strong Jewish presence there. By 1887, *Zoria* would be writing more generally about "our Galicia," noting that "Galician Rus had always been a threshold between Western Europe and the East."[88] In the 1880s, Ruthenians thus met the Polish presumption of civilized rule with a reciprocal Ruthenian claim to the province, favoring the eastern aspect of the delicately constructed identity of Galicia between east and west.

The year 1883 offered a bicentennial occasion of irresistible ideological implications in Galicia, the two hundredth anniversary of the liberation of Vienna from the Ottoman Turkish siege by the Polish king Jan Sobieski in

1683. There was a historical exhibit of Turkish tents and Western armor in the Sukiennice in Cracow, and a huge historical painting of "Sobieski at Vienna" was completed by the foremost Cracow artist, Jan Matejko. On 12 September, the anniversary date of the assault on the Ottomans, there was a ceremonial procession to the Wawel Cathedral, where Sobieski was entombed; the procession then descended from the Wawel to the Rynek, where a bronze monument to Sobieski was unveiled, and a cantata, composed for the occasion by Władysław Żeleński (the father of Tadeusz), was performed.[89]

In addition to the urban public of Cracow, there were thousands of peasants who came to the city for the celebration, prompted especially by the populist priest Stanisław Stojałowski. Historian Keely Stauter-Halsted has suggested that commemorative pageantry in the final decades of the nineteenth century was conceived as a means for promoting Polish national identity among the Galician peasantry, which had been so emphatically non-national in 1846.[90] The commemoration of 1883 was, at the same time, nationally Polish, imperially Habsburg, and provincially Galician. The Poles had been of invaluable assistance to Austria in 1683, even as the Galicians remained crucial political associates in the governing of Cis-Leithania in 1883, supporting the conservative ministry of Eduard Taaffe in Vienna. The souvenir postcard of the occasion, representing Sobieski, as drawn by the Cracow artist Juliusz Kossak, offered side-by-side texts in Polish and Ruthenian, emphasizing the fully Galician nature of the public.[91] Matejko's canvas of "Sobieski at Vienna" was sent to Vienna for display, and eventually ended up in the Vatican.

The lyrics to the Żeleński cantata were penned by the Cracow writer Władysław Ludwik Anczyc; born in 1823, Anczyc was old enough to have participated in the Cracow insurrection of 1846. In 1848 he published in Cracow a poem on "The Galician Brigand of 1846," about Jakub Szela. Yet, in his Galician lyrics of 1883, Anczyc enthusiastically celebrated the defense of Vienna:

> The invincible courage of Polish knights,
> brought down the power of the crescent moon—
> And Christ gave victory to Sobieski
> and the imperial capital was rescued.[92]

No Polish national commemoration could have been more ideologically Galician.

In early 1884, *Czas* cited the recently deceased Anczyc with reference to the increasingly alarming issue of emigration to America. Anczyc had composed popular dramas on peasant themes, such as *Peasant Emigration* and *Kościuszko at Racławice*, a historical drama about Polish peasants fighting with scythes against the Russians in 1794. *Czas* mentioned Anczyc as one who had brought the issue of emigration before the public, while now, after his death, a new wave of emigration was anticipated for the spring of 1884: peasants were reported to be selling their plots and homes in order to collect the cash for the voyage. "It is difficult to believe to what degree they have responded in recent years to the awakening of various desires and needs, not only among those who are going to America, but among those who remain in the country," wrote *Czas*. "Our peasantry [*lud nasz*] is becoming Americanized [*amerykanizuje się*]—if only it were not just with respect to material instincts, but also with respect to the spirit of initiative and the sense of work."[93] *Czas* seemed to recognize that the identity of a Galician peasant was sufficiently amorphous to permit Americanization.

Czas noted that in Galicia there was a particular region that was most susceptible to emigration, a triangle of territory in central Galicia from Tarnów to Jasło to Rzeszów. This region, according to *Czas*, lacked strong folk traditions and colorful local costumes.

> As with dress, so also in human type, there is here no local singularity or original-ity. Szujski, in his well-known work *The Poles and Ruthenians in Galicia*, calls the people of this region deaf-and-dumb Germans and denies their Slavic origin. It seemed to us that there must also be some significant admixture of Tartar cap-tives in those who became settlers here. In any event this is a population which, among all the breeds populating Galicia, shows the least attachment to tradition and custom, and also to the land—in this region emerged that type of peasant who became imperial, and about whom they say in Vienna, "Der Bauer wacht in Galizien" ["The peasant stands guard in Galicia"]. Though the storm of 1846 spread into other regions with equal violence, it was in this corner of the country that it had its original flame, and here emerged its hero Szela.[94]

Czas emphasized that this seemed to reflect the circumstances of one par-ticular locality, characterized by "the worst traditions of the Galician peas-antry." Elsewhere in the province, by implication, better Galician traditions prevailed.

The paradox was that the peasant most inclined to leave Galicia was also the peasant who was, in some sense, most Galician—that is, of such amor-phous identity as to feel truly "imperial." The same lack of "attachment" that made possible the massacres of 1846 now seemed to encourage the abandon-ment of Galicia by emigration. Szela, removed from Galicia to Bukovina in the aftermath of 1846, was rediscovered as the emblematic Galician emigrant, originating in the geographical triangle of peasant detachment from the land. The deep ambivalence of conservative organs like *Czas*, contemplating the peasantry, was reflected in its perspective on emigration, which, on the one hand, had to be regretted, and, on the other, might be secretly welcomed—if the peasant emigrant was spiritually related to Jakub Szela.

"In Word and Image"

The posthumous publication of Metternich's memoirs in the 1880s enabled the Galician public to appreciate the tenuousness of Galicia itself during its early decades of existence. *Czas* revealed, in an article of April 1884, that Metternich had contemplated giving up Galicia altogether after Napoleon created the Grand Duchy of Warsaw. It seemed to the Habsburg chancellor that if Poland were actually to be restored, Galicia would be surely lost to Austria: "So we can either lose Galicia without compensation, or surrender it voluntarily with compensation." The memoirs revealed Metternich's unedifying indifference to the possession of a province whose Habsburg identity, since that time, had come to seem almost self-evident, from the reign of Franz to the reign of Franz Joseph.[95]

In 1884, *Czas* was already looking toward the next Habsburg reign, and noted with interest the publication in that year of Crown Prince Rudolf's travel account, *An Oriental Voyage* (*Eine Orientreise*), about southeastern Europe and the Ottoman Empire. The prince's rumored liberalism could not have been altogether to the taste of *Czas* and its conservative editors, but they respected his intellectual curiosity as a traveler:

> The inquiring intellect, dedicated to science, of our heir to the throne has inclined him already to undertaking distant journeys, which he has willingly pursued, since he loves nature and wants to investigate it. But voyages have an unappreciated side of immeasurable value for a prince, in that they allow him to know better the most important part of nature, the human part. Knowledge of humanity, that is the foundation of wise governments.[96]

The hint was delicate, but nevertheless public in the pages of *Czas*. If the curiosity of the crown prince could take him as far as the Orient, then he might also want to undertake a voyage to the semi-Orient of *Halb-Asien*, where he could learn to know the Galicians who anticipated his visit no less than his eventual rule. Habsburg visits were always welcome occasions for affirming the ideology of Galicia.

Joseph Redlich, in his classic account of the reign of Franz Joseph, emphasized the creative and liberal intellectual endeavors of Crown Prince Rudolf during the 1880s, the last decade of his life, which would end in the scandalous double suicide at Mayerling in 1889. "About the middle of the eighties, he formed a great literary plan and carried it through with all the temperamental zest native to him," wrote Redlich, concerning Rudolf's sponsorship of the multivolume series of books on *The Lands of Austria-Hungary in Word and Image* (*in Wort und Bild*). According to Redlich, "an exhaustive description of the whole realm in all its parts and of all its nationalities was to be produced by the cooperation of distinguished authors and scholars."[97] Already in 1884 there appeared in Vienna, in German, the Galician volume *The Kingdom of Galicia and Lodomeria* in 150 pages, with *The Duchy of Bukovina*, now a separate crownland, discussed as an addendum of 40 pages. The author was Julius Jandaurek, who was teaching German in the gymnasium in Lviv—by title a "professor," though teaching high school students. His previous publications from the 1870s had included texts for teaching German in Galician middle schools. In other words, he was a teacher whose pedagogical expertise had been rendered somewhat marginal by Galician autonomy, when Polish displaced German as the basic language of instruction in the province. Now, under the special patronage of the crown prince, he would sum up Galicia as an imperial possession for the Viennese public.

Beginning with a "historical overview," Jandaurek related Polish history as Galician history, from "the oldest legends of the Slavs on the upper Vistula." These legends involved the mythological dragon-slaying founder of Cracow, Krak, and his daughter Wanda, who supposedly refused to marry a German prince and killed herself by jumping into the Vistula.[98] Jandaurek was sentimentally attached to the Galician landscape, whose principal features he presented as the Carpathian Mountains and the great rivers, Vistula and Dniester. The Vistula was fondly described with attention to the harmony between the natural and the human, the river and the traditional "Galician raftsmen" with their straw hats: "Life and movement is here from first dawn to the onset of dark night. You see at various distances red fire shining on the rafts, and you hear happy fiddle tones." Peace came to the Vistula at night, when the moon arose to gaze upon itself in the Vistula-mirror [*Weichselspiegel*].[99]

Concerning nationality, Jandaurek cited the recent census figures of 1880: the total population of Galicia at almost 6 million, including 3 million Poles, 2.5 million Ruthenians, and 300,000 Germans. This census was based on language, and therefore did not include the Galician Jews as a separate category, for Yiddish was not one of the authorized language choices. For this reason, Jews tended to be counted as Poles, and the percentage of Poles in Galicia was correspondingly overstated in the census. The survey by religion, also cited by Jandaurek, clarified the breakdown: 2.7 million Roman Catholics, 2.5 million Greek Catholics, and 700,000 Jews.[100]

For Jandaurek, simple nationality was less interesting than complex ethnography, and his book presented a great variety of Galician ethnographic communities, with an emphasis on different folk costumes, generously illustrated. He divided the population into general Polish and Ruthenian categories, but also into people of the plains and people of the mountains. Among the latter there were Mazurs and Krakowiaks; among the former there were

Hutsuls and Boykos. One image presented a "Krakusse" or "Krakowiak," with a plumed cap and embroidered cape.[101] According to Jandaurek, this community was famous for its enthusiastic style of singing.

> Joyously singing, the Krakusse cultivates his native earth, and, singing, he hero-
> ically stands up for the same; music and song so rightly characterize his essence;
> he too, like the Galician in general [*wie überhaupt der Galizianer*], is an excellent
> rider. When Emperor Franz Joseph gladdened Galicia with his visit in the fall of
> 1879 [*sic*], it was mounted troops of Krakusse, riding boldly, who led the beloved
> monarch's coach on its excursions in the surroundings of Cracow.[102]

The book included a picture of Franz Joseph in his carriage—in 1880, not 1879—surrounded by Krakowiaks on horseback, raising their plumed caps in the emperor's honor. Their gallantry and loyalty were emphasized as aspects of character and custom that were, in some respects, intended to be representative of "the Galician in general." Jandaurek was committed to representing the diversity of Galicians, but also to discovering some general aspects of what it meant to be Galician.

The sharp distinction between Ruthenians and Poles was effaced as Jandaurek, assuming a relatively nonpartisan German perspective, explored the more subtle differences between Krakowiacy and Górale (as in Bogusławski's famous musical drama of the 1790s) or between Hutsuls and Boykos. Still, some generalizations could be made about Ruthenians and Poles:

> The Ruthenian peasant is taller and more slender than the Pole. He is by nature
> also slower and more thoughtful in business. Good-natured and gentle, not bois-
> terous, he knows though how to avenge injuries done to him, often after a long
> time has passed. The sad past has marked his whole being with a melancholy
> aspect, and has made him mistrustful and reserved.[103]

For Jandaurek, as for Szujski, melancholy was an essential part of the Ruthenian character, in this case implicitly contrasted with the cheerfully singing Krakowiak. The ethnography of Galicia involved multiple anthropological distinctions, undercutting the polarizing political conception of the province in strictly national terms.

"Up to this point, dear reader," wrote Jandaurek, "I have described to you the Galicians [*die Galizianer*] in their exterior appearance; now I want to let you have a look into their souls, into their emotional life, and I believe that there is no better way to be able to do that than to make you acquainted with their folk songs, because the Pole and Ruthenian, rich in song, accompany all the occurrences of life with a song."[104] Thus Jandaurek sought to synthesize the Poles and Ruthenians as Galicians in their souls, emotional lives, and folk songs. The apostrophized "dear reader" was clearly neither one nor the other, but perhaps someone who occupied a perspective of civilized and gracious

Franz Joseph visiting Galicia in 1880, surrounded by Galicians on horseback in folkloric costume. From Julius Jandaurek, *Das Königreich Galizien und Lodomerien* (Vienna: Karl Graeser, 1884).

condescension toward peoples whose wealth could be calculated in songs: perhaps the Viennese public, perhaps Crown Prince Rudolf himself. From folk songs it was a natural transition to folk celebrations, like Holy Evening, Christmas Eve, which Jandaurek associated with pagan Slavic religious occasions. "Now we want to see the Galician Slavs in their folk festivals," he wrote, synthesizing the Poles and Ruthenians as Galician Slavs. Ancient paganism, with its modern survivals, was part of the Slavic legacy that bound both nations together: "The Galician people [*das galizische Volk*] has still other usages originating in venerable pagan times; here and there women still perform the hemp dance on Ash Wednesday in the village tavern, so that the hemp will grow well in the coming year."[105] By focusing on peasants and mountaineers as the characteristically Galician people, Jandaurek emphasized the unmodern, even pagan, aspects of the province, and, from a German perspective, the backwardness of Eastern Europe.

His treatment of the Germans of Galicia followed that logic explicitly.

Jandaurek explained that a great number of German colonists came in the age of Joseph II, who invited them "so that the Slavic peasant might imitate the advanced culture of the German peasant." Here again the Poles and Ruthenians were synthesized as Slavic peasants vis-à-vis the German colonists.[106] Jandaurek regarded the Jews, like the Germans, as distinctive from other Galicians. A picture, labeled "Galizischer Jude," brought that figure into the array of ethnographic illustrations in typical folk costume. "The dress of the normal Jew is old Polish: a long black silk coat, black sash, fur cap, stockings and. shoes. This costume is now increasingly displaced by normal town dress. Once all Jews had beards, and long locks of hair [*Peissen*] at the temples. Married women cut their hair off, and wear a wig." Switching between the past tense and the present tense, Jandaurek suggested that the Galician Jews were living through a generation of uneven modernization, like Galicia itself, with some Jews still dressed in the style of "old Poland," while others were becoming assimilated to modern customs and costumes. Surveying Jewish customs, from Hamantaschen at Purim, to the broken wine glass of the Jewish wedding, Jandaurek made clear that the Galician Jews were different from other Galicians, who were, for that very reason, more like one another.[107]

The last fifty pages of the book offered a sort of guided tour around the province, concluding in far eastern Galicia with a visit to the Carpathian forests, famous for bandits and bears. The author was being guided by an old Hutsul, "a mighty bear hunter," who spoke from his own expertise.

> "The bear, dear sirs," he began, with great eyes fixed upon me, "is not nearly so dangerous as people think. On the contrary, he is by nature good-hearted, and harms neither men nor cattle without need. It is only hunger that compels him to go hunting, and he also shows, when he must, his great cunning and courage."[108]

There was a picture of a bear hunter in folk costume, with a long rifle, but no picture of a bear. The Hutsul bear hunter addressed the "dear sirs" of his visiting party, but Jandaurek transmitted that message to a broader public of "dear sirs," the civilized urban public of Vienna, for whom the remote forests of eastern Galicia must have seemed wild and dangerous, full of bears and Hutsuls. The message was meant to be reassuring in the liberal spirit of Crown Prince Rudolf himself: the bears of Galicia were only dangerous when they were hungry. Galicia in the past decades had been a land of recurrent famines when not only bears but also humans had been hungry and needy. Their poverty would be increasingly recognized as the definitive Galician trait.

In 1887, Rudolf did actually come to Galicia, together with his wife, the Crown Princess Stephanie, and on 28 June they were in Cracow, visiting the

Hutsul bear hunter in the Carpathians: "The bear, dear sirs, is not nearly so dangerous as people think. On the contrary, he is by nature good-hearted, and harms neither men nor cattle without need. It is only hunger that compels him to go hunting." From Jandaurek, *Das Königreich Galizien und Lodomerien* (Vienna: Karl Graeser, 1884).

Wawel Cathedral and royal tombs, the Jagiellonian University, the Academy of Learning, and the Czartoryski Museum, where it was possible to see some of the spectacular Turkish items seized by Sobieski's Polish army at Vienna in 1683. While Rudolf thus reaffirmed the Habsburg commitment to Galicia, Ivan Franko in 1887 addressed the history of Galicia's relation to the Habsburg dynasty, looking back to the revolutionary year of 1848 in his epic poem on "The Passing of Serfdom." Rudolf toured the impressive Polish cultural institutions of Cracow, but Franko reflected that Habsburg rule in Galicia had not brought about either national justice for Ruthenians or social justice for the peasantry.

Franko's poem recorded the moment of conflict in 1848 between a Polish

feudal noble and the Habsburg official who brought to eastern Galicia the
proclamation of the emancipation of the peasantry from feudal obligations,
with the local Ruthenian peasantry forming the Greek (Catholic) chorus of
the drama. The peasants could not understand the proclamation when it
was read to them—in German—and then could not believe that the Polish
lord would ever accept their emancipation. They therefore addressed the
Habsburg official with more Ruthenian reserve than Galician enthusiasm:

> We wish the Tsisar [Caesar] many years,
> And may his glory never wane!
> But we poor folk so much in vain
> Have suffered and wept bitter tears,
> That we much fear lest this time too,
> We may deluded be. So you,
> Kind sir, we humbly ask to go
> With us up to the Hall, and show
> That paper with the Tsisar's seal
> Unto our lord.[109]

The emperor was Ferdinand, in the springtime of 1848, and the Ruthenians
acknowledged the bond of gratitude to the Habsburg fatherland for their
promised emancipation, but also recognized that imperial intentions could
be provincially frustrated in the execution.

The Polish lord, for his part, vividly recalled the peasant massacres of 1846,
which made him angrily mistrustful of the emperor. The official confronted
the lord with the Habsburg perspective on Galician history:

> 'Twere best today
> No more of "forty-six" to say.
> 'Twas you yourselves, you Polish lords,
> Who first shot down the serfs, poor folk!
> Yourselves brought down the storm which broke
> Upon your heads, as your just due.
> Yes, noble sir! Had lords like you
> But looked upon your serfs as men,
> They never would have tried to do
> You harm, but would have helped you then.[110]

After their confrontation, the Polish lord would lock up the Habsburg official in the dog kennels, but ultimately the official was able to have the lord
arrested by the authority of the state. Although Franko could recognize in
historical retrospect the great promise of the revolution of 1848, he could
not enthusiastically accept the Galicia of Franz Joseph, which was also the
Galicia of *Czas* and the Polish conservatives.

THE MISERY OF GALICIA IN STATISTICS

While Franko recognized the poverty of ordinary Galicians in his poetry, in 1888, Stanisław Szczepanowski published in Lviv a landmark work of economics and sociology: *The Misery of Galicia in Statistics* (*Nędza Galicyi w Cyfrach*), which presented numerical data to show that Galicia could be considered the poorest part of Europe. Because Galicia existed as a distinct political entity, invented by the Habsburgs in 1772, autonomous since the 1860s, now it was possible to assess its statistical character across a meaningful and measurable socioeconomic domain. Szczepanowski, however, further believed that Galicia, after a century of provincial existence, possessed a characteristic and disastrous economic tradition of its own. In the preface he apostrophized his readers—"Honorable Gentlemen!"—and urged them to "break free from the Galician tradition, but join the Polish tradition." Szczepanowski's argument was historical: that Galicia had been separated from Poland by the first partition of 1772, and had therefore failed to be influenced by the inauguration of a civic Polish tradition with the Four-Year Sejm of 1788–92 and the Constitution of 3 May 1791—"tending toward the comparability of our society with civilized nations." Galicia lacked the tradition of "civic work" that led to economic development in such nations, and therefore, inevitably, fell further behind, becoming "the most unhappy, most oppressed province."[111] Poverty, underdevelopment, and economic drag were, in Szczepanowski's view, so deeply rooted in Galicia that they defined a Galician tradition and therefore the Galician identity. His title would brand the epithet "Galician Misery" onto the body of Polish political culture, giving Galicia a tragic economic identity to associate with its cherished political autonomy.

Born in Russian Poland in the Galician year of crisis, 1846, Szczepanowski lived in England for years, learning about economic progress, and finally settled in Galicia where he played a leading role in the development of the province's oil fields.[112] He was elected as a representative to the Galician Sejm and the Austrian Reichsrat. *The Misery of Galicia* was published in Lviv, but *Czas* in Cracow publicized the book with a long series of articles about it, citing, summarizing, and reflecting.

> About Galician poverty and misery much has already been written, lamenting and moralizing incessantly. This author calculates our misery with statistical figures, and does not fall into pessimism. The sad account of the present day is joined with the hope, almost the certainty, of a better tomorrow.[113]

The subtitle of the book, in fact, promised a "program of energetic economic provincial development" based on Szczepanowski's confidence that an authentic Polish tradition of "civic work" would invigorate "organic work" in Galicia and put the province on the economic path that pointed toward English prosperity. Szczepanowski was a political and economic liberal, differing from the conservatism of *Czas*, but his critical historical perspective made him enthusiastic about the Cracow historical school, and *Czas* responded favorably to his liberal appreciation of the Stańczyk conservatives. "None have better understood, or now understand, their own century than Szujski, Kalinka, or Stanisław Tarnowski," wrote Szczepanowski. "They are Europeans in the full sense of the word. That is, their diagnosis of social ills is incomparable."[114] Szczepanowski was interested in associating his own liberal economic criticism with the conservative Cracow school of historical revisionism—in pursuit of the paradoxical ideal of Galician progress.

Szczepanowski ranked Galicia against a variety of European countries and Habsburg provinces. According to the statistics, the Polish kingdom—that is, Russian Poland—with none of Galicia's political advantages, seemed to possess a more advanced economy. When Szczepanowski counted the number of people working in agriculture for each square kilometer, he found England with twenty-seven people, then, increasingly numerous, France, Hungary, Germany, Russian Poland, the Czech lands, Ireland, Belgium, Italy, and finally, last of all, Galicia, with sixty people for each square kilometer. In the whole world, only China and Bengal had greater agricultural congestion. When Szczepanowski measured agricultural production per capita, England was first again, now tied with Belgium, and followed by France, Germany, Ireland, Hungary, Russian Poland, and, last again, Galicia. In fact, Galicia was last in Europe according to every cited economic indicator, with the exception of railway tracks with respect to territorial size: in that regard Galicia was just ahead of Hungary.[115] Back in the 1840s, Fredro had mortified his Polish pride to call upon Salomon Rothschild in Vienna and lobby for the building of railways in Galicia; by the 1880s the modest result was that Galicia was, in this single regard, not absolutely last in Europe.

In Szczepanowski's analysis the diverse peoples of Galicia were statistically synthesized into the figure of "the average Galician," whose principal characteristic was neither his nationality nor his religion, nor even his folk costume, but rather his extreme poverty. The average Galician was undernourished and underemployed:

> The statistical figures show that the average Galician [*przeciętny Galicjanin*] eats for half, and works for a quarter, of a person. We see it equally among our peasants, among our artisans, among our clerks. But if it applies to any and every level of our population, then certainly it applies to the Jews.[116]

In a climate of rising anti-Semitism, there were those who insisted upon the alien nature of the Jews in Galicia, and insinuated that Jews exploited

Poles and Ruthenians. Szczepanowski, however, argued that Jews were average Galicians, characterized on the whole by the same poverty, misery, and malnutrition as their neighbors. In this sense, Jews were already economically assimilated in Galicia, and Szczepanowski was liberally confident that they would be more generally assimilated if the province could discover the path to economic progress.

Czas conservatively dissented—"as for the Jewish question, the views of the author are somewhat optimistic"—and suggested that Jews were truly different.

> The author does not seem to doubt the success of assimilation, emancipation, and the reform of the Jews, even without baptism. . . . He insufficiently considers, however, the higher reasons for the separation and antagonism in difference of religion. We are not anti-Semites, but we do not share the hope of Mister Szczepanowski, especially as it seems to us, that, evaluating the question only from the economic point of view, he does not fathom its depths.[117]

We are not anti-Semites, declared *Czas*, at a time when populist currents among average Galicians—like the peasant movement inspired by Father Stojałowski—were openly anti-Semitic. *Czas* simply recognized—or even insisted—that Jews were anthropologically and sociologically different, meaning that Galician Jews were not necessarily Galicians, and certainly not typical or average Galicians. Szczepanowski's liberal emphasis on the economic coherence of the province, transcending national and religious differences, posed the question of Galician identity in radically modern form.

Michał Śliwa has argued that *The Misery of Galicia* was not simply a statistical representation of the province, but achieved the status of "myth"—serving to rally diverse forces for social and political change.[118] The statistics on poverty were closely related to the mythology of civilization, and Szczepanowski analyzed the condition of Galicia accordingly:

> We have acquired the needs and pretenses of civilization, but not its power and production. We work with the incapacity of barbarians, and we have European tastes and needs. . . . We feel the need for European goods and elegance, but we do not know how to provide them ourselves in the province. . . .[119]

The attractions of European civilization thus paradoxically exercised a negative economic impact on the semicivilized society of the Slavic Orient. What was at stake in Szczepanowski's economic analysis was Galicia's entire relation to Europe.

"Galicia is not surrounded by a Chinese wall," declared Szczepanowski, and, inasmuch as the railways were one of the province's least feeble features, he recommended that his readers take a train to Warsaw, to Budapest, even to Bucharest, and "observe societies which not long ago were just as backward and barbarous [*zacofane i barbarzyńskie*] as ours."[120] His economic analysis rested upon assumptions about the backwardness of Eastern Europe that dated back to the age of Enlightenment, and had helped to furnish an ideology for Habsburg rule in Galicia during the reign of Joseph II. The Galician conservatives had made "civilization" into the ideological foundation of their declaration of loyalty to the Habsburg emperor in 1866, and Szczepanowski now challenged them to act economically in the name of civilization, against the statistically demonstrable features of backwardness and barbarism. If Warsaw, Budapest, and Bucharest could manage to become more like Paris and London, then Cracow and Lviv could also aspire to rise on the continental slope—statistically measured by Szczepanowski—that was supposed to define the complementary relation between Eastern Europe and Western Europe.

The conservative philosopher Antoni Molicki published in Cracow in 1890 a response to *The Misery of Galicia*, denouncing its conclusions as "the fruits of fever, morbid like shrieks in delirium, scarecrows of an imagination in pathological condition, fantastic phantoms which do not correspond to reality." Such nearly hysterical reaction suggests how much was at stake in the representation of Galicia. According to Molicki, Szczepanowski's ideas "defame our country abroad, completely without foundation, and spread poison internally, and demoralize weaker minds, filling them with bitterness and despondency."[121] By the end of the 1880s it was possible to maintain that Galicia possessed a provincial reputation at home and abroad, a sense of its own provincial honor and integrity that could be cultivated, enhanced, diminished, or defamed, entirely within the public sphere of intellectual criticism.

Czas in 1888, though certainly conservative, nevertheless accepted Szczepanowski's challenge, and publicized the book among its readers who were, in fact, the Polish cultural elite of Galicia. The misery of Galicia was not pleasant news, to be sure, but it suggested a provincial and providential mission that transcended national and religious controversy and therefore implicitly affirmed the assumptions and institutions of Galician autonomy. The statistics of Szczepanowski were not like the letters of Belshazzar, wrote *Czas*, alluding to the Babylonian prophecy of doom in the Hebrew Bible. The Galicians, however miserable, were not *perduta gente*, wrote *Czas*, with an allusion to Dante, not "lost people" condemned to the various levels of the inferno.[122] Rather, Szczepanowski situated the Galicians according to the graded levels of European economic development, which, by definition, allowed for the possibility of improvement.

Czas would not despair over *The Misery of Galicia*, because the remedy to misery could be economically envisioned and actively pursued, while giving purpose to the Polish political elites who governed autonomous Galicia. The Cracow conservatives accepted Szczepanowski's comparison of his own economic criticism to the historical revisionism of the Cracow historical school. *Czas*, after referencing both the Bible and Dante, needed only an allusion to ancient Greek philosophy to complete its appreciation of Szczepanowski: "Just as knowledge of oneself [*znajomość siebie samego*] is the beginning of wisdom for a person, inasmuch as it leads to correction and improvement, so historical criticism and the diagnosis of social ills are positive to the extent that they do not lead to pessimism."[123] In Szczepanowski's statistics Galicia could discover its identity by responding to the classical Socratic injunction: "Know thyself!"

CHAPTER SEVEN

Fin-de-siècle Galicia

Ghosts and Monsters

≈⟩

INTRODUCTION: THE WEDDING

On 16 March 1901 there was performed in Cracow the premiere of perhaps the most important work of Polish literary modernism, *Wesele* (*The Wedding*) by Stanisław Wyspiański. The drama concerned the wedding between a poet from Cracow and a peasant girl from a Galician village, with a whole Cracovian party of urban intellectuals arriving in the village for the celebration of the union. Modeled on an actual marriage that had taken place in 1900, Wyspiański re-created the occasion in verse and interpolated a series of fantastic encounters with ghosts from the Polish past. *The Wedding* was almost immediately recognized as a masterpiece, and the poet Kazimierz Tetmajer, writing about *The Wedding* in *Tygodnik Ilustrowany* in 1901, compared Wyspiański to Mickiewicz in Polish literary stature. Tetmajer declared that "Wyspiański has struck the nation in the heart, and the nation has responded to him with its heart."[1] The nationally Polish appreciation of Wyspiański has perhaps obscured the ways in which *The Wedding* may also be interpreted as a profoundly Galician masterpiece.

Wyspiański was one of the giant figures of the literary movement called Młoda Polska (Young Poland), and his concerns were Polish national concerns, to be sure: the tensions and affinities between intellectuals and peasants, between Christians and Jews, between historical pasts and haunted presents. Yet there were elements of the drama that made it unmistakably Galician, such as the encounter between the character called "The Journalist" (modeled on Rudolf Starzewski, an editor of *Czas*) and the ghost of the mythological jester Stańczyk. Rachel, the local Jewish beauty who fascinates

the visiting urban poet (probably modeled on Tetmajer), was unmistakably
Galician:

> at Vienna she's been to the opera,
> but at home she still plucks chickens,
> she knows all of Przybyszewski . . . .[2]

Stanisław Przybyszewski was the charismatic cult leader of the modernist
movement in Cracow. He was dedicated to Chopin, Nietzsche, and literary
Satanism, and was the author of the essay "The Synagogue of Satan" and the
novel *Satan's Children*. Poised between the opera in Vienna and Przybyszewski
in Cracow, Rachel in *The Wedding* was the feminine emblem of fin-de-siècle
Galicia.

The most intensely Galician aspect of Wyspiański's *The Wedding* was the
drama's traumatic fixation on the memory of the massacres of 1846, which
had occurred more than half a century before the premiere in 1901. The
host of the wedding was perhaps modeled on Włodzimierz Tetmajer—the
artist and brother of the poet—who himself married a peasant woman in
1890, and the groom in *The Wedding* was obviously modeled on the writer
Lucjan Rydel, the actual groom of 1900. On the eve of the wedding the host
and the groom, both of them intellectuals who had chosen to marry into
the peasantry, were historically preoccupied with the murderous role of the
Galician peasants in the massacres of 1846:

> HOST: just let them see a flashing knife,
>   and they forget the name of God—
>   just like it was in forty-six—
>   the Polish peasants are like that. . . .
> GROOM: I know it only
>   from the tales, but I believe them,
>   for it poisons my thoughts about
>   the Polish village: they were dogs,
>   who poisoned water with their breaths,
>   and the blood still clings to their shirts,
>   as I look at the village today. . . .
> HOST: What is past may come again.
> GROOM: We have forgotten all of that;
>   they sawed my grandfather in two;
>   we have forgotten all of that.
> HOST: They stabbed my father to death,
>   they beat him down with sticks and picks,
>   chased the bloody man through the snow. . . .
>   we have forgotten all of that.[3]

Myśmy wszystko zapomnieli—we have forgotten all of that—except that the drama demonstrated precisely the reverse, that everything was remembered in excruciating detail, even by the host and the groom who had not yet been born in 1846. It was this remembered horror that made the marriage between an intellectual and a peasant, in the Galician context, something far more complex than a pastoral idyll, something more like a nervously fraught declaration of historic rapprochement. Modernist culture in Paris and Vienna was also tinged with anxiety at the turn of the century, but, in Wyspiański's *The Wedding*, the memory of 1846 constituted an anxiety that was very specifically Galician.

An old beggar among the dramatis personae of *The Wedding* can still remember the massacre of 1846 after half a century, and it is he who recognizes the ghost of Jakub Szela when it appears on stage. Thus it was that the Galician public of 1901 was confronted with the nightmarish apparition of Galicia's most notorious historical actor.

> BEGGAR: Get out of here, hell-hound!
> GHOST: Don't curse me, you're my brother—
>   Tremble! It is me—Szela!!
>   I came here to the Wedding [*przyszedłem tu do Wesela*].[4]

Nowhere else in Europe—only in Galicia—could this particular ghost have been conjured on stage to provoke in the public both horror and catharsis. Only in Galicia could the name of Szela be made to rhyme with the genitive form of the wedding: *Wesele, do Wesela*. The promised intimacy between intellectuals and peasants, on the occasion of the wedding, was laced with anxiety over the blood-stained history that lay behind them. The dawning twentieth century was haunted by the ghosts of the nineteenth century not yet dead and buried.

> BEGGAR: Get out of here, you're a corpse!
> GHOST: You see, I've worn my medal.[5]

This was the medal that, according to unconfirmable but irrepressible rumor, had been awarded to Szela by the Habsburg government for inciting the peasants to thwart the Polish insurrectionaries in Galicia—that is, the incitement to massacre. Szela was not a corpse at all, but a potent spirit still hovering over the fin-de-siècle psychic landscape of Habsburg Galicia.

The 1890s would compel Galicians—like other Europeans—to confront their own particular anxieties as the century turned, to reflect anew upon the unresolved issues of identity that the nineteenth century had posed. Franz Joseph visited Galicia again in 1894 at the moment of the General Provincial Exhibition, where the ethnographic pavilion obliquely addressed the volatile and violent tensions among the national communities of the province. The triangular intimacy and enmity of Poles, Jews, and Ruthenians became increasingly explosive in the context of the late-nineteenth-century Habsburg political scene, amid the alarming intimations of mass politics that Carl Schorske, writing about fin-de-siècle Vienna, has characterized as "politics in a new key." Violence was a subject of profound fascination in Galicia at the turn of the century, from the remote assassination of the Habsburg empress Elisabeth by an Italian anarchist on the shores of Lake Geneva in 1898, to the intimately domestic assassination of the Galician *namiestnik* Andrzej Potocki in Lviv by a Ruthenian student in 1908. The appearance of Jakub Szela as a ghost in *The Wedding* served as a reminder that violence and murder were an inseparable part of Galician history, and the history of Galicia would become a crucial forum for exploring the identity of the province at the turn of the century. Mykhailo Hrushevsky came to the university in Lviv from Ukraine in 1894 to preside over the cultivation of Ukrainian history among the Galician Ruthenians. In the first decade of the twentieth century Majer Bałaban began to publish, in Polish, histories of the Galician Jews. In that decade Michał Bobrzyński, one of the masters of the Cracow historical school, actually became the *namiestnik* of Galicia.

The history of fin-de-siècle Galicia would be narrated later, after the war, in the memoirs of its anxious, emotional, decadent, inebriated actors, and most famously in the memoirs of the literary critic and cabaret poet Tadeusz Żeleński, known always as "Boy" in perennial tribute to his youth. It was Boy who would recall, in the 1920s, the circumstances surrounding the creation of *The Wedding* in the context of the *chłopomania*, peasant-mania, of the 1890s. It was Boy in the 1930s who would recall the bohemian cultural explosion in fin-de-siècle Cracow, publishing his memoirs under the title *Znaszli ten kraj?* [*Do You Know the Land?*]. It was a Polish rendering of Goethe's "Kennst du das Land?" Goethe meant Italy, of course, the land where the lemon trees bloom, the Mediterranean land of magical atmospheric appeal, but Boy was thinking of a different land with a different appeal. For every Galician, the word *kraj* meant Galicia. Boy was remembering the spiritual land of Bohemia, which he had relished in his boyish youth, *la vie de bohème*, but he was also remembering Galicia, a land that no longer existed when he wrote his memoirs. By then Galicia had passed forever from the geopolitical map of European history, had become a disembodied land of ghosts. *Znaszli ten kraj?*

Galicia in 1894, the year of the General Provincial Exhibition in Lviv. From the map of
Austria-Hungary in *Rand-McNally's Indexed Atlas of the World* (Chicago, 1894).

S

Krasnystaw

Zamost Hrubleszow Vladimir-Volyask Lutsk Sdolbunow

Ostrog

Krasnobrod Dubno

Sokal Tartakow

Kremenetz

omascow Betzec Ostrow Krystynopol Witkow Szczurowice Lesniow

Plazow Korezow Bole River Radziwillow
Werchrata Rawa Ruska Kamionka Lipnik Toporow Brodywy Zablotze
Baszna Horyniec Kamionka Sirzumil Busa
CAR. River Dobrosin Zkwadow Zoltunce Ozydow Podkamien Uhlosce
Niemitroc Zolkiew Kulikow Knlaze Zloczow Jezierna Zbaraz Medyn
aw Krakowiec Jaworow Zaszkow Busk Krasne Podwoloczliska Woloczliska
aski Mosciska Sadowa Janow Grodek Zadworze Pluchow Zborow Storo
I GALICIAN Barszczovice Siechow Gologury Hluboczek Bogdanowka Skalat Proskure
Hussakow LEMBERG Winniki Staresiolo Kozlow Tarnopol Maxymowka Mikulince Trembowla
enice Nawa Swicz Bobrka Koszowa Kupczynce Toste Tinna
Wykoty River Mikolajow Wybranowke Brzezany Zlotniki Czortkow Husiatyn
Sambor Roxdzil Borynicze Chodorow Bukaezowke Podhayee Buzacz Przybusua Jagielnica
Dublany Bystrica Bilcze Bort. lki Nowosiele Bursztyn Halicz Jeslouieny Dzaryn Jezierzany
Drohobyez Uhersko Zurawna Czeaow Stanislau Monasterzyska Jitlowci
Borysław Zawadow Stryj Morszyn Kalusz Tysmen Korosciatyn Tluste Borszcow
Stryi Kontuuchow Liso River Oleszow Usciecko Krzywca
PATHIANS Skole Holyn Lysec Markowce Zaleszczyki
Bolechow Raclin Boharodczany Otynia Kolomea Miel ika
Tuchla Dolina Wlgoda Holoskow Korszow Rozwa Nowoselica
Slawsko Kamionka Nadworna Matyjowce Kobotechin River
Ludwikocka Pinsko Sopow Zabiotow Kotsman Cho
Mt. 1.75 Nepolokoutz Luzan
Kalusahi przezutyn Sloboda rung. Czernowitz Zuezka
KACS Mikliczyn Kozmae Storozynetz Luzan
Okormelo Rusky Mt. Berhon Kuczurmare
Bilke 9.981 feet Serth Hliboka
Huszt Zabie Merchody Petroutz Czerokoutz
Stepna Czudin Ruda
Bustyahaz Teresulpatak Czerna Glora Mt. Krasna Palti Radauta
Ardo Tecso Podpler Raho 5.581 Suczaw Hadikfalva Hatna
Thur Taraczkoz Hoszimezo BUKOWINA Istenazegi Suczava Strigols
Aranyos Medgyes M. Sziget Mars-Mind Radauta Komanestio
Szinyervaralja Sikarlo Kippol Kucumora Moldava Falticeni
Nagybanya Stulpikany Watro Borna
Fetsa Banya Diak Lip
Kapolnok Magyar Lupsa

The General Provincial Exhibition:
"This Wealth of Ethnographic Forms"

Fin-de-siècle Galicia could present a fashionable European pose of world-weary ennui, as in 1891 when the poet Kazimierz Tetmajer—then only twenty-six but destined to remain forever young as a poet of Young Poland—published in Cracow the poem "I Believe in Nothing" ("Nie wierzę w nic"). Although the poet claimed to desire "nothing in the world," he longingly looked beyond this world:

> the only thing that remains to me is the desire
> for Nirvana in which all of existence is overwhelmed
> by inertia, in sleepy, mysterious languor,
> and, without feeling it, passes slowly into non-existence.[6]

This stance of almost obligatory world-weariness was adopted by poets of the decade, in fin-de-siècle Galicia as elsewhere in Europe. Even Ivan Franko would write a hymn to Buddha and Nirvana, though in the context of his active political life the sentiment might have seemed not entirely convincing.[7]

In 1894, in the collection of poetry that made his reputation, Tetmajer published a poem—"The End of the Nineteenth Century" ["Koniec wieku XIX"]—wondering how a poet of his generation should respond to the fin-de-siècle moment: with curses? with contempt? with struggle? with resignation?

> Struggle? but can an ant who is cast upon the rails
> struggle with the train approaching at full speed?
> Resignation? but would one suffer less
> if one submissively bent down beneath the guillotine?[8]

Speaking for his generation at the end of the century—"we who know everything, we for whom none of the faiths of the past suffice"—the poet concluded that he could only "hang his head in silence."[9] The railway that had been so hopefully projected for Galicia way back in the 1840s, by Aleksander Fredro and Leon Sapieha, was now the metaphorical train of modernity, relentlessly advancing through the province and bringing alarming intimations of violence, upheaval, even revolution. The delicately balanced ambiguities of nineteenth-century Galician identity now conditioned a tensely wrought complex of fin-de-siècle Galician anxieties.

In 1894, as Tetmajer heralded the end of the nineteenth century, Wyspiański returned to Galicia after having spent the earlier years of the decade, since 1890, traveling around Europe and working, for the most part, in Paris. From Paris he had prepared the designs for a set of stained glass windows to be installed in Lviv in the Roman Catholic cathedral: a glittering historical representation of the seventeenth-century Polish king Jan Kazimierz as he dedicated Poland to the Virgin Mary, and a lush allegorical vision of the sleeping, dreaming female form of Poland on a field of floral glory, related perhaps to the contemporary fin-de-siècle images of Beardsley and Klimt.[10] The designs were not accepted for the Lviv cathedral, but their vivid floral intensity would be immediately carried over into Wyspiański's masterpiece of stained glass in the Franciscan Church in Cracow, begun in 1895, and his historical Polish fantasies would find poetic form in his modernist dramas, including *The Wedding*. Also in 1894, as Wyspiański returned to Galicia, the young Ukrainian historian Mykhailo Hrushevsky left Kiev and the Russian Empire to settle in Galicia and occupy a new chair of history at the Lviv university. In 1890 a Polish-Ruthenian "compromise" had seemed to promise a "new era" of better relations and brought some Polish concessions in the field of education, including the university chair for Hrushevsky. Although in Vienna the Austrian minister of education, Baron Paul Gautsch, considered that "Ruthenian history is not real scholarship," the chair was authorized for "universal history with special reference to the history of Eastern Europe."[11] Hrushevsky hoped to find in Galicia a refuge from the censorship of the Russian Empire and an opportunity to teach Ukrainian history to Galician Ruthenian students, whom he already envisioned as the Ukrainians of the twentieth century.

In his inaugural lecture in 1894, Hrushevsky argued that "all periods of Rus history are closely and inseparably joined together." For Hrushevsky, the nation was "the alpha and omega of historical discourse," and "with its ideals and struggles" became "the sole hero of history."[12] Both Wyspiański and Hrushevsky, born in the 1860s, would find themselves engaged in fin-de-siècle anxieties and struggles of their own in Galicia in the 1890s, but for both of them its political, ethnographic, and natural landscape would become the cultural platform for projecting deep historical fantasies—about Poland, about Ukraine—onto the political imagination of the impending twentieth century.[13]

Znaszli ten kraj? Do you know the land? That was the question that Boy would pose as the title of his memoir of turn-of-the-century Cracow. It was the title of a song by the Polish composer Stanisław Moniuszko, setting Goethe's poem, but it also summed up the imperative of Habsburg imperial government and Galician provincial government: to know the land, for the exercise of imperial rule or for the articulation of provincial identity. This would have been fundamental in any of the lands of the Habsburg empire but was perhaps all the more so in Galicia, where geopolitical artifice made

"Peasant and Jewish Types." Drawing by Włodzimierz Tetmajer, from Bolesław Limanowski, *Galicya przedstawiona słowem i ołówkiem* (Warsaw: Wydawnictwo Przeglądu Tygodniowego, 1892).

provincial identity particularly problematic. In 1884, Galicia was comprehensively represented, in the spirit of positivism, by Jandaurek's volume in the Viennese series on the lands of the monarchy "in word and image." In 1892 another book on Galicia appeared in Warsaw, *Galicya przedstawiona słowem i ołówkiem*, represented in word and pencil.[14] The prose by Bolesław Limanowski sought to sum up the character, complexity, and contradictions of the province, still in a positivist spirit, but the sometimes stylized images, drawn by Włodzimierz Tetmajer, brother of the poet, offered intimations of fin-de-siècle modernism. The drawing of "Peasant and Jewish Types in Galicia"—with figures that seemed almost carved from wood, works of folk art, with swirling lines of anxious portent in the Galician sky—might have been a scene from *The Wedding*. Włodzimierz Tetmajer became a character in *The Wedding* in 1901, when Wyspiański made him the model for the Host.

To know the land was the fundamental impetus of the Galician General Provincial Exhibition—*Powszechna Wystawa Krajowa*—of 1894, the year of Wyspiański's return and Hrushevsky's move to Galicia. Laid out in Stryjski

Park in Lviv, the pavilions of the exhibition—"more than a hundred pavilions in various historical styles," notes historian Ihor Zhuk—celebrated progress and modernity, "the successes of the autonomous kingdom of Galicia and Lodomeria in the social, economic, and cultural spheres."[15] The exhibition thus served as a kind of ideological counterblast to the already proverbial "misery" of Galicia, as publicized by Szczepanowski in 1888. The emphasis on progress, however, did not displace a powerful focus on understanding Galicia through the most traditional aspects of the province, notably in the ethnographic exhibit of folk culture.

In the catalogue of the ethnographic exhibit the introductory remarks, by Volodymyr Shukhevych (writing in Polish as Włodzimierz Szuchiewicz), introduced Galicia as deeply "diverse [*różnorodny*]" in many aspects, including the "life, clothing, occupations, dwellings, and customs of the people"—that is, the anthropological substance of the ethnographic exhibits. "Passing over the national differences between the Polish and Ruthenian people, there are still differences among Polish mountaineers, Ruthenian Hutsuls, Bojkos, and Lemkos on the one hand, and among Polish Mazurs, Krakowiaks, and Ruthenian Podgórzany, Pokuts, and Podolaks on the other hand." The ethnographic exhibit was thus conceived as undercutting the divisive national distinction between Poles and Ruthenians by insisting on the complicating topographical ethnography of mountaineers versus lowlanders. "This wealth [*bogactwo*] of ethnographic forms, which till now has still not been scientifically mastered and exhausted in full, offers to ethnography an immensely rewarding terrain." The challenge of the exhibit was, thus, to try to represent, and make sense out of, such dramatic diversity: "to exhaust all the forms, to show in a systematic collection all the varieties of ethnographic types of our land."[16] Proverbial Galician poverty was transmuted into the "wealth" of Galician ethnography. The fin-de-siècle exhibition acknowledged the difficulty of a "scientifically" positivist representation of these riches, and promised instead a kaleidoscopic show of colorful forms in shifting patterns of similarity and difference. Shukhevych would later make his own turn-of-the-century ethnographic contribution with a three-volume study of the Hutsuls, *Hutsulshchyna*, the first volume appearing in 1899, and the whole study eventually published in both Ukrainian and Polish.

At the Chicago World's Fair of 1893 there was an ethnographic section that involved the building of a Samoan village and an Aztec temple, both rather exotic and remote from the perspective of Chicago. At the Lviv exhibition of 1894 the ethnographic focus was on the communities of Galicia itself. In a report to the Viennese folklore journal, *Zeitschrift für österreichische Volkskunde*,

Hutsuls, from Jandaurek,
*Das Königreich Galizien und
Lodomerien* (Vienna: Karl
Graeser, 1884).

a schoolteacher, Adele Pfleger, from the little Galician town of Trzebinia,
declared that "the ethnographic pavilion is the glory [*Glanzpunkt*] of the
whole exhibition." The pavilion was designed by the leading Lviv architect,
Julian Zachariewicz, and was architecturally complemented by the construction of an adjoining "village" of characteristic Galician folk buildings. "Every
visitor who enters the extensive grounds of the exhibition," reported Adele
Pfleger, "must be immediately struck by the Ruthenian church," surrounded
by different kinds of peasant houses, "in pleasing irregularity," representing
different parts of Galicia. The church itself was constructed by a "simple
carpenter"—and Pfleger noted that it was furnished with "a great number
of religious objects and carvings that clearly betray Byzantine influence."[17] If
there was an element of exoticism at work in the exhibition—as reported in
German to the journal in Vienna—it was Byzantine, rather than Samoan or

Aztec. The condition of "pleasing irregularity" seemed to sum up both the exhibition and Galicia itself, where divisive diversity was rendered pleasant and benign in the staged circumstances of ethnographic representation.

Julian Zachariewicz, the designer of the pavilion, represented the nineteenth-century architecture of Viennese historicism as rector and professor at the Lviv Polytechnic School, where he himself designed the school's neo-Renaissance palace. His son Alfred Zachariewicz would become in the next generation the leading figure in Lviv modernist architecture. His work was influenced by Art Nouveau and by the modernism of the Viennese architect Otto Wagner, but historian Jacek Purchla also notes that Alfred Zachariewicz made modernist use in Lviv of "architectural motifs derived both from Zakopane and Hutsul folklore."[18] These specifically Galician twists in the evolution of Lviv modernism were already present in 1894 in the juxtaposition of the historically styled exhibition pavilions with the museum village of Ruthenian folk architecture. Historian Markian Prokopovych has observed that at the exhibition there was even a promiscuously Galician collaboration among Polish and Ruthenian architects working across the supposed barrier of nationality: "Thus, for example Julian Zachariewicz and Ivan Levynskyi together drew up the plans for the pavilion of Ukrainian art. In parallel, Zachariewicz also designed the Ruthenian wooden church, another architectural curiosity, and Levynskyi built the Matejko pavilion."[19] That the Ruthenian architect Levynskyi worked on the pavilion of the Polish artist Jan Matejko, and that the Polish architect Zachariewicz worked on the church for the Ruthenian village, served to underline that the exhibition was in some ways successfully Galician even in a decade of mounting national tensions.

"Leaving the village we pass an old statue," reported Adele Pfleger, "and an old man sits at the foot of the statue, and entices us with the incomprehensible tunes of a fiddle." The old Galician man tempted the visitors onward to the ethnographic pavilion, where displays of excavated prehistoric artifacts, weavings, wooden carvings, and musical instruments culminated in an arrangement of thirty-two costumed mannequins. These mannequins, according to the Polish catalogue, "represent the true image of the types of the Ruthenian people."[20] The statue and the old man, the visitors and the mannequins: the exhibition staged a tantalizing fin-de-siècle encounter between art and reality.

Adele Pfleger lavished upon the mannequins a detailed aesthetic account of their costumes, contrasting especially the Hutsul mountaineers with the village lowlanders. Around the neck of the female Hutsul mannequin was hanging "a multitude of strings of glass beads and a number of brass crosses," and one of the male lowland mannequins wore "a hat richly decorated with peacock feathers and embroidered bands."[21] The aestheticism of ornament and color thus conveyed the ethnographic identity of Galicia to a Viennese public that, in 1894, was already under the influence of Jung-Wien, the writers of the Café Griensteidl, and the poetry of the young Hugo von Hofmannsthal.

Aestheticism was enhanced by exoticism at the Lviv exhibition, not only in the ornamentation of folkloric Galician costumes but also in the culturally Byzantine influence manifested in the many works of religious art on display. The Uniate or Greek Catholic religion of most Ruthenians in Galicia, based on the compromise achieved at the Union of Brest in 1596, largely preserved the religious liturgy, observances, and traditions of Orthodoxy. The religious art of the Uniate Ruthenians in Galicia thus resembled that of the Orthodox Church, and Byzantine style was noted as an exotic aspect of folk art at the Lviv exhibition of 1894. Just as Pfleger noted the Byzantine influence in the Ruthenian Church, so Shukhevych, in the catalogue, remarked that it was "the purpose of this part of the exhibition to show that cultural peculiarity of Galician Rus which resulted from the mutual rubbing against each other of the influences of Byzantine tradition and Western civilization."[22] Such was the mixed cultural character of "Galician Rus" in Lviv in 1894, the very year when Hrushevsky arrived from Kiev to bring his Ukrainian historical interpretation of Ruthenian nationality.

According to the catalogue, some Ruthenians had actively opposed the contribution of religious objects to the exhibition and had "terrorized" the more sympathetic segment of the clergy. Julian Pelesz, the sympathetic bishop of Przemyśl and historian of the Uniate Church, contributed religious objects from his personal collection. Yet, according to the catalogue, "the loss of objects over the course of five months created a significant void in the churches, and the people themselves, not understanding the purposes of the exhibition, opposed sending things, even engaging in active resistance, as for instance at Bohorodchany."[23] There was a certain irony here in noting that "the people themselves" did not understand the significance of the folk art created within their own popular culture, and Shukhevych was perhaps suggesting that a Galician elite of civilized visitors to the exhibition could better appreciate Ruthenian folk art than could the Ruthenian folk. Bohorodchany, as later described in the guidebook to Galicia of 1914, was a small town of 5,000 (800 Poles, 1,800 Ruthenians, 2,400 Jews) near Stanyslaviv, with oil wells in the vicinity. The drilling for oil would unearth, in 1907, a well-preserved prehistoric mammoth, but the touristic highpoint of the town was "the most valuable ikonostas in Galicia," from the seventeenth century, showing "Flemish influence" in the landscape painting.[24] The guidebook thus stressed the same combination of Byzantine tradition and Western civilization that had been emphasized at the exhibition of 1894, when the Ruthenians of Bohorodchany had actively opposed the dispatch and display of their religious objects.

In the end, there was an ikonostas on display at the exhibition, borrowed from a Basilian monastery, and there was also a sixteenth-century painting of the Last Judgment from Kamenka Strumilova, representing the condemnation of Tartars, Germans, and Jews. Kamenka Strumilova was also known for the frescoes of its old wooden synagogue, "one of the most precious in Galicia," though Jewish religious art was not mentioned in the catalogue as part of the exhibition in Lviv.[25] The exhibition of 1894 was ready to relish Byzantine exoticism in Galicia, but perhaps not quite ready to countenance the aesthetic appreciation of popular Judaism. By 1914, the guidebook to Galicia had taken that next step in provincial self-appreciation, and could recommend both Ruthenian churches and Jewish synagogues for their aesthetic value. Visitors to the town of Buchach (Buczacz), for instance, were sent to see the ikonostas of the Uniate Church of St. Nicholas—"of high artistic value"—but were also urged to appreciate the general "picturesqueness [*malowniczność*]" of the houses arranged alongside the Strypa River ravine: "especially on Friday evening, *shabbas*, when hundreds of candles gleam in the windows."[26] The powerful presence of anti-Semitism in the province could be momentarily made to vanish in the twinkling of the Sabbath lights, when Judaism was represented as aesthetically picturesque in the spirit of fin-de-siècle Galicia.

The ethnographic pavilion at the Lviv exhibition of 1894 displayed a whole library of relevant books, collected by Ivan Franko. This collection reached back into the early history of Galician folk culture, including a copy of the *Pieśni polskie i ruskie ludu galicyjskiego*, published by "Wacław z Oleska" in 1833, and folk collections by Iakiv Holovatsky, one of the original members of the Ruthenian Triad. More recent works included a book by the Viennese rabbi Adolf Jellinek, *Der jüdische Stamm in nicht-jüdischen Sprich-Wörtern* (1881), about the Jewish people in non-Jewish proverbs—such as Polish and Ruthenian proverbs—and another book by the Cracow anthropologist Izidor Kopernicki, *O góralach ruskich w Galicyi: zarys etnograficzny* (1889), about the Ruthenian highlanders in Galicia, an ethnographic outline.[27] These were the same highlanders who, as mannequins, displayed their folk costumes at the exhibition.

In 1894, the aesthetic appreciation of folk art in the ethnographic pavilion served to evade the increasing national and religious tensions within Galicia. Yet the layout of the exhibition was arranged geographically according to the eastern and western parts of the province, thus implicitly acknowledging the crucial opposition between Poles and Ruthenians. Polish national pride also found expression at the exhibition in the panoramic painting of Polish peasants engaged in the Battle of Racławice against the Russians, marking the centennial of the Kościuszko insurrection of 1794. Painted by Wojciech Kossak and Jan Styka, in a style of historical realism uninfluenced by contemporary modernist art, the panorama survived not only the exhibition but also Galicia itself, and was on display in Lviv up until World War II, to be transferred to Wrocław after the war. The explicitly Polish nationalism of the Racławice panorama contrasted with the "diversity" and "pleasing irregularity" of Galician folk forms in the ethnographic pavilion. When Emperor Franz Joseph came to Lviv for five days to see the exhibition—his last official visit to Galicia, excepting military maneuvers—he was hosted by the Polish elite who governed autonomous Galicia. According to the research of Daniel Unowsky, the emperor also visited the Uniate Ruthenian seminary and a Jewish orphanage, while becoming acquainted with all his Galician subjects—the live public and the costumed mannequins—at the Lviv exhibition.[28] The exhibition of 1894 offered to the emperor and to the Galicians themselves a complex, colorful, and kaleidoscopic representation of the province in the final decade of the nineteenth century.

ART FOR ART'S SAKE: "ALCOHOLIC VARIATIONS ON A THEME BY CHOPIN"

"Here in Cracow it is boring [*nudno*] for me, in spite of every occupation," wrote Wyspiański in a letter of 31 October 1895; it was the eve of All Saints Day, sometimes known as the Day of the Dead in Poland, when Poles visit the dead in the cemeteries. In Wyspiański's dramas, and notably in *The Wedding*, the ghosts of the dead would often appear on stage to visit the living. Almost a year later, on 8 August 1896, he was determined to return to Paris: "In Cracow I absolutely will not remain any longer." He had a "life program" planned out in his mind, to occupy him in Paris until 1905: "and earlier than that I would not return to this country [*do kraju*]." This was to be a departure not only from Cracow, the city, but also from Galicia, the country. Wyspiański noted that "Lucjan Rydel, alter ego, has left for Zakopane."[29] It was thus possible to leave Cracow without leaving Galicia, like Rydel, who, as the groom in *The Wedding*, was the dramatist's alter ego. In the 1890s the town of Zakopane, in the Tatra Mountains, became a literary and artistic center, where the folk style of the Galician highlands influenced poets like

Jan Kasprowicz and Kazimierz Tetmajer, the artist and architect Stanisław Witkiewicz, and, later, his more famous son of the same name, the writer and artist known as Witkacy.

Wyspiański would, for the most part, remain in Cracow until his death, and the city would become less boring, not least because of his own contributions, already in progress in 1895 and 1896. Wyspiański was writing modernist verse drama, inspired by Wagner to make use of mythology, symbolism, and thematic motifs. In the letter of 8 August, 1896, he noted that he was at work on the drama *Legenda*, about the Vistula River in the mythological times of the king Krak and the princess Wanda.[30] At the same time he was preparing the designs for his greatest artistic project: the painted murals and stained glass for the church of the Franciscans in Cracow. Wyspiański's brilliantly colored floral and geometric motifs, already sketched in 1895 and 1896, would define the character of his modernist masterpiece of church decoration.

While Wyspiański wrestled with the limitations of Cracow in 1895, Franko found frustration in Lviv. He had recently received a doctorate from the University of Vienna, with a dissertation on the medieval tale of Barlaam and Josaphat. When Franko applied for a lectureship at the university in Lviv, however, the *namiestnik* of Galicia, Kazimierz Badeni, intervened in Vienna to block the academic appointment, on account of Franko's political radicalism. "Because of the viceroy's report the ministry has not confirmed my appointment as lecturer of Ukrainian-Rus literature," wrote Franko; he also blamed his Ruthenian political enemies: "who have blackened my name in every possible way in order to prevent my appointment to a chair." According to historian Thomas Prymak, it was Hrushevsky, favoring Franko, who now made Lviv livable for the greatest Ruthenian writer of his age, by involving him in the work of the Shevchenko Scientific Society—especially in ethnography and folklore—and paying him for his contributions. The convergent courses of the controversial Galician poet and the recently arrived Ukrainian historian—at the moment when the Polish-Ruthenian political compromise was breaking down in the elections of 1895—indicated the reshuffling of fin-de-siècle affiliations. "He correctly surmised," wrote Hrushevsky of Franko, "that I, as a man not tied down by Galician complications, and armed, so to speak, with a pan-Ukrainian mandate, would cross the Galician wattled fences, and especially in the Scientific Society, which was the center of my work, would not be hemmed in by its traditions."[31] The identity of modern Ukraine would emerge from the Galician crossings and complications of the 1890s.

Boy dated the fresh breath of a modernist "wind over Cracow" to 1893, the year that Tadeusz Pawlikowski assumed the directorship of the Municipal Theater and began to introduce the dramatic modernism of Ibsen,

Strindberg, Wilde, Chekhov, Gorky, and Maeterlinck. Pawlikowski remained in Cracow until 1899, when he moved across Galicia to modernize the theatrical life of Lviv. In 1894, Kazimierz Tetmajer published a landmark volume of verse in Cracow—including the poem "The End of the Nineteenth Century." In 1897 the founding of the literary journal *Życie* (*Life*) created a forum for aestheticism at precisely the moment when the violently contested "bloody elections" of 1897 made Galician political reality—and Polish-Ruthenian relations—a far from pretty picture. In Boy's memoirs, however, he remembered the crucial year for modernism as 1898, the year that Stanisław Przybyszewski arrived in Cracow from Berlin and took over the editing of *Życie* in a spirit of full-throttled, uninhibited, alcoholic fin-de-siècle decadence. That year was also one of multiple commemorations in Galicia, creating occasions to reflect upon the history and identity of the province: the hundredth birthday of Adam Mickiewicz for Poles, the Ivan Kotliarevsky Ukrainian literary centennial for Ruthenians, the fiftieth anniversary of the emancipation of the Galician serfs in 1848, and also the fiftieth jubilee year of the reign of Emperor Franz Joseph. The Habsburg imperial connection was crucial to Galician identity, and the anarchist assassination of the empress Elisabeth in Geneva in 1898 provided a traumatic impetus to reflect upon the condition of the province, as the nineteenth century approached its anxious conclusion.

Schorske, writing about fin-de-siècle Vienna, argued that the rise of a modernist culture of aestheticism, of art for art's sake, was nourished by intellectuals who would not, or could not, confront the ugly contemporary political reality of illiberal mass politics. Scott Spector, reconsidering Schorske, has suggested that "the 'retreat into culture' was always already ideological," that "the aestheticist center was the eye of a hurricane which it could not ignore."[32] The Viennese artistic Sezession of 1897, led by Gustav Klimt, coincided with the triumph of popular anti-Semitism in mass politics when Karl Lueger became mayor of Vienna. Przybyszewski came to Cracow in 1898, with a message of art for art's sake; during that year, Galicia was not only electorally polarized between Poles and Ruthenians but also, in the spring of 1898, deeply unsettled by eruptions of anti-Semitic riots, the most extensive in the whole history of the province.

Przybyszewski, arriving in the province in the year of the riots, settling in Cracow to take over *Życie*, had a completely different, preeminently aesthetic, relation to the Jews of Galicia. In his memoirs he remembered himself as the cult leader of Cracow's bohemians, staying up all night long:

> One listened till morning in some Jewish tavern to Jewish music, which one had never known before, and it was rather expensive music, because it was necessary

to induce in the musicians a state of trance in which one could feel their music as something unheard of, something never before experienced. Och! how they played, how they played! Sometimes I had the impression that I had come to a home for the insane: like the time when four Jewish musicians played to me in that half drunken trance, which does not paralyze the fingers . . . Jewish songs: Kol Nidre—and songs of the Last Judgment—I was gripped by the chills.[33]

Elsewhere, Galician taverns were being attacked by anti-Semitic village mobs, while Przybyszewski was losing himself in an alcoholic trance of Jewish music, in the thrilling musical intimations of Kol Nidre and Yom Kippur. Such was the strange engagement—or escape—of modernist aestheticism in a climate of modern anti-Semitism.

Just by chance, in 1898, the year of Przybyszewski's arrival, there was also present in Galicia the most precious gem of fin-de-siècle Viennese aestheticism, the poet Hugo von Hofmannsthal. He was performing his military service in Chortkiv, the hometown of Karl Emil Franzos, in the easternmost part of the province, near the Russian border. Hofmannsthal, who had been discovered as a poet at the age of sixteen, back in 1890, a teenage prodigy, was regarded as one of the great lyric poets in the German language; he was already an adult of twenty-four in 1898, and perhaps the most celebrated figure in Viennese fin-de-siècle culture. He had spent time in military service in Galicia once before, in 1896 in Tlumach near Stanyslaviv, and had reported with deep distress to his friend Leopold Freiherr von Andrian in Vienna:

Everything around me is more ugly than you can imagine. Everything is ugly, miserable, and dirty [*hässlich, elend und schmutzig*], the people, the horses, the dogs, even the children. I am very low and dispirited. Yesterday, in the evening twilight, an old beggar crawled into my room on all fours and kissed my feet, and I was so terrified that afterwards I was exhausted and embittered as if I had experienced some pointlessly great danger. I also can not sleep very well.[34]

The Viennese poet reacted to Galicia with aesthetic horror, while he himself was treated as some kind of royalty, or even divinity, by the prostrate Galicians. Among other things, his direct exposure to the Galician Jewish shtetl community was a part of what Hofmannsthal, like so many other travelers to the province, found distressing; he himself had one Jewish grandfather who converted to Catholicism, and the family had been formally ennobled, completely assimilated, and finally aestheticized by his own poetic vocation. An encounter with the Galician Jews, who fit into the ugly, miserable, dirty context of Tlumach, might well have been disturbing to the poet. While Hofmannsthal was suffering the ugliness of Galicia in 1896, Wyspiański was completing the floral designs for the Franciscan Church in Cracow.

Whether in Tlumach in 1896 or in Chortkiv in 1898, Hofmannsthal was unsettled by the experience of his military service in Galicia. He had to struggle to maintain his equanimity, as suggested in one letter to his father mentioning the Galician Jews:

> In the evenings I walk up and down the only road where there is no deep shit: namely a long plank between the houses of Elias Rizer and Chaim Dicker. This is in the middle of the marketplace: here stand the Ruthenian peasants with their miserable horses, the size of dogs, and let themselves be cheated by the Jews. . . . For hours I walk up and down amidst this swarm as if I were alone upon a silent mountain peak, and I read Plato or the beautiful serious poems of Hölderlin.[35]

The Galician Jews were clearly one of the provincial elements disturbing to Hofmannsthal, who balanced his Viennese aesthetic identity on the plank that separated two Jewish houses. The elevated sphere of Romantic poetry and Platonic forms, including the form of ideal beauty, had to be maintained in the face of the human swarm, the ugliness of mundane reality, here represented by the experience of Galicia. "I am correcting my conception of life," noted Hofmannsthal. "What life is for most people is much more joyless and low than one would like to think."[36] For Hofmannsthal this experience of Galicia may have helped to precipitate his artistic crisis at the turn of the century—described in the Chandos letter of 1902—as he sought to negotiate his own artistic balance between the aesthetic cult of sublime beauty and the disturbing reality of deep shit. After completing his service in 1898, Hofmannsthal packed up his Plato and headed home for Vienna, but Przybyszewski was about to arrive in Galicia, preaching the aesthetic religion of art for art's sake.

Przybyszewski was born in Prussian Poland and ended up as a student in Berlin, where, in the 1880s, he lived at the center of modernist circles as the friend of Edvard Munch and August Strindberg, eventually marrying the glamorous Norwegian Dagny Juell, whom they also both loved. Dedicated to the philosophy of Nietzsche and the music of Chopin, Przybyszewski pursued the vocation of a literary decadent, but in German rather than his native Polish, publishing *Totenmesse* (*Mass for the Dead*) in 1893, and *Satans Kinder* (*Satan's Children*) in 1897. By then, however, he was thinking about being decadent in Polish, and fantasizing about a future in Galicia. In May 1897 he wrote from Norway to Arnošt Procházka, the editor of the *Moderní Revue* in Prague:

> I have now begun to write in Polish. In the younger generation I have found such strong support that I can venture to do it. I am dreaming about going somewhere in Galicia and founding there in Lviv or Cracow a journal in the style of *Moderní Revue*. I am dreaming that afterwards both of those journals would join fraternal hands in the name of Satan and all infernal powers.[37]

Przybyszewski would realize his dream of coming to Galicia and editing a journal, *Życie*, that he himself would imbue with the satanic force of his own personality. The circle that gathered around him would be dubbed by Boy as "Satan's Children," and they would listen to Jewish music all night long, as the nineteenth century drew to a close.

When Przybyszewski arrived in Cracow in 1898 his first gesture was to extend a fraternal hand, not to Prague, but to Lviv, where the poet Jan Kasprowicz had settled in the 1890s, also coming from Prussian Poland and Germany. In 1898, Kasprowicz published a volume of verse including the verse drama "Na wzgórzu śmierci" ("On the Hill of Death"). Przybyszewski promptly wrote a letter to Kasprowicz, across Galicia, from Cracow to Lviv:

> My beautiful and great one—Never have I bowed down before anyone or anything—I bow down before you, because you have created the most powerful thing that I know—"On the Hill of Death"—I am rereading it for the hundredth time—it is a miracle, a revelation. For the first time in my life I feel profound joy that I can bow and kiss your hand.[38]

It was an extravagant expression of fin-de-siècle Galician literary solidarity, and an even more extravagant gesture would soon be forthcoming when Przybyszewski came to Lviv in person, to begin his dramatic love affair with Jadwiga Kasprowicz, the poet's wife.

Życie had been originally founded in 1897 by the poet Ludwik Szczepański, very much influenced by his education in Vienna in the 1890s, and inspired by the literary world of fin-de-siècle Vienna with its literary journal *Die Zeit*. Alois Woldan has shown that especially some of the cover art for the early issues of *Życie* in 1897 emerged from a distinctly Austrian-Polish Galician perspective, like the allegorical symbolism of Heinrich Rauchinger (born in Cracow, studied in Vienna) and the Art Nouveau floralism of Ephraim Moses Lilien (born in Drohobych, educated in Lviv, Cracow, Vienna, and Munich, later a dedicated Zionist).[39] Hans Bisanz has further shown that in the celebrated Viennese artistic Sezession, dating from 1897 under the modernist leadership of Gustav Klimt, Galician artistis, including Wyspiański, were a significant presence.[40] In Cracow, after 1898, the leading roles of Przybyszewski and Wyspiański, with their respective backgrounds in Berlin and Paris, made fin-de-siècle Galicia more culturally independent from the influences of imperial Vienna.

Przybyszewski spent only two years in Cracow, at the helm of *Życie*, but his comet struck with sufficient force to transform the cultural life of the city, which Wyspiański had found so stifling and dull in 1895. In fact, Wyspiański worked together with Przybyszewski on the editing of *Życie*, between 1898 and 1900, and by the time the latter had moved on, the former was ready to create in *The Wedding* the quintessential Galician character of Rachel, the young Jewish woman at the wedding: "She knows all of Przybyszewski." Indeed, the fin-de-siècle spirit that Przybyszewski stoked to such intensity in Cracow, between 1898 and 1900, conditioned the theatrical public that would appreciate Wyspiański's Galician masterpiece in 1901.

Przybyszewski inaugurated his editorship with his "Confiteor," a bold "confession" of principles—that is, the radical intellectual implications of his one fundamental principle: art for art's sake, *sztuka dla sztuki*. Art, according to Przybyszewski, recognized "neither limits nor laws," was, in fact, "the highest religion," while "the artist becomes its high priest." This meant that art aspired to a realm beyond politics, patriotism, and even morality:

> Tendentious art, art-pleasure, art-patriotism, art possessing a moral or a social aim ceases to be art. . . . To act upon society in an instructive or moral sense, to foster patriotism or social instincts through art means to humiliate art, to throw it down from the summits of the Absolute into the miserable accidentality of life, and the artist who proceeds that way does not deserve the name of artist.[41]

Such aestheticism also made it possible for the fin-de-siècle artist to try to rise above the political, national, social, and religious tensions that were forcefully present in Galicia in the 1890s. Przybyszewski, arriving in troubled Galicia at the very end of the century, came just in time to inspire an ideological movement of art for art's sake.

Przybyszewski's memoirs of the period appeared after his death in 1927, published as a book in Warsaw in 1930, when Warsaw was the capital of independent Poland and Galicia no longer existed. Boy's memoirs then appeared serially in 1930 and 1931 as reflections inspired by Przybyszewski's memoirs. Boy remembered the melody of Moniuszko's song—"Znaszli ten kraj?"—played on a violin during long nights of alcoholic excess with Przybyszewski as the satanic messiah, Stach, among his disciples.

> And that melody incessantly plays in my head when I read the memoirs of Stach from the Cracow period. Strange book! although written not long ago, barely several years ago, it gives the impression of an excavation, in which past time has been preserved like the fossilized imprint of a shell on rock. . . . The present-day reader would not easily understand . . . if he picked up the old journal *Życie*—today an antiquarian rarity—and read in it all those clamorous manifestos. It would be necessary for the whole thing to be soaked in alcohol and set to music. In fact, to speak about the influence of Przybyszewski and not to speak about alcohol would be like writing the history of Napoleon and forgetting the wars.[42]

Boy mentioned Przybyszewski's "Confiteor" among the clamorous manifestos of *Życie*, and argued, thirty years later, that the whole thing made no sense unless it was read under the dual sign of "alkohol i muzyka." Fin-de-siècle aestheticism became all the more intense when "alcohol and music" made art into a kind of cultivated "trance." Sometimes Przybyszewski himself played on the piano his "alcoholic variations on a theme by Chopin," and Boy still remembered those occasions decades later:

> These were the true manifestos, alongside which those printed in *Życie* seemed dull and a little comical. Those were good for export, for the provinces, but not for us, the intimates, who had the good fortune to drink from the source. Alcohol combined with music in one elixir was like the essence of the Dionysian element—according to Nietzsche's terminology—of Stach's art.[43]

If the manifestos in *Życie* were deemed suitable "for the provinces," that might have metaphorically reflected the snobbism of Przybyszewski's elite inner circle of bohemians, who saw the ordinary public as mere provincials. Galicia, however, was a real province, not just a metaphorical one, and Przybyszewski's manifestos were aimed at a Galician provincial public that was challenged to reflect on its own cultural relation to art, society, morality, politics, and patriotism. *Znaszli ten kraj?* By the time that Boy's and Przybyszewski's memoirs were published in independent Poland, the twentieth century was entering its fourth decade, and fin-de-siècle Galicia, like the province of Galicia itself, had been swept away by history, though it could still be brought to mind by a poignantly remembered melody.

Assassination: "Monsters and Reptiles"

Przybyszewski arrived in Galicia in September 1898, a great event in the alcoholic nightlife of bohemian circles, but the event that actually dominated the headlines of Galician newspapers during that month was the anarchist assassination of the Habsburg empress Elisabeth in Geneva on 10 September. *Czas*, in Cracow, reacted with great emotion to the assassination:

> The crime committed in Geneva shocks the whole world with aversion and repugnance, calls forth curses in the entire monarchy, and intensifies the feeling of filial loyalty and attachment, when for the lonely monarch the peoples under the Habsburg scepter remain his nearest family. Such feelings have taken hold deeply in every level of the population in our society and country. Some years ago there flashed for us for a moment the hope of greeting the enchanting empress, who everywhere spread grace and charm. A concurrence of contraries deprived us of the possibility of paying homage to her in our land, and this regret increases the mourning of our country.[44]

The assassination immediately became an occasion for affirming the solidarity of "every level of the population in our society and country"—that is, in Galicia. At the same time, the integrating Galician quality of loyalty to the Habsburg dynasty made the assassination into an occasion for affirming the

Emperor Franz Joseph and Empress Elisabeth in 1898, the fiftieth anniversary year of his reign and the year of her assassination. From the author's collection.

identity of Galicia itself, now a country in mourning. There were funeral masses in the churches and black crepe in the streets. While Franz Joseph's visits to Galicia—in 1851, in 1880, and in 1894 for the Lviv provincial exhibition—had been important occasions for articulating Galician identity, the fact that the empress had never set foot in Galicia was not an obstacle to a Galician apotheosis after her death. Indeed, the unconsummated connection between the empress and the province seemed to encourage the rhetorical intensification of Galician sentiment in the posthumous homage to Elisabeth.[45]

On 17 September, the funeral of the empress took place in Vienna, with Galician delegates representing the province in the funeral procession, placing Galician wreaths on the imperial coffin. Galician journalists reported back to the province on the great funereal occasion in the capital, and *Czas* reflected on the "psychological truth" of Habsburg loyalism that reinforced

Galician identity in the circumstances of the tragedy. Habsburg subjects in mourning experienced their dynastic sentiments for Franz Joseph all the more acutely:

> Millions of these hearts beat in time with the heart of the aching monarch. May this sympathy become balsam. . . . The treasury of dynastic feelings, gathered through fifty years of fatherly rule, are multiplied more by the days of mourning than could be done by the most brilliant intoxication of jubilee celebrations. Often the bonds formed by tears are stronger than those joined by joy.[46]

Aching hearts, flowing tears, and healing balsam became the emotional imagery of an "intoxication" of mourning, articulated in the emotionally overwrought language of fin-de-siècle literature. The tragedy of the assassination was almost to be cherished in its intensity, more sentimentally potent than any anticipated celebration of the emperor's upcoming, now overshadowed, jubilee. Internal Galician tensions could be fancifully dissolved while Galicia as a whole was envisioned as part of a single imperial organism, with millions of loyal hearts beating in unison.

Any dissent would need to be suppressed, and at the end of October there took place a secret trial in Cracow of a postman named Gimpel Goldberg, charged with lèse-majesté and condemned to fourteen days of imprisonment. According to *Czas*, which gave only the briefest report, "The accused used words praising a criminal act after the death of Her Majesty, and on account of the denunciation was immediately suspended from service by the direction of the post and telegraph."[47] The secrecy of the trial concealed the details of this one dissident note in the supposedly unified exaltation of mourning over the assassination of the empress. One presumably Jewish postman in Galicia had failed to conform to the seemingly mandatory mourning, and was promptly fired, charged, condemned, and imprisoned.

The assassin was an Italian anarchist, Luigi Luccheni. *Czas* published an informative historical account of "The Origin and Development of Anarchism" while also, on the front page, meditating about the imminent end of the nineteenth century.

> The nearer the end of the century, the more threatening the clouds which veil the future. In whatever direction we look, everywhere is unrest and discord. . . . The force of racial, social, even confessional hatred is increasing in the world. It is as if, following the angel of faith, the good spirits have flown from the earth—the angel of hope and the angel of love, the spirit of freedom, of right, the spirit of progress. Instead monsters and reptiles are crawling out from every side.[48]

Anarchist assassins were to be counted among those monsters and reptiles, as the assassination of the empress in 1898 followed the anarchist killing of French President Sadi Carnot in 1894, and would in turn be followed by assassinations of Italian King Umberto in 1900 and U.S. President William McKinley in 1901. *Czas* explicitly linked such assassinations to the fin-de-siècle spiritual crisis, envisioning an apocalyptic encounter between angels and spirits, on the one hand, and monsters and reptiles on the other. In 1894, Tetmajer asked, "What is your shield against the spear of evil, man of the end of the century?" In 1898, after the murder of the empress, *Czas* recognized the dagger of the anarchist assassin as the instrument of a monstrous evil hovering over the century's end. Likewise, Cracow conservatism did not hesitate to identify the only operative shield as "the finger of God and the hand of Providence." *Czas* declared that "our century is not thoroughly perverted," and, in spite of "moments of eclipse, of decline, of discord, of danger," there was nevertheless reason to believe in the ultimate triumph of redemptive Christianity.[49]

In Galicia the reptilian origins of anarchism could be understood to date back to 1846, when murderous social forces were called forth by the Habsburg government against the Polish national insurrection. Fredro had not hesitated to use the term "anarchy" at that time. Half a century later, the events of 1846 had not been forgotten in Galicia, and in 1899, when *Czas* reviewed the work of the historian Bronisław Łoziński concerning 1846, the newspaper recognized the massacre of the nobles under the name of anarchy.[50] In 1900, as the century turned, *Czas* reviewed the work of the Polish philosophy professor Henryk Struve and evaluated the concept of "anarchism of the spirit [*anarchizm ducha*]." Struve traced the history of philosophical anarchism from Baudelaire through Nietzsche and, finally, to the epicenter of fin-de-siècle literary anarchism, Cracow itself, where Młoda Polska was in the intellectual thrall of the notoriously self-proclaimed Satanist Przybyszewski. Struve remarked upon Przybyszewski's "naked erotomania" as evidence of his anarchism.[51] The assassination of the empress focused public attention on the sensational assaults of political anarchism, but in Galicia it was also possible to discern traces of anarchism in the nineteenth-century history of the province and in its contemporary cultural life.

In 1898, Elisabeth's assassination exercised a perverse fin-de-siècle dramatic fascination of its own, and even *Czas* was not immune to the aesthetic and sentimental aspects.

> The tragic death of the Empress Elżbieta on foreign territory, by the hand of a foreigner, is among the series of dramas which have played continuously in our century on the steps of thrones—but exceptional in its historical significance, we would dare to say [*śmielibyśmy powiedzieć*], it has a strange poetry and beauty [*ma dziwną poezyę i piękność*]; it also arouses exceptional suffering and terror.[52]

The almost Aristotelian aspects of the tragedy were articulated in the fin-de-siècle formulas of morbid modern aestheticism. Even while deploring the monstrosity of the crime, *Czas* could not help feeling that the tragedy was artistically admirable, suffused with "strange poetry and beauty." The convergence between the older generation of Galician dynastic conservatism and the younger generation of artistic modernism was consummated in a daring ideological concession to the poetry of violence.

On the first of March 1899, Arthur Schnitzler's one-act play *Der grüne Kakadu (The Green Cockatoo)* was first performed in Vienna at the Burgtheater, and before the end of that month it was reviewed in *Czas*, keeping Galicia up to date on the important dramatic phenomena of fin-de-siècle Vienna.[53] Schnitzler's play was all about the theatricality of violence, about the ways in which violence, even murder, could produce a poetic titillation in the fantasy of susceptible spectators. The play was set in a Paris cabaret called the Green Cockatoo, in which decadent aristocrats went to watch actors playing the parts of violent criminals. The date of the action was 14 July 1789, and outside in the streets the people of Paris were storming the Bastille, so that real revolutionary violence became confused with theatrical violence inside the club.

The assassination of the empress in Geneva in 1898 was sufficiently remote from Galicia to be appreciated as horrific drama. At the same time, however, in Galicia itself there were manifestations of violence that could be neither apocalyptically philosophized nor aesthetically poeticized, and, still less, comprehended and confronted. Most notably, Galicia was the scene of a wave of anti-Semitic pogroms during the summer of 1898, involving the looting and destruction of Jewish shops and taverns by Polish peasants in the villages of western Galicia. The spreading riots led to the declaration of martial law, with eventually more than three thousand arrests, and a thousand trials of the peasant rioters. The rioters, provoked by the anti-Semitic rhetoric of the populist priest Stanisław Stojałowski, were also moved by rumors that Crown Prince Rudolf, who committed murder and suicide with his young lover at Mayerling in 1889, was secretly still alive and encouraging attacks upon the Jews of Galicia. Alternatively, some Galician peasants held the bizarre conviction that the Jews had murdered Rudolf, and that now Emperor Franz Joseph himself was somehow encouraging the pogroms.[54] A certain Stanisław Szeliga was charged with lèse-majesté, because he told his fellow villagers that he had been to Vienna, where the emperor informed him personally that it was permissible to beat up Jews.[55] These allegedly loyalist Galician motivations for the riots were historically reminiscent of the massacre of the nobles in 1846, which also had been supposedly instigated by the Habsburgs and carried out in the name of the emperor. Indeed, the region of the pogroms of 1898 to some extent overlapped with that of the massacres of 1846.

The articles in *Czas* during the first week of September 1898 revealed the violent events that were promptly displaced in the press by the assassination of the empress on 10 September. On 5 September the trial began in Cracow of forty-four people accused of theft and criminal violence against Jews in various villages of the region. Reporting under the heading "Anti-Semitic Disturbances," *Czas* told the unsavory story of a village mob, armed with axes and cudgels, smashing windows and breaking into Jewish taverns in order to destroy the premises, help themselves to vodka, and steal whatever could be carried away. On 9 September four more defendants were accused in court of public violence and putting people at risk of bodily injury; they broke the windows of Jewish establishments in Wieliczka, not far from Cracow. At the same time *Czas* was following a murder trial in Sanok, east of Cracow, where a peasant was charged with stabbing to death his wife and her uncle, who happened to be a priest; the defendant claimed to have committed the murder on account of the incestuous relation between the two victims.[56] Such were the stories of unpoetic village violence in Galicia that were conveniently swept aside by the sensational news of the assassination of the empress, far away in Geneva, by the hand of a satanic anarchist.

By October it was violence as usual, as a case came to court in Cracow that involved a Jew accused of murdering the agent of the noble Zamojski family in a village near Nowy Targ, in consequence of a dispute over the *propinacja*, the alcohol monopoly, on the Zamojski estate.[57] In general, the violent crimes reported in the pages of *Czas* involved peasant villagers, with bloody murder occurring in the context of bitter poverty, often within families, and sometimes reflecting the terrible tensions between Christians and Jews in the villages of Galicia. In November, around the same time that Luccheni went on trial in Geneva, a peasant was tried in Cracow for the village murder of his son-in-law, in a case that also involved suspicions of father-daughter incest. In February 1899 another man came to trial for murdering his brother, and a nineteen-year-old boy was tried for killing a woman who was struck on the forehead while he and his friends were throwing stones at the windows of a Jewish tavern.[58] Such crimes of violence were without any glimmering of beauty or poetry, and though they compelled the attention of the press, they could hardly inspire any "exaltation" in the Galician public. All of the issues that were raised in connection with the assassination of Empress Elisabeth—imperial solidarity in mourning, the menace of satanic anarchism, and the poetics of violence—were, in fact, all the more compelling inasmuch as they evaded the everyday regional recurrence of violent crime in Galicia and focused on the rare and remote sensation of Habsburg tragedy.

In Wyspiański's drama the encounter between urban and rural contingents at the wedding was fraught with misconceptions. The most striking urban misconception was perhaps the notion that Galician village life was idyllically peaceful. "Oh, this peace; oh, this quiet," the groom exclaimed, while the journalist remarked to the peasant Czepiec:

> Yes, but here your village is peaceful.
> Let there be war the whole world over,
> as long as the Polish village is quiet,
> as long as the Polish village is peaceful.[59]

Czepiec belligerently replied, "We're ready for any kind of a fight," and later he appeared as the very model of a violent villager:

> CZEPIEC: Well, then just look at my fists;
> 　　　just you whistle for me sometime,
> 　　　you'll hear the sound of breaking ribs.
> HOST: Like with that Jew![60]

Then, when a Jew and a priest arrived upon the scene, the former remarked, "Look, good Father, what's going on, the peasants beat each other up." Czepiec owed money to the Jew, and addressed the priest in a rage:

> Good Father don't be mad at me,
> but I'm in such a dogged fever
> that, dammit, I could even break
> the neck of my own brother.[61]

Wyspiański could have taken this fratricidal sentiment from the pages of *Czas*, which reported on just such a case of murder in February 1899. More generally, the conception of unpeaceful peasants fighting among themselves, and then assaulting the Jews, could have come from the regularly reported cases of village violence in Galicia.

Within the play, it was the Host, himself an urban artist living in the countryside, who acknowledged the peasant inclination to violence: "You only have to give them arms/ and they're afire just like dry straw." He also recognized the historical significance of peasant inflammability: "Just like it was in forty-six [*taki rok czterdziesty szósty*]."[62] The context of village violence at the turn of the century, like the sinister and murderous manifestations of international anarchism, excited very particular Galician memories of the massacre of the nobles in 1846. Sensational journalism and modernist literature compulsively circled around this excruciatingly sensitive subject that lay at the heart of darkness in fin-de-siècle Galician identity.

CHAPTER EIGHT

The Land of Impossibilities

Another Chapter Beginning

Introduction: "Pathological Fantasy"

"Whoever deeply considers the position of our country," wrote *Czas* on 7 October 1898, "whoever looks into himself and before himself, must admit that one chapter in the history of Galicia is already closing and another is beginning." The progress achieved in the age of autonomy since the 1860s now pointed toward a new chapter, the twentieth century, with newly urgent concerns: "It is time to look into the depths of society and the country, where there are many sins of omission, many disturbing symptoms, many ominous signs." The turn of the century, after all, was the moment of reptiles and monsters, and they were not all external to Galicia, for some might also be harbored deep within. The politics of the future would have to seek social solidarity on the basis of a new foundation, by reaching down to the masses, but in the meantime Habsburg authority offered a reassuring guarantee of Galician order. The martial law that followed the anti-Semitic riots of 1898 was not unwelcome to *Czas*: "The state of emergency, indispensable as a means of pacification after stormy commotions, has however a momentary and passing influence, and, having reminded people of the element of power defending order, leaves behind a trace in the sobered consciousness of the peasants."[1] To know Galicia at the turn of the century meant looking within, and *Czas* in Cracow was interested in exploring the deep traces in Galician consciousness, even as Sigmund Freud in Vienna was articulating the principles of psychoanalysis.

Gazing deeply within was also related to gazing deeply into the historical past, and the many coincident jubilees of 1898, most of them celebrated in the final months of the year, were shadowed by disturbing complications. The jubilee of Franz Joseph in December, the fiftieth anniversary of his reign, was already overshadowed by the tragic death of the empress in September. The anniversary of the emancipation of the serfs in 1848—celebrated especially by Ruthenians—inevitably recalled social and national divisions that continued to trouble Galicia at the end of the century. Adam Mickiewicz became a sort of honorary Galician in 1890, thirty-five years after his death, when his remains were brought from France to Cracow for reburial in the Wawel cathedral, and the Mickiewicz centennial in 1898 produced a bronze monument in the Cracow Rynek.[2] The Mickiewicz centennial, however, as a Polish national occasion, also became an occasion for national rivalry in Galicia, and was paralleled by the Ruthenian celebration of the writer Ivan Kotliarevsky from Poltava: Kotliarevsky had published in 1798 a mock epic, *Eneida*, which represented Aeneas as a Cossack, and marked the beginning of modern Ukrainian literature.

In the exclamations of a Ruthenian journal, eastern Galicia responded to western Galicia: "The Poles not only in their own country, but also here in Rus, have in nearly every city a celebration to honor their poet Adam Mickiewicz. Is it not a disgrace for us Ruthenians that we, in our own land, pay less honor to our own prophet? We should celebrate the anniversary of the death of Shevchenko in every city and in every village reading room."[3] The fiftieth anniversary of Taras Shevchenko's death, however, would not come until 1911, nor the hundredth anniversary of his birth until 1914, so Hrushevsky helped to organize the Kotliarevsky centennial of 1898, the Mickiewicz year.

Franko had published in Vienna in 1897 a controversial article on Mickiewicz as "a poet of treason" who advocated feigned loyalty and ultimate insurrection. The Romantic Lithuanian Mickiewicz was, in this regard among others, the least Galician of all Polish cultural figures; Franko managed to make this point in a manner that purposefully antagonized all his Polish literary, journalistic, and political colleagues in Galicia, just as the year of the Mickiewicz centennial was about to begin. This meant the opening of a new chapter for Franko, as he became more closely bound than ever before to Hrushevsky and the Ukrainian political movement in Galicia. In 1898, Hrushevsky and Franko together created a new Ukrainian-Ruthenian literary journal, *Literaturno-naukovyi vistnyk* (*Literary-Scientific Herald*), and Hrushevsky published the first volume of his *History of Ukraine-Rus*. Furthermore, Franko celebrated a personal anniversary, twenty-five years since he wrote his first poems as a teenage Ruthenian writer. One of those poems, dating from 1873, was a sonnet in honor of Kotliarevsky.[4]

The nineteenth century thus ended in a jumbled concatenation of cultural commemorations whose rituals and formulas were undercut by the anxieties and tensions of the century's turn. Franko in 1899 published an essay in Vienna on "The Impossible in the Land of Impossibilities" ["Unmögliches in dem Lande der Unmöglichkeiten"]. With deep bitterness toward the Austrian imperial government and the Polish provincial politicians—especially the "Polish Club" in Vienna—Franko decried the "impossibility" for Ruthenians of participating in fair elections in Galicia. In fact, an unfair franchise based on the curial system, the gerrymandering of Polish districts, and intimidation during elections all guaranteed Polish domination of the Sejm in Lviv and the Galician delegation to the Reichsrat in Vienna. Even as commemorative occasions compelled Galicians to look deep into their provincial past to unravel the complexities of their historical identity, Franko acknowledged his despair over Galicia in the political present: "The land of impossibilities, which I would like to speak about in a few words, is Galicia." Like *Czas*, Franko believed that Galicia was concluding a chapter in its history, the chapter of Habsburg constitutionalism and Galician autonomy dating from the 1860s, but his fin-de-siècle pessimism held out little hope for the twentieth century. Only honest elections could salvage constitutional politics in Galicia and the whole Habsburg monarchy, but that was precisely the "impossible" scenario:

> One single legal electoral campaign could effect the miracle, but miracles do not happen in our times, and so these lines may be regarded not as a suggestion, not as a pious hope on my part, but rather, as far as I am concerned, as something exuded by a pathological fantasy [*als ein Exsudat krankhafter Phantasie*].[5]

Nothing could have been more true to the spirit of fin-de-siècle culture than the decadent affirmation of the poet's "pathological fantasy"—which Przybyszewski would have seen as the essential condition for artistic creation. Franko, a more sober artist who did not particularly admire Przybyszewski, nevertheless invoked such fantasy as an apt perspective for exploring the identity of Galicia, the land of impossibilities.

The new chapter represented by the twentieth century would involve bold intellectual efforts to plumb the depths of Galicia's internal impossibilities, and would witness dramatic undertakings, both in culture and politics, to cut through the provincial contradictions. In 1903, Bertha Pappenheim, Viennese social activist, set out to visit and study Galicia, to publicize its problems, and especially the circumstances of the Galician Jews. In 1905, Boy inaugurated in Cracow the violently irreverent cabaret the Green Balloon, while Franko in Lviv published his epic and messianic treatment of Galician Ruthenian destiny in a biblical poem about Moses. The coming of universal male suffrage to the whole Habsburg monarchy in 1907 suddenly gave the Ruthenians a greatly increased presence in the Reichsrat in Vienna, and created new pressures for a greater Ruthenian role in the Galician provincial government. In 1908, however, the Polish governor, or *namiestnik*, Andrzej Potocki, personal viceroy of the emperor and aristocratic representative of the Polish Galician elite, was assassinated by a Ruthenian student in Lviv. It was an act of political violence that, in some ways, anticipated the assassination of Archduke Franz Ferdinand in Sarajevo in 1914 and challenged the fundamental premises of both the province of Galicia and the Habsburg monarchy itself. With the assassination in Lviv in 1908 it became clear that the very existence of Galicia was at stake in the increasingly feverish encounter of its contradictory impossibilities. The new chapter that opened with the twentieth century would, in fact, become the last chapter of Galicia's provincial history.

Bertha Pappenheim: Immorality in Galicia

In 1901, in Lviv, a bronze statue was erected to honor Agenor Gołuchowski, who had been the confidant and minister of Franz Joseph as well as the viceroy and political architect of autonomous Galicia. Gołuchowski had died in 1875, when it was still possible to believe in his own formulas for Polish predominance, before Galicia had become too obviously a land of impossibilities. The statue of Gołuchowski, with a female allegory of Galicia at its pedestal, gazed steadily, obliviously backward into the nineteenth century.[6] In *The Wedding* in 1901, by contrast, Wyspiański dramatically confronted the impossibilities of Galicia, searching for a cathartic reconciliation of its social tensions. In 1901 the impossible contradictions of Galicia could also be reconciled in the ecclesiastical person of Andrzej Szeptycki, the grandson of Aleksander Fredro, for Szeptycki became the metropolitan archbishop of the Greek Catholic Church, supreme pastoral leader of the Ruthenians of Galicia even as, more and more, they began to think of themselves nationally as Ukrainians.[7] As Andrei Sheptytsky he would transform his family's Polish Galician legacy from the nineteenth century, the legacy of Fredro, into the Ukrainian Galician perspective of the twentieth century, reigning as metropolitan until his death in 1944—and today a likely candidate for future sainthood. Himself the personal synthesis and reconciliation of Polish and Ukrainian perspectives, Sheptytsky also reached out to Galician Jews, and tried to save Jewish lives during World War II.

In 1901, Bertha Pappenheim, born in Vienna, based in Frankfurt as an activist for Jewish women's causes, lectured on the supposed "immorality" of Galician Jewish women—their reputation for involvement in prostitution both at home in Galicia and at large in Austria and Germany. The category of the *Galizianerin* represented Jewish Galician women as a distinctive and recognizable sociological group. Pappenheim argued that it was the dire conditions of the province—poverty and ignorance—that made the *Galizianerin* so susceptible to prostitution, that Jewish women were not immoral by nature. In 1901 a sympathetic representative of the *Galizianerin* appeared on the Cracow stage in Wyspiański's *The Wedding* as Rachel, the beautiful Jewess who went to the opera in Vienna, plucked chickens at home, and knew all of Przybyszewski. If she knew all of Przybyszewski, then she knew the biblical first line of his decadent Mass for the dead, *Totenmesse* of 1895: "Am Anfang war das Geschlecht." In the beginning, there was sex. The Polish translation would appear in 1904: "Na początku była chuć." In 1903, Bertha Pappenheim made a tour of Galicia, and in 1904 she published her account of the province. She explored the Galician underworld of illicit sex, including Galicia's white slave trade. Pappenheim, herself of the prosperous Viennese Jewish middle class, had been a psychiatric patient of Joseph Breuer, and then an early psychoanalytic case history in the *Studies on Hysteria* by Freud and Breuer in 1895. In Galicia Pappenheim would recognize the *Galizianerinnen* as her sisters and dedicate herself to publicizing their plight.[8]

In 1888, the year that Szczepanowski published *The Misery of Galicia*, the Brussels financier Baron Maurice de Hirsch established a foundation for the education and social betterment of Galician Jews, to alleviate Jewish misery in the province. In 1889 the Jews of Vienna published a journal of Jewish studies with regular reports from Galicia, giving particular attention to the "redemptive" philanthropy of the Hirsch Foundation, while defining their own metropolitan relation to the provincial Galician Jews: "The Israelitische Allianz in Vienna heralded loud and clear, that they, in the interest of civilization, wanted to develop their activity among their religious comrades [*Glaubensgenossen*] in Galicia."[9] This double-edged perspective of solidarity and condescension, from the self-assumed civilization of Jewish Vienna to the emphatically imputed backwardness of Jewish Galicia, coincided with a spirit of messianic redemption, heightened by the generosity of the Hirsch Foundation. "With this foundation a new era begins for the Galician Jews," reported the Vienna journal. Without sufficient funding the Israelitische Allianz in Vienna "could only develop its civilizing activity to a modest extent," and therefore the report from Galicia ("Aus Galizien") heralded the advent of Hirsch "like an angel from heaven."[10] The spirit of Josephine messianism was born again, and during the course of the 1890s the Hirsch Foundation especially funded schools for Jewish children in Galicia. Yet, when Pappenheim visited Galicia in 1903, she would be interested to note how little the educational efforts of the foundation had achieved, especially for Jewish girls, who still languished in ignorance and then fell into immorality. The spirit of messianism could be infinitely renewed as long as the land itself remained eternally unredeemed.

During the 1890s the Hirsch Foundation's philanthropic efforts in Galicia were paralleled by the political engagements of Galician Jews themselves within the province. Historian Joshua Shanes has traced the emergence of Jewish national politics in Galicia, noting the discontinuation in 1892 of the Polish Jewish journal *Ojczyzna* (*Fatherland*), which supported assimilation in Galicia, and the advent of the new journal *Przyszłość* (*Future*). *Ojczyzna* was edited by the author Alfred Nossig in the 1880s to support the cause of Polish Jewish assimilation, a cause also enthusiastically endorsed by the critic Wilhelm Feldman, but Nossig "converted" to Zionism in 1886, and by 1892 one journal declared assimilationism to be completely "played out in Galicia." Instead, Jews sought to establish a national identity of their own within the province, organizing a Jewish National Party of Galicia. The statutes of the party, as formulated in 1893, affirmed the importance of Jewish settlement in Palestine—that is, the program of modern Zionism—but also affirmed a distinctly Galician provincial program: "The Jewish National Party in Galicia recognizes the necessity to defend the political, social, and economic interests of the Jews in the land, and considers it therefore its duty to pursue an independent Jewish politics in Galicia." Mordechai Ehrenpreis, representing an organization called "Zion," spelled out this dual program in a publication in Lviv in 1895: "On the one hand, we want to work with those who want the Jewish people freed from exile, who want to acquire our own home in the land of Israel for our poor emigrants; on the other hand, we want to work with all our powers to improve our position here in the land."[11] In other words, the Promised Lands of Galician Zionism were both Palestine and Galicia itself.

In 1898 the early Zionist Saul Landau published in Vienna an account of his travels in Galicia and Russian Poland, *Unter jüdischen Proletariern* (*Among Jewish Proletarians*). He visited Kolomiya, Stanyslaviv, and Boryslav in Galicia, exploring the Jewish aspect of Galician misery [*das Massenelend*], and he puzzled over the relative significance of socialism and Zionism, as in this exchange with a worker in Stanyslaviv:

"What party do you belong to?"
"The Social Democratic Party. I want to work. I want to work all day to earn what's necessary for myself and my family."
"Where do you stand concerning Zionism?"
"Whether I would go to Palestine? Immediately. There we would have no anti-Semitism. There we would live among ourselves."[12]

"Żydzi galicyjscy," Galician Jews. Drawing by Włodzimierz Tetmajer, from Bolesław Limanowski, *Galicya przedstawiona słowem i ołówkiem* (Warsaw: Wydawnictwo Przeglądu Tygodniowego, 1892).

Galician Jews, alarmed by the level of anti-Semitism, contemplated leaving Galicia at the turn of the century. While *Czas* in 1898 meditated conservatively about the anarchist assassination of the empress, worrying about "monsters and reptiles" in the modern world, populist journals like *Głos Narodu* (*Voice of the Nation*), the newspaper of the National Democrats in Cracow, had no hesitation about identifying those monsters as the Jews, intent upon world domination. Apocalyptic intimations in fin-de-siècle Galicia could provide the ideological context for vicious and violent anti-Semitism.[13]

Contemporary anti-Semitism also conditioned the purposes of Bertha Pappenheim, as she set out to explore and explain the reputation for "immorality" of Jewish women in Galicia. In 1903, together with her colleague Sara Rabinowitsch, she made a five-week tour of inspection. "Above all, I must guard myself against wanting to count as an expert [*Kennerin*] on the province after only a five-week stay in Galicia," she wrote. Yet, that of course was precisely the perspective she adopted, like so many Viennese visitors before her, dating back to Emperor Joseph II touring Galicia in 1773 at the moment of its creation. Pappenheim published her report in Frankfurt in 1904 under the title "On the Situation of the Jewish Population in Galicia: Travel Impressions and Proposals for the Improvement of Conditions." She cited her own "Austrian fellow citizenship [*Landsmannschaft*] and orthodox Jewish upbringing," as well as her record of social involvement on issues of poverty, as her qualifications for studying Galicia. Pappenheim was quite certain that the province had a distinctive, though elusive, character all its own: "the individuality of the land that in its mixture of German-Austrian, Polish, and Jewish elements has a very definite character."[14] Perhaps her lack of expertise was evident in her seeming failure to notice the Ruthenians who made up almost half the population of Galicia.

In 1903, Pappenheim's particular charge was to comprehend the Jews of Galicia, and she drew her conclusions based upon limited but graphic experience:

> When we, for instance, are sitting in the room at the home of a wonder-working rabbi—he opposes the necessity of boys' schools—and while we speak there falls from the ceiling into the lap of my traveling companion a large vermin [*Ungeziefer*], I don't need to eat a lot of salt in that house to form an approximately correct image of the spirit of the inhabitants, man and wife.[15]

This Kafkaesque encounter with the Hasidic rabbi and the verminous insect (Gregor Samsa became an *Ungeziefer* in Kafka's *Metamorphosis*, published in 1915) contributed to Pappenheim's broader generalizations about "the physiognomy of the land," as reflected in "the negative moral and hygienic conditions of impoverished homes."[16] The "moral" and "hygienic" aspects of Galicia were connected to one another in the civilizing and reforming perspective of the traveler from Western Europe as she generalized about the shocking backwardness of Eastern Europe.

Galician Jews: "Hunger Artists"

A dedicated social activist, Pappenheim was still enough of a fin-de-siècle aesthete to be repulsed by the ugliness of Galicia.

> The sense of beauty among Galician Jews seems to have died, under the mental pressure and terrible distress of daily life. The women and girls dress strikingly and tastelessly, but they do not adorn themselves. To want to make aesthetic demands on the living spaces, in their hygienic inadequacy, would sound like mockery. Also the synagogues are bare of every decoration, even those which the interpretation of religious law would allow. Here and there a pretty brass candlestick, and in Brody a true treasury of splendid old silver Torah crowns, testify to better times in the past.[17]

Even the dedicated social reformer, evaluating Galician poverty, expressed herself in aesthetic terms at the turn of the century. Indeed, Pappenheim seemed to struggle self-consciously with her own aesthetic impulses.

> There is something unusually poetic, atmospheric [*Poetisches, Stimmungsvolles*] in the Sabbath peace that falls upon the Jewish houses with the evening twilight—but when critical thought dispels the mood, one says to oneself: The Sabbath celebration in this venerable form is only possible where contact with the advancing world has ceased for the greatest part of the Jewish population, and the curse of unemployment makes the Sabbath peace so easy.[18]

The poetic charm of traditional life thus momentarily seduced the critical observer from bearing witness to Galician misery.

Pappenheim supposed that the Galicians became accustomed to their distasteful circumstances through the blunting or deadening of their general sensibilities.

> I believe that for the subjective feeling of the Galician population the blessing of habituation [*Gewohnheit*] is far outweighed by the curse of deadened sensibility [*Abstumpfung*]. For every human being refined by civilization [*durch die Kultur verfeinerten Menschen*], a sojourn under the prevailing conditions there in that land would be like staying in a torture chamber [*Folterkammer*] that was set up to damage all our senses and sensations.[19]

Thus fin-de-siècle sensibility became a part of the mental equipment by which the refined foreign visitor distinguished herself from the Galician circumstances at the beginning of the twentieth century. The perceived abyss that separated civilization from Galicia made the province seem like a torture chamber for the visitor of civilized sensibility.

Pappenheim, having made herself enough of an expert to enter into the "subjective feeling of the Galician population," recognized that the objective problem was poverty, the misery of Galicia. She puzzled over how Galician anti-Semites could so insistently attribute riches to the Jews, when Galician Jews were apparently as poor as everyone else.

> Aside from a very small number of relatively prosperous merchants, the commercially active Jews in Galicia belong to the poorest proletariat in the world. I was repeatedly assured that the weekly earnings of some family fathers were only just enough to buy the Sabbath bread and candles. The whole manner of life of these Jews—in the jargon of the anti-Semites, "vampires who suck the blood of Christian children"—is such that no Christian farmer or craftsman needs to feel any stirring of envy. The Jews are hunger artists [*Hungerkünstler*] whose frugality has so depressed the simplest conditions of existence that for most of them a situation of constant undernourishment prevails.[20]

Well before Franz Kafka made the "hunger artist" into one of the most fascinating figures in modern European literature, Pappenheim had already conjured that figure as the quintessential Galician Jew. The aesthetic Western observer found artistry even in Galicia, the artistry of hunger.

Mere survival was the most that Galicians could manage, Pappenheim supposed, just going on living [*dahinleben*] without any sense of how to improve their condition.

> I consider it very characteristic of the condition of dull survival of the great mass of the Jewish people in Galicia that ideas for advancing their condition must be brought from outside. Suggestions for improving circumstances by their own power did not come to my attention, neither in the province itself, nor from Galicians who live outside the province.[21]

In 1903 a series of destructive summer fires in Galician villages and towns led to a relief effort among Galician Jewish immigrants in New York, who banded together in 1904 to form the Federation of Galician and Bucovinean Jews of America.[22] This organization confirmed Galician Jewish identity in New York, while mobilizing resources to assist Galician Jews in need, both in the Old World and the New World.

In 1903, the year of Pappenheim's visit to Galicia, the great Polish magnate Andrzej Kazimierz Potocki became *namiestnik*. Aristocratically conservative in his political approach, he was deeply committed to maintaining social order in the face of the mounting Polish-Ruthenian tensions that would ultimately lead to his own assassination. In 1903, Ivan Franko contributed to those tensions by publishing a commentary on the letter to the Galicians by Mickiewicz, which dated back to the 1830s. Franko, who had already burned his Polish bridges in 1897 by writing about Mickiewicz as a poet of treason, now criticized the Polish national poet for his naiveté in affirming harmonious solidarity between peasants and nobles in Galicia. Franko wondered whether Mickiewicz was altogether ignorant about Galicia, whether "his knowledge of the history of the Polish peasantry was very scant and superficial." Writing in 1903, Franko cited the "unpleasantness" of 1846 as evidence that Mickiewicz was far from comprehending the Galician peasantry and Galician class relations.[23] Franko at the turn of the century, like Pappenheim, sought to fathom some of the cultural and economic tensions that traumatized the land of impossibilities.

Pappenheim seemed hardly confident that her own recommendations for better education, especially education for girls, would bring about the transformation of a province that seemed to her a torture chamber. Although she enthusiastically proposed nursery schools and kindergartens for Galicia, she could hardly have felt confident that they would regenerate a society of hunger artists.[24] She recognized that the two forces that truly appealed to the Jews of Galicia were traditional Hasidism and modern Zionism. Her encounter with the wonder-working rabbi and the verminous insect that fell from the ceiling indicated her general distaste for Hasidism, and she felt that some such rabbis were charlatans who publicized their miracles to drum up business. Religious Judaism, she believed, "hangs like a lead weight upon everyday life and flattens, swamps, and oppresses people."[25]

Zionism, on the other hand, Pappenheim recognized as a force for liberation, but she doubted it would do anything for the Jews in Galicia except, ultimately, remove them from the province. She further doubted that the Galician Jews she encountered on her visit were sufficiently enlightened to form a modern nation. Returning to the problem that had originally claimed her attention, the prostitution of Jewish women in Galicia, Pappenheim regretfully concluded that "the morality question" was inextricably bound up with the problems of poverty, unemployment, and ignorance.[26] The civilized visitor discovered the confirmation of backwardness that she had fully anticipated from the beginning. With her emphasis, however, on the desperate plight of the Galician Jews, she contributed to the increasing recognition of their distinctively Galician sociological and ethnographic existence among the Jews of Eastern Europe.

In 1903, Gustav Mahler, director of the Vienna opera, also visited Galicia. He traveled to Lviv to conduct a concert that would include his own first symphony. Mahler, who had just enjoyed a modernist triumph in Vienna with a new production of Wagner's *Tristan und Isolde*, in collaboration with the stage designer Alfred Roller, now approached his Lviv assignment with Viennese condescension and distaste. According to his biographer, Henry-Louis de la Grange, the thirteen-hour train trip from Vienna gave Mahler headaches and nausea, and Lviv itself seemed dirty and "repulsive" to him. When Metternich had been in Lviv eighty years before, in 1823, he had written to his wife in a tone of arch and disdainful amusement: "There necessarily occurred some funny things. I will recount them to you, and they will make you laugh." Mahler's Viennese perspective, in his letters to Alma, seemed not so dissimilar in tone: "Today I took a marvelous stroll during which I had some strange experiences. . . . I shall tell you about it when we're together." Invited to dinner by "the prototype of a provincial theater director," and honored with an award, Mahler commented to Alma, "I had to accept the invitation, and the public award of a laurel wreath (was it silver or gold? I don't know). You can imagine the face I made!"[27] Alma Mahler might not have been able to imagine, but Bertha Pappenheim certainly could have.

Yet the two concerts that Mahler conducted with the Lviv orchestra were successful, including the performance of his own symphony—reviewed in *Gazeta Lwowska* with reference to Mahler's "hypermodernism." The performances also included orchestral works by Beethoven and Wagner, and Mahler took the opportunity to see his first performance of Puccini's *Tosca* in Lviv—"admirably performed for a provincial city"—though the visitor walked out before the end, hating the opera. After his second concert, Mahler did not stay another night but went to the train station and took the 12:45 A.M. train back to Vienna, where he conducted the following evening. His most powerful impression in Galicia was a sort of extreme distress at his encounter with the Galician Jews—"who run around here like the dogs elsewhere." Mahler, a Jew from Moravia who converted to Christianity when he became director of the opera in Vienna, was horrified at his own presumptive kinship with the Jews of Galicia: "My God! So I am supposed to be related to these people! I can't tell you how absurd racial theories seem to me in the face of such evidence!"[28] From a "civilized" Viennese perspective, like that of Mahler or Pappenheim, the Galician Jews constituted a completely distinctive and disturbingly primitive anthropological community.

In spite of Mahler's musical and personal reservations about Galicia in 1903, that very same year the Galician Ruthenian opera diva Salomea Krusceniski (Solomiya Krushelnytska), who came from a village near Ternopil and received her musical training in Lviv, made her triumphant La Scala debut as Aida. In 1904 in Brescia she would star in the successfully revised version of Puccini's *Madama Butterfly*. In 1906 she would give voice to the spirit of turn-of-the-century decadence when she portrayed her operatic namesake in Richard Strauss's *Salome*, in a landmark performance at La Scala under the baton of Arturo Toscanini. The provincial obscurity of her Galician origins did not prevent her from enjoying a dazzling international career as an artist, and perhaps added an element of exoticism to her operatic appearances. One musical commentator has remarked that "she was guided by original and subtle ideas which in roles such as Aida and Salome led her to a highly stylized characterization, marked by hieratic attitudes or an enigmatic Oriental languor."[29] She died in Soviet Lviv in 1952, but her international celebrity during the first decade of the twentieth century might have given Mahler some cause to reconsider his artistic condescension toward Galicia in 1903.

FRANZ JOSEPH: "THE FANTASY OF THE JEWISH PEOPLE"

In 1903 the *Zeitschrift für österreichische Volkskunde*, the Austrian folklore journal in Vienna, published a contribution of two Jewish "folk tales [*Volkssagen*]" concerning Emperor Franz Joseph, submitted by Benjamin Segel of Lviv. "Among the Jews of the Kingdom of Galicia, which Emperor Franz Joseph

Franz Joseph at cavalry
maneuvers in Galicia in
1903. From the author's
collection.

has often visited," wrote Segel, "he has become almost a legendary figure,
surrounded by a whole array of very poetic tales, which are notable for the
way that the personality of the Emperor and many of his magnanimous
traits are mirrored in the fantasy of the Jewish people."[30] Indeed, it was the
Habsburg monarchy, in some sense, that created the Galician Jews (by creating Galicia), and it was therefore entirely appropriate that the fantasy of the
Galician Jews should act as a mirror, reflecting back to Vienna the image of
the Habsburg monarchy. In 1815, Metternich's policy, or fantasy, was to try
"to make true Galicians." The spirit of fantasy moved in both directions,
from the Habsburgs to the Galicians, from the Galicians to the Habsburgs.
Even the anti-Semitic rioters of 1898 fantasized that the emperor, or the dead
crown prince, had endorsed their pogroms.

Benjamin Segel, in 1903, couched his contribution in the language of
scientific folklore, and noted the precise circumstances under which he had

collected his specimens of fantasy. Himself a Galician Jew, Segel had heard the tales in 1894 from an old Jew who had served in the Habsburg army. That was the year of the Galician exhibition in Lviv, and the old Jew's tales would have fit the folkloric agenda of the ethnographic pavilion. Segel must have taken careful notes, since he was now able to report verbatim these specimens of fin-de-siècle fantasy, preserved for the record of the early twentieth century. Segel's sensitivity to the power of fantasy was such that much later, in Berlin in 1924, he would publish the pioneering exposé of the fabrication of the anti-Semitic text *The Protocols of the Elders of Zion*.[31] In 1903, however, he was occupied not with fantasies about Jews, but the fantasies of the Jews themselves.

The first tale of the old Jew referred back to the time when he himself was a young man, serving in the army, and along with other Jewish soldiers on leave for Yom Kippur, heard an old man telling a story about Franz Joseph. This tale thus reached back across several generations, dating to the period before Franz Joseph actually became emperor, before 1848, when he was just an imperial nephew. He was hunting in the mountains in wintertime, in a sleigh, and his coachman became completely lost in the drifting snow.

"All at once the prince looked around and saw a hunched over little man, with a walking stick in his hand, and a bundle on his shoulders; he wore a threadbare coat, and his whole body shivered from the cold so that his teeth were chattering. The emperor called out, 'Halt!' He didn't ask questions, but sprang out of the sleigh, took off his fur, and threw it around the little old man, saying, 'Climb in with me, or you'll freeze!' And as he spoke thus, the emperor suddenly saw before him a tall old man with a long white beard, all dressed in white, and in his hand he held a walking stick with a silver knob. What is this? the emperor thought to himself, for he was very much amazed. But the old man said: 'Do you know that I am Elijah the Prophet, and I have come to seek you out. For it has been decided in heaven that you will be emperor one day. So I have come down, to learn for myself what kind of heart you have, because you will have to command over many, many people. Because I have seen that you are so merciful, I promise you that I will protect you from all those who may seek to take your life.' Then he sat down beside the emperor in the sleigh, showed him the right path, and disappeared. And Elijah the prophet held to his word. It happened that an enemy of the emperor—for every emperor has many enemies—crept up behind him to take his life, but Elijah the prophet was there, and invisibly guarded him from misfortune."[32]

The historical setting of the fantasy was prior to Franz Joseph's accession in 1848, at the age of eighteen. If he was, nevertheless, old enough to be hunting in the mountains with only a coachman for his companion, he was perhaps not much younger than sixteen, which would date the fantasy to the period right around 1846, the moment when the peasants of Galicia demonstrated their supreme loyalty to the Habsburg dynasty. The Jewish fantasy suggested that Galician Jews were likewise supremely loyal. Franz Joseph, whose reign witnessed the full emancipation of the Jews as citizens in the 1860s, offering them the full protection of the law, was regarded as a guardian of the Galician Jews. The anti-Semitic rioters of 1898 were brought to trial according to the law of the land. In fantasy the Jews reciprocated this imperial protection, and provided Franz Joseph with a supernatural guardian, the Old Testament prophet Elijah, whose efficacy was all the more necessary in an age of anarchist assassinations. If the tale was recorded in 1894, there would have been no need to explain Elijah's failure to protect the Empress Elisabeth in 1898.

This tale was supposedly first told on the holy day of Yom Kippur, narrated among the Galician Jewish soldiers of the Habsburg monarchy who were directly involved in the protection of the emperor's lands, and sometimes associated with the protection of his person. Jews had been conscripted into the Habsburg army since the reign of Joseph II, and Jewish communities had regarded military service with great apprehension. "Those Jews who will be called on to serve in the army will in time forget God's Torah," lamented the Galician Jews in a circular of 1788. "They will have to desecrate the Sabbath. . . . They will mix with Gentiles and learn their ways."[33] One century later, the folk tales suggested that some of these same anxieties still remained, to be becalmed by the beneficent legend of Franz Joseph. The second tale also concerned Yom Kippur and was also set among Galician Jewish soldiers in the Habsburg army.

"In earlier times, everything was different, and Jewish soldiers did not yet have leave on Yom Kippur to go to synagogue, but had to perform their duties. So it happened once that a Jewish soldier was standing watch on the evening of Kol Nidre, and directly across from him was a synagogue. The soldier saw through the window how all the lights were burning, and the Jews were gathered, and he heard how they prayed, covered with the tallis [prayer shawl] and the kittel [ceremonial robe], and he had to stand before the guard's station with his rifle on his shoulder, and was not supposed to move. And as the Jews went on praying, it began to pull at the soldier's heart, and he could resist no longer. He himself did not know how it was with him, and what was happening to him. He let the rifle slip down, and moved a little away, step by step, until he was standing right at the synagogue next to the window, and he prayed along, and he forgot completely that he was a soldier, and that he was supposed to be on watch. Our emperor, however, is a good master, and does not rely on his subordinates, but loves to look after the laws himself. So this time also he was going around, dressed as an ordinary officer, in order to see whether the soldiers were dutifully guarding the city from the enemy. When he came now to our guard post—and saw everything—what did our emperor do? He took up the rifle, set himself at the guard post, and waited until the poor soldier was finished. You can imagine how our soldier was frightened to death, when he returned and saw who was standing watch in his place. Now there is a law that whoever abandons the watch will be punished by death. The soldier was supposed to be shot two days later. In the military it is no joke when one has broken the rules, and so he had forfeited his life. When he was led to the place of execution, and they had already covered his eyes, he thought to himself: It's all finished with me, the only thing I still need to do is acknowledge my sins and call out 'Shema Yisrael.' But then suddenly the emperor appeared, riding up on a horse, and laid his hand on the head of the soldier. And he whom the emperor has touched may not be executed. So the soldier's life was spared, but from that time the emperor commanded that all Jewish soldiers should be given leave on Yom Kippur, and that is how it has been up to the present day."[34]

In this second tale the fantasy of Franz Joseph held him to be both interested and involved in the details of Jewish ritual observance, and supremely magnanimous in his indulgence and amnesty of even the erring members of his Jewish flock. The year 1894, when the tale was collected, was the year of Franz Joseph's last extensive tour of Galicia, on the occasion of his visit to the Galician Provincial Exhibition, when he was also present for the opening of a Jewish orphanage in Lviv.[35] His presence in the province might have stimulated Galician Jewish fantasy to the telling of such tales. Indeed the timing of his visit, in September 1894, may have particularly promoted some sort of fantastic association of the person of the emperor with the ritual celebration of Yom Kippur. Segel's contribution to the Viennese folklore journal seemed to suggest that Yom Kippur, the most solemn day in the Jewish religious calendar, had also become, in Galicia, an occasion for gratefully recognizing the benevolence of Franz Joseph. Yom Kippur is a day of ritual fasting, atonement for sins; Jews pray to be inscribed by God in the Book of Life for the coming year—that is, to live and not to die. The tale of the derelict Jewish watchman seemed to emphasize the emperor's worldly power of life and death, exercised analogously to the mercy of God.

When the tale was published in 1903, Franz Joseph had very recently and very dramatically intervened to spare the life of a Jew condemned to death, Leopold Hilsner, bizarrely accused and convicted of the ritual murder of two Christian girls in Bohemia. While anti-Semites in Bohemia, but also in Galicia, urged and relished the condemnation of Hilsner in 1900, Franz Joseph intervened in 1901 to commute the death sentence to life imprisonment. The fantasy of the emperor's sympathy for the Galician Jews generated preposterous fables, like those collected and published by Benjamin Segel, but they were certainly based on the more or less plausible perception that Franz Joseph regarded Jews, like Christians, as his subjects and therefore entitled to his imperial protection. For Galician Jews the fantasized relation to Franz Joseph made them all the more Galician in their identity, the Galician identity that made them distinct from the Jewish subjects of the Russian czar. Esther Kurtz, born a Galician subject of Franz Joseph at the turn of the century in the village of Dąbrowa near Tarnów, would still remember him favorably three-quarters of a century later, in New York City, and would comment, "He was good to the Jews." She further recalled learning in school how to draw, free hand, the geographical outline of the province of Galicia.[36]

While the Viennese Pappenheim explored the misery of Galician Jews in 1903, and Mahler brought the highest culture of the capital, including his own first symphony, to the provincial Lviv symphony orchestra, Vienna published folkloric accounts of Galicia to relish its exotic, primitive, and fantastic provincial aspects. The same 1903 issue of the journal that published the two tales of the Galician Jews also included a description of folkloric research projects among the Galician Ruthenians; these projects were sponsored by the Shevchenko Scientific Society, under the auspices of Hrushevsky in Lviv. Volodymyr Shukhevych, who wrote the catalogue for the ethnographic exhibit in 1894, was busy in 1902 collecting materials, and taking photographs, for his ongoing study of the Hutsuls; some of the volumes of his *Hutsulshchyna* had already been published in Lviv, and had been reviewed in the Viennese folklore journal by none other than Ivan Franko. The year 1902 was a year of huge agrarian strikes in eastern Galicia, but also a year of intensive folkloric self-study. While Shukhevych employed photography, Osyp Rozdolsky was making use of a phonograph, and had recorded some fifteen hundred Galician folk songs; this was very early in the history of phonograph technology, as Caruso made his first operatic recording only in 1902. Volodymyr Hnatiuk in 1902 was busy in the region around Buchach, writing down folkloric accounts, including songs, legends, and fables, with six about devils, eight about vampires, and fourteen about witches.[37]

The Viennese folklore journal did not specify whether any of Hnatiuk's Ruthenian accounts concerned Jews, but Franko's essay about "My Jewish Acquaintances" (solicited by Buber in 1903) made clear that superstitions about Jews, including the blood-libel—and like beliefs about devils, vampires, and witches—played a part in Galician Ruthenian fantasy.[38] The tensions among Poles, Jews, and Ruthenians in Galicia involved their long-standing communal fantasies about one another, reinforced by modern tensions over politics and language. In 1904 a Galician Jew wrote to a Yiddish journal to describe the tensions in his hometown:

> A hired Jew traveling through our town asked his foreman something in Polish in the middle of the Ringplatz. A Ruthenian peasant who happened to be standing nearby fell on the Jew murderously and shouted, "Cursed Jew, you live on Ruthenian land, you eat Ruthenian bread and you speak Polish!" He began to beat the Jew with a big stick. . . .[39]

Historian John-Paul Himka has written about the tense "triangle" of Polish-Ukrainian-Jewish relations in Galicia, tense for reasons of religious as well as national conflict, and Himka has noted that the Greek Catholic Metropolitan Sheptytsky, Fredro's grandson, was already trying to play a Galician conciliatory role during this first decade of the twentieth century. The tensions between Ruthenians and Jews in the oil fields of Boryslav, described by Franko in his fiction, such as *Boa Constrictor* back in 1878, conditioned the class struggle in the Boryslav oil workers' strike of 1904.[40]

Historian Maciej Janowski has analyzed the emergence of a civil society and public sphere in autonomous Galicia, conditioned by the liberal constitutional framework of the monarchy after the 1860s, and in spite of poverty and economic backwardness. Yet this Galician public sphere was also increasingly nationalized by the end of the century. The Sokol (Falcon) athletic association, founded in Bohemia in 1862, also served as a Czech civic association; the Sokół established in Galicia in 1867 was Polish, and therefore led to the parallel creation of the Ukrainian Sokil in 1894. The unifed Galician Social Democratic Party, founded in 1890, was divided into Polish and Ukrainian parties by the end the decade, with a separate Jewish party to follow in 1905. Janowski notes that even coffee houses, potentially neutral public spaces, and part of a common Habsburg café culture with Vienna at its center, were subtly divided in Lviv by the Ruthenian affinity for tea.[41]

For Jews and Ruthenians the turn of the century was an important moment for cultivating the cultural identity of their respective communities. In 1901 at the university in Lviv the Polish dean tried to prevent Hrushevsky from addressing a faculty meeting in Ukrainian, and protesting students demanded the formation of a separate Ukrainian university.[42] In 1904, Galician Yiddish culture made a major public advance with the establishment of the first Yiddish daily newspaper in Lviv, the *Lemberger Tageblatt*. According to scholar Solomon Liptzin, this journal then played a central role in the development of the Yiddish literary movement that he calls "Galician

Neoromanticism." The Yiddish poets Shmuel Imber, Melech Chmelnitzky, and David Königsberg constituted "Young Galicia," modeled on "Young Vienna" and "Young Poland" at the turn of the century. Chmelnitzky, just like Hrushevsky, had moved from Kiev to Lviv, from the Russian Empire to Galicia—although Chmelnitzky ended up living in Vienna. "In his youth, under the influence of the decadent, satanic Polish novelist Stanisław Przybyszewski, he wrote in Polish and translated Yiddish poetry into Polish," notes Liptzin about Chmelnitzky, "but with the founding of the *Lemberger Tageblatt* in 1904, he turned to Yiddish and translated Polish and German poets into Yiddish."[43] Hrushevsky was busy cultivating Ukrainian culture in Lviv in 1904, the year that he established a summer school program for Ukrainian students from the Russian Empire; he himself taught them national history while Franko offered the course in literature.[44] Three-quarters of a century later, in Cambridge, Massachusetts, Professor Omeljan Pritsak, first holder of the Mykhailo Hrushevsky Chair of Ukrainian History at Harvard, would create the Harvard Ukrainian Summer Institute, as a program for the encouragement of Ukrainian culture at a time when Lviv and Kiev were both cities of the Soviet Union.

Martin Buber, born in Vienna in 1878, grew up in the home of his Galician Jewish grandfather in Lviv, but then became a university student in fin-de-siècle Vienna. He became a young Zionist, inspired by Herzl, and then at the age of twenty-six—that is, in 1904, the year of Herzl's death—Buber had his turn-of-the-century spiritual epiphany, and it was altogether Galician.

> I opened a little book entitled the Zevaat Rivesh—that is the testament of Rabbi Israel Baal-Shem—and the words flashed toward me, "He takes unto himself the quality of fervor. He rises from sleep with fervor, for he is hallowed and become another man and is worthy to create and is become like the Holy One, blessed be He, when he created his world." It was then that, overpowered in an instant, I experienced the Hasidic soul.[45]

Returning to his own family origins as a Galician Jew, Buber would now make it a large part of his life's work to explore Galician Jewish fantasy through the tales of the Hasidim.

THE GREEN BALLOON

Just as Buber in Vienna was turning to the Hasidic soul of Galicia, in 1905 the bohemian spirit of Galicia found a fervid and frenzied expression in the opening of a Cracow cabaret, the Green Balloon (Zielony Balonik), at the coffee house "Jama Michalika" on Floriańska Street. Like the explosive advent of Przybyszewski in 1898, the opening of the Green Balloon in 1905 was a defining moment for a whole generation, the young Cracovians. Przybyszewski's disciples, or "Satan's children," were now coming of age in the early twentieth century—like Boy, the presiding spirit of the cabaret. He wrote the cabaret songs, inspired by the spirit of bohemian Paris transposed to the Vistula, and celebrated the whole historic experience under the rubric "madness [*szał*]." There were satiric songs and puppet shows, while the walls of the cabaret were covered with caricatures and graffiti, taking on a whole range of targets and earning the rage or disapproval of everyone from Stanisław Tarnowski, the old Cracow conservative, to Wilhelm Feldman, the Lviv leftist and advocate of Polish-Jewish assimilation.[46]

The invitation to the opening of the Green Balloon in 1905 was almost a manifesto with its outrageous stipulations:

> During the "numbers" people are expected to howl. . . .
> Improvisers should make known that a creative and humoristic madness has seized them and that they want to show people their bare souls. . . .
> Death to Rats and Palefaces![47]

The director, Jan August Kisielewski, embraced his fellow spirits: "I love the boundlessness of your idiocy, I adore the effrontery of your silliness."[48] Thus, in the satirical spirit of mockery and merriment, the Green Balloon turned its back, indeed its bare buttocks, on the crisis of social and political tensions that engulfed Galicia at the turn of the century. Yet, in their inebriated madness, the initiates of the Green Balloon remained ultimately Galician, as expressed in a phrase whose first usage Boy credited to the artist Jan Stanisławski: "At the moment of ecstasy he formulated the often repeated exclamation, 'So, just let the Emperor Franz Joseph try to have as much fun as this!'"[49] At the Green Balloon it was perhaps difficult to distinguish the blasphemy of lèse-majesté from the perverse indulgence in hyperbolic Habsburg loyalism.

Boy himself did not doubt that the Green Balloon had an impact on the rest of Galicia: the infectious laughter became "epidemic" so that "there was almost no little town in Galicia where a handful of young intellectuals did not attempt to create their own cabaret."[50] Clearly, there was some hint of condescension here, in the Cracow bohemian perspective on the rest of Galicia, but at the same time Boy recognized that the Green Balloon was not only a cultural landmark of Young Poland but also a beacon to the provincial disciples who potentially constituted a sort of Young Galicia.

As the Green Balloon was opening in 1905, on the other side of Cracow Wyspiański was finally finishing his fin-de-siècle masterpiece of murals and stained glass in the Franciscan Church. The last piece of the project was the giant stained glass representation of Bóg Ojciec, God the Father, venerable, bearded, and dazzlingly colored in blues, greens, and purples as he brought forth life on earth. "Here in Cracow it is boring," Wyspiański had complained ten years earlier in 1895, at the beginning of the project, and now, as he finished it, Cracow had certainly become a more colorful city, the city of the Green Balloon.[51] In the Franciscan Church, however, Wyspiański eschewed irreverence, offering walls of lavish floral tribute to Franciscan spirituality, finally dominated by the regally purple presence of the creator from the Old Testament. Wyspiański's Jehovah of 1905 offered a unifying authority, looking down from the heavens upon the internecine tensions of Galicia.

The God of the Old Testament communicated directly with the man who climbed Mt. Sinai to confront him face to face, Moses, the prophet of the Hebrews, who also appeared in Galicia in 1905, conjured in Ukrainian epic verse by Ivan Franko. In *Moses (Moisei)*, Franko imagined a prophet supremely venerable and supremely visionary, but, at the very end of his life, consumed by tormenting doubts about what would happen after his death. Franko's Moses could be understood to be the prophet of the Ruthenians, and his problems were those of Galicia at the beginning of the twentieth century.

The poem began with a dedication to "my people, tortured, overpowered"—Franko's Ruthenians, like Moses' Hebrews.

> Oh, no! You are not doomed just to dejection
> And tears! I still believe in will, its power,
> In your uprising day and resurrection!
> If one could but create a moment's fraction,
> And then a word which would in such a moment
> Inflame the people into life and action!
> Or just a song with fire and living passion
> Which would grip millions and lend them wings
> For action leading them to self-expression!
> Yes, if! But we on whom all worries settle,
> And torn apart with doubt, with shame inflicted.
> We are not fit to lead you into battle![52]

Franko might have been comparing himself to Moses, both of them belonging to an older generation of intellectual leaders who had failed to find the word of inspiration that would enable them to lead their respective nations into the Promised Land.

Franko represented Moses beset by doubts, as an insidious voice within himself formulated the most painful questions.

> Perhaps midst tortures as Egyptian slaves,
> Once multiplied throughout their lands,
> They, growing stronger, might have taken hold

> Of all the country in their hands?
> In leading them into the desert land
> From homes where they have lived that long,
> Did you once think; perhaps in doing this
> I may be doing them a wrong?[53]

Moses can not find the inspirational word to bring his people into the Promised Land of Palestine, a seemingly poor land that could become, Moses knows, a "paradise on earth." Franko's mapping of Moses' spiritual reference points—from the slavery of Egypt, through the doubts of the desert, to the liberty of Palestine—would have been perfectly recognizable in Galicia in 1905 as the biblical counterpart of modern Zionism.

For the most fervid Zionists Galicia itself was, in some sense, Egypt—Mitzrayim in Hebrew—the land of slavery, and Palestine remained the Promised Land, as in biblical times. In Landau's travel account of 1898 he interviewed workers in Boryslav, center of the oil industry, and they typically replied: "We work harder than our forefathers did under Pharaoh in Mitzrayim. It is high time for God to send us a new Moses to lead us out of the Galician Mitzrayim."[54] Galician Jews were ready to equate modern Zionism with the biblical Exodus, and Egypt was equated with Galicia. In fact, Franko was very much aware of Herzl, and Herzl of Franko. According to Vasyl Shchurat, who was Franko's fellow student in Vienna in the 1890s when Franko was completing his doctorate, there was a meeting between Franko and Herzl as early as 1893. They supposedly discussed Herzl's idea for a Jewish state, and the possible analogy between movements for a Jewish state and for a Ukrainian state. When Herzl's *Jewish State* was published in 1896, Franko immediately reviewed it with great interest for a Polish journal in Lviv. He was skeptical about whether Zionism could immediately achieve its goal:

> The plan, however, undoubtedly has a future before itself; and if the present generation turns out to be yet immature for it, it is bound to survive to see, in the course of time, young people who will be willing and able to implement it.[55]

Franko may already have been thinking about the difficulties that Moses faced in inspiring his people to reach the Promised Land.

In Franko's poem, the biblical geography had to possess a parallel Ruthenian meaning. After all, Galicia was, also for the Ruthenians, a sort of Egypt in which they had suffered the slavery of oppressive serfdom up until 1848. They might have hoped, someday—by imperial magnanimity or national self-assertion or suffrage reform—to achieve their national rights and to find political satisfaction in Galicia. What then was their Promised Land, their Palestine? It could only have been Ukraine. Of course, the analogy did not actually demand the human displacement of three million Ruthenians from Habsburg Galicia to Russian Ukraine, but rather the spiritual reorientation of the Ruthenians to a new identity as Ukrainians, looking beyond the borders of Galicia and the Habsburg monarchy. This was the same reorientation that Franko himself had undergone in recent years, partly inspired by Hrushevsky, and while Hrushevsky himself had come to Galicia in 1894 to benefit from the greater liberty of the Habsburg monarchy, the Russian Revolution of 1905 made the balance of liberty between the two empires seem suddenly less uneven.

Franko, born in 1856, had, like Moses in the Sinai desert, traveled for many decades with his people after their emancipation from the bondage of serfdom. Yet he himself remained ultimately a Galician Ruthenian, and though, like a prophet, he recognized the paradise of Palestine across the Jordan, he himself was not destined to enter into the Promised Land of Ukrainian nationhood. Jehovah spoke thus to Moses:

> And since, for a moment, you dared to doubt
> The meaning of my spoken will,
> Having once seen the promised fatherland
> Your foot will never pass this hill.[56]

Wyspiański, who dared to represent the majestical image of Jehovah in the Franciscan Church of Cracow, died in 1907, not yet forty years old. Franko, who dared to write the dialogue between Moses and Jehovah, suffered a complete physical collapse in 1908, succumbed to paralysis that prevented him from using his hands, and began to hear strange voices in his head, as Moses did in the poem. He died in 1916—while Galicia still existed, though not for long—the same year that Emperor Franz Joseph died. Actually, the Ruthenian writer died six months before the Habsburg emperor, so that Franko, like Wyspiański, lived his whole life as the Galician subject of Franz Joseph.

Franko's poem did not quite end with the death of Moses. The Hebrews fell into paralyzed dejection, even guilt, over their failure to heed him in his lifetime. And then the younger generation of Joshua rose up to make themselves heard:

> A stamping sound! Is that a hurricane?
> Perhaps he prophesied the truth?
> It is Joshua, the herdsmen's chosen prince
> Who is followed by the faithful youth. . . .
> From spiritual hunger, solitude,
> From chaos of the past, they flee,
> While Joshua is rending his command:
> "To arms! To arms and liberty!"[57]

As in turn-of-the-century Vienna, where radical politics, according to Schorske, was a matter of generational revolt, so in turn-of-the-century Galicia, the younger generation turned to what Schorske called "politics in a new key"—a violent new key. Ruthenian students at the university in Lviv were outraged that their university remained largely Polish, and disgusted at the Polish political domination of elections to the Galician Sejm.[58] In 1908, while Franko's aging hands succumbed to paralysis, the twenty-one-year-old Ruthenian student Miroslav Sichynsky took up arms in Lviv and shot dead the Polish *namiestnik*, the governor of Galicia, Andrzej Kazimierz Potocki. The generation of Joshua had taken Galician politics into its own hands.

THE MURDER OF THE VICEROY: "BRAVO!"

The Potocki family was one of the greatest magnate families of the Polish-Lithuanian Commonwealth in the eighteenth century, and was likewise preeminent in Galicia in the nineteenth century. Two cousinly branches of the family flourished on the respective estates of Łańcut and Krzeszowice, owning vast lands, dominating Galician agricultural and economic life, playing leading roles in both the imperial government in Vienna and the provincial government in Lviv. Prominent members of the Potocki family helped to shape the emergence of Galician autonomy based on Habsburg loyalism in the 1860s. In 1880 it was Alfred Potocki, the cousin of the father of Andrzej Kazimierz, who, as governor of the province, welcomed Franz Joseph to Galicia; in Cracow the emperor lodged in the Potocki palace, "Pod Baranami [Under the Rams]," in the main square. When Andrzej Kazimierz Potocki became governor in 1903 it was the culmination of a political career that had already taken him into the Galician Sejm and the Viennese Reichsrat. He thus governed the province that, in fact, he partially owned, from agricultural estates, to coal mines and oil refineries, as well as spectacular collections of coins, manuscripts, tapestries, rugs, and pictures. In a spirit of noblesse oblige, shaping a policy of tactical conciliation, Potocki, the noble Polish conservative, tried to engage the radical new political players of the turn of the century: socialists, peasant populists, and Ruthenians aroused by a new Ukrainian nationalism. He sought to navigate the fierce currents of social and national tension that surrounded the outbreak of the great oil strike at Boryslav in 1904 and the advent of universal male suffrage in Austria in 1907.[59] The tragedy of his assassination underlined the failure of his policy.

The bullets that killed Potocki in 1908 were aimed at the very existence of Galicia itself. Functioning as a governor, he was actually appointed by the emperor as *namiestnik*, or viceroy, and was thus the embodiment of Habsburg imperial rule in the province. From the naming of Gołuchowski as *namiestnik* in 1866, that office was crucial to the functioning of autonomy in Galicia. When the Empress Elisabeth was assassinated in Geneva in 1898, it was an assault on the dynasty that was marked with demonstrations of mourning and affirmations of loyalty in the provinces, including Galicia. When the *namiestnik* Potocki was assassinated in Lviv ten years later, in 1908, it was an assault on the political constitution of the province and was interpreted with dire foreboding in Vienna, the imperial capital. The assassination of Potocki in Lviv in 1908 anticipated, in notable ways, the assassination of the Archduke Franz Ferdinand in Sarajevo in 1914, which proved to be ultimately fatal to the Habsburg monarchy. Both assassinations expressed the violent rejection of the politics of Habsburg rule, in Galicia and in Bosnia, respectively, and both reflected the national tensions that rendered Habsburg rule ultimately untenable.

On 12 April, when Potocki as *namiestnik* was holding a public audience, Sichynsky entered the hall and immediately fired five shots, one of which entered the head above the left eye. On 13 April the great liberal newspaper of Vienna, the *Neue Freie Presse*, reported the assassination to the public of the imperial capital.

> The viceroy of Galicia, Count Andreas Potocki was murdered yesterday by a Ruthenian student. The political blindness, the insane passion, and the boiling national hatred which were the motives for the crime, can not moderate the revulsion at the deed, which is without precedent in Austrian history. The national struggles have called forth the sharpest discord and the greatest bitterness between the rival peoples in this monarchy. . . . Certainly this assassination, that was hatched in an immature and confused head, is a sign of the tension between Poles and Ruthenians. The murder of the viceroy was made psychologically possible by the relation between these two nations in Galicia, and even in this madness the history of that land in the last forty years remains recognizable. . . . No less terrible is the misfortune that now a bloody ghost stands between Poland and Ruthenia. Both peoples inhabit Galicia, and both must share the destiny of this land. . . .[60]

From the perspective of Viennese liberalism, the violence of Galicia seemed shockingly alien but nevertheless dangerously relevant to the political life of the whole monarchy. From the perspective of Freud's Vienna, at the turn of the century—and the *Neue Freie Presse* was Freud's newspaper—the insanity of Galicia cried out for psychological explanation. In 1901, Wyspiański had conjured ominous Galician ghosts on the Cracow stage in *The Wedding*, and now those ghosts could be seen from as far away as Vienna.

Historian Hans-Christian Maner has studied the metropolitan perception of Galicia as a border region of the Habsburg monarchy. On the eve of the assassination, in 1907, there were Galicians who claimed that the viceroyalty actually functioned as if Galicia were the Orient, like the British viceroyalty in India—that "we are regarded as Asia." In the aftermath of the assassination, in 1908, members of the parliamentary "Polish club" in Vienna, representatives to the Reichsrat, claimed that Galicia remained "terra incognita" for most Austrians. In the Reichsrat there allegedly prevailed "perfect ignorance of Galicia" among most representatives: "They have no interest in it, and only hear from a faraway land, where the peoples fight with each other, news that does not concern them and is as amusing as a telegram from Manchuria."[61] With the assassination of 1908 the internecine struggles of the Galicians began to seem less remote and more relevant to political life in Vienna.

The *Neue Freie Presse* noted that Potocki himself, ironically, had pursued a conciliatory policy toward the Ruthenians of Galicia, and the newspaper recalled his father, Adam Potocki (possibly confusing him with Alfred Potocki), as a figure in the Viennese government—"and always respected and cherished as a Gentleman, even by his opponents." Andrzej Kazimierz was supposed to have his father's character as Gentleman (the Viennese newspaper used the English word, with a capital G): "All the deeper was the painful sympathy with which the report of the tragic fate of Count Potocki was received in Vienna." Sichynsky, by contrast, was no gentleman but a madman, and his deed was neither English nor Austrian in its style: "This is not Austrian, but Russian." For it was Russian influence and example that was presumed to motivate the Galician Ruthenians of the Ukrainian party. The campaign of assassination attempts by the Russian revolutionaries of Narodnaya Volya were supposed to have shaped Sichynsky's political consciousness.

> Accusations of injustice were absorbed by an unbalanced mind and fermented there until the idea established itself of imitating the admired example of the Russian assassination heroes and giving up one's own life to destroy another's. With this exaltation the murderer was hereditarily burdened. At least it is being said that also his mother—which is almost unbelievable—confirmed the son in his intention, and had declared herself to be in agreement. Through such confused and unrestrained seething of an overwrought brain was this deed, the senseless copy of Russian propaganda, brought to Austria.[62]

The Galician assassination conjured, in Vienna, a clash of civilizations between Austria and Russia, a vision that would be further intensified by the Bosnian annexation crisis later that year. The protagonists of the Galician drama illustrated a hereditary chasm between the victim Potocki, whose father was a gentleman, and the murder Sichynsky, whose mother was a monster.

As Potocki lay dying, he was reported to have said, "Telegraph to the emperor that I have always been his loyal servant." When he was shot he was wearing his decoration of the Habsburg order of the Golden Fleece. Potocki's final affirmation of Galician loyalty and identity was put before the Viennese public, and the *Neue Freie Presse* further emphasized both Potocki's absolute devotion to the dynasty and his complete identification with the province that he governed. His contributions to the Galician Provincial Exhibition of 1894 were particularly noted: "When he in his own special exhibition revealed the natural treasures of Galicia to the astonished view of the visitors, he did it with the proud consciousness of a magnate who wants to show the whole world what the land can achieve."[63] Galicia itself, as proudly represented to the world with all its provincial treasures in the exhibition of 1894, now appeared to be politically prostrate.

While Sichynsky could be represented as both a madman and a vessel of foreign influence, the life of the assassin was also intimately embedded in the context of the province and the monarchy. The *Neue Freie Presse* found his sister in Vienna, the wife of a Galician Ruthenian representative to the Reichsrat, and she gave a tearful interview about her brother and her family from the district of Zbarazh: "My father was a priest. In our house much was said about the suffering of our nation. We were six sisters and two brothers. Miroslav was also a diligent and very talented student." He had studied in the gymnasium in Kolomyia and in Przemyśl; he had taken courses at the university in Vienna as well as in Lviv, where he was frequently involved in student protests on behalf of Ruthenian political causes. He had participated in hunger strikes, had led demonstrations, and had even been arrested. There was an older brother with a nervous condition, who had shot himself. According to their sister, Miroslav was much affected by his older brother's suicide, and was heard to utter, "If someone is going to renounce his life, he should first achieve some great deed, a deed for the whole people." The assassination of Potocki was Sichynsky's great deed, and he confessed to it fully, without regrets, promising that future assassins would follow in his footsteps if the Ruthenians of Galicia remained unsatisfied: "There will be another Ruthenian who will clear the next viceroy out of the way." His mother, arrested as an accomplice, remarked, "What is there to be secretive about? I have nothing against Count Potocki, but only held against the viceroy that he oppressed the Ruthenian people. I spoke with my son about his assassination plan. I encouraged him to carry out the assassination, and gave him the necessary money."[64] What the Viennese public was learning, along with the news of the deed itself, was that the Ruthenian perspective allowed for no regrets.

The *Neue Freie Presse* quoted earlier editions of the Polish newspapers in Galicia which claimed that, when Sichynsky was delivered to the courthouse in Lviv, there were Ruthenian students in the streets crying out, "Bravo!" In Arthur Schnitzler's drama *The Green Cockatoo*, performed in Vienna in 1899, about criminal violence enacted as theatrical entertainment, one of the characters remarked, "In the moment when you cry bravo, you make everything into theater." The theatricality of political violence in Galicia was fully registered in Vienna, where the *Neue Freie Presse* noted even the details of costume, such as Potocki's order of the Golden Fleece. Sichynsky, in the vestibule before the audience hall, supposedly "smoothed his black salon jacket and stepped before the mirror to put his hair in order."[65] Then he entered the hall, and began to shoot.

In Freud's Vienna the *Neue Freie Presse* pondered the psychological circumstances of the assassination. "The student Sichynsky is probably a sick man," observed the paper on the front page on 14 April, noting the medical mysteriousness of "illnesses of the soul."[66] In order to fathom the context of his sickness, the *Neue Freie Presse* made use of a special correspondent, who described the approach to Lviv for the funerary ceremonies of Potocki:

> A dreary wet cold morning. Patches of snow still lie scattered over the steppe landscape as the train passes through; bare fields alternate with scrubby woods, and fearfully poor villages fly past and seem to sink into the morass. Then city houses appear in the distance, towers rise up, and we are in Lemberg.[67]

The correspondent spoke with Polish officials of the Galician government in Lviv, and they hoped that the assassination would make an impression in Vienna: "Now people will finally believe us in Vienna." The assassination, they believed, should prove that it made no sense to reproach the Galician government for being unsympathetic to the Ruthenians. "It is a wild people who live here," one official explained. "Galicia is not Lower Austria, and Lviv is not Vienna."[68] The correspondent himself, describing the train's passage through the "steppe landscape" of Galicia, had already sought to make visibly evident to the Viennese public that there was a notable difference between their own metropolitan experience and the "morass" of Galicia. The backwardness of Eastern Europe thus appeared as the context for an act of sick and monstrous violence.

On 14 April, Potocki's funeral bier traveled from Lviv to Cracow, and from there to the family estate at Krzeszowice, where he was to be interred. The correspondent of the *Neue Freie Presse* reported that the whole urban life of Lviv came to a halt for four hours, while people paid tribute to Potocki's

bier, and from Cracow to Lviv the route of the train was lined with Galicians
paying their bare-headed last respects to Potocki: "People in urban clothes,
peasants in rough sheepskins, and orthodox Jews, all stood in colorful combination to offer the quickly passing train their greeting."[69] Missing from
this colorful, multicultural Galician picture were, of course, the Ruthenians.
There was, however, a provocative Ruthenian poster that appeared in Lviv:
"The spreading report that the murderer of the viceroy was a Ruthenian
must be designated as lying and false. The murderer Sichynsky is a typical Ukrainian barbarian." The poster thus suggested that those who called
themselves Ruthenians still recognized themselves as civilized Galicians, and
those, like Sichynsky, who called themselves Ukrainians, were dedicated to
the destruction of Galicia. The assassination of the *namiestnik*, however,
revealed that the Ukrainian perspective was already pervasive, as the *Neue
Freie Presse* reported news from places in eastern Galicia where money was
being collected to support Sichynsky. Supposedly, peasants were celebrating
the assassination with "joy," refusing to work in the fields, and commenting
enthusiastically that Potocki had been "shot down like a dog."[70] For the liberal
Neue Freie Presse, even though the paper had some sympathy for Ruthenian
national concerns in Galicia, it was difficult not to feel that such expressions
of joy and enthusiasm were closely related both to mental illness and social
barbarism.

"The Spirit of Wildness and Anarchy"

The Polish perspective in Galicia sought to make itself known in Vienna,
and was not inclined to rely on Viennese special correspondents to get the
story right, especially correspondents for the liberal press. Polish hegemony
in the province had been politically conservative, dating back to the achievement of autonomy in the 1860s. The long-standing alliance between political
conservatives and historical revisionists of the Cracow school—like Kalinka
and Szujski—underlined the importance of historians and historical work for
the ideology of Galicia. In 1908 the assassination of Potocki was immediately
taken up by the young historian Stanisław Zieliński, who published in Vienna,
in German, his account of *The Murder of the Viceroy Count Andrzej Potocki: Materials for the Judgment of Ukrainian Terrorism in Galicia.* The historical problem
that Zieliński set himself was to explain how the Ukrainian movement had
succeeded in transforming "the Ruthenian people who formerly appeared
as a model of adherence to law, peace, and order," so that now they offered
"a sad picture of anarchy, the release of the lowest passions, contempt for

authority, and disregard for the law."[71] Zieliński emphasized the issues of law and authority in Galicia, and he insisted that the assassination constituted an act of terrorist anarchism.

The Empress Elisabeth in 1898 had, in fact, been assassinated by a self-proclaimed anarchist who thus demonstrated his commitment against all political authority. Now, in 1908, with Zieliński's historical treatment, the assassination of Potocki was linked to earlier excesses of violence in an allegedly ongoing tradition of monstrous violence undertaken for the sole purpose of undermining social order. Sichynsky's explicitly national aims were thus reinterpreted in the extreme spirit of apocalyptic, satanic, and barbarous anarchism.

The Ukrainian movement was supposed to be seeking to produce "instead of peaceful, friendly relations, only a greater confusion and anarchy in the land," so as to achieve the "ruin [*Zerfall*] of the land." Anarchism thus aimed at the destruction of Galicia itself. Zieliński was quick to pick up on the lexicographical issues of being "Ruthenian" and being "Ukrainian," arguing that it was Hrushevsky who had purposefully and sophistically introduced into Galician discourse such mixed terms as "Galician Ukraine" and "Ukrainian-Ruthenian," intended to undermine the provincial identity of Galician Ruthenians.[72] Putting the word "Ukrainian" in quotation marks, Zieliński bitterly resented the "newly discovered 'Ukrainian' people in Galicia," and saw this semiotic move as inevitably bound up with the political purposes of a "party of anarchy and subversion"—the subversion of Habsburg Galicia by redefining its politics in terms of "extra-Galician relations" with Russian Ukraine.[73]

The Polish-Ruthenian compromise of 1890, according to Zieliński, had led to the establishment of Ruthenian schools in Galicia, including secondary schools, or gymnasiums, at Kolomiya, Przemyśl, Ternopil, Stanyslaviv, and Lviv. These Ruthenian schools, however, nourished Ukrainian culture, even as Hrushevsky advocated Ukrainian identity at the university in Lviv. Putting "Ukrainian culture" in quotation marks, Zieliński represented it from the Polish perspective:

> It was a culture of the rabble, pervaded by the spirit of wildness and anarchy. As history education, students in these schools were indoctrinated with the glorification of the Cossacks and the deification of their sacrilege and murder. As national hero there was Bogdan Khmelnytsky, a man who, as leader of rebellious Cossack bands, summoned Tartars, desolated the land with fire and sword, and gave over all of Ukraine into the hands of the Russians.[74]

The phrase "with fire and sword" alluded to the epic Polish historical novel of Henryk Sienkiewicz, *Ogniem i Mieczem*, which graphically represented the wildness and savagery of Poland's Ukrainian frontier during the seventeenth century. Zieliński seemed to suggest that the Ukrainians of the twentieth century might similarly desolate (and betray to the Russians) the Ruthenian frontier of the Habsburg monarchy. Hrushevsky was particularly cited for seeking "to link the present Ruthenians with the traditions of the Ukrainian Cossacks and Haidamaks," and for making Khmelnytsky into "the greatest hero of Ukrainian history." When Hrushevsky went to St. Petersburg after the Russian Revolution of 1905, he brought back "greetings to the Ukrainian youth of Lviv" and proposals for a common Ukrainian struggle for "freedom and equality"—in Russian Ukraine and in Galician Ukraine. The latter place name—"Galician Ukraine"—was regarded by Zieliński as Hrushevsky's pernicious political invention.[75] Among the Galician youth to whom this greeting was addressed would have been, of course, young Miroslav Sichynsky.

In Hrushevsky's "Galicia and Ukraine" ("Halychyna i Ukraina"), published in 1906, he worried anxiously that these two lands were moving in separate directions, especially after the recent revolution in Russia.

> Now Ukraine will go along its own separate road, and its distance from Galicia will grow with each step if care is not taken to shorten the distance between these roads. Should each go along its own road and rapprochement not be secured, in twenty or thirty years we will have before us two nationalities on one ethnographic base. This would be similar to the position of the Serbs and Croatians.[76]

The very political existence of Galicia was thus an obstacle to Ukrainian national unity, and Zieliński quoted Hrushevsky's "Galicia and Ukraine" to demonstrate that the reasoning was implicitly subversive, even treasonous, to Galicia and the Habsburg monarchy. According to Hrushevsky, "It is in Galicia's interest to draw closer to Ukraine, for the security of its future, for the liberation from its present slavery and misery."[77] Galician economic "misery" had been a byword ever since Szczepanowski, but now that misery, imbued with a national dimension, was viewed not as a motive for reform but as an argument against the political existence of Galicia altogether.

In 1901, Hrushevsky had created fierce university controversy by defiantly refusing to speak in Polish at a faculty meeting. In 1908, Zieliński emphasized the particular atmosphere of "wild anarchy" that had developed at the university in Lviv; students were demanding a separate Ukrainian university or, at least, greater priority for the Ukrainian language alongside Polish at the existing university. In student protests there was massive destruction—tables, armchairs, sofas, lamps, glasses, electrical wires, windows, and portraits of past rectors—while Ruthenian students proclaimed socialist and revolutionary slogans. Zieliński was shocked:

But let the curtain fall upon such scenes, which must fill every friend of law and legality with horror. The few features that we have presented here are sufficient to give the dark picture of the desperate relations which prevail at the Lviv university, and to characterize the bestial barbarization and anarchy of Ukrainian youth, which, at one of the focal points of culture and civilization, have created circumstances reminiscent of the terrible scenes of Russian Ukraine. In such a milieu was educated the student who would become the murderer of the viceroy of Galicia. He was a student of the third year in philosophy. He studied history (under Professor Hrushevsky) and geography.[78]

History and geography, which had been invoked to explain and justify the invention of Galicia back in the eighteenth century, were now, in the twentieth century, being employed to question the assumptions and undermine the foundations that maintained the political existence of Galicia. Zieliński wanted the Viennese public to see this not as a national struggle but rather as an apocalyptic encounter between barbarism and civilization, between bestiality and humanity, between society and anarchy.

Zieliński was eager to put before the public of Vienna the Ukrainian reaction to the assassination in Lviv, which "not only called forth no movement of horror and indignation" but was rather "received with calm and forbearance, yes even with appreciation and joy." He suggested that the newspaper *Dilo (The Deed)* was virtually responsible for the crime:

> Every day, for a month and a half before the murder, *Dilo* reviled Count Potocki, stirred up its readers against him, and put the murder weapon in the hands of dehumanized Ukrainian youth, filled with fanaticism in the infected atmosphere of hatred. What profound relief and immeasurable joy lay in the words—"It has been accomplished!"—with which the political editor of *Dilo* began his first article dedicated to the murder, when finally the long-desired deed had been carried out.[79]

While the *Neue Freie Presse* sought to characterize Sichynsky as an individual madman, Zieliński wanted the Viennese public to see the assassination as a crime committed by an entire political movement, the Ukrainian Ruthenians. *Dilo*, he noted, actually defended the general phenomenon of assassination, arguing that "political murders pass into history and art, as poets and artists make them eternal."[80] At the time of the anarchist assassination of the Empress Elisabeth in 1898, *Czas* had found a "strange poetry and beauty" in the fin-de-siècle tragedy, and now, ten years later, *Dilo* dared to invoke art and poetry with regard to the assassination of Potocki. After all, there were supposedly already Ruthenian students crying, "Bravo!"

Zieliński provided abstracts from the Polish press, where *Czas* in Cracow explored the "tragedy" of the assassination, and *Słowo Polskie (The Polish Word)* in Lviv denounced "the spirit of anarchy." This latter theme was developed at length in *Słowo Polskie* and quoted at length by Zieliński for the Viennese public:

> The Ukrainian movement is not the movement of a national struggle, not the striving of a developing culture toward independence, not the fighting for special rights and public institutions in order to raise itself to higher levels of cultural development. This, in its essence, is a movement of social and political anarchy. It has found a good social basis, namely the masses of the Ruthenian people, filled with the traditions of the Haidamaks, organically incapable of an independent state culture, a people whose soul has been formed in the atmosphere of wild barbarism, the struggles of the uncontrollable Cossacks with the Tartar nomadic hordes. And herein lies the special danger of Ruthenian Ukrainianism, that appears under the name of the Ukrainian party. It is dangerous for the political life of the whole state, into which it brings the element of subversion and barbarism, and above all it is dangerous for us, for our national interests in Galicia. . . . While we guard our culture, our national rights, we must at the same time defend from anarchy the social order of the land, at whose helm we stand.[81]

The good ship Galicia was in danger, and the Poles of Galicia stood at the helm guiding it to safety. The Poles of the old Commonwealth had prided themselves on their role as the *antemurale*, the bulwark, of Roman Catholic Europe, and now the Poles of Galicia adopted the same role, defending not only themselves but also the whole Habsburg monarchy from the dangerously corrosive forces of anarchy and barbarism.

Galicia's political preservation now appeared historically urgent, more so than ever before, as the "monsters and reptiles" of the new century made their presence known. Galicia would know how to defend itself, according to *Słowo Polskie*: "We do not ask the central government for the protection of our society from anarchy, but we have the right to demand that the government should not come to agreements with that anarchy, at the cost of our social order."[82] Ultimately, the purpose of Zieliński's work was to put the Polish perspective before the Viennese public, in the hope that the Habsburg government would not try to placate the Ruthenians in Galicia. Thus, he insisted that the Ukrainian party was not a national movement for national rights, but an anarchist assault on the whole social order and political existence of the province.

Zieliński was pleased to be able to report that Emperor Franz Joseph himself seemed to take a politically sympathetic position, with a handwritten personal note to the widowed Countess Potocki, gratefully acknowledging that the viceroy, "even in the face of death, assured me of his loyalty." *Czas* in Cracow declared that the emperor's note "called forth in the land not just a touching emotion, not just gratitude and an inner union between the emperor and the land in mourning for the departed—but also reassurance for the future."[83] As *Czas* saw it, not just the widow, but all of Galicia was in mourning, and the emperor's note was to be understood as a message of sympathy for Galicia itself. *Czas*, back in the 1860s, had helped to articulate the public expressions of loyalty to Franz Joseph that accompanied concessions of autonomy in Galicia, and had led the Galician chorus of mourning for the Empress Elisabeth in 1898. Now *Czas* returned to the theme of mourning and loyalty, of the bond between emperor and province, when the very existence of Galicia seemed to be at stake.

Michał Bobrzyński: "Our Own Internal Disorder"

Poles like Zieliński, and Polish journals like *Słowo Polskie*, worried that the government in Vienna, in spite of Franz Joseph's personal message to the widow, would decide that the politically expedient reaction to the assassination was to conciliate the Ruthenians. This was precisely the liberal perspective of the *Neue Freie Presse*, which, while abhorring the assassination, never equated Ruthenian nationalism with wanton anarchism. The Viennese newspaper noted on 18 April that "in Galicia the dangerously explosive masses of national dynamite lie stockpiled, so that the opposition between Poles and Ruthenians can not bear any further deepening or sharpening."[84] The crucial question to be imminently decided was the succession to Potocki, and whether the new *namiestnik* would be more or less conciliatory toward the Ruthenians. The *Neue Freie Presse* certainly wanted conciliation—"to pacify the land, to curb and soften the agitation"—a matter that would have implications for the entire Habsburg monarchy with its complex problems of nationality.

> A fateful chance has placed the crownland Galicia in the front line, and made it a necessity to apply practically in this crownland for the first time those principles that later may bring to the whole state the possibility of the peaceful coexistence [*Nebeneinanderleben*] of nations. The policy of pacification [*Beruhigung*] and mutual understanding is here also the only means to achieve the end.[85]

For conservative Poles, Galicia was the bulwark, the *antemurale*, of order against anarchy, while for liberal Austrians in Vienna, Galicia represented the crucial test case of peaceful multinational coexistence. From both perspectives, the future of Galicia was meaningful for the monarchy as a whole, and fatefully uncertain in the aftermath of the assassination. The first step toward the next stage would be the naming of Potocki's successor.

The *Neue Freie Presse*, on 18 April, already spoke of an "interregnum" in Galicia—a province temporarily without a viceroy—and considered possible candidates. The paper reviewed the powerful viceroys of the past half-century, including Agenor Gołuchowski, Alfred Potocki, and Kazimierz Badeni, all of whom also served in important positions in the emperor's central government in Vienna. The *Neue Freie Presse* speculated that Gołuchowski's son, also Agenor, might be called to succeed the murdered Potocki as viceroy, after recently completing a decade of service as the emperor's foreign minister and presiding over improved relations with Russia. It was doubtful, however, whether he would now accept the viceroyalty, and the *Neue Freie Presse* recognized that one of the most likely possibilities was Michał Bobrzyński, the celebrated Cracow historian, regarded as "one of the cleverest minds among the Polish politicians." He seemed all the more likely, inasmuch as the *Neue Freie Presse* actually located Gołuchowski in Rome, pressed him to respond to the rumors of his possible appointment, and received an emphatic denial in the aesthetic mode of the turn of the century: "The Polish world has become alien to me. I enjoy undisturbed my well-earned peace in the dreamlike beauty of this unique city, and I am not thinking about renouncing that." Galicia was certainly less tranquil, and the *Neue Freie Presse* reported, quoting *Słowo Polskie*, that in Przemyśl twenty-five Ruthenian high school students had been arrested for chanting "Long live Sichynsky! Let Potocki rot!"[86] The next Galician viceroy was obviously not going to be able to enjoy any sort of dreamy peace.

"Ein Komplott?" was the heading on one report to Vienna from Lviv, for this assassination, like so many others, produced a troubling uncertainty about whether the assassin had acted alone or as part of a conspiracy: *ein Komplott.*[87] Sichynsky, in his cell, was being closely watched to prevent him from committing suicide, while Sheptytsky, the Uniate metropolitan, was said to be considering resigning his post in despair. Sheptytsky supposedly remarked, "I see that my hand has been too weak. There is nothing else that remains for me to do, except to resign my pastoral dignity, and retreat into a monastery."[88] In fact, Sheptytsky would preside over the Uniate Church until his death in 1944, but his reported despair reflected the traumatic intensity of the moment in 1908. Potocki, the emperor's viceroy, had tried and failed to govern Galicia by conciliating Poles and Ruthenians, while Sheptytsky, the pope's vicar, was seeking to conciliate Roman and Greek Catholics in Galicia. Aleksander Fredro in 1832 had written despairingly, "How gladly I would sign myself today: Gin-Li-Kia-Bo-Bu, a Chinese Mandarin."[89] Likewise, Andrei Sheptytsky, Fredro's grandson, fantasized in 1908 about simply withdrawing from the public life of Galicia.

On 21 April the *Neue Freie Presse* took a liberal stand against the anticipated appointment of Bobrzyński, arguing that he was too much of a hard-liner in his conservative approach to the Ruthenians. "Since what matters is that both nationalities should live in peace in the land and that the hostile mood should not be sharpened," editorialized the newspaper, "so this appointment would be a great political mistake." In Galicia the Easter season was dominated by a mood of "general nervousness," as unconfirmed rumors of new violence circulated.[90] Conspiracy theories mounted when a slip of paper was found in Lviv with a black border, a death's head, and the text of a Russian revolutionary song. Sichynsky was placed under special guard with bayonets, no longer for fear that he would kill himself, but, reportedly, out of concern that there might be a Ruthenian conspiracy to help him escape from prison.[91] In fact, he did escape in 1911, immigrated to America, and died in Detroit in 1979, long outliving Galicia, the province whose political life he had so violently traumatized in 1908.

In spite of the reservations of the *Neue Freie Presse*, the appointment of Bobrzyński, to succeed Potocki, was announced on 25 April, two weeks after the assassination. The interregnum was over; the political life of Galicia, violently interrupted, now continued under a new *namiestnik*, but the future was full of foreboding. Bobrzyński, in any event, was a Galician who harkened back to earlier provincial traditions and more stable times. Born in Cracow in 1849, he had studied at the Jagiellonian University, a student of Józef Szujski. Bobrzyński himself became a history professor there in the 1870s, and a Cracow conservative delegate to the Sejm in Lviv and the Reichsrat in Vienna in the 1880s. Historian Philip Pajakowski, writing about Bobrzyński, notes that "for his contemporaries, Bobrzyński's defining political feature was his Habsburg loyalism," inasmuch as "the Habsburgs represented a bridge to West European civilization, which, for Bobrzyński, was Poland's cultural community."[92] He was thus a quintessential Galician who carried on, into the twentieth century, the Stańczyk political conservatism that underlay the creation of Galician autonomy in the 1860s. As a historian, he remained similarly committed to the midcentury principles of the Cracow school, publishing in 1879 an "outline history" of Poland (*Dzieje Polski w zarysie*) that rejected Romanticism and made the Poles fully responsible for their national misfortunes. Bobrzyński believed in the historical importance of the state and its institutions, and, an admiring reader of Herbert Spencer, he subscribed to a sort of social Darwinism in which national survival meant, in part, the survival of the fittest.[93]

"Neither our borders nor our neighbors, but only our own internal disorder, brought about the loss of our political existence," wrote Bobrzyński, reflecting on the history of Poland.[94] It was a classic formulation of the Cracow historical school with reference to the partitions of Poland, but by

1908, when Bobrzyński became viceroy, the message was coming to seem relevant to contemporary Galicia as well as the former Commonwealth. The "internal disorder" of the eighteenth century was echoed in the "anarchy" that Polish conservatives saw looming over the political scene in the twentieth century. For some Galicians the "anarchist" violence of the assassination in 1908 recalled the massacres of the Polish nobles in 1846, while for others the assault on Galician political institutions, like the viceroyalty, served as a reminder that the weakening of state institutions in the Commonwealth led to the complete collapse of the state. Bobrzyński would look to both Galician and Habsburg institutions as remedies to political disorder, but in a Darwinian struggle between Poles and Ukrainians he also knew where he stood. It was under his governorship, beginning in 1908, that Józef Piłsudski would organize in Galicia his Polish paramilitary clubs of riflemen that would eventually evolve into the Legions of World War I, bringing Polish independence—and, at the same time, dissolving Galicia.

Bobrzyński, in his memoirs, remembered that he too was in Italy at the time of the assassination in April 1908, that he read about it in the Italian newspapers and then traveled to Galicia, to Krzeszowice, for the funeral. Soon after, he was summoned by Franz Joseph in Vienna, who told him that he would be the next viceroy.

> You should know that you were my only candidate for the viceroyalty. Of course I allowed my ministers to discuss this matter with me, but as soon as I heard of the death of Potocki I immediately took the decision to name you as his successor. Remember above all that you are the guardian of the relation by which I have bound myself personally to the Poles.[95]

For Bobrzyński, to be entrusted with the governorship of Galicia was a matter of mediating the emperor's relations with the Poles, and from such a Polish perspective the Ruthenians could only appear as a problem of proper management. After accepting the emperor's offer, Bobrzyński brought the news to the members of the parliamentary Polish Club in Vienna:

> Having been graciously called by His Highness to the position of *namiestnik* of Galicia, I accept that office at a moment when heartfelt pain and grief oppresses the heart after the loss of the remarkable man who fell at his post, leaving to us the unforgettable example of his loyalty to the monarchy and patriotic feeling of duty. I accept this office at a hard and difficult moment which can only lead to a sober evaluation of relations. . . .[96]

He did not specify what those "relations" were, presumably the relations between Poles and Ruthenians in Galicia. The tragedy of Potocki's assassination, however, compelled Poles like Bobrzyński to seek solace in their own Polish conception of Galicia, for which the supremely important relation, trumping all others, was that between the emperor and the Poles. In 1866 they had stood by the emperor—"We stand with you, Your Majesty, and we wish to stand with you"—and now they needed the emperor to stand by the Poles, to preserve their conception of Galicia, and to save the province from anarchy.

While Poles and Ruthenians in Galicia were traumatically polarized in 1908, the Jews of the province explored the meaning of their own Galician identity. During the first week of September 1908, Jews from all over Eastern Europe, including Galicia, met in Czernowitz, in Bukovina, for the first international Yiddish conference, sponsored by Nathan Birnbaum from Vienna. For Galician Jews, the conference offered an opportunity to recognize their own distinctiveness as Galitzianer, evident in their Yiddish pronunciation. For the Russian Jews, Galician Yiddish had such notable German inflections that there were rude cries of "Yiddish! Yiddish!" when Galicians took the floor—as if they were speaking German.[97]

By 1908 the Jews of Galicia had a history of their own, and the Lviv historian Majer Bałaban marked Franz Joseph's sixtieth jubilee with a publication in Polish on the Jews of Austria under his reign, from 1848 to 1908, "with particular regard to Galicia." Bałaban, who would become an eminent historian in Lviv and would die in the Warsaw Ghetto in 1942, began his career with a book about the Jews of Lviv in 1906, and published another in 1912 on the Jews of Cracow. Yet already in 1906 he was thinking about an integral history of Galician Jews when he published an account of Herz Homberg and Jewish education in Galicia under Joseph II. This was followed by an account of the Austrian Jews under Franz Joseph, which appeared in 1909, and culminated in a history of the Jews in Galicia (*Dzieje Żydów w Galicyi*) published in Lviv in 1914 with the outbreak of the war that would ultimately undo Galicia altogether. This latter book was also published in New York, the home of immigrant Galician Jews who still thought of themselves as Galitzianer.[98]

In 1907, when universal male suffrage came to the Habsburg monarchy, *The New York Times* reported that "an interesting premonitory symptom of the effect of universal suffrage on the electoral situation in Austria is reported from Lemberg, the capital of Galicia, where many hundred representative Jews met yesterday and resolved to create a provincial organization for the defense of the political rights and economic interests of Jews." The *Times* particularly applauded the fact that these Jews—Jewish nationalists, in fact, though focused on Galicia rather than Palestine—were frankly affirming their identity, whereas "hitherto the Jews of Austria have preferred to masquerade as members of other races, preferably as Germans." The article declared, in conclusion, that "the Galician Jews are to be congratulated upon setting a good example to their fellow-Semites elsewhere."[99] From as far away as New York the Galician Jews were of interest, not only as immigrants but also in relation to their Galician homeland.

In 1908, the year of the Yiddish conference in Czernowitz, Martin Buber offered his earliest exploration of the religious mythology and folklore of Galician Jews with the publication, in Frankfurt, of his *Legend of the Baal-Shem*. Buber claimed to speak from the authority of his own Galician childhood and his own Galician ancestors.

> The Hasidic legend does not possess the austere power of the Buddha legend nor the intimacy of the Franciscan. It did not grow in the shadow of ancient groves nor on slopes of silver-green olive-trees. It came to life in narrow streets and small, musty rooms, passing from awkward lips to the ears of anxious listeners. A stammer gave birth to it and a stammer bore it onward—from generation to generation. I have received it from folk-books, from note-books and pamphlets, at times also from a living mouth, from the mouths of people still living who even in their lifetime heard this stammer. I have received it and told it anew. . . . I bear in me the blood and the spirit of those who created it, and out of my blood and spirit it has become new.[100]

For Buber, the Viennese Jew with family from Lviv, Galicia was a sort of Sarnath or Assisi, the homeland of a great mystical phenomenon, offering to him a very particular philosophical perspective, carried in his own blood and spirit, for confronting modernity and the twentieth century. The *namiestnik* was assassinated in 1908, and the province confronted the irresolvable contradictions of its political condition, but Buber was entranced by Galician myths and legends of past centuries. The *namiestnik* was dead, but the Baal Shem still lived. In the 1890s, Tetmajer and Franko wrote fin-de-siècle poetry of exotic mysticism, invoking Buddhism and longing for Nirvana; Buber would discover for Galicia an indigenous Buddha of its own.

"The Comet"

At the beginning of the twentieth century Galicia appeared as an ancestral homeland of mystical roots for the modern Jews of turn-of-the-century Vienna. Sigmund Freud was born in Moravia, but his father came from Galicia, from the town of Tysmenitz (Tysmenytsia). "I have reason to believe that my father's family were settled for a long time on the Rhine (at Cologne)," wrote Freud in his autobiographical sketch, "that, as a result of the persecution of the Jews during the fourteenth and fifteenth centuries, they fled eastwards, and that, in the course of the nineteenth century, they migrated back from Lithuania through Galicia into German Austria." It thus required circuitous explanation and contorted speculation for Freud to acknowledge his Galician origins. In a letter of 1930 he went further: "It may interest you to hear that my father did indeed come from a Hasidic background. He was forty-one when I was born and had been estranged from his native environment for almost twenty years."[101] As Freud was born in 1856, his father would have become "estranged" from Galicia· right around the time of the death of Emperor Franz in 1835, around the time that Fredro stopped writing comedies. Freud wrote from the perspective of his own secularism and modernity, but he still acknowledged his family origins in Hasidic Galicia.

In 1894, while Freud was studying hysteria in Vienna, Kazimierz Tetmajer wondered how a poet of fin-de-siècle Galicia should face the end of the century. He struck the note of nervous anticipation, which sounded all over Europe at the turn of the century, but Galicia had sensitive nerves and anxieties of its very own. In 1901, in the concluding scenes of the third act of Wyspiański's *The Wedding*, the assembled company anxiously awaited the coming of the legendary Ukrainian bard Wernyhora, who had supposedly prophesied the destruction and eventual rebirth of Poland.

> HOST: Quiet—dawn, dawn, Aurora!
> It's almost daylight—It's Him—My God!
> It's Him, it's Him—Sh!—Wernyhora.
> Bow your heads—it's a living truth,
> a Phantom, a Spirit, a Vision that's real.
> POET: He summons the dawn with his lyre—
> GROOM: Hoofbeats.
> BRIDE: They're coming.
> WIFE: Hoofbeats.
> HEADMAN: They're charging.
> (All listen, leaning toward the door and window—in complete silence—as if in a trance.)[102]

The wedding party wonders what might be taking place in Cracow, even as they wait transfixed in the village, their nerves taut with anticipation, their imaginations filled with the sound of spectral hoofbeats.

The ghost of Wernyhora haunted the Host already in the second act, recalling the bloodshed between Poles and Ukrainians in the past:

> WERNYHORA: Do you remember the bloody glow,
> the groan of bells and thunder,
> the bloody slaughter and river of blood?
> HOST: And the dream, the somehow distant dream,
> those bells still ring in my ears—[103]

They were probably recalling the massacres of Uman in 1768, when thousands of Poles and Jews were killed by Ukrainian Haidamaks in the troubled times leading up to the first partition of Poland. Those same Haidamaks—irregular military bands of Cossacks and peasants—were invoked by the Polish press in 1908 when Sichynsky assassinated Potocki. Memories of violence in *The Wedding* also brought the nervous fear of future violence. At the conclusion of the third act, waiting for Wernyhora's return, the company of wedding guests was suddenly armed, according to Wyspiański's stage direction:

> (All are bent down, genuflecting, listening, strongly grasping their scythes in their right hands; they grab for the swords hanging on the wall as well as for the flint-locks and pistols; listening as if their souls were entranced, hands cupped over their ears. We can now hear the sound of real hoofbeats, which grow suddenly closer and closer—then stop. . . .)[104]

The play concluded with mysterious anticipation, leaving the audience baffled about what great events might be about to unfold. There was some suggestion that the company was listening for the signs of Poland's coming resurrection, and the image of peasants with scythes certainly alluded to the Kościuszko insurrection of 1794, so recently commemorated in the centennial of 1894. Yet, peasants with scythes inevitably also called to mind the massacres of 1846 in Galicia, explicitly invoked in *The Wedding* with the spectral appearance of Jakub Szela in the second act. Could the peasants ever again turn their scythes upon the Galician nobles? In any event, there was no doubt that they could turn upon their neighbors the Galician Jews, as demonstrated in the widespread pogroms of 1898, very fresh in memory at the moment of the premiere of *The Wedding* in 1901. If the company at the conclusion of the play, however, was waiting for some dramatic signal to shatter the silence, to announce with violence the advent of the twentieth century in Galicia, then the fateful report for which they waited, "hands cupped over their ears," might have turned out to be the shots that murdered the *namiestnik* in Lviv in 1908.

Wernyhora was only a ghost at the turn of the century, but in 1894 another custodian of memory came from Ukraine to Galicia, Mykhailo Hrushevsky, historian and political prophet. In 1898, Satan himself came to fin-de-siècle Galicia in the human form of Przybyszewski and electrified the province for a few tumultuous years before moving on. Gustav Mahler, the great maestro of imperial Vienna, appeared upon the Galician scene in Lviv for just a few days in 1903. The Green Balloon had its sensational opening in 1905 in Cracow. Galicia had its heralds of modernism and modernity at the turn of the century, while those who awaited messianic manifestations might have found them in 1905 in the stained-glass window of God the Father by Wyspiański or the poetic rendering of Moses the Prophet by Franko. Yet both great Galician artists, Wyspiański and Franko, on the eve of the former's death in 1907 and the latter's paralysis in 1908, were already looking beyond Galicia, to

Poland and to Ukraine, respectively. Bertha Pappenheim preached Viennese civilization as the remedy for the backwardness of the Jews of Galicia, but she was not surprised to find them more responsive to the mystical ecstasies of Hasidism and the political promises of Zionism.

Znaszli ten kraj? That was the song that later haunted Boy when he recalled the turn of the century. Do you know the land? Cracow artists and poets went to the countryside to learn to know the Galician peasants, while Viennese reformers, like Pappenheim, went to the shtetls to learn to know the Galician Jews, while Lviv scholars and officials set up the ethnographic pavilion of 1894 so that the public could learn to know Galician folk culture. Yet to know Galicia with all its complexities and contradictions was to recognize the menacing fault lines that underlay the geopolitical surface of the province. And so the Galicians waited, "hands cupped over their ears," for a sign of what was to come, messianic exaltation or apocalyptic cataclysm.

In "The Comet," published in 1938, Bruno Schulz recalled the Galician world of his childhood in the town of Drohobych. Almost all his fiction involved the conjuring of that world, but "The Comet" can be most precisely dated by the astronomical phenomenon of the title, presumably referring to Halley's comet, which was visible in 1910 (or possibly the so-called Great Daylight Comet, also visible in 1910, and sometimes confused with Halley's comet in that year). Halley's comet had been visible only once before during Galicia's historical existence, in 1835, the year of the death of Emperor Franz, and in 1910 the comet was seen once again as an astronomical portent by those who witnessed its passage. Schulz, born in Drohobych in 1892, was one such witness, and he described the mood of nervous anticipation in 1910:

> From Twelfth Night onward we sat night after night over the white parade
> ground of the table gleaming with candlesticks and silver, and played endless
> games of patience. Every hour, the night beyond the windows became lighter,
> sugar coated and shiny, filled with sprouting almonds and sweetmeats. The moon,
> that most inventive transmogrifier, wholly engrossed in her lunar practices, ac-
> complished her successive phases, and grew continually brighter and brighter.[105]

As in the Galician company of the final scene of Wyspiański's *The Wedding*, so in Schulz's story the Galician Jewish family of the narrator waited anxiously for signs from the heavens. The advent of the comet bred strange terrors: "One day my brother, on his return from school, brought the improbable and yet true news of the imminent end of the world." The comet itself might be the agent of apocalypse:

> Again the sky opened above us, with its vastness strewn with stellar dust. In that
> sky, at an early hour of each night appeared that fatal comet, hanging aslant, at the
> apex of its parabola, aimed unerringly at the earth and swallowing many miles per

second. . . . How difficult it was to believe that that small worm, innocently glow-
ing among the innumerable swarms of stars, was the fiery finger from Belshazzar's
feast, writing on the blackboard of the sky the perdition of our globe.[106]

Yet, they almost did believe it in Drohobych, where in 1910, two years after
the assassination of the *namiestnik* in Lviv, anticipations of the future were
fraught with anxiety, and any ominous manifestation—like the comet—might
be fearfully viewed as potentially cataclysmic. In fact, the moment of the
publication of the story in 1938, even without a comet, was also one of grim
anticipation. Just as Schulz's Galician world would be swept away by World
War I, soon after the appearance of the comet, so his Polish world would
be destroyed by World War II, fatal for him, as for so many other Galician
Jews; he was murdered by the Nazis in Drohobych in 1942.

Tadeusz Żeleński, the ever-youthful Boy, left Cracow after World War I,
after the abolition of Galicia, and settled in Warsaw, the Polish capital, where
he lived as an eminent literary and cultural critic, a controversial social commentator, and a brilliant translator of French literature into Polish. With the
outbreak of World War II, Boy, age sixty-five, fled Warsaw, which quickly fell
to the Nazis; he moved to Lviv, which was occupied by the Soviet Union according to the terms of the Molotov-Ribbentrop Pact. Boy taught at the university in Lviv, the old Galician university, which Stalin was going to make over
into a Ukrainian university, as the Galician Ruthenian students had demanded
at the beginning of the century. In 1941, however, Hitler invaded the Soviet
Union and occupied Lviv, where a reign of terror ensued, including the mass
murder of Polish university professors. One of them was Boy. There is some
evidence that Ukrainian students, the successors to alumnus Sichynsky, helped
to draw up the list of Polish professors to be purged from the university.[107]

In 1942, the year that Schulz was murdered in Drohobych, Metropolitan
Andrei Sheptytsky, Fredro's grandson, issued the pastoral letter "Thou Shalt
Not Kill." Sheptytsky appealed in vain for an end to the hatred and bloodshed
in Galicia, as he had back at the beginning of the century, under the scepter
of Franz Joseph, when Sichynsky assassinated Potocki. In fact, hundreds
of thousands of Galicians were murdered during World War II, including
almost all the Galician Jews. Boy too was murdered in Galicia during the war,
in former Galicia, the land of his birth in 1874—he whose boyish spirit had
been formed by fin-de-siècle Galicia, who had made himself into one of
"Satan's children" at the side of Przybyszewski in 1898, who had witnessed
the premiere of Wyspiański's *The Wedding* in 1901, and who had irreverently
celebrated the contradictions of Galicia in the satirical songs of the Green
Balloon during the first decade of the twentieth century. *Znaszli ten kraj?*

CHAPTER NINE

Geopolitical Conclusion

The Liquidation of Galicia

INTRODUCTION: "BEYOND HUMAN COMPREHENSION"

"Right after the outbreak of hostilities, the Russian army overran Galicia," wrote the Yiddish writer S. Ansky, who visited Galicia from the Russian Empire soon after the outbreak of World War I.[1] Later famous as the author of the Yiddish drama *The Dybbuk*, Ansky, during the war, made himself into the witness and chronicler of the wartime fate of the Galician Jews. In fact, the Russian occupation of most of Galicia in September 1914 would, in some sense, mark the beginning of the end of Galicia's political existence as a Habsburg province. The retaking of Galicia from the Russians in 1915 would be a joint Austrian-German military achievement, and the German command tended to have the upper hand in such joint ventures. After World War I, Piłsudski's victory in the Polish-Soviet war meant that Galicia was entirely incorporated into independent Poland, but its entirety was severed forever from the Habsburg sovereignty that had defined the province's political existence ever since 1772; that sovereignty anyway ceased to exist with the abdication of the last Habsburg emperor in November 1918.

During the war itself the ultimate fate of Galicia remained a matter of speculation, for no one could predict the circumstances of the eventual peace. The wartime period in some ways paralleled that of the Napoleonic military presence in Galicia, a hundred years earlier, when Metternich had noted the "uncertainty of possession" that made Galicia's political future indeterminable. Yet Ansky's interest in Galicia, and especially Galician Jews under Russian occupation, demonstrated already in 1914 that the province would still be capable of provoking and compelling attention, even as its political existence was being challenged—indeed, even long after it ceased to exist.

Ansky, born as Shloyme Rappaport in 1863 in Vitebsk, was a subject of the Russian czar who became a Russian socialist. Beginning around 1905, in St. Petersburg, he began to study Jewish ethnography and folklore, and to write in Yiddish. His studies of the Jews of the Russian Empire stimulated his interest in Jewish life in Galicia on the other side of the Russian-Habsburg border, and when the Russian army advanced in 1914, St. Petersburg was suddenly as relevant as Vienna for everything that pertained to Galicia. Ansky heard unsettling rumors:

> There were vague, murky reports that the Russians, especially the Cossacks and Circassians, were savaging the Jewish population in these occupied areas. . . . "My arms go numb and my eyes fill with tears," wrote one Jewish soldier, "when I think of the horrors I've seen in Galicia, when I remember the soldiers' and the Cossacks' atrocities."[2]

Galicia in World War I, as later in World War II, would appear as a theater of horrors, even as Galicia itself became a historical ghost. It would become the site of murderous atrocities and, ultimately, of Nazi genocide.

Ansky in 1914 was hearing reports of brutal rape and slashing murder, perpetrated by soldiers in the Russian army against the Jews of Galicia:

> From these and other dismaying reports, we realized that things beyond human comprehension were going on in Galicia. A vast region of one million Jews, who only yesterday, under Austrian rule, had enjoyed human and civil rights, was trapped in a cordon of blood and iron. Severed from the rest of the world, they were at the mercy of Cossack and Russian soldiers provoked like wild beasts. It was as if an entire people were perishing.[3]

Not yet: an entire people would perish one generation later in World War II, but for Ansky, writing about World War I, genocide in Galicia was already imaginable. In fact, the province was not severed from the world, but merely severed from the Habsburg monarchy—from constitutional and multinational government—and without the political presence of the monarchy there suddenly hovered the possibility of horrors beyond human comprehension. From the beginning of Ansky's mission in 1914, to Isaac Babel's account of traveling with the Red Cavalry in Galicia during the Polish-Soviet war in 1920, it was possible to observe the social collapse that accompanied the geopolitical conclusion of Galicia's existence. The province's defining relation to the Habsburg monarchy was rendered tenuous and uncertain by the war, and, in November 1918, with the conclusion of the war, the institutions of Habsburg Galicia were formally "liquidated" by the Polish Liquidation Commission. The abolition of Galicia, however, could not suppress postwar political controversy concerning the contested future of what had become the former Galicia.

"Bitter Tears"

Ansky's account, *The Destruction of Galicia* (*Khurbn Galitsye*), would not be published until the year of the author's death in 1920, after the abolition of Galicia itself. Yet, writing during the war, Ansky composed his work in the vivid present tense, creating a summation of Galicia and Galician Jews at the endpoint of Galician history. He began his summation where Szczepanowski left off in 1888:

> Galicia is one of the poorest regions of central Europe, if not the poorest. . . . The deeply rooted Galicians, especially the Ruthenians in the eastern part, are barely educated and live roughly. . . . Even though Jews in the Austrian Empire enjoy equal rights, with equal access to all the professions and government jobs, those in Galicia are very poor and unsophisticated. . . . Galicia's Hasidism degenerated into blind faith in wonder rabbis, while Orthodoxy waged an especially savage and relentless war against the Enlightenment. . . .[4]

Like other travelers before him Ansky noted the backwardness of Galician Jews—blindly credulous, savagely unenlightened, hopelessly unassimilated—and also appreciated the context of the general backwardness of the entire province. For Ansky the paradox of Galician history, now coming to an end, was that in spite of all the political advantages offered by Habsburg constitutional government, the backwardness of Galicia remained irremediable and irredeemable. In fact, that backwardness had always been ideologically essential to the Habsburg sense of a civilizing imperial mission, and continued to be affirmed right up to the moment of Galicia's geopolitical cancellation in 1918.

The perception of social and economic backwardness was reinforced by the intensity of national rivalries in the province. Ansky certainly noted "the fierce national struggles of various ethnic groups" in Galicia, and the consequent problems for Galician Jews, trying to maintain their balance among the Germans, Poles, and Ruthenians of the province, in shifting sympathy or alliance with one or another of these nationalities. "Because of these shifts, the various ethnic groups resented the Jews all the more and viewed their behavior as treacherous," wrote Ansky. He understood that the fundamental political identity of the Jews was one of non-national loyalty to the Habsburg monarch, making them the quintessential Galicians:

> The generally favorable political situation gave Galician Jews a feeling of self-worth and security, a conscious sense of being full-fledged citizens. Their Austrian patriotism was strong, and their dedication to the old Kaiser, Franz Joseph, was cultlike. They loved him deeply and respected him as their protector and helper. At the start of the war, Austria's Poles were in an ambiguous position,

while the Ruthenians stood apart from everyone. The Galician Jews, however, stuck to their pro-Austrian orientation, flaunting it in the most delicate of circumstances, with no concern for horrible consequences. Their self-sacrificing allegiance was extraordinary. I saw Jews shedding bitter tears when they heard about the fall of Przemyśl to the Russians.[5]

What Ansky witnessed, without quite realizing it, was the recognition that Galicia might be coming to a historical end, marked with bitter tears by the Galician Jews who feared that the end of Galicia could be catastrophic for them.

Yet they still preserved their identity as Galician Jews, and would continue to preserve it long after the end of Galicia. Ansky noted with fascination the gulf between them and the Jews of the Russian Empire.

They were alien to each other, even inimical, and always cool. The Galician Jews looked down on the Russians as disenfranchised Jews and were unable to grasp how anyone could live and breathe under arbitrary rule, deadly pogroms, and random persecutions. The Orthodox among them saw Russian Jews as licentious and heretical. For their part, the Russians despised the Galicians as backward, fossilized—an ignorant mass without culture or aspirations.[6]

The proud Galician Jews were about to discover their own extreme vulnerability without the security of Habsburg Galicia. They too would experience deadly pogroms, more savage than the anti-Semitic riots that had sometimes occurred under the Habsburg monarchy before the war. The passing of Galicia during World War I would be punctuated by pogroms, first during the Russian occupation in 1914, and then with the inauguration of Polish independence in 1918, especially in Lviv. During the war an enormous number of Galician Jews fled to Vienna as refugees, and after the war many more emigrated from Poland to America.

By 1915 some 150,000 Galician Jews were refugees, and half of them were in Vienna. There they received assistance from Viennese Jewish organizations such as the Israelitische Allianz, founded in 1872, and dedicated since the 1890s to improving Jewish education in Galicia. Historian Marsha Rozenblit has described how new wartime organizations, such as the Hilfsverein für die notleidende jüdische Bevölkerung in Galizien, the Aid Society for the Suffering Jewish Population of Galicia, were specifically focused on the catastrophe of Galicia. Yet the presumption of civilization from the Viennese perspective—so evident in the humanitarian writings of Bertha Pappenheim at the turn of the century—still underlay a sense of difference from Galician Jews. Charity sought to bridge that gap, as in this Viennese address to Galician Jews at a Passover seder hosted in a soup kitchen in Vienna in 1915: "You were foreign to us, and your culture did not appear to be like ours. . . .

But our contact with you has brought us closer, and the bearing and dignity with which you bear your tragedy fills us with sincere admiration."[7] There was clearly a significant sense of difference between Viennese and Galician Jews, as there was between Galician and Russian Jews.

In 1916, in the middle of the war, the most famous Yiddish writer in the world, Ansky's contemporary Sholem Aleichem, died in New York City, leaving incomplete his novel on the adventures of Mottel, the cantor's son. The novel told the story of a Jewish boy from the Russian Empire who immigrated to America by way of Galicia. Sholem Aleichem himself had traveled that route before the war, and Mottel's reactions to Galicia offered a naively comical perspective on what was distinctive about the province:

> Guess where we are? In Brody! We must be quite close to America. Brody is a nice city. City, streets, and people are nothing like those back home. Even the Jews here are different. That is, they are Jews like ours back home—and maybe the Jew here is even more of a Jew than ours at home: their earlocks are much longer, their coats almost reach the ground, they wear strange caps, belts, shoes, and socks, and the women wear wigs—but it's their language. My, what a language! The words are the same, but they have broad A's and sound like German. And the way they talk! They don't really talk—they sing. It sounds as if they are always chanting psalms. . . .[8]

Sholem Aleichem, for whom the Yiddish language was central to his literary vocation, was naturally sensitive to variations in dialect. So he could not help noticing that the Jews of Galicia were different in this regard, and the difference was noticeable as soon as one crossed the border of the Russian Empire and arrived at Brody.

Mottel brought with him a certain prejudice against Galicia: "It's because of a saying we have back home about 'Cracow and Lemberg.' When you eat something very sour, you say, 'It's so sour that it makes you see Cracow and Lemberg.'" Mottel, however, was not a sour fellow, and he could not help admiring what he saw in Brody, and, even more so, what he saw in Lemberg— "clean, spacious, handsome"—the next stop on his journey. Mottel reported that "our friend Pinney explains to us that Lemberg is better than Brody just because it is farther away from the frontier and closer to America."[9] Pinney comically prided himself on having studied geography, and therefore could recognize the supposed proximity of Lemberg and America. Each step away from Russia brought the emigrants closer to America, and Galicia thus appeared—as it sometimes did to the Galicians themselves—as an outpost of Western civilization.

In Cracow, still further west, Mottel thought the Jews did not even look like Jews: "They twist their moustaches upwards and put on airs." Galician women presumed to compare themselves to empresses, and Mottel reflected about his own mother: "If we hadn't been swindled out of our things at the frontier, she would be quite a 'Kaiserin' now. I recall mother's silken yellow kerchief in which she really did look like a Kaiserin." The Kaiserin Elisabeth was assassinated in 1898, and so there was no empress in the Habsburg monarchy for the rest of Franz Joseph's reign, until 1916, but Galician presumption seemed to allow any woman to give herself imperial airs. Pinney remarked that "there is more 'civilization' here," and Mottel thought, "I'd like to know just what is this 'civilization' without which our friend Pinney can not live."[10] Sholem Aleichem was inclined to find humor in the presumption of civilization, but he was certainly aware that the word played a role in defining the differentiated perspectives of Galician Jews and Russian Jews.

THE ASHES OF POMPEII

Marsha Rozenblit, writing about Habsburg Jews and World War I, has observed that it became a kind of "holy war" for Jews, fighting to demonstrate their loyalty to Franz Joseph in battle against czarist Russia, perceived as an empire of barbarism, anti-Semitism, and pogroms. Rozenblit has described, from memoirs, the immediate reaction of Galician Jews to the outbreak of war in 1914:

> Minne Lachs, who was seven years old, remembered that her father took her downtown at night (in Trembowla, Galicia) to see "how a war begins." At the city hall, Austrian and Galician flags waved in the breeze, torches glowed, a man read Franz Joseph's manifesto to his peoples. . . . Similarly, Manes Sperber, nine years old at the beginning of the war, recalled that Max the trumpeter, who announced the mobilization in the Galician town of Zabłotów, appeared intensely joyful as he announced the great news. "Looking at him," Sperber wrote, "you would have thought he had announced that the Messiah had come."[11]

The families of both Minne Lachs and Manes Sperber would end up leaving Galicia among the Jewish refugees who fled from the Russian occupation, and both families ended up in Vienna.[12] The war itself quickly became, for Habsburg Jews as for the Habsburg army, a war for the liberation of Galicia from Russia.

When Ansky came to Brody in 1914, it had been recently torched by the Russian occupying army, and the "nice city" that Sholem Aleichem had admired before the war—"we must be quite close to America"—was in ruins. "The town looked like the ancient, mossy remnants of Pompeii," observed Ansky. "I noticed the scorched wall of a synagogue." The Russians claimed that a Jewish girl had fired upon them from a window in Brody, and that constituted the excuse for the burning of the town: "Later in the war, this crime was repeated in dozens, indeed hundreds, of Galician towns and villages, becoming normal, not worthy of notice. The burning of Brody, however, was the first such atrocity . . . and so the soldiers felt the need to devise an excuse, to rationalize the savagery."[13] Like Pompeii, the city destroyed by volcanic eruption, the province of Galicia, suffering a sudden eruption of savagery, was being transformed into a smoking landscape of charred ruins. The Habsburg infrastructure of the province was being dismantled by the Russian occupiers, as Ansky observed: "I spent several days in Brody because I had to transfer my load of medicine to non-Russian freight cars on the Austrian tracks. . . . The Austrian railroad gauge had been widened to Russian specifications only within five or ten miles from the border."[14] The nineteenth-century cultivation of provincial connections by the construction of Habsburg railroads was now coming undone according to the military exigencies of World War I.

"I found Lviv to be an elegant, cultivated European city," wrote Ansky. "There were no signs of war, no burned or shattered houses." The Habsburg train station—completed in 1904 in the modernist architectural spirit of the Viennese Jugendstil—made a particular impression on Ansky: "The largest and most glorious structure was the train terminal, one of the most beautiful in all Europe. Later on, while pulling out, the Russians blew it up, totally destroying it." Baedeker's *Oesterreich-Ungarn*, published in Leipzig in 1910, mentioned a good restaurant in the Lviv train station, and invited visitors to appreciate the sights of the Galician capital: good views from the tower of the Town Hall and from the Franz-Joseph-Berg (that is, the Castle Hill). Baedeker mentioned Juliusz Hochberger's building for the Galician Sejm, the assembly hall decorated with Jan Matejko's historical painting of the Union of Lublin. Outside in the Stadtpark (or Jesuit Gardens) stood the bronze statue of Agenor Gołuchowski, erected in 1901. Near the university the visitor might note the monument to Aleksander Fredro, erected in 1897. Baedeker estimated the population of Lviv at 200,000 in 1910, before the war, and counted 11 percent as Jews.[15]

Ansky in 1914 was frustrated in his encounters with the Lviv Jewish leaders who were not eager to accept the war relief that he proposed to them. According to the prominent lawyer Yankev Diamant, "We were and remain Austrian citizens. We are loyal to our fatherland and to our gracious monarch, to whom we Jews especially have a lot to be thankful for. If we went along with the proposal to establish a Russian-Jewish committee, we'd be entering into an official relationship with the Russian authorities."[16] The Galician Jews remained punctiliously Galician.

According to the rabbi whom Ansky interviewed, there had been one sole pogrom in Lviv when the Russians arrived in September, at the time of Yom Kippur. The synagogues were therefore closed—"the Jews were too frightened to attend synagogue for the Yom Kippur Kol Nidre prayers"—but, according to Ansky, Jewish soldiers in the Russian army protested. They themselves wished to attend religious services, and therefore the synagogues were reopened under Russian military protection.[17]

Jews were not the only Galicians who stayed at home in fear of violence during the Russian occupation, as Ansky learned:

> The instant the Russians occupied a section of Galicia, they were followed by whole armies of priests. . . . The Ruthenian peasants belong to the Uniate Church, and the black army instantly began working on them, trying to bring them back to the Orthodox faith. And the proselytizers . . . threatened to confiscate the land belonging to the obstinate Ruthenians and to forcibly take away their children and induct them into the Orthodox creed. . . . One doctor told me that the Ruthenian woman in whose home he was billeted had locked herself in during the past few days and refused to admit anyone because of a rumor that the children of the Uniates were to be taken away.[18]

Like Jewish Galicians, Uniate Ruthenians had developed a particular identity within the provincial cocoon of Habsburg Galicia. While many Ruthenians had already revised their identity to become Ukrainians before the war, associating themselves nationally with the Ukrainians of the Russian Empire, the Uniate religion remained fundamentally Galician, defining a distinctive Galician perspective. Over the course of the twentieth century, Stalin would make eastern Galicia into western Ukraine, and would completely suppress the Uniate Church, but the former Galicians would enthusiastically reclaim their identity as Uniates in independent Ukraine in the 1990s.

From Lviv Ansky traveled west to Tarnów, where the embattled front lines were only a few miles away, and the booming and banging of artillery fire could be heard in the town. Yet everyone grew accustomed to the percussive reports, and Ansky observed that "life was virtually normal," that "two cafés were open, and they were constantly packed, especially with officers." Ansky's Russian military contact in Tarnów, Igor Platonovich Demidov, was nevertheless perturbed by the Galician Jews: "The Galicians aren't like our Russian Jews. They are very unappealing." Asked to explain, Demidov could only observe that the Galician Jews were hostile to the Russian occupation, and that some were profiting from the presence of the Russian troops.[19]

Ansky was distressed to discover in the streets of Tarnów a poster, unsigned but presumably authorized by the Russian military, concerning the Jews of the town:

> Our experience in the present war has revealed the open hostility toward us on the part of the Jewish populations in Poland, Galicia, and Bukovina. Whenever we leave a place and our enemy marches in, he inflicts all sorts of punishments upon our pro-Russian friends mainly because of denunciations by Jews, who stir up the Austrian and German authorities.[20]

The poster proposed the hanging of Jewish hostages in retaliation for such denunciations, and the banning of Jews from the region around the military front. This was, as Ansky noted, "virtually a call for a pogrom."[21] He concluded that the authorities encouraged pogroms and persecution because "the Russians wanted to annex Galicia," and, therefore, "they wanted to reduce the Galician Jews to the level of Russian Jews as far as rights were concerned." Interestingly, as Galician Jews adapted to Russian occupation, especially in Lviv, they made the opposite calculation: "They believed that if Russia gained control of Galicia, it would, under the pressure of the peace conference, be forced to grant the Galician Jews the same rights they had under Austria."[22] What was at stake in Galicia was, fundamentally, the civic emancipation of the Jews, and it was possible to envision the entire Galician population, all of them voters since the universal suffrage reform of 1907, as a potentially transformative social element within the Russian Empire. Russia, of course, was on the brink of a far more transformative revolution of its own.

In the spring of 1915, when the military balance shifted, the Russians prepared to withdraw from Lviv. Ansky observed that the Poles too had been rendered more Galician by their experience under Russian occupation.

> They furtively prepared to welcome the Austrians, conferring in secret and waiting for the moment when they could express their ferocious hatred of the Russians. . . . An acquaintance told me that his maid had asked him for her salary in advance; she had to buy a new hat, because her priest had told his parishioners to greet the Austrian army with flowers and in their Sunday best.[23]

By the end of the war she would be wearing her hat to celebrate Polish independence, but in 1915, with Franz Joseph still reigning in Vienna, the Poles, Ruthenians, and Jews of Lviv all still maintained some sense of Galician identity.

According to Marsha Rozenblit, the reconquest of Galicia by the Habsburg army was carried out with particular fervor by Jewish soldiers in the ranks.

> One Jewish solider described the Austrian attack on Tarnów, Galicia, the signal for which came just after some men in his company had finished morning prayers. A young yeshiva student stormed forth wearing his *tefillin*, which saved his life when a bullet lodged within it. Another letter reported how *tefillin* in a soldier's backpack saved his life by preventing a bullet from entering his lungs.

> The *Jüdische Volksstimme* in Brünn reported with pride that in the reconquest of
> Lemberg, Galician Jews went forth to battle wearing their *tefillin* and reciting the
> *shema*, the central prayer of the Jewish liturgy.[24]

Such wondrous tales of *tefillin* (little black boxes strapped to the hand and
the head during morning prayers) might almost have come from the folklore
of Jewish loyalty to Franz Joseph, even as the war provided the occasion for
new legends in the making. The *Jüdische Volksstimme* further declared, with
the retaking of Galicia in 1915, that "Jewish national interests and Austrian
imperial interests urgently require that Galicia be tightly united with the
other parts of the monarchy and that Galicia be ruled from Vienna for all
eternity."[25] Such affirmations of eternal Habsburg loyalty would be rendered
meaningless with the dissolution of the Habsburg monarchy itself at the
end of the war.

  Since Ansky was himself associated with the Russian occupation in 1915,
he left Lviv two days before the Austrian army returned and just before the
Russians blew up the beautiful train station. Ansky departed on 6 June, taking with him the last issue of the Russian occupation newspaper, *Tshervonaya
Rus*, which harkened back to the medieval name for the territory of eastern
Galicia, Red Ruthenia, back before it was annexed to Poland, long before it
was reconceived as part of Galicia. The resurrection of such names was also
a part of the cultural cancellation of the province's Habsburg identity.

> It [the newspaper] didn't contain the slightest allusion to the withdrawal. The
> tone was cheerful and victorious. The gazette listed a whole week of productions
> at the Russian theater: "Saturday, June 8, *Cavalleria Rusticana*; Sunday, June 9, *La
> Belle Hélène*." But the most interesting thing of all was a decree put out by the ad-
> ministrator of Galicia: "All Jews are to be excluded from all juridical institutions
> in Galicia." The province was slipping through Russia's fingers, but the persecu-
> tion of Jews was still going full-throttle![26]

In fact, the dismantling of the civic rights of Galician Jews was not incidental,
but fundamental, to the Russian assault on the identity of Habsburg Galicia.
The occupation could be more casual about such Habsburg inclinations as
Italian opera and French operetta; it would not be until the next world war
that the Nazis would do away with Offenbach as a Jewish composer. As for
Cavalleria Rusticana, Mascagni's verismo representation of village passions
and violence—ending with a fatal duel of honor—must have seemed quaint-
ly innocuous in the context of military occupation, national hatred, religious
persecution, and savage pogroms in the villages of wartime Galicia.

  The Russian army continued to occupy the eastern districts of Galicia,
around Chortkiv, the native region of Karl Emil Franzos, where he first
envisioned Galicia as *Halb-Asien*. Now Ansky pursued relief work in this

area, and in the town of Khorostkiv he encountered the world of Galician Hasidism:

> An elderly woman burst in, came over to me, and began in a bold, rattling tone: "I'm a granddaughter of Rabbi Zusye of Anipolye and a great-granddaughter of Rabbi Leyvik Yitskhik of Berditshev, and on my mother's side I'm a descendant of the Baal Shem Tov. Our family includes seventeen rebbes, and I'm third cousins with the great rabbi of Brody." Having poured out her entire lineage, she stood there, eyeing me sharply to gauge how shaken I was.[27]

Unimpressed, Ansky explained that there was no special war relief for persons of illustrious religious descent. That evening he was far more sympathetic in his dealings with the needy town cantor:

> The amount he asked for was so minuscule and so equitable that I instantly agreed. I asked whether he knew any Hasidic stories. Now he livened up and enthusiastically launched into tale after tale. And what a storyteller he was! Filled with rapture, teeming with marvelous details like a true poet. . . . Characteristically, all his stories were about the Messiah. Later on, I concluded that elderly Jews throughout Galicia were deeply interested in the Messiah.[28]

Like Buber, who had collected tales of the Baal Shem Tov, Ansky was fascinated by the folklore of Galicia. The cantor of Khorostkiv was placed in the position of performing his Galician identity, through the narration of Hasidic tales, in exchange for war relief. That same evening in Khorostkiv, Ansky heard a klezmer musician playing the violin, and, like Przybyszewski listening in a trance to Jewish musicians in Cracow at the turn of the century, Ansky responded emotionally to the wartime performer: "His gentle strains told me about his harsh plight, about his misery and anguish. It was very touching to hear his violin weeping, to see the hungry man's tears."[29] Thus, at the very end of Galicia's existence, the province appeared in the crucible of war as the land of earthly tears and messianic fantasies. It was in Chortkiv that Ansky encountered a celebrated rabbi who was convinced that "the sufferings portending the Messiah would begin in the year 5674 (1914) and that the Messiah would come in 5684 (1924)."[30] By this prophetic calculation, the end of Galicia would coincide with the coming of the Messiah.

"THE SPIRIT OF THE CARPATHIANS"

In February 1914, six months before the outbreak of the war, Poles and Ruthenians reached a historic agreement on sharing power in Galicia, with Ruthenians to be guaranteed 62 seats out of 228 in the Sejm and representation on all its principal committees. The agreement had been brokered partly by the previous Polish viceroy Michał Bobrzyński and the Uniate metropolitan Andrei Sheptytsky.[31] While the numbers did not fully reflect the percentage of Ruthenian population in the province, this was the first serious breach in Polish predominance since the achievement of autonomy in the 1860s, and made it possible to believe in some sort of national coexistence in the province. The advent of war, of course, suspended the implementation of this agreement, and when the war was finally over Galicia no longer existed.

The dissolution of Galicia was implicit in the promises of Polish unity, autonomy, or outright independence offered from both sides during the war, as the belligerents bid for the loyalty of their Polish subjects and soldiers. The Russians promised Polish unity and autonomy—within the Russian Empire, of course—to be obtained by conquering Galicia and joining it to Russian Poland. The Germans and Austrians, as the war progressed, made their own promises of Polish independence, in association with Piłsudski, who had made his Galician riflemen into a Polish legion, fighting alongside the Central Powers against Russia. Reciprocal to the Russian approach, the Central Powers hoped to conquer Russian Poland and unite it with Galicia, and in 1915, soon after the Austrian reconquest of Lviv, the Germans took Warsaw from the Russians. In 1916 the Central Powers went so far as to proclaim the independence of the "Kingdom of Poland," though, with the German General Paul von Hindenburg as commander in the region, the meaning and extent of Polish independence was at best ambiguous.

The competitive stoking of Polish national hopes by the opposing powers was complicated by the simultaneous encouragement of Ukrainian national aspirations. Historian Mark von Hagen, studying the policies of both Russia and the Central Powers, has shown how the advances and reverses of the opposing armies inspired Ruthenian and Ukrainian national leaders to envision a political future that transcended the former separation of Habsburg Galicia and Russian Ukraine. Historian Timothy Snyder has further shown that Wilhelm von Habsburg, a much younger cousin of Franz Joseph, was already styling himself as a Ruthenian leader—"Vasyl" rather than "Wilhelm" to the Ruthenian soldiers in his regiment—as he participated in the retaking of Galicia in 1915. In 1916, when he was only twenty-one, Wilhelm proposed himself as the presiding dynastic figure of a new Ruthenian or Ukrainian crownland within the Habsburg monarchy. His father, Stefan von Habsburg, who had lived in Galicia and had many Polish connections, envisioned himself in an analogously important role in the newly proclaimed Kingdom of Poland. Among the Polish Galicians who played a leading military role in the occupation of the former lands of Russian Poland was Stanisław

Szeptycki, the brother of the Uniate metropolitan Andrei Sheptytsky, both of them grandsons of Aleksander Fredro. One brother sought to promote the national future of the Poles, while the other attempted to advance the prospects of the Ruthenians. The metropolitan gave particular encouragement to Wilhelm von Habsburg.[32]

The declaration of the Kingdom of Poland in 1916 could have been considered a decisive blow to the political existence of Galicia, which would be absorbed into the kingdom, but it was also possible to imagine this absorption the other way around: Galicia expanded to include all of Poland and renamed as Poland. Dating back to the achievement of autonomy in the 1860s the Polish conservative loyalists, the Stańczyk party, had permitted themselves the fantasy of a Habsburg monarch ruling over a united Poland, thus reconciling the sentiments of Galician provincialism, Habsburg loyalism, and Polish nationalism. Back in 1867, as Galician autonomy was being established, the editors of *Czas* dared to dream of "a triad of three crowns under the Austrian scepter of the Habsburg dynasty": Hungarian, Bohemian, and Polish crowns.[33] Such a Galician fantasy could be fitted to the Kingdom of Poland as articulated in 1916, but amid the massive fatalities of the war, one death was particularly problematic for this particular scenario. The Kingdom of Poland was declared on 5 November 1916, and on 21 November the Emperor Franz Joseph died at the age of eighty-six, in the sixty-eighth year of his reign. Both as political ruler and as political symbol he was the crucial figure for eliciting Habsburg loyalism throughout the monarchy, and in Galicia, as elsewhere, there were very few Habsburg subjects who could remember any other emperor. The "dream" of three crowns, dating back to the 1860s, referred to the imperial brow of Franz Joseph, and was certainly less sentimentally compelling without his living presence.

With a Habsburg ruler the Kingdom of Poland might indeed have been considered a kind of conceptual enlargement of Galicia, but no king was ever chosen for that crown in wartime; the decision was postponed for the duration, and, of course, the Central Powers lost the war in the end. In January 1918, when Woodrow Wilson issued his Fourteen Points concerning war aims, the thirteenth specified that "an independent Polish state should be erected which should include the territories inhabited by indisputably Polish populations." This point was doubly fatal to the existence of Galicia, which not only would be superseded by an independent Poland but also certainly did not possess an indisputably Polish population, and would therefore appear politically illegitimate according to the Wilsonian principle of national self-determination. Indeed, the Ruthenians of Galicia would have taken national encouragement not only from Wilsonian principles but also—in January

1918—from the declaration of a sovereign Ukrainian state in Kiev, resisting the Bolsheviks and supported by the Central Powers. The aims and promises of both competing sides in World War I thus served to undermine the logic and legitimacy of Galicia's political existence.

When the Viennese poet Hugo von Hofmannsthal came to Galicia for military service in the 1890s, he found everything "ugly, miserable, and dirty"—but he returned to Galicia during World War I.[34] In 1915 he was working for the Austrian war effort, writing about what it meant to be Austrian in time of war, and he was sent to Cracow in May and June, just as the Austrian army was about to move forward and chase the Russians out of Lviv. Hofmannsthal was given a glimpse of the Carpathian front, and wrote a patriotic article for the *Neue Freie Presse* called "The Spirit of the Carpathians." The poet, who had once found everything in Galicia so ugly, was now powerfully moved by the mountain landscape and the soldiers who manned the Carpathian lines between Galicia and Slovakia.

> The sound of destiny will be forever associated with the Carpathian rivers; whenever we hear Dunajec, or Biala, Ondawa and Orawa and Laborcza, Ung or Stryj, something in us will shudder at the deepest level. We pronounce these names and we feel that they instill something sublime in us, not we in them, something that we were accustomed to feel and to seek only in past times. This mountain forest curved toward the east, this eastern mountain wall of the monarchy, has by a monstrous destiny become a heroic landscape like no other.[35]

These names—some associated with Galicia, some with Slovakia—were to be pronounced with sacramental piety, because they were associated with terrible battles for the defense of the monarchy and the massive fatalities of World War I. They meant for Austria what such names as Verdun and the Somme would mean for the French and the British. The Galician names from Hofmannsthal's military service in the 1890s—Tlumach, Chortkiv—had signified only ugliness and poverty, but now Galician place names—the Stryj, the Dunajec rivers—were imbued with sublime and tragic meaning.

In August 1915 Hofmannsthal published in the *Neue Freie Presse* an essay on "Our Military Administration in Poland," acknowledging that Austria's current and future holdings in the region might have different contours from those of Galicia before the war.[36] He believed that the Habsburgs had a particular wartime role to play in Poland, which was directly connected to their prewar rule in Galicia: "the gift of our army for being able to live with people of all sorts of soils." Hofmannsthal affirmed that the Austrians possessed a special "tact" in dealing with the "coexistence of nations," and that "more than the Germans it has been given to us to live with strangers: as neighbors, as masters, as temporary administrators, as friends." The Polish occupation zone consisted of many elements: "Among these elements—peasants, noble-men, townspeople, industrialists, Jews—our organs of administration, our officers and soldiers, move with effortless tact."[37] Catholic Austrian soldiers, for instance, would have the necessary tact to deal with Polish monks at Czę-stochowa. Although his own prewar experience of Galicia had been less than enthralling, Hofmannsthal now affirmed that Austria's general experience of Galician government was particularly relevant to some sort of current and future relation to Polish territory—even if Galicia itself, in its prewar form, were to lapse, change, or be somehow transmogrified. In 1916, Hofmannsthal traveled to Warsaw, now occupied by the Central Powers after a century of Russian rule, and gave a lecture on "The Austrian Idea." That idea, over the course of centuries, was based on the principle of "elasticity," of a "flowing border [*fliessende Grenze*]"—not simply a barrier—between Europe and "the chaotically driven miscellany of peoples of Half-Europe, Half-Asia [*Halb-Europa, Halb-Asien*]."[38] Austria was allegedly able to reconcile these eastern and western cultural vectors. Hofmannsthal, using the term *Halb-Asien*, was certainly aware that Franzos had made the phrase famous with reference to Galicia.

By the time of World War I, Hofmannsthal was not only recognized as a great poet but also celebrated as an opera librettist, notably for his work with composer Richard Strauss. Their joint masterpiece *Der Rosenkavalier* had its premiere in 1911, and when the war broke out they were working on the fairy tale opera *Die Frau ohne Schatten (The Woman without a Shadow)*. The tale was set in two separate spheres: in the elevated world of a mythological emperor and empress and in the lower mundane world—brutal, impoverished, and often repulsively ugly—of ordinary people. The world of the imperial couple could have been Vienna, the home of the emperor and empress in Hofmannsthal's Viennese childhood, and the fabulous empress might even have been mod-eled on the Kaiserin Elisabeth, assassinated in Geneva in 1898, soon after Hofmannsthal's return from his term of service in Galicia. In that year, the young poet himself clearly understood the chasm between upper and lower worlds to be represented by the difference, as he experienced it, between the civilization of Vienna and the ugliness of Galicia. Some remembered strands of that antithesis must have lingered in his artistic consciousness as he completed the libretto for *Die Frau ohne Schatten* in 1915, a year when Galicia was very much present in public consciousness as a theater of war.

After the war Hofmannsthal wrote the play *Der Schwierige (The Difficult One)*, first performed in 1921, about an Austrian nobleman who could not adjust to normal civilian life in postwar Vienna. Hans Karl had been traumatized by his experience in the war, and remained psychically fixed in the landscape and comradeship of his military service: "We were together, in the winter of 1915, for twenty weeks, on assignment in the Carpathian forest."[39] Hofmannsthal's post-Habsburg Austrian hero was somehow never able to get over Galicia, though by 1921 Galicia, along with the Habsburg monarchy, had ceased to exist.

While Hofmannsthal visited Cracow in 1915 to cover the war effort in Galicia, the taking of Warsaw from the Russians in that year gave rise to considerable Galician excitement. A poster signed with the name of the longtime mayor of Cracow, Juliusz Leo, addressed his fellow Cracovians with the "most joyful news" that "after a hundred years of Russian bondage Warsaw has been liberated." Poles could rejoice that "there will no longer exist the border which for a century has separated the two ancient capitals of Poland, Cracow and Warsaw." That was, of course, also the border that defined Galicia's geopolitical existence. The taking of Warsaw was clearly a Polish national occasion, but the mayor was careful also to acknowledge it as a matter of Habsburg and Galician concern: "May omnipotent God bless our most august monarch and heroic armies. . . . May the present celebration increase in our hearts the burning flame of love for the fatherland."[40] The precise designation of the fatherland was perhaps left purposefully ambiguous—Poland or the Habsburg monarchy—though that term, *ojczyzna*, usually had Polish associations in Galician public discourse. The poster reminded the citizens of Cracow that, even now, their brothers and sons were risking their lives "for the fatherland and the beloved emperor," a phrase that both associated and confused those two crucial political terms. For Juliusz Leo, born near Drohobych, educated at the Jagiellonian University, professor at the Jagiellonian University, mayor of Cracow since 1904, Galicia was still meaningful in 1915—but the breaking down of the barrier between Cracow and Warsaw was clearly a momentously Polish development.

In November 1915, the eighty-fifth anniversary of the Warsaw November Insurrection of 1830 was commemorated in Cracow. At the Teatr Wielki on 29 November the program included a Chopin polonaise, the so-called military polonaise in A-major with its passionately national associations—and also the recitation of a poem by Tetmajer and dramatic verse by Wyspiański.[41] Thus, after the taking of Warsaw, with the intensification of Polish national hopes, the grand figures of fin-de-siècle Galicia—Tetmajer and Wyspiański—were placed on a program with Chopin and recited in the nationally Polish spirit that was destined soon to displace Galicia from the hearts and minds of Central Europe.

THE POLISH LIQUIDATION COMMISSION: "UNNECESSARY PORTRAITS"

At the beginning of November 1918, that displacement was about to be consummated on the map. On 1 November the newspaper *Kuryer Codzienny* (*Daily Courier*) appeared in Cracow with the headline "Polish Liquidation Commission Takes Over Civil and Military Power in Galicia." The commission—Polska Komisja Likwidacyjna—was created in Cracow during the last week in October, for the purpose of "liquidating" Galicia's political relation to the Habsburg monarchy, by assuming responsibility for military, administrative, and judicial institutions, and thus joining Galicia to independent Poland. This was a transitional commission, proposed on 24 October, formally established on 28 October, two weeks before the abdication of Emperor Karl on 11 November.[42] During these weeks, as the committee sought to liquidate Galicia's relations to the monarchy, the *namiestnik*, the very last one, Karl Georg Huyn, still claimed to govern Galicia, and contested the authority of the liquidation commission. *Kuryer Codzienny* reported unsympathetically on Huyn's attempt to resist liquidation:

> General Huyn, occupying still the office of *namiestnik* of Galicia, published yesterday a circular to officials "subject" to him, in which he calls the realization of the joining of Galicia to Poland "presently quite impossible," and at the same time he announces also that in the future "he will keep state power firmly in hand" in our country [*w naszym kraju*]. And therefore the leading power in our country is today already the official of a foreign state. . . . The circular of General Huyn of course does not rest on anything but the right of might. It has absolutely no legal or moral basis, and as such can not be sustained.[43]

Putting strategic quotation marks around the words of the *namiestnik* served not only as a means of citation but also to emphasize the newspaper's rejection of his now alien perspective, that of a foreign official. *Kuryer Codzienny* effectively denied the existence of Galicia, and hence the validity of its viceregal government, without actually going so far as to put quotation marks around "Galicia"—for the newspaper still accepted as meaningful the notion of "our country." As long as Galicia was not yet severed from Austria, not yet joined to Poland, the concept of Galicia remained relevant; once the severing and joining had been consummated, Galicia would be effectively liquidated, and would cease to exist along with the moral and legal authority of the Habsburg governor.

The liquidation commission was established in Cracow and operated in western Galicia, but it could not effectively exercise its function in eastern Galicia, where the formation of a Ukrainian National Council meant that liquidation might take a different direction. In Lviv the Ukrainians, the former Galician Ruthenians, claimed to establish a West Ukrainian (rather than East Galician) National Republic, which they sought to join to the independent Ukrainian state established in Kiev in January 1918. The Polish Liquidation Commission, based in Cracow, which sought to join Galicia to Poland, found its intentions contested by an alternative vision of post-Habsburg liquidation in Lviv.

The founding figures of the Polish Liquidation Commission included such Polish Galician leaders as Ignacy Daszyński, the socialist, and Wincenty Witos, the peasant populist, both of whom would go on to play prominent political roles in independent Poland. Also participating in the establishment of the liquidation commission was an almost legendary Galician figure: Włodzimierz Tetmajer, the artist, who had married a peasant girl, lived in a country village, and served as the literary model for the Host in Wyspiański's *The Wedding*. In the 1890s, together with his brother the poet, Tetmajer had been among the leading figures of fin-de-siècle Galicia. In 1918, together with Witos, Tetmajer served as a representative of the peasant party at the founding of the liquidation commission. Now the artist stepped outside the Galician scenario of *The Wedding*, and looked beyond the final scene in which the whole company tensely contemplated the fearful portent of fire over Cracow; now he played a part in the apocalyptic liquidation of Galicia and its messianic incorporation into independent Poland.[44]

The liquidation commission existed for the express purpose of liquidating Galicia's relation to Austria, and therefore, paradoxically, existed only with reference to Galicia, whose existence the commission endeavored to erase. Thus the full absorption of Galicia into Poland came about, as historian Michał Śliwa has suggested, with the liquidation of the liquidation commission, carried out by the Polish government of Ignacy Paderewski in March 1919. Not until the conclusion of the Polish-Soviet war in 1920 would the entirety of Galicia, eastern and western, be made part of the Polish state, ironically ceasing to exist at the moment that it was forcefully united again. Śliwa has noted the determination "finally after the creation on September 1, 1921, of administrative voivodships in Cracow, Lviv, Ternopil, and Stanyslaviv, to abolish the legal, political, and administrative distinctiveness of former Galicia."[45] Thus, with the eventual liquidation of the liquidation commission, Galicia definitively became part of Poland, and became "former Galicia."

This was, in fact, a gradual process, and *Kuryer Codzienny*, on 2 November 1918, already described the work of liquidation in progress. In Cracow, and in the surrounding region, the Austrian eagle and the Habsburg black-and-yellow colors came down, and "in the eyes of the whole world a miracle took place," the miracle of Polish freedom and Polish independence. The miracle was represented by works of decorative and symbolic liquidation: "Down from the exterior walls came the hated eagles, today indifferent to us—while from the interior walls of offices there disappeared unnecessary portraits." Hated, indifferent, unnecessary [*nienawidzone, obojętne, niepotrzebne*]: thus appeared the Habsburg symbols that, ever since 1772, had marked the political identity of Galicia.[46] It was perhaps emotionally easier to take down a portrait of the Emperor Karl, his reign only two years old, than it might have been to remove the image of Franz Joseph, which had hung on so many walls for so many decades until his death in 1916. The hated double-headed Habsburg black eagles might simply have been replaced by single-headed Polish white eagles, thus reversing in 1918 the aquiline substitutions of 1772.

From Vienna, the *Neue Freie Presse* had a different perspective on events in Galicia. On 3 November the news from Cracow was not about miracles but rather simply a report of "perfect calm," in contrast to Lviv, which was said to be occupied by "Galician-Ukrainian" troops. Indeed, they had occupied the post office and train station, so that between Vienna and Lviv there was no telephone or telegraph connection, and therefore very little news. On 4 November the *Neue Freie Presse* announced in its front page headline "The End of the War," but it noted in another heading the advent of a new war: "The Battle between Poles and Ukrainians in Galicia."[47] Even as Galicia itself was being liquidated, it was also the object of a fierce struggle, eventually a new war. Galicia's place on the map and in the news remained meaningful even with the passing of Habsburg rule. On 6 November there might have been a hint of relief and good riddance when the *Neue Freie Presse* noted in its front page headline "Peace in All of Austria," but, in another headline, "Street Fighting in Lemberg: More than Sixty Dead."[48]

On 11 November, Armistice Day, Emperor Karl abdicated, ten days after his portraits had been taken down from the office walls of Cracow. The Habsburg monarchy ceased to exist. Galicia, which had been defined, from the moment of its invention in 1772, by its relation to that monarchy, should have logically ceased to exist as well on 11 November, and certainly it could have no further political connection to Austria. By 18 November, one week later, the *Neue Freie Presse* had a correspondent in Lviv, reporting, as if from a foreign city, on an urban and provincial landscape that had so recently seemed politically inseparable from Vienna. The front page headline was "Days of Horror [*Schreckenstage*] in Lemberg," describing the battle between Poles and Ukrainians. It began with the Ukrainian "liquidation" of Habsburg power in Lviv, the Galician capital, their occupation of its public buildings: the train station, the residence of the *namiestnik*, the palace of the Sejm, the police headquarters, the post and telegraph office, the branch of the Austro-Hungarian bank, the Galician Provincial Bank.[49] This was an enumeration of the public buildings that had constituted Galicia's institutional existence. There was the palace of the Sejm crowned by the female personification of Galicia, a goddess of provincial autonomy. There was the palace of the viceroys—like Andrzej Potocki and Michał Bobrzyński—who had presided over autonomous Galicia.

These buildings still existed in November 1918—as many of them still exist today—architectural landmarks of Galicia, but they lost their Galician political aspect with the abdication of the emperor, as the province itself was liquidated and its institutions were "occupied" in the Polish-Ukrainian contest for control of the former Galicia. "As soon as the public buildings were occupied by the Ukrainians," noted the *Neue Freie Presse*, "the viceroy Count Huyn, the military commander Field Marshal Pfeffer, and the police chief Hofrat Dr. Reinländer were interned, measures were taken for the Ukrainization of the administration and its personnel, and the Poles quickly collected themselves for resistance." The street fighting that ensued in Lviv, "the days of horror," also occurred in Przemyśl, Stanyslaviv, and Kolomiya: Galician towns that were, as the fighting proceeded, becoming former Galician towns, the objects of post-Habsburg national struggle.[50]

A week later the Polish forces had retaken Lviv, and on 27 November the *Neue Freie Presse* in Vienna reported a new kind of violence: "Der Judenpogrom in Lemberg." The newspaper, under the long-standing editorship of Moriz Benedikt, himself Jewish, described the advent of the pogrom in the context of complex Galician tensions.

> Lemberg was one of the most tortured, most horribly tormented cities during the world war. It had to endure the alien Russian conqueror marching drunk with victory through the streets. . . . But the full misery of unleashed unrestraint broke over Lemberg only when the country's own children [*Landeskinder*] turned their weapons upon one another, when Poles and Ukrainians struggled over the possession of this city with grim hatred, a centuries-old national rivalry. Last Friday the Poles succeeded in mastering their adversaries, and hoisting the red and white flag upon the towers of Lemberg. This victory was celebrated by a three-day pogrom against the Jews. . . . Hundreds of men, women, and children stained the streets of Lemberg with their red blood . . . three days during which, in this great, densely populated city, the seat of important authorities, the site of a centuries-old historical culture, scenes were played out that would have brought eternal shame and disgrace to any remote and godforsaken provincial town of the Russian steppe.[51]

From the Viennese perspective Lviv now offered one last retrospective vision of the lapsed Habsburg civilizing mission in Galicia, for, no sooner were the

Habsburgs removed from the political scene, than the province collapsed into barbarism. Lviv had been the seat of important authorities—Habsburg Galician authorities—and now there was no longer any authority to protect its population from savage assaults. Indeed, the *Neue Freie Presse* concluded that the Polish military authorities had actually encouraged the pogrom. Thus the children of the province—that is, the children of Galicia—were left to murder one another as the province itself lapsed into liquidation.

Historian William Hagen has written about the pogrom of Lviv in November 1918, noting that Polish soldiers believed that they were entitled to punish Jews for having remained neutral in the preceding Polish-Ukrainian struggle. As in the case of the Russian pogroms in Galicia in 1914, the assaults became even more savage with the circulation of rumors that Jews were shooting to defend themselves from their attackers. Hagen suggests that a carnivalesque spirit of violence presided, a world turned upside down, with the furious desecration of Torahs in synagogues, and the burning of synagogues with Jews inside them.[52] It was Galicia turned upside down, no longer under Habsburg rule, and the pogrom, like the Polish-Ukrainian struggle, involved a settling of Galician accounts. Hagen cites a ranting declaration from a Polish vigilante organization called the Red Guard: "The Red Guard Committee demands you leave Lwów free of Jews by New Year's. And all your grand gentlemen can travel with you to Palestine. Leave! All your assets will be devoted to rebuilding Galicia, for without your millions, without your Kaiser with his Jewish mistresses, no such misfortune as now prevails would have come into the world."[53] In this vision the liquidation of Galicia was to be followed by the "rebuilding of Galicia," a new Galicia without the emperor, without the Jews, and without the Ukrainians, a new Galicia paradoxically defined as Galician only by the absence of those essential Galician elements.

On 28 November the *Neue Freie Presse* reported pogroms in Rzeszów, Przemyśl, and elsewhere: "The Jewish population in all Galicia [*in ganz Galizien*] finds itself in the highest agitation." Galicia existed still in a condition of conceptual entirety, as a site of anti-Semitic violence. The Israelitische Allianz in Vienna took up the cause of their Galician brethren, no longer joined by any political Habsburg connection, but only by the bond of common religion and former imperial affiliation. The Allianz sought to mobilize international pressure, even as far off as America, against the Galician pogroms, and also appealed to what seemed the most plausibly effective institutional body in Galicia: the Polish Liquidation Commission. With its mission to sever all ties to Vienna, to displace Habsburg government, the commission now became the object of Viennese appeals to maintain civil order and legal norms, just as the Habsburg government would have done in former Galicia.[54]

The liquidation commission, however, represented the Polish perspective on the Galician pogroms. On 29 November the *Neue Freie Presse* cited the commission's dubiously exculpatory insistence that the Ukrainians had freed criminals from the former Habsburg prisons of Lviv, and that those criminals, not Polish soldiers, had instigated the pogroms. The liquidation commission set up a committee to investigate the pogroms, including a certain Dr. Diamant, probably the same Jewish community leader in Lviv who had declined to work together with Ansky on war relief in 1914.[55] It was Diamant, under Russian occupation, who had declared, "We were and remain Austrian citizens. We are loyal to our fatherland, to our gracious monarch, to whom we Jews especially have a lot be thankful for." By the end of November 1918 the Jews of Lviv were no longer Austrian citizens, and painfully aware of how much they formerly had to be thankful for as Galician Jews and Habsburg subjects. Jewish refugees from Galicia, like the family of Manes Sperber, were trying to stay in Vienna—because "our old homeland would become foreign"—because Galicia would no longer be Galicia.[56]

On 30 November the *Neue Freie Presse* published a feuilleton, not a news story but a meditative reflection, entitled "The Pogrom in Lemberg," by an anonymous eyewitness, presumably the newspaper's special correspondent. Now he was leaving Lviv behind:

> On the journey from Lemberg through all of Galicia [*durch ganz Galizien*] I had the opportunity to speak with people belonging to the most different professions and social circles. They all made no secret of their radical perspective of hatred. No one condemned the riots. They all said that the Jews had been the aggressive and provocative ones, and that the Polish soldiers had only defended themselves. A middle school teacher expressed himself most clearly. He said: "At the moment when the liquidation commission was established in Cracow, all Galicia became Polish state territory. The Ukrainians, who openly opposed the Poles, and the Jews who called themselves neutral, committed the crime of high treason. The Poles sent a punishment expedition for the punishment of state criminals. What happened in Lemberg was only the carrying out of a frankly deserved punishment. Should the Jews, through protests and reports abroad, attempt to slander the Polish people, they will be even more harshly punished."[57]

The correspondent, who still felt that he was traveling through "all of Galicia," acknowledged that, from the Polish perspective of his interlocutors, it was not Galicia any longer. The middle school teacher believed that "all Galicia became Polish" with the founding of the liquidation commission. From that moment all the inhabitants of Galicia became former Galicians and—in the case of Jews and Ukrainians—potential traitors to the emerging Polish state.

"This teacher is not an isolated figure in Polish society," observed the cor-respondent.[58] Poles generally insisted on Polish mastery over allegedly Polish territory, and sought the subordination of "foreign nationalities" who had been Galician citizens and Habsburg subjects up until the month before. The teacher was perhaps a typical figure in Polish society, but, until very recently, he had served in the educational institutions of Galicia, himself a subject of the Habsburg monarch. It was the work of the liquidation commission to make him over, from a Galician middle school teacher into a Polish middle school teacher, and that work was carried out over the course of November 1918. Mentally, emotionally, culturally, however, that work had been long in progress, and would continue for a long time after Galicia ceased to exist. As the *Neue Freie Presse* correspondent traveled across "all of Galicia" at the end of November he was witnessing a society that was reorienting itself, rethinking its identity, revising its history.

On 1 December the *Neue Freie Presse* printed a telegram that the Viennese Jewish community had sent to Woodrow Wilson, pleading for his interven-tion against the pogroms: "the appeal from the depths of the soul of the Jews of the whole world, concerning the monstrous, scandalous occurrences in Galicia."[59] Three days later Wilson sailed for the Paris Peace Conference. While he surely sympathized with the murdered Jews of Lviv, Wilson would have also recognized some aspects of the schoolteacher's reasoning, the sometimes twisted logic of national self-determination. What Wilson might not have recognized in the appeal of the Viennese Jews was the non-national notion of Galicia, the provincial fiefdom of an antiquated dynasty ruling over motley populations. There was no place in Woodrow Wilson's postwar Europe for Galicia.

On 11 December another feuilleton in the *Neue Freie Presse* reflected on "Scenes from the Days of Murder in Lemberg," and began with this meta-geographical reflection: "Never has Lemberg been so far from us as it is today [*Nie war Lemberg so weit von uns wie heute*]." The disruptions of the Nordbahn railway network were part of the problem, a mechanical issue of transpor-tation—the Nordbahn railway, which had been created back in the 1830s, exciting the interest of Galicians like Fredro. The disruption of transporta-tion, however, was not the only aspect of the newly remote distance from Vienna to Lviv in 1918. There was also, of course, the political dimension, the fact that Lviv was no longer a Habsburg provincial capital, subordinate and bound to Vienna within the monarchy. What made Lviv seem so truly remote, however, was the unrestrained violence of civil war between Poles and Ukrainians, and the savage assault of the triumphant Poles upon the Jews of the city. In Vienna it was difficult to imagine such "Scenes from the Days of Murder" in a city that had so recently been ruled by Franz Joseph. Even one single murder—the assassination of the *namiestnik* in Lviv in 1908—had shocked the Viennese, and now, ten years later, Lviv appeared as an unimaginably monstrous scene of barbarous bloodshed. The only palliating factor was the pretense that Lviv was now, all at once, very far away from Vienna, connected only by the remembered thread of a formerly common history, the history of Galicia. The feuilleton of 11 December concluded that, with the triumph of the Poles, "anarchy and mass murder" came to Lviv.[60]

For decades, "anarchy" had been the most fearful specter haunting Galicia, dating back to the massacres of 1846, but long remembered across the nineteenth century and frighteningly confronted at the turn of the century at the moment of the anarchist assassination of the Empress Elisabeth in 1898. The whole ideology of Galicia, as cultivated in the age of autonomy, envisioned the province not just as a bulwark against barbarism, looking east to Russia, but also as a bulwark against anarchy, looking inward to the province's own irreconcilable tensions. So it was that from Vienna, at the end of 1918, it was possible to discern in far-away Lviv the dreaded eruption of anarchy that occurred with the passing of Galicia.

THE PARIS PEACE CONFERENCE: "STATISTICS OF GALICIA"

The West Ukrainian National Republic, created on 1 November 1918, lost Lviv to the Poles before the end of November, but the republic, with its "Ukrainian Galician Army," continued to fight a Polish-Ukrainian war in eastern Galicia during the first half of 1919. The Ukrainian Galician Army, with many former Habsburg troops, enjoyed the support of Wilhelm von Habsburg, while its small air force was led by Petro Franko, the son of the writer.[61] The Polish-Ukrainian war overlapped with the Polish-Soviet war that began in 1919, and Galicia became the crucially contested area for determining the boundary between Piłsudski's independent Poland and Soviet Ukraine. The Paris Peace Conference in 1919 thus considered the future of Galicia, even as Polish and Ukrainian armies, and then Polish and Soviet armies, sought to settle the issue on the ground.

The memorandum *Mémoire sur la Galicie*, published in Paris in 1919, was sponsored by the Polish Commission of Preparatory Work for the Peace Conference, and principally authored by Eugeniusz Romer, a leading geographer from the university in Lviv. The *Mémoire* put the Polish case before the Big Four of Wilson, Lloyd George, Clemenceau, and Orlando: "The Poles demand that all of Galicia [*la Galicie entière*], detached [*desannexée*] from the

Austrian empire, be attributed entirely to the new Polish state; they base their revindication on historic, ethnographic, economic, and territorial reasons."[62] The language of revindication and annexation, which played its part in the invention of Galicia in 1772, was now revived at the moment of the abolition and liquidation of Galicia and its reabsorption into Poland. The epoch of the Habsburg annexation of 1772 was closed by the Polish "disannexation" of 1918, in both cases legitimated under the term "revindication." The Poles of 1918 accepted entirely the Habsburg proposition of 1772 that "Galicia" possessed a meaningful geopolitical coherence: historic, ethnographic, economic, and territorial. This proposition, which was plainly false in 1772, a mere pretext of self-justification, had gradually, over the course of a century and a half, acquired historical plausibility. Yet, especially from an ethnographic perspective, it was clear that the Poles of 1918 were also concocting a fictive picture of Galicia, to be used polemically against the Ukrainians in the context of the peace conference.

The importance of 1772 was made absolutely explicit in the *Mémoire* of 1919: "Since 1772, all of Galicia with the exception of Cracow and the district of Tarnopol, belonged in constant fashion to Austria; with Austria's disappearance Galicia must revert completely [*tout entière*] to the Polish fatherland." Thus the twentieth-century disappearance of Austria, and the liquidation of Galicia, was interpreted in terms of the eighteenth-century disappearance of Poland and invention of Galicia. The "historical" reasoning for Galicia's "reversion" to Poland was supplemented by ethnographic data—notably false—insisting that the province was 59 percent Polish and 40 percent Ruthenian.[63] This must have involved counting all the Galician Jews as Poles, a brazen statistical maneuver after the Polish pogroms of November 1918. These statistics were reiterated in a pamphlet with the misleadingly positivist title *Statistics of Galicia*, published in Paris in English, perhaps to make a more emphatic impression on President Wilson with regard to statistical national self-determination. This pamphlet, also written principally by Romer for the Polish Commission on the Peace Conference, went well beyond statistics, when it preposterously affirmed that "the great tolerance of the former Polish government and of Polish society can be seen also from the good mutual understanding between the Poles and Ruthenians in Galicia." Furthermore, *Statistics of Galicia* presumed to evaluate the "civilization of the Poles and Ruthenians," predictably assuming "the much higher civilization of the Poles," while observing that "to the primitive social structure of the Ruthenians corresponds also their civilization."[64] The designation "Ukrainian" was studiously avoided here, as the Poles produced, perhaps for the last time, their Polish version of the Habsburg civilizing mission in Galicia.

The French *Mémoire* also divided Galicia ethnographically between Poles and Ruthenians, while insisting that "the two races are so reciprocally penetrated" as to constitute an "ethnographic mélange," produced by numerous mixed marriages. Therefore, integral Galicia should not, and could not, be divided ethnographically between east and west. Both medieval chronicles and archaeological evidence were cited to prove that Poles were, in fact, "autochthonous" throughout the province, even in the east, where they allegedly demonstrated "civilizational superiority." The *Mémoire* insisted that in Galicia "the Poles direct all the intellectual and economic work."[65] To sweeten the argument, Polish representatives in Paris promised a British oil company continued access to Galician economic resources: "The Polish government—as soon as it has the power to do so—is prepared to use all legal means it possesses to return to the Premier Oil and Pipe Line Company possession of those oil terrains in Galicia that were exploited before the war."[66] Considerations of ethnography, culture, and economy were all invoked in order to claim Galicia in its entirety for postwar Poland.

Eugeniusz Romer, as a geographer, offered in the *Mémoire* a further geographical argument for claiming Galicia. Citing the courses of Polish rivers between the Baltic Sea and the Black Sea, Romer insisted that "from this character of Poland derives the fact that all of Galicia, from the point of view of general geography, belongs to Poland," and that "Galicia, resting on the Carpathians, gives Poland a natural frontier." Geography was, of course, supposed to be a matter of nature, and, by geographical reasoning, one could determine the "natural" affiliation of Galicia.

> The reunion of Galicia with Poland, and, if we wish to express it geographically, its reattachment to the basin of the Vistula as well as that of the Dniester, is well founded inasmuch as it is based upon the ensemble of natural conditions and the physiographical structure of the country.[67]

While Galicia originated in the artifice of partition in 1772, its reunion with Poland after 1918 was declared entirely "natural."

While Romer made his sometimes pedantic geographical contributions to the Polish position at the peace conference, the Poles were more spectacularly represented by Ignacy Paderewski, the internationally famous pianist. The British diplomat Harold Nicolson noted in his diary a night at the Paris opera in April 1919:

> A coup de théâtre provided by the entry of Paderewski into the Presidential box: the Polish national anthem: handkerchiefs and cheers amid a risen audience: "Bravo! Bravo!": I stand up limply: Paderewski bows and smiles. Not a presidential bow: a concert-platform bow. His wife looks like hell in orchids.[68]

Paderewski's diplomatic showmanship in Paris in April was followed by the May publication of the *Mémoire sur la Galicie* and *Statistics of Galicia*. In June, however, the Poles published another pamphlet in Paris, this time virtually eliminating the name of Galicia in the *Memorandum on the North and South Eastern Frontiers of Restored Poland*. The more cries of bravo for Poland, the less important it may have seemed to emphasize the distinctiveness of Galicia, which had to be revindicated only to be absorbed and effaced. Galicia was on the way to becoming South Eastern Poland.

"The crime of the partitions of Poland must necessarily be atoned," according to the June memorandum, "for otherwise it would be impossible to find a good foundation for the renewal of the world according to the sacred principles of right and justice. It is therefore necessary to go back to the state of things before the partitions, when we deal with the question of the territories and frontiers of future Poland."[69] The state of things before the partitions, of course, did not involve Galicia, which had not yet come into existence. The frontiers of Galicia, including eastern Galicia, thus became the once and future "South Eastern Frontiers" of Poland. In capital letters, the memorandum spelled out the axiom: RED RUTHENIA IS NOT THE UKRAINE. True, Ruthenia was inhabited by a large population of Ruthenians—not Ukrainians—but "the Ruthenian people are not yet a nation in the political sense of the word, and therefore not ripe enough for independence."[70] Ruthenia and Ruthenians had belonged to the Polish-Lithuanian Commonwealth before the eighteenth-century partitions and were now to be restored to the new Polish state. Furthermore, "the Poles inhabiting the country are autochthones as much as the Ruthenians," and Polishness provided, according to the memorandum, the region's only force for civilization: "Every time the country was devastated and pillaged by the Tartars or the Ukrainian Cossacks, the Poles came to restore order and agriculture. For these reasons the Poles have a right to consider themselves at home in the Ruthenian lands." Ruthenia had always been "under the influence of Polish civilization," and therefore rightly belonged to Poland.[71]

One dissenting voice appeared in the *New York Times*, which published in May 1919 a letter to the editor from none other than Miroslav Sichynsky. When he had first surfaced in the United States in 1915, the *Times* had run a small article under the headline "SLAYER SEEKS CITIZENSHIP." The *Times* had noted that the slain Potocki had been governor of Galicia, that he "was regarded with enmity by the Ruthenian peasants," and that the assassination was analogous to that of Franz Ferdinand in 1914, having "arisen out of the same general conditions in the Slav provinces of Austria." By the time of Sichynsky's letter to the editor in 1919, Potocki was forgotten, his assassination was not mentioned, and the heading for the letter read "WAR IN EAST GALICIA: Disputed Claims of Poles and Ukrainians Now Before the Conference"—with no reference to Ruthenians. Sichynsky cited statistics to demonstrate the Ukrainian predominance in East Galicia, denouncing Polish "imperialism," and noting that the Poles were boosting their numbers by counting Jews as Poles. "The annexation of Eastern Galicia by Poland," concluded Sichynsky, "instead of acting as a check on the spread of Bolshevism, as Paderewski predicts, will prepare another hotbed for its propagation."[72] The voice of violence in Galicia from before the war now warned of the menace of revolution in Galicia after the war was over.

In 1920, as the new League of Nations prepared to establish itself in Geneva, Mykhailo Hrushevsky published in Geneva an address *To the Civilized Nations of the World*, on behalf of the Committee of the Independent Ukraine. Hrushevsky had played a leading role in the declaration of Ukrainian independence in Kiev in January 1918, and then again in January 1919, when representatives from eastern Galicia participated in an Act of Union that theoretically affirmed a unified Ukraine—until the Bolshevik army took Kiev in February. In 1920, Hrushevsky, in exile from Ukraine, was writing about his outrage at the Polish domination of eastern Galicia, and he denounced the outcome of the Paris Peace Conference for having too easily accepted Galicia—including Lviv where he had lived and taught for so long—as part of Poland.[73]

While the Polish pamphlets insisted that twentieth-century Ukrainians were still Habsburg Galician Ruthenians, Hrushevsky projected the modern Ukrainian designation backward into the Middle Ages.

> East Galicia has been a Ukrainian country from times immemorial, and lived an independent national life, first as a part of the Ukrainian State of Kiev and later as a kernel of the Galician-Volhynian State. Conquered by Poland in 1349, East Galicia, after the secular domination of the Poles, fell to the lot of Austria. . . .[74]

While the Polish revindication of Galicia referred back to 1772, the Ukrainian revindication of East Galicia was a matter of medieval history, and Hrushevsky, as an historian, was just the man to make the case. The abdication of the Habsburg monarch in 1918 meant, in Hrushevsky's long historical view, that East Galicia reverted to independent Ukraine.

Poland's determination to incorporate all of Galicia made the Soviet Union, in reaction, an advocate of Galicia during the course of the Polish-Soviet war. For a few months in 1920 the Soviet Union sponsored a Galician Soviet Socialist Republic, based in Ternopil, and dedicated to the multicultural concerns of Ukrainians, Poles, and Jews. Thus affirming the existence of Galicia in defiance of Poland, the Soviet Union conjured the Galician phantom from the brink of oblivion. Had the Soviet Union fared better in the war, Lenin might, hypothetically, have had to encourage the development of Ukraine and Galicia as adjoining socialist republics. Much later, after the collapse of the Soviet Union in 1991, Galicia, like Ukraine, might have emerged as an independent country on the map of Europe in the twenty-first century.

ISAAC BABEL: "THESE PITIFUL GALICIANS"

The Polish-Soviet war, just by chance, brought to Galicia one of the greatest Russian writers of the twentieth century, Isaac Babel, who accompanied the Soviet cavalry as a journalist and later published his Red Cavalry stories. These stories suggested Babel's fascination with the sometimes brutal conduct of the Cossack cavalrymen, his outrage at the supposedly feudal privilege of Poland, and, at times, his sympathy with the suffering of the Jews in the path of the armies. All this played out against the landscape of Galicia.

One of the stories was set in the town of Sokal, where Babel's narrator observed the funeral rites for one of the Cossack commanders: "I touched my lips on an unblemished patch of forehead crowned by his saddle, and then left to go for a walk through the town, through Gothic Sokal, which lay in its blue dust and in Galicia's dejection." On his walk the narrator was distracted by a gathering of Hasids who—"ignoring war and gunfire"—were busy denouncing the Lithuanian Orthodox rabbinate of Vilnius. There then appeared another striking figure: "I suddenly saw a Galician before me, sepulchral and gaunt as Don Quixote."[75] Galicia, for Babel, was a land of poverty and death, with a whiff of demented fantasy.

The gaunt Galician Quixote led an equally gaunt cow: "The pitiful little cow tagged along behind the Galician. He led her with importance, and his lanky body cut into the hot brilliance of the sky like a gallows." Babel's narrator felt pity for the cow, but he hoped to harden himself in Galicia, to learn to be brutal, a man of war and revolution, like the Cossacks in the Red Cavalry:

> I staggered off into the village of Czesniki, which was sliding around in the relentless Galician rain. The village floated and bulged, crimson clay oozing from its gloomy wounds. The first star flashed above me and tumbled into the clouds. The rain whipped the willow trees and dwindled. The evening soared into the sky like a flock of birds, and darkness laid its wet garland upon me. I was exhausted, and, crouching beneath the crown of death, walked on, begging fate for the simplest ability—the ability to kill a man.[76]

Isaac Babel, born a Russian Jew in Odessa in 1894, lived through the Odessa pogrom of 1905 but was still trying to learn lessons about death in Galicia in 1920. He could not kill a man. Stalin would have no such hesitations to overcome when he sent Babel to his death in the purges of the 1930s.

Galicia, the constant scene of warfare in World War I, of assault upon the Jews, of Polish-Ukrainian war, and finally of Polish-Soviet war, offered sepulchral coloring to Babel's stories. Indeed, Galicia itself was about to be buried in its own geopolitical tomb. Babel's diaries show, even more than the stories, that the writer was deeply aware of the distinctiveness of Galicia and fascinated by the qualities that distinguished it from the Russian Empire. On 25 July 1920, he found himself in Leshniv:

> A Catholic church, a Uniate church, a synagogue, beautiful buildings, miserable life, a few spectral Jews, a revolting landlady, a Galician woman, flies and dirt . . . leaflets about Soviet Galicia . . . . How unimaginably sad this all is, and these piti-ful Galicians gone wild, and the destroyed synagogues, and trickles of life against a backdrop of horrifying events. . . .[77]

The former Habsburg ensemble of Galicia—the trio of two churches and a synagogue—could only barely be appreciated after the violence and de-struction of war, ongoing since 1914. While the Cossack fighters, whom Babel found so fascinating, casually found soldiers' sex in Galicia, sometimes paid, sometimes compelled, the author noted in his diary on 28 July, with metaphorical intensity, the omnipresence of syphilis: "The whole of Galicia is infected."[78] Once again, the integrity of Galicia was affirmed, this time its medical integrity, as a provincial whole.

"Galicia is unbearably gloomy, destroyed churches and crucifixes, overcast low-hanging sky, the battered, worthless, insignificant population," noted Babel in Leshniv, and he wondered, "Are the Slavs the manure of history?"[79] Galicia induced in Babel a sort of ethnographic despair, concerning everyone around him, including the Soviet Cossack cavalrymen and the local Galician populations, as they encountered each other in brutal, oppressive, dismis-sive, or even syphilitic relations. His own sympathies and identifications, his repulsions and alienations, seemed to fluctuate between the Soviet cavalry and the Galicians, and also among the ethnographic varieties of Slavs and Jews. In Brody on 30 July he noted "the terrible bazaars, the dwarves in long coats," and "nine synagogues, everything half destroyed." His injunction to himself, as a Russian writer, was to try to identify what was distinctive about Galicia:

> This is a Jewish town, this is Galicia, describe. Trenches, destroyed factories, the Bristol, waitresses, "Western European" culture, and how greedily we hurl our-selves onto it. Pitiful mirrors, pale Austrian Jews—the owners.[80]

Babel found Galicia an incongruous jumble of eastern and western aspects, and, with self-conscious grammatical precision, placed "Western Europe" in ironic quotation marks. The Austrian Jews of Brody offered an alarming spectacle of mirrors, with Eastern Europe and Western Europe reflecting back and forth, into the receding distance of mirrored space, from Oriental bazaars to the Hotel Bristol.

His writerly injunction to himself—"describe"—was complemented by an almost moral injunction to remember: "Must not forget Brody and the pitiful figures, and the barbershop, and the Jews from the world beyond, and the Cossacks in the streets."[81] Then, however, he found a Polish bookstore, and suddenly he began to believe that he really was in Western Europe: "All marvelous uncut books, albums, the West, here it is, the West and chivalrous Poland, a chrestomathy, a history of all the Boleslaws, and for some reason this seems to me so beautiful: Poland, glittering garments draped over a decrepit body." He found a volume of the poetry of Kazimierz Tetmajer, a souvenir of fin-de-siècle Galicia, for Babel an intimation of the West.[82] Galicia, as it lay dying in 1920, evoked East and West, the world beyond and the world behind, chivalry and decrepitude, the manure of history and the delusions of Don Quixote. On 1 August, Babel noted a surreal procession of "solemn, barefoot, spectral Galicians" walking through wheat fields.[83] Already phantoms, the Galicians still walked onward into the twentieth century, while Galicia itself was translated from history into fantasy.

From the village of Lashkiv—"a green, sunny, quiet, rich Galician village"—Babel tried to follow the course of the Polish-Soviet war and its international implications, wondering, "Will we have to go to war against the whole world?" Then a fire broke out in Lashkiv, and suddenly the whole village was all smoke and flames, as Babel witnessed the destruction of yet one more surviving village of Habsburg Galicia. The Cossacks seemed to feel no Ukrainian solidarity with the Galician Ruthenian peasants, and set about plundering the Uniate church. The sacred objects of booty seemed fascinating and exotic to Babel:

> Our Cossacks, a sad sight, dragging loot out over the back porch, their eyes burning, all of them looking uneasy, ashamed, this so-called habit of theirs is ineradicable. All the church banners, ancient saints' books, icons are being carried out, strange figures painted whitish pink, whitish blue, monstrous, flat-faced, Chinese or Buddhist, heaps of paper flowers, will the church catch fire, peasant women are wringing their hands in silence. . . . The soldiers are circling around the priest's trunks like rapacious, overwrought beasts, they say there's gold in there, one can take it away from a priest, a portrait of Count Andrei Sheptytsky, the metropolitan of Galicia. A manly magnate with a black ring on his large aristocratic hand.[84]

Babel was suddenly confronted with this image of Sheptytsky, still reigning as metropolitan in Lviv through the horrors of the war; indeed, he would reign until his death in 1944, living just long enough to witness the Soviet army's arrival at the end of World War II, when Stalin incorporated eastern Galicia into Soviet Ukraine. In 1920, Babel asked an old Uniate priest about Sheptytsky, and was told that the metropolitan came from an originally Ruthenian noble family, and that now he had "returned to the Ruthenians."[85] Babel, conversing with the old priest, seemed to feel some sympathy for the Ruthenians and the metropolitan of Galicia, even as the Cossacks carried out their Galician plundering.

Riding at night through the town of Busk—"silent, dead Busk"—Babel wondered, "What is special about Galician towns? The mixture of the dirty ponderous East (Byzantium and the Jews) with the beer-drinking German West." In Adamy he noticed the presence of "frightened Ruthenians," but the Poles remained excluded from his Byzantine-Jewish-Germanic conception of Galicia. Babel clarified this point when he noted the cavalrymen's even greater expectations of plunder up ahead: "In Poland, where we are heading, there's no need to hold back—with the Galicians, who are completely innocent, we had to be more careful."[86] The innocence of Galicia—excluding the Poles—added pathos to the martyrdom of the province, and Babel seemed to suffer along with Galicia. "The pitiful Galicians," he noted, concisely, on 22 August, and then, on 26 August, "Poor Galicia, poor Jews."[87] Babel, though eager to establish himself as a comrade among the Cossack cavalry, discovered in "poor Galicia"—in its poor earth, its poor Jews, its relentless rain, and the "crimson clay oozing from its gloomy wounds"—that which is indispensable to any great writer, a rich reserve of human sympathy.

CHAPTER TEN

Haunted Epilogue

Galicia after Galicia

⤸

INTRODUCTION: "A GEOGRAPHIC EXPEDITION"

Piłsudski's triumph in the Polish-Soviet war guaranteed that Galicia would be absorbed as a whole into the independent Polish republic. Within Poland the framework of Galicia officially disappeared in 1921 with the division of its territory into the administrative voivodships of Kraków, Lwów, Tarnopol, and Stanisławów. Thus Poland was able, according to historian Michał Śliwa, "to abolish the legal-political and administrative distinctiveness of the former Galicia."[1] The internal national tensions of Galicia now became Poland's own tensions, monitored by the League of Nations according to its guarantee of minority protection.

Gaining Galicia, Piłsudski established a multinational Poland with large minorities, which was consistent with his own left-leaning and inclusive "Jagiellonian" conception of what it meant to be Polish. His political archrival, the National Democrat Roman Dmowski, preached a more exclusive brand of integral nationalism, in which the Polish state was presumed to be the preserve of ethnic Poles, based on a national identity that encouraged political animosity toward minorities, including Jews and Ukrainians. Thus Piłsudski favored, and actually brought about, the inclusion of all of Galicia in Poland, while Dmowski encouraged the internal national tensions that characterized the province already under Habsburg rule. In 1922 the election to the Polish presidency of Gabriel Narutowicz, with the support of the minorities, was promptly followed by his assassination, which was carried out by a fanatical follower of Dmowski. In 1923 the League of Nations accepted Poland's rule over eastern Galicia on the understanding that the Ukrainians would be granted some sort of autonomy. On the contrary, in 1924 the National Democrat Stanisław Grabski, as Polish minister of education, legislated restrictions on education in the Ukrainian language—the Lex Grabski—setting back the progress made in that sphere during the final decade of Habsburg rule in Galicia.

In 1924, Alfred Döblin, the German writer who would later become famous as the author of the novel *Berlin Alexanderplatz*, made a journey to Poland and published his account in Weimar Germany in the following year. Born into a German Jewish family in Stettin, today Polish Szczecin, Döblin became a Berliner, and was interested in traveling to Poland particularly for the purpose of learning about the Jews of Eastern Europe. Already by 1921 he had noted ironically the general ignorance in Germany about those Jews, who seemed so alien and remote from the world of the Alexanderplatz. "We would have to determine whether millions of East European Jews really do live in Poland and Galicia," he commented wryly. "A geographic expedition would have to be fitted out to confirm this question."[2] In 1921 he seemed not quite certain about the distinction between Poland and Galicia, and when he finally set out on his expedition in 1924 the distinctiveness of the former Galicia would become one of his subjects of exploration.

Galicia in the twentieth century without the Habsburg monarchy—Galicia after Galicia—was a phantom of its former provincial self. Yet the political instability and ethnic tension of late Habsburg Galicia continued to spiral unstably, destructively, murderously, under the diverse sovereignties that governed those territories and peoples, the former Galicia and the former Galicians. Russian and German armies occupied all or part of Galicia in the course of two world wars; Polish and Ukrainian, Soviet and post-Soviet regimes sought to impose their political programs upon its peoples. Even after Habsburg rule the poverty of the region continued to send Galician emigrants all over the world. Whether they stayed at home or emigrated across the ocean, some of the former Galicians would maintain their Galician identity as Galician Ukrainians, as Galician Poles, and especially as Galician Jews, who constituted an ethnographic category of their own: Galitzianer. Bruno Schulz and Joseph Roth, both born as Galician Jews in the 1890s, in the reign of Franz Joseph, would come of age as writers in post-Habsburg Europe, exploring the Galician legacy in Polish and in German literature, respectively. Shmuel Yosef Agnon, born in Galicia in the 1880s, would win the Nobel Prize in the 1960s as an Israeli novelist, writing in Hebrew.

The League of Nations, overseeing the postwar treaties on minority protection, would try to guarantee the security of the former Galicians in independent Poland, with only limited success. Perceived Polish oppressions, however, would give way to the greater horrors that Hitler and Stalin brought to Galicia during and after World War II. The Molotov-Ribbentrop Pact of 1939 partitioned not only Poland but also Galicia, divided into Nazi and Soviet spheres. While Hitler and Stalin, with their unprecedented and murderous brutalities, would pass from the scene in 1945 and 1953, respectively, the geopolitical division of Galicia that they consummated would persist. The territories of the former Galicia remain today divided between Poland and Ukraine. With the collapse of communism first in Poland in 1989, then in Ukraine in 1991, pictures of the Emperor Franz Joseph began to appear in Cracow and Lviv, as Galician nostalgia conjured the phantom province—like the ghosts in Wyspiański's *The Wedding*—for one last spectral visitation at the very end of the twentieth century.

ALFRED DÖBLIN: "PRIMEVAL PHANTASMAGORIA"

In 1924, when Döblin was traveling, Galicia remained still a meaningful place name, a well remembered, only recently effaced, geopolitical entity. Setting out from Berlin, Döblin traveled to Warsaw, Vilnius, and Lublin before proceeding to Lviv—then Lwów in Poland—and discovering the former Galicia. Immediately he claimed that he could discern the Austrian influence in Lviv.

> This Galician city is completely different from the cities of Congress Poland. The people here are soft and friendly: the people of Warsaw were rigid, drilled, in the Russian style. Who could that man be, made of red sandstone, sitting on a chair up there? "Aleksander Fredro," it says on the monument. I hear the message well, but I lack the knowledge. He must be long dead, for he has no steel pen, but a goose feather for writing in his hand.[3]

Galicia was a name that Döblin still knew in 1924, though the name of Fredro was unknown to him. Fredro had been writing comedies a hundred years before, and the Polish language and Galician context of his literary career were both alien to Döblin.

Lviv felt like Europe to Döblin, as he listened to a band playing Viennese waltzes, just six years after the imperial connection to Vienna had been severed. Yet this European aspect of Galicia now repelled him, and made him long for Warsaw with its Russian rigidity. "These Europeans, these half and whole ones, these horribly colorless ones," he wrote about the Galicians of Lviv. "I already fear that there will be cafés here, that people will follow literature, that they will talk about Tagore." And of course there were cafés, European style, with pretty girls and amiable music. "Again and again, the

Viennese waltz," he noted. "In the hall they are singing along. Is there a heart or soul in them?"[4] The half-European aspect of Galicia, which Franzos had summed up half a century earlier, reciprocally, as half-Asian, disturbed Döblin as some sort of offensive mimicry of the Europe he knew and mistrusted. Franzos, who wrote in German, would not have been as unknown as Fredro to the traveler from Berlin; in fact, there had been a Berlin silent movie in 1920, *Judith Trachtenberg*, based on a Franzos story about a Galician Jewish girl who married a Galician Polish nobleman, with tragic consequences.[5]

In Lviv, Döblin learned about Uniates and Ukrainians: "Besides the Roman Catholic archbishop, there is the Greek Catholic one, for the Ruthenians or Ukrainians. And that is another story in itself." Döblin did not know that the Greek Catholic archbishop was the grandson of the writer with the goose feather, but he was interested in the story of the Ruthenians or Ukrainians, with their "terrible, blind, numb hatred, an entirely animal hatred of the Poles." This antagonism shadowed Lviv's European aspect:

> Lemberg is a lively modern Western town, with peace and activity in its streets. And yet there is a strange thing that I suddenly came up against. This town rests in the arms of two rivals, who are struggling for it. In the background and underground there are hostility and violence [*Feindschaft und Gewalt*].[6]

It was not difficult for Döblin to identify this "background" and "underground" as the historical circumstances of Habsburg Galicia:

> The Ukrainians were already fighting against the Poles during the Austrian period. Count Potocki, the Austrian viceroy, was murdered here in 1911 [*sic*]. Someone shows me the old viceregal palace on a rampartlike rise behind trees. Potocki was wearing the Golden Fleece at his death.[7]

The site of the assassination in 1908 had become almost a tourist destination, to be pointed out to foreign visitors as a landmark in the history of former Galicia.

Döblin had come to Poland to learn about the Jews, but in Galicia, perhaps unexpectedly, he was discovering the Ukrainians. He went to visit the Ukrainian national museum, established by the Greek Catholic archbishop, and he admired a Last Judgment full of "naïve figures." He visited a private Ukrainian school, where students were learning about "a polymath, Ivan Franko"—seemingly as unknown as Fredro to the German tourist. Döblin made an excursion from Lviv: "I travel to the countryside, and I see these Ukrainian men, women, their children. An extraordinarily robust human breed, rich in anthropological types." He heard about the Hutsuls as an unusual community of Ukrainian mountaineers, and though he did not travel to the mountains to study them, Döblin admired Hutsul crafts in Lviv:

There are Hutsul ceramics, weapons, musical instruments, wood carving, embroidery, weaving, furniture, toys. This mountain people possesses unbelievable manual skill and an original sense of form. In their customs there are supposedly many "pagan" elements. Astonishing is their inventiveness in cutting out silhouettes, in painting Easter eggs. The war changed many things among them; they were brought into contact with modern civilization, and their specific character has been blurred.[8]

Galicia, in retrospect, had been a marvelous museum of ethnography and folklore, and the end of Galicia coincided with the coming of "modern civilization," the endangerment of its anthropological treasures, the effacement of its ethnographic variety in the crucible of modern national antagonisms. In former Galicia, Döblin observed that the contemporary Polish state was haunted by a "primeval phantasmagoria [*eine Phantasmagorie aus der Urzeit*]," by collective "delirium," by historical memories that had become pathological "delusions [*Wahnideen*]."[9] There were perhaps Freudian intimations in Döblin's sense that present Poland rested unstably upon its historical components and legacies, its fantasies and memories, which the state might attempt to liquidate, abolish, and repress—but not necessarily with lasting success, and perhaps at some psychic cost.

Döblin's tour of Lviv taught him the traumatic story of the Polish-Ukrainian war and the pogrom against the Jews in 1918:

> The band of the dead rests in the Jewish cemetery. You can see their graves. But another monument is visible in the city, more terrible and disturbing than any that could ever be built: the burnt houses. They still stand as they did then, after the fire and plunder.[10]

The very recent memories of 1918, the end of Galicia, still visibly marked Lviv in 1924. It was a city in which three peoples still lived together "side by side [*nebeneinander*]"—as Döblin observed—but in a state of sustained tension and wariness, haunted by the past, nervous about the future.[11]

Very much interested in the Jews and the Ukrainians, Döblin in 1924, like Babel in 1920, seemed least sympathetic to the politically dominant Poles, but was willing to enjoy their hospitality and appreciate their legacy.

> A refined old count, a former viceroy in Austrian Poland, chats with me over tea, shows me his Italian paintings, complains about what he has lost to the Bolsheviks. Then he, a university professor of law, gives me his card, so that I can easily visit the collections at the Ossolineum. It is a library and a museum created about a hundred years ago by a Count Ossoliński and a Prince Lubomirski. There are 700,000 books. . . .[12]

The former viceroy of the former Galicia was probably Leon Piniński, who had served as *namiestnik*—now an extinct office—between 1898 and 1903, presiding over turn-of-the-century Galicia: when Przybyszewski came to Cracow, when Wyspiański wrote *The Wedding*, when Franko wrote about Galicia as "the land of impossibilities," when Sheptytsky first became the Uniate metropolitan of Galicia, when Franz Joseph passed the fifty-year mark in his epic reign. In 1924, Wyspiański and Franko were no longer alive, and Piniński must have seemed to Döblin like a relic of the phantasmagorical Galician past. Yet, assisted by Piniński's card and courtesy, Döblin gazed even further back into the ghostly history of Galicia, to the turn of an even earlier century, when Ossoliński was collecting books in Vienna during the reign of Franz, finally moving his collection to Lviv after the conclusion of the Napoleonic Wars.

The Polish science-fiction writer Stanisław Lem was born in Lviv in 1921, and his childhood there coincided with the post-Galician period of the 1920s. One particular treat that he recalled was the purchase of gas balloons in different colors: "They were sold by a vendor in front of the University, but the University then was still called Parliament, perhaps out of inertia, from the Austrian time, when the building housed the Galician parliament."[13] Indeed, it was the architectural expression of Galicia's geopolitical integrity, and Lem's balloons, if carelessly released, would have floated upward past the allegorical sculpture of the lady Galicia who stood (and still stands), flanked allegorically by the rivers Vistula and Dniester, atop the palace of the Galician Sejm. Robbed of its political meaning, the palace still preserved its allegorical sculptures and its symbolic Galician significance in public memory. The Polish poet Zbigniew Herbert, born in Lviv in 1924, and still writing poetry in Poland in the 1990s, remembered his childhood in verse: Mr. Cogito, who learned calligraphy "in the first grade of Saint Anthony's elementary school, seventy years ago in Lwów."[14] It would have been an elegant Habsburg calligraphy as taught in Galicia, which had only just ceased to exist.

Döblin in 1924 traveled from Lviv to Drohobych and Boryslav, to observe the former Galician oil industry. That industry was in deep decline from its former boom days before the war, and Döblin described the town of Drohobych itself in ruins:

> Frightening [*fürchterlich*] there stands in the middle of the market square a high rectangular tower with a clock. The tower is alone, no church, no house attached. It is a leg that has been torn from the body. A bombardment must have taken place here. . . . In front of a public building, there is an empty pedestal: this was Mickiewicz, the Polish national poet. The Ukrainians shattered the bust several years ago during their advance.[15]

Thus the ruins of Habsburg Drohobych survived in independent Poland, and Döblin actually decided that the condition of ruin was appropriate to the site. He saw the town's renovated synagogue: "And I can not escape the thought that it should not have been renovated." He visited the oil refinery in Drohobych and the oil fields in Boryslav, was repelled by the circumstances of exploitation, and concluded, "I have the impression of the Wild West, haste, speculation. An American creation that remains stuck in the swamp [*im Sumpf*]."[16] In fact, the oil industry was a Galician creation that outlived both its own economic boom and the geopolitical existence of Galicia itself, surviving into the twentieth century as a ruined reminder of the amputated past, a leg without a body, a pedestal without a bust. Such was Döblin's phantasmagoria of Galicia.

Joseph Roth also traveled from Germany to Galicia in 1924, though for him, born in Brody, it was a return to the familiar territory of his native province. Writing for the *Frankfurter Zeitung*, Roth reflected on the still persistently negative images of Galicia in Western Europe, even after Galicia itself had ceased to exist: "The cheap and lazy wit of civilized arrogance brings a crude association with vermin, filth, and dishonesty." Galicia belonged by reputation to Eastern Europe, and was somehow not ennobled as the battlefield of fallen soldiers during World War I. Roth himself reported on Galicia as a backward land of poverty and superstition: "So it was when Franz Joseph reigned, and so it is today. There are other uniforms, other eagles, other badges, but the essential things do not change." Roth also observed "the eternal mud [*der unsterbliche Schlamm*]" in the streets—an almost aestheticized mud which, by night, reflected the moon and the stars "as in a very dirty crystal." In the markets he watched people buying "primitive wooden puppets, as in Europe two hundred years ago"—and he asked himself, "Does Europe stop here?" Then he saw English and French books for sale in the bookstores, and concluded that Galicia was Europe after all, but somehow estranged from Europe: "Galicia lies in loneliness [*Einsamkeit*] lost to the world, and yet is not isolated; it is exiled [*verbannt*] but not cut off." Although Galicia no longer actually existed, Roth believed that it still possessed "its own pleasures, its own songs, its own people, and its own splendor: the sad splendor of the reviled."[17] Roth had been born Galician himself, and still identified with Galicia: the essential things do not change.

"THE DANGER SPOT OF EUROPE"

In 1926, the year that Piłsudski's coup d'état imposed an authoritarian government on the Polish republic, the communist poet Bruno Jasieński reached deep into the Galician past to produce his epic poem *The Song of*

Jakub Szela. Jasieński, who moved artistically from futurism to communism, and geographically from Cracow to Lviv, in the early 1920s, took some appreciation of Galicia along with him when he immigrated to Paris in 1925, and it was there, looking back to Galicia, that he wrote and published his poem about Szela. From Jasieński's communist perspective, the notorious instigator of the Galician massacres of 1846 was nothing less than a revolutionary hero: "Even if the historical Szela had not existed, one would have had to invent him for the benefit of the peasant class consciousness. Even if the existing Szela had not been a hero, one would have had to make a hero out of him in the name of peasant martyrdom and injustice."[18] Like his fellow communist Isaac Babel, Jasieński found in Galicia the object of his profound revolutionary sympathies, and commemorated Szela on behalf of the Galician peasantry. For Wyspiański in *The Wedding,* in 1901—the year of Jasieński's birth—Szela was still a figure of horror, the foundational nightmare of nineteenth-century Galician history, but for Jasieński, writing after the demise of Galicia itself, it was possible to rehabilitate Szela in the name of a new post-Galician revolutionary politics.

Literary critic Nina Kolesnikoff, discussing Jasieński, has emphasized the folkloric aspects of his *Song of Jakub Szela,* the ways in which the poem appeared as a mock-folkloric work of an invented oral tradition: "sustained in the tradition of Polish folk songs: its motifs, images, stylistic figures, and metric form were all inspired by folk couplets and ditties."[19] Kolesnikoff notes that one of Jasieński's works of reference in Paris was Żegota Pauli's *Pieśni ludu polskiego w Galicji (Polish Folk Songs in Galicia),* published in Lviv in 1838.[20] In other words, the folk idiom was as much Galician as Polish, and, in fact, the whole lesson of the massacres of 1846 was precisely that the Galician peasants did not identify themselves as nationally Polish.

In folkloric fashion Szela encountered Jesus Christ, but the Galician peasant proved to be more Christian than Christ himself. He accused Jesus of not valuing peasant blood—*nie ceniłeś ty krwi chłopskiej*—of favoring instead the noble masters. Szela confronted Jesus with the fact of "peasant misery [*chłopska nędza*]," which in the 1920s might have still been recognized as the proverbial Galician misery from Szczepanowski's title in the 1880s.[21] In Jasieński's folkloric vision, the peasants of 1846, with Habsburg encouragement, engaged their noble masters in a terrible dance of death, only to be sent back to work by the Habsburg emperor, returned to the forced labor of serfdom. The poem, steeped in the Galician legacy, mimicked the emperor's address to the peasants after the massacre—"We the Emperor in Lodomeria"—ordering them to return to their masters' fields. The peasants, naive enough to believe in Habsburg beneficence, were sold back to their feudal masters—"the emperor took us and sold us to the lords [*wziął nas cesarz sprzedał panom*]"—for thirteen coins.[22]

The Habsburgs were the dynasty of Judas in this communist and folk-loric celebration of Jakub Szela, as Jasieński discovered his poetic sympa-thies with the Galician victims of the nineteenth century. These particular victims—the Galician peasantry—actually played the part of murderers in 1846, but Jasieński discerned and celebrated the revolutionary righteousness behind the massacres. He too was sometimes capable of misplaced revolu-tionary enthusiasm. In 1938, Jasieński was purged by Stalin as an enemy of the revolution and sent to his death in a Siberian labor camp.

The peasant revolutionary violence represented by Szela in 1846 was not actually perceived as the most potentially explosive aspect of the former Galicia in the 1920s; much more menacing were the national tensions among Poles, Ukrainians, and Jews. These national tensions were summed up in a booklet whose title focused attention upon "The Danger Spot of Europe"—published by the Ukrainian Bureau in London. A Labour member of the British Parlia-ment, Cecil Malone (who had briefly been a communist in the early 1920s) introduced the work with reference to "reports of a reign of terror inflicted by the militarist dictatorship of Marshal Piłsudski on the three Provinces of Eastern Galicia, inhabited largely by Ukrainians, who were handed over to the newly-constituted State of Poland, under the protection of the Minorities Trea-ties." These reports focused on systematic government brutality, the "Polish terror" deployed during the Polish elections of 1930, including the imprison-ment of Ukrainians and the closing of Ukrainian schools and libraries.[23]

The "danger spot of Europe" was none other than "the problem of Eastern Galicia," which Malone described as "a question of the desire or ability of the modern world, of the League of Nations, to insist that the Mi-norities, the members of one nation or race, placed in subjection to another race, shall receive justice and equality of treatment." Malone declared that the Ukrainians were "the largest and worst treated Minority in Europe," and reproached the Poles for refusing them "even the right to the name Ukrai-nian which, according to the *Encyclopaedia Britannica*, they have used since the Middle Ages." There was perhaps something perversely pedantic about making the *Encyclopaedia Britannica* into the arbiter of nationality—Ukrainian or Ruthenian—in Galicia, but Malone was notably sensitive to the ways in which certain names were used and not used. Most strikingly, he protested against the Polish elimination of the name of Galicia itself, as if it were intended as a semantic blow against the Ukrainians. "The historic name of Galicia is to disappear," he observed, with outrage, "and the name 'Little Eastern Poland' is given to Eastern Galicia."[24] More than a decade after the liquidation of Habsburg rule in Galicia, a British member of parliament was affirming the political importance of Galicia, as a name and an entity, even as he conceptually partitioned the province into national components.

Malone's preface led into the report on Eastern Galicia written by Mary Sheepshanks, who had gone to Poland as a representative of the Women's International League for Peace and Freedom, which was based in Geneva, along with the League of Nations. Sheepshanks had been a suffragette before the war, a pacifist during the war, and an advocate of disarmament afterward. In 1930 she made a pet project out of the Ukrainians in Poland, and she became a particular fan of "their Metropolitan Archbishop, Count Szeptycki, a man of great culture and learning" and "champion of their civil rights." Sheepshanks described the Polish brutalization of the Ukrainians in Eastern Galicia, and, with all the zeal of Western civilization, declared that "this so-called 'pacification' was carried out with a ferocity which can only be compared to the previous atrocities carried out in the early nineteenth century by the Bashi-Bazouks in the old Turkish territories." In the nineteenth century it was William Gladstone who denounced the "atrocities" of the Ottoman irregular troops, the Bashi-Bazouks, in southeastern Europe, and Sheepshanks now embraced with Gladstonian moral fervor the oppressed population of the former Galicia.[25]

The report of Mary Sheepshanks, the foreign visitor, was followed by a dissenting report from the Polish Section of the Women's International League for Peace and Freedom, discussing "events in Little Eastern Poland (formerly Eastern Galicia)." The Polish women took issue with Sheepshanks, and stood largely in solidarity with the Polish government in a negative view of Ukrainian political activity. The Polish women claimed for themselves the expertise concerning the region that foreign visitors, even equipped with the *Encyclopaedia Britannica*, presumably lacked:

> We have found it absolutely essential to give a short account of the territory where the incidents took place, and of the population by which it is inhabited. The territory annexed under the Partition of Poland by the Austro-Hungarian Monarchy, was given the name of "Galicia" with Lwów (Leopol) as the capital, in order to stamp out Poland even as its name. . . . Up to the end of the XIXth century the two nationalities in this country lived harmoniously together, intermingling and forming politically one nation. The Ruthenians considered themselves as part of the Polish nation . . . in the same way as the Bretons regard themselves as French, and the Welsh as English. Discord and separatism were provoked by the Austrian Government following the maxim *divide et impera*. For centuries the Ruthenians have, in their own language, called themselves, "Ruthenians."[26]

Like Malone, the Polish women were also sensitive to the power of names for making a political case. Most notably, they needed to explain the name

"Galicia"—how it originated in the partitions of Poland—in order to make the case for abolishing the name and absorbing the region into the Polish state as Eastern Little Poland [Małopolska Wschodnia]. The Poles needed to put "Galicia" in quotation marks in order to identify the semantic danger spot in the geopolitical lexicon, the better to explain why the designation should no longer be employed. At the same time they argued forcefully for the name "Ruthenian" over the name "Ukrainian," insisting that Poles and Ruthenians formed a single nation. The British public was urged to appreciate the merely regional variation of the Ruthenians by analogy to the Welsh within a national community of Britons.

The Polish women argued that Poland was, in fact, living up to its commitments under the Minority Protection Treaty, granting "Ruthenians" equality before the law, and allowing them their churches and schools and newspapers, as well as positions in the state civil service. According to the Polish women, there were "Ukrainian extremists" at large, committing acts of terror and sabotage against the Polish population in Eastern Little Poland, while "from 1918 onwards they insisted on calling it 'Western Ukraine' and strove to introduce the use of this name abroad."[27] The Ukrainian extremists were identified as members of the UVO, Ukrainian Military Organization—which in 1929 gave way to the OUN, Organization of Ukrainian Nationalists, militantly engaged in the struggle for Ukrainian independence. The Polish Section of the Women's International League for Peace and Freedom, citing the pacifism of the organization, denounced the actions of "the Ukrainian terrorists," and issued an invitation to "Ukrainian sisters" to join in future reconciliation between, at least, the female part of the two nations.[28]

There was, however, no sisterly indulgence for Mary Sheepshanks, who appeared as a black sheep indeed from the pastoral perspective of the Polish women.

> Miss Sheepshanks announced, although a little vaguely, that she had come to Poland in a more or less private capacity, and we gladly awaited her arrival. We only asked her to be good enough to come to Warsaw, if only for a day, before going to Lwów, desiring that she should be accompanied there by one of our delegates. . . . However, Miss Sheepshanks, without replying in any way to our letter, went all alone to Lwów without even informing us. . . . She cut herself off from Polish society at Lwów, so that no one knew anything about her stay. . . . Unfortunately, Miss Sheepshanks would have nothing but information from a chauvinistic group of Ukrainians.[29]

Döblin, traveling to Lviv after Warsaw, was sensitive to the different circumstances of the former Galicia, and discovered, among other things, the "whole other story" of the Ruthenians or Ukrainians. Mary Sheepshanks also

heard that story in Lviv, for Galicia continued to preserve, indeed with growing intensity, the multinational circumstances and animosities that had given
the province its particular political character in the age of Franz Joseph.

Mary Sheepshanks was undaunted by the criticism of the Polish women,
and rejected the analogy between the Ruthenians and the Welsh with a differently pointed analogy: "I believe in the case of East Galicia, as in the case
of Ireland and other disturbed countries, the people themselves are unhappy
and discontented." Thus the Ruthenian rejection of Poland was to be compared to the Irish rejection of England, which resulted in the establishment
of the Irish Free State in 1922. Sheepshanks showed some sympathy with
the former Habsburg monarchy, especially concerning its government of the
former Galicia: "I think it is generally admitted, and it was the impression I
had in making comparisons between East Galicia as it is now and as I saw it
in 1913, that it is at present much less well treated and much less happy than
under Austria."[30] Her reply to the Polish women concluded with an enumeration of brutalities allegedly committed by the Polish military or police in the
so-called pacification of 1930.

Finally, all within the same booklet, the Ukrainians themselves gave their
reply to the report of the Polish women, beginning with an affirmation of
the right to be called Ukrainians rather than Ruthenians, and the right to use
the name of East Galicia:

> The guilt of the Ukrainians is shown first of all in the refusal of the Ukrainians
> of Galicia to accept the name of Ruthenians for themselves, or the name of
> Little Poland for East Galicia . . . although in our opinion every one should be
> free to adopt the name that suits them and that is no concern of other peoples.
> The Ukrainians of East Galicia gave unmistakable expression of their intention
> to call themselves Ukrainians before they were joined to Poland. In 1918, after
> the collapse of Austria, they founded their own independent State on the former
> territory of East Galicia, and called it West Ukraine. This action was based on the
> principle of the right of every nation to self-determination, proclaimed by Presi-
> dent Wilson.[31]

The question of the free deployment of names for peoples and places was
of utmost importance for the notion of national self-determination, which
sought to discover the authentic correspondence between nations and territories. Yet these names were as slippery as any unstable signifier—like
"Galicia"—in attempting to capture the reality of phenomena, of assigning
identity, of designating space.

"It is a universally recognized fact that the Ukrainians who are Polish
citizens do not differ in any respect from their brothers of the same race
living in Soviet Ukraine," wrote the Ukrainians, though such issues of identity were peculiarly elusive of factual acknowledgment, let alone universal

recognition. The Ukrainians claimed to possess a ruptured tradition of state independence dating back to the Middle Ages, and, furthermore, traced their claim to Galicia back to that same period. Whereas Poles in 1918 looked back to 1772 to reclaim the territory they had lost to Austria under the name of Galicia, Ukrainians looked back to the fourteenth century to reclaim the territory they had lost to Poland: "In 1341 Galicia was sundered from the Ukrainian kingdom Halitsch (Galicia)."[32] The name of Galicia thus continued to circulate in the claims and counterclaims of the postwar world, designating the "danger spot of Europe," but dangerous precisely because of its nonexistence, because of its liquidation in 1918 and the still contested post-Habsburg succession. The Ukrainians insisted on articulating the name "Galicia" as a rejection of Poland, but, in fact, they too sought the semantic effacement and political absorption of Galicia, the transformation of East Galicia into West Ukraine, as ultimately occurred.

CAFÉ HABSBURG: "OUR OWN FANTASY"

Galicia was still being invoked in the political controversies of the 1930s, while in literature and culture it was already entering into the realm of mythology. The literary legacy of Galicia richly emerged in the 1930s, with the fictional works of Shmuel Yosef Agnon, born in Buchach in 1888, Bruno Schulz, born in Drohobych in 1892, and Joseph Roth, born in Brody in 1894. All three were born as Galician Jewish subjects of Franz Joseph, and all three became famous as writers in different languages, Agnon in Hebrew, Schulz in Polish, and Roth in German. Although none of them wrote in Ukrainian, the birthplaces of all three are today located in Ukraine.

Agnon, who emigrated from Weimar Germany to British Palestine in the 1920s, created a historical novel of Galicia set in the early nineteenth century, *The Bridal Canopy*, published in 1931; in 1938 he published *A Guest for the Night*, about an emigrant Galician's return to the former Galicia in the early twentieth century. Roth, educated in Brody, Lviv, and Vienna, was also writing in Weimar Germany in the 1920s, and published the novel *Radetzky March* in Berlin in 1932, a historical novel about Habsburg loyalism during the last fifty years of the monarchy; the novel concluded in Galicia, on the Russian frontier, at the outbreak of World War I. Galicia was also the crucial setting for Roth's celebrated story of Habsburg loyalism, "The Bust of the Emperor," published in 1935, and the province played an important part in the novel *The Emperor's Tomb*, published in 1938. Schulz never left Drohobych, but become a Polish citizen with the lapsing of Habsburg rule; in 1934 he published the collection of stories *Cinnamon Shops* (known in English as *The Street of Crocodiles*), and, in 1937, *Sanatorium under the Sign of the Hourglass*, landmarks of modernist Polish literature that conjured with dreamlike mythological intensity the Galician town of Schulz's childhood. Schulz was murdered by the Nazis in Drohobych in 1942, while Roth died in Paris in 1939; Agnon lived long enough to win the Nobel Prize in literature in 1966 as the first Hebrew laureate, four years before his death in Jerusalem in 1970. Such was the far-flung, multilingual, and mythologizing literary legacy of Galicia.

In *Radetzky March*, Roth evoked Galicia as the mysterious frontier of the Habsburg monarchy. He brought to that frontier not only his young soldier hero of the Slovenian Trotta family, but also, in an act of bold fictional conjuring, the ancient emperor, Franz Joseph himself, on a tour of military inspection. Roth seemed to suggest that the idea of Galicia existed most fully and meaningfully in the consciousness of the emperor, who embodied its fundamental relation to the Habsburg dynasty. Roth described, from the emperor's point of view, the homage of the Galician Jews, as Franz Joseph met them on horseback:

> They swarmed toward him, a dark cloud. Like a field of strange black grain stalks in the wind, this congregation of Jews did obeisance to the Emperor. He saw their bent backs from the saddle. Then he rode up closer and made out the long, fluttering beards, silver, pitch-black, or flame-red, stirring in the light autumn wind.[33]

In this postimpressionist rendering of Galicia from the emperor's perspective—a swirling, swarming canvas of color and light—the province seemed already on the point of dissolving into incoherence, held together for the moment only by the emperor's point of view. The Jews approached the emperor:

> The patriarch stopped three paces from the Emperor. In his arms he bore a large purple Torah scroll decorated with a gold crown, its little bells softly jingling. Then the Jew lifted the Torah scroll toward the Emperor. And his widely bearded, toothless mouth gabbled in an incomprehensible language the blessing which Jews utter in the presence of an emperor.[34]

Yet, incomprehensibility became meaningful and coherent as Franz Joseph received the Galician blessing that pertained only to him, that had been his prerogative alone in Galicia ever since his accession to the throne in 1848.

> The wind carried to his ears a remark made by Captain Kaunitz to a friend riding at his side: "I couldn't make out a word that Jew was saying." The Emperor turned in his saddle. "Well, my dear Kaunitz," he said, "he was speaking only to me." And he rode on.[35]

Roth, who was born a Galician subject of Franz Joseph in 1894, remembered the empire of his youth in which the already mythological figure of the still living emperor rendered comprehensible the relation of the Habsburg monarchy to its Galician subjects.

In "The Bust of the Emperor," Roth set his story just a little bit later, in the postwar world, on the other side of the historical upheaval that had made ghosts out of Galicia and the Habsburg monarchy. "In what used to be Eastern Galicia, and today is Poland, far indeed from the solitary railway line which links Przemyśl with Brody, lies the small village of Lopatyny, about which I intend to tell a remarkable tale."[36] This was the tale of Count Morstin, a Galician nobleman who could not come to terms with the passing of the Habsburg monarchy, could not forget his loyalty to the Habsburg emperor, could not adjust to political life in the postwar world. Deciding to ignore the current political reality of postwar Poland, Count Morstin displayed in front of his home a stone bust of Franz Joseph that had been made years before on the occasion of the emperor's visit to the district for military maneuvers. Now Galicia and the Habsburg monarchy came to life again, in the realm of fantasy and delusion:

> . . . as though there had been no war and no Polish Republic, as though the old Emperor had not been long laid to rest in the Kapuzinergruft; as though this village still belonged to the territory of the old Monarchy; every peasant who passed by doffed his cap to the sandstone bust of the old Emperor, and every Jew who passed by with his bundle murmured the prayer which a pious Jew will say on seeing an Emperor.[37]

When the Polish government became aware of this bizarre anachronism—which seemed implicitly treasonous—the bust was ordered removed from public view. Therefore, with all due solemnity, with the religious support of the local Jewish rabbi, Roman Catholic priest, and Uniate priest, with the participation of the local Jewish, Polish, and Ukrainian populations, Count Morstin carried out the funeral interment of the stone bust, as if it were the body of the emperor himself. "So the old Emperor was laid to rest a second time in the village of Lopatyny, in what had once been Galicia," wrote Roth, who seemed to suggest that the province survived in phantom form, wherever the memories and fantasies of former Galicians still lingered in the Habsburg historical past.[38]

In Bruno Schulz's story "Spring," published in 1937 in the collection *Sanatorium under the Sign of the Hourglass*, the circumscribed domain of a Habsburg childhood was suddenly shattered by the discovery of a postage stamp album, with the Emperor Franz Joseph reduced to the size of a postage stamp and surrounded by the leaders and emblems of every other country on earth as represented in philatelic form.

> At that time the world was totally encompassed by Franz Joseph I. On all the horizons there loomed this omnipresent and inevitable profile, shutting the world off, like a prison. And just when we had given up hope and bitterly resigned ourselves inwardly to the uniformity of the world—the powerful guarantor of whose narrow immutability was Franz Joseph I—then suddenly, Oh God, unaware of the importance of it, you opened before me that stamp album, you allowed me to cast a look on its glimmering colors. . . . What a dazzling relativism, what a Copernican deed, what flux of all categories and concepts![39]

Suddenly, Schulz's young Galician protagonist, Joseph, his fictional alter ego, had to question his own inculcated loyalty to the emperor. Joseph wondered whether perhaps Franz Joseph might be, not a benign deity, but an oppressive force that denied the thrilling colors of the world and cut off the subservient loyalist from a true glimpse of God in a universe of dazzling diversity.

> The world at that time was circumscribed by Franz Joseph I. On each stamp, on every coin, and on every postmark his likeness confirmed its stability and the dogma of its oneness. This was the world, and there were no other worlds besides, the effigies of the imperial-and-royal old man proclaimed. Everything else was make-believe, wild pretense, and usurpation. Franz Joseph I rested on top of everything and checked the world in its growth. By inclination we tend to be loyal, dear reader. . . . If that authoritarian old man threw all his prestige on the scales, one could do nothing but give up all one's aspirations and longings, manage as well as one could in the only possible world—that is, a world without illusions and romanticism—and forget.[40]

Looking back from the perspective of 1937, twenty years after the emperor's death, Schulz's portrait of the young artist, himself, represented his youthful relation to the emperor's omnipresent image as the struggle of poetry against prose, of creativity against authority, of freedom against repression.

Like Roth's loyalist Count Morstin, Schulz's rebellious young artist was completely embedded and circumscribed within the Habsburg world of imperial busts and imperial postage stamps. The album, however, offered an emancipatory perspective:

> How greatly diminished you have become, Franz Joseph, and your gospel of prose! I looked for you in vain. At last I found you. You were among the crowd, but how small, unimportant, and grey. You were marching with some others in the dust of the highway, immediately following South America, but preceding Australia, and singing together with the others: Hosanna![41]

Franz Joseph was only one stamp among many, saluting the God whose poetic presence encompassed all the stamps of the world in all their colors.

Joseph, the protagonist of "Spring," concluded that Franz Joseph was not a divinity, but perhaps the demiurge who presided over the material universe, cut off from its spiritual aspect. Joseph joined the secret countercult of Franz Joseph's younger brother Maximilian, the murdered and martyred emperor of Mexico. The principle most opposed to the prosaic reign of Franz Joseph was embodied in the ill-fated Maximilian: "full of fantasy and imagination, enticed by the hope of creating a new, happier world on the Pacific."[42] Joseph was convinced that Franz Joseph conspired with Napoleon III to send Maximilian to his death in Mexico in 1867, twenty-five years before Bruno Schulz was born. Maximilian appeared in the story as a wax figure in a traveling wax museum in Galicia, an exhibit that also included the figure of Luigi Luccheni, who assassinated the Empress Elisabeth in 1898, when Bruno Schulz was six years old. In the end Joseph burned down the exhibit of wax figures, and was about to shoot himself when he was placed under arrest by a Habsburg officer for his prophetic dreams:

> "I can not answer for my dreams," I said.
> "Yes, you can. I am arresting you in the name of His Majesty the Emperor-and-King!"
> I smiled. "How slow are the mills of justice. The bureaucracy of His Majesty the Emperor-and-King grinds rather slowly."[43]

In the 1930s, Franz Joseph, the former Emperor of Austria and King of Hungary, was still weighing upon the dreams of Bruno Schulz in the former Galicia.

In the story "August," in *Cinnamon Shops*, Schulz evoked with mythological intensity the town of Drohobych in the days of his Galician childhood.

> Market Square was empty and white-hot, swept by hot winds like a biblical desert. The thorny acacias, growing in this emptiness, looked with their bright leaves like the trees on old tapestries. Although there was no breath of wind, they rustled their foliage in a theatrical gesture, as if wanting to display the elegance of the silver lining of their leaves that resembled the fox-fur lining of a nobleman's coat. The old houses, worn smooth by the winds of innumerable days, played tricks with the reflections of the atmosphere, with echoes and memories of colors scattered in the depth of the cloudless sky.[44]

Schulz, like Roth, represented Galicia as a postimpressionist ensemble of color and light, of echoes and memories, of rustlings and reflections. Such was the surreal setting for his semimythological characters. The old houses of Market Square still haunted Schulz as he wrote in the 1930s, reflecting the light of Galician history from his childhood in the 1890s. Those houses preserved the echoes and memories from still earlier generations, perhaps from the 1860s, when Ivan Franko came to Drohobych as a child to go to school.

Roth, in *The Emperor's Tomb*, had a Galician Jew propose to some Viennese acquaintances a voyage to the Galician town of Zlotogrod, the town of gold [*złoto*]:

> Gradually this journey became for us a passion, even an obsession. We thus began, quite deliberately, to paint ourselves a picture of little, distant Zlotogrod, but in such a way that even as we described Zlotogrod, we were convinced that we were painting an entirely false portrait of it, yet could not stop picturing this place which none of us knew. In other words we furnished it with all sorts of characteristics which we knew from the start were deliberate creations of our own fantasy. . . . We talked so urgently of Zlotogrod, at such length and with such intensity, that I was gripped by fear that the town would one day suddenly disappear, or that my friends might begin to think that Zlotogrod had become unreal and no longer existed, that it was just a tale I had told.[45]

Indeed, the invented town of Zlotogrod was just a tale told by Joseph Roth, and the fictional visit, finally consummated in the summer of 1914, coincided with the eruption of World War I, which led to the destruction of the fictional town.

In Agnon's *Guest for the Night* a visitor returned to his Galician hometown in the aftermath of the war, as witness to the physical and personal ruins of Habsburg Galicia. Agnon's hometown of Buchach (or Buczacz) was renamed Szibucz, and announced at the train station by a man who had lost his left arm in the war:

> "Szibucz!" It was many years since I had heard the name of Szibucz coming from the lips of a man of my town. Only he who is born there and bred there and lives there knows how to pronounce every single letter of that name.[46]

Of course, the pronunciation and orthography—which would once have varied among the Polish, Ruthenian, and Jewish populations of Buczacz/Szibucz—was rendered in Hebrew letters by Agnon in his novel, published in Jerusalem. The narrator encountered a character in Szibucz who reminded him of his grandmother, and who was called by the mocking nickname, Kaiserin, the Empress.

> "Why should I be offended?" asked she. "Everyone calls me the Kaiserin and I am not ashamed. But tell me yourself, sir, am I really a Kaiserin? Woe is me, may all the enemies of Israel have a life like mine. Now that the Kaiser is no longer Kaiser, what does it matter?"[47]

Thus the Galician Jews continued to live in a parodic, remembered relation to the Habsburg past, even when Galicia itself was no longer Galicia. Schulz's Drohobych, Roth's Zlotogrod, Agnon's Szibucz, all served as mythological sites in the literary remembering of Galicia in the 1930s.

When Roth's narrator arrived in Zlotogrod in 1914 he paused at the Café Habsburg, in the Hotel of the Golden Bear, and took note of "a confidence-inspiring cashier, blonde and buxom as only cashiers used to be when I was young, an honest form of the latter-day Goddess of Depravity."[48] Billy Wilder, born a Galician Jew in the town of Sucha in the Carpathians in 1906, twelve years younger than Joseph Roth, also made his way to Vienna and Berlin, but then ended up in Hollywood in the 1930s. He wrote such masterpieces as *Ninotchka* for Greta Garbo and *Ball of Fire* for Barbara Stanwyck, then directed *Double Indemnity* for Stanwyck and *Sunset Boulevard* for Gloria Swanson. Perhaps his greatest film, however, was the comedy *Some Like It Hot* in 1959, with its sublime blonde goddess of innocent depravity, transposed from the Café Habsburg to the Café Hollywood. It was the Galician Billy Wilder whose fantasy made Marilyn Monroe into a Polish goddess, Sugar Kane Kowalczyk, the girl who always ends up with the fuzzy end of the lollipop. Kowalczyk! "Only he who is born there and bred there and lives there knows how to pronounce every single letter of that name."

FORMER GALICIANS: "PHANTOMOLOGY"

When Billy Wilder died in Beverly Hills in 2002, at the age of ninety-five, Galicia had been gone for more than eight decades. The *New York Times* obituary tried to sum up his remote origins, under the heading "Roots in Mitteleuropa," but "Mitteleuropa" required some further explication:

> Billy Wilder was born Samuel Wilder on June 22, 1906, in Sucha, a village in Galicia, an Austro-Hungarian province that is now part of Poland. His father was Max Wilder, who ran a railway cafe, and his mother was the former Eugenia Baldinger, whose family owned a resort hotel. Recalling his childhood in a big hotel, he remarked, "I learned many things about human nature—none of them favorable."[49]

This was a family background that could have come out of one of Joseph Roth's novels, featuring the Hotel of the Golden Bear, but Galicia itself had to be explained (incorrectly) as being "now part of Poland"—though half of it was part of Ukraine in 2002.

In fact, Billy Wilder's Galician origins were worth noting in the *New York Times*, inasmuch as Galician identity survived for decades beyond the existence of the Austro-Hungarian province among the communities of Galician Jews who immigrated to America, and especially to New York City. Around the time of Wilder's birth at the beginning of the twentieth century there were more than 800,000 Jews in Galicia, and almost 900,000 on the eve of World War I, but their numbers were constantly being depleted by emigration. They left Galicia for other Habsburg lands, emigrated to the German Empire, and, above all, they came to America. It has been estimated that 380,000 Jews came to America from the Habsburg monarchy between 1881 and 1914, mostly from Galicia.[50] This emigration continued after the war, until strict limitations were imposed by the U.S. Immigration Act of 1924. There were also, in America, hundreds of thousands of Polish and Ruthenian emigrants from Galicia, but the Jews most particularly found a Galician identity as the Galitzianers, the cultural counterparts, and sometimes adversaries, of the Litvaks, the Lithuanian Jews who emigrated from the Russian Empire. These two ethnographic types were articulated in conceptual opposition to each other, based on differing Yiddish pronunciations, religious perspectives, and domestic cultures. The Galitzianers were more comfortable with their fellow immigrants from Galicia: their language sounding more like German, their religious practice less strictly rabbinical and Orthodox than the Lithuanians, their cuisine closer to that of Central Europe. The Galitzianer would caricature his Litvak neighbor in the New World as a man "with a herring in one hand and a prayer book in the other."

Although differences between these two huge populations of the Jews of Eastern Europe were also noted in the Old World—as for instance at the Yiddish Language Congress in Czernowitz in 1908—it was in America that the Galitzianer and the Litvak ended up living side by side, becoming conscious of their cultural difference, far more than when they lived remote from each other in Galicia and Lithuania. Historian Daniel Soyer has noted this encounter in his book on Jewish immigrant associations in New York, citing a journalist's report from 1906:

> Jews from all over Eastern Europe met in New York. Though they shared the same culture, spoke the same language, and appeared to outsiders to be a homogenous group, they sometimes seemed very different to one another. . . . When asked by a journalist what she thought of her Russian-Jewish neighbors, one Galician woman responded: "A strange sort of people. You can't understand a word they say. They always shout and talk with their hands. . . . And their cooking! Dishes which one should never even see in a Jewish house! They put sugar in everything and call everything by the wrong name."[51]

The name that the Russian Jews called their Austrian Jewish neighbors was "Galitzianer," and though it was intended negatively to stigmatize, the Galicians were able to appropriate it as a term of identity for themselves. Their Galician hometown associations—*Landsmanshaftn*—were mocked in a spirit of parody by their neighbors for overweening Austrian presumption: First Lemberger Gentlemen's and Ladies' Support and Sick and Death Benefit Society under the Patronage of the Godly Late Austrian Empress Elisabeth.[52]

Back in 1903, the same year that Bertha Pappenheim was visiting Galicia

and reporting on the miserable condition of Galician Jews, there were disastrous summer fires in Galician towns that attracted the attention of the
Galitzianer emigrants far away in New York. As they tried to organize aid to
their native Jewish communities, the New Yorkers banded together in 1904 to
form a united federation of Jews from Galicia and Bukovina. The members
were overwhelmingly from Galicia, rather than Bukovina, and the organization proceeded to open a Galician hospital in New York in 1908. Bringing
together the many hometown associations, the broader Galician federation
had the stated purpose "to support the members of the societies in times
of need, to help unfortunate towns in Galicia and Bukovina, and in general
to protect the interests of the tens of thousands of Austrian Jews in this
country."[53] In 1912 the Viennese Jewish leader Joseph Bloch came to New
York as the guest of the United Galician Jewish Societies, and was described
in the *New York Times* as "the Moses of Galician Jews." In his Mosaic role,
Bloch sought to assist Jewish emigration out of Galicia and into America,
while encouraging emigrants to consider other American destinations besides New York City, where Galicians were already very well established.
Such Viennese sponsorship of Galician emigration was complemented by
Bloch's proposal for a special bank to safeguard the money that American
Jews sent back across the ocean to their Galician families: "Millions of dollars, according to Dr. Bloch, which are sent unregistered by immigrants to
poor relatives in Galicia alone, are stolen by postal officials there, it having
come to such a pass that nearly all letters received in the small towns there
from America are suspected of containing money and as such are opened and
looted."[54] Bloch thus sought to encourage both emigration and remittance
for the benefit of Galicia, while the *Times* emphasized the circumstances of
Galician poverty and the sense of identity that connected the immigrants to
their Galician homeland. Galician Jewish identity in America was forged in
solidarity with fellow Galician Jewish immigrants, and also, at the same time,
with the Galician Jews who remained behind in Galicia.

While Galician Jews in New York recognized the poverty and need of
those in Galicia, they also felt embattled in their own right on the emigrant turf of New York City. In a letter to the advice column—"A Bintel
Brief"—of the *Forward*, the Yiddish newspaper of New York, a Galician gar-
ment worker claimed that the Russian Jews regarded Galicians as "inhuman
savages."[55] Galitzianer identity was further consolidated during World War
I, as Galician Jewish immigrants in America tried to send aid to their native
province, ravaged by war and pogroms. They were also aware that the future
of Galicia was uncertain, and someone commented in August 1914 that "the
new sign which the Galician Federation recently made for its office reads only

'Federation Office,' because no one knows in whose hands Galicia will fall, and what name the 'Federation' will have to take."[56] Implicitly aware of the geopolitical contingency of Galicia's historical existence, the Galician Jewish immigrant community nevertheless discovered its identity as Galitzianer, and preserved that identity in America for a whole generation after Galicia itself disappeared from the map of Europe. In 1923 the Yiddish film "East and West," made in Vienna, represented a family of Galician New Yorkers, including the famous Yiddish theater comedienne Molly Picon, returning to their hometown in Galicia for a traditional family wedding, the occasion for the encounter between East and West.[57]

In 1927, almost a decade after Galicia ceased to exist, the *Jewish Lexicon* (*Jüdisches Lexikon*), which appeared in Berlin, included an article on Galicia that confidently, and anachronistically, insisted that Galician Jews already formed a coherent community in the eighteenth-century age of the Polish partitions: "The Galician Jews then formed, by their distinctiveness of language and ritual, as well as their characteristic way of life, a closed world unto itself [*in sich geschlossene Welt*]."[58] The lexicon included old drawings of "Jewish Types from Galicia" and more recent photographs to suggest typical costumes and aspects. In fact, the "world unto itself" of ethnographic and anthropological coherence among Galician Jews had developed along with the history of Galicia itself, over the course of the nineteenth century, but it still remained culturally meaningful after Galicia's abolition in the twentieth century.

While the memory of Galicia was cultivated in literature, lexicons, and cinema, from New York to Drohobych to Jerusalem, the territory of Galicia was geopolitically absorbed and administratively integrated into the postwar Polish republic. Galicia had been consumed in its entirety by Poland after World War I, but with the conclusion of the Molotov-Ribbentrop Pact in 1939, just before the outbreak of World War II, Stalin and Hitler agreed to divide Poland between them and mapped out the division of the former Galicia. With the invasion of Poland by Hitler on 1 September, and the corollary invasion by Stalin on 17 September, Galicia was effectively partitioned between the Soviet Socialist Republic of Ukraine and the General Government of Nazi-occupied Poland. The boundary lay at the River San, roughly where it was first proposed by the Ruthenian Council to divide Galicia in 1848, and, furthermore, where the border of Poland and Ukraine still stands today. Galicia, abolished in 1918, was demolished in 1939, and just as its invention dated back to the partition of Poland in 1772, so its demolition in 1939 came about through a new partition of Poland.

In February 1939, more than thirty years after he assassinated Potocki in Lviv, Miroslav Sichynsky, now based in Scranton, Pennsylvania, and representing the "Ukrainian Defense Association," wrote a letter to the *Washington Post*. He affirmed Ukrainian national aspirations by remembering Galicia: "The Ukrainians of Galicia, who were governed by Polish landlords and their officials in spite of the allegiance of that rich wheat, oil, and timber-producing land to Austria, claimed the right to govern themselves since the Austrian revolution of 1848." This Austrian and Galician history of the Ukrainians also indicated that "the Ukrainians are more freedom-loving than the Russians and of an entirely different political tradition." In September, after the war had begun, Sichynsky wrote to the *Post* again, this time on behalf of the "Ukrainian Workingmen's Association," to refute the insinuation that Ukrainians welcomed the Nazi attack on Poland, and again to denounce the Poles by recalling the history of Galicia: "Very little has been written in English about the history of Polish administration of eastern Galicia before 1914 and about the government of Ukrainian provinces forcibly annexed by Poland after the Great War, when Woodrow Wilson's ideal of Polish democracy was betrayed."[59] Sichynsky did not mention his own dramatic role in that history as the assassin of the viceroy of Galicia.

In September 1939, left-leaning Polish writers preferred to take refuge in Stalin's Lviv, rather than wait to find out what Hitler had in store for occupied Poland. This was the moment when Boy, who had left Cracow for Warsaw after World War I, returned to Lviv and Galicia for what would prove to be the final years of his life. Historian Marci Shore has described the pathos of Boy in Lviv, suddenly confronted by the Soviet authorities with the demand that he put his signature to a writers' resolution approving the annexation of eastern Galicia, as western Ukraine, by the Soviet Union. He was given fifteen minutes to make up his mind.[60]

The younger writer Aleksander Wat, born in Warsaw in 1900, also found refuge in Galicia in 1939, and was also required to sign the resolution. Wat was sensitive to the Habsburg character of Lviv, and claimed, in his memoirs, that he could immediately discern the deterioration of that character under Soviet influence:

> Did you know Lwów before the war? Lwów was one of the loveliest Polish cities in the sense that it was a merry city. Not so much the people, but the city itself. Very colorful, very exotic, it had none of the greyness of Warsaw, or even Cracow or Poznań. Its exoticism made it a very European city. Vienna, of course, had influenced Cracow, but its influence made Cracow an Austrian bureaucratic city, a city with an Austrian bureaucracy and an Austrian bureaucratic university. Lwów was a bit more like the Vienna of operetta, the Vienna of *joie de vivre*. . . . Well, the Soviets had barely arrived, and all at once everything was covered in mud (of course it was fall), dirty, gray, shabby. People began cringing and slinking down the streets.[61]

Wat stressed the lingering Viennese atmospheres of Lviv and Cracow before World War II, very different cities, but each in its way a little like Vienna, as a consequence of their shared Habsburg history in Galicia. According to Wat's impressions, the Molotov-Ribbentrop Pact not only decisively partitioned the former Galicia but also, with the advent of the Soviet occupation in Lviv, immediately liquidated the Galician spirit that had survived for more than two decades after the liquidation of Galicia.

Wat's memoirs were narrated on tape, in dialogue with Czesław Miłosz, in Berkeley in the 1960s, when Wat would ask, "Did you know Lwów before the war?" From the perspective of the 1960s, the decades before World War II still seemed retrospectively Galician, but when Polish refugees arrived in Lviv in 1939, Boy might have been asking, with an analogous historical implication, "Did you know Lwów before the war?" Boy would have meant World War I, and would have clearly remembered when Galicia actually existed. *Znaszli ten kraj?*

In 1940 Wat was arrested in Lviv by the Soviet authorities. By 1941 he was being held in the Lubyanka prison in Moscow, Stalin's chamber of horrors, but, strange to say, the Lubyanka was a relatively safer place for him to be than Lviv during that year; in June 1941 Hitler tore up the Molotov-Ribbentrop Pact, invaded the Soviet Union, and almost immediately took Lviv, where Wat, a Polish Jewish intellectual, would have certainly been targeted for death. The Nazi invasion of the Soviet Union had the incidental effect of reuniting Galicia for the last time—under hellish circumstances—within the General Government of occupied Poland, and the Nazis even revived the name of Galicia as an administrative unit, Distrikt Galizien, which covered the eastern part of Galicia seized from Stalin in 1941. In 1943, Distrikt Galizien became the site for the creation of SS Galizien, an SS division of Ukrainian soldiers under German command. SS Galizien fought against the Soviet army in 1944 in the region around Brody, precisely where the Russian Empire once bordered Habsburg Galicia. Hitler had been born a subject of Franz Joseph in Upper Austria in 1889, and, according to historian Dieter Pohl, in the Nazi discussions about administering Galicia, "the reestablishment of the former Austrian governmental domain was important for Hitler."[62] Galicia was a name that remained meaningful to him.

Pohl's research on the murder of the Jews in Galicia indicates that, with the outbreak of the Nazi-Soviet war, even before the arrival of the Nazi occupiers, pogroms against Jews broke out in eastern Galicia, perpetrated largely by Ukrainians in the name of revenge for supposed Jewish complicity in the Soviet occupation. Pohl concludes that "the background of the pogroms appears to have come from traditional Ukrainian-Jewish tensions"—that is, tensions dating back to the circumstances of Habsburg Galicia.[63] On the other hand, Andrei Sheptytsky, the Uniate metropolitan of Galicia ever since 1901, nominated by Franz Joseph, made use of his power, his influence, and his residence to hide and shelter Jews from the Nazis during World War II. The national tensions that survived from Habsburg times were, in any event, radically superseded by the genocidal aims of the Nazis, who, in 1941, immediately began to carry out the mass murder of the Jews of eastern Galicia, and eventually killed almost all the Galician Jews as part of Hitler's Final Solution. Bruno Schulz, who was briefly protected in Drohobych by a Gestapo officer who admired his artwork, was murdered in the streets of his town by another Nazi in 1942. At the end of the war, the town of Oświęcim, located in the western part of the former Galicia, would become very well known to the world under its German name of Auschwitz. The long list of Habsburg titles had represented the emperors not only as kings of Galicia and Lodomeria but also—in a strained attempt to cover the territory of Galicia with legitimate titles—as dukes of Auschwitz.

The end of the war brought about the restoration of the Molotov-Ribbentrop division of Galicia, now between Soviet Ukraine and communist Poland, both halves behind the Iron Curtain, and both regimes oblivious, or even hostile, to the name and legacy of Galicia. Sheptytsky, the last Uniate metropolitan of Galicia, died in 1944, and in 1946, Stalin suppressed altogether the Uniate Church—once the foundation of Ruthenian identity within the Habsburg monarchy—and imposed "reunification" with the Orthodox Church. During these same years, at the end of the war, the massive transfer of populations that reshaped the demography of Central Europe also completely transformed the demographic face of the former Galicia. Some 800,000 Poles were moved from Soviet Ukraine, mostly from the former Galicia, and more than 100,000 from Lviv alone.[64] At the same time the government of communist Poland undertook its Operation Vistula, the violent forcible resettlement of more than 100,000 Ukrainians, to be scattered around Poland and thus isolated from Ukrainian national resistance to the government. Poles from eastern Galicia, as well as Ukrainians from western Galicia, were most frequently resettled in Poland's new western territories, especially Silesia, which had been left demographically vacant by the forcible deportation of its German population. Whole communities moved from Galicia to Silesia, and even a new Ossolineum library was established in Wrocław with the transfer from Lviv of a portion of the library's famous Galician collection.

Back in eastern Galicia, now western Ukraine, the Ukrainian Insurgent Army (UPA) fought a guerrilla war against the Soviet government until

1947, with some resistance continuing into the 1950s. The Galician legacy of Ukrainian nationalism, once nourished in Habsburg Lviv by Hrushevsky, then intensified in the adversity of interwar Polish rule, now strengthened the nationalist cause in Soviet Ukraine. According to Ivan Rudnytsky, "The emergence of a vocal national dissidence in the Ukrainian SSR in the course of the 1960s is difficult to account for without taking into consideration the Western Ukrainian factor." Professor Roman Szporluk, who held Harvard's Mykhailo Hrushevsky Chair of Ukrainian History, suggested that "the inclusion of West Ukraine into the Soviet body politic may have been one of Stalin's most fateful decisions"—fateful because the former Galicians proved ultimately indigestible and would contribute to the eventual demise of the Soviet Union itself.[65]

After World War II—after the murder of the Galician Jews, after the division of Galicia's territories between Poland and Soviet Ukraine, after the transfer and resettlement of Polish and Ukrainian populations—Galicia no longer existed either as an ethnographic or a geographic entity in any relation to its former Habsburg form and complexion. Western Galicia and Eastern Galicia, now Southern Poland and Western Ukraine, faced each other as relatively compact Polish and Ukrainian population blocs. The Jews of Galicia were all dead and gone. Habsburg Lviv was, before World War I, 50 percent Polish, 27 percent Jewish, and 20 percent Ruthenian. After World War II, the population of Soviet Lviv was 60 percent Ukrainian, 27 percent Russian, 4 percent Polish, and 4 percent Jewish.[66] "Did you know Lwów before the war?" asked Wat in Berkeley in the 1960s. He himself could probably not have imagined how much the city had been transformed. Galicia seemed finally to have ceased to exist, to have altogether lost its former geopolitical character and identity. In 1948, after the demolition of Galicia, the Yiddish comedian Leo Fuchs (born in Warsaw, and therefore not Galician) had a Yiddish theater hit in London with the show *Galitzianer Cowboy*, just for laughs.

Meanwhile, former Galicians—such as Billy Wilder in Hollywood—still played a part on the world stage, often unrecognized as Galicians. In 1960, the year that Wilder (born in Sucha in 1906) won the Academy Award for *The Apartment*, Simon Wiesenthal (born in Buchach in 1908) was making his contribution to the capture of Adolf Eichmann in Buenos Aires, with Wiesenthal on the way to becoming the world's most famous Nazi-hunter. Salo Baron (born in Tarnów in 1895) appeared as a witness for the prosecution at Eichmann's Jerusalem trial in 1961, testifying as perhaps the world's foremost scholar of Jewish history, professor at Columbia University and author of the monumental, multivolume *Social and Religious History of the Jews*. Hannah Arendt, herself a German Jew, reported from Jerusalem on the

Eichmann trial: "On top, the judges, the best of German Jewry. Below them, the prosecuting attorneys, Galicians, but still Europeans. . . . And outside the doors, the Oriental mob, as if one were in Istanbul or some other half-Asiatic country."[67] In Israel in 1961, as once upon a time in the Habsburg monarchy, Galicia was still conceived as the barely European frontier of *Halb-Asien*.

In 1961, Stanisław Lem (born in Lviv in 1921) published in Poland his most famous science fiction novel, *Solaris*. In 1964, Lem published a philosophical work, *Summa Technologiae*, that discussed "phantomology [*fantomologia*]," his term for virtual reality; in that same year, Lem's post-Galician contemporary Karol Wotyła (born in Wadowice in 1920) became archbishop of Cracow. Martin Buber (born in Vienna in 1878, raised in Lviv in the 1880s), religious philosopher and collector of Hasidic tales, died in Jerusalem in 1965, one year before Agnon (born in Buchach in 1888, living in Jerusalem in the 1960s) won the Nobel Prize in literature in 1966.

There were some small tokens of Galician reconciliation during the Cold War. Anthropologist Christopher Hann has noted that, with the passing of Stalin and Stalinism in the 1950s, Ukrainians in Poland were able to worship according to the Uniate rite in Przemyśl, making use of the Jesuit Church.[68] By the 1980s, in the age of Gorbachev and glasnost in the Soviet Union, some Ukrainians in Lviv were demonstratively attending to Polish graves in the Lychakivsky cemetery. Historian Padraic Kenney has noted the conciliatory role of the Lion Society in Lviv in the 1980s, and quotes activist Iurii Voloshchak at a public meeting:

> Today in the city I met some girls from Poland. I told them about how the Lion Society is taking care of the graves of Polish cultural figures in the Lychakivsky cemetery here in Lviv. I asked that they do the same for the neglected graves of well-known Ukrainian cultural figures in Cracow or Przemyśl.[69]

This vision reached across the former Galicia, from Lviv to Cracow, just as the Lychakivsky cemetery itself summed up the history of the province with its complex and conflicting legacies. Ivan Franko was buried there, as was Seweryn Goszczyński, the Polish critic who denounced Fredro in 1835 for being a "non-national" writer. Stanisław Szczepanowski, the Polish author of the *Misery of Galicia* was laid to rest in the same cemetery, as was Salomea Krusceniski, the Ruthenian opera singer who glamorously sang *Salome* with Toscanini at La Scala. The ghosts of Galician history were waiting there in the cemetery, through the twentieth century, for anyone who dared, or cared, to confront them.

In 1985 the Polish poet Adam Zagajewski, then living in Paris, published in London a poetry collection under the title *To Go to Lwów* (*Jechać do Lwowa*), and the title poem soon become his most celebrated work. Zagajewski was born in Lviv in 1945—the last historical moment when a Polish poet could have been born in Lviv—and, together with his family, was subject to the transfer of populations during his earliest childhood. He grew up in Silesia in a community of transplanted Galicians, and his poem about Lviv gave voice to the potent fantasy of Galicia that was nourished among the emigrants as they lived through the grim decades of postwar communist Poland. These Silesian Galicians were cut off from the world of their own early lives and the lives of their parents and grandparents, of whole Galician generations left behind in the untended Lviv cemetery. The poem was dedicated to Zagajewski's parents.

> To go to Lwów. Which station
> for Lwów, if not in a dream . . .[70]

The poet hesitated: "If Lwów exists . . . " [*Jeżeli Lwów istnieje* . . .]. For the emigrants in Silesia, it became difficult to believe in the real existence of the city, which they preserved in memories, dreams, fantasies: a phantom city, just like Galicia the phantom province, which really did not exist in the 1980s. Lwów and Galicia appeared all the more fantastic to the poet who had heard about them only as part of his family's history; he had been taken from Lwów too young to be able to remember anything at all.[71] Which station for Lwów? Even the Habsburg line—finally completed in 1861 after decades of planning and lobbying—had been drastically disrupted by the alteration of the railroad tracks at the Soviet border. Galicia was gone, and Lwów—especially under its Polish name—had become so remote that a poet might even doubt its existence.

Literary critic George Grabowicz has written about Zagajewski's work in the context of "Mythologizing Lviv/Lwów."[72] Zagajewski conjured the landmarks of the almost mythological city: the towering cathedral, the ghost of Fredro. Like Schulz's Drohobych, like Roth's Zlotogrod, so Zagajewski's Lwów in the 1980s was a legend, full of life in the poet's imagination: "There was always too much of Lwów. . . ." Born in 1945, he could only conjure the city in the poetic spirit of fantasy and nostalgia, the nostalgia for a place he had never known. He had been part of the great exodus, the transfer of populations, a babe in arms, but he could not remember, only imagine:

> and the cathedral trembled, people bade goodbye
> without handkerchiefs, no tears, such a dry
> mouth, I won't see you anymore, so much death
> awaits you, why must every city
> become Jerusalem and every man a Jew,
> and now in a hurry just
> pack, always, each day,

and go breathless, go to Lwów, after all
it exists, quiet and pure as
a peach. It is everywhere.[73]

The peach, entirely perfect in the imagination, could be consumed only in fantasy, which still left the fruit as perfect as before. The Jews of Lviv had been murdered during the war, the Poles deported only after the war. In Zagajewski's poetic conceit Lviv became the city of exodus, the city of destroyed temples, the city of messianic anticipation and longing: the peach, Jerusalem. Zagajewski's poetic conjuring of Lviv in the 1980s occurred, ironically, as history was about to take another breathlessly lurching turn, as Poland and Ukraine, Cracow and Lviv, were about to receive a rush of new life at the end of the twentieth century. Even Galicia itself, haunting the region like a phantom, would emerge from the realm of privately cherished emigrant fantasy into the public sphere of historical reckoning with the past and future of Central Europe.

Mythology and Nostalgia: "A Matter of Simple Relativity"

The end of communism in Poland in 1989, and the emergence of independent Ukraine in 1991 with the collapse of the Soviet Union, encouraged new ways of thinking about the character and construction of Europe. During the Cold War it was entirely conventional to describe the continent as divided politically between Eastern Europe and Western Europe. Already in the 1980s there had emerged a discussion about Central Europe which somewhat subverted the Cold War paradigm by insisting, in the famous phrase of Milan Kundera, that Central Europe had been "kidnapped" by Stalin and forcibly alienated from its true home within Western civilization. The Habsburg legacy was a crucial part of what defined Central Europe, and after 1991, with the re-emergence of free intellectual life in Lviv and the amazing resurgence of the previously suppressed Uniate Church, it was possible to rediscover the most thoroughly abducted and forgotten corner of the former Habsburg monarchy, eastern Galicia, hidden away for decades in Soviet Ukraine.[74] Now suddenly, after 1991, portraits of the Emperor Franz Joseph appeared in the cafés of Lviv, a reminder that this city had been intimately connected to Vienna—not to Moscow, or even Kiev—for 150 years, from 1772 to 1918, the historical duration of Galicia. The website of the Viennese Café in Lviv notes that the café was established in 1829, and "hasn't lost its authentic Austrian atmosphere, Polish charm, or Ukrainian hospitality."[75]

That combination of cultural elements could only be Galician, and, founded in 1829, the café was actually one year older than Franz Joseph himself.

Luiza Bialasiewicz has written about the nostalgic rediscovery of the myth of "Galicia Felix" in Poland after 1989, when the end of communism encouraged the search for more appealing historical legacies. Delphine Bechtel has also written about "the myth of Galicia" and its "resurrection" in the 1990s. Dietlind Hüchtker has further analyzed the literary construction of the Galicia myth (*Mythos Galizien*) in relation to the multicultural society of the province. Lidia Stefanowska has written about the Galician "discourse of nostalgia" in the 1990s. According to Bialasiewicz, Galicia was idealized as a land of imperial political benevolence, economically and culturally integral to Central Europe. The fierce national tensions of Galicia were effaced in historical memory and rewritten as a triumph of multicultural coexistence.

> Galicia was born of myth, and from myth it would rise again. When new myths were so sorely needed, in the years after 1989, Galicia Felix proved particularly attractive. The re-materialization of Galicia first became apparent in the early 1990s through the sudden proliferation of its name. Shops, restaurants, and bars in the principal towns of the province (at least those on the much more prosperous Polish side of the border) carried the name Galicia. Evocations of Galicia and the Habsburg past were used in promoting a variety of new consumer goods. There was mineral water from Przemyśl called *Galicja*, blessed by the emperor's smile.[76]

Bialasiewicz notes that the picture of Emperor Franz Joseph could be found in bars, restaurants, and coffee houses of the former Galicia in postcommunist Poland, and that was also true for the less prosperous establishments of Lviv in postcommunist Ukraine.[77]

Even more striking was the fact that Galicia seemed to possess its own political character in the 1990s, in both Poland and Ukraine. It was statistically notable in the Polish elections of the 1990s that voters from the former Galicia were more likely to support the Solidarity parties of the center-right. After the election of the former communist Aleksander Kwaśniewksi to the presidency in 1995, there was a theatrical Cracovian protest that involved setting up border crossing stations where the borders of Galicia had been in the nineteenth century, as if to declare independence from Warsaw: "a cordon sanitaire separating us from the barbarians." One of the protesters commented that it was "finally time to admit that the people who live here [Galicia] are different, have different traditions, a different way of thinking."[78] At the same time, there was a notable political difference between Western Ukraine—the former Galicia—and Eastern Ukraine, with its former Russian imperial associations. In the 1990s the Galician region around Lviv was measurably more committed to Ukrainian national ideals and post-Soviet transformation, while the eastern part of the country was more inclined to preserve Soviet political culture and solidarity with Russia.[79] Michael Moser has studied "anti-Galician" postings on the internet, analyzing the hostile perception that there is a Galician language distinct from Ukrainian: characterized, for instance, as "this Polish-German-Yiddish Galician dialect." Roman Szporluk, looking back into Galician Ukrainian history, has posed the question, "Ukraine—One Nation or Two?" Why had the Galician Ruthenians not become a distinctive Galician nation?[80] This sense of historical difference would crystallize around the opposing camps in the Orange Revolution of 2004, when Viktor Yushchenko received overwhelming support from western Ukraine, and the incumbent Viktor Yanukovych drew upon electoral support (and probably electoral fraud) from eastern Ukraine.

In 1998 a publisher in Zakopane undertook the unusual venture of republishing the last Polish-language *Illustrated Guide to Galicia* (*Ilustrowany Przewodnik po Galicji*), originally published in Lviv in 1914, with Europe on the brink of war. The original guidebook was created by Mieczysław Orłowicz, the president of the Academic Tourist Club in Lviv, and had been dedicated to "Polish youth who want to go touring in their own country [*zwiedzić swój kraj*]." Republished in 1998, eighty years after that country had been politically liquidated in 1918, the guidebook, complete with the original photographs and advertisements, served as an invitation to postcommunist Poles to enter into a realm of history, of nostalgia, of mythology, that was, at the same time, the geographical space in which they actually lived. For young Poles of the 1990s, "Galicia" was as much the remote "world of our fathers," or rather grandfathers, as it was for American Jews on the other side of the Atlantic Ocean. The republished guidebook preserved the multinational diversity of the province, meticulously recorded. Bruno Schulz's Drohobych, a Ukrainian city in the 1990s, still appeared in the guidebook with a population of 12,000 Poles, 7,500 Ruthenians, and 15,500 Jews, as in 1914, before the murder of the Jews and the departure of the Poles. The illustrated sight to see was the Uniate Church of St. George, "the most beautiful wooden church of Galicia." Salo Baron's Tarnów, a Polish city in the 1990s, was presented in the guidebook as a town of 37,000, including 15,000 Jews—with its Gothic town hall, its monument to native son Józef Szujski, and its ultramodern electric streetcars.[81] In the guidebook the multinational Galicia of the Habsburg era was conjured into existence once again, half a century after the Nazis murdered the Galician Jews, half a century after the transfer of populations separated Poles and Ukrainians in the postwar political settlement.

The Jews of Cracow were most vividly remembered with the making of Steven Spielberg's film *Schindler's List* in 1993, and the somewhat deso-

late former Jewish quarter of Kazimierz underwent a decade of resurgence
and renovation in the aftermath of the film's success; the Galician legacy
was evoked as a tourist phenomenon with restored synagogues, kosher restaurants, klezmer bands—and even trendy nightclubs for Polish youth. In
Kazimierz, Galician nostalgia was adapted to urban renewal and modern
tourism such as to make a mark on the guidebooks of the 1990s, not just the
republished Galician guidebook of 1914.

In 1998, in Cracow, there appeared a work entitled *Austrian Chatter or
Galician Encyclopedia*. As if parodying the encyclopedia project of Antoni
Schneider from the 1870s, *Austrian Chatter* consisted of just one single vol-
ume, mixing equal measures of kitsch and history, and published on the
assumption that Galician nostalgia was sufficiently developed to create a
reading public for such a work in 1998. The back of the book jacket showed
Franz Joseph dressed in "Krakowiak" peasant folk costume, and the intro-
duction noted that "Austrians are often surprised at our weakness for Franz
Joseph."[82] The loyalist Habsburg nostalgia began with A for Audience (with
Franz Joseph, of course), and B for Beau Rivage (the hotel in Geneva where
Elisabeth stayed just before her assassination, a place of "pilgrimage" for
Galicians), C for the Café Habsburg ("the most elegant café in Przemyśl"),
D for Demonstrations at train stations (cheering for Franz Joseph), E for
Elisabeth herself, and F for Franz (Franciszek Dobry, Franz the Good), and
of course Franz Joseph. Eventually one arrives at Z for Złote Runo (the
Golden Fleece, the ultimate Habsburg decoration) and for Empress Zita, the
wife of the last Habsburg emperor, Karl. A more scholarly Galician project
is the multivolume series *Galicia and Its Legacy* (*Galicja i jej dziedzictwo*), whose
first volume appeared in Rzeszów in 1994.[83]

In Austria and Germany there was also growing interest in Galicia, and
already in 1984, around the time of Kundera's affirmation of Central Europe, Martin Pollack published in Vienna a book about Galicia, billed as
"a voyage through the vanished world of East Galicia and the Bukovina."
The book was republished in 1994, and then again in 2001, with a prefatory
remark in the spirit of Goethe's *Kennst du das Land?* to formulate the mystery
of the subject: "Who today still knows Galicia? Who still knows where it
lies—or rather where it lay? For Galicia no longer exists. It has disappeared
from the map."[84] Yet, as Pollack's multiple editions demonstrated, it had not
disappeared from the minds, memories, and fantasies of the Austrian and
German public in the late twentieth century. Omer Bartov, writing about
post-Soviet Ukraine, has observed the reciprocal process of collective forgetting in his travelogue account: *Erased: Vanishing Traces of Jewish Galicia in
Present-Day Ukraine*.[85]

In 1990 there was republished in Berlin, the reunited city, the 1786 edition of Franz Kratter's *Letters about the Present Situation of Galicia.*[86] The "present" moment of Galicia was obviously long past in 1990, but the revival of interest overflowed the borders of the former province and touched some larger public of Central Europe. In 1995 there appeared in Germany the posthumous memoirs of Soma Morgenstern, who died in New York in 1976, leaving behind his recollections, written in German, of his early life in eastern Galicia. The time had come again for Galicia in 1995, when there seemed to be a reading public for the long-gone Jewish life of Ternopil, where a young boy was thrilled to be taken to see Buffalo Bill's Wild West Circus, which had come all the way from America to the eastern frontier of Galicia. The writer Józef Wittlin published his Polish memoirs of Lviv (*Mój Lwów*) in New York in 1946; the German translation (*Mein Lemberg*) was published in 1994. Wittlin too remembered the Buffalo Bill Circus in Galicia in 1905, when he was nine, and recalled that it was as thrilling for him as a glimpse of the Emperor Franz Joseph.[87]

In Lviv in 2000 a group of self-proclaimed Galician Ukrainians ostentatiously celebrated the 170th birthday of Franz Joseph, whose birthday had indeed been marked in Galicia every August 18 throughout the seven decades of his reign. Yaroslav Hrytsak has observed that this group actually envisioned some sort of Galician autonomy within post-Soviet Ukraine.

> Lviv artist Volodymyr Kostyrko currently is probably the most outspoken Galician autonomist. He is best known as a cartoonist for the influential Ukrainian newspapers *Postup* and *Krytyka*. In one of his pictures, popularized in a mass-produced pocket calendar for the year 2000, Galicia is presented as a young woman—not unlike Joan of Arc perhaps—clad in shining armor. In her hand she holds the Ukrainian national flag, while at her feet lies a sleeping lion (symbol of Lviv). Encircling her image are the portraits of Galician historical heroes King Danylo and Stepan Bandera.[88]

Remarkably, at the beginning of the twenty-first century, Galicia was still being culturally invented and reinvented, constructed and reconstructed; after almost a century of phantom existence, Galicia was allegorized as a young woman, young again after her resurrection from the graveyard of history. In 2000, however, even while celebrating Franz Joseph's birthday, the Ukrainians revised the meaning of Galicia to make her less fundamentally a Habsburg heroine: King Danylo ruled over the Rus principality of Halych-Volhynia in the thirteenth century, while Stepan Bandera was a leader of the OUN during World War II. In another work of art, entitled "Galicia and Ukraine," Kostyrko provocatively allegorizes them both as naked men, with "Galicia" holding and guiding the penis of "Ukraine," thus taking the directing role in their intimate union.

The celebration of Franz Joseph's birthday in 2000 was accompanied by a petition for a monument to the emperor in Lviv. The petition proposed that "this monument should become a very special symbol, a testimony to our choosing Europe and to our will to coexist in the circle of free and independent nations of Central Europe." The writer Yuri Andrukhovych has emphasized Galicia's Habsburg relation to Central Europe, recalling the historical connection "not with Tambov and Tashkent, but with Venice and Vienna!" Political scientist and political officeholder Taras Batenko has observed that "the generation which is able to form its opinion of Austria only on the basis of proverbs and reprints feels a certain nostalgia for these good old days," and "this nostalgia is supported by the portrait of Franz Joseph."[89] Certainly, the 1990s was a decade of proverbs, reprints, and portraits in the former Galicia, and the historical connection to Franz Joseph was explicitly understood to signify a political relation to Central Europe and therefore to Europe more broadly. Poland, together with several other postcommunist countries of Central Europe, was admitted into NATO in 1999, and would be accepted into the European Union in 2004. Western Ukraine, which had once been so intimately bound to southern Poland, the two halves of the former Galician whole, would be left out in the post-Soviet cold, on the other side of the Schengen border that marked the boundary between Europe and not-Europe. The proposed monument to Franz Joseph might serve as a reminder that Lviv once lay within the border of his European empire, that he had personally visited Lviv on several occasions, as did the Buffalo Bill Circus. There were Lviv intellectuals who looked even more deeply into their Galician legacy and, controversially, advocated a monument to Leopold von Sacher-Masoch. It would have been a worthy European subject: to represent the masochist's bare back, cruelly lacerated by the whip of his beloved Wanda.

In 2004 the Orange Revolution illustrated the still meaningful divide between Galician West Ukraine and Soviet East Ukraine. Yet in 2004 the EU expansion, including Poland, excluding Ukraine, confirmed the ever more meaningful border between Ukrainian East Galicia and Polish West Galicia. In 2004, Pope John Paul II, born in Wadowice in 1920, two years after Galicia ceased to exist in 1918, presided over the beatification of the last Habsburg emperor, Karl, who abdicated in 1918, marking the end of Galicia and the Habsburg monarchy.

At the beginning of the twenty-first century the spirit of Galicia was elusive, illusory, mythological, contradictory, but very much alive. In 2001 a

German filmmaker was making a movie about Bruno Schulz, and traveled to Drohobych where Schulz spent his entire life, born in Habsburg Galicia in 1892, murdered in Nazi Galicia in 1942. The filmmaker made the remarkable discovery, in the pantry of an apartment, of some wall murals painted by Schulz for Felix Landau, the SS officer who protected and patronized Schulz after the Nazis conquered East Galicia in 1941. Schulz, though he published his brilliant stories before the war, actually supported himself as an art teacher in Drohobych and was himself a talented artist. The murals, which had been covered over for decades, were fairy tale scenes painted for the nursery of Landau's young children. The uncovering of the murals in 2001 came at a moment of general interest in Schulz as a cultural figure of the Galician legacy, revealed both figuratively and literally as a sort of pentimento, hidden behind the surfaces of contemporary Ukraine. In February the murals were discovered; in May they suddenly disappeared.[90]

It was soon revealed that the frescoes had been removed from the walls in Drohobych and transported to Jerusalem by representatives of the Yad Vashem Holocaust Museum, who had negotiated the removal with local Ukrainian authorities in Drohobych and paid the owners of the apartment a hundred dollars. Thus the removal was not unequivocally illegal, but for some who cared about Schulz, especially in Poland, the actions of Yad Vashem appeared as a sort of grand artistic theft, an absconding with national treasure, an illegitimate highjacking of the regional legacy. These murals were hardly the Elgin marbles, but their furtive transfer to Israel aroused considerable intellectual outrage—internationally, but especially in Poland. The Polish perspective on national literary custodianship was complicated by the fact that Drohobych—which belonged to Poland between the world wars—was a Ukrainian town in 2001, where Poles themselves were foreigners. The Ukrainian perspective—somewhat lesser outrage than that of the Poles, and indeed some degree of local complicity in the removal—was complicated by the fact that Schulz wrote his masterpieces in Polish and was therefore only tenuously a figure of Ukrainian literature and culture. The perspective of Yad Vashem was blunt and uncomplicated, though not unchallenged: Schulz was a Jew, and a victim of the Nazis, and therefore his legacy rightly belonged in Jerusalem at the Holocaust memorial museum, where it would, in any event, receive better curatorial care and better public exposure than in a provincial Ukrainian town.[91] The landscape of the region around Drohobych is marked by the debris of the defunct Galician oil industry, which was booming when Schulz was born in 1892.

Yad Vashem thus assumed custodianship over murals that Schulz had originally painted for the children of the Gestapo officer Felix Landau, himself a leading figure in the murder of Galician Jews. Landau's protection of Schulz indirectly brought about the writer's death in 1942, for, after Landau shot a Jewish dentist, it was a rival Gestapo officer who murdered Schulz during a Nazi "wild action"—supposedly exclaiming, "You killed my Jew—I killed yours."[92] Whose Jew was Schulz? Polish literature has claimed him for its own, and all the more intently since the removal of the frescoes from Drohobych in 2001. Ukrainian intellectuals in Lviv, considering a monument for Franz Joseph and perhaps even for Sacher-Masoch, also took an interest in Schulz, and regretted the carelessness (or venality) by which his legacy had slipped through the provincial fingers of Drohobych. Yad Vashem has claimed him in the name of the Holocaust, which brought about his death in 1942, but if he was anyone's Jew at the time of his birth in 1892 he was a subject of Emperor Franz Joseph. Schulz never forgot the liquidated world of Habsburg bureaucrats who had served Franz Joseph: "He standardized the servants of heaven, dressed them in symbolic blue uniforms, and let them loose upon the world, divided into ranks and divisions—angelic hordes in the shape of postmen, conductors, and tax collectors. The meanest of those heavenly messengers wore on his face a reflection of age-old wisdom borrowed from his Creator and a jovial, gracious smile framed by sideburns."[93] It was Franz Joseph whose image appeared on every coin, on every stamp of Schulz's childhood, Franz Joseph whose "prosaic reign" Schulz wrestled with when he discovered the revelation of poetry in a postage stamp album.

In Schulz's story "Sanatorium under the Sign of the Hourglass," the protagonist goes to visit his father at a very special sanatorium, a sanatorium for the dead who do not know that they are dead. The presiding doctor explains:

> None of our patients know it or can guess. The whole secret of the operation . . . is that we have put back the clock. Here we are always late by a certain interval of time of which we can not define the length. The whole thing is a matter of simple relativity. Here your father's death, the death that has already struck him in your country, has not occurred yet.[94]

This was a realm of indeterminate existence that must have been very familiar to the inhabitants of the former Galicia, where the relativity of time allowed for the intermingling of identities. "I am a public employee," wrote Schulz, "an Austrian, a Jew, a Pole—all in the space of an afternoon."[95] He even lived for two years, between 1939 and 1941, under Stalin's rule in Soviet Ukraine, without ever leaving Drohobych, and the Soviet literary journal in Lviv rejected one of Schulz's stories with the comment, "We don't need any more Prousts."[96] The crisis over the removal of the murals in 2001 elicited a cacophony of claims to Schulz and his legacy: Polish, Jewish, Ukrainian,

Austrian. To reconcile these competing claims and assorted identities one must follow them back to their point of origin, the time and place of Schulz's birth in Habsburg Galicia as a subject of Franz Joseph. The fairy tale frescoes—a woman who might have been a queen, a coachman who might have been Schulz himself—testify to the now fading pigment, but the still abiding figment, of the once and future Galicia.

Notes

INTRODUCTION

Translations, unless otherwise specified in the notes, are by the author, Larry Wolff.

Place names are generally given either in their standard English forms—like Vienna, Cracow, and Lviv—or else in the spelling of their current political affiliations, Polish or transliterated Ukrainian. However, in quoted passages, Galician place names match the original language of the source material. For instance, when a Polish writer is being quoted, the city will be named as Lwów, and when the original source is German, the city will be Lemberg.

1. Benjamin Segel, "Zwei jüdische Volkssagen über Kaiser Franz Josef," *Zeitschrift für österreichische Volkskunde* 9 (1903): 124.

2. Isaac Babel, *1920 Diary*, in *The Complete Works of Isaac Babel*, ed. Nathalie Babel, trans. Peter Constantine (New York: W. W. Norton, 2002), p. 422, diary entry of 1 August 1920.

3. Benedict Anderson, *Imagined Communities: Reflections on the Origin and Spread of Nationalism* (1983; London: Verso, 1991), p. 53.

4. Edward Said, *Culture and Imperialism* (1993; New York: Vintage Books, 1994), pp. xi, 12.

5. Ostap Sereda, "From Church-Based to Cultural Nationalism: Early Ukrainophiles, Ritual-Purification Movement, and Emerging Cult of Taras Shevchenko in Austrian Eastern Galicia in the 1860s," *Canadian American Slavic Studies* 40, no. 1 (Spring 2006): 22–23; see also Krzysztof Zamorski, *Informator statystyczny do dziejów społeczno-gospodarczych Galicji: Ludność Galicji w latach 1857–1910* (Cracow: Uniwersytet Jagielloński, 1989), pp. 69–71.

6. *Korespondencja Józefa Maksymiliana Ossolińskiego*, ed. Władysława Jabłońska (Wrocław: Zakład Narodowy imienia Ossolińskich, 1975), p. 267, letter of Joseph Mauss, 29 December 1817.

7. Józef Szujski, *Die Polen und Ruthenen in Galizien* (Wien and Teschen: Verlag von Karl Prochaska, 1882); Andrzej Wierzbicki, "Józef Szujski," in *Nation and History: Polish Historians from the Enlightenment to the Second World War*, ed. Peter Brock, John Stanley, and Piotr Wróbel (Toronto: University of Toronto Press, 2006), pp. 85–100; Philip Pajakowski, "Michał Bobrzyński," in *Nation and History: Polish Historians from the Enlightenment to the Second World War*, pp. 141–64.

8. Stefan Kaczala [Kachala], *Polityka Polaków względem Rusi* (Lviv: Nakładem Autora, 1879), p. 14.

9. Jan Kozik, *The Ukrainian National Movement in Galicia, 1815–1849*, trans. Andrew Gorski and Lawrence Orton (Edmonton: Canadian Institute of Ukrainian Studies, 1986); Andrei Markovits and Frank Sysyn, eds., *Nationbuilding and the Politics of Nationalism: Essays on Austrian Galicia* (Cambridge: Harvard Ukrainian Research Institute, 1982); Larry Wolff, review of *The Ukrainian National Movement in Galicia 1815–1849* by Jan Kozik, in *Harvard Ukrainian Studies* 11 (June 1987).

10. John-Paul Himka, *Socialism in Galicia: The Emergence of Polish Social Democracy and Ukrainian Radicalism* (Cambridge: Harvard Ukrainian Research Institute, 1983); Himka, *Galician Villagers and the Ukrainian National Movement in the Nineteenth Century* (New York: St. Martin's Press, 1988); Himka, *Religion and Nationality in Western Ukraine: The Greek Catholic Church and Ruthenian National Movement in Galicia, 1867–1900* (Montreal: McGill-Queen's University Press, 1999); Paul Robert Magocsi, *Galicia: A Historical Survey and Bibliographic Guide* (Toronto: University of Toronto Press, 1983).

11. Maria Kłańska, *Daleko od Wiednia: Galicja w oczach pisarzy niemieckojęzycznych, 1772–1918* (Cracow: Towarzystwo Autorów i Wydawców Prac Naukowych UNIVERSITAS, 1991); *Polin: Studies in Polish Jewry*, Vol. 12, *Focusing on Galicia: Jews, Poles, and Ukrainians, 1772–1918*, ed. Israel Bartal and Antony Polonsky (London: Littman Library of Jewish Civilization, 1999); *Galicia: A Multicultured Land*, ed. Christopher Hann and Paul Robert Magocsi (Toronto: University of Toronto Press, 2005).

12. Keely Stauter-Halsted, *The Nation in the Village: The Genesis of Peasant National Identity in Austrian Poland, 1848–1914* (Ithaca, NY: Cornell University Press, 2001); Alison Fleig Frank, *Oil Empire: Visions of Prosperity in Austrian Galicia* (Cambridge: Harvard University Press, 2005); Daniel Unowsky, *The Pomp and Politics of Patriotism: Imperial Celebrations in Habsburg Austria, 1848–1916* (West Lafayette, IN: Purdue University Press, 2005); Daniel Mendelsohn, *The Lost: A Search for Six of Six Million* (New York: Harper Collins, 2006); Omer Bartov, *Erased: Vanishing Traces of Jewish Galicia in Present-Day Ukraine* (Princeton: Princeton University Press, 2007).

13. Jacek Purchla, ed. *Kraków i Lwów w cywilizacji europejskiej* (Cracow: Międzynarodowe Centrum Kultury, 2003); Yaroslav Hrytsak, *Prorok u svoii vitchyzni: Franko ta ioho spilnota 1856–1886* (Kiev: Krytyka, 2006); Christoph Augustynowicz and Andreas Kappeler, eds., *Die galizische Grenze 1772–1867: Kommunikation oder Isolation* (Vienna: LIT Verlag, 2007); Michael Moser, *"Ruthenische" (ukrainische) Sprach- und Vorstellungswelten in den galizischen Volksschullesebüchern der Jahre 1871 und 1872* (Vienna: LIT Verlag, 2007); Hans-Christian Maner, *Galizien: Eine Grenzregion im Kalkül der Donaumonarchie im 18. und 19. Jahrhundert* (Munich: Institut für deutsche Kultur und Geschichte Südosteuropas, 2007); Michael Stanislawski, *A Murder in Lemberg: Politics, Religion, and Violence in Modern Jewish History* (Princeton: Princeton University Press, 2007); Danuta Sosnowska, *Inna Galicja* (Warsaw: Elipsa, 2008); Markian Prokopovych, *Habsburg Lemberg: Architecture, Public Space, and Politics in the Galician Capital, 1772–1914* (West Lafayette, IN: Purdue University Press, 2009).

14. Julian Ursyn Niemcewicz, *Pamiętniki czasów moich* (Leipzig: F. A. Brockhaus, 1868), pp. 63–65.

15. Leopold von Sacher-Masoch, *Graf Donski: Eine galizische Geschichte: 1846*, 2nd ed. (Schaffhausen: Friedrich Hurter, 1864), pp. iii–iv.

16. Joseph Roth, *The Emperor's Tomb*, trans. John Hoare (London: Chatto and Windus, Hogarth Press, 1984), pp. 34–35.

1. Inventing Galicia

1. Alfred Ritter von Arneth, ed. *Maria Theresia und Joseph II: Ihre Correspondenz sammt Briefen Joseph's an seinen Bruder Leopold*, Band II (Vienna: Carl Gerold's Sohn, 1867), Joseph to Leopold, 23 July 1773, p. 12; some of the material in this chapter has appeared in an article: Larry Wolff, "Inventing Galicia: Messianic Josephinism and the Recasting of Partitioned Poland," *Slavic Review* 63, no. 4 (Winter 2004): 818–40.

2. Stanisław Grodziski, *Historia ustroju społeczno-politycznego Galicji, 1772–1848* (Wrocław: Zakład Narodowy imienia Ossolińskich, 1971); Horst Glassl, *Das Österreichische Einrichtungswerk in Galizien, 1772–1790* (Wiesbaden: Otto Harrassowitz, 1975); Roman Rosdolsky, *Untertan und Staat in Galizien: Die Reformen unter Maria Theresia und Joseph II*, ed. Ralph Melville (Mainz: Verlag Philipp von Zabern, 1992); Henryk Lepucki, *Działalność kolonizacyjna Marii Teresy i Józefa II w Galicji, 1772–1790* (Lviv: L. Wiśniewski, 1938); Wacław Tokarz, *Galicya w początkach ery józefińskiej w świetle ankiety urzędowej z roku 1783* (Cracow: Akademia Umiejętności, 1909).

3. Alfred Ritter von Arneth, *Maria Theresia's letzte Regierungszeit, 1763–1780*, Band II (Vienna: Wilhelm Braumüller, 1877), p. 595.

4. Arneth, *Maria Theresia's letzte Regierungszeit, 1763–1780*, Band II, p. 596.

5. Grodziski, p. 27; Stanisław Hubert, *Poglądy na prawo narodów w Polsce czasów Oświecenia* (Wrocław: Zakład Narodowy imienia Ossolińskich, 1960), pp. 207–50.

6. Arneth, *Maria Theresia und Joseph II: Ihre Correspondenz*, Band II, Maria Theresa to Joseph, 20 June 1773, pp. 9–10.

7. Ibid., Joseph to Maria Theresa, 1 August 1773, p. 14.

8. Johann Polek, "Joseph's II. Reisen nach Galizien und der Bukowina und ihre Bedeutung für letztere Provinz," *Jahrbuch des Bukowiner Landes-Museums* 3(Czernowitz: H. Pardini, 1895).

9. Arneth, *Maria Theresia und Joseph II: Ihre Correspondenz*, Band I, Joseph to Maria Theresa, 1 August 1773, p. 14.

10. Ibid., Joseph to Leopold, 1 August 1773, p. 16.

11. Larry Wolff, *Inventing Eastern Europe: The Map of Civilization on the Mind of the Enlightenment* (Stanford: Stanford University Press, 1994), p. 197.

12. Hans-Christian Maner, *Galizien: Eine Grenzregion im Kalkül der Donaumonarchie im 18. und 19. Jahrhundert* (Munich: Institut für deutsche Kultur und Geschichte Südosteuropas, 2007), pp. 35–36.

13. Glassl, *Das Österreichische Einrichtungswerk in Galizien*, pp. 39, 44; Franz Szabo, "Austrian First Impressions of Ethnic Relations in Galicia: The Case of Governor Anton von Pergen," in *Polin: Studies in Polish Jewry*, Vol. XII, *Focusing on Galicia*, pp, 49–60; see also Franz Szabo, *Kaunitz and Enlightened Absolutism 1753–1780* (Cambridge: Cambridge University Press, 1994), pp. 66–69.

14. Glassl, *Das Österreichische Einrichtungswerk in Galizien*, 44; see also Hugo Lane, "Szlachta Outside the Commonwealth: The Case of Polish Nobles in Galicia," *Zeitschrift für Ostmitteleuropa-Forschung* 52, no. 4 (2003): 530–33.

15. Glassl, *Das Österreichische Einrichtungswerk in Galizien*, pp. 62–64.

16. Stanisław Grodziski, "The Jewish Question in Galicia: The Reforms of Maria Theresa and Joseph II, 1772–1790," in *Polin: Studies in Polish Jewry*, Vol. XII, *Focusing on Galicia: Jews, Poles, and Ukrainians, 1772–1918*, ed. Israel Bartal and Antony Polonsky (London: Littman Library of Jewish Civilization, 1999), pp, 61–72; Wolfgang Häusler, *Das galizische Judentum in der Habsburgermonarchie: Im Lichte der zeitgenössischen Publizistik und Reiseliteratur von 1772–1848* (Vienna: Verlag für Geschichte und Politik, 1979), pp. 18–45; Nancy Sinkoff, *Out of the Shtetl: Making Jews Modern in the Polish Borderlands* (Providence, RI: Brown Judaic Studies, 2004), pp. 203–24.

17. Glassl, *Das Österreichische Einrichtungswerk in Galizien*, p. 70; Szabo, "Austrian First Impressions," pp. 49–60; Ludwik Finkel, "Memoryal Antoniego hr. Pergena, pierwszego gubernatora Galicyi o stanie kraju," *Kwartalnik Historyczny* 14, no. 1 (Lviv, 1900): 24–43.

18. Polek, "Joseph's II. Reisen," pp. 27–28; Arneth, *Maria Theresia und Joseph II: Ihre Correspondenz*, Band III, Joseph to Maria Theresa, 19 May 1780, p. 243; Derek Beales, *Joseph II*, Vol. I, *In the Shadow of Maria Theresa, 1741–1780* (Cambridge: Cambridge University Press, 1987), p. 435.

19. Maner, *Galizien*, pp. 206–7.

20. [Franz Kratter], *Briefe über den itzigen Zustand von Galizien* (Leipzig: Verlag G. Ph. Wucherers, 1786; rpt. Berlin: Helmut Scherer Verlag, 1990), Erster Theil (I), "An den Leser"; Maria Kłańska, *Daleko od Wiednia: Galicja w oczach pisarzy niemieckojęzycznych, 1772–1918* (Cracow: Towarzystwo Autorów i Wydawców Prac Naukowych UNIVERSITAS, 1991), pp. 27–38; "Franz Kratter," in Constant von Wurzbach, *Biographisches Lexikon des Kaiserthums Oesterreich*, XIII (Vienna: Druck und Verlag der k. k. Hof- und Staatsdruckerei, 1865), pp. 144–45; Gustav Gugitz, "Franz Kratter: Ein Beitrag zur Geschichte der Tagesschriftstellerei in der josephinischen Zeit," *Jahrbuch der Grillparzer-Gesellschaft*, 24 (1913), pp. 245–49; Volkmar Braunbehrens, *Mozart in Vienna 1781–1791*, trans. Timothy Bell (1986; New York: Grove Weidenfeld, 1990), pp. 247–49; see also Maria Kłańska, "Erkundungen der neuen österreichischen Provinz Galizien im deutschsprachigen Schrifttum der letzten Dezennien des 18. Jahrhunderts," in *Galizien als Gemeinsame Literaturlandschaft*, ed. Fridrun Rinner and Klaus Zerinschek (Innsbruck: Innsbrucker Beiträger zur Kulturwissenschaft, 1988), pp. 35–48; Jan Papiór, "Kontexte des Galizienerlebnisses von Franz Kratter," in *Galizien als Gemeinsame Literaturlandschaft*, pp. 83–94; Stanisław Schnür-Pepłowski, *Galiciana 1778–1812* (Lviv: Nakładem Księgarni H. Altenberga), pp. 15–43.

21. Kratter, *Briefe*, I, "An den Leser."

22. Ibid., p. 154.

23. Wolff, *Inventing Eastern Europe*, p. 62.

24. Maner, *Galizien*, p. 55.

25. Kratter, *Briefe*, I, pp, 159, 165.

26. Ibid., pp. 170–71, 176–78.

27. Ibid., pp. 185, 191–92.

28. Tadeusz Namowicz, "Galizien nach 1772: Zur Entstehung einer literarischen Provinz," in *Galizien als Gemeinsame Literaturlandschaft*, pp. 68–69.

29. Kratter, *Briefe*, I, pp. 192–93; see also Tadeusz Cegielski, "Der Josephinismus," in *Polen-Österreich: Aus der Geschichte einer Nachbarschaft*, ed. Walter Leitsch and Maria

Wawrykowa (Vienna and Warsaw: Österreichischer Bundesverlag and Wydawnictwa Szkolne i Pedagogiczne, 1988), pp. 41–76.

30. Kratter, *Briefe*, Zweiter Theil (II), p. 15.

31. Norbert Elias, *The History of Manners*, trans. Edmund Jephcott (New York: Pantheon Books, 1978), pp. 144–48.

32. Kratter, *Briefe*, II, pp. 15–16.

33. Ibid., pp. 1–2.

34. Ibid., pp. 2–3.

35. Ibid., p. 14.

36. Ibid., p. 5.

37. Ibid., pp. 168–70.

38. Ibid., pp. 13, 27–28.

39. Ibid., I, pp. 226–30; II, pp. 193–94.

40. Grodziski, "The Jewish Question in Galicia," p. 66.

41. Kratter, *Briefe*, II, pp. 37–40.

42. Ibid., p. 42.

43. Ibid., pp. 42–43.

44. Grodziski, "The Jewish Question in Galicia," p. 68.

45. Ibid., pp. 61–72; Häusler, *Das galizische Judentum*, pp. 43–49; see also Michael Stanislawski, *A Murder in Lemberg: Politics, Religion, and Violence in Modern Jewish History* (Princeton: Princeton University Press, 2007), pp. 9–17; Schnür-Pepłowski, *Galiciana*, p. 15.

46. Michael Silber, "From Tolerated Aliens to Citizen-Soldiers: Jewish Military Service in the Era of Joseph II," in *Constructing Nationalities in East Central Europe*, ed. Pieter Judson and Marsha Rozenblit (New York: Berghahn Books, 2004), p. 25; Raphael Mahler, *Hasidism and the Jewish Enlightenment: Their Confrontation in Galicia and Poland in the First Half of the Nineteenth Century* (Philadelphia: Jewish Publication Society of America, 1985), pp. 3–7.

47. Kratter, *Briefe*, II, pp. 54, 59; Häusler, *Das galizische Judentum*, pp. 43–49; Kłańska, *Daleko od Wiednia*, pp. 42–44.

48. Kratter, *Briefe*, II, p. 153.

49. Ibid., pp. 154–55.

50. Ibid., I, pp. 129–30.

51. Ibid., II, pp. 184–85.

52. Glassl, *Das Österreichische Einrichtungswerk in Galizien*, pp. 220–34; see also Isabel Röskau-Rydel, *Galizien: Deutsche Geschichte im Osten Europas* (Berlin: Siedler Verlag, 1999), pp. 22–38.

53. Kratter, *Briefe*, I, pp. 248, 274–76.

54. Polek, "Joseph's II. Reisen," pp. 45–46.

55. Kratter, *Briefe*, II, "An den günstigen Leser."

56. [Alphons Heinrich Traunpaur], *Dreissig Briefe über Galizien: oder Beobachtungen eines unpartheyischen Mannes, der sich mehr als nur ein paar Monate in diesem Königreiche umgesehen hat* (Vienna and Leipzig: G. Wucherer und E. Beer, 1787; rpt. Berlin: Helmut Scherer Verlag, 1990); Jürgen Habermas, *The Structural Transformation of the Public Sphere: An Inquiry into a Category of Bourgeois Society*, trans. Thomas Burger (Cambridge: MIT Press, 1993).

57. Traunpaur, *Dreissig Briefe*, pp. 1–4.
58. Ibid., pp. 5–9.
59. Ibid., pp. 66, 170–71.
60. Ibid., pp. 26, 31–32, 47.
61. Ibid., pp. 109–14.
62. Ibid., p. 117.
63. Ibid., p. 121.
64. Ibid., pp. 123–24.
65. [Ernst Traugott von Kortum], *Magna Charta von Galizien: oder Untersuchung der Beschwerden des Galizischen Adels pohlnischer Nation über die österreichische Regierung* (Jassy 1790).
66. *Korespondencja Józefa Maksymiliana Ossolińskiego*, ed. Władysława Jabłońska (Wrocław: Zakład Narodowy imienia Ossolińskich, 1975), p. 188, letter of Ossoliński, 20 May 1789; Władysława Jabłońska, *Józef Maksymilian Ossoliński: szkic biograficzny* (Wrocław: Zakład Narodowy imienia Ossolińskich, 1967), pp. 42–50; see also Lane, "Szlachta Outside the Commonwealth," pp. 535–38.
67. "Ernst Traugott Kortum," in *Polski Słownik Biograficzny*, XIV (Wrocław: Zakład Narodowy imienia Ossolińskich, 1968–69), pp. 120–21; "Ernst Traugott von Kortum," in Constant von Wurzbach, *Biographisches Lexikon des Kaiserthums Oesterreich*, XII (Vienna: Druck und Verlag der k. k. Hof- und Staatsdruckerei, 1864), pp. 471–73.
68. [Kortum], *Magna Charta*, p. 238.
69. Ibid., pp. 268–69.
70. Ibid., pp. 241–44.
71. Ibid., p. 252.
72. Ibid., pp. 264–65, 270–72.
73. Ibid., p. 265.
74. Arneth, *Maria Theresia und Joseph II: Ihre Correspondenz*, Band III, Joseph to Maria Theresa, 19 May 1780, p. 244.
75. [Kortum], *Magna Charta*, pp. 277–78.
76. Ibid., p. 292.
77. Ibid., pp. 292–93.
78. Ibid., p. 295.
79. Ibid.
80. James Van Horn Melton, *The Rise of the Public in Enlightenment Europe* (Cambridge: Cambridge University Press, 2001), pp. 81–122.
81. [Kortum], *Magna Charta*, p. 312.
82. Edmund Burke, *Reflections on the Revolution in France*, ed. Conor Cruise O'Brien (London: Penguin Books, 1973), p. 195.
83. [Kortum], *Magna Charta*, pp. 301–8, 322–25, 329–32.
84. Ibid., pp. 343–45.
85. Ibid., pp. 349, 358.
86. Ibid., pp. 347, 349–50.
87. Wolff, *Inventing Eastern Europe*, pp. 110–11.
88. [Kortum], *Magna Charta*, p. 365.
89. Ibid., pp. 11–13, 22–23.

90. Ibid., pp. 74–75.

91. Ibid., p. 109.

92. Ibid., p. 111.

93. Ibid., pp. 3, 8.

94. Ibid., pp. 32–33.

95. Ibid., p. 184.

96. Ibid., p. 203.

97. "Ernst Traugott von Kortum," in *Biographisches Lexikon des Kaiserthums Oesterreich*, XII, pp. 471–73.

98. Johann Christian von Engel, *Geschichte der Ukraine und der ukrainischen Cosaken wie auch der Königreiche Halitsch und Wladimir* (Halle: Gebauer, 1796); Paul Robert Magocsi, *Galicia: A Historical Survey and Bibliographic Guide* (Toronto: University of Toronto Press, 1983), pp. 27–28.

99. [Kortum], *Magna Charta*, p. 205.

100. Ibid., pp. 200–201.

101. Ibid., pp. 18–19.

102. Ibid., pp. 205–6.

103. Ibid., pp. 206, 231–32.

104. [Voltaire], *Der Kirchenzwist der Pollen: historisch kritisch beleuchtet aus dem Französischen des Herrn Bourdillon, Professor des Jus publikums, übersetzt von einem deutschen Pollaken* (Lviv, 1781).

105. *Skutki dzieł Woltera, przez Gallicyana* (1792), Biblioteka Jagiellońska, Cracow, p. 3.

106. Ibid.

107. Ibid., p. 10.

108. Ibid., pp. 11, 18.

109. Ibid., p. 20.

110. Balthasar Hacquet, *Neueste physikalisch-politische Reisen in den Jahren 1788 und 1789 durch die Dacischen und Sarmatischen oder Nördlichen Karpathen*, Erster Theil (Nuremberg: Verlag der Raspischen Buchhandlung, 1790), "Vorrede"; Zweiter Theil (1791), "Vorrede."

111. Grodziski, *Historia ustroju społeczno-politycznego Galicji*, p. 28.

112. Izabela Kleszczowa, *Ceremonie i parady w porozbiórowym Krakowie, 1796–1815* (Cracow: Wydawnictwo Uniwersytetu Jagiellońskiego, 1999), pp. 17–18, 23, 33; Gustav Seidler, *Studien zur Geschichte und Dogmatik des Oesterreichischen Staatsrechtes* (Vienna: Alfred Hölder, 1894), p. 181, n. 26; Maner, *Galizien*, p. 57;

113. Kajetan Koźmian, *Pamiętniki: obejmujące wspomnienia od roku 1780 do roku 1815*, Oddział I (Poznań: Nakład Jana Konstantego Żupańskiego, 1858), pp. 241, 248, 252–53.

114. Andrzej Jezierski and Cecylia Leszczyńska, *Historia gospodarcza Polski* (Warsaw: Wydawnictwo Key Text, 2003), p. 100; Norman Davies, *God's Playground: A History of Poland*, Volume 2 (New York: Columbia University Press, 1982), p. 142.

115. *Geographisch-historische Nachrichten von Westgalizien oder den neu erlangten österreichisch-polnischen Provinzen* (Vienna: Johann Otto, 1796), pp. 145–46.

116. Ibid., pp. 35, 67, 79–80, 84.

117. Ibid., pp. 54, 125.

118. Ibid., p. 51.

119. Wojciech Bogusławski, *Dzieie teatru narodowego* (Warsaw: N. Glücksberg, 1820), pp. 85–86.

120. Ibid., p. 99; Zbigniew Raszewski, *Bogusławski*, II (Warsaw: Państwowy Instytut Wydawniczy, 1972), pp. 7–50.

121. Bogusławski, *Dzieie teatru narodowego*, p. 107.

122. Ibid., p. 100; Jerzy Got, *Na Wyspie Guaxary: Wojciech Bogusławski i Teatr Lwowski, 1789–1799* (Cracow: Wydawnicto Literackie, 1971), pp. 113–16.

123. Got, *Na Wyspie Guaxary*, p. 405.

124. Wojciech Bogusławski, *Cud Mniemany czyli Krakowiacy i Górale*, ed. Juliusz Kijas (Cracow: Wydawnictwo M. Kot, 1949), p. 74.

125. Jolanta Pekacz, *Music in the Culture of Polish Galicia, 1772–1914* (Rochester, NY: University of Rochester Press, 2002), p. 157.

126. Got, *Na Wyspie Guaxary*, pp. 176–89.

127. Ibid., pp. 62–63, 220, 390.

128. Pekacz, *Music in the Culture of Polish Galicia*, p. 94; Got, *Na Wyspie Guaxary*, pp. 222–50.

129. Got, *Na Wyspie Guaxary*, p. 112.

130. Ibid., pp. 141–42, 186; Pekacz, *Music in the Culture of Polish Galicia*, p. 183.

131. Franz Kratter, *The Maid of Marienburg: A Drama in Five Acts, From the German of Kratter* (London: M. Allen, 1798), p. 73; Gugitz, "Franz Kratter," pp. 267–68.

132. Julian Ursyn Niemcewicz, *Pamiętniki czasów moich* (Leipzig: F. A. Brockhaus, 1868), pp. 63–65.

133. Norman Davies, *God's Playground: A History of Poland*, Vol. I (1982; New York: Columbia University Press, 1984), p. 542.

134. "Ernst Traugott von Kortum," in *Biographisches Lexikon des Kaiserthums Oesterreich*, XII, pp. 471–73; Pekacz, *Music in the Culture of Polish Galicia*, p. 183.

135. Maner, *Galizien*, p. 208.

136. Willibald Swibert Joseph Gottlieb von Besser, *Primitiae Florae Galiciae Austriacae Utriusque*, Parts I and II (Vienna: Sumptibus Ant. Doll., 1809), pp. iv–v.

2. Galicia Restored

1. Klemens Wenzel von Metternich, *Mémoires, documents, et écrits divers*, ed. Richard de Metternich, Part I (1773–1815), Vol. II (Paris: E. Plon, 1880), pp. 418–420; some of the material in this chapter has previously appeared in an article: Larry Wolff, "Kennst du das Land? The Uncertainty of Galicia in the Age of Metternich and Fredro," *Slavic Review* 67, no. 2 (Summer 2008): 277–300.

2. Metternich, *Mémoires*, Part I (1773–1815), Vol. II, pp. 420–21.

3. Ibid., pp. 432–33, 436–37.

4. *Intelligenzblatt zu den Annalen der Literatur und Kunst in dem österreichischen Kaiserthum* (September 1811, January 1812), in Gertraud Marinelli-König, *Polen und Ruthenen in den Wiener Zeitschriften und Almanachen des Vormärz* (Vienna: Verlag der Österreichischen Akademie der Wissenschaften, 1992), p. 103; *Stulecie Gazety Lwowskiej 1811–1911*, ed. Wilhelm Bruchnalski, Tom 1 (Lviv: Nakładem Redakcyi Gazety Lwowskiej, 1911), pp.

52–54; Jerzy Łojek, Jerzy Myśliński, and Wiesław Władyka, *Dzieje prasy polskiej* (Warsaw: Wydawnictwo Interpress, 1988) p. 40; Władysław Zawadzki, *Literatura w Galicji* (Lwów: Władysław Łozinski, 1878), pp. 42–43; Jan Papiór, "Kontexte des Galizienerlebnisses von Franz Kratter," in *Galizien als Gemeinsame Literaturlandschaft*, ed. Fridrun Rinner and Klaus Zerinschek (Innsbruck: Innsbrucker Beiträger zur Kulturwissenschaft, 1988), p. 85. Although there is some confusion in the secondary literature over the two roughly contemporary figures named Franz Kratter, and some have supposed that the author of the *Briefe* of 1786 was also the editor of *Gazeta Lwowska* in 1811, a careful examination suggests that these were two different men (probably cousins) with the same name. In particular, Wilhelm Bruchnalski's centennial study of *Gazeta Lwowska*, published in Lviv in 1911, is unequivocal about the distinction between these two men, who died in 1830 (the author and dramatist) and 1838 (the bureaucrat and editor) respectively. Bruchnalski cites the obituary published in 1838 in *Gazeta Lwowska*, to honor its founding editor, and the Habsburg bureaucratic career described in that obituary was clearly different from the life and career of the author and dramatist. It is, of course, not impossible, given their family relation, that there was some contact and collaboration between these two men with the same name.

    5. *Gazeta Lwowska*, 7 February, 11 February 1812.

    6. Ibid., 11 February 1812.

    7. Ibid., 7 February 1812.

    8. Ibid., 24 March 1812.

    9. Ibid., 11 February, 28 February 1812.

    10. Ibid., 3 March 1812.

    11. *Intelligenzblatt zu den Annalen der Literatur und Kunst in dem österreichischen Kaiserthum* (February 1811, May 1811, May 1812), in Marinelli-König, *Polen und Ruthenen*, pp. 88–91.

    12. *Gazeta Lwowska*, 3 March 1812.

    13. Ibid.

    14. Ibid., 24 April, 19 May, 14 July 1812.

    15. Ibid., 28 July 1812.

    16. Aleksander Fredro, *Sans queue ni tête*, trans. Elisabeth Destrée-Van Wilder (Montricher, Switzerland: Les Editions Noir sur Blanc, 1992), pp. 10, 82; Fredro, *Trzy po trzy*, in *Proza*, XIII, Part 1 (Warsaw: Pańtswowy Instytut Wydawniczy, 1968), pp. 71, 123.

    17. Fredro, *Sans queue ni tête*, pp. 80, 105; *Trzy po trzy*, pp. 121, 139–40.

    18. Fredro, *Sans queue ni tête*, pp. 104, 196; *Trzy po trzy*, pp. 139, 205.

    19. Fredro, *Sans queue ni tête*, p. 158; *Trzy po trzy*, p. 178.

    20. H. C. Robbins Landon, *1791: Mozart's Last Year* (New York: Schirmer Books, 1988), p. 187.

    21. Walter Hummel, *W. A. Mozarts Söhne* (Kassel and Basel: Bärenreiter-Verlag, 1956), pp. 61–62; letters of Constanze Mozart: 4 September, 7 December 1808; letters of F. X. W. Mozart: 19 November, 15 December 1808; see also Isabel Röskau-Rydel, *Galizien: Deutsche Geschichte im Osten Europas* (Berlin: Siedler Verlag, 1999), pp. 54–56.

    22. Hummel, *W. A. Mozarts Söhne*, p. 63, letter of F. X. W. Mozart, 22 January 1809.

    23. Ibid., pp. 64–65, letter of Constanze Mozart, 29 July 1809, letter of F. X. W. Mozart, 18 October 1809.

24. Ibid., p. 66, letter of F. X. W. Mozart, 8 February 1810; there was more than one place in Galicia called Podkamień, and Mozart was, apparently, not living in the town of Podkamień near Brody, but rather in a village by the same name near Lviv.

25. Ibid., letter of F. X. W. Mozart, 8 February 1810.

26. "Die Einsamkeit," from *The Other Mozart: Franz Xaver Mozart, The Songs*, recording by Barbara Bonney and Malcolm Martineau (Decca, B0005505–02, 2005).

27. Hummel, *W. A. Mozarts Söhne*, p. 68, letter of F. X. W. Mozart, 22 November 1810.

28. Ibid., pp. 68–72; letters of F. X. W. Mozart, 20 February 1811, 22 June 1811, 22 August 1812; see also ibid., pp. 280–81.

29. Ibid., p. 74, letter of F. X. W. Mozart, 6 September 1816.

30. Ibid., pp. 316–17; Wolfgang Amadeus Mozart Sohn, *12 Polonaisen für Klavier*, ed. Joachim Draheim (Heidelberg: Willy Müller, Süddeutscher Musikverlag, 1980).

31. *Gazeta Lwowska*, 8 September, 12 September, 29 September, 2 October, 6 October 1812.

32. Ibid., 3 November, 13 November 1812.

33. Ibid., 20 November, 18 December, 29 December 1812.

34. Fredro, *Sans queue ni tête*, pp. 22, 195, 202; *Trzy po trzy*, pp. 79, 205, 210; Krystyna Poklewska, *Galicja romantyczna, 1816–1840* (Warsaw: Pańtswowy Instytut Wydawniczy, 1976), pp. 148–49; see also Jarosław Rymkiewicz, *Aleksander Fredro jest w złym humorze* (Warsaw: Czytelnik, 1977).

35. Hummel, *W. A. Mozarts Söhne*, pp. 73–74; letters of F. X. W. Mozart, 22 May, 6 December 1817.

36. Ibid., pp. 75–76.

37. Fredro, *The Major Comedies of Alexander Fredro*, ed. and trans. Harold B. Segel (Princeton: Princeton University Press, 1969), *Ladies and Hussars*, pp. 123–24.

38. Ibid., p. 184; Fredro, *Damy i Huzary*, in *Pisma Wszystkie*, ed. Stanisław Pigoń, Tom III (Warsaw: Państwowy Instytut Wydawniczy, 1955), p. 117.

39. Arthur Haas, *Metternich: Reorganization and Nationality, 1813–1818: A Story of Foresight and Frustration in the Rebuilding of the Austrian Empire* (Wiesbaden: Franz Steiner Verlag, 1963), p. 167: "Vortrag des Fürsten Metternich an Kaiser Franz über die Situation in Galizien," 18 April 1815.

40. Ibid., pp. 167–68.

41. Ibid., pp. 168–69.

42. Ibid.

43. Stanisław Grodziski, *Historia ustroju społeczno-politycznego Galicji 1772–1848* (Wrocław: Zakład Narodowy imienia Ossolińskich, 1971), pp. 149–50.

44. Jan Kozik, *The Ukrainian National Movement in Galicia, 1815–1849*, trans. Andrew Gorski and Lawrence Orton (Edmonton: Canadian Institute of Ukrainian Studies, 1986) p. 32.

45. *Korespondencja Józefa Maksymiliana Ossolińskiego*, ed. Władysława Jabłońska (Wrocław: Zakład Narodowy imienia Ossolińskich, 1975), p. 188, letter of Kaiser Franz, 23 February 1809; Władysława Jabłońska, *Józef Maksymilian Ossoliński: szkic biograficzny* (Wrocław: Zakład Narodowy imienia Ossolińskich, 1967), pp. 66–67.

46. *Korespondencja Józefa Maksymiliana Ossolińskiego*, pp. 220–23, letter of Ossoliński, 19 November 1815.

47. Ibid., pp. 248–49, 253–54, letter of Jozef Erdödy, 5 May 1817, letter of Franz Krieg, 6 June 1817, letter of Ossoliński, 30 August 1817.

48. Ibid., pp. 254–57, letter of Ossoliński, 1 September 1817, letter of Franz Krieg, 3 September 1817.

49. Ibid., p. 264, letter of Joseph Mauss, 29 December 1817.

50. Ibid., pp. 265–66, letter of Joseph Mauss, 29 December 1817.

51. Ibid., p. 267, letter of Joseph Mauss, 29 December 1817.

52. *Rozmaitości*, 7 February; Zawadzki, *Literatura w Galicji*, pp. 44–45.

53. *Rozmaitości*, 18 February, 11 March, 6 June, 10 October 1818.

54. *Korespondencja Józefa Maksymiliana Ossolińskiego*, pp. 261–64, letters of Ossoliński, 3 December, 24 December 1817, letter of Joseph Mauss, 29 December 1817.

55. Kozik, *The Ukrainian National Movement in Galicia*, pp. 52–56; Larry Wolff, *The Uniate Church and the Partitions of Poland: Religious Survival in an Age of Enlightened Absolutism* (Cambridge: Harvard Ukrainian Research Institute, 2007), in *Harvard Ukrainian Studies* 26: 179–92.

56. Kozik, *The Ukrainian National Movement in Galicia*, pp. 54–58; Stanisław Stępień, "Borderland City: Przemyśl and the Ruthenian National Awakening in Galicia," in *Galicia: A Multicultured Land*, ed. Christopher Hann and Paul Magocsi (Toronto: University of Toronto Press, 2005), pp. 55–60; Michael Moser, "Die sprachliche Erneuerung der galizischen Ukrainer zwischen 1772 und 1848/1849 im mitteleuropäischen Kontext," in *Comparative Cultural Studies in Central Europe*, ed. Ivo Pospišil and Michael Moser (Brno: Ustav Slavistiky Filozofické Fakulty Masarykovy Univerzity, 2004), pp. 88–89.

57. Stępień, "Borderland City," p. 57.

58. Zorian Chodakowski, *O Sławiańszczyźnie przed Chrześcijaństwem: oraz inne pisma i listy* (Warsaw: Państwowe Wydawnictwo Naukowe, 1967), p. 214.

59. Markian Prokopovych, *Habsburg Lemberg: Architecture, Public Space, and Politics in the Galician Capital, 1772–1914* (West Lafayette, IN: Purdue University Press, 2009), p. 182, n. 27.

60. *Pamiętnik Galicyjski*, Tom I: July, August, September 1821 (Lviv: Nakładem Karola Wilda, Drukiem Józefa Sznaydera, 1821), pp. 3–4.

61. Ibid., p. 140.

62. Poklewska, *Galicja romantyczna*, pp. 58–83.

63. *Pamiętnik Galicyjski*, Tom II: October, November, December 1821, pp. 196–202.

64. Ibid., Tom I: July, August, September 1821, p. 206.

65. Ibid., Tom II: October, November, December 1821, pp. 175–76.

66. Joseph Perl, *Revealer of Secrets*, trans. Dov Taylor (Boulder, CO: Westview Press, 1997), pp. xxv–xxxii; Michael Stanislawski, *A Murder in Lemberg: Politics, Religion, and Violence in Modern Jewish History* (Princeton: Princeton University Press, 2007), pp. 16–17, 31–32; Israel Bartal and Antony Polonsky, "Introduction: The Jews of Galicia under the Habsburgs," in *Polin: Studies in Polish Jewry*, Vol. XII, *Focusing on Galicia*, ed. Israel Bartal and Antony Polonsky (London: Littman Library of Jewish Civilization, 1999), pp. 12–13; Nancy Sinkoff, *Out of the Shtetl: Making Jews Modern in the Polish Borderlands* (Providence, RI: Brown Judaic Studies, 2004), pp. 25–40; Paul Robert Magocsi, *Galicia: A Historical Survey and Bibliographic Guide* (Toronto: University of Toronto Press, 1983),

p. 230; Raphael Mahler, *Hasidism and the Jewish Enlightenment: Their Confrontation in Galicia and Poland in the First Half of the Nineteenth Century* (Philadelphia: Jewish Publication Society of America, 1985), pp. 121–48.

67. *Pamiętnik Galicyjski*, Tom II: October, November, December 1821, pp. 3–12.

68. Ibid.

69. Ibid., Tom I: July, August, September 1821, pp. 57–64.

70. Poklewska, *Galicja romantyczna*, pp. 116–21.

71. Jan Nepomucen Kamiński, *Zabobon, czyli Krakowiacy i Górale: Zabawka dramatyczna z śpiewkami* (Lviv: K. B. Pfaff, 1821), pp. 3, 7, 34.

72. Ibid., p. 154.

73. Fredro, *Husband and Wife*, in Segel, *The Major Comedies*, p. 75; *Mąż i żona*, in Fredro, *Komedie: Wybór* (Warsaw: Państwowy Instytut Wydawniczy, 1972), p. 82.

74. Fredro, *Husband and Wife*, in Segel, *The Major Comedies*, pp. 75–76; *Mąż i żona*, in Fredro, *Komedie: Wybór*, p. 83.

75. Metternich, *Mémoires*, Part II (1816–48), Vol. IV, p. 15, letter of 25 September 1823.

76. Ibid., pp. 16, 19; letters of 28 September, 17 October 1823.

77. Ibid., pp. 19–20, letter of 17 October 1823.

78. Ibid., pp. 16–17, letter of 29 September 1823.

79. Ibid., p. 19, letter of 17 October 1823.

80. Ibid., pp. 20–21, letter of 21 October 1823.

81. Ibid.

82. Ibid., pp. 21–22, letter of 27 October 1823.

83. Ibid., p. 23, letter of 30 October 1823.

84. *Gazeta Lwowska*, 3 January, 31 January 1825.

85. Ibid., 11 March 1825.

86. Ibid., 13 April 1825.

87. *Korespondencja Józefa Maksymiliana Ossolińskiego*, p. 474, letter of Ossoliński, 6 March 1826.

88. Fredro, *Korespondencja*, ed. Krystyna Czajkowska, in *Pisma Wszystkie*, Tom XIV (Warsaw: Państwowy Instytut Wydawniczy, 1976), pp. 72–73, letter of Fredro, undated.

89. Marinelli-König, *Polen und Ruthenen*, pp. 347–48.

90. *Hymn śpiewany przez aktorów sceny polskiej w wigilią urodzin najjaśniejszego cesarza i króla Galicyi i Lodomerii* (Lviv: J. Schnajder, 1828); Moser, "Die sprachliche Erneuerung der galizischen Ukrainer," pp. 91–92.

91. Julian Horoszkiewicz, *Notatki z życia*, ed. Henryk Wereszycki (Wrocław: Zakład Narodowy imienia Ossolińskich, 1957), p. 18.

92. Ibid., p. 22.

93. Ibid., pp. 26–27.

94. Ibid., pp. 27–28.

95. C. A. Macartney, *The Habsburg Empire, 1790–1918* (New York: Macmillan, 1969), p. 234.

96. Horoszkiewicz, *Notatki z życia*, pp. 28–29.

97. Józef Reitzenheim, *Galicia: Pamiętnik* (Paris: Maistrasse, Place Cambrai, 1845), pp. 3–4.

98. Ibid., pp. 4–5.

99. Ibid., p. 6.

100. Ibid., pp. 7–11.

101. Ibid., p. 14.

102. Ibid., pp. 25, 30.

103. Prokopovych, *Habsburg Lemberg*, pp. 136–37.

104. Macartney, *The Habsburg Empire*, p. 234.

105. Fredro, *Korespondencja*, p. 77, letter of Fredro, 2 January 1832.

106. Antoni Cetnarowicz, "Metternich in den Augen der zeitgenössischen Polen und in der polnischen Historiographie," in *Polen-Oesterreich: Aus der Geschichte einer Nachbarschaft*, ed. Walter Leitsch and Maria Wawrykowa (Vienna and Warsaw: Oesterreichische Bundesverlag and Wydawnictwa Szkolne i Pedagogiczne, 1988), p. 89.

107. Adam Mickiewicz, "Do przyjaciół Galicyjskich," in *Pisma filomackie, pisma polityczne: z lat 1832–1834* (Warsaw: Czytelnik, 2000), pp. 316–17.

108. Marinelli-König, *Polen und Ruthenen*, pp. 60–61.

109. Fredro, *Maidens' Vows*, in Segel, *The Major Comedies*, p. 210.

110. Reitzenheim, *Galicia: Pamiętnik*, p. 32.

111. Anna Zeńczak, "Piotr Michałowski: sa vie, son oeuvre," in *Piotr Michałowski: Peintures et dessins* (Paris: RMN, 2004), pp. 10–19; Jan Ostrowski, "Pomiędzy Paryżem i galicyjską prowincją," in *Piotr Michałowski 1800–1855* (Cracow: Muzeum Narodowe w Krakowie, 2000), pp. 15–31.

112. Fredro, *The Life Annuity*, in Segel, *The Major Comedies*, pp. 353, 367; Fredro, *Dożywocie*, in *Pisma Wszystkie*, ed. Stanisław Pigoń, Tom VI (Warsaw: Państwowy Instytut Wydawniczy, 1956), pp. 212, 237.

113. Seweryn Goszczyński, "Nowa epoka poezyi polskiej," in *Dzieła zbiorowe*, Tom III, *Podróże i rozprawy literackie*, ed. Zygmunt Wasilewski (Lviv: H. Altenberg, 1911), p. 229.

114. Fredro, *The Life Annuity*, in Segel, *The Major Comedies*, p. 379; Fredro, *Dożywocie*, in *Pisma Wszystkie*, VI, pp. 264–65.

115. Prokopovych, *Habsburg Lemberg*, pp. 152–53.

3. The Galician Childhood of Sacher-Masoch

1. Leopold von Sacher-Masoch, *Venus in Furs*, trans. Joachim Neugroschel (New York: Penguin, 2000), p. 73, "Introduction," Larry Wolff, pp. vii–xxviii; Sacher-Masoch, *Venus im Pelz* in *Venus im Pelz und Die Liebe des Plato* (Munich: Delphin Verlag, 1987), pp. 11, 109.

2. [Franz Kratter], *Briefe über den itzigen Zustand von Galizien* (Leipzig: Verlag G. Ph. Wucherers, 1786; rpt. Berlin: Helmut Scherer Verlag, 1990), Erster Theil (I), pp. 169–70; Larry Wolff, *Inventing Eastern Europe: The Map of Civilization on the Mind of the Enlightenment* (Stanford: Stanford University Press, 1994), pp. 50–88.

3. Wanda von Sacher-Masoch, *The Confessions of Wanda von Sacher-Masoch*, trans. Marian Phillips, Caroline Hébert, and V. Vale (San Francisco: Re/Search Publications, 1990), p. 33.

4. Sacher-Masoch, *Venus im Pelz*, p. 113.

5. Richard von Krafft-Ebing, *Psychopathia Sexualis*, trans. Franklin S. Klaf (New York: Arcade Publishing, 1998), p. 87.

6. Sacher-Masoch, *Souvenirs: Autobiographische Prosa* (Munich: Belleville, 1985), pp. 23–24; Maria Kłańska, *Daleko od Wiednia: Galicja w oczach pisarzy niemieckojęzycznych, 1772–1918* (Cracow: Towarzystwo Autorów i Wydawców Prac Naukowych UNIVER-SITAS, 1991), pp. 120–34.

7. Sacher-Masoch, *Souvenirs*, p. 17.

8. Ibid., p. 34.

9. Bernard Michel, *Sacher-Masoch 1836–1895* (Paris: Robert Laffont, 1989), p. 143.

10. Jan Kozik, *The Ukrainian National Movement in Galicia, 1815–1849*, trans. Andrew Gorski and Lawrence Orton (Edmonton: Canadian Institute of Ukrainian Studies, 1986), p. 31; see also Danuta Sosnowska, *Inna Galicja* (Warsaw: Elipsa, 2008).

11. Kozik, *The Ukrainian National Movement in Galicia*, pp. 30–32; Fredro, *The Major Comedies of Alexander Fredro*, ed. and trans. Harold B. Segel (Princeton: Princeton University Press, 1969), p. 23; Władysław Zawadzki, *Literatura w Galicji* (Lwów: Władysław Łoziński, 1878), pp. 43–53.

12. Kozik, *The Ukrainian National Movement in Galicia*, pp. 34–36; Michael Moser, "Die sprachliche Erneuerung der galizischen Ukrainer zwischen 1772 und 1848/1849 im mitteleuropäischen Kontext," in *Comparative Cultural Studies in Central Europe*, ed. Ivo Pospišil and Michael Moser (Brno: Ustav Slavistiky Filozoficke Fakulty Masarykovy Univerzity, 2004), pp. 102–3.

13. Wolff, *Inventing Eastern Europe*, p. 307.

14. Wacław z Oleska [Wacław Zaleski], *Pieśni polskie i ruskie ludu galicyjskiego* (Lviv: Franciszek Piller, 1833), p. iv.

15. Wacław z Oleska, *Pieśni polskie i ruskie ludu galicyjskiego*, pp. x, xxvii, xxx.

16. Ibid., p. xxxii.

17. Ibid., p. xlii.

18. Ibid., pp. xliii, xlviii.

19. Kozik, *The Ukrainian National Movement in Galicia*, p. 35.

20. Włodzimierz Mokry, *Ruska Trójca: Karta z dziejów życia literackiego Ukraińców w Galicji w pierwszej połowie XIX wieku* (Cracow: Wydawnictwo Uniwersytetu Jagiellońskiego, 1997), pp. 51–52.

21. *Rusalka Dnistrovaia (The Dnister Nymph)*, photocopy of the 1st ed., ed. Mykhailo Marunchak (Winnipeg: Markian Shashkevych Centre, 1987), pp. x–xi; Mokry, *Ruska Trójca*, p. 62; Kozik, *The Ukrainian National Movement in Galicia*, pp. 69–73.

22. Sacher-Masoch, *Souvenirs*, p. 19.

23. Ibid., pp. 20–21.

24. Ibid., p. 43.

25. Sacher-Masoch, *Don Juan of Kolomea*, in *Love: The Legacy of Cain*, trans. Michael T. O'Pecko (Riverside, CA: Ariadne Press, 2003), p. 18.

26. *Galicia: Zeitschrift zur Unterhaltung, zur Kunde des Vaterlandes, der Kunst, der Industrie und des Lebens*, Lviv, 2 January 1841.

27. *Allgemeine Theaterzeitung* 182 (31 July 1841), in Gertraud Marinelli-König, *Polen und Ruthenen in den Wiener Zeitschriften und Almanachen des Vormärz* (Vienna: Verlag der Österreichischen Akademie der Wissenschaften, 1992), pp. 117–18.

28. *Galicia: Zeitschrift,* 7 January, 14 January, 21 January 1841.

29. Ibid., 28 January, 6 February 1841.

30. Sacher-Masoch, *Souvenirs,* pp. 60–61.

31. Ibid., p. 91.

32. Julian Horoszkiewicz, *Notatki z życia,* ed. Henryk Wereszycki (Wrocław: Zakład Narodowy imienia Ossolińskich, 1957), pp. 153–59.

33. Raphael Mahler, *Hasidism and the Jewish Enlightenment: Their Confrontation in Galicia and Poland in the First Half of the Nineteenth Century* (Philadelphia: Jewish Publication Society of America, 1985), pp. 134–35, 139–41, 144–45.

34. Mahler, *Hasidism and the Jewish Enlightenment,* pp. 99–103, 148.

35. Sacher-Masoch, *Souvenirs,* p. 91.

36. Sacher-Masoch, *Don Juan of Kolomea,* pp. 19–20.

37. *Rusalka Dnistrovaia,* pp. 89–90; Mokry, *Ruska Trójca,* pp. 156–62; Kozik, *The Ukrainian National Movement in Galicia,* pp. 120–21.

38. *Galicia: Zeitschrift,* 23 February 1841.

39. Józef Korzeniowski, *Karpaccy Górale,* in *Dzieła Wybrane,* VII, *Dramaty* (Cracow: Wydawnictwo Literackie, 1954), p. 208; see also Patrice Dabrowski, "Discovering the Galician Borderlands: The Case of the Eastern Carpathians," *Slavic Review* 64, no. 2 (Summer 2005): pp. 380–402.

40. *Galicia: Zeitschrift,* 4 March 1841.

41. Ibid., 12 January 1841.

42. Ibid., 6 February 1841.

43. Moser, "Die sprachliche Erneuerung der galizischen Ukrainer," pp. 89–90.

44. *Dennitsa-Jutrzenka* (Warsaw), Number 6, March 1842.

45. Kozik, *The Ukrainian National Movement in Galicia,* pp. 164–66.

46. Ibid., pp. 110–11, 162–63.

47. Sacher-Masoch, *Venus im Pelz,* p. 94.

48. *Das Projekt der Wien—Bochnia—Eisenbahn in technischer, kommerzieller und finanzieller Hinsicht betrachtet* (Vienna: Carl Gerold, 1836).

49. Aleksander Fredro, *Pisma Polityczno-Społeczne: Aneksy,* ed. Krystyna Czajkowska and Stanisław Pigoń, in *Pisma Wszystkie,* Tom XV (Warsaw: Państwowy Instytut Wydawniczy, 1980), p. 114.

50. Fredro, *Korespondencja,* ed. Krystyna Czajkowska and Stanisław Pigoń, in *Pisma Wszystkie,* Tom XIV (Warsaw: Państwowy Instytut Wydawniczy, 1976), p. 544, letter of Franz Krieg, 11 October 1839.

51. Leon Sapieha, *Wspomnienia z lat od 1803 do 1863,* ed. Bronisław Pawłowski (Lviv: H. Altenberg, G. Seyfarth, E. Wende, 1912), p. 189.

52. Fredro, *Korespondencja,* p. 92, letter of Fredro, 26 December 1839.

53. Ibid., pp. 554–55, letter of Henryk Fredro, 30 September 1840.

54. Ibid., p. 566, letter of Leon Sapieha, 23 December 1840; p. 96, letter of Fredro, 24 December 1840.

55. Ibid., pp. 562–63, letter of Henryk Fredro, 21 December 1840; p. 563, note 1; *Galicia: Zeitschrift,* 5 January 1841.

56. Fredro, *Korespondencja,* pp. 572–73, letter of Henryk Fredro, 13 February 1841; see also Andrzej Walicki, *Russia, Poland, and Universal Regeneration: Studies on Russian and*

Polish Thought of the Romantic Epoch (Notre Dame: University of Notre Dame Press, 1991), pp. 107–57; Wiktor Weintraub, *Profecja i profesura: Mickiewicz, Michelet i Quinet* (Warsaw: Państwowy Instytut Wydawniczy, 1975).

57. Fredro, "O możności i potrzebie założenia banku i kolei żelaznej w Galicji," in *Pisma Polityczno-Społeczne: Aneksy*, pp. 65–66.

58. Ibid., pp. 69, 78.

59. Marinelli-König, *Polen und Ruthenen*, p. 11.

60. Fredro, *Korespondencja*, p. 112, letter of Fredro, 13 September 1842.

61. Ibid., p. 108, letter of Fredro, 20 November 1841.

62. Ibid.

63. Ibid., p. 116, letter of Fredro, 20 May 1844; Hans-Christian Maner, *Galizien: Eine Grenzregion im Kalkül der Donaumonarchie im 18. und 19. Jahrhundert* (Munich: Institut für deutsche Kultur und Geschichte Südosteuropas, 2007), pp. 256–57.

64. Sapieha, *Wspomnienia*, pp. 205–6.

65. Sacher-Masoch, *Venus im Pelz*, pp. 75–76.

66. Sapieha, *Wspomnienia*, p. 201.

67. Stefan Kieniewicz, *The Emancipation of the Polish Peasantry* (Chicago: University of Chicago Press, 1969), p. 115.

68. Fredro, "Aperçus sur les progrès de la démoralisation en Galicie, de sa cause et des moyens d'y contrevenir," in *Pisma Polityczno-Społeczne: Aneksy*, p. 77.

69. Ibid., pp. 78–79.

70. Ibid., p. 79.

71. Ibid., p. 81.

72. Ibid.

73. *Galicia: Zeitschrift*, 27 February 1841.

74. Marinelli-König, *Polen und Ruthenen*, p. 95.

75. *Galicia: Zeitschrift*, 27 February 1841.

76. Sacher-Masoch, *Souvenirs*, p. 63.

77. Michel, *Sacher-Masoch*, p. 51; see also Thomas Simons, Jr., "The Peasant Revolt of 1846 in Galicia: Recent Polish Historiography," *Slavic Review* 30 (December 1971): 795–817; see also Kai Struve, *Bauern und Nation in Galizien: Über Zugehörigkeit und soziale Emanzipation im 19. Jahrhundert* (Göttingen: Vandenhoeck und Ruprecht, 2005), pp. 78–85.

78. Piotr Wandycz, *The Lands of Partitioned Poland* (Seattle: University of Washington Press, 1974), p. 135; C. A. Macartney, *The Habsburg Empire, 1790–1918* (New York: Macmillan, 1969), p. 308; Simons, "The Peasant Revolt of 1846," p. 795; Keely Stauter-Halsted, *The Nation in the Village: The Genesis of Peasant National Identity in Austrian Poland, 1848–1914* (Ithaca, NY: Cornell University Press, 2001), p. 1.

79. Sacher-Masoch, *Souvenirs*, p. 63.

80. Ibid., pp. 63–64.

81. Alan Sked, "Benedek, Breinl and the 'Galician Horrors' of 1846," *Resistance, Rebellion, and Revolution in Hungary and Central Europe*, ed. Laszlo Peter and Martyn Rady (London: Studies in Russia and Eastern Europe, University College London, 2008), pp. 87–98; see also Arnon Gill, *Die polnische Revolution 1846: zwischen nationalem Befreiungs-kampf des Landadels und antifeudaler Bauernerhebung* (Munich: Oldenbourg, 1974).

82. Michel, *Sacher-Masoch*, pp. 56, 63.

83. Kozik, *The Ukrainian National Movement in Galicia*, pp. 120–21.

84. Kłańska, *Daleko od Wiednia*, pp. 93–94.

85. Leopold von Sacher-Masoch, *Graf Donski: Eine galizische Geschichte: 1846*, 2nd ed. (Schaffhausen: Friedrich Hurter, 1864), p. 343.

86. Ibid.; [Franz Kratter], *Briefe über den itzigen Zustand von Galizien*, I, p. 185; [Alphons Heinrich Traunpaur], *Dreissig Briefe über Galizien: oder Beobachtungen eines unpartheyischen Mannes, der sich mehr als nur ein paar Monate in diesem Königreiche umgesehen hat* (Vienna and Leipzig: G. Wucherer und E. Beer, 1787; rpt. Berlin: Helmut Scherer Verlag, 1990), pp. 31–32.

87. Sacher-Masoch, *Graf Donski*, pp. 402.

88. Ibid., pp. 344–47.

89. Ibid., pp. iii–iv.

90. Ibid., pp. iv–v.

91. Klemens Wenzel von Metternich, *Mémoires, documents, et écrits divers*, ed. Richard de Metternich, Part II (1816–48), Vol. VII (Paris: E. Plon, 1883), pp. 193–94.

92. Ibid., p. 194.

93. *Gazeta Krakowska*, 24 February 1846.

94. Metternich, *Mémoires*, Part II (1816–48), Vol. VII, pp. 197–98.

95. Ibid., p. 198.

96. Ibid.

97. Ibid.

98. Ibid., p. 200.

99. *Gazeta Krakowska*, 10 March 1846.

100. Ibid.

101. Ibid., 14 March 1846.

102. Ibid., 16 March 1846.

103. Ibid., 23 March 1846.

104. Metternich, *Mémoires*, Part II (1816–48), Vol. VII, p. 211.

105. Ibid., p. 213–14.

106. Ibid., p. 213.

107. Maner, *Galizien*, pp. 89–90.

108. Metternich, *Mémoires*, Part II (1816–48), Vol. VII, pp. 214–15.

109. *Gazeta Krakowska*, 23 March 1846.

110. Ibid., 30 March 1846; *Archiwum Państwowe w Krakowie: Inwentarz Tymczasowy*, register 927a (1846–48), "Wyrok śmierci . . . przeciw Teofilowi Wiśniowskiemu," 31 July 1847.

111. *Gazeta Krakowska*, 6 April 1846.

112. Maner, *Galizien*, pp. 210–11.

113. *Gazeta Krakowska*, 30 May 1846.

114. Ibid., 28 July 1846.

115. Ibid., 17 November 1846.

116. Ibid.

117. Ibid.

118. Gabriele Rossetti, "All'Austria" (November 1846), in *Cracovia: Carmi* (Lausanne: S. Bonamici e Compagni, 1847), pp. 15–16.

4. GALICIAN VERTIGO

1. Antoni Cetnarowicz, "Metternich in den Augen der zeitgenössischen Polen und in der polnischen Historiographie," in *Polen-Oesterreich: Aus der Geschichte einer Nachbarschaft* (Vienna and Warsaw: Oesterreichische Bundesverlag and Wydawnictwa Szkolne i Pedagogiczne, 1988), p. 100.

2. [Aleksander Wielopolski], "Lettre d'un gentilhomme polonais sur les massacres de Galicie: adressée au prince de Metternich," in Henry Lisicki, *Le Marquis Wielopolski: sa vie et son temps, 1803–1877*, Tome I (Vienna: Faesy und Frick, 1880), p. 315.

3. Ibid.

4. Ibid., pp. 317–19.

5. Ibid., pp. 319–20, 323–24.

6. Ibid., p. 325.

7. Ibid.

8. Ibid., pp. 325–26.

9. Ibid., p. 326.

10. Ibid.

11. Ibid., p. 329.

12. Ibid., p. 331.

13. Ibid.

14. Ibid., pp. 332–33.

15. Ibid., p. 337.

16. Aleksander Fredro, *Korespondencja*, ed. Krystyna Czajkowska and Stanisław Pigoń, in *Pisma Wszystkie*, Tom XIV (Warsaw: Państwowy Instytut Wydawniczy, 1976), p. 124, letter of Fredro, late April/early May 1846.

17. Ibid.

18. Ibid., pp. 124–25, letter of Fredro, late April/early May 1846.

19. Ibid., pp. 125–26, letter of Fredro, late April/early May 1846.

20. Ibid., p. 619, letter of Alfred Potocki (fragment), May 1846.

21. Ibid., p. 129, letter of Fredro, 16 May 1846.

22. Ibid.

23. Ibid., p. 130, letter of Fredro, 16 May 1846.

24. Ibid., p. 622, letter of Alfred Potocki, 25 May 1846.

25. Ibid., p. 132, letter of Fredro, 27 July 1846.

26. Ibid., pp. 132–33, letter of Fredro, 27 July 1846.

27. Ibid., p. 133, letter of Fredro, 27 July 1846.

28. Fredro, *Pisma Polityczno-Społeczne: Aneksy*, ed. Krystyna Czajkowska and Stanisław Pigoń, in *Pisma Wszystkie*, Tom XV (Warsaw: Państwowy Instytut Wydawniczy, 1980), pp. 122–26.

29. Fredro, "Uwagi nad stanem socjalnym w Galicji," *Pisma Polityczno-Społeczne: Aneksy*, p. 95.

30. Ibid., pp. 99–100.

31. Ibid., pp. 102–5.

32. Ibid., p. 107.

33. Fredro, *Pisma Polityczno-Społeczne: Aneksy*, p. 123.

34. Bernard Michel, *Sacher-Masoch 1836–1895* (Paris: Robert Laffont, 1989), pp. 18–19; Maria Kłańska, *Daleko od Wiednia: Galicja w oczach pisarzy niemieckojęzycznych, 1772–1918* (Cracow: Towarzystwo Autorów i Wydawców Prac Naukowych UNIVERSITAS, 1991), pp. 91–92.

35. [Leopold von Sacher-Masoch], *Polnische Revolutionen: Erinnerungen aus Galizien* (Prague: F. A. Credner, 1863), pp. v, 5.

36. Sacher-Masoch, *Souvenirs*, p. 17; Michel, *Sacher-Masoch*, p. 15.

37. *Polnische Revolutionen*, pp. 63–64.

38. Ibid., p. 4.

39. Ibid., p. 5.

40. Ibid., p. 6.

41. Ibid., p. 7.

42. Ibid., pp. 7–9.

43. Ibid., pp. 14–15.

44. Ibid., p. 16.

45. Ibid., pp. 22–24.

46. Ibid., p. 23.

47. Ibid., pp. 22, 26.

48. Michael Stanislawski, *A Murder in Lemberg: Politics, Religion, and Violence in Modern Jewish History* (Princeton: Princeton University Press, 2007), p. 57.

49. *Polnische Revolutionen*, p. 66.

50. Ibid., pp. 52, 73.

51. Ibid., p. 75.

52. Ibid., p. 95.

53. Ibid., pp. 103–4.

54. Ibid., p. 108.

55. Ibid.

56. Ibid., pp. 108–9.

57. Ibid., pp. 109–13.

58. Ibid., p. 107.

59. Ibid., p. 108.

60. Ibid., p. 116; Michel, *Sacher-Masoch*, p. 56.

61. *Polnische Revolutionen*, pp. 370–71.

62. Ibid., p. 386.

63. Jan Kozik, *The Ukrainian National Movement in Galicia, 1815–1849*, trans. Andrew Gorski and Lawrence Orton (Edmonton: Canadian Institute of Ukrainian Studies, 1986), pp. 178–80; C. A. Macartney, *The Habsburg Empire, 1790–1918* (New York: Macmillan, 1969), pp. 368–69; see also *Galicja w 1848 roku*, ed. Andrzej Bonusiak and Marian Stolarczyk, in series *Galicja i jej dziedzictwo*, Vol. XII (Rzeszów: Wydawnictwo Wyższej Szkoły Pedagogicznej, 1999).

64. Kozik, *The Ukrainian National Movement in Galicia*, pp. 189–90, 211–13.

65. Ibid., p. 185.

66. *Gazeta Tarnowska*, 1 April 1848.

67. Ibid.

68. Ibid., 8 April 1848.

69. Marta Bohachevsky-Chomiak, *The Spring of a Nation: The Ukrainians in Eastern Galicia in 1848* (Philadelphia: Shevchenko Scientific Society, 1967), pp. 37–40.

70. Wyspiański, *The Wedding*, trans. Gerard Kapolka (Ann Arbor, MI: Ardis Publishers, 1990), p. 112.

5. After the Revolution

1. Jerzy Łojek, Jerzy Myśliński, Wiesław Władyka, *Dzieje prasy polskiej* (Warsaw: Wydawnictwo Interpress, 1988), pp. 40–43.

2. Joseph Redlich, *Emperor Francis Joseph of Austria* (New York: Macmillan, 1929), pp. 32–33.

3. *Czas*, 3 November, 9 November 1848; C. A. Macartney, *The Habsburg Empire, 1790–1918* (New York: Macmillan, 1969), pp. 404–5.

4. *Czas*, 30 November 1848.

5. Ibid., 7 December 1848.

6. Jan Kozik, *The Ukrainian National Movement in Galicia, 1815–1849*, trans. Andrew Gorski and Lawrence Orton (Edmonton: Canadian Institute of Ukrainian Studies, 1986), pp. 231–32, 265–73; see also Marta Bohachevsky-Chomiak, *The Spring of a Nation: The Ukrainians in Eastern Galicia in 1848* (Philadelphia: Shevchenko Scientific Society, 1967).

7. *Czas*, 9 December 1848.

8. Ivan Rudnytsky, "The Ukrainians in Galicia under Austrian Rule," in *Essays in Modern Ukrainian History* (Edmonton: Canadian Institute of Ukrainian Studies, 1987), p. 321; Macartney, *The Habsburg Empire*, pp. 419–21; Bohachevsky-Chomiak, *The Spring of a Nation*, pp. 47–49; Kozik, *The Ukrainian National Movement in Galicia*, pp. 276–78.

9. *Czas*, 13 January 1849.

10. Ibid.

11. Ibid.

12. Ibid., 5 March 1849.

13. Kozik, *The Ukrainian National Movement in Galicia*, pp. 273–74; Macartney, *The Habsburg Empire*, pp. 404–5.

14. *Czas*, 5 March 1849.

15. Ibid., 22 March 1849, 31 March 1849.

16. Maciej Janowski, *Polish Liberal Thought before 1918* (Budapest: Central European University Press, 2004), pp. 81–87; Brian Porter, *When Nationalism Began to Hate: Imagining Modern Politics in Nineteenth-Century Poland* (Oxford: Oxford University Press, 2000), pp. 48–57.

17. Hipolit Stupnicki, *Das Königreich Galizien und Lodomerien, sammt dem Grossherzogthume Krakau und dem Herzogthume Bukowina: in geographisch-historisch-statistischer Beziehung* (Lviv: Peter Piller, 1853), pp. 9–10, 13.

18. Ibid., pp. 18, 24–25.

19. *Czas*, 3 October 1849.

20. Ibid., 1 November 1849.

21. Ibid., 27 March 1850.

22. Ibid.

23. Ibid.

24. Ibid., 7 October 1850.

25. Macartney, *The Habsburg Empire*, p. 424; see also Konstanty Grzybowski, *Galicja 1848–1914: historia ustroju politycznego na tle historii ustroju Austrii* (Cracow: Zakład Narodowy imienia Ossolińskich, 1959).

26. Józef Buszko, "Gołuchowski, Agenor," in *Polski Słownik Biograficzny*, Tom VIII (Wrocław: Zakład Narodowy imienia Ossolińskich, 1959–60), p. 258.

27. *Czas*, 25 October 1850.

28. Ibid.

29. Ibid., 11 November 1850.

30. Ibid.

31. Ibid., 2 January 1851.

32. Ibid.

33. Ibid., 3 January 1851.

34. Ibid., 10 June 1851.

35. Ibid., 27 June 1851.

36. Ibid., 30 July 1851.

37. Ibid., 13 October 1851.

38. Daniel Unowsky, *The Pomp and Politics of Patriotism: Imperial Celebrations in Habsburg Austria, 1848–1916* (West Lafayette, IN: Purdue University Press, 2005), pp. 33–46.

39. *Czas*, 14 October 1851.

40. Unowsky, *The Pomp and Politics of Patriotism*, p. 45.

41. Michael Stanislawski, *A Murder in Lemberg: Politics, Religion, and Violence in Modern Jewish History* (Princeton: Princeton University Press, 2007); Wolfgang Häusler, *Das galizische Judentum in der Habsburgermonarchie: Im Lichte der zeitgenössischen Publizistik und Reiseliteratur von 1772–1848* (Vienna: Verlag für Geschichte und Politik, 1979), pp. 76–78.

42. Walerian Kalinka, *Galicja i Kraków pod panowaniem austriackim: Wybór pism*, ed. Włodzimierz Bernacki (Cracow: Ośrodek Myśli Politycznej, 2001), pp. x–xi.

43. Ibid., pp. 8–9.

44. Aleksander Fredro, *Korespondencja*, ed. Krystyna Czajkowska, in *Pisma Wszystkie*, Tom XIV (Warsaw: Państwowy Instytut Wydawniczy, 1976), pp. 159–60, letter of Fredro, 6 December 1855; "Sprawa Aleksandra Fredry przed sądem kryminalnym o zdradę stanu," in Fredro, *Pisma Polityczno-Społeczne: Aneksy*, ed. Krystyna Czajkowska and Stanisław Pigoń, in *Pisma Wszystkie*, Tom XV (Warsaw: Państwowy Instytut Wydawniczy, 1980), pp. 257–88; Fredro, *The Major Comedies of Alexander Fredro*, ed. and trans. Harold B. Segel (Princeton: Princeton University Press, 1969), pp. 38–39.

45. Fredro, *Korespondencja*, p. 651, letter of Zofia Fredrowa, 25 August 1853; p. 660, letter of Jan Fredro, 30 June 1856; p. 165, letter of Aleksander Fredro, 12 June 1857.

46. Leopold von Sacher-Masoch, *Souvenirs: Autobiographische Prosa* (Munich: Belleville, 1985), p. 66.

47. Ibid.

48. Sacher-Masoch, *A Light for Others: And Other Jewish Tales from Galicia*, ed. Michael O'Pecko (Riverside, CA: Ariadne Press, 1994), p. 6.

49. Ibid., pp. 2–3.

50. Ibid., p. 7.

51. Ibid., pp. 10–11.

52. Macartney, *The Habsburg Empire*, p. 511.

53. Stefan Kieniewicz, ed. *Galicja w dobie autonomicznej (1850–1914): Wybór tekstów w opracowaniu* (Wrocław: Zakład Narodowy imienia Ossolińskich, 1952), pp. 59–61.

54. Maksymilian Nowicki, *Insecta Haliciae* (Cracow: Typis Universitatis Jagiellonicae, 1865); Nowicki, *Motyle Galicyi* (Lviv: Nakładem Włodzimierz hr. Dzieduszyckiego, w drukarni Instytuta Stauropigiańskiego, 1865); Nowicki, *Beitrag zur lepidopteren fauna Galiziens* (Vienna: K. K. Zoologisch-Botanischen Gesellschaft, 1865); Nowicki, *O rybach dorzeczy Wisły, Styru, Dniestru i Prutu w Galicyi* (Cracow: Nakładem Wydziału Krajowego, w drukarni Czasu, 1889).

55. *Czas*, 11 August 1866.

56. Ibid., 26 September 1866.

57. Ibid., 29 September 1866.

58. John-Paul Himka, *Religion and Nationality in Western Ukraine: The Greek Catholic Church and the Ruthenian National Movement in Galicia, 1867–1900* (Montreal: McGill-Queen's University Press, 1999), pp. 23–44; Ostap Sereda, "From Church-Based to Cultural Nationalism: Early Ukrainophiles, Ritual-Purification Movement, and Emerging Cult of Taras Shevchenko in Austrian Eastern Galicia in the 1860s," *Canadian American Slavic Studies* 40, no. 1 (Spring 2006): 21–47; Paul Robert Magocsi, *The Roots of Ukrainian Nationalism: Galicia as Ukraine's Piedmont* (Toronto: University of Toronto Press, 2002), pp. 99–118.

59. *Czas*, 8 November 1866.

60. Ibid.

61. Ibid.

62. Kieniewicz, ed. *Galicja w dobie autonomicznej*, p. 98; see also Larry Wolff, "*Czas* and the Polish Perspective on the Austro-Hungarian Compromise of 1867," *Polish Review* 27, nos. 1/2 (1982): 65–75.

63. Kieniewicz, ed. *Galicja w dobie autonomicznej*, p. 99.

64. *Czas*, 11 December 1866, 20 December 1866.

65. Ibid., 19 January 1867.

66. Henryk Michalak, *Józef Szujski, 1835–1883* (Łódź: Wydawnictwo Łódzkie, 1987), pp. 24–27; Andrzej Wierzbicki, "Józef Szujski," in *Nation and History: Polish Historians from the Enlightenment to the Second World War*, ed. Peter Brock, John Stanley, and Piotr Wróbel (Toronto: University of Toronto Press, 2006), pp. 85–100.

67. Michalak, *Józef Szujski*, pp. 118–19.

68. Józef Szujski, "Kilka prawd z dziejów naszych: ku rozważeniu w chwili obecnej," in *O fałszywej historii jako mistrzyni fałszywej polityki: rozprawy i artykuły*, ed. Henryk Michalak (Warsaw: Państwowy Instytut Wydawniczy, 1991), pp. 190–91.

69. Ibid., pp. 192, 195, 200.

70. Ibid., pp. 203, 206.

71. *Czas*, 20 January 1867.

72. Ibid., 9 February 1867.

73. Ibid., 14 May 1867; Piotr Wandycz, *The Lands of Partitioned Poland, 1795–1918* (Seattle: University of Washington Press, 1974), p. 223.

74. *Czas,* 19 June 1867.

75. Ibid., 5 July, 6 July 1867.

76. Ibid., 8 August 1867.

77. Ibid.

78. Ibid., 23 January, 15 February 1868.

79. Szujski, "Mowy na Sejmie galicyjskim," in *O fałszywej historii,* p. 237.

80. Macartney, *The Habsburg Empire,* pp. 575–77; Hans-Christian Maner, *Galizien: Eine Grenzregion im Kalkül der Donaumonarchie im 18. und 19. Jahrhundert* (Munich: Institut für deutsche Kultur und Geschichte Südosteuropas, 2007), pp. 139–42.

81. *Teka Stańczyka,* in *Stańczycy: Antologia myśli społecznej i politycznej konserwatystów krakowskich,* ed. Marcin Król (Warsaw: Instytut Wydawniczy Pax, 1982), p. 80.

82. Stanisław Koźmian, "Szkoła patriotyzmu politycznego," in *Stańczycy,* pp. 214, 224; *Czas,* 13 January 1849.

83. *Czas,* 17 January 1869.

84. Maner, *Galizien,* pp. 190–94.

85. *Czas,* 19 February 1869.

86. Ibid., 25 February 1869; Ivan Rudnytsky, "Franciszek Duchiński and His Impact on Ukrainian Political Thought," in *Essays in Modern Ukrainian History,* pp. 192–93.

87. *Czas,* 28 February 1869.

88. Ibid., 11 March 1869.

89. Ibid.

90. Ibid., 21 April 1869.

91. Patrice Dabrowski, *Commemorations and the Shaping of Modern Poland* (Bloomington: Indiana University Press, 2004), pp. 1–2.

92. *Czas,* 11 August 1869.

93. Markian Prokopovych, *Habsburg Lemberg: Architecture, Public Space, and Politics in the Galician Capital, 1772–1914* (West Lafayette, IN: Purdue University Press, 2009), pp. 208–22; Pawel Sierżęga, "Obchody rocznicy Unii Lubelskiej na terenie Galicji w 1869 roku," in *Galicja i jej dziedzictwo,* Tom 15, *Działalność wyzwoleńcza,* ed. Jadwiga Hoff (Rzeszów: Wydawnictwo Uniwersytetu Rzeszowskiego, 2001), pp. 168–70, 179–92.

94. *Czas,* 24 August 1869, 1 September 1869.

95. Apollo Korzeniowski, *Conrad under Familial Eyes,* ed. Zdzisław Najder, trans. Halina Carroll-Najder (Cambridge: Cambridge University Press, 1983), letter of Apollo Korzeniowski, 5/17 March 1868, p. 113.

96. Ibid., letter of Apollo Korzeniowski, 29 May 1868, p. 117.

97. Ibid., letter of Apollo Korzeniowski, 12 October 1868, p. 121.

98. Ibid., pp. xvii–xviii.

6. The Average Galician in the Age of Autonomy

1. Antoni Schneider, "Zaproszenie do przedpłaty na dzieło pod tytułem: Encyklopedya do krajoznawstwa Galicyi" (1868), Biblioteka Czartoryskich, Cracow; some of the material in this chapter is to appear in an article: Larry Wolff, "The Encyclopedia

of Galicia: Provincial Synthesis in the Age of Galician Autonomy," *Journal of Ukrainian Studies* 33 (2010).

2. Ihor Zhuk, "The Architecture of Lviv from the Thirteenth to the Twentieth Centuries," *Harvard Ukrainian Studies* 24 (2000): 114; Markian Prokopovych, *Habsburg Lemberg: Architecture, Public Space, and Politics in the Galician Capital, 1772–1914* (West Lafayette, IN: Purdue University Press, 2009), pp. 109, 113–15; Paul Robert Magocsi, *Galicia: A Historical Survey and Bibliographic Guide* (Toronto: University of Toronto Press, 1983), p. 228.

3. Daniel Unowsky, *The Pomp and Politics of Patriotism: Imperial Celebrations in Habsburg Austria, 1848–1916* (West Lafayette, IN: Purdue University Press, 2005), pp. 48–50.

4. Wiesław Bieńkowski, "Schneider (Szneider, Sznejder), Antoni Julian," in *Polski Słownik Biograficzny*, Tom XXXV (Warsaw: Polska Akademia Nauk, 1994), pp. 571–73.

5. Antoni Schneider, *Encyklopedya do krajoznawstwa Galicji*, Tom I (Lviv: Zakład Narodowy imienia Ossolińskich, 1871), p. iii; Tom II (Lviv: z drukarni J. Dobrzańskiego i K. Gromana, 1874).

6. *Archiwum Państwowe w Krakowie, Wawel: Teka Schneidra* 1782, "Żurawno."

7. Ibid., *Teka Schneidra* 515, "Gedrängte statistische Übersicht des Königreiches Galizien (1822)"

8. Ibid., "Quandoquidem circumspecto (1772)"; *Teka Schneidra* 442, "Drohobycz: Żydzi."

9. Jan Hulewicz, "Majer, Józef," in *Polski Słownik Biograficzny*, Tom XIX (Warsaw: Polska Akademia Nauk, 1974), pp. 161–64; Stefan Kieniewicz and Paweł Sikora, "Kopernicki, Izydor," in *Polski Słownik Biograficzny*, Tom XIV (Warsaw: Polska Akademia Nauk, 1994), pp. 1–3.

10. Józef Mayer and Izydor Kopernicki, *Charakterystyka Fizyczna Ludności Galicyjskiej* (Cracow: Uniwersytet Jagielloński, 1876), pp. 3–6.

11. Ibid., pp. 15, 36.

12. Ibid., pp. 36–38.

13. Ibid., pp. 64, 77, 88, 90.

14. Ibid., pp. 123, 137, 175.

15. C. A. Macartney, *The Habsburg Empire, 1790–1918* (New York: Macmillan, 1969), p. 518.

16. Yad Vashem Central Database of Shoah Victims' Names; Leiser Erber was the author's great-grandfather, and the name "Larry" was intended as a rough American remembrance of "Leiser."

17. Macartney, *The Habsburg Empire*, pp. 562–63.

18. "Contract between Frau Fanny von Pistor and Leopold von Sacher-Masoch," in Leopold von Sacher-Masoch, *Venus in Furs*, ed. Joachim Neugroschel, intro. by Larry Wolff (New York: Penguin, 2000), p. 121.

19. Cited in Sacher-Masoch, *Don Juan von Kolomea: Galizische Geschichten*, ed. Michael Farin (Bonn: Bouvier Verlag Herbert Grundmann, 1985), pp. 195–96.

20. Cited in Sacher-Masoch, *A Light for Others: And Other Jewish Tales from Galicia*, ed. Michael O'Pecko (Riverside, CA: Ariadne Press, 1994), p. 334.

21. Carl Steiner, *Karl Emil Franzos, 1848–1904: Emancipator and Assimilationist* (New York: Peter Lang, 1990), pp. 11–13; Maria Kłańska, *Daleko od Wiednia: Galicja w oczach*

pisarzy niemieckojęzycznych, 1772–1918 (Cracow: Towarzystwo Autorów i Wydawców Prac Naukowych UNIVERSITAS, 1991), pp. 179–86.

22. Steiner, *Karl Emil Franzos*, pp. 53–54.

23. Larry Wolff, *Inventing Eastern Europe: The Map of Civilization on the Mind of the Enlightenment* (Stanford: Stanford University Press, 1994), p. 19; [Ernest Traugott von Kortum], *Magna Charta von Galizien: oder Untersuchung der Beschwerden des Galizischen Adels pohlnischer Nation über die österreichische Regierung* (Jassy, 1790), pp. 18–19; Metternich, *Mémoires, documents, et écrits divers*, ed. Richard de Metternich, Part II (1816–48), Vol. IV (Paris: E. Plon, 1881), pp. 20–21, letter of 21 October 1823.

24. Steiner, *Karl Emil Franzos*, p. 62.

25. Jan Kozik, *The Ukrainian National Movement in Galicia, 1815–1849*, trans. Andrew Gorski and Lawrence Orton (Edmonton: Canadian Institute of Ukrainian Studies, 1986), p. 118.

26. Karl Emil Franzos, *The Jews of Barnow: Stories*, trans. M. W. MacDowall (New York: D. Appleton and Company, 1883), pp. 130–32.

27. Ibid., pp. 128, 135.

28. Ibid., pp. 182.

29. Ibid., pp. 205.

30. Ibid., pp. 76–78.

31. John-Paul Himka, "Dimensions of a Triangle: Polish-Ukrainian-Jewish Relations in Austrian Galicia," in *Polin: Studies in Polish Jewry*, Vol. XII, *Focusing on Galicia: Jews, Poles, and Ukrainians, 1772–1918*, ed. Israel Bartal and Antony Polonsky (London: Littman Library of Jewish Civilization, 1999), p. 36.

32. Josef Ehrlich, *Der Weg meines Lebens: Erinnerungen eines ehemaligen Chassiden* (Vienna: Verlag von L. Rosner, 1874), p. 1; Mary McCarthy, "My Confession" (1953), republished in *The Humanist in the Bathtub* (New York: Signet, 1964), p. 130.

33. Ehrlich, *Der Weg meines Lebens*, p. 12.

34. Mieczysław Orłowicz, *Ilustrowany Przewodnik po Galicyi* (Lviv: Akademicki Klub Turystyczny, 1914), p. 87.

35. Ehrlich, *Der Weg meines Lebens*, p. 30.

36. Ibid., pp. 42, 106–8; see also *Kultura Żydów Galicyjskich: z zbiorów Muzeum Etnografii i Rzemiosła Artystycznego we Lwowie*, ed. Elżbieta Skromak, Anna Garbacz, Marek Wiatrowicz (Stalowa Wola: Drukarnia Marlex, 2006); Suzan Wynne, *The Galitzianers: The Jews of Galicia 1772–1918* (Tucson, AZ: Wheatmark, 2006).

37. Ivan Franko, *Beiträge zur Geschichte und Kultur der Ukraine: Ausgewählte deutsche Schriften des Revolutionären Demokraten, 1882–1915*, ed. E. Winter and P. Kirchner (Berlin: Akademie Verlag, 1963), pp. 503–4, letter of Buber to Franko, 3 April 1903.

38. Franko, "Meine jüdischen Bekannten," in ibid., pp. 50–51; see also Yaroslav Hrytsak, *Prorok u svoii vitchyzni: Franko ta ioho spilnota 1856–1886* (Kiev: Krytyka, 2006), pp. 335–63.

39. Franko, "Meine jüdischen Bekannten," in *Beiträge zur Geschichte und Kultur der Ukraine*, pp. 51–53.

40. Ibid., pp. 57–58; John-Paul Himka, *Socialism in Galicia: The Emergence of Polish Social Democracy and Ukrainian Radicalism* (Cambridge: Harvard Ukrainian Research Institute, 1983), pp. 115–21; Hrytsak, *Prorok u svoii vitchyzni*, pp. 275–302.

41. Alison Fleig Frank, *Oil Empire: Visions of Prosperity in Austrian Galicia* (Cambridge: Harvard University Press, 2005), pp. 126–29.

42. Franko, *Boa Constrictor: And Other Stories*, trans. Fainna Solasko (Moscow: Foreign Languages Publishing House, n.d. [1957?]), p. 213; see also Yaroslav Hrytsak, "Franko's Boryslav Cycle," *Journal of Ukrainian Studies* 29, nos. 1–2 (Summer–Winter, 2004).

43. Franko, *Boa Constrictor*, pp. 253–54.

44. Franko, "Meine jüdischen Bekannten," in *Beiträge zur Geschichte und Kultur der Ukraine*, p. 58.

45. Leonid Rudnytzky, "The Image of Austria in the Works of Ivan Franko," in *Nationbuilding and the Politics of Nationalism: Essays on Austrian Galicia*, ed. Andrei Markovits and Frank Sysyn (Cambridge: Harvard Ukrainian Research Institute, 1982), p. 246.

46. Ibid., pp. 243–46.

47. Jan Lewicki [Ivan Levytsky], *Ruch Rusinów w Galicji: w pierwszej połowie wieku panowania Austrii, 1772–1820* (Lviv: Nakładem Autora, 1879), p. 5.

48. Paul Robert Magocsi, *Galicia: A Historical Survey and Bibliographic Guide* (Toronto: University of Toronto Press, 1983), pp. 6, 23.

49. John-Paul Himka, *Religion and Nationality in Western Ukraine: The Greek Catholic Church and the Ruthenian National Movement in Galicia, 1867–1900* (Montreal: McGill-Queen's University Press, 1999), pp. 108–9; Julian Pelesz, *Geschichte der Union der ruthenischen Kirche mit Rom von den ältesten Zeiten bis auf die Gegenwart* (Vienna: Verleger der Mechitharisten,1878–80; Würzburg: Leo Woerl, 1881).

50. Stefan Kaczala [Kachala], *Polityka Polaków względem Rusi* (Lviv: Nakładem Autora, 1879), p. 1.

51. Ibid., p. 5.

52. Ibid., p. 14.

53. Ibid., p. 17.

54. Ibid., pp. 286, 306–7, 354; see also Himka, *Socialism in Galicia*, pp. 40–70; Ivan Rudnytsky, "The Ukrainians in Galicia under Austrian Rule," in *Essays in Modern Ukrainian History* (Edmonton: Canadian Institute of Ukrainian Studies, University of Alberta, 1987), pp. 315–52; Ostap Sereda, "Whom Shall We Be?" Public Debates over the National Identity of Galician Ruthenians in the 1860s," in *Jahrbücher für Geschichte Osteuropas*, Band 49, Heft 2 (Stuttgart: Franz Steiner Verlag, 2001), pp. 200–212; Anna Veronika Wendland, "Die Rückkehr der Russophilen in die ukrainische Geschichte: Neue Aspekte der ukrainischen Nationsbildung in Galizien, 1848–1914," in *Jahrbücher für Geschichte Osteuropas*, Band 49, Heft 2, pp. 178–99.

55. *Czas*, 18 February 1880; see also Jerzy Myśliński, "Prasa Polska w Galicji w dobie autonomicznej (1867–1918)," in *Prasa Polska w latach 1864–1918*, ed. Jerzy Łojek (Warsaw: Państwowe Wydawnictwo Naukowe, 1976), pp. 114–76.

56. *Czas*, 18 February 1880.

57. *Czas*, 19 March 1880; see also Keely Stauter-Halsted, *The Nation in the Village: The Genesis of Peasant National Identity in Austrian Poland, 1848–1914* (Ithaca, NY: Cornell University Press, 2001), pp. 97–114.

58. *Conrad under Familial Eyes*, ed. Zdzisław Najder, trans. Halina Carroll-Najder

(Cambridge: Cambridge University Press, 1983), letter of Apollo Korzeniowski, 11/23 March 1868, p. 115.

59. Franko, "Spring Scene," in *Selected Poems*, trans. Percival Cundy, ed. Clarence Manning (New York: Greenwood Press, 1968), p. 109.

60. Franko, "National Hymn," in *Selected Poems*, p. 115.

61. *Czas*, 7 July 1880.

62. Tadeusz Żeleński (Boy), *Znaszli ten kraj? i inne wspomnienia* (Cracow: Wydawnictwo Literackie, 1956), p. 34; Myśliński, "Prasa polska w Galicji," pp. 121–28.

63. *Czas*, 13 July 1880.

64. Ibid., 18 August 1830.

65. Daniel Unowsky, "Celebrating Two Emperors and a Revolution: The Public Contest to Represent the Polish and Ruthenian Nations in 1880," in *The Limits of Loyalty: Imperial Symbolism, Popular Allegiances, and State Patriotism in the Late Habsburg Monarchy*, ed. Laurence Cole and Daniel Unowsky (New York: Berghahn Books, 2007), pp. 124–31.

66. *Czas*, 22 August 1880; Patrice Dabrowski, "Discovering the Galician Borderlands: The Case of the Eastern Carpathians," *Slavic Review* 64, no. 2 (Summer 2005): 380–402; see also Dabrowski, "Constructing a Polish Landscape: The Example of the Carpathian Frontier," *Austrian History Yearbook* 39 (April 2008): 45–65.

67. *Czas*, 1 September 1880.

68. Ibid.

69. *Archiwum Państwowe w Krakowie: Inwentarz Tymczasowy 872, Uroczystości (Franz Joseph)*, 1880.

70. Unowsky, *The Pomp and Politics of Patriotism*, pp. 56–57.

71. *Archiwum Państwowe w Krakowie: Inwentarz Tymczasowy 872, Uroczystości (Franz Joseph)*, *Gazeta Lwowska*, 1 September 1880.

72. "Program podróży," *Czas*, 22 August 1880.

73. Ibid., "Program podróży"; *Archiwum Państwowe w Krakowie: Inwentarz Tymczasowy 872, Uroczystości (Franz Joseph)*, *Czas*, 5 September 1880.

74. *Czas*, 8 September 1880.

75. Unowsky, *The Pomp and Politics of Patriotism*, pp. 65–69; Michael Moser, *"Ruthenische" (ukrainische) Sprach- und Vorstellungswelten in den galizischen Volksschullesebüchern der Jahre 1871 und 1872* (Vienna: LIT Verlag, 2007), p. 139.

76. *Czas*, 15 September 1880.

77. Walerian Kalinka, *Galicja i Kraków pod panowaniem austriackim: Wybór pism*, ed. Włodzimierz Bernacki (Cracow: Ośrodek Myśli Politycznej, 2001), pp. xvii–xviii.

78. Himka, *Religion and Nationality*, p. 70.

79. Ibid.

80. Józef Szujski, *Die Polen und Ruthenen in Galizien* (Wien and Teschen: Verlag von Karl Prochaska, 1882), p. 1; Andrzej Wierzbicki, "Józef Szujski," in *Nation and History: Polish Historians from the Enlightenment to the Second World War*, ed. Peter Brock, John Stanley, and Piotr Wróbel (Toronto: University of Toronto Press, 2006), pp. 85–100.

81. Szujski, *Die Polen und Ruthenen in Galizien*, p. 19.

82. Ibid., pp. 20–21.

83. Ibid., pp. 26–27.

84. Ibid., p. 29.

85. Ibid., pp. 28–29.

86. Ibid., pp. 30–31.

87. Ibid., p. 81.

88. Prokopovych, *Habsburg Lemberg*, pp. 109, 115.

89. Patrice Dabrowski, *Commemorations and the Shaping of Modern Poland* (Bloomington: Indiana University Press, 2004), pp. 52–58; see also Paweł Sierżęga, *Obchody 200. rocznicy odsieczy wiedeński w Galicji*, Vol. XVII, *Galicja i jej dziedzictwo* (Rzeszów: Wydawnictwo Uniwersytetu Rzeszowskiego, 2002).

90. Stauter-Halsted, *The Nation in the Village*, pp. 208–215; see also Dabrowski, *Commemorations*, pp. 114–32.

91. Dabrowski, *Commemorations*, p. 67.

92. *Kantata na pamiątkę dwóchsetnej rocznicy zwycięstwa Króla Jana III pod Wiedniem*, W. L. Anczyc, W. Żeleński (1883), Biblioteka Czartoryskich, Cracow.

93. *Czas*, 27 January 1884.

94. Ibid.

95. Ibid., 26 April 1884.

96. Ibid., 2 May 1884.

97. Joseph Redlich, *Emperor Francis Joseph of Austria: A Biography* (New York: Macmillan, 1929), pp. 414–15.

98. Julius Jandaurek, *Das Königreich Galizien und Lodomerien: und das Herzogthum Bukowina* (Vienna: Verlag von Karl Graeser, 1884), pp. 5–6.

99. Ibid., pp. 37–39.

100. Ibid., p. 44; Himka, "Dimensions of a Triangle," p. 26.

101. Jandaurek, *Das Königreich Galizien und Lodomerien*, pp. 44–45.

102. Ibid., pp. 46–48.

103. Ibid., p. 55.

104. Ibid., p. 60.

105. Ibid., pp. 63–65.

106. Ibid., pp. 72–73.

107. Ibid., pp. 74–76.

108. Ibid., p. 154.

109. Franko, "The Passing of Serfdom," in *Selected Poems*, p. 141.

110. Ibid., p. 144.

111. Stanisław Szczepanowski, *Nędza Galicyi w cyfrach i program energicznego rozwoju gospodarstwa krajowego* (Lviv: Gubrynowicz i Schmidt, Drukiem Pillera, 1888), pp. v–vii.

112. Frank, *Oil Empire*, pp. 82–89.

113. *Czas*, 4 February 1888.

114. Ibid.

115. Ibid., 5 February 1888.

116. Szczepanowski, *Nędza Galicyi*, p. 125.

117. *Czas*, 11 February 1888.

118. Michał Śliwa, "Nędza Galicyjska: mit i rzeczywistość," in *Galicja i jej dziedzic-*

two, I, *Historia i polityka*, ed. Włodzimierz Bonusiak and Józef Buszko (Rzeszów, 1994), pp. 145–53.

119. Szczepanowski, *Nędza Galicyi*, p. 61; Śliwa, "Nędza Galicyjska," p. 146.

120. Szczepanowski, *Nędza Galicyi*, p. 178.

121. Śliwa, "Nędza Galicyjska," p. 148.

122. *Czas*, 15 February 1888.

123. *Czas*, 15 February 1888.

7. FIN-DE-SIÈCLE GALICIA

1. Kazimierz Tetmajer, "Wielki poeta," in *Wesele we wspomnieniach i krytyce*, ed. Aniela Łempicka (Cracow: Wydawnictwo Literackie, 1961), p. 133.

2. Stanisław Wyspiański, *The Wedding*, trans. Gerard Kapolka (Ann Arbor, MI: Ardis Publishers, 1990), p. 50 (Act I, Scene 17); see also Aniela Łempicka, *Wyspiański: pisarz dramatyczny: idee i formy* (Cracow: Wydawnictwo Literackie, 1973), pp. 279–345; Alicja Okońska, *Stanisław Wyspiański* (Warsaw: Wiedza Powszechna, 1971), pp. 235–72; Claude Backvis, *Le Dramaturge Stanislas Wyspiański* (Paris: Presses Universitaires de France, 1952), pp. 213–35; Artur Hutnikiewicz, *Młoda Polska*, (Warsaw: Wydawnictwo Naukowe PWN, 1994), pp. 7–214.

3. Wyspiański, *The Wedding*, pp. 72–73 (Act I, Scene 30).

4. Ibid., p. 112 (Act II, Scene 15).

5. Ibid., p. 113 (Act II, Scene 15).

6. Kazimierz Tetmajer, "Nie wierzę w nic," in *Antologia liryki Młodej Polski*, ed. Ireneusz Sikora (Wrocław: Zakład Narodowy imienia Ossolińskich, 1990), p. 136.

7. Ivan Franko, "Hymn to Buddha," in *Ivan Franko: The Poet of Western Ukraine: Selected Poems*, trans. Percival Cundy, ed. Clarence Manning (New York: Philosophical Library, 1948), pp. 189–90.

8. Kazimierz Tetmajer, "Koniec wieku XIX," in *Antologia liryki Młodej Polski*, pp. 237–38.

9. Ibid.

10. Marta Romanowska, "Katedra Lwowska," in *Stanisław Wyspiański: Opus Magnum* (Cracow: Muzeum Narodowe, 2000), pp. 79–81.

11. Thomas Prymak, *Mykhailo Hrushevsky: The Politics of National Culture* (Toronto: University of Toronto Press, 1987), p. 29; Ivan Rudnytsky, "The Ukrainians in Galicia under Austrian Rule," in *Essays in Modern Ukrainian History* (Edmonton: Canadian Institute of Ukrainian Studies, University of Alberta, 1987), pp. 339–40.

12. Prymak, *Mykhailo Hrushevsky*, pp. 29–31.

13. Czesław Miłosz, *The History of Polish Literature*, 2nd ed. (1969; Berkeley: University of California Press, 1983), pp. 351–58; Timothy Snyder, *The Reconstruction of Nations: Poland, Ukraine, Lithuania, Belarus 1569–1999* (New Haven, CT: Yale University Press, 2003), pp. 125–32; Serhii Plokhy, *Unmaking Imperial Russia: Mykhailo Hrushevsky and the Writing of Ukrainian History* (Toronto: University of Toronto Press, 2005), pp. 23–211; Jacek Purchla, "Kraków i Lwów: zmienność relacji w XIX i XX wieku," in Jacek Purchla, ed. *Kraków i Lwów w cywilizacji europejskiej* (Cracow: Międzynarodowe Centrum Kultury, 2003), pp. 81–90; Maciej Janowski, "Galizien auf dem Weg zur

Zivilgesellschaft," in *Die Habsburgermonarchie 1848–1918*, Band 8, *Politische Öffentlichkeit und Zivilgesellschaft*, Teilband 1 (Vienna: Verlag der Österreichischen Akademie der Wissenschaften, 2006), pp. 840–45.

14. Bolesław Limanowski, *Galicya przedstawiona słowem i ołówkiem* (Warsaw: Wydawnictwo Przeglądu Tygodniowego, 1892).

15. Ihor Zhuk, "The Architecture of Lviv from the 13th to the 20th Centuries," *Harvard Ukrainian Studies* 24 (2000): 116; *Architektura Lwowa: XIX wieku*, ed. Jacek Purchla (Cracow: International Cultural Center, 1997), figures 89–108.

16. *Katalog działu etnograficznego: Powszechna Wystawa Krajowa w Lwowie 1894* (Lviv: Piller, 1894), pp. 1–2.

17. *Zeitschrift für österreichische Volkskunde*, I. Jahrgang 1895 (Vienna and Prague: Verlag von F. Tempsky, 1896), p. 15.

18. Jacek Purchla, "Patterns of Influence: Lviv and Vienna in the Mirror of Architecture," *Harvard Ukrainian Studies* 24 (2000): 139; Markian Prokopovych, *Habsburg Lemberg: Architecture, Public Space, and Politics in the Galician Capital, 1772–1914* (West Lafayette, IN: Purdue University Press, 2009), pp. 247–53.

19. Prokopovych, *Habsburg Lemberg*, p. 252.

20. *Zeitschrift für österreichische Volkskunde*, I. Jahrgang 1895, pp. 15–16; *Katalog działu etnograficznego*, p. 37.

21. *Zeitschrift für österreichische Volkskunde*, I. Jahrgang 1895, p. 16.

22. *Katalog działu etnograficznego*, p. 67.

23. Ibid., p. 68.

24. Mieczysław Orłowicz, *Ilustrowany Przewodnik po Galicyi* (Lviv: Akademicki Klub Turystyczny, 1914), p. 136.

25. *Katalog działu etnograficznego*, pp. 74, 83; Orłowicz, *Ilustrowany Przewodnik po Galicyi*, p. 92.

26. Orłowicz, *Ilustrowany Przewodnik po Galicyi*, p. 141.

27. *Katalog działu etnograficznego*, pp. 23–24.

28. Daniel Unowsky, *The Pomp and Politics of Patriotism: Imperial Celebrations in Habsburg Austria 1848–1916* (West Lafayette, IN: Purdue University Press, 2005), pp. 72–75.

29. *Listy Stanisława Wyspiańskiego: do Józef Mehoffera, Henryka Opieńskiego i Tadeusza Stryjeńskiego*, I, ed. Maria Rydlowa (Cracow: Wydawnictwo Literackie, 1994), p. 184–85 (31 October 1895); pp. 209–10 (8 August 1896).

30. Ibid., pp. 209–10 (8 August 1896).

31. Prymak, *Mykhailo Hrushevsky*, pp. 38–40; see also Harald Binder, *Galizien in Wien: Parteien, Wahlen, Fraktionen und Abgeordnete im Übergang zur Massenpolitik* (Vienna: Verlag der Österreichischen Akademie der Wissenschaften, 2005); Anna Veronika Wendland, *Die Russophilen in Galizien: Ukrainische Konservative zwischen Österreich und Russland* (Vienna: Verlag der Österreichischen Akademie der Wissenschaften, 2001).

32. Carl Schorske, "Politics and the Psyche: Schnitzler and Hofmannsthal," in *Fin-de-siècle Vienna: Politics and Culture* (1980; New York: Vintage Books, 1981), pp. 3–23; Scott Spector, "Beyond the Aesthetic Garden: Politics and Culture on the Margins of Fin-de-Siècle Vienna," *Journal of the History of Ideas* 59, no. 4 (October 1998): 695.

33. Stanisław Przybyszewski, *Moi współcześni: wśród swoich* (Warsaw: Instytut Wydawniczy "Biblioteka Polska," 1930), p. 50.

34. Hofmannsthal to Leopold von Andrian, 4 May 1896, in *Europa Erlesen: Galizien*, ed. Stefan Simonek and Alois Woldan (Klagenfurt: Wieserverlag, 1998), pp. 153–55; see also Stefan Simonek, "Hugo von Hofmannsthals Galizische Implikationen," in *Kakanien Revisited*, March 2004, http://www.kakanien.ac.at.

35. Werner Volke, *Hugo von Hofmannsthal in Selbstzeugnissen und Bilddokumenten* (Reinbek bei Hamburg: Rowohlt, 1967), p. 54.

36. Ibid., p. 55.

37. Stanisław Przybyszewski, *Listy*, Tom I (1879–1906) (Warsaw: Parnas Polski, 1937), p. 155, letter of May 1897.

38. Ibid., p. 207, letter of 8 October 1898.

39. Alois Woldan, *"Życie (Leben)*: Kunstzeitschrift und Ort der Begegnung," in *Kunst und Humanismus*, ed. Wolfgang Augustyn and Eckhard Leuschner (Passau: Dietmar Klinger Verlag, 2007), pp. 563–79; Tomasz Weiss, "Die Krakauer Zeitschrift *Życie* und die Österreichischen modernistischen Zeitschriften," *Studia Austro-Polonica* 2, *Zeszyty Naukowe Uniwersytetu Jagiellońskiego* DLXXXII, Prace Historyczne, Zeszyt 68 (1980), pp. 179–94.

40. Hans Bisanz, "Polnische Künstler in der Wiener Sezession und im Hagenbund," *Studia Austro-Polonica* 2, *Zeszyty Naukowe Uniwersytetu Jagiellońskiego* DLXXXII, Prace Historyczne, Zeszyt 68 (1980), pp. 29–41.

41. Miłosz, *The History of Polish Literature*, p. 330.

42. Tadeusz Żeleński (Boy), *Znaszli ten kraj? i inne wspomnienia* (Cracow: Wydawnictwo Literackie, 1956), pp. 98–99.

43. Ibid., pp. 99–100.

44. *Czas*, 13 September 1898; see also Jerzy Myśliński, "Prasa Polska w Galicji w dobie autonomicznej (1867–1918)," in *Prasa Polska w latach 1864–1918*, ed. Jerzy Łojek (Warsaw: Państwowe Wydawnictwo Naukowe, 1976), pp. 114–76.

45. Larry Wolff, "Dynastic Conservatism and Poetic Violence in Fin-de-siècle Cracow: The Habsburg Matrix of Polish Modernism," *American Historical Review* 106, no. 3 (June 2001): 735–64.

46. *Czas*, 20 September 1898.

47. Ibid., 28 October 1898.

48. Ibid., 22 September 1898.

49. Tetmajer, "Koniec wieku XIX," in *Antologia liryki Młodej Polski*, pp. 237–38; *Czas*, 22 September 1898.

50. *Czas*, 7 July 1899; 8 July 1899.

51. Ibid., 23 March 1900.

52. Ibid., 18 September 1898.

53. Ibid., 23 March 1899; see also Schorske, "Politics and the Psyche: Schnitzler and Hofmannsthal," pp. 11–12.

54. Piotr Wróbel, "The Jews of Galicia under Austrian-Polish Rule, 1869–1918," *Austrian History Yearbook* 25 (1994): 130–31; Unowsky, *The Pomp and Politics of Patriotism*, p. 177; see also Keely Stauter-Halsted, "Jews as Middleman Minorities in Rural Poland: Understanding the Galician Pogroms of 1898," in *Antisemitism and Its Opponents in Modern Poland*, ed. Robert Blobaum (Ithaca, NY: Cornell University Press, 2005), pp. 39–59; Frank Golczewski, "Rural Anti-semitism in Galicia before World War I," in *The Jews in Poland*, ed. Chimen Abramsky, Maciej Jachimczyk, and Antony Polonsky (Ox-

ford: Basil Blackwell, 1986), pp. 97–105; Frank Golczewski, *Polnisch-Jüdische Beziehungen 1881–1922: Eine Studie zur Geschichte des Antisemitismus in Osteuropa* (Wiesbaden: Franz Steiner Verlag, 1981), pp. 60–84.

55. *Archiwum Państwowe w Krakowie: Sąd Krajowy Karny w Krakowie*, register 590 (1898), file 905.

56. *Czas*, 3 September 1898; 6 September 1898; 10 September 1898.

57. Ibid., 13 October 1898.

58. Ibid., 5 November 1898; 7 November 1898; 9 November 1898.

59. Wyspiański, *The Wedding*, p. 28 (Act I, Scene 1).

60. Ibid., p. 63 (Act I, Scene 25).

61. Ibid., pp. 69, 72 (Act I, Scenes 28, 29).

62. Ibid., pp. 72–73 (Act I, Scene 30).

8. THE LAND OF IMPOSSIBILITIES

1. *Czas*, 7 October 1898.

2. Patrice Dabrowski, *Commemorations and the Shaping of Modern Poland* (Bloomington: Indiana University Press, 2004), pp. 77–100, 133–56; see also Keely Stauter-Halsted, *The Nation in the Village: The Genesis of Peasant National Identity in Austrian Poland 1848–1914* (Ithaca, NY: Cornell University Press, 2001), pp. 209–14; and Kai Struve, *Bauern und Nation in Galizien: Über Zugehörigkeit und soziale Emanzipation im 19. Jahrhundert* (Göttingen: Vandenhoeck und Ruprecht, 2005), pp. 323–62.

3. Kai Struve, "Peasants and Patriotic Celebrations in Habsburg Galicia," in *Galicia: A Multicultured Land*, ed. Christopher Hann and Paul Magocsi (Toronto: University of Toronto Press, 2005), p. 114; see also Struve, *Bauern und Nation in Galizien*, pp. 362–81.

4. Dabrowski, *Commemorations*, pp. 145–46; Thomas Prymak, *Mykhailo Hrushevsky: The Politics of National Culture* (Toronto: University of Toronto Press, 1987), pp. 48–53; Yaroslav Hrytsak, "A Ukrainian Answer to the Galician Ethnic Triangle: The Case of Ivan Franko," in *Polin: Studies in Polish Jewry*, Vol. 12, *Focusing on Galicia: Jews, Poles, and Ukrainians, 1772–1918*, ed. Israel Bartal and Antony Polonsky (London: Littman Library of Jewish Civilization, 1999), pp. 141–42; George Grabowicz, "Franko et Mickiewicz: le wallenrodisme et la crainte de l'influence," in *Le Verbe et l'Histoire: Mickiewicz, la France et l'Europe*, ed. François-Xavier Coquin and Michel Masłowski (Paris: Institut d'études slaves, 2002), pp. 96–103.

5. Ivan Franko, "Unmögliches in dem Lande der Unmöglichkeiten," in *Beiträge zur Geschichte und Kultur der Ukraine: Ausgewählte deutsche Schriften des Revolutionären Demokraten, 1882–1915*, ed. E. Winter and P. Kirchner (Berlin: Akademie Verlag, 1963), pp. 370–72; see also Ivan Rudnytsky, "The Ukrainians in Galicia under Austrian Rule," in *Nationbuilding and the Politics of Nationalism: Essays on Austrian Galicia*, ed. Andrei Markovits and Frank Sysyn (Cambridge: Harvard Ukrainian Research Institute, 1982), pp. 60–65.

6. Markian Prokopovych, *Habsburg Lemberg: Architecture, Public Space, and Politics in the Galician Capital, 1772–1914* (West Lafayette, IN: Purdue University Press, 2009), pp. 165–70.

7. John-Paul Himka, *Religion and Nationality in Western Ukraine: The Greek Catholic Church and the Ruthenian National Movement in Galicia, 1867–1900* (Montreal: McGill-Queen's University Press, 1999), p. 146.

8. Bertha Pappenheim, *Sisyphus: Gegen den Mädchenhandel—Galizien*, ed. Helga Heubach (Freiburg: Kore Verlag, 1992), pp. 11–24; Melinda Guttmann, *The Enigma of Anna O: A Biography of Bertha Pappenheim* (Wickford, RI: Moyer Bell, 2001), pp. 129–52; see also Marion Kaplan, *The Jewish Feminist Movement in Germany: The Campaigns of the Jüdischer Frauenbund, 1904–1938* (Westport, CT: Greenwood Press, 1979); Elizabeth Loentz, *Let Me Continue to Speak the Truth: Bertha Pappenheim as Author and Activist* (Cincinnati, OH: Hebrew Union College Press, 2007).

9. *Monatsschrift für die Literatur und Wissenschaft des Judenthums*, Jahrgang 1889, ed. Arthur Weissmann (Vienna: Selbstverlag, 1889), p. 3.

10. Ibid., pp. 8–9.

11. Joshua Shanes, "Neither Germans nor Poles: Jewish Nationalism in Galicia before Herzl, 1883–1897," *Austrian History Yearbook* 34 (2003): 205–9; Ezra Mendelsohn, "Jewish Assimilation in L'viv: The Case of Wilhelm Feldman," in *Nationbuilding and the Politics of Nationalism*, ed. Andrei Markovits and Frank Sysyn, pp. 94–110.

12. S. R. Landau, *Unter jüdischen Proletariern: Reiseschilderungen aus Ostgalizien und Russland* (Vienna: Buchhandlung L. Rosner, 1898), pp. 3, 25.

13. Brian Porter, "Antisemitism and the Search for a Catholic Identity," in *Antisemitism and Its Opponents in Modern Poland*, ed. Robert Blobaum (Ithaca, NY: Cornell University Press, 2005), pp. 107–8.

14. Pappenheim, "Zur Lage der jüdischen Bevölkerung in Galizien: Reiseeindrücke und Vorschläge zur Besserung der Verhältnisse" (1904), in *Sisyphus*, p. 44.

15. Ibid., p. 45.

16. Ibid., p. 64.

17. Ibid., p. 47.

18. Ibid., p. 48.

19. Ibid., p. 65.

20. Ibid., p. 66.

21. Ibid., p. 76.

22. Daniel Soyer, *Jewish Immigrant Associations and American Identity in New York, 1880–1939* (Cambridge: Harvard University Press, 1997), pp. 147–48.

23. Ivan Franko, "Do przyjaciół galicyjskich [Adama Mickiewicza]: próba analizy," in *O literaturze polskiej*, ed. Mikołaj Kuplowski (Cracow: Wydawnictwo Literackie, 1979), p. 81.

24. Pappenheim, "Zur Lage der jüdischen Bevölkerung in Galizien," p. 92.

25. Ibid., pp. 79–80.

26. Ibid., pp. 81–84.

27. Henry-Louis de la Grange, *Gustav Mahler*, Vol. 2, *Vienna: The Years of Challenge, 1897–1904* (Oxford: Oxford University Press, 1995), pp. 598–602; Klemens Wenzel von Metternich, *Mémoires, documents, et écrits divers*, ed. Richard de Metternich, Part II (1816–48), Vol. IV (Paris: E. Plon, 1881), pp. 21–22, letter of 27 October 1823.

28. De la Grange, *Gustav Mahler*, Vol. 2, pp. 599–602.

29. Rodolfo Celletti, "Krusceniski, Salomea," in *The New Grove Dictionary of Opera*, Vol. 2 (Oxford: Oxford University Press, 1997), pp. 1053–54.

30. Benjamin Segel, "Zwei jüdische Volkssagen über Kaiser Franz Josef," *Zeitschrift für österreichische Volkskunde* [Vienna] 9 (1903): 124.

31. Binjamin [Benjamin] Segel, *A Lie and a Libel: The History of the Protocols of the Elders of Zion*, trans. Richard S. Levy (Lincoln: University of Nebraska, 1995).

32. Segel, "Zwei jüdische Volkssagen über Kaiser Franz Josef," p. 125.

33. Michael Silber, "From Tolerated Aliens to Citizen-Soldiers: Jewish Military Service in the Era of Joseph II," in *Constructing Nationalities in East Central Europe*, ed. Pieter Judson and Marsha Rozenblit (New York: Berghahn Books, 2004), p. 28.

34. Segel, "Zwei jüdische Volkssagen über Kaiser Franz Josef," p. 125.

35. Daniel Unowsky, *The Pomp and Politics of Patriotism: Imperial Celebrations in Habsburg Austria 1848–1916* (West Lafayette, IN: Purdue University Press, 2005), p. 73.

36. Personal communication. Esther Kurtz (1899–1987) was the author's paternal grandmother; she grew up in Dąbrowa Tarnowska, near Tarnów, in Galicia.

37. "Ševčenko-Gesellschaft der Wissenschaften in Lemberg," *Zeitschrift für österreichische Volkskunde* [Vienna] 9 (1903): 176.

38. Franko, "Meine jüdischen Bekannten," in *Beiträge zur Geschichte und Kultur der Ukraine*, pp. 50–51.

39. Shanes, "Neither Germans nor Poles," p. 195.

40. John Paul Himka, "Dimensions of a Triangle: Polish-Ukrainian-Jewish Relations in Austrian Galicia," in *Polin: Studies in Polish Jewry*, Vol. 12, *Focusing on Galicia*, pp. 41–43; Alison Frank, *Oil Empire: Visions of Prosperity in Austrian Galicia* (Cambridge: Harvard University Press, 2005), pp. 157–58.

41. Maciej Janowski, "Galizien auf dem Weg zur Zivilgesellschaft," in *Die Habsburgermonarchie 1848–1918*, Band 8, *Politische Öffentlichkeit und Zivilgesellschaft*, Teilband 1 (Vienna: Verlag der Österreichischen Akademie der Wissenschaften, 2006), pp. 811–12, 841–44.

42. Prymak, *Mykhailo Hrushevsky*, p. 59; Serhii Plokhy, *Unmaking Imperial Russia: Mykhailo Hrushevsky and the Writing of Ukrainian History* (Toronto: University of Toronto Press, 2005), p. 47.

43. Solomon Liptzin, *A History of Yiddish Literature* (Middle Village, NY: Jonathan David Publishers, 1972), pp. 237–41.

44. Prymak, *Mykhailo Hrushevsky*, p. 64.

45. Martin Buber, *Tales of the Hasidim* (New York: Schocken Books, 1991), p. viii.

46. Harold Segel, *Turn-of-the-Century Cabaret* (New York: Columbia University Press, 1987), pp. 221–53; David Crowley, "Castles, Cabarets, and Cartoons: Claims on Polishness in Kraków around 1905," in *The City in Central Europe: Culture and Society from 1800 to the Present*, ed. Malcom Gee, Tim Kirk, and Jill Steward (Brookfield, VT: Ashgate, 1999), pp. 107–14; Tadeusz Żeleński (Boy), *Znaszli ten kraj? i inne wspomnienia* (Cracow: Wydawnictwo Literackie, 1956), pp. 141–50.

47. Segel, *Turn-of-the-Century Cabaret*, p. 229.

48. Ibid., p. 230.

49. Boy, *Znaszli ten kraj?* p. 149.

50. Ibid., pp. 412–13.

51. Marta Romanowska, "Kościół Franciszkanów w Krakowie," in *Stanisław Wyspiański: Opus Magnum* (Cracow: Muzeum Narodowe, 2000), pp. 94–97; *Listy Sta-*

nisława Wyspiańskiego: do Józef Mehoffera, Henryka Opieńskiego i Tadeusza Stryjeńskiego, I, ed. Maria Rydlowa (Cracow: Wydawnictwo Literackie, 1994), p. 184–85 (31 October 1895).

52. Ivan Franko, *Moses*, trans. Waldimir Semenyna (New York: United Ukrainian Organizations of the United States, 1938), pp. 28–29.

53. Ibid., pp. 70–71.

54. Landau, *Unter jüdischen Proletariern*, p. 34.

55. Asher Wilcher, "Ivan Franko and Theodor Herzl: To the Genesis of Franko's *Mojsej*," *Harvard Ukrainian Studies* 6, no. 2 (June 1982): 236–37, 242–43.

56. Franko, *Moses*, p. 90.

57. Ibid., p. 92.

58. Carl Schorske, "Politics in a New Key: An Austrian Trio," in *Fin-de-siècle Vienna: Politics and Culture* (1980; New York: Vintage Books, 1981), pp. 116–80; Torsten Wehrhahn, "Die 'Junge Ukraine': Nationalismus und Sozialismus als Aspekte eines Generationskonflikts im politischen Leben Ostgaliziens (1899–1903)," in *Jahrbücher für Geschichte Osteuropas*, Band 49, Heft 2 (Stuttgart: Franz Steiner Verlag, 2001), pp. 213–29.

59. "Andrzej Potocki," in *Polski Słownik Biograficzny*, Tom XXVII / I, Zeszyt 112 (Warsaw: Polska Akademia Nauk, 1982), pp. 778–81.

60. *Neue Freie Presse*, 13 April 1908.

61. Hans-Christian Maner, *Galizien: Eine Grenzregion im Kalkül der Donaumonarchie im 18. und 19. Jahrhundert* (Munich: Institut für deutsche Kultur und Geschichte Südosteuropas, 2007), pp. 153–55.

62. *Neue Freie Presse*, 13 April 1908.

63. Ibid.

64. Ibid.

65. Ibid.; Arthur Schnitzler, *Der grüne Kakadu* (1899), in *Das dramatische Werk*, Vol. 3 (Frankfurt: Fischer Taschenbuch, 1978), p. 40.

66. *Neue Freie Presse*, 14 April 1908.

67. Ibid.

68. Ibid.

69. Ibid., 15 April 1908.

70. Ibid.

71. Stanislaus Zieliński, *Die Ermordung des Statthalters Grafen Andreas Potocki: Materialen zur Beurteilung des Ukrainischen Terrorismus in Galizien* (Vienna and Leipzig: C. W. Stern, 1908), p. 1.

72. Ibid., pp. 2–3.

73. Ibid., pp. 12–13.

74. Ibid., pp. 18–19.

75. Ibid., pp. 21–22; see also Plokhy, *Unmaking Imperial Russia*, pp. 281–345.

76. Prymak, *Mykhailo Hrushevsky*, pp. 79–80.

77. Zieliński, *Die Ermordung*, p. 22.

78. Ibid., p. 28.

79. Ibid., pp. 16, 36.

80. Ibid., p. 39.

81. Ibid., pp. 51–54, 57.
82. Ibid., pp. 61–62.
83. Ibid., pp. 64–66.
84. *Neue Freie Presse*, 18 April 1908.
85. Ibid.
86. Ibid.
87. Ibid.
88. Ibid., 19 April 1908.
89. Aleksander Fredro, *Korespondencja*, ed. Krystyna Czajkowska, in *Pisma Wszyst-kie*, Tom XIV (Warsaw: Państwowy Instytut Wydawniczy, 1976), p. 77, letter of Fredro, 2 January 1832.
90. *Neue Freie Presse*, 21 April 1908.
91. Ibid., 22 April 1908.
92. Philip Pajakowski, "Michał Bobrzyński," in *Nation and History: Polish Historians from the Enlightenment to the Second World War*, ed. Peter Brock, John Stanley, and Piotr Wróbel (Toronto: University of Toronto Press, 2006), p. 157.
93. Ibid., pp. 144–47.
94. Ibid., p. 151.
95. Michał Bobrzyński, *Z moich pamiętników*, ed. Adam Galos (Wrocław: Wydaw-nictwo Zakładu imienia Ossolińskich, 1957), p. 9.
96. Ibid., p. 10.
97. Gabrielle Kohlbauer-Fritz, "Yiddish as an Expression of Jewish Cultural Identity in Galicia and Vienna," in *Polin: Studies in Polish Jewry*, Vol. 12, *Focusing on Gali-cia*, p. 168.
98. Majer Bałaban, *Dzieje Żydów w Galicyi: i w Rzeczypospolitej Krakowskiej, 1772–1868* (Lviv: Księgarnia Polska B. Połonieckiego; New York: Polish Book Importing Com-pany, n.d. [1914?]); Paul Robert Magocsi, *Galicia: A Historical Survey and Bibliographic Guide* (Toronto: University of Toronto Press, 1983), pp. 231–39.
99. *New York Times*, 8 January 1907.
100. Martin Buber, *The Legend of the Baal-Shem*, trans. Maurice Friedman (Prince-ton: Princeton University Press, 1995), p. 10.
101. Marianne Krull, *Freud and His Father*, trans. Arnold Pomerans (1979; New York: W. W. Norton, 1986), pp. 89–90.
102. Wyspiański, *The Wedding*, trans. Gerard Kapolka (Ann Arbor, MI: Ardis Pub-lishers, 1990), p. 191 (Act 3, Scene 33).
103. Ibid., p. 127 (Act 2, Scene 24).
104. Ibid., p. 192 (Act 3, Scene 33).
105. Bruno Schulz, "The Comet," in *The Street of Crocodiles*, trans. Celina Wieniew-ska (New York: Penguin Books, 1977), pp. 139–40.
106. Ibid., pp. 152, 157.
107. Barbara Winklowa, *Boy we Lwowie, 1939–41* (Warsaw: Pokolenie, 1992), p. 182.

9. Geopolitical Conclusion

1. S. Ansky, *The Enemy at His Pleasure: A Journey through the Jewish Pale of Settlement during World War I*, trans. Joachim Neugroschel (2002; New York: Henry Holt, Metropolitan/Owl Books, 2004), p. 7.

2. Ibid., pp. 7–8; see also Gabriella Safran and Steven Zipperstein, eds., *The Worlds of S. An-sky: A Russian-Jewish Intellectual at the Turn of the Century* (Stanford: Stanford University Press, 2006).

3. Ansky, *The Enemy at His Pleasure*, p. 9.

4. Ibid., pp. 63–64.

5. Ibid., p. 64.

6. Ibid., pp. 64–65.

7. Marsha Rozenblit, *Reconstructing a National Identity: The Jews of Habsburg Austria during World War I* (Oxford: Oxford University Press, 2001), pp. 66–68, 74–75.

8. Sholem Aleichem, *Adventures of Mottel the Cantor's Son*, trans. Tamara Kahana (New York: Collier Books, 1961), p. 88.

9. Ibid., p. 94.

10. Ibid., pp. 99, 102.

11. Rozenblit, *Reconstructing a National Identity*, pp. 4, 42, 44–45.

12. Ibid., p. 66.

13. Ansky, *The Enemy at His Pleasure*, pp. 67–68.

14. Ibid., p. 73.

15. Ibid., pp. 74–75; Karl Baedeker, *Oesterreich-Ungarn: Handbuch für Reisende* (Leipzig: Verlag von Karl Baedeker, 1910), pp. 366–68.

16. Ansky, *The Enemy at His Pleasure*, pp. 74–75.

17. Ibid., p. 78.

18. Ibid., pp. 73–74.

19. Ibid., pp. 86–88.

20. Ibid., p. 94.

21. Ibid.

22. Ibid., pp. 106, 122.

23. Ibid., p. 121.

24. Rozenblit, *Reconstructing a National Identity*, p. 101.

25. Ibid., p. 53.

26. Ansky, *The Enemy at His Pleasure*, pp. 149–50.

27. Ibid., p. 246.

28. Ibid.

29. Ibid., p. 247.

30. Ibid., p. 259.

31. Ivan Rudnytsky, "The Ukrainians in Galicia under Austrian Rule," in *Essays in Modern Ukrainian History* (Edmonton: Canadian Institute of Ukrainian Studies, University of Alberta, 1987), pp. 344–45.

32. Mark von Hagen, *War in a European Borderland: Occupations and Occupation Plans in Galicia and Ukraine, 1914–1918* (Seattle, WA: Donald W. Treadgold Studies on Russia, East Europe, and Central Asia, 2007), pp. 19–71; Timothy Snyder, *The Red Prince: The Secret Lives of a Habsburg Archduke* (New York: Basic Books, 2008), pp. 77–98; Jan Le-

wandowski, "Okupacja austriacka w Królestwie Polskim (1914–1918)," *Dzieje najnowsze* 30, no. 4 (1998): 32.

33. *Czas*, 9 February 1867.

34. Hugo von Hofmannsthal to Leopold von Andrian, 4 May 1896, in *Europa Erlesen: Galizien*, ed. Stefan Simonek and Alois Woldan (Klagenfurt: Wieserverlag, 1998), pp. 153–55; see also Stefan Simonek, "Hugo von Hofmannsthals Galizische Implikationen," in *Kakanien Revisited*, March 2004, http://www.kakanien.ac.at.

35. Hofmannsthal, "Geist der Karpathen," in *Gesammelte Werke: Reden und Aufsätze, II, 1914–1924* (Frankfurt: Fischer Taschenbuch Verlag, 1979), pp. 412–13.

36. Hofmannsthal, "Unsere Miltärverwaltung in Polen," in ibid., p. 422.

37. Ibid., pp. 426–28.

38. Hofmannsthal, "Die Oesterreichische Idee," in ibid., p. 456.

39. Hofmannsthal, *Der Schwierige* (Frankfurt: Fischer Bücherei, 1958), p. 15 (Act I, Scene 3).

40. *Archiwum Państwowy w Krakowie: Inwentarz Tymczasowy*, file 1611 (1914–18).

41. Ibid.

42. Michał Śliwa, "Pierwsze ośrodki władzy polskiej w Galicji w 1918 r.," *Dzieje najnowsze* 30, no. 4 (1998): 67–68.

43. *Kuryer Codzienny*, 1 November 1918, in *Archiwum Państwowy w Krakowie: Inwentarz Tymczasowy*, file 1611 (1914–18).

44. Śliwa, "Pierwsze ośrodki władzy polskiej," p. 67.

45. Ibid., p. 72.

46. *Kuryer Codzienny*, 2 November 1918; in *Archiwum Państwowy w Krakowie: Inwentarz Tymczasowy*, file 1611 (1914–18).

47. *Neue Freie Presse*, 3 November 1918; 4 November 1918.

48. Ibid., 6 November 1918; 8 November 1918.

49. Ibid., 11 November 1918; 18 November 1918.

50. Ibid., 18 November 1918.

51. Ibid., 27 November 1918.

52. William Hagen, "The Moral Economy of Popular Violence: The Pogrom in Lwów, November 1918," in *Antisemitism and Its Opponents in Modern Poland*, ed. Robert Blobaum (Ithaca, NY: Cornell University Press, 2005), pp. 124–47.

53. Ibid., p. 146.

54. *Neue Freie Presse*, 28 November 1918.

55. Ibid., 29 November 1918.

56. Rozenblit, *Reconstructing a National Identity*, pp. 135–36.

57. *Neue Freie Presse*, 30 November 1918.

58. Ibid.

59. Ibid., 1 December 1918.

60. Ibid., 11 December 1918.

61. Snyder, *The Red Prince*, p. 118; see also Philipp Ther, "War versus Peace: Interethnic Relations in Lviv during the First Half of the Twentieth Century," *Harvard Ukrainian Studies* 24 (2000): 259–60.

62. *Mémoire sur la Galicie* (Paris: Commission Polonaise des Travaux Préparatoires au Congrès de la Paix, May 1919), p. 3.

63. Ibid., p. 4.

64. *Statistics of Galicia* (Paris: Polish Commission of Preparatory Work to the Conference of Peace, Imprimerie Levé, May 1919), pp. 2–5.

65. *Mémoire sur la Galicie*, pp. 4, 7, 14–15.

66. Alison Frank, *Oil Empire: Visions of Prosperity in Austrian Galicia* (Cambridge: Harvard University Press, 2005), pp. 220–21.

67. *Mémoire sur la Galicie*, pp. 15, 19.

68. Harold Nicolson, *Peacemaking 1919* (New York: Grosset and Dunlap, Universal Edition, 1965), pp. 313–14, diary entry of 16 April 1919.

69. *Memorandum on the North and South Eastern Frontiers of Restored Poland* (Paris: Polish Office of Political Publications, Imprimerie Levé, June 1919), p. 3.

70. Ibid., pp. 8–9.

71. Ibid., pp. 10–11.

72. *New York Times*, 28 September 1915, 25 May 1919.

73. Thomas Prymak, *Mykhailo Hrushevsky: The Politics of National Culture* (Toronto: University of Toronto Press, 1987), pp. 186–95.

74. Mykhailo Hrushevsky, *To the Civilized Nations of the World* (Geneva: Committee of the Independent Ukraine, 1920), p. 1.

75. Isaac Babel, *The Red Cavalry Stories*, in *The Complete Works of Isaac Babel*, ed. Nathalie Babel, trans. Peter Constantine (New York: W. W. Norton, 2002), p. 291.

76. Ibid., pp. 291, 327.

77. Babel, *1920 Diary*, in *The Complete Works of Isaac Babel*, p. 412, diary entry of 25 July 1920.

78. Ibid., p. 416, diary entry of 28 July 1920.

79. Ibid., pp. 416–17, diary entry of 29 July 1920.

80. Ibid., p. 418, diary entry of 30 July 1920.

81. Ibid., p. 419, diary entry of 30 July 1920.

82. Ibid., pp. 419–20, diary entry of 31 July 1920.

83. Ibid., p. 422, diary entry of 1 August 1920.

84. Ibid., pp. 434–37, diary entries of 9 August and 10 August 1920.

85. Ibid., pp. 436–37, diary entry of 10 August 1920.

86. Ibid., p. 450, diary entries of 18 August and 21 August 1920.

87. Ibid., pp. 452, 455, diary entries of 22 August and 26 August 1920.

10. Haunted Epilogue

1. Michał Śliwa, "Pierwsze ośrodki władzy polskiej w Galicji w 1918 r.," *Dzieje najnowsze* 30, no. 4 (1998): 72.

2. Alfred Döblin, *Journey to Poland*, trans. Joachim Neugroschel, ed. Heinz Graber (London: I. B. Tauris, 1991), p. xiv; see also Werner Stauffacher, "Polen 1924—eine Erfahrung: Zu Alfred Döblins *Reise in Polen*," in *Galizien als Gemeinsame Literaturlandschaft*, ed. Fridrun Rinner and Klaus Zerinschek (Innsbruck: Innsbrucker Beiträge zur Kulturwissenschaft, 1988), pp. 131–42; Regina Hartmann, "Faszination Ostjudentum: Alfred Döblin auf dem Weg zu den Wurzeln des Herkommens," *Transversal: Zeitschrift für Jüdische Studien* 1 (2007): 49–62.

3. Alfred Döblin, *Reise in Polen* (1926; Olten und Freiburg im Breisgau: Walter-Verlag, 1968), p. 184; Döblin, *Journey to Poland*, p. 139.

4. Döblin, *Reise in Polen*, pp. 186–88; Döblin, *Journey to Poland*, pp. 141–42.

5. J. Hoberman, *Bridge of Light: Yiddish Film between Two Worlds* (New York: Museum of Modern Art and Schocken Books, 1991), p. 61.

6. Döblin, *Reise in Polen*, pp. 191–92; Döblin, *Journey to Poland*, p. 145.

7. Döblin, *Reise in Polen*, p. 193; Döblin, *Journey to Poland*, p. 146.

8. Döblin, *Reise in Polen*, pp. 194–97; Döblin, *Journey to Poland*, pp. 147–49.

9. Döblin, *Reise in Polen*, pp. 200–201; Döblin, *Journey to Poland*, p. 152.

10. Döblin, *Reise in Polen*, p. 202; Döblin, *Journey to Poland*, p. 154.

11. Döblin, *Reise in Polen*, p. 205; Döblin, *Journey to Poland*, p. 156.

12. Döblin, *Reise in Polen*, pp. 216–17; Döblin, *Journey to Poland*, p. 166.

13. Stanisław Lem, *Highcastle*, trans. Michael Kandel (1975; New York: Harcourt Brace/A Harvest Book, 1995), p. 92.

14. Zbigniew Herbert, "Pan Cogito: Lekcja kaligrafii" ("Mr. Cogito: Calligraphy Lesson"), in *The Collected Poems 1956–1998*, ed. and trans. Alissa Valles (New York: Harper Collins, 2007), pp. 559–60.

15. Döblin, *Reise in Polen*, pp. 230–31; Döblin, *Journey to Poland*, p. 176.

16. Döblin, *Reise in Polen*, pp. 231, 235; Döblin, *Journey to Poland*, pp. 176, 179.

17. Joseph Roth, *Werke*, Band 2, *Das journalistische Werk, 1924–1928*, ed. Klaus Westermann (Cologne: Kiepenheuer und Witsch, 1990), pp. 281–85.

18. Nina Kolesnikoff, *Bruno Jasieński: His Evolution from Futurism to Socialist Realism* (Waterloo, Ontario: Wilfrid Laurier University Press, 1982), p. 6.

19. Ibid., p. 63.

20. Ibid., pp. 63–64, footnote 11.

21. Bruno Jasieński, *Słowo o Jakóbie Szeli* (Paris: Imprimerie Menilmontant, 1926), Part 3 (no page numbers).

22. Ibid.

23. *The Danger Spot of Europe: Poland and Ukraine: A Report on the Polish Terror*, foreword by Cecil Malone (London: Ukrainian Bureau, n.d. [1932?]), p. 3.

24. Ibid., pp. 5–6.

25. Ibid., pp. 9, 15, 19.

26. Ibid., pp. 21–22.

27. Ibid., p. 29.

28. Ibid., p. 39.

29. Ibid., pp. 40–41.

30. Ibid., p. 46.

31. Ibid., pp. 56–57.

32. Ibid., pp. 57–58.

33. Joseph Roth, *The Radetzky March*, trans. Eva Tucker (Woodstock, NY: Overlook Press, 1974), p. 215.

34. Ibid.

35. Ibid., p. 216.

36. Roth, "The Bust of the Emperor," in *Hotel Savoy, Fallmerayer the Stationmaster, The Bust of the Emperor*, trans. John Hoare (Woodstock, NY: Overlook Press, 1986), p. 157.

37. Ibid., p. 176.

38. Ibid., p. 182.

39. Bruno Schulz, "Spring," in *The Fictions of Bruno Schulz: The Street of Crocodiles & Sanatorium under the Sign of the Hourglass*, trans. Celina Wieniewska (London: Picador, 1988), pp. 158–59.

40. Ibid., p. 159.

41. Ibid., p. 160.

42. Ibid., p. 182.

43. Ibid., p. 206.

44. Schulz, "August," in *The Fictions of Bruno Schulz*, p. 16.

45. Roth, *The Emperor's Tomb*, trans. John Hoare (London: Chatto and Windus, Hogarth Press, 1984), pp. 34–35.

46. S. Y. Agnon, *A Guest for the Night*, trans. Misha Louvish (Madison: University of Wisconsin Press, Terrace Books, 2004), p. 1.

47. Ibid., p. 78.

48. Roth, *The Emperor's Tomb*, p. 39.

49. *New York Times*, 29 March 2002.

50. Daniel Soyer, *Jewish Immigrant Associations and American Identity in New York, 1880–1939* (Cambridge: Harvard University Press, 1997), pp. 23, 27.

51. Ibid., p. 51.

52. Ibid., p. 53.

53. Ibid., pp. 147–48.

54. *New York Times*, 4 January 1912.

55. Soyer, *Jewish Immigrant Associations*, pp. 147, 254.

56. Ibid., pp. 159–60.

57. Hoberman, *Bridge of Light*, pp. 66–67.

58. "Galizien," in *Jüdisches Lexikon: Ein enzyklopädisches Handbuch des jüdischen Wissens in vier Bände*, Band II (Berlin: Jüdischer Verlag, 1927; rpt. Königstein: Jüdischer Verlag im Athenäum Verlag, 1982), pp, 867–68.

59. *Washington Post*, 11 February 1939; *Washington Post*, 22 September 1939.

60. Marci Shore, *Caviar and Ashes: A Warsaw Generation's Life and Death in Marxism, 1918–1968* (New Haven: Yale University Press, 2006), p. 159.

61. Aleksander Wat, *My Century: The Odyssey of a Polish Intellectual*, trans. Richard Lourie (1977; New York: W. W. Norton, 1990), p. 104.

62. Dieter Pohl, *Nationalsozialistische Judenverfolgung in Ostgalizien 1941–1944: Organisation und Durchführung eines staatlichen Massenverbrechens*, 2nd ed. (Munich: R. Oldenbourg Verlag, 1997), p. 75; see also Isabel Röskau-Rydel, *Galizien: Deutsche Geschichte im Osten Europas* (Berlin: Siedler Verlag, 1999), pp. 209–11.

63. Pohl, *Nationalsozialistische Judenverfolgung in Ostgalizien*, pp. 56–57.

64. Philipp Ther, "War versus Peace: Interethnic Relations in Lviv during the First Half of the Twentieth Century," *Harvard Ukrainian Studies* 24 (2000): 270–71; Timothy Snyder, *The Reconstruction of Nations: Poland, Ukraine, Lithuania, Belarus 1569–1999* (New Haven, CT: Yale University Press, 2003), pp. 187–88.

65. Ivan Rudnytsky, "Soviet Ukraine in Historical Perspective," in *Essays in Modern Ukrainian History* (Edmonton: Canadian Institute of Ukrainian Studies, University of Alberta, 1987), p. 470; Roman Szporluk, "The Soviet West—or Far Eastern Europe"

(1991), republished in *Russia, Ukraine, and the Breakup of the Soviet Union* (Stanford: Hoover Institution Press, 2000), pp. 266–67.

66. Ther, "War versus Peace," pp. 253, 271.

67. Adam Kirsch, "Beware of Pity: Hannah Arendt and the Power of the Impersonal," *New Yorker,* 12 January 2009, p. 66.

68. Christopher Hann, "The Limits of Galician Syncretism: Pluralism, Multiculturalism, and the Two Catholicisms," in *Galicia: A Multicultured Land,* ed. Christopher Hann and Paul Magocsi (Toronto: University of Toronto Press, 2005), p. 221; see also Hann, "Postsocialist Nationalism: Rediscovering the Past in Southeast Poland," *Slavic Review* 57, no. 4 (Winter 1998): 839–63.

69. Padraic Kenney, "Lviv's Central European Renaissance, 1987–1990," *Harvard Ukrainian Studies* 24 (2000): 308.

70. Adam Zagajewski, "To Go to Lwów," trans. Renata Gorczyńska, in Zagajewski, *Without End: New and Selected Poems* (New York: Farrar, Straus and Giroux, 2002), pp. 79–81.

71. Zagajewski, "Two Cities," in *Two Cities: On Exile, History, and the Imagination,* trans. Lillian Vallee (1991; New York: Farrar, Straus, Giroux, 1995), pp. 3–68.

72. George Grabowicz, "Mythologizing Lviv/Lwów: Echoes of Presence and Absence," *Harvard Ukrainian Studies* 24 (2000): 313–42; see also Alois Woldan, "Literacki mit Krakowa i Lwowa w XX wieku," in Jacek Purchla, ed. *Kraków i Lwów w cywilizacji europejskiej* (Cracow: Międzynarodowe Centrum Kultury, 2003), pp. 91–106.

73. Zagajewski, "To Go to Lwów," pp. 79–81.

74. Milan Kundera, "The Tragedy of Central Europe," *New York Review of Books,* 26 April 1984, pp. 33–38; originally published in French as "Un Occident kidnappé ou la tragédie de l'Europe centrale," *Le Débat,* November 1983.

75. http://www.wienkaffe.lviv.ua/indexua_e.html.

76. Luiza Bialasiewicz, "Back to *Galicia Felix?*" in *Galicia: A Multicultured Land,* p. 173; Dietlind Hüchtker, "Der 'Mythos Galizien': Versuch einer Historisierung," in *Die Nationalisierung von Grenzen: Zur Konstruktion nationaler Identität in sprachlich gemischten Grenzregionen,* ed. Michael Müller and Rolf Petri (Marburg: Verlag Herder-Institut, 2002), pp. 81–107; Lidia Stefanowska, "Back to the Golden Age: The Discourse of Nostalgia in Galicia in the 1990s," in *Contemporary Ukraine on the Cultural Map of Europe,* ed. Larissa Zaleska Onyshkevych and Maria Rewakowicz (London: M. E. Sharpe, 2009), pp. 219–30; Delphine Bechtel, "Le mythe de la Galicie, de la disparition à la résurrection (virtuelle)," *Cultures d'Europe centrale,* no. 4, CIRCE, 2003: http://www.circe.paris4.sorbonne.fr/rubriques/5publications/cec4_bechtel.html; see also Alois Woldan, *Der Oesterreich-Mythos in der polnischen Literatur* (Vienna: Böhlau Verlag, 1996).

77. Bialasiewicz, "Back to *Galicia Felix?*" p. 174.

78. Ibid., p. 175.

79. Yaroslav Hrytsak, "Historical Memory and Regional Identity among Galicia's Ukrainians," in *Galicia: A Multicultured Land,* p. 188; Roman Szporluk, "The Western Dimension of the Making of Modern Ukraine," in *Contemporary Ukraine on the Cultural Map of Europe,* pp. 13–14.

80. Michael Moser, "Colonial Linguistic Reflexes in a Post-Soviet Setting: The Galician Variant of the Ukrainian Language and Anti-Ukrainian Discourse in Con-

temporary Internet Sources," in *Contemporary Ukraine on the Cultural Map of Europe*, pp. 317–21; Szporluk, "Ukraine: From an Imperial Periphery to a Sovereign State," in *Russia, Ukraine, and the Breakup of the Soviet Union*, pp. 384–85.

81. Mieczysław Orłowicz, *Ilustrowany Przewodnik po Galicyi* (Lviv: Akademicki Klub Turystyczny, 1914), pp. 248–49, 336–40.

82. Mieczysław Czuma and Leszek Mazan, *Austriackie Gadanie czyli Encyklopedia Galicyjska* (Cracow: Oficyna Wydawniczo-Handlowa ANABASIS, 1998), p. 5.

83. *Galicja i jej dziedzictwo*, ed. Włodzimierz Bonusiak and Józef Buszko (Rzeszów: Wydawnicto Wyższej Szkoły Pedagogicznej w Rzeszowie, 1994–).

84. Martin Pollack, *Galizien: Eine Reise durch die verschwundene Welt Ostgaliziens und der Bukowina* (Frankfurt: Insel Verlag, 2001).

85. Omer Bartov, *Erased: Vanishing Traces of Jewish Galicia in Present-Day Ukraine* (Princeton: Princeton University Press, 2007).

86. [Franz Kratter], *Briefe über den itzigen Zustand von Galizien* (Leipzig: Verlag G. Ph. Wucherers, 1786; rpt. Berlin: Helmut Scherer Verlag, 1990).

87. Soma Morgenstern, *In einer anderen Zeit: Jugendjahre in Ostgalizien* (1995; Berlin: Aufbau Taschenbuch Verlag, 1999), pp. 226–27; Józef Wittlin, *Mój Lwów* (New York: Biblioteka Polska, 1946), pp. 14–15.

88. Hrytsak, "Historical Memory and Regional Identity among Galicia's Ukrainians," p. 201; Stefanowska, "Back to the Golden Age," pp. 223–24.

89. Stefanowska, "Back to the Golden Age," pp. 219, 224–25; Andriy Zayarnyuk, "On the Frontiers of Central Europe: Ukrainian Galicia at the Turn of the Millennium," in *Spaces of Identity: Tradition, Cultural Boundaries, and Identity Formation in Central Europe*, Vol. 1 (2001), http://www.yorku.ca/soi/Vol_1/_HTML/Zayarnyuk.html.

90. Jerzy Ficowski, *Regions of the Great Heresy: Bruno Schulz*, trans. Theodosia Robertson (New York: W. W. Norton, 2003), pp. 168–72.

91. Benjamin Paloff, "Who Owns Bruno Schulz?" *Boston Review*, December 2004/January 2005.

92. Ficowski, *Regions of the Great Heresy*, p. 138.

93. Schulz, "Spring," p. 181.

94. Schulz, "Sanatorium under the Sign of the Hourglass," in *The Fictions of Bruno Schulz*, p. 241.

95. Bialasiewicz, "Back to *Galicia Felix*?" p. 169.

96. Ficowski, *Regions of the Great Heresy*, p. 130.

Index

Academy of Learning (Akademia Umiejętności), Cracow, 219, 237, 260, 265, 273
Adams, John Quincy, 98
administration, of Galicia, 14, 64, 79, 81,
112, 139, 160, 202, 244; administrative
circles (*Kreise*), 18, 19; and bureaucratic
absolutism of the 1850s, 210, 216, 259;
Fredro on, 170–73; Josephine, 38, 41,
43, 52, 221; language of, 39, 46–47, 172,
184, 210, 222, 223; officials, bureaucracy,
53, 71, 75, 100, 101, 138, 149, 161, 226, 235,
405, 418; suspicion of complicity in
1846, 143–44, 154, 162, 170–71, 177–78,
179, 181, 182
Adriatic Sea, 7, 64, 130
aestheticism, fin-de-siècle, 292, 293, 296–
98, 300, 304–5, 315–16
Africa, 264
Agnon, Shmuel Yosef, 8, 384, 395–96, 409;
A Guest for the Night, 395, 400
agriculture, 67, 68, 96, 124, 133–34, 195, 198,
238, 256, 276, 324, 331, 377
alcohol: drunkenness, 25, 27, 31, 50, 138,
177; propinacja, 27, 236, 306; and Przybyszewski, 297, 300–301
Alexander I, czar, 95–96
allegory of Galicia, sculpture for Sejm,
232–34, 370, 388
Allgemeine musikalische Zeitung (Vienna), 78
Allgemeine Theaterzeitung (Vienna), 123, 134
Allgemeines Europaeisches Journal (Brno), 59
anarchism, anarchist assassinations, 283,
301–5, 306, 337. *See also* Elisabeth; Luccheni
"anarchy," attributed to Commonwealth,

219, 344; attributed to Galicia after
partitions, 16, 22, 32, 41–42; attributed
to Galicia in 1918, 374; as problem discussed in *Czas*, 190, 303–4; in relation to
1846 massacres, 166–67, 170; in relation
to Potocki assassination, 336–37, 338,
339, 340, 341, 344
Anatolia, *see* Ottoman empire
Anczyc, Władysław, 266
Anderson, Benedict, 6
Andrian, Leopold Freiherr von, 297
Andrukhovych, Yuri, 416
Anhelovych, Antin, Uniate metropolitan
of Galicia, 86
Ankwicz, Andrzej, Roman Catholic metropolitan of Galicia, 83
anniversaries, historical commemorations,
225–26, 308–10; bicentennial of Sobieski
at Vienna, 265–66; centennial of accession of Joseph II, 258, 261; of death of
Casimir the Great, 227; of emancipation of serfs, 296, 309; Franz Joseph
jubilee in 1898, 296, 302, 303, 309; Franz
Joseph jubilee in 1908, 345; Kościuszko
centennial, 294, 348; Kotliarevsky centennial, 296, 309; Mickiewicz centennial,
296, 309; of November Insurrection,
257–58, 366; of Union of Lublin,
225–26, 227–28
Ansky, S. (Shloyme Rappaport), *Destruction
of Galicia*, 351–55, 356–61
antemurale, Commonwealth as, 102–3, 224,
340; Galicia as, 173, 224, 340, 341, 374
anthropology, 45, 88, 248, 264–65, 270,
319, 386–87; physical anthropology of

Galicia, 6, 236–39, 243, 251, 263. *See also* ethnographic exhibits
anti-Semitism, 29, 239, 249, 276–77, 293, 307, 313–14, 316, 321, 354, 406; Lviv pogrom of 1918, 370–74; *Neue Freie Presse* interview with Polish teacher, 372–73; riots, pogroms of 1898, 296, 297, 305–6, 308, 320, 322, 348; of Russians, 352, 354, 356
Apponyi, Anton, and Metternich, 147
archaeology, 265, 376
architecture, 10, 88, 97, 203, 233, 290–91, 370; Jugendstil, modernism, 291, 357
Arendt, Hannah, 408
Armenians, 195, 208, 235, 236
Arneth, Alfred Ritter von, 221
Augustynowicz, Christoph, 10
Auschwitz, Oświęcim, 133, 258, 260, 407; Duchies of Auschwitz and Zator, 200, 201, 407
Australia, 264
Austrian Chatter or Galician Encyclopedia (1998), 414
Austro-Hungarian compromise of 1867, dualism, 189, 212–13, 218, 220
Austro-Prussian War, 194, 212, 224
autonomists, Galician, post-Soviet, 11, 415–16
autonomy, of Galicia, 8, 182, 188, 200, 216–21, 226, 227, 230, 231–79, 289, 331, 343; Gołuchowski and, 213–14, 220, 311, 332; Polish hegemony, 8, 212, 222, 223, 229, 236, 246, 255, 259, 269, 294, 310, 362; as "special position," 133, 189, 213, 220, 227, 228, 257
Aztecs, 289, 291

Baal Shem Tov, 19, 208, 326, 346, 361
Babel, Isaac, 4, 352, 379–82, 387, 390; and Red Cavalry, 352, 379; on "spectral Galicians," 4, 380, 381
Bach, Alexander, 210
backwardness of Galicia, 7, 33, 67, 69, 134, 160, 198, 217, 244, 256, 325, 349, 353, 354; discussed in Szczepanowski, 275–79; of Galician Jews, 243, 264, 312, 315–18
Badeni, Kazimierz, 295, 342

Baedeker's *Oesterreich-Ungarn*, 357
Bałaban, Majer, history of Galician Jews, 9, 283, 345
Baltic Sea, 376
Bandera, Stepan, 415
banks, banking, in Galicia, 132–35, 220, 249, 370, 403
barbarism: attributed to Galicia, 7, 22–23, 29, 33, 36, 49, 113, 148, 152–53, 160, 242, 277, 278, 371; attributed to Metternich and the Habsburgs in 1846, 159, 165, 168; attributed to Russia, 59, 76, 103, 150, 356, 374; attributed to Ukrainians by Poles, 339
Baron, Salo, 408, 413
Baroni-Cavalcabò, Josephine, and Franz Xaver Wolfgang Mozart, 75
Bartal, Israel, 10
Bartov, Omer, 10, 414
Batenko, Taras, 416
Baworowski, Wiktor, and Franz Xaver Wolfgang Mozart, 72–74
bears, 26, 99, 110, 125, 128, 131, 272
Bechtel, Delphine, 412
Beethoven, Ludwig van, 122, 319
Belcredi, Richard, 213
Bellini, Vincenzo, 124, 132
Belshazzar, 278, 350
Belz, 247
Bengal, 251, 276
Besser, Wilibald, on botany of Galicia, 61–62
Bialasiewicz, Luiza, 412
Bible, 278–79, 328–30
Binder, Harald, 10
Birnbaum, Nathan, 345
Bisanz, Hans, 299
Bismarck, Otto von, 212, 217
Black Sea, 133, 376
Bloch, Joseph, 403
Bobrzyński, Michał, namiestnik, 283, 342–44, 362, 370
Bochnia, and railroad, 130–31, 132, 136
Bogusławski, Wojciech, 55–59; *Krakowiacy i Górale*, 14, 55–57, 59, 91–92, 103, 127, 196
Bogusz family, in 1846, 144, 161, 181

Bohemia, 29, 55, 98, 103, 105, 106, 174, 212, 276, 324, 325; crown of, 5, 43, 174, 218, 220, 363

Bohorodchany, ikonostas and religious art, 292, 293

Bolivar, Simon, 98

Boris Godunov, 263

Borodino, Battle of, 71, 76, 166

Boryslav, oilfields, 8, 249–52, 275, 313, 325, 329, 376, 388–89, 405, 417; Boryslav Wars of 1884, 250; oil workers' strike of 1904, 325, 331

Bosnia, 332, 333

Boston, 86

botany of Galicia, 5, 61–62

"Boy," *see* Żeleński, Tadeusz

Boyko highlanders, 270, 289

Bredetzky, Samuel, 68

Breinl, Joseph, 170–71, 181

Breitkopf and Härtel, music publishers, 72, 73, 75

Bretschneider, Franz, 132

Breuer, Joseph, 312

brigands, bandits, 116, 125, 126, 127, 128, 144

Brno, publications in, 68; *Allgemeines Europaeisches Journal*, 59; *Jüdische Volksstimme*, 360

Brocki, Eugeniusz, "Brigands of the Carpathians," 116, 126; "Short Sketch of the History of Galicia," 91

Brody, 100, 132, 356, 380–81, 389, 395, 397; compared to Pompeii, by Ansky, 356–57; elements of "Western Europe" noted by Babel, 380–81; Jews in, 151, 247–48, 355, 361

Buber, Martin, 8, 248–49, 252, 324, 326, 346, 361, 409

Buber, Solomon, 249, 326

Buchach, Buczacz, 293, 324, 395, 400, 408, 409; Jewish sabbath candles in, 293

Bucharest, 277, 278

Budapest, 119, 120, 224, 277, 278

Buddha, Buddhism, 286, 346, 381

Buffalo Bill's Wild West Circus, in Galicia, 415, 416

Bukovina, 52, 96, 182, 208, 217, 241, 242, 267, 269, 345, 403, 414; separated from

Galicia in 1849, 5, 64, 201. *See also* Czernowitz; Sadagora

Burke, Edmund, 38, 40, 41, 42, 160

Busk, 382

Buszko, Józef, 199

Byzantine influence: on Ruthenian religious art, 290, 292, 293; aspects of Byzantium in Galicia, 382

café culture, in Galicia, 155, 325, 358, 400–401, 411, 412, 414

California, 192, 401, 406, 408

Capuchin crypt, in Vienna, *see* Kapuzinergruft

carnival, 55, 57, 124, 126, 138, 140, 141, 178

Carnot, Sadi, assassinated, 303

Carpathians, 4, 5, 15, 52, 62, 91, 99, 110, 112, 175, 177, 258, 269, 272, 401; literary subject, 89, 95, 116, 126; military front in World War I, 364, 365; Tatra range, 55, 57, 127, 294. *See also* Boyko highlanders; brigands; *górale*; Hutsuls

Casimir the Great (Kazimierz Wielki), 19, 54–55, 160, 227, 236, 238, 244, 254, 261, 265

Castiglione, Heinrich, Field Marshal, 156

Catherine the Great, 15, 16, 20, 50, 52

censorship, 64, 65, 92, 95, 120, 126, 172, 188; in Russian empire, 287

Central Europe, and Habsburg legacy, 411, 416

charity, 67, 77, 98, 102, 124, 138, 140, 141, 171. *See also* Roman Catholicism, Sisters of Charity

Charles V, Holy Roman Emperor, 173

Chicago World's Fair, 289

Chłędowski, Walenty, 116

Chmelnitzky, Melech, 326

Chodakowski, Zorian, 87–89, 117

Chopin, Frédéric (Fryderyk), 76, 104, 196–97, 366; and Przybyszewski, 281, 298, 301

Chortkiv, 241, 242, 243, 297–98, 360, 361, 364

Circassians, 150, 177, 352

Cis-Leithania, constitutional government, 220, 233, 239–40, 325; crownlands of, 212, 213, 216, 220; national rights in, 239–40, 258, 261 civilization, as standard for judging Galicia, 49, 97, 113, 139, 149, 209, 228, 316, 318, 339, 365, 375, 389; and Galician Jews, 242–46, 264, 312, 318; and ideology of empire, 139, 153, 159, 165; in Kratter, 22, 25–26, 29; in Szczepanowski, 277–78

civilization, as standard for judging Habsburg government in 1846, 138, 159

civilization, Galicia representing Western civilization, 216–17, 224, 228, 243, 247, 265, 278, 343

civilizing imperial project in Galicia, 22, 49, 97, 152, 155, 217, 353, 370; adopted by Poles after World War I, 375–76, 377

Clemenceau, Georges, 374

Cold War, 409, 411

Columbia University, 408

comedy, comical perception of Galicia, 74, 78, 81, 96, 97; comic drama, *see* Fredro, Aleksander

Commonwealth of Poland-Lithuania, 14, 17, 19, 41, 82, 88, 145, 171, 175, 206, 218, 261, 263, 331, 338, 344; antemurale, 102–3, 224, 340; ruling over Ruthenian lands, 17, 25, 176, 377; Szujski on, 219. *See also* partitions of Poland

communism, 246, 390; Bolshevism, 364, 378; of Karl Marx, 147, 190; noted by Metternich in 1846, 147–48, 150, 158. *See also* Poland, communist; Soviet Union; Soviet Ukraine

Congress of Vienna, 59, 62, 64, 77, 79, 172, 194

Congress Poland, *see* Russian Poland

Conrad, Joseph, 229–30

conservatism, Galician: reaction to Josephinism, 38–43; reaction to the Enlightenment, 49–51. *See also* Cracow conservatism

Considerations on the Galician Government (*Uwagi*), 37–38

conspiracies, Polish, 124, 125, 126

Constitution (Habsburg) of 1849, 199, 200, 210

Constitution (Polish) of May 3, 1791, 48, 51, 52, 275

constitutional government, Habsburg: in 1848–49, 183, 184, 186, 191; after 1867, 220, 233, 239–40, 325, 352, 353. *See also* Cis-Leithania; elections

Cook, Captain James, 21

corporal punishment, flogging, whipping, 113, 124, 139, 145. *See also* Sacher-Masoch (writer), and masochism

Cossacks, 47, 116, 126, 150, 247, 309, 337, 338, 340, 348, 352, 377; with Babel in Galicia, 379–82

Cracow bohemians, 283, 296, 300–301, 326–27. *See also* Green Balloon; Przybyszewski

Cracow conservatism, 189, 201, 205, 214, 223–24, 303–4. *See also Czas*; Stańczyk

Cracow historical school, 9, 194, 205, 206, 219, 254, 261, 275, 279, 283, 336, 343. *See also* Bobrzyński; Kalinka; Szujski

Cracow, Kraków, Krakau: Academy of Learning (Akademia Umiejętności), 219, 237, 260, 265, 273; annexation in third partition of Poland, 52–54, 194; Czartoryski Museum, 260, 273; Franciscan church, work by Wyspiański, 287, 295, 297, 327–28, 330, 348; Franz Joseph visits, 203, 259, 260–61; Jagiellonian University, 194, 212, 218, 219, 237, 248, 260, 265, 273, 343, 366; Kazimierz, Jewish quarter, 203, 413–14; Mariacki church, St. Mary's, 53, 156, 192, 193, 203, 228, 260; municipal archive, 259; Rudolf, Crown Prince, visits, 272–73; Rynek, Market Square, 150, 156, 202, 260–61, 309, 331; St. Anne's, school, 218, 260; Sukiennice, 203, 260–61, 266; theater, 280, 295–96; Wawel hill, castle, cathedral, 53, 156, 164, 227, 235, 260, 266, 273, 309; Wyspiański, bored in Cracow, 294, 295. *See also* Cracow bohemians; Cracow conservatism; *Czas*

Cracow, urban republic of: Free, Independent, and Strictly Neutral City of, 64, 131, 141; its abolition in 1846, joined to Galicia, 147–56, 164–65, 194

Croatia, Croatians, 338

Cyrillic alphabet, 119, 130

Czartoryski, Adam Kazimierz, 70, 234

Czartoryski family, 32, 75, 87, 260

Czartoryski Museum, in Cracow, 260, 273
Czas, 188–94, 196–206, 213–22, 224–29, 243, 255–61, 262, 266–67, 280, 306–7, 308, 363; "About Galicia," 191–92; on anarchism, 190, 303–4; on assassination of Empress Elisabeth, 301–5, 314, 339, 341; on assassination of Potocki, 339, 340–41; on Christianity, 218, 304; conservatism, 201, 205, 214, 232, 257, 268, 274, 276, 303–4; on Jews, 222, 277; and loyalism, 200, 215, 216, 218, 220, 257; "monsters and reptiles," 303–4, 308, 314, 340; on Russia, 224, 225; on Russia and Ruthenians, 190, 214; on Ruthenians, 190, 221, 225, 255, 257; on Szczepanowski's *The Misery of Galicia*, 275–79
Czernowitz, Chernivtsi, 240, 241, 242, 245; meeting of Franz and Alexander at, 95–96, 105; Yiddish conference of 1908, 345, 346, 402
Czesniki, 379
Częstochowa, 365

Dąbrowa Tarnowska, 324, 454n36
Dąbrowski, Jan Henryk, 58–59, 103
Dabrowski, Patrice, 258
Dalmatia, 7, 64, 67, 212
"The Danger Spot of Europe" (Eastern Galicia), 391–95
Dante, 278–79
Danylo, king, 415
Da Ponte, Lorenzo, 78
Daszyński, Ignacy, 368
Declaration of the Rights of Man and the Citizen, 38, 39
Delamarre, Casimir, on Ruthenians, 225
Dembowski, Edward, 141
Demidov, Igor, 358
Denisko, Joachim, 58
Dennitsa-Jutrzenka, in Russian and Polish, 129
Deym, Moritz, 156
Diamant, Yankev, 357, 372
Dilo, on Potocki assassination, 339
Dmowski, Roman, 384
Dniester River, 4, 115, 119, 121, 132–33, 136, 175, 212, 235, 251, 269, 376; allegory of

Dniester, as part of Galicia allegory, 233–34, 370, 388
Döblin, Alfred, in Galicia, 384–88, 393; "primeval phantasmagoria," 387, 389
Dolina, 131
Donizetti, Gaetano, 124, 132
Don Quixote, in Galicia: in Babel, 379, 381; in Szujski, 265
dragons, 92, 269
Drohobych, 236, 258, 299, 366, 388–89, 404, 413; and Franko, 250, 251; and Schulz, 11, 349–50, 395, 396, 399, 407, 410, 413, 417–19
Dunajec River, 146, 364
Dunin Borkowski, Leszek, 116
Dziennik Literacki, 235

eagles, Habsburg (two-headed), 54, 110, 368–69, 389
eagles, Polish, 54, 369, 389
Easter eggs, painted, 386
Eastern Europe, idea of, 7, 11, 59, 67, 97, 113, 148, 159, 217, 271, 278, 315, 335, 389, 411; in Kortum, 45, 48–49; in Kratter, 22, 25, 26. *See also* Enlightenment, and Eastern Europe
education, schools, 65, 86, 373, 384, 386, 388, 391; German language, 30, 86, 152, 269; Jewish education, 29, 125, 312–13, 345; Polish language, 172, 222, 223, 269; Ruthenian language, 65, 86–87, 337
Egypt, Egyptians, 28, 328–29
Ehrenpreis, Mordechai, 313
Ehrlich, Josef, *Memoirs of a Former Hasid*, 246–48
Eichmann, Adolf, 408–9
elections, in Galicia, 295, 296, 310, 331; Habsburg universal male suffrage, 310–11, 331, 345, 359; in interwar Poland, 391; in postcommunist Poland, 412
Elias, Norbert, civilizing process, manners, 24
Elisabeth, Empress, 207, 356, 365, 400, 402; assassination, 283, 296, 301–6, 309, 314, 322, 332, 337, 339, 341, 374, 399, 414
Elżanowski, Seweryn, 211

emigration, from Galicia to America, 234–35, 248, 256, 264, 267, 384, 401–2

emigration, Polish, in Paris, 102, 104, 133, 141, 148, 205, 234

empire, ideology of, 6, 7, 49, 59, 139, 153, 159, 165, 178, 181, 182. *See also* civilizing imperial project in Galicia

Encyclopaedia Britannica, 391, 392

Encyclopedia of Expertise on Galicia, 231–36, 414. *See also* Schneider

Encyclopédie, of Diderot and D'Alembert, 36

Engel, Johann Christian von, 47

England, Britain, 217, 222, 275, 276; British publications on Eastern Galicia, 391–95

enlightened statecraft, 13, 64

Enlightenment, 36, 69, 74, 117; and Eastern Europe, 7, 16, 21, 22, 25, 26, 45, 48–49, 67, 97, 113, 152, 234, 242, 243, 278; hostility to the Enlightenment, 49–51. *See also* Josephinism; Voltaire

Erber, Leiser, 239, 444n16

Erdödy, Jozef, 83

essay contests, 67–68, 155

ethnographic exhibits, at the General Provincial Exhibition, 282, 289–94, 321, 324, 349

"ethnographic mélange," in Galicia, 376

European Union, 416

exhibition, General Provincial Exhibition of 1894, 6, 282, 284, 288–94, 321, 323, 334

famine, 255, 256, 257, 259, 264, 272

fantasy, 11, 85, 162, 180, 220, 242, 260, 287, 321, 325, 326, 363, 379, 387, 400, 401; and Fredro, 104, 110, 135, 166; of Galicia, 4, 11, 241, 260, 263, 310, 361, 381, 397, 410, 414; Jewish fantasy of Franz Joseph, 4, 319–23, 324; Josephine fantasy, 17, 30, 32, 36, 141; and Sacher-Masoch, 112, 122, 181–82, 208–9, 241, 263; Zagajewski's Lwów, 410–11

fatherland: Galicia as, 36, 39, 42–43, 91, 123, 140, 232; Poland as (*ojczyzna*), 70–71, 83–84, 163, 188, 189, 192, 194, 211, 366, 375; Habsburg, Austrian fatherland, 83–84, 100, 123, 140, 154, 262–63, 357, 366, 372

February Patent of 1861, 211, 212

federalism, Habsburg, 191, 210–11

Feldman, Wilhelm, 313, 327

Ferdinand, Emperor, 123, 130, 157, 390–91; his birthday, 154–55; as object of loyalty in 1846, 142, 146, 156, 162; and revolution of 1848, 183, 184, 185, 188–89, 190, 274

Ferdinand d'Este, Archduke, governor, 61, 104, 131, 136, 140, 170, 178

fin-de-siècle Cracow, *see* Cracow bohemians; Przybyszewski; Wyspiański; Żeleński, Tadeusz

fin-de-siècle Vienna, 283, 292, 296, 297–98, 299, 305. *See also* Hofmannsthal; Klimt; Schnitzler; Sezession

folk costume, 263, 267, 270, 271, 291, 292, 293, 294

folk songs, folk poetry, 87, 89, 114, 128, 147, 197, 270, 324, 390; Ruthenian, 116, 120, 176, 192–93; and Sacher-Masoch, 122, 143, 146; Wacław z Oleska, Galician folk songs, 117–19, 293

folklore, *see* ethnographic exhibits; folk costume; folk songs; *Zeitschrift für österreichische Volkskunde*

Four-Year Sejm (Warsaw, 1788–92), 48, 52, 70, 275

"Franco-Galician army," (as described by Fredro), 71, 72, 76, 78, 79, 107

Frank, Alison, 10, 250

Franko, Ivan, 4, 8, 10, 116, 119, 233, 248–52, 256–57, 286, 293, 324, 346, 386, 409; "Boa Constrictor," 248–49, 251–52, 325; "The Impossible in the Land of Impossibilities," 310, 388; "Moses," 8, 310, 328–30, 348; "My Jewish Acquaintances," 249–50, 324; "The Passing of Serfdom," 273–74; and Hrushevsky, 295, 309; and Mickiewicz, 309, 317

Franz, Emperor, 22, 52, 62, 83, 86, 104, 252, 388, 414; his birthday, 53, 59, 66, 67, 71, 76, 98, 99, 119; in Czernowitz, 95–96; his death in 1835, 107, 110, 347, 349; and Metternich, 63–64, 79; visits Galicia in 1817, 81, 83–84, 103

Franz Ferdinand, Archduke, 311, 332, 377

Franz Joseph, Emperor, 234, 252, 268, 320, 327, 344, 350, 356, 359, 362, 366, 369, 374, 384, 389, 395, 406, 407, 419; his accession in 1848, 188–89, 204; and assassination of Empress Elisabeth, 301–3; and Austro-Hungarian compromise, 212–13; his birthday, 228, 257–58, 415–16; his death, 330, 363; and declaration of loyalty in Sejm (1866), 216–17; in fiction of Bruno Schulz, 397–99, 418; in fiction of Joseph Roth, 396–97; and Gołuchowski, 199–200, 210, 213; and Jews, 1, 4, 203, 205, 305, 319–24, 345, 353, 360, 371; jubilee in 1898, 296, 302, 303, 309, 388; jubilee in 1908, 345; and Potocki assassination, 340–41, 344; remembered in postcommunist Poland and Ukraine, 11, 385, 411, 412, 414, 415–16, 418; visits Galicia in 1851, 194, 201, 202–5, 207, 216, 218, 228, 255, 257; visits Galicia in 1880, 234, 255, 257–61, 262, 270, 271, 331; visits General Provincial Exhibition in 1894, 294, 323

Franzos, Karl Emil, 233, 241–46, 263, 297; *Halb-Asien*, 242–43, 245–46, 263, 264, 360, 365, 386, 409

Frederick the Great, 15, 50, 124

Fredro, Aleksander, 77–79, 102, 106, 116, 131, 134, 141, 154, 206–7, 239, 311, 325, 347, 350, 363, 410; *Husband and Wife*, 92–95; *Ladies and Hussars*, 78–79; *Life Annuity*, 107–10, 132, 136; and banking, 132–35; and bears, 99, 110; charged with treason after 1848, 173, 183, 206; denounced as "non-national" in 1835, 7, 65, 108–9, 129, 133, 196, 409; on events of 1846, 165–73, 186, 304; "a flowering oasis in the Sahara," 77, 93, 109; and Galician identity, 65, 71, 109, 110, 169; hunting, 131–32; and Jews, 71–72, 135, 136, 171; his Mandarin identity, 104, 106, 109, 110, 342; memorial statue in Lviv, 357, 385; as Napoleonic soldier, 71–72, 76, 77, 80, 93, 166, 206, 228; "The Progress of Demoralization in Galicia," 136–40; and railroad, 131–36, 198, 276, 286, 373; and reform of serfdom, 131, 136, 161, 167, 172; and Sejm, 131, 132, 133, 134, 135, 206;

his sense of vertigo, 170; on Slavs and Slavdom, 173

Fredro, Henryk, 131–33

Fredro, Jan, 206–7

Fredrowa, Zofia, 207

French Revolution, 38–40, 42–43, 48, 51, 221, 305

Freud, Sigmund, 112, 308, 312, 332, 335; family origins in Galicia, 346–47

Fuchs, Leo, *Galitzianer Cowboy*, 408

Galicia, the newspaper, 123–24, 128, 133, 138, 140, 141

Galician Soviet Socialist Republic, 378–79, 380

Galicja i jej dziedzictwo, publication series, 414

Galitzianer, *see* Jewish Galicians

Gallenberg, Joseph Sigmund, 56

Gallicjan, anonymous poet of 1792, 6, 49–51, 62; his Galician identity, 50–51, 60, 80

Garbo, Greta, 401

Gautsch, Paul, 287

Gazeta Krakowska, 53, 148–51, 153–56

Gazeta Lwowska, 65–70, 76–77, 82, 98, 101, 133, 171, 236, 260, 318, 428–29n4. *See also Rozmaitości*

Gazeta Tarnowska, 185–86

General Provincial Exhibition, in Lviv, 1894, *see* exhibition

Geneva: and assassination of Elisabeth, 283, 296, 301, 305, 306, 332, 365, 414; and League of Nations, 378, 392

geography, 23, 52, 133, 262; *Geographical-Historical Report*, 53–54; maps of Galicia, 2–3, 18, 284–85; and Paris Peace Conference, 376

geology, 52, 68

German culture in Galicia, 65, 152, 228, 242, 246; alongside Polish culture, 69, 75, 128, 129, 245

German immigrants in Galicia, 31, 48, 68, 153, 224–25, 264, 271–72; *Niemiec galicyjski* (as described by Fredro), 71, 72

Gibbon, Edward, 47

Gladstone, William, 392

glasnost, 409

Głos Narodu (*Voice of the Nation*), anti-
Semitism of, 314

Goess, Peter, governor, 66, 67, 79–81

Goethe, 124, 128, 129, 165, 209; *Kennst du das
Land?* 96, 283, 287, 414

Goldbaum, Wilhelm, on Sacher-Masoch,
240

Golden Fleece, Order of, 70, 260, 334, 335,
386, 414

"Golicia and Głodomeria," 256

Gołuchowski, Agenor (namiestnik), 182,
193–94, 198–200, 202, 203, 210–11, 235,
236, 252, 342; and Galician autonomy,
213–14, 220, 311, 332; as minister in
Vienna, 210–11; his statue in Lviv, 311,
357

Gołuchowski, Agenor (foreign minister),
342

górale, highlanders, 55–57, 126–27, 196, 237,
270, 289, 293. *See also* Carpathians; ethnographic exhibits; Hutsuls

Gorbachev, Mikhail, glasnost, 409

Goszczyński, Seweryn, denounces Fredro,
108–9, 129, 131, 196, 409

Got, Jerzy, 56, 58

"Gott erhalte," Habsburg anthem (Haydn),
53, 59, 67, 99, 100, 105, 156, 203, 260

Grabowicz, George, 410

Grabski, Stanisław, Lex Grabski, 384

Grand Duchy of Warsaw, 52, 61, 63, 66, 70,
72, 147, 156, 268

Grande Armée, of Napoleon, 66, 70–71,
75, 93

Graz, and Sacher-Masoch, 115, 145, 146,
207, 240, 242

Greek Catholic Church, *see* Uniates

Green Balloon (Zielony Balonik), cabaret,
310, 326–27, 328, 348, 350

Grodziski, Stanisław, 82

guidebook to Galicia (1914), 292, 293, 413,
414

Guizot, François, 147

Gypsies, Roma, 195, 236, 237, 249

Habermas, Jürgen, 32

Habsburg, Stefan von, 362

Habsburg, Wilhelm von, and Ukrainian
politics, 362, 363

Hacquet, Balthasar, 30, 52

Hagen, William, 371

Haidamaks, 338, 340, 347

Haliczanin, 116, 126; and Ruthenian literary
culture, 116

Halych, medieval, 1, 15, 23, 47, 52, 60, 91, 95,
116, 176, 184, 254, 265, 378, 395, 415

Halych and Vladimir, Latinized as "Galicia
and Lodomeria," 15, 23, 47, 52, 60, 91

Hann, Christopher, 10, 409

Hann, Wacław, 69, 73, 75

Harrison, William Henry, 123

Harvard University, Mykhailo Hrushevsky
Chair of Ukrainian History, 326, 408

Hasidism, 19, 30, 65, 90–91, 125–26, 205,
210, 240, 264, 347, 353, 379; and Ansky,
361; and Buber, 248, 326, 346, 409; and
Ehrlich, 246–48; and Pappenheim, 315,
317–18, 349; and Sacher-Masoch, 208–9

Haskalah, *see* Jewish Enlightenment

Hauer, Franz, governor, 86

Haydn, Joseph, "Gott erhalte," 53, 59,
67, 99, 100, 105, 156, 203, 260; "The
Seasons," 77

Herbert, Zbigniew, 388

Herder, Johann Gottfried, 46, 89, 117

Herzl, Theodor, 326, 329

Hilsner, Leopold, 323–24

Himka, John-Paul, 9, 325

Hindenburg, Paul von, general, 362

Hirsch, Maurice de, his philanthropy in
Galicia, 312–13

history writing in Galicia, 9; medieval
history of Galicia, 85, 91, 196, 255. *See
also* Cracow historical school; Bałaban;
Bobrzyński; Hrushevsky; Kachala;
Kalinka; Szujski

Hitler, Adolf, 350, 404, 405, 406, 407

Hnatiuk, Volodymyr, 324

Hochberger, Juliusz, architect, 233, 357

Hoffmann von Fallersleben, August
Heinrich, 123

Hofmannsthal, Hugo von, 292; military
service in Galicia, 297–98, 364, 365; and
World War I, 364–66; "The Austrian

Idea," 365; "Our Military Administration in Poland," 364–65; "The Spirit of the Carpathians," 364; *Die Frau ohne Schatten*, 365; *Der Rosenkavalier*, 365; *Der Schwierige*, 365–66

Hölderlin, Friedrich, 298

Holocaust, 48, 311, 350, 352, 406–7, 411, 413, 417–18

Holovatsky, Iakiv, 119–20, 129, 243, 293

Holovatsky, Ivan, 130

Holy Alliance, 95

Holy Roman Empire, 21, 37

Homberg, Herz, and Jewish education, 29, 345

Horoszkiewicz, Julian, and insurrection of 1830–31, 100–101, 105, 125

Hotel Lambert, Paris, 234

Hrushevsky, Mykhailo, 9, 324, 325, 326, 329, 337, 338, 339, 348, 408; comes to Lviv in 1894, 283, 287, 288, 292; and Franko, 295, 309, 330; "Galicia and Ukraine," 338; "To the Civilized Nations of the World," 378

Hrytsak, Yaroslav, 10, 415

Hüchtker, Dietlind, 412

Hummel, Walter, 75

Der Humorist (Vienna), 140

Hungary, 276; crown of, 5, 40, 43, 218, 220, 363; and dualism, 212, 213; medieval claim to Galicia, 15, 17, 23, 39–40, 42, 44, 64; resistance to Joseph, 37, 40; in Revolution of 1848, 184, 235

Hutsuls, 126–27, 177, 195, 237, 258, 270, 272, 273, 289, 290, 291, 324, 386–87

Huyn, Karl Georg, namiestnik, 367, 370

Iakhymovych, Hryhorii, 191

Imber, Shmuel, 326

independence of Poland, 189, 190, 344; discussed in *Czas*, 191–92, 194, 224; and World War I, 351, 359, 363, 367–68

Insurrection of 1830–31 (November Insurrection), 99–105, 108, 109, 110, 116, 125, 131, 132, 134, 158, 199, 237, 262; commemorated, 257–58, 366

Insurrection of 1846, by nobles, 113, 125, 141–42, 205, 266, 282, 304; in Cracow, 147–48. *See also* massacres of 1846

Insurrection of 1863, 158, 174, 182, 211, 212, 216, 218, 219, 223, 237

Ireland, 222, 276, 394

Iron Curtain, 407

Israel, Israelis, 1, 384, 395, 396, 409, 417–18. *See also* Zionism

Israelitische Allianz, in Vienna, 312, 354, 371

Italy, Italians, 58, 96, 112, 156–57, 183, 195, 210, 276, 283, 319, 344. *See also* Lombardy and Venetia; Rome

Jackson, Andrew, 98

Jagiellonian University, 194, 212, 218, 219, 237, 248, 260, 265, 273, 343, 366

Jan Kazimierz, king, 287

Jandaurek, Julius, *Das Königreich Galizien und Lodomerien*, 35, 67, 121, 127, 180, 197, 269–72, 273, 288, 290

Janowski, Maciej, 325

Jasieński, Bruno, *The Song of Jakub Szela*, 389–91; describes Szela encountering Jesus Christ, 390

Jasło, 267

Jaszowski, Stanisław, 89

Jellinek, Adolf, rabbi, 293

Jerusalem, 11, 396, 400, 404, 408–9, 410–11, 417–18

Jesuits, 20, 236, 254, 357, 409

Jewish blood libel, concerning ritual murder, 244, 250, 323–24

Jewish Enlightenment, Haskalah, 65, 90–1, 140, 205, 242, 345, 353. *See also* Homberg; Perl

Jewish Galicians, Galician Jews, 272, 277, 312, 314, 317, 318, 319, 345–46, 396, 400; in Ansky, 351–61; difference from Jews in Russian empire, 354, 355, 356, 402, 403; difference from Litvaks, Lithuanian Jews, 248, 379, 402; emancipation, equality before the law, 29, 38, 239, 322, 353, 359, 360; family names, 29, 241, 245, 246; and Franz Joseph, 1, 4, 203, 205, 305, 319–24, 345, 353, 360, 371; Galitzianer identity, 1, 210, 248, 345, 384, 402, 403, 404, 408; hostility to Russia during World War I, 356, 358, 359, 360; as immigrants in America, 1, 317, 354, 371, 401–4,

413; and Josephine reform, 19, 27–30, 34, 36, 177, 236, 345; loyalty to Habsburgs, 177–78, 322, 353, 356, 357, 360, 372; and the Messiah, 34, 356, 361; military service, 29, 321–23, 359–60; as non-national Galicians, 135; *Pamiętnik Galicyjski* and the history of the Jews, 89–90; Passover, 244, 250, 354; Polish-Jewish assimilationism, 264, 313, 327; refugees in Vienna during World War I, 354–55, 356; Sabbath observance, 29, 30, 293, 316, 322; in Szujski, 264–65; viewed by Franko, 248–52; viewed by Franzos, 241–46; viewed by Fredro, 71–72, 135; viewed by Kratter, 27–30; viewed by Majer and Kopernicki, 237–39, 243; viewed by Pappenheim, 311–12, 314–19, 349; Yom Kippur, 297, 321, 322, 323, 358. *See also* Hasidism; Holocaust; Yiddish; Zionism

Jewish music, 296–97, 299, 361, 414

Jewish political parties, 313, 345

Jewish women in Galicia: Pappenheim on, 311–12, 314, 315, 318; Sholem Aleichem on, 355–56; Wyspiański's Rachel in *Wesele*, 280–81, 300, 312

John Paul II, Pope, *see* Wojtyła

Joseph II, emperor, 62, 82, 119, 172, 228, 245, 246, 261, 264, 272, 278, 322; death, 36, 38, 44; remembered by peasants, 4, 178, 228, 252; remembered by Ruthenians, 258, 261; visiting Galicia, 13–16, 19–20, 31–32, 68, 204, 221, 314

Josephinism, Josephine Enlightenment, 7, 13–50, 59, 64, 65, 113, 125, 221, 228, 234; and Jews, 19, 27–30, 34, 36, 177, 236, 345; messianism in Galicia, 4, 7, 28, 34, 36, 64, 85, 140–41, 312–13; "recasting" of Galicia, 23, 28, 30, 31, 32, 60, 97, 141; reform of serfdom, 16, 20, 136, 142, 149, 160–61, 162, 176, 180, 183, 258; and religion, criticized and reformed, 24–27, 33, 38; religious toleration, 29, 31, 50

Josephinism after Joseph, the legacy, 53, 54–55, 57, 92, 138, 152, 174, 178

Journal de Paris, 76

journalism, press, in Galicia, 64, 66, 128–29, 183, 185, 229, 280, 302, 307; and assassination of Potocki, 339–41, 342, 348. *See also Czas; Dilo; Gazeta Lwowska; Galicia; Gazeta Tarnowska; Kuryer Codzienny; Słowo Polskie; Zoria*

journalism, press, in Vienna, 211, 220, 221, 224–25. *See also Neue Freie Presse; Oesterreichische Beobachter; Wiener Zeitung*

Jüdische Volksstimme, Brno, 360

Juell, Dagny, 298

Jung-Wien, Young Vienna, 292, 326

Juvenal, 49

Kachala, Stefan, 9, 233, 254–55, 262

Kaczkowski, Joachim, 75

Kafka, Franz, 315, 316

Kalinka, Walerian, 9, 194, 205, 206, 219, 262, 276, 336; *Galicia and Cracow under Austrian Rule*, 205

Kamenka Strumilova, Last Judgment from, 293; synagogue in, 293

Kamiński, Jan Nepomucen, author of *Zabobon*, 91–92, 102, 105, 116

Kant, Immanuel, 38, 45, 46

Kappeler, Andreas, 10

Kapuzinergruft, Capuchin crypt, in Vienna, 20, 162, 164, 258, 397

Karadžić, Vuk, 117

Karaites, 196

Karl, Archduke (brother of Emperor Franz), 58, 59

Karl, Emperor, 369, 414; his abdication, 351, 367, 369, 370, 416; his beatification, 416

Kasprowicz, Jan, 295, 299

Kaunitz, Wenzel Anton, 14–17, 37, 64, 162

Kazimierz, Jewish quarter of Cracow, 203, 413–14

Kazimierz Wielki, *see* Casimir the Great

Kenney, Padraic, 409

Khmelnytsky, Bogdan, 126, 337, 338

Khorostkiv, 361

Kieniewicz, Stefan, 137

Kiev, 287, 292, 326, 364, 368, 378, 411; Kievan Rus, 1, 17, 176, 378

Kingdom of Poland, created by Central Powers during World War I, 362, 363

Kisielewski, Jan August, 327

kissing: in patriotic enthusiasm, 71; in religious ritual, 27

Klimt, Gustav, 287, 296, 299

Kłańska, Maria, 9

Kohn, Abraham, rabbi, 205

Kolberg, Oskar, on folklore, 237

Kolesnikoff, Nina, 390

Kolomiya, 256, 258, 313, 337, 370. *See also* Sacher-Masoch (writer), *Don Juan von Kolomea*

Kolowrat, Franz Anton, 152

Königgrätz (Sadowa), battle of, 212

Königsberg, David, 326

Kopernicki, Izydor, 237, 293. *See also* Majer and Kopernicki, *The Physical Characteristics*

Kortum, Ernst Traugott von, 38–49, 61; *Examination of the Grievances of the Galician Nobility*, 44–49; ventriloquizes Galician nobility, 44–45, 47–48. *See also Magna Charta of Galicia*

Korzeniowski, Apollo, 229–30, 256

Korzeniowski, Józef, *Carpathian Mountaineers*, 126–27, 128

Korzeniowski, Józef Teodor Konrad, *see* Conrad, Joseph

Kościuszko, Tadeusz, insurrection of, 52, 55, 57, 103, 261, 266, 348; centennial, 294, 348

Kossak, Juliusz, 266

Kossak, Wojciech, 294

Kostyrko, Volodymyr, 415–16; "Galicia and Ukraine," 415–16

Kotliarevsky, Ivan, 296, 309

Kozik, Jan, 9, 87

Koźmian, Kajetan, 53

Koźmian, Stanisław, 218, 223–24; "different degrees of national existence," 223–24

Krafft-Ebing, Richard von, *Psychopathia Sexualis*, 113–14, 209

kraj, the country, Galicia, 132, 134, 172, 216, 260, 283, 295, 367, 413; in *Czas*, 188, 195, 199, 202, 203, 206, 213, 214, 220

Kraków, *see* Cracow

Krakowiacy i Górale, 14, 55–57, 59, 91–92, 103, 127, 196, 197; as Galician drama, 57, 59, 92. *See also* Bogusławski; Kamiński

Krakowiak, 55–57, 92, 147, 196, 197, 269–70, 289, 414

Kratter, Franz (author of the *Briefe*); as distinguished from the editor Franz Kratter, 65–66, 428–29n4; *Briefe (Letters about the Present Situation of Galicia)*, 21–33, 80, 82, 113, 145, 264, 415; *Das Mädchen von Marienburg*, 59

Kratter, Franz (founding editor of *Gazeta Lwowska*), 65–66, 428–29n4

Krieg, Franz, 83, 84, 131–32, 138, 140, 155, 174, 175, 178

Krusceniski, Salomea (Krushelnytska, Solomiya), 319, 409

Krzeszowice, Potocki family estate, 331, 335, 344

Kufstein fortress and prison, 105, 125

Kundera, Milan, on Central Europe, 411, 414

Kürnberger, Ferdinand, on Sacher-Masoch, 115

Kurtz, Esther, 324, 454n36

Kuryer Codzienny, in 1918, 367, 368–69

Kuzemsky, Mykhailo, 115, 184

Kwaśniewski, Aleksander, 412

La Grange, Henry-Louis de, 318

La Scala, 319, 409

Lachs, Minne, 356

Landau, Felix, and Bruno Schulz, 417–18

Landau, Saul, *Unter jüdischen Proletariern*, 313–14, 329

Lashkiv, 381

Lavrovsky, Ivan, 87; Ruthenian-Polish-German dictionary, 65, 87

League of Nations, 378, 383, 392; minority protection, 384–85, 391–93

leases, economic, 134; and Jews, 27, 28, 29

legitimacy, legitimation of Habsburg Galicia, 15, 54, 64, 66, 81, 113, 163; "revin-dication" of Galicia, 15, 17, 20, 23, 62, 63–64, 156, 163

Leipzig, battle of, 74

Leitha River, 212

Lem, Stanisław, 388, 409; "phantomology," 409

Lemberger Zeitung, 65

Lemkos, 289
Lenin, Vladimir, 379
Leo, Juliusz, mayor of Cracow, 366
Leonardo da Vinci, "Lady with Ermine," 260
Leopold II, emperor, 36–39, 42, 43, 44, 52, 138; corresponds with Joseph, 13, 16
lèse-majesté, 303, 305, 327
Leshniv, 380
Lessing, Gotthold Ephraim, *Nathan the Wise*, 34, 36
Levynsky, Ivan, architect, 291
Levytsky, Ivan, *The Ruthenian Movement in Galicia*, 252–53
Lilien, Ephraim Moses, 299
Limanowski, Bolesław, *Galicya przedstawiona słowem i ołówkiem*, 193, 288, 314
Lipiński, Karol, 75
Liptzin, Solomon, 325, 326
"liquidation" of Galicia, *see* Polish Liquidation Commission
Lithuania, 74, 88, 89, 191, 263, 346. *See also* Vilnius
"Little Russians," meaning Ruthenians or Ukrainians, 114–15, 130, 240
Litvaks, Lithuanian Jews, 72, 248, 379, 402
Lloyd George, David, 374
Lobkovic, Prince August, governor, 98–99, 100, 103, 104, 106, 131
Lodomeria, in title "Kingdom of Galicia and Lodomeria," from "Halych and Vladimir," 15, 17, 19, 23, 33, 39, 53, 61, 99, 189, 200, 201, 256, 269, 289, 407
Lombardy and Venetia, Habsburg Italian lands, 81, 157, 210
loneliness, *Einsamkeit, samotność*, 74, 94, 389
Louis-Philippe, king, 148
loyalty to Habsburgs, 8, 51, 61, 63, 99, 106, 153, 156, 173, 178, 179, 200, 255, 261, 327, 331, 343, 363, 414; after assassination of Elisabeth, 301–3, 332; and *Czas*, 215, 216, 218, 220, 226, 257, 301–3, 341; declaration of Sejm in 1866, 194, 216–17, 259, 265, 278, 345; fidelity and infidelity in Fredro's *Husband and Wife*, 94–95; of Jews, 177–78, 322, 353, 356, 357, 360, 372; Ossoliński and Franz, 83–84; peas-

ant loyalism in 1846, 113, 138, 142, 146, 149, 150–51, 154–55, 162–63, 175, 180–81, 185–86, 322; of Andrzej Potocki, dying, 334, 340, 344; in Roth's "Bust of the Emperor," 397, 398; Ruthenian, 87, 184, 252, 258, 261. *See also* "Gott erhalte"
Lubomirski family, 32, 387
Luccheni, Luigi, assassin of Elisabeth, 303, 306, 399
Lueger, Karl, 296
Lviv, Lwów, Lemberg: balls, 57–58, 96, 124, 129, 140, 141, 178, 230; cafés, 155, 325, 385, 411–12; carnival, 55, 57, 124, 126, 138, 140, 141, 178; Castle Hill, 31, 228, 357; cathedral, Roman Catholic, 287, 410; Döblin in, 385–88; Korzeniowski (Apollo) in, 229–30; Lychakivsky cemetery, 409; Mahler in, 318–19; Metternich in, 95–97; musical life, 74–75, 76, 77–78, 124, 318–19, 324, 360; pogrom of 1918, 370–74; and Polish-Ukrainian war, 369–70; population, 114, 357, 408, 411; and railroad in Galicia, 132–33, 136, 198, 207, 211, 213, 410; railroad station, 357, 360, 369; receives Franz Joseph in 1880, 261; receives Gołuchowski in 1850, 199–200; Rynek, Market Square, 66, 67, 110; sanitation, 30, 31; under Soviet rule, 405–6, 408–9; Stryjski Park, 288–89; Town Hall, 67, 110, 199, 357; urban landscape, 67, 97, 129, 357; Viennese/Austrian atmosphere, 385–86, 405–6, 411; Wat, "Did you know Lwów before the war?" 405, 406, 408; weather, 66; in Wittlin's memoirs, 415; in Zagajewski's poem, 409–11. *See also* *Gazeta Lwowska*; Ossolineum
Łańcut, Potocki family estate, 95, 168, 331
Łoziński, Bronisław, 304
Łubieński, Roger, *Scarcity and Famine in Galicia*, 256

Macartney, C. A., 101, 104, 211
Maeterlinck, Maurice, 296
Magna Charta of Galicia (Magna Charta von Galizien), 7, 37–40, 42, 44, 49, 82, 138, 160, 172, 183
Magocsi, Paul Robert, 9, 10

Mahler, Alma, 318
Mahler, Gustav, in Lviv, 318–19, 324, 348
Mahler, Raphael, 30, 90–91
Majer, Józef, 237
Majer and Kopernicki, *The Physical Characteristics of the Population of Galicia*, 236–39, 243, 251, 260
Malone, Cecil, introduces "The Danger Spot of Europe," 391–92
Małopolska, Little Poland, 17, 102
Małopolska Wschodnia, Eastern Little Poland (Eastern Galicia), 393
Maner, Hans-Christian, 10, 224, 332–33
manners, of Galicia, 33, 222; criticized by Kratter, 24–25
Margelik, Johann Wenzel, 53
Maria Theresa, empress, 41, 42, 64, 149, 162, 164, 218, 228; her conscience, 15, 52; her death, 20; and partition of Poland, 1, 14–15, 23, 200, 221, 236, 244; and Uniate Church, 25, 86, 253
Marie Antoinette, queen of France, 220–21
Markovits, Andrei, 9
Marx, Karl, 147, 190
Mary, Queen of Poland, Queen of Galicia, 53, 287
Mascagni, Pietro, *Cavalleria Rusticana*, 360
Masons, Masonic symbolism, 21, 69
Massachusetts, 85–86
massacres of 1846, 8, 112, 113, 137, 141–57, 185–87, 217, 226, 261, 317, 344, 348, 374; in *Czas*, 189–90, 191, 201, 267, 304; in Franko's "The Passing of Serfdom," 274; Fredro on, 165–73; in Jasieński's *The Song of Jakub Szela*, 390–91; Metternich on, 147–49, 151–52, 158; remembered in relation to anarchism, 304–5, 307; and Revolution of 1848, 183–87; Sacher-Masoch, police chief, on, 173–83; Sacher-Masoch, writer, on, 141–47, 157, 162, 173–74, 207; Wielopolski's letter on, 158–65; in Wyspiański's *Wesele*, 281–82
Matejko, Jan, 228, 266, 291, 357
Mauss, Joseph, professor, 9, 84–85, 86; his New Year's wish for Galicia, December 1817, 84–85

Maximilian, emperor of Mexico, 220–21, 399
Mayerling, 268, 305
Mazurs, 101, 147, 152, 175, 269, 289
McCarthy, Mary, 246
McKinley, William, 304
Mehoffer, Joseph, editor of *Galicia*, 123
melancholy, as Ruthenian characteristic, 122, 146, 147, 177, 263–64, 270
Mendelsohn, Daniel, 10
Mendelssohn, Moses, and Jewish Enlightenment, 34
messianism in Galicia: Jewish, 34, 356, 361; Josephine, 4, 7, 28, 34, 36, 64, 85, 140–41, 312–13
Metternich, Klemens Wenzel, 69, 77, 79–81, 109, 112, 131, 155, 157, 268, 351; and censorship, 64, 95, 98, 124, 126; correspondence concerning events of 1846, 147–53; fall from power in 1848, 183, 186; as "hangman of Poland," 105, 110; and Jews, 90, 95, 97, 205; "to make true Galicians," 65, 79–80, 85, 88, 99–100, 110, 320; and Napoleon, 63–64, 97; and police, 64, 79, 108, 124, 206; on Polishness (*polonisme*), 151–52, 158, 163; visits Galicia in 1823, 95–98, 105, 107, 112, 318; Wielopolski's letter to Metternich, 158–65
Michalewicz, Mikołaj, 82, 116
Michałowski, Piotr, 106–7; painting Napoleon, 107
Mickiewicz, Adam, 66, 89, 93, 104, 134, 183, 219, 280, 388; addressing the Galicians, 105, 142; centennial, 296, 309; at Collège de France, 133, 165, 234; and Franko, 309, 317; *Pan Tadeusz*, 66, 106, 191
military service, Habsburg, 177, 237; Galician Jews, 29, 321–23, 359–60; Hofmannsthal, 297–98
Miłosz, Czesław, 406
minorities, national, in interwar Poland, 383–84, 391–93
Młoda Polska, Young Poland, 280, 286, 304, 326, 327
modernism, literary, 280–83, 287, 295–96, 304–5, 307, 318. *See also* Przybyszewski; Wyspiański

Mohylnytsky, Ivan, 87
Moldavia and Wallachia, 37, 48, 133, 201, 236
Molicki, Antoni, 278
Molière, influence on Fredro, 93, 132, 136, 138
Molotov-Ribbentrop pact, 350, 385; partition of Poland and Galicia, 385, 404, 406, 407
Moniuszko, Stanisław, 287, 300
Monroe, Marilyn, as Sugar Kane Kowalczyk, 401
Montenegro, 89, 90, 95
Moravia, 97, 118, 170, 191, 212, 228, 276, 346
Morawski, Tadeusz, on Metternich, 158
Morgenstern, Soma, 415
Moscow, 219, 229, 255, 263, 406, 411; and Napoleonic wars, 76–77, 80, 94
Moser, Michael, 261, 413
Moses, 28, 31, 403; Franko's *Moses*, 8, 310, 328–30, 348
Mozart, Constanze, 72–73
Mozart, Franz Xaver Wolfgang, 65, 72–76, 77–78, 79, 88, 99
Mozart, Karl, 72–74
Mozart, Wolfgang Amadeus, 43, 74, 99, 122; *Cosi fan tutte*, 78, 93; *Le Nozze di Figaro*, 77; *Die Zauberflöte*, 58, 69, 72
Mułkowski, Stefan, 105
Munch, Edvard, 298
Munchausen, Baron, 26
Münchengrätz, agreement of, 105, 106
mythology of Galicia, 410, 412–13, 416. *See also* allegory of Galicia; nostalgia

name of Galicia, 1, 33, 43, 46, 60, 62, 72, 116, 152, 174, 412, 413; adopted with partition of Poland in 1772, 15–17; discussed in "The Danger Spot of Europe," 391–95
Napoleon, Napoleonic wars, 52, 63–79, 82, 91, 92, 106–7, 300, 351, 388; centennial birthday, 228; invasion of Russia, 63, 66, 70–71, 75, 76–77, 101, 106; and Metternich, 63–64; and Polish national sentiment, 66, 70–71, 133, 134. *See also* Grand Duchy of Warsaw; Fredro, Aleksander, as Napoleonic soldier

Napoleon III, 399
Narodnaya Volya, 333
Narutowicz, Gabriel, assassinated, 383
nation, Galician, 39, 46, 66, 83, 84–85, 88, 117
National Democrats, Polish, 314, 383–84
nationality: ambiguous, cryptic, 39, 83, 92, 163–64, 175, 196, 215, 229, 235; discussed by Fredro, 171–72; discussed by Metternich, 79–80; and national rights, 239–40, 258, 261; non-national identity, 6–7, 108–10, 133–35, 141, 196, 224, 229, 353, 373; and peasants, 6, 172, 175, 266, 294, 390; transcendent, synthetic, 5–7, 79–80, 86, 103–4, 129, 259, 418. *See also* nation, Galician
NATO, 416
natural space, natural history, 5–6, 124, 128; and construction of Galicia, 61–62, 68, 128, 195, 211–12, 220, 238–39, 376
Nazi occupation, of Poland and Galicia, 188, 237, 404, 405–7, 417–18; Distrikt Galizien, 406; General Government, 404, 406; SS Galizien, 406
Netherlands, Austrian, 33, 37
Neue Freie Presse (Vienna), 224–25, 242, 364; on assassination of Potocki, 332–36, 339, 341; on choosing the successor to Potocki, 341–43; on the former Galicia, after World War I, 369–74
New York City, Galician emigrants in, 1, 244, 248, 317, 324, 345–46, 401–4, 415
New York Times, 345, 377, 401, 403
Nicholas, Saint, 26, 293
Nicholas I, czar, 105, 110
Nicolson, Harold, 376
Niemcewicz, Julian, 11, 60
Nietzsche, Friedrich, 281, 298, 301, 304
Nirvana, 286, 346
Nobile, Pietro von, architect, 88
nobility, *szlachta*, in Galicia, 17, 20, 54–55, 160, 172, 199, 243, 261, 274; feudal privileges, 22, 37–38, 41–43; and Jews, 23, 27–28, 244; Kratter's negative view of, 22–24, 28, 36, 113; and Magna Charta of 1790, 37–49; reaction against Josephinism, 37–44; rebels and victims in 1846, 141–57, 159, 175, 179, 180–81

noses: blowing, 24–25; physiognomy, 237–38; in Sacher-Masoch's fiction, 241
Nossig, Alfred, 313
nostalgia, for Galicia, 11, 385, 410, 412–16
November Insurrection, *see* Insurrection of 1830–31
Nowicki, Maksymilian, on natural history, 212
Nowy Targ, 306
nursing, wet nursing, breast milk and national culture, 114, 116, 117, 119, 120–22, 192–93, 241

October Diploma of 1860, 210–11
Oesterreichische Beobachter (Vienna), on events of 1846, 150, 154
Offenbach, Jacques, 360
oil fields, oil industry, *see* Boryslav
opera, in Lviv, 69, 77, 78, 124, 129, 319, 360. *See also* Bogusławski; *Krakowiacy i Górale*
Operation Vistula, 407
Orange Revolution, 413, 416
organic work, 195, 196, 219, 224, 256, 275
Organization of Ukrainian Nationalists (OUN), 393, 415
Orient, Orientalism, in Galicia, 177, 251, 268, 319, 333, 409; in Babel, 381–82; Franzos and *Halb-Asien*, 242–43, 245–46, 263, 264, 298, 360, 365, 386, 409; Fredro's Mandarin identity, 104, 106, 109, 110, 342; Metternich's Orient, 97; Sacher-Masoch's Orient, 115, 130, 137, 208–9, 240–41; and Sarmatians, 16, 30, 47–48, 49, 52, 69, 174
Orlando, Vittorio Emanuele, 374
Orłowicz, Mieczysław, 413. *See also* guidebook to Galicia (1914)
Orthodox Christianity, 26, 214, 254, 292, 358, 407
Ossolineum Library, 37, 65, 81–85, 98–99, 104, 131, 195, 261; Döblin visits, 387–88; as "Parnassus Ossolinius," 85; supports Schneider and encyclopedia, 235–36; in Wrocław, 407
Ossoliński, Józef Maksymilian, 86, 87, 388; author of *Magna Charta* and

Considerations (Uwagi), 37, 40, 82, 138; and Ossolineum, 65, 81–85, 98–99, 387
Ostrow, Moritz Ritter von, 226
Ottoman empire, 42, 78, 102, 224, 235, 268, 392; siege of Vienna in 1683, 164, 265–66, 273

Pacific Ocean, South Seas, 21, 45
Paderewski, Ignacy, 368, 376–77, 378
Pajakowski, Philip, 343
Pamiętnik Galicyjski, 65, 88–91, 94–95
Pamiętnik Lwowski, 88
Pan-Slavism, 129–30; Slavic Congress in Prague (1848), 186, 190
Pappenheim, Bertha, 310, 311–12, 314–18, 324, 349, 354; on Galician Jewish women, 311–12, 314, 318; on Jews as hunger artists, 316–17
Paris Peace Conference, 373–78
partition of Galicia, proposed, considered, 152, 184, 186, 190, 191, 192, 200–201, 213–14, 225, 376, 404
partitions of Poland, 100, 152, 195, 218, 219, 221, 225, 343; first partition, 1, 13, 42, 68, 81, 102, 148, 160, 174, 201, 236, 347, 404; second partition, 52; third partition, 52, 60, 64, 147, 194; to be undone at the Paris Peace Conference, 375, 377
Paul, Saint, 105
Pauli, Żegota, on folk songs, 390
Pawlikowski, Tadeusz, 295–96
peasants, 54–55, 70, 126, 196, 272, 288, 317, 336, 349; and anti-Semitism, 305–6, 308, 325; "der Bauer wacht," 182, 267; *Czas* on, 221, 226, 267; and emigration, 256, 267; and Franz Joseph, 203–4; Fredro and feudal reform, 136–39; Jasieński on, 390–91; and Josephine reform, 4, 16, 20, 45, 57, 142, 149, 178; and massacres of 1846, 141–57, 163, 174, 175, 179–83, 185–86, 261, 267, 274, 391; and nationality, 6, 172, 175, 266, 294, 390; "Peasant and Jewish Types," 288; in Wyspiański's *Wesele*, 280–83. *See also* serfdom
Pelesz, Julian, *History of the Union of the Ruthenian Church with Rome*, 253; and General Provincial Exhibition, 292

Pergen, Johann Anton, governor, 14–17, 19
Perl, Joseph, 90; against Hasidism, 65, 125–26
Persia, 85, 89, 244
Peru, Galicia as "a new Peru," 33
Peter the Great, 59
Pfleger, Adele, writing about the General Provincial Exhibition, 290–91
piano music, 72, 73, 75, 78, 79, 94, 301, 366
Picon, Molly, 404
Piłsudski, Józef, 344, 351, 362, 374, 383, 391; coup d'état of 1926, 389, 391
Piniński, Leon, namiestnik, 387–88
Plato, 298
Podkamień, 73, 74, 430n24
Podolia, 60, 91, 102, 132
Poetic Almanac for Galicia, 69, 73, 75
pogrom in Lviv (1918), 370–74, 375, 387
Pohl, Dieter, 406
Poklewska, Krystyna, 89
Poland, communist, 407–9
Poland, interwar, 383–89, 391–95, 397
Poland, postcommunist, 411–14, 416
police, *see* Metternich, and police; Sacher-Masoch, police chief
Polish claims to Galicia, after World War I, 374–78
Polish Galician perspective, identity, 211, 228, 260; of *Czas*, 188, 194, 215
Polish incorporation of Galicia, after World War I, 351, 368, 378, 383, 404, 405; as "Little Eastern Poland" or "Eastern Little Poland," 391–93; as "South Eastern Poland," 377
Polish Liquidation Commission, liquidating Galicia, 352, 367–68, 371–72, 373
Polish national culture, preserved in Galicia, 14, 215
Polish-Ruthenian agreement of 1914, 361
Polish-Ruthenian compromise of 1890, 287, 295, 337
Polish-Soviet war (1919–20), 4, 351, 352, 368, 374, 383; and Babel in Galicia, 379–82
Polish-Ukrainian war (1918–19), 369–70, 371, 378, 380, 387; struggle for Lviv, 369–70, 373–74
Pollack, Martin, 414

polonaises, 75, 76, 366
Polonsky, Antony, 10
Poltava, 309
Poniatowski, Józef, occupies Lviv in 1809, 61, 71
Popiel, Paweł, 205
population of Galicia, 6, 64, 173, 195–96, 236, 249, 264, 269, 315; and Paris Peace Conference, 375–76; physical anthropology, 236–39; physiognomy, 175; transfer of populations, after World War II, 407–8, 410–11, 413
positivism, Polish, 195
Potocki, Alfred, Fredro's correspondent, 166–71, 260
Potocki, Alfred, namiestnik, 260, 331, 333, 342
Potocki, Andrzej, namiestnik, 317; assassination, 283, 311, 331–41, 342, 343, 344, 346, 348, 350, 374, 377–78, 386, 404, 405
Potocki, Jan, author, 166
Potocki family, 23, 32, 95, 96, 100, 260, 331, 333
poverty, misery, of Galicia, 96, 138, 221, 234–35, 256, 259, 264, 275–79, 306, 325, 353, 384, 390; of Galician Jews, 264, 277, 297, 315, 316, 353, 403. *See also* Szczepanowski, *Misery of Galicia*
Poznań, 405
Prague, 43, 72, 212, 298; and Sacher-Masoch family, 111, 116, 173, 174, 183, 186, 207; Slavic Congress, 186, 190
Pritsak, Omeljan, 326
Procházka, Arnošt, editor of *Moderní Revue*, 298
Prokopovych, Markian, 10, 291
Promised Land, Galicia as, 28, 31, 33, 313
property rights, in Galicia, 38, 42, 45, 100, 168, 176
prostitution, 27, 124, 311–12, 318
Protestantism, 31, 68, 264
Proust, Marcel, 418
Prussian Poland, 129, 195, 206, 298, 299
Prut River, 212
Prymak, Thomas, 295
Przegląd Polski, 218, 223
Przemyśl, 23, 97, 128, 258, 334, 354, 370, 371,

397, 412, 414; as center of Ruthenian culture and nationality, 86–87, 119, 129, 254, 337, 342; and Uniates, 124, 253, 292, 409

Przybyszewski, Stanisław, 281, 296–97, 298–301, 310, 312, 326, 348, 350, 388; his "anarchism of the spirit," 304; in Berlin, 298, 299; his "satanism," 281, 298–99, 300, 304, 326, 327, 348, 350; and *Życie*, 296, 297, 298–301

public sphere, European, concerning Galicia, 158–59, 179, 263

public sphere, German, concerning Galicia, 21–22, 25, 37, 43–44, 129, 244

public sphere, public opinion, Galician, 64, 215, 222, 231–2, 282, 301, 325; in Lviv, Polish and German, 56–58

Puccini, Giacomo, 319

Purchla, Jacek, 10, 291

Rabinowitsch, Sara, 314

Racławice, Kościuszko at, 266, 294

railroad, trains, in Galicia, 130–36, 243, 258, 260, 276, 357, 397, 410, 414; Kaiser-Ferdinands-Nordbahn, 130, 132, 373; the line to Lviv, 131, 136, 198, 207, 211, 213, 318–19, 335; as metaphor in poetry, 286; in *Venus in Furs*, 130

Raphael of Urbino, 120, 122

Rapoport, Solomon Judah, rabbi, 125

Rauchinger, Heinrich, artist, 299

Red Ruthenia, Red Rus, 60, 91, 102, 236, 254, 360, 377

Redlich, Joseph, biography of Franz Joseph, 268

Reichsrat, of Cis-Leithania, in Vienna, 217, 228, 239, 275, 331, 343; Polish Club, 310, 333, 344; Ruthenians in, 252, 310–11, 334

Reichstag, at Kremsier (1848–49), 191

Reitzenheim, Józef, memoirs of insurrection of 1830–31, 101–4

Revolution of 1848, 125, 137, 160, 173, 174, 182, 183–87, 201, 235; defeat of revolution, 186, 188, 189; "The Passing of Serfdom," by Franko, 273–74; Polish political program, Polish National Council, 183, 186, 190–91, 203, 206; Ruthenian

political program, Supreme Ruthenian Council, 116, 184–85, 186, 190–91, 243, 255, 404, 405

"Robinson Crusoe" (Traunpaur) in Galicia, 34–36

Roller, Alfred, 318

Roman Catholicism, 228, 269, 297; bishops, 38, 43, 83, 235; Brothers of the Resurrection, 262; Kratter's hostility, 24–25, 50; Sisters of Charity, 68, 98, 102

Romanticism, 69, 89, 93, 103, 144, 164, 196, 343; attack on Fredro, 108–9, 133; musical, 74, 76; poetry, 89, 93, 108, 298; and Polish national sentiment, 104, 134, 189, 195, 206; rejected by Cracow historical school, 206, 343. *See also* Chopin; Mickiewicz

Rome, ancient, 47; modern, 262, 342

Romer, Eugeniusz, geographer, 374; *Mémoire sur la Galicie* (1919), 374–77; *Statistics of Galicia* (1919), 375, 377

Rossetti, Gabriele, poem addressed to Metternich, 157

Rossini, Gioachino, 79, 124

Roth, Joseph, 384, 395–97, 401; "The Bust of the Emperor," 395, 397; *The Emperor's Tomb*, 11, 395, 399–400, 410; Franz Joseph in Roth's work, 396–97; *Radetzky March*, 395, 396; visits Galicia in 1924, 389

Rothschild, Salomon, and Fredro, 136, 198, 276

Rothschild family, 130

Rousseau, Jean-Jacques, 38, 39

Rozdolsky, Osyp, 324

Rozenblit, Marsha, 354, 356, 359

Rozmaitości, 81, 82, 85–86, 87, 128; and Ruthenian literary culture, 116

Rubens, Peter Paul, 122

Rudnytsky, Ivan, 408

Rudnytzky, Leonid, 252

Rudolf, Crown Prince, 258, 271, 305; in Cracow, 272–73; patron of *The Lands of Austria-Hungary in Word and Image*, 256, 258

Rudolf of Habsburg, Rudolf I, 164

Rusalka Dnistrovaia, 111, 116, 119–21, 122

Russian occupation of Galicia, during

World War I, 351–54, 356–60, 370; hostility to Jews, pogroms, 352, 354, 358–60

Russian Poland, Congress Poland, 64, 93, 99–105, 112–13, 142, 158, 229, 275, 276, 362, 385; Jews of, 210, 248, 313. *See also* Insurrection of 1830–31; Insurrection of 1863

Russian Revolution of 1905, 330, 338

"Ruthenian," as national classification, 130, 393–94, 413

Ruthenian National Institute, in Lviv, 261

Ruthenian Triad, 65, 116, 119–20, 126, 129, 243, 293

Rydel, Lucjan, and *Wesele*, 281, 294

Rzeszów, 36, 95, 97, 140, 258, 267, 371, 414

Sacher, Johann Nepomuk von, 111–12, 174

Sacher-Masoch, Leopold von, writer, 8, 11, 111–16, 126, 128, 263, 416, 418; Galicia as his "homeland," 11, 114, 146, 186, 207–8; and Jews, 208–9, 240–41; and Little Russians, Ruthenians, 114–16, 120–22, 192–93, 241; and masochism, 111–12, 113–14, 139, 145, 147, 165, 167, 181–82, 207–8, 240; and the massacres of 1846, 141–47, 157, 162, 173–74; return to Galicia in 1857, 207–10; *Don Juan von Kolomea*, 115, 122, 126; *A Galician History of 1846* or *Graf Donski*, 145–47, 173–74, 207; *Venus in Furs*, 112, 113, 130, 137, 139, 146, 209, 240, 241, 242, 245

Sacher-Masoch, Leopold von, police chief, 111–12, 124–28, 132, 138, 140, 141, 183, 184, 186, 208; in 1846, 143, 162; writing about 1846, *Polish Revolutions*, 159, 173–83, 226

Sacher-Masoch, Wanda von, 113

Sacher-Masoch family, 111–12, 114, 115, 123

Sadagora, zaddik in, 208–9, 240

Sade, Marquis de, 24

Said, Edward, 6, 108

St. George party, Old Ruthenians, 14

St. Stephen, Order of, 61, 84

Samoa, 289, 290

San River, 132, 152, 404

Sanok, 254, 306

Saphir, Moritz Gottlieb, 184

Sapieha, Leon, 131, 132, 136, 137, 155, 161, 167, 175, 198, 286

Sarajevo, 311, 332

"Sarmatians" in Galicia, 16, 30, 47–48, 49, 52, 69, 174

satanism, and Przybyszewski, 281, 298–99, 300, 304, 326, 327, 348, 350

Schengen border, of European Union, 416

Schiller, Friedrich, 91, 105–6, 225, 246

Schneider, Antoni, his encyclopedia, 231–36, 414

Schnitzler, Arthur, *The Green Cockatoo*, 305, 335

Schorske, Carl, on fin-de-siècle Vienna, 283, 296; "politics in a new key," 283, 331

Schulz, Bruno, 8, 246, 350, 384, 395–99, 410, 413, 417–19; "August," 399; "The Comet," 349–50; "Sanatorium under the Sign of the Hourglass," 418; "Spring," 397–99, 418; murals in Drohobych, 11, 417–19; murdered in 1942, 350, 396, 407, 417

Segel, Benjamin, 319–21, 324

Ségur, Louis-Philippe, 243

Sejm of Galicia, 183, 198, 199, 210, 212, 213, 220, 260, 275, 331, 343; and autonomy, 222–23, 234; and declaration of loyalty in 1866, 216–17, 218; discusses reform of feudalism in 1840s, 111, 112, 131, 137, 139; Fredro in, 131, 132, 133, 134, 135, 172, 206; palace of, with allegorical sculpture, 232–34, 357, 369–70, 388; reestablished in 1817, 81–82, 84; and Ruthenians, 225, 255, 262, 310, 331, 361; supports Schneider and encyclopedia, 235, 236. *See also* elections

Serbia, Serbs, 117, 338

serfdom, 22, 38, 40, 42, 119, 136–37, 141, 172, 181, 183; emancipation, 92, 112, 142, 185, 186, 239, 273–74, 296, 309; "The Passing of Serfdom," by Franko, 273–74; as "slavery," 22, 112–13, 137–39, 141, 240, 329. *See also* Josephinism; peasants

Sezession, in Viennese art, 296, 299

Shakespeare, William, *Hamlet*, 58, 209

Shanes, Joshua, 313

Shashkevych, Markiian, 119–20

Shaw, George Bernard, 248
Shchurat, Vasyl, 329
Sheepshanks, Mary, in Eastern Galicia, 392–94
Sheptytsky, Andrei, 311, 325, 342, 362, 363, 388, 392; and Babel, 381–82; and World War II, 350, 407
Shevchenko, Taras, 214, 309
Shevchenko Scientific Society, 295, 324
Sholem Aleichem, on Galicia, 355–56; on "Cracow and Lemberg," 355–56
Shore, Marci, 405
shtetl communities, 4, 297–98, 349
Shuisky, Vasily, tsar, 263
Shukhevych, Volodymyr: and catalogue of ethnographic exhibits, 289, 292; and Hutsuls, 289, 324
Sichynsky, Miroslav, 331–38, 342, 343, 348, 350; in America, 343, 377–78, 404–5
Sieniawa, Czartoryski estate, 70, 87, 88
Sienkiewicz, Henryk, 337–38
Silber, Michael, 29
Silesia, 38; resettled with former Galicians, 407, 410
Sked, Alan, 144
Slavic character, of Poles and Ruthenians in Galicia, 254, 264–65
"Slavic civilization" (Wielopolski), 165
Slavic Congress, in Prague (1848), 186, 190
Slavic mythology: Popiel, 103; Krak and Wanda, 269, 295
"Slavic Orient," 240, 242, 254, 277
Slavs, ancient, pagan: Chodakowski's "On Slavdom before Christianity," 87–89; in Jandaurek, 271; in *Pamiętnik Galicyjski*, 88–89; in *Rusalka Dnistrovaia*, 120
Slovakia, Slovaks, 118, 364
Slovenia, Slovenes, 254, 396
Słowo Polskie, on Potocki assassination, 339–40, 341, 342
Snihursky, Ivan, 87
Snyder, Timothy, 362
Sobieski, Jan, king, 164, 235, 265–66, 273
socialism, in Galicia, 250, 313, 325, 327, 331, 338
Socrates, 124, 236, 279
Sokal, 379

Sokół, Sokil, athletic associations, 325
Solferino, battle of, 210
Solidarity, 412
Sosnowska, Danuta, 10
Soviet Ukraine, 374, 382, 404, 407, 408, 418; incorporates eastern Galicia, 382, 404
Soviet Union: Bolshevism, 350, 364, 378–79, 380, 404–9, 410; collapse of the Soviet Union, 408, 411
Soyer, Daniel, 402
Spanish Galicia, 1
Spector, Scott, 296
Spencer, Herbert, Social Darwinism, 343–44
Sperber, Manes, 356, 372
Spielberg, Steven, *Schindler's List,* 413–14
Stadion, Franz, 170, 183, 184, 185, 191, 192, 199
Stadion, Rudolf, 170
Stalin, Joseph, 350, 382, 385, 391, 404, 405, 406, 407, 409, 411, 418
Stańczyk, political perspective, 223–24, 259, 276, 280, 343, 363
Stanisław August, king, 38, 50–51
Stanislawski, Michael, 10, 205
Stanisławski, Jan, artist, 327
Stanwyck, Barbara, 401
Stanyslaviv (Ivano-Frankivsk), 253, 292, 297, 313, 337, 368, 370
Starzewski, Rudolf, editor of *Czas,* 280
Stauter-Halsted, Keely, 10, 266
Stefanowska, Lidia, 412
Stephanie, Crown Princess, wife of Rudolf, 272
Stojałowski, Stanisław, 266, 277, 305
Strauss, Richard, 319, 365
Strindberg, August, 296, 298
Struve, Henryk, 304
Stryj River, 364
Strypa River, 293
Stupnicki, Hipolit, *Galicia,* 195–96, 197, 198, 203, 211
Sturm und Drang, 32
Styka, Jan, artist, 294
Styr River, 212
Styria, 146, 212. *See also* Graz
Sucha, 401, 408

Swanson, Gloria, 401
Switzerland, 156. *See also* Geneva
syphilis, 380
Sysyn, Frank, 9
Szczepanowski, Stanisław, *Misery of Galicia in Statistics* (*Nędza Galicyi w Cyfrach*), 234–35, 275–79, 289, 312, 338, 390, 409; "the average Galician," 234, 276; and Jews, 276–77
Szczepański, Ludwik, 299
Szczyrzyc, 203
Szela, Jakub, 144, 161–62, 170, 171, 179–82, 217, 266, 267; as "Galician Spartacus," 144, 179; in Jasieński's *Song of Jakub Szela*, 389–91; in Wyspiański's *Wesele*, 187, 282–83, 348, 390
Szeptycki, Stanisław, 362–63
Szporluk, Roman, 408, 413
Szujski, Józef, 194, 218, 223, 226, 233, 260, 276, 336, 343, 413; *The Poles and Ruthenians in Galicia*, 9, 262–65, 267; on Polish Don Quixote and Ruthenian Sancho Panza, 265; on Russia, 219; in Sejm, 222–23; "Several Truths from our History," 218–20
Śliwa, Michał, 277, 368
Śniadecki, Jan, 84

Taaffe, Eduard, 266
tabula rasa, in Galicia, 4, 17, 19
Tagore, Rabindranath, 385
Tarnów, 97, 205, 258, 267, 324, 358, 359, 408, 413; in 1846, 142, 144, 148, 150, 153, 155, 162, 171, 179, 180, 218, 219, 226; in 1848, 185–86
Tarnowski, Stanisław, 218, 223, 276, 327
Tartars, Tartary, 48, 102, 243, 265, 267, 293, 337, 340, 377
taxation in Galicia, 19, 29, 31, 108
Terence, "Slavus sum," 129
Ternopil, Tarnopol, 90, 125–26, 241, 244, 319, 337, 368, 375, 378, 415
Tetmajer, Kazimierz, 280, 281, 295, 346, 366, 381; "The End of the Nineteenth Century," 286, 296, 304, 347; "I Believe in Nothing," 286
Tetmajer, Włodzimierz, 193, 281, 288, 314, 368

textbooks, Ruthenian, 65, 87
theater, drama: Bogusławski in Lviv, 55–59; Kamiński in Lviv, 91–92; Korzeniowski in Lviv, 126–27; Pawlikowski in Cracow and Lviv, 295–96. *See also* Fredro, Aleksander; Wyspiański
Thugut, Franz, 82
Tlumach, 297, 364
Toscanini, Arturo, 319, 409
Traunpaur, Alphons Heinrich, *Dreissig Briefe* (*Thirty Letters*), 14, 32–36, 41, 54, 60, 145
Trembowla, 356
Trieste, 130
Trzebinia, 290
Turteltaub, Wilhelm, "Some Words from Galicia," 140–41
Tygodnik Ilustrowany, on *Wesele*, 280
Tysmenytsia, 346
Tysmenytsia (Tismennitsa) River, 251
Tyssowski, Jan, 141

Ukraine, in Russian Empire, 47, 117, 130, 214, 283, 339
Ukraine, post-Soviet, 411–17
Ukrainian claims to Galicia, after World War I, 378–79
Ukrainian identity and Galician Ruthenians, 9, 130, 214, 336, 337, 358, 378, 392–93, 413; and Franko, 256–57, 295, 309, 329–30; and Hrushevsky, 287, 295, 309, 330, 337, 378; discussed in *Słowo Polskie*, 339–40
Ukrainian Insurgent Army (UPA), 407–8
Ukrainian language, Galician Ruthenian language, 10, 47, 86–87, 116, 119, 130, 413
Ukrainian national politics during World War I, 362–63, 364
Ukrainian national politics following World War I, 368, 374, 378–79; Committee of the Independent Ukraine, 378; Ukrainian National Council, 367–68; West Ukrainian National Republic, 368, 374
Ukrainian summer school, 326
Uman, massacre, 347
Umberto I, king of Italy, 304

Uniates, Greek Catholic Church, 228, 253–54, 269, 342, 358, 388, 413; Babel on, 381–82; Barbaraeum, St. Barbara's, in Vienna, 86, 87, 253; Basilian Order, 293; bishops, hierarchy, 191, 235, 253, 311, 386; clergy, 25–26, 87, 105, 123–24; Döblin on, 386; *History of the Union*, by Pelesz, 253; Kratter's hostility, 25–27; metropolitanate of Halych established, 86, 253; Mickiewicz on, 105; news reports on Greek Catholic criminals, 76, 141; Orthodox aspects, 25, 214, 254, 292; in post-Soviet Ukraine, 358, 411; religious art on exhibit, 290, 291, 292, 293, 386; Roman Catholic aspects, 214, 253–54, 262; and *Rusalka Dnistrovaia*, 120; and Ruthenian nationality, 17, 19, 114, 116, 214; St. George's Cathedral, in Lviv, 99, 261; seminaries, 25, 26, 32, 86, 119, 120, 294; Society of Greek Catholic Priests in Galicia, 87; suppressed in Soviet Union, 407. *See also* Sheptytsky

Union of Brest, and Uniates, 25, 292

Union of Lublin, in 1569, commemorated in 1869, 225–26, 227–28, 357

United States of America, 98, 113, 217; Immigration Act of 1924, 402; Wild West, compared to Galicia, 389. *See also* Buffalo Bill's Wild West Circus; California; emigration, from Galicia to America; New York City; *New York Times*; *Washington Post*

University of Lviv, 62, 81, 82, 84–85, 253, 295, 350, 374, 388, 405; chair in Polish language and literature, 82–85, 103; Hrushevsky at, 283, 287, 325, 337, 338, 339; Ruthenian/Ukrainian students, 331, 338–39, 350

University of Vienna, 10, 242, 245, 295, 326, 334

Unowsky, Daniel, 10, 203, 259, 294

Vahylevych, Ivan, 119–20

Vatican, 254, 266

Vienna, siege of (1683), 164, 265–66, 273. *See also* Ottoman empire; Sobieski

Viennese perspective on Galicia, 4,

78, 112, 123, 312, 319, 335, 369–74; Hofmannsthal, 297–98, 365; Mahler, 318–19; Pappenheim, 314, 315, 319, 349; on Potocki assassination, 332–33, 334–35, 339, 340; public for Jandaurek, 269, 271, 272; Viennese-Jewish perspective on Galician Jews, 312, 315, 354–55. *See also Neue Freie Presse*

Vilnius, Wilno, 70, 84, 93, 126, 379, 385

Virgil, 124, 309

Vistula River, 4, 92, 115, 146, 176, 212, 233–34, 269, 295, 376, 388

Vladimir, *see* Halych and Vladimir

voivodships of Cracow, Lviv, Ternopil, Stanyslaviv (former Galicia), 368, 383

Volhynia, 91, 378, 415

Voltaire, 16, 59; "Consequences of the Works of Voltaire," 49–51, 80; "Dissensions of the Churches of Poland," 50; against Roman Catholic fanaticism, 50

Von Hagen, Mark, 362

Wacław z Oleska, *see* Zaleski

Wadowice, 409, 416

Wagner, Otto, 291

Wagner, Richard, 295, 318, 319

Warsaw, 88, 100, 129, 182, 194, 198, 300, 350, 393; and Bogusławski, 55–57; different from Galicia, 57, 70, 230, 277–78, 366, 385, 405, 408, 412; taken by Central Powers during World War I, 362, 365, 366

Warsaw Ghetto, 345

Washington Post, 405

Wat, Aleksander, 405–6, 408

Waterloo, battle of, 74

Wawel hill, castle, cathedral, in Cracow, 53, 156, 164, 227, 260, 266, 273, 309; state archive, 235

Weimar Germany, 321, 384, 395, 404

Wernyhora, 347–48

Wesele (The Wedding), *see* Wyspiański

West Galicia (after 1795), 52–55, 61, 64, 158

Western Europe, idea of: in Babel's observations of Galicia, 380–81; compared to Eastern Europe, 14, 67, 176, 217, 265, 315,

411; as perspective on Eastern Europe, 159, 315, 389

Western Ukraine, 394, 405, 408, 412–13, 416

Wieliczka, 4, 64, 130, 150–51, 203, 306

Wielopolski, Aleksander, on the massacres, 158–65, 166, 167, 168, 170, 173, 186; and Russia, 164–65, 182

Wiener Zeitung, 31–32

Wiesenthal, Simon, 408

Wilde, Oscar, 296

Wilder, Billy, 401, 408

Wilson, Woodrow, 373, 374, 405; Fourteen Points, 363; and principle of national self-determination, 363, 373, 375, 394

Windischgrätz, Alfred, 186

Wiśniowski, Teofil, 154

Witkiewicz, Stanisław (artist and architect), 295

Witkiewicz, Stanisław (writer and artist, Witkacy), 295

Witos, Wincenty, 368

Wittlin, Józef, 415

Wojtyła, Karol, Pope John Paul II, 409, 416

Woldan, Alois, 299

Women's International League for Peace and Freedom, 392–94

World War I, 344, 350, 351–66, 380, 384, 389, 395, 400, 403, 406, 408

World War II, 350, 352, 382, 384, 385, 404–8, 415

Wrocław, 294

Wyspiański, Stanisław: and commemoration of November Insurrection, 366; on Cracow, 294, 295; and Paris, 286, 294, 299; and Przybyszewski, 299–300; stained glass and murals for Cracow Franciscan church, 287, 295, 297, 327–28, 330, 348; stained glass designs for Lviv cathedral, 286–87; *Wesele (The Wedding)*, 187, 280–83, 287, 288, 294, 300, 306–7, 311, 312, 332, 347–48, 349, 350, 368, 385, 388, 390

Yad Vashem: and Schulz, 11, 417–18; and Shoah victims, 444n16

Yanukovych, Viktor, 413

Yiddish, language and culture, 269, 325–26, 351–51, 402–4, 408; Czernowitz conference (1908), 345, 346, 402; Galitzianer pronunciation, 247–48, 355, 402; Young Galicia, 326. *See also* Ansky; Sholem Aleichem

YIVO Institute for Jewish Research, 4

Yushchenko, Viktor, 413

Zabłotów, Zabolotiv, 356

Zachariewicz, Alfred, architect, 291

Zachariewicz, Julian, architect, 290–91

Zagajewski, Adam, "To Go to Lwów," 409–11

Zakopane, 291, 294, 413

Zaleski, Wacław: as Wacław z Oleska, collector of Galician folk songs, 117–19, 192, 197, 293; as governor of Galicia, 192–93, 199

Załuski, Józef, 134

Zawadzki, Aleksander, on Galician fauna, 128, 195

Zbarazh, 334

Zeitschrift für österreichische Volkskunde: on General Provincial Exhibition, 289–92; on Jews and Franz Joseph, 4, 319–23; on Ruthenian folklore, 324

Zhuk, Ihor, 289

Zieliński, Stanisław, *The Murder of the Viceroy*, 336–40, 341

Ziemiałkowski, Florian, 191

Zionism, 299, 313, 317–18, 326, 329, 349

Zita, Empress, 414

Zolochiv, 76, 154

Zoria Halytska, 184, 186

Żeleński, Tadeusz, "Boy," 257, 295; Green Balloon, 310, 327; murdered by Nazis, 350; on Przybyszewski, 299, 300–301; in Soviet Lviv, 405; *Znaszli ten kraj?* 283, 287, 300–301, 349, 350, 406

Żeleński, Władysław, 266

Żurawno, Zhuravno, 235, 239

Życie (Life), 296–301